Frommer's®
Cancún, Cozumel & the Yucatán

My Yucatán

by David Baird

THE YUCATAN PENINSULA, TOGETHER WITH TABASCO AND CHIAPAS, is only a modest section of Mexico, but it offers almost all that makes this country special: beautiful beaches, mysterious ruins, thick jungles, tall mountains, and thriving Indian cultures. As with any part of Mexico, it has its own regional culture and cuisine. A trip here is not a substitute for a trip to central Mexico; rather it's a great way to get acquainted with the country.

Once I've had enough beach time (but how much is enough?), what I most like to do is rent a car and drive the back roads of the peninsula. Scattered about the area are the small villages of the Yucatek Maya, ruins, colonial convents, and many of those strange natural features known as cenotes, natural wells where water from underground rivers rises up close to the surface. If I have more time, I take a break from the lowland heat and head for the cool mountains in the central highlands of Chiapas. Here, myriad Indian villages surround the colonial city of San Cristóbal de las Casas, and each boasts a different handicrafts specialty, whether it's weaving, pottery, or embroidery.

In these pages, you'll see photos that show the Yucatán at its best—from the jungle ruins of Palenque to the eco-friendly water park at Xel-Ha to the beachfront megaresorts of Cancún.

© Danita Delimont/Alamy

SNORKELING (left) is my favorite water-sport, and I particularly love exploring the Yucatán coast. It has the second longest reef in the world and offers plenty of places to dive. For beginners, there are also numerous sheltered areas where swimmers are protected from the currents and the waves. Here you see a snorkeler in Chankanaab National Park.

The gorgeous, natural lagoon at **XEL-HA MARINE PARK (above)** is the park's main attraction. This ecological park was established to preserve the area's beauty and provide access to visitors. You can catch a ride on a miniature train up to the innermost part of the lagoon and then drift or paddle down with your snorkel gear to where it meets the sea. Along the way you'll see lots of fish and sea life, and caves and cenotes.

It's always fun to see kids dress up on holidays in the local garb. These children are dancing around a **MAYPOLE IN MERIDA (above)**.

Mexicans have a genius for working with their hands. When given the opportunity, many artisans shine, but more often they produce the everyday goods that demand dictates. I try to seek out the less commonplace work that arises from the need for personal expression. This **MAYA VENDOR IN SAN CRISTOBAL DE LAS CASAS (right)** is selling nontraditional garments to tourists. She may have other, more interesting pieces, but the highland Maya are often difficult to engage in conversation.

I always enjoy visiting **MARKETS** when I have the chance, even when I'm not buying anything. You see a variety of produce and foodstuffs in most of them that would put a supermarket to shame. They also serve as the place where friends and neighbors meet, eat, and chat with each other about things of interest, such as local events and the latest scandals.

Chiapas is wetter than the Yucatán peninsula, and the water mostly stays above ground. There are some beautiful spots not far from Palenque where you can go for a refreshing swim in lush surroundings. This one, known as **AGUA AZUL (left)**, is one of them. I enjoy it most when 3 or 4 days have passed without rain and the water does actually get blue, as its name suggests.

Of the many cenotes I've seen, **CENOTE DZITNUP IN VALLADOLID (above)** is one of the most beautiful. It has retained its ceiling, as many do, and the roots of trees have penetrated the chamber and grown down to the water. The contrast between the bright, hot outside and the cool, dark chamber is almost otherworldly. It's no wonder that the Maya considered cenotes sacred places.

The megalithic **OLMEC HEADS** (above) are some of the most intriguing pre-Colombian artifacts. Most are in out-of-the-way places like Villahermosa and Xalapa, but this modern reproduction can be found at Chankanaab National Park on the island of Cozumel.

Like much of Chichén Itzá's art and architecture, this statue of **CHACMOOL** (right) at the Temple of the Warriors reflects a style that originated in the faraway central highlands of Mexico. That it displays little or no Maya influence has raised questions regarding the true rulers of the city.

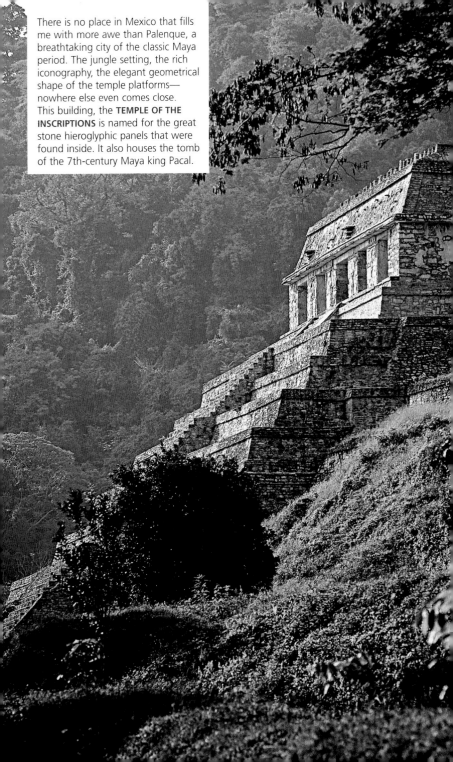

There is no place in Mexico that fills me with more awe than Palenque, a breathtaking city of the classic Maya period. The jungle setting, the rich iconography, the elegant geometrical shape of the temple platforms—nowhere else even comes close.

This building, the **TEMPLE OF THE INSCRIPTIONS** is named for the great stone hieroglyphic panels that were found inside. It also houses the tomb of the 7th-century Maya king Pacal.

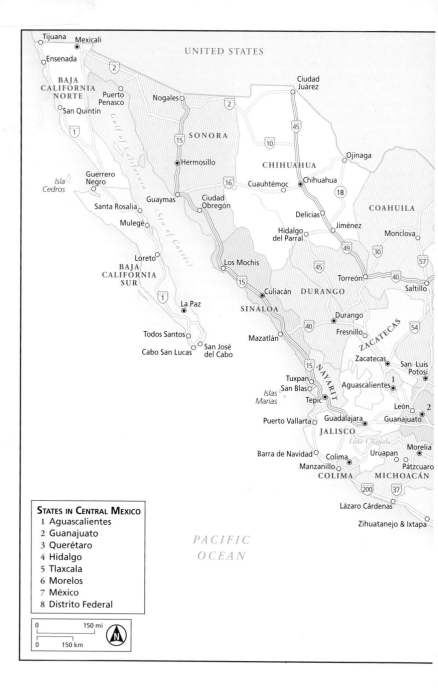

Tijuana
Mexicali
Ensenada

UNITED STATES

BAJA
CALIFORNIA
NORTE
Puerto
Penasco
San Quintin

Nogales

Ciudad
Juárez

2

45

SONORA

10

CHIHUAHUA

Ojinaga

Hermosillo

Isla
Cedros

Guerrero
Negro

16

Cuauhtémoc

Chihuahua

18

COAHUILA

Santa Rosalia
Guaymas
Mulegé

Ciudad
Obregón

Delicias

Jiménez

Monclova

Hidalgo
del Parral

49

30

57

Loreto
BAJA
CALIFORNIA
SUR

Los Mochis

1

15

45

Torreón

40

Saltillo

Culiacán

DURANGO

La Paz

SINALOA

Durango

40

Fresnillo

54

Todos Santos

San José
del Cabo

Mazatlán

Zacatecas

Cabo San Lucas

San Luis
Potosí

15

Tuxpan
San Blas

Aguascalientes

1

Islas
Marias

Tepic

León

2

Puerto Vallarta

Guadalajara

Guanajuato

JALISCO

Lake Chapala

Morelia

Barra de Navidad

Colima

Uruapan

Manzanillo

Pátzcuaro

COLIMA

MICHOACÁN

200

37

STATES IN CENTRAL MEXICO
1 Aguascalientes
2 Guanajuato
3 Querétaro
4 Hidalgo
5 Tlaxcala
6 Morelos
7 México
8 Distrito Federal

Lázaro Cárdenas

Zihuatanejo & Ixtapa

PACIFIC
OCEAN

0   150 mi
0   150 km

Gulf of California
(Sea of Cortés)

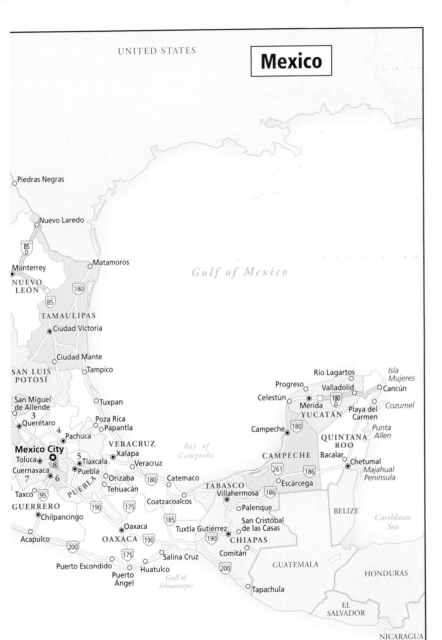

Mexico

UNITED STATES

Gulf of Mexico

Piedras Negras

Nuevo Laredo

85
D

Monterrey
Matamoros

NUEVO
LEÓN

180

85

TAMAULIPAS

Ciudad Victoria

Ciudad Mante

SAN LUIS
POTOSÍ

Tampico

San Miguel
de Allende

3

Querétaro

Tuxpan

Poza Rica

Papantla

4

Pachuca

VERACRUZ

Bay of
Campeche

Río Lagartos

Isla
Mujeres

Progreso

Celestún

Valladolid

Cancún

180
D

Mérida

YUCATÁN

Playa del
Carmen

Cozumel

Campeche

180

Punta
Allen

QUINTANA
ROO

Mexico City

Toluca

Xalapa

8

5

Tlaxcala

Veracruz

Cuernavaca

Puebla

7

6

PUEBLA

Orizaba

CAMPECHE

Bacalar

Chetumal

180

Catemaco

261

186

Majahual
Peninsula

Taxco

95

Tehuacán

TABASCO

Escárcega

186

GUERRERO

190

175

Coatzacoalcos

Villahermosa

BELIZE

Caribbean
Sea

Chilpancingo

185

Palenque

Acapulco

200

Oaxaca

OAXACA

190

Tuxtla Gutiérrez

San Cristóbal
de las Casas

190

CHIAPAS

Puerto Escondido

175

Salina Cruz

Comitán

GUATEMALA

HONDURAS

Puerto
Ángel

Huatulco

Gulf of
Tehuantepec

200

Tapachula

EL
SALVADOR

NICARAGUA

The Yucatán Peninsula

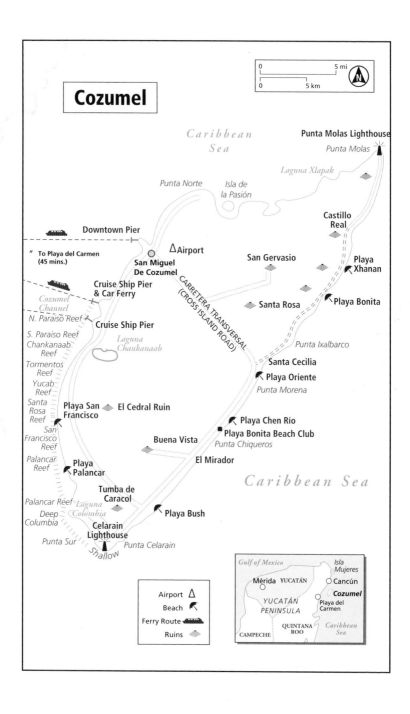

Cozumel

Caribbean Sea

Punta Molas Lighthouse
Punta Molas

Laguna Xlapak

Punta Norte

Isla de la Pasión

Castillo Real

Downtown Pier

" To Playa del Carmen (45 mins.)

△ Airport

San Gervasio

Playa Xhanan

San Miguel De Cozumel

Cruise Ship Pier & Car Ferry

CARRETERA TRANSVERSAL (CROSS ISLAND ROAD)

Santa Rosa

Playa Bonita

Cozumel Channel

N. Paraíso Reef

Cruise Ship Pier

Punta Ixalbarco

S. Paraíso Reef
Chankanaab Reef

Laguna Chankanaab

Santa Cecilia

Playa Oriente

Punta Morena

Tormentos Reef

Yucab Reef

Santa Rosa Reef

Playa San Francisco

El Cedral Ruin

Playa Chen Río

San Francisco Reef

Buena Vista

Playa Bonita Beach Club

Punta Chiqueros

Palancar Reef

El Mirador

Playa Palancar

Caribbean Sea

Tumba de Caracol

Palancar Reef

Laguna Colombia

Playa Bush

Deep Columbia

Celarain Lighthouse

Punta Sur *Shallow* *Punta Celarain*

Airport △
Beach
Ferry Route
Ruins

Gulf of Mexico

Isla Mujeres

Mérida YUCATÁN

Cancún

YUCATÁN PENINSULA

Cozumel

Playa del Carmen

CAMPECHE

QUINTANA ROO

Caribbean Sea

Chichén Itzá Ruins

Snack bar and toilets

Well of Sacrifice
(Sacred Cenote)

Sacred Way
(Sacbé)

North Temple

Main Ball Court

PARKING

Temple of Jaguars

"NEW" CHICHÉN

Main Tourist Entrance

Temple of the Skulls
(Tzompantli)

Temple of the Warriors

Platform of the Eagles

Platform of Venus

180

Pyramid of Kukulkán
(El Castillo)

Ball Court

Councillor's House

Group of the Thousand Columns

Tomb of the High Priest
(Tumba del Gran Sacerdote)

Northeast Colonnade

Temple of the Grinding Stones

Ball Court

Ball Court

"OLD" CHICHÉN

The Market

Steambath 2

Temple of the Deer

Little Holes
(Chichan-Chob)

Ball Court

Cenote Xtoloc

Secondary Tourist Entrance

The Observatory
(El Caracol)

Temple of Obscure Writing
(Akab Dzib)

Hotel Mayaland

Steambath 1

Temple of the Sculptured Panels

Hotel Hacienda Chichén

Edifice of the Nuns
(Edificio de las Monjas)

Villas Arqueológica
Chichén Itzá

Church

0   330 ft
0   100 m

Uxmal Ruins

↑ To Mérida

0   330 ft
0   100 m

North Group
(Grupo Norte)

261   Hotel Hacienda Uxmal

Northwest Group
(Grupo Noroeste)

261   To Puuc Route & Campeche →

Platform of the Stelae
(Plataforma de las Estelas)

Columns Group
(Grupo de las Columnas)

Quadrangle of the Nuns
(Cuadrángulo de las Monjas)

Villa Arqueológica Uxmal

PARKING

Cemetery Group
(Grupo del Cementerio)

Ball Court
(Juego de Pelota)

Pyramid of the Magician
(Pirámide del Advino)

House of the Doves

House of the Turtles
(Casa de las Tortugas)

West Group
(Grupo Oeste)

Governor's Palace
(Palacio del Gobenador)

South Temple
(Templo Sur)

Great Pyramid
(Gran Pirámide)

House of the Old Woman
(Pirámide de la Vieja)

To Temple of the Phallus ↓

To Chimez Temple ↓

Information ⓘ

Cobá Ruins

To Valladolid

Hotel Villa Archeológica

Hotel El Bocadito

Lake Cobá

La Iglesia

Tickets

GRUPO CHUMUC MUL

GRUPO COBÁ

El Castillo

GRUPO NOHOCH MUL

GRUPO DE LA PINTURAS

Lake Macanxoc

To Grupo Macanxoc

0 — 200 yds
0 — 200 m

— — — Sacbé

Palenque Archaeological Site

North Group
(Grupo Norte)

Temple of the Count
(Templo del Conde)

Temple 10

Ball Court
(Juego de Pelota)

Bridge
(Puente)

Entrance

Tickets

Temple 11

Rio Otulum

The Palace
(El Palacio)

Temple 12

Temple 13

Temple of the Inscriptions
(Templo de las Inscripciones)

Temple 14

Temple of the Sun
(Templo del Sol)

Temple of the Cross
(Templo de la Cruz)

Temple of the Foliated Cross
(Templo de la Cruz Foliada)

Temple 18

Temple 18A

House of the Jaguar
(Casa del Jaguar)

0 — 100 yds
0 — 100 m

Frommer's®

Cancún & the Yucatán 2010
with Tabasco & Chiapas

by David Baird, Shane Christensen & Christine Delsol

Here's what the critics say about Frommer's:

"Amazingly easy to use. Very portable, very complete."
—**BOOKLIST**

"Detailed, accurate, and easy-to-read information
for all price ranges."
—**GLAMOUR MAGAZINE**

"Hotel information is close to encyclopedic."
—**DES MOINES SUNDAY REGISTER**

"Frommer's Guides have a way of giving you
a real feel for a place."
—**KNIGHT RIDDER NEWSPAPERS**

WILEY
Wiley Publishing, Inc.

Published by:

WILEY PUBLISHING, INC.

111 River St.
Hoboken, NJ 07030-5774

ISBN 978-0-470-48730-3
Editor: Melinda Quintero
Production Editor: Eric T. Schroeder
Cartographer: Nick Trotter
Photo Editor: Richard Fox
Production by Wiley Indianapolis Composition Services

Front cover photo: Tanning in the Yucatán. ©Chris Cheadle / Alamy Images
Back cover photo: Olmec Head in Villahermosa, Museo la Venta. ©Adalberto Rios Szalay / Sexto Sol / Photodisc / Alamy Images

For information on our other products and services or to obtain technical support, please contact our Customer Care Department within the U.S. at 877/762-2974, outside the U.S. at 317/572-3993 or fax 317/572-4002.

Wiley also publishes its books in a variety of electronic formats. Some content that appears in print may not be available in electronic formats.

Manufactured in the United States of America

5 4 3 2

CONTENTS

LIST OF MAPS	**vi**

WHAT'S NEW IN CANCÚN & THE YUCATÁN	**1**

1 THE BEST OF CANCÚN & THE YUCATÁN   4

1 The Best Beach Vacations 4	**7** The Best Shopping.................10
2 The Best Cultural Experiences 5	**8** The Hottest Nightlife..............10
3 The Best Archaeological Sites 5	**9** The Most Luxurious Hotels 11
4 The Best Active Vacations 8	**10** The Best Inexpensive Inns.........12
5 The Best Places to Get Away from It All..........................9	**11** The Best Unique Inns 13
6 The Best Museums.................9	**12** The Best Restaurants.............13

2 THE YUCATÁN, TABASCO & CHIAPAS IN DEPTH   15

1 The Yucatán, Tabasco & Chiapas Now 15	*A Debt of Gratitude* 28
	Dining Service Tips..................32
2 A Look at the Past.................18	**4** Art & Architecture.................33
It's All in the Game 19	**5** Religion, Myth & Folklore.........35
Of Henequén & Haciendas..........24	*The Maya Pantheon* 36
A Tale of Two Hurricanes............26	**6** The Lay of the Land...............37
A Sticky Habit 27	**7** Books, Film & Music 39
3 Eating & Drinking 27	

3 PLANNING YOUR TRIP TO THE YUCATÁN, TABASCO & CHIAPAS   43

1 When to Go......................43	**3** Getting There & Getting Around ...50
Calendar of Events 44	**4** Money & Costs....................55
What's Biting When?.................47	**5** Health 57
2 Entry Requirements 48	*Smoke-Free Mexico?* 60

6 Safety............................60

*One More Author Gives His
Two Cents: Safety in Mexico*.........61

7 Specialized Travel Resources 62

8 Sustainable Tourism...............64

General Resources for Green Travel...67

9 Special Interest Trips & Escorted
General Interest Tours.............67

10 Staying Connected................69

11 Tips on Accommodations.........70

4 SUGGESTED YUCATÁN ITINERARIES   72

1 The Regions in Brief...............72

If You Have Even Less Time 77

2 Northern Yucatán in a Week.......77

3 The Yucatán in 2 weeks 78

4 An Eco-Adventure for the
Entire Family......................80

5 La Ruta Maya 82

5 CANCÚN   85

1 Orientation 86

The Best Websites for Cancún.......87

Fast Facts: Cancún 89

2 Where to Stay....................91

3 Where to Dine 100

4 Beaches, Watersports &
Boat Tours 106

5 Outdoor Activities & Attractions ... 110

6 Shopping 111

7 Cancún After Dark 112

6 ISLA MUJERES & COZUMEL   115

1 Isla Mujeres 115

*The Best Websites for Isla Mujeres
& Cozumel*............................118

Fast Facts: Isla Mujeres..............119

2 Cozumel 128

*An All-Inclusive Vacation in
Cozumel*............................130

Fast Facts: Cozumel................132

Anatomy of the Coral Reef.........134

7 THE CARIBBEAN COAST: THE RIVIERA MAYA   145

1 Puerto Morelos & Vicinity........ 149

2 Playa del Carmen 154

Fast Facts: Playa del Carmen........156

*Choosing an All-Inclusive in the
Riviera Maya*.......................162

3 South of Playa del Carmen 163

4 Tulum, Punta Allen & Sian Ka'an... 170

5 Cobá Ruins....................... 175

6 Majahual, Xcalak & the
Chinchorro Reef 178

7 Lago Bacalar 180

8 Chetumal 181

9 Side Trips to Maya Ruins from
Chetumal...................... 183

8 MÉRIDA, CHICHÉN ITZÁ & THE MAYA INTERIOR   190

*The Best Websites for Mérida,
Chichén Itzá & the Maya Interior*...191

1 Mérida: Gateway to the Maya
Heartland....................... 192

Daily Festivals & Special Events in Mérida....................................196

Fast Facts: Mérida 197

Haciendas & Hotels 200

2 Side Trips from Mérida 214

3 The Ruins of Uxmal 220

4 The Puuc Maya Route & Village of Oxkutzcab 224

5 Campeche........................ 229

Fast Facts: Campeche..............232

6 The Ruins of Chichén Itzá 236

7 Valladolid 243

9 TABASCO & CHIAPAS 249

1 Villahermosa 250

2 Palenque......................... 256

3 San Cristóbal de las Casas 264

The Zapatista Movement & Chiapas.............................266

Fast Facts: San Christóbal de las Casas 267

4 Tuxtla Gutiérrez 278

FAST FACTS 283

1 Fast Facts: Yucatán, Tabasco & Chiapas.......................... 283

Online Traveler's Toolbox...........286

2 Airline, Hotel & Car Rental Websites 287

APPENDIX: SURVIVAL SPANISH 289

1 English-Spanish Phrases......... 289

INDEX 297

General Index.................... 297

Accommodations Index 310

Restaurant Index................ 312

LIST OF MAPS

Mexico. 6

The Yucatán, Tabasco & Chiapas
in Depth. 20

The Yucatán Peninsula. 74

Tabasco & Chiapas 76

Northern Yucatán in a Week 78

The Yucatán in Two Weeks 79

An Eco-Adventure for the
Entire Family 81

La Ruta Maya 83

Isla Cancún (Zona Hotelera). 93

Ciudad Cancún. 95

Isla Mujeres 117

Cozumel 129

San Miguel de Cozumel. 135

The Yucatán's Upper Caribbean
Coast. 147

Playa del Carmen. 155

Tulum Ruins 173

The Yucatán's Lower Caribbean
Coast. 179

Yucatán State 193

Where to Stay & Dine in Mérida. . . 199

What to See & Do in Mérida. 209

Kabah Ruins 225

Sayil Ruins 227

Labná Ruins. 228

Campeche 231

Chichén Itzá Ruins. 239

Villahermosa. 251

Where to Stay & Dine in
Palenque 261

San Cristóbal de las Casas 265

The Chiapas Highlands 279

HOW TO CONTACT US

In researching this book, we discovered many wonderful places—hotels, restaurants, shops, and more. We're sure you'll find others. Please tell us about them, so we can share the information with your fellow travelers in upcoming editions. If you were disappointed with a recommendation, we'd love to know that, too. Please write to:

Frommer's Cancún & the Yucatán 2010 with Tabasco & Chiapas
Wiley Publishing, Inc. • 111 River St. • Hoboken, NJ 07030-5774

AN ADDITIONAL NOTE

Please be advised that travel information is subject to change at any time—and this is especially true of prices. We therefore suggest that you write or call ahead for confirmation when making your travel plans. The authors, editors, and publisher cannot be held responsible for the experiences of readers while traveling. Your safety is important to us, however, so we encourage you to stay alert and be aware of your surroundings. Keep a close eye on cameras, purses, and wallets, all favorite targets of thieves and pickpockets.

ABOUT THE AUTHORS

A writer, editor, and translator, **David Baird** has lived several years in different parts of Mexico. Now based in Austin, Texas, he spends as much time in Mexico as possible. A former resident of Mexico City, **Shane Christensen** has written extensively for Frommer's throughout Mexico, and is the author of *Frommer's Dubai* and *Frommer's Grand Canyon*. He resides in New York, and goes back to Mexico at every chance he gets. Author of *Pauline Frommer's Cancún & the Yucatán,* **Christine Delsol** has been traveling to Mexico at every opportunity for 30 years. She has spent most of her career in newspapers and is the recipient of an Associated Press award and two Lowell Thomas awards.

Other Great Guides for Your Trip:

Frommer's Spanish Phrasefinder & Dictionary
Frommer's Cancún & the Yucatán Day by Day
Frommer's Mexico 2010
Pauline Frommer's Cancún & the Yucatán, 1st Edition

FROMMER'S STAR RATINGS, ICONS & ABBREVIATIONS

Every hotel, restaurant, and attraction listing in this guide has been ranked for quality, value, service, amenities, and special features using a **star-rating system.** In country, state, and regional guides, we also rate towns and regions to help you narrow down your choices and budget your time accordingly. Hotels and restaurants are rated on a scale of zero (recommended) to three stars (exceptional). Attractions, shopping, nightlife, towns, and regions are rated according to the following scale: zero stars (recommended), one star (highly recommended), two stars (very highly recommended), and three stars (must-see).

In addition to the star-rating system, we also use **eight feature icons** that point you to the great deals, in-the-know advice, and unique experiences that separate travelers from tourists. Throughout the book, look for:

Finds	Special finds—those places only insiders know about
Fun Facts	Fun facts—details that make travelers more informed and their trips more fun
Kids	Best bets for kids and advice for the whole family
Moments	Special moments—those experiences that memories are made of
Overrated	Places or experiences not worth your time or money
Tips	Insider tips—great ways to save time and money
Value	Great values—where to get the best deals
Warning!	Warning—traveler's advisories are usually in effect

The following **abbreviations** are used for credit cards:

AE	American Express	DISC	Discover	V	Visa
DC	Diners Club	MC	MasterCard		

TRAVEL RESOURCES AT FROMMERS.COM

Frommer's travel resources don't end with this guide. **Frommers.com** has travel information on more than 4,000 destinations. We update features regularly, giving you access to the most current trip-planning information and the best airfare, lodging, and car-rental bargains. You can also listen to podcasts, connect with other Frommers.com members through our active-reader forums, share your travel photos, read blogs from guidebook editors and fellow travelers, and much more.

What's New in Cancún & the Yucatán

As with other destinations, Mexico's tourism industry has been hit hard by the global financial crisis as many would-be travelers tighten their belts and await a stronger economy. Since Mexico relies on tourism for much of its income, the country has redoubled its efforts to attract visitors and enticing specials abound. For the American traveler, Mexico remains a budget destination, as the dollar continues to rise against the peso at press time. For Brits and Canadians, Mexico remains an outright bargain.

In late April 2009, an outbreak of A(H1N1) influenza known as "swine flu" appeared to have originated in Mexico. It spread to numerous countries around the world (including throughout North America), leading the **World Health Organization** (WHO) to declare a global pandemic with a moderate severity as of press time. On May 15, 2009, the U.S. Centers for Disease Control and Prevention (CDC) lifted its recommendation that American citizens avoid all non-essential travel to Mexico, discontinuing the State Department's Mexico travel alert regarding the swine flu outbreak. The CDC has suggested precautions that travelers in Mexico (especially those at high risk for complications of influenza) should take to reduce their risk of infection while there. Following the outbreak, some countries imposed quarantines and other screening procedures for travelers coming from Mexico. Travelers going directly to another country after Mexico (other than their home country) may wish to check the website of the foreign country's embassy to learn what procedures may be in place for that destination. For the latest information regarding the risks of A(H1N1) when traveling to Mexico, please consult the **U.S. State Department**'s website at www.travel.state.gov, or the website of the **World Health Organization** at www.who.int. Complete CDC guidelines regarding A(H1N1) influenza can be found at the following: www.cdc.gov/travel. For more information on the A(H1N1) influenza, turn to p. 57.

Public safety remains a challenge, with the government locked in combat against narco-traffickers in a number of areas of the country. The government seems to be making advances and improving its intelligence, but violence has increased just as the government has made headway. Most of the conflict is well removed from the popular tourist destinations, except for some areas along the U.S. border. Visitors should pay close attention to travel alerts and advisories, such as those published by the U.S. Department of State (www.state.gov).

PLANNING YOUR TRIP TO MEXICO
Under the Western Hemisphere Travel Initiative (WHTI), all persons traveling by air outside of the United States are required to present a passport or other valid travel

document to enter or re-enter the United States. On June 1, 2009, the U.S. government implemented the full requirements of the land and sea phase of WHTI. The rules require most U.S. citizens entering the United States at sea or land ports of entry to have a passport, passport card, or other travel document approved by the Department of Homeland Security. For full information on entry requirements for returning to the U.S., see p. 48.

Travelers to Mexico are now able to make tax-free purchases while vacationing, thanks to a law passed by Mexico's Congress. The law grants international visitors a full refund of the tax added to purchases if the buyer adheres to certain criteria. The merchandise must be purchased in Mexico and verified by airport or seaport Customs, and be verified with a receipt presented at time of departure to be worth at least 1,200 Mexican pesos. Reimbursement to tourists is contingent upon any added costs a possible return may generate.

CANCÚN Cancún's International Airport has expanded to three terminals and offers greatly improved facilities. All flights in and out of the United States now go through Terminal 3.

Fully reopened in 2008 after having been destroyed by Hurricane Wilma, **Aqua** (© **800/343-7821;** www.feel-aqua. com; p. 92) once again reigns as one of Cancún's most tempting resorts. The spa-resort includes spacious oceanview rooms, eight oceanfront pools, an invigorating spa, world-class cuisine, and extremely gracious service. The high-tech rooms feature flatscreen TVs with DVD/CD players, large bathrooms with Molton Brown goods, and aromatherapy kits for private spa treatments.

Situated adjacent the Nichupté Lagoon, **Harry's** (© **998/840-6550;** www.harrys. com.mx; p. 102) is the hottest new addition to Cancún's dining scene. This prime steak-house and raw bar serves huge portions and offers extremely attentive service; you're unlikely to find a better steak in Cancún.

ISLA MUJERES & COZUMEL   Cozumel The Reef Club, an all-inclusive resort on the southern end of the island, has changed management and is now a member of the Wyndham chain of properties. The new name is **Wyndham Cozumel Resort and Spa** (www.wyndham. com). And its neighbor, the Allegro Cozumel Resort, has become the **Holiday Village White Sands,** under the First Choice label (www.firstchoice.co.uk). The all-inclusive resort Costa Club has changed names and is now **Hotel Cozumel & Resort** (www.hotelcozumel.com.mx).

The cruise ship pier **Puerta Maya,** destroyed by Hurricane Wilma in 2005, was the last of the three piers to return to full functionality. The long delay was caused by the fact that very little of the original pier could be saved.

THE RIVIERA MAYA   Puerto Morelos There's a new beach restaurant in town called **La Suegra** (no phone; p. 153), which offers great casual food (burgers, sandwiches, and the like) and a full bar. It's near the lighthouse.

Mayakobá (www.mayakoba.com), the golf course residential resort development between Playa del Carmen and Puerto Morelos, has continued to grow. If you're interested in buying a resort villa, you can choose between the Fairmont, Rosewood (opened in 2008), Banyan Tree (opening in 2009), and Viceroy (opening in 2010).

PLAYA DEL CARMEN Two things of interest: The great beach hotel—the Shangri-La Caribe, which was scheduled to be replaced by a condo project—has been given a reprieve (finance troubles, don't you know). Chances are it won't have the same name or the same webpage, but it will work with the same reservations agency, **Turquoise Reefs** (© **800/538-6602**). Also, a good little *taquería,* **Los**

Carboncitos (© 984/873-1382; p. 163) was slated to close, but merely changed owners. It's on calle 4 and sells tacos, soup, and a few traditional dishes, and does a good job of it.

TULUM Construction work on Hwy. 307 will be completed by summer 2009. It will then be four lanes all the way to Tulum.

MÉRIDA, CHICHÉN ITZÁ & THE MAYA INTERIOR Mérida Plans to tear down the old municipal market and convert the land to an urban green space have stalled. Market vendors have been reluctant to move to the new market across the way. The city government is still trying to persuade them.

CHICHÉN ITZÁ The state government is making an effort to curb the large number of peddlers who operate at the ruins. Over the last few years these have grown into the hundreds. They are well organized and will be difficult to dislodge. Tourists to the site might see banners protesting the actions of the state police.

COSTA MAYA The cruise ship pier in Majahual is now up and running. Cruise ship crowds have returned to the area.

TABASCO & CHIAPAS Villahermosa The **Museo Regional de Antropología Carlos Pellicer Cámara** is still closed for repairs after it was damaged by floods in 2007.

The Best of Cancún & the Yucatán

by David Baird & Shane Christensen

The Yucatán Peninsula welcomes more visitors than any other part of Mexico. Its tremendous variety attracts every kind of traveler with an unrivaled mix of sophisticated resorts, rustic inns, ancient Maya culture, exquisite beaches, and exhilarating adventures. Between the two of us, we've logged thousands of miles crisscrossing the peninsula, and these are our personal favorites—the best places to visit, the best hotels and restaurants, plus must-see, one-of-a-kind experiences.

1 THE BEST BEACH VACATIONS

- **Cancún:** In terms of sheer beauty, Cancún has always been the site of Mexico's most alluring beaches. The powdery, white-sand beaches are complemented by warm Caribbean waters the color of a Technicolor dream; it's so clear that you can see through to the coral reefs below. It's also one of the world's most popular entertainment destinations. Cancún offers Mexico's widest selection of beachfront resorts, with more restaurants, nightlife, and activities than any other resort destination in the country. See chapter 5.

- **Isla Mujeres:** If laid-back is what you're after, this island affords peaceful, small-town beach life at its best. Most accommodations are small, inexpensive inns, with a few one-of-a-kind, luxury places tossed in. Bike—or take a golf cart—around the island to explore rocky coves and sandy beaches, or focus your tanning efforts on the wide beachfront of Playa Norte. Here you'll find calm waters and *palapa* restaurants, where you can have fresh-caught fish for lunch. If all that tranquillity starts to

get to you, you're only a ferry ride away from the action in Cancún. See chapter 6.

- **Cozumel:** It may not have lots of big, sandy beaches, but Cozumel has something the mainland doesn't: the calm, flat waters of the sheltered western shore. It's so calm that it's like swimming in a pool, only this pool has lots of fish, so take your snorkeling mask even if you don't plan to do any diving. See chapter 6.

- **Playa del Carmen:** This is one of our absolute favorite Mexican beach vacations. Stylish and hip, Playa del Carmen has a beautiful beach and an eclectic assortment of small hotels, inns, and cabañas. The social scene focuses on the beach by day and the pedestrian-only Quinta Avenida (Fifth Avenue) by night, with its fun assortment of restaurants, clubs, sidewalk cafes, and shops. You're also close to the coast's major attractions, including nature parks, ruins, and cenotes (sinkholes or natural wells). Enjoy it while it's still a manageable size. See chapter 7.

- **Tulum:** Fronting some of the best beaches on the entire coast, Tulum's small *palapa* hotels offer guests a little slice of paradise far from the crowds and megaresorts. The bustling town lies inland; at the coast, things are quiet and remain so because all these small hotels must generate their own electricity. If you can pull yourself away from the beach, there are ruins to marvel at and a vast nature preserve to explore. See chapter 7.

2 THE BEST CULTURAL EXPERIENCES

- **Exploring the Inland Yucatán Peninsula:** Travelers who venture only to the Yucatán's resorts and cities miss the rock-walled inland villages, where women wear colorful embroidered dresses and life seems to proceed as though the modern world (with the exception of highways) didn't exist. The adventure of seeing newly uncovered ruins, deep in jungle settings, is not to be missed. See chapter 8.
- **Street & Park Entertainment in Mérida:** Few cities have so vibrant a street scene as Mérida. Throughout the week you can catch music and dance performances in plazas about town, but on Sunday, Mérida really gets going—streets are closed off, food stalls spring up everywhere, and you can enjoy a book fair, a flea market, comedy acts, band concerts, and dance groups. At night, the main plaza is the place to be, with people dancing to mambos and rumbas in the street in front of the town hall. See chapter 8.

- **San Cristóbal de las Casas:** The city of San Cristóbal is a living museum, with 16th-century colonial architecture and pre-Hispanic native influences. The highland Maya live in surrounding villages and arrive daily in town wearing colorful handmade clothing. A visit to the villages is a window into another world, giving visitors a glimpse of traditional Indian dress, religious customs, churches, and ceremonies. See chapter 9.
- **Regional Cuisine:** A trip to the Yucatán allows for a culinary tour of some of Mexico's finest foods. Don't miss specialties such as *pollo* or *cochinita pibil* (chicken or pork in savory *achiote* sauce), great seafood dishes, the many styles of *tamal* found throughout Chiapas and the Yucatán, and Caribbean-influenced staples such as fried bananas, black beans, and yucca root. For a glossary of popular regional dishes, see Appendix A.

3 THE BEST ARCHAEOLOGICAL SITES

- **Calakmul:** Of the many elegantly built Maya cities of the Río Bec area, in the lower Yucatán, Calakmul is the broadest in scope and design. It's also one of the hardest to reach—about 48km (30 miles) from the Guatemalan border and completely surrounded by jungle (actually, the Calakmul Biological Reserve). Calakmul is a walled city with the tallest

pyramid in the Yucatán—a city whose primary inhabitants are the trees that populate the plazas. Go now, while it remains infrequently visited. See "Side Trips to Maya Ruins from Chetumal" in chapter 7.
- **Tulum:** Some dismiss Tulum as less important than other ruins in the Yucatán Peninsula, but this seaside Maya

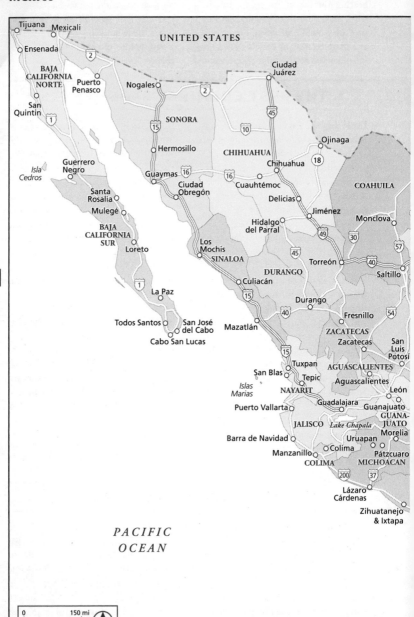

UNITED STATES

Tijuana
Mexicali
Ensenada
BAJA CALIFORNIA NORTE
Puerto Penasco
Nogales
Ciudad Juárez
San Quintin
SONORA
Hermosillo
CHIHUAHUA
Ojinaga
Chihuahua
Isla Cedros
Guerrero Negro
Guaymas
Cuauhtémoc
COAHUILA
Santa Rosalia
Ciudad Obregón
Delicias
Mulegé
Hidalgo del Parral
Jiménez
Monclova
BAJA CALIFORNIA SUR
Loreto
Los Mochis
SINALOA
Torreón
Saltillo
La Paz
Culiacán
DURANGO
Durango
Fresnillo
Todos Santos
San José del Cabo
Mazatlán
ZACATECAS
Zacatecas
San Luis Potosí
Cabo San Lucas
San Blas
Tuxpan
AGUASCALIENTES
Islas Marias
Tepic
Aguascalientes
León
NAYARIT
Puerto Vallarta
Guadalajara
Guanajuato
GUANA-JUATO
JALISCO
Lake Chapala
Morelia
Barra de Navidad
Uruapan
Pátzcuaro
Manzanillo
Colima
MICHOACAN
COLIMA
Lázaro Cárdenas
Zihuatanejo & Ixtapa

PACIFIC OCEAN

0   150 mi
0   150 km

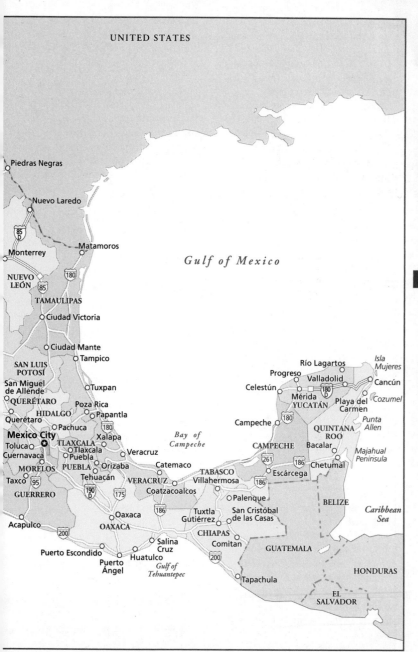

fortress is still inspiring. The stark contrast of its crumbling stone walls against the clear turquoise ocean just beyond is an extraordinary sight. See "Tulum, Punta Allen & Sian Ka'an" in chapter 7.

- **Uxmal:** No matter how many times we see Uxmal, the splendor of its stone carvings remains awe-inspiring. A stone rattlesnake undulates across the facade of the Nunnery complex, and 103 masks of Chaac—the rain god—project from the Governor's Palace. See "The Ruins of Uxmal" in chapter 8.

- **Chichén Itzá:** Stand beside the giant serpent head at the foot of the El Castillo pyramid and marvel at the architects and astronomers who positioned the building so precisely that shadow and sunlight form a serpent's body slithering from peak to the earth at each equinox (Mar 21 and Sept 21). See "The Ruins of Chichén Itzá" in chapter 8.

- **Ek Balam:** In recent years, this is the site where some of Mexico's most astounding archaeological discoveries have been made. Ek Balam's main pyramid is taller than Chichén Itzá's, and it holds a sacred doorway bordered with elaborate stucco figures of priests and kings and rich iconography. See "Ek Balam: Dark Jaguar" in chapter 8.

- **Palenque:** The ancient builders of these structures carved histories in stone that scholars have only recently deciphered. Imagine the magnificent ceremony in A.D. 683 when King Pacal was buried deep inside his pyramid—his tomb unspoiled until its discovery in 1952. See "Palenque" in chapter 9.

4 THE BEST ACTIVE VACATIONS

- **Scuba Diving in Cozumel & Along the Yucatán's Caribbean Coast:** The coral reefs off the island, Mexico's premier diving destination, are among the top five dive spots in the world. The Yucatán's coastal reef, part of the planet's second-largest reef system, affords excellent diving all along the coast. Diving from Isla Mujeres is quite spectacular. Especially beautiful is the Chinchorro Reef, lying 32km (20 miles) offshore from Majahual or Xcalak. See chapters 6 and 7.

- **Fly-Fishing off the Punta Allen & Majahual Peninsulas:** Serious anglers will enjoy the challenge of fly-fishing the saltwater flats and lagoons on the protected sides of these peninsulas. See "Tulum, Punta Allen & Sian Ka'an" and "Majahual, Xcalak & the Chinchorro Reef" in chapter 7.

- **Cenote Diving on the Yucatán Mainland:** Dive into the clear depths of the Yucatán's cenotes for an interesting twist on underwater exploration. The Maya considered the cenotes sacred—and their vivid colors do indeed seem otherworldly. Most are between Playa del Carmen and Tulum, and dive shops in these areas regularly run trips for experienced divers. For recommended dive shops, see "Cozumel" in chapter 6, and "Playa del Carmen" and "South of Playa del Carmen" in chapter 7.

- **Birding:** The Yucatán Peninsula, Tabasco, and Chiapas are ornithological paradises. Two very special places are Isla Contoy, with more than 70 species of birds as well as a host of marine and animal life (p. 122), and the Huitepec Cloud Forest, with its flocks of migratory species (see p. 272).

- **An Excursion to Bonampak & Yaxchilán:** Bonampak and Yaxchilán—two remote, jungle-surrounded Maya sites along the Usumacinta River—are now accessible by car and motorboat. The experience could well be the highlight of any trip. See "Road Trips from San Cristóbal" in chapter 9.

5 THE BEST PLACES TO GET AWAY FROM IT ALL

- **Isla Mujeres:** Isla Mujeres in low season is about as low-key as you can get. You'll find an ample selection of hotels and restaurants, and they're as laid-back as their patrons. Here life moves along in pure *mañana* mode, with little sign of the bustling commercialism that exists just across the bay. Visitors stretch out and doze beneath shady palms or languidly stroll about. In fact, Isla Mujeres feels worlds removed from Cancún, yet remains comfortably close for those who choose to reconnect. See "Isla Mujeres" in chapter 6.

- **The Yucatán's Riviera Maya:** Away from the busy resort of Cancún, a string of quiet getaways, including Paamul, Punta Bete, and a portion of Xpu-ha, offer tranquillity on beautiful beaches at low prices. See "North of Playa del Carmen" and "South of Playa del Carmen" in chapter 7.

- **Tulum:** Near the Tulum ruins, about two dozen beachside *palapa* inns offer some of the most peaceful getaways in the country. This stretch just might offer the best sandy beaches on the entire coast. Life here among the birds and coconut palms is decidedly unhurried. See "Tulum, Punta Allen & Sian Ka'an" in chapter 7.

- **Rancho Encantado Cottage Resort** (Lago Bacalar; www.encantado.com):

The attractive *casitas* are the best place to unwind at this resort, where hammocks stretch between trees. The hotel is on the shores of placid Lago (Lake) Bacalar, south of Cancún near Chetumal, and there's nothing around for miles. But if you want adventure, you can head out to the lake in a kayak, follow a birding trail, or take an excursion to Belize and the intriguing Maya ruins on the nearby Río Bec route. See p. 181.

- **Hotel Eco Paraíso Xixim** (Celestún; www.ecoparaiso.com): In these crowded times, space is a luxury that's getting harder to come by. Space is precisely what makes this place so great: Fifteen bungalows and 5km (3 miles) of beach bordering a coconut plantation. Throw in a good restaurant, a pool, and a couple of hammocks, and you have that rare combination of comfort and isolation. See p. 216.

- **Hacienda San José Cholul** (www.luxury collection.com): Operated by Starwood Hotels, this hacienda is only an hour east of the bustling city of Mérida, toward Izamal, but it feels like another world. The quiet, unhurried manner of both guests and staff, and the beautiful tropical surroundings make it the perfect place to recoup some of the silence and slow time lost to the modern world. See "Haciendas & Hotels" on p. 200.

6 THE BEST MUSEUMS

- **Museo de la Cultura Maya** (Chetumal; © 983/832-6838): This modern museum, one of the best in the country, explores Maya archaeology, architecture, history, and mythology. It has interactive exhibits and a glass floor that allows visitors to walk above replicas of Maya sites. See p. 182.

- **Museo Regional de Antropología** (Mérida; © 999/923-0557): Housed in the Palacio Cantón, one of the most beautiful 19th-century mansions in the city, this museum showcases local archaeology and anthropological studies in handsome exhibits. See p. 211.

- **Museo Regional de Antropología Carlos Pellicer Cámara** (Villahermosa; ℗ 993/312-6344): This anthropology museum addresses Mexican history in the form of objects found at archaeological sites, with particular emphasis on the pre-Hispanic peoples of the Gulf coast region. See p. 252.
- **Parque–Museo La Venta** (Villahermosa; ℗ 993/314-1652): The Olmec, considered Mexico's mother culture, are the subject of this park/museum, which features the magnificent stone remains that were removed from the La Venta site not far away. Stroll through a jungle setting where tropical birds alight, and examine the giant carved stone heads of the mysterious Olmec. See p. 253.

7 THE BEST SHOPPING

Some tips on bargaining: Although haggling over prices in markets is expected and part of the fun, don't try to browbeat the vendor or bad-mouth the goods. Vendors won't bargain with people they consider disrespectful unless they are desperate to make a sale. Be insistent but friendly.

- **Resort Wear in Cancún:** Resort clothing—especially if you can find a sale—can be a bargain here. And the selection may be wider than what's available at home. Almost every mall on the island contains trendy boutiques that specialize in locally designed and imported clothing. The best is La Isla Shopping Center. Less expensive local fashions are widely available in the original downtown known as El Centro. See "Shopping" in chapter 5.
- **Duty-Free in Cancún:** If you're looking for European perfume, fine watches, or other imported goods, you'll find the prices in Cancún's duty-free shops (at the major malls on the island and in downtown Cancún) hard to beat.
- **Quinta Avenida, Playa del Carmen:** This pedestrian-only street offers leisurely shopping at its best—no cars, no hassle. Simply stroll down the street and let your eye pick out objects of interest. Expect a good bit of merchandise popular with counterculture types, such as batik clothing and fabric, Guatemalan textiles, and inventive jewelry and artwork. But you'll also find quality Mexican handicrafts, premium tequilas, and Cuban cigars. See "Playa del Carmen" in chapter 7.
- **Mérida:** This is *the* marketplace for the Yucatán—the best place to buy hammocks, *guayaberas,* Panama hats, and Yucatecan *huipiles.* See "Exploring Mérida" in chapter 8.
- **San Cristóbal de las Casas:** Deep in the heart of the Maya highlands, San Cristóbal has shops, open plazas, and markets that feature the distinctive waist-loomed wool and cotton textiles of the region, as well as leather shoes, handsome pottery, and Guatemalan textiles. Highland Maya Indians sell direct to tourists from their armloads of textiles, dolls, and attractive miniature likenesses of Subcomandante Marcos—complete with ski masks. See "San Cristóbal de las Casas" in chapter 9.

8 THE HOTTEST NIGHTLIFE

Although, as expected, Cancún is the source of much of the Yucatán's nightlife, that resort city isn't the only place to have a good time after dark. Along the Caribbean coast, beachside dance floors with live bands and extended happy hours in seaside bars dominate the nightlife. Here are some favorite hot spots, from live music in hotel lobby bars to hip techno dance clubs.

- **Cancún:** Longstanding Cancún favorites **Carlos 'n' Charlie's** and **Dady'O** offer potent drinks, hot music, and wild (if sometimes sloppy) dance floors. For a more cosmopolitan setting, **La Madonna** is a fashionable martini bar and restaurant in the La Isla Shopping Village, while **Bling,** with its outdoor terrace overlooking the lagoon, is the city's most chic cocktail venue. See chapter 5.

- **Forum by the Sea:** This seaside entertainment center in Cancún has it all: a dazzling array of dance clubs, sports bars, fast food, and fine dining, with shops open late as well. You'll find plenty of familiar names here, including the Hard Rock Cafe and Rainforest Cafe. It's also the home of what remains Cancún's hottest club, **CoCo Bongo,** which regularly packs in up to 3,000 revelers. See p. 113.

- **The City:** One of Cancún's hottest nightclubs, the City is a raging day-and-night club, offering a Beach Club with a pool, beach activities, and food and bar service, and the sizzling Club, at which the world's top DJs have spun through the night until the sun once again rises over the turquoise waters. This is truly a City that never sleeps. See p. 113.

- **Quinta Avenida (Playa del Carmen):** Stroll along lively, pedestrian-only Fifth Avenue to find the bar that's right for you. With live-music venues, tequila bars, sports bars, and cafes, you're sure to find something to fit your mood. See p. 146.

- **San Cristóbal de las Casas:** This city, small though it may be, has a live-music scene that can't be beat for fun and atmosphere. The bars and clubs are all within walking distance, and they're a real bargain. See "San Cristóbal de las Casas" in chapter 9.

9 THE MOST LUXURIOUS HOTELS

- **Aqua** (Cancún; www.feel-aqua.com): This is the trendiest resort in Cancún, a privileged spa-retreat for the urban jet-set. Completely rebuilt after having been destroyed by Hurricane Wilma, Aqua features spacious oceanview rooms, eight beachfront pools, an invigorating spa, world-class cuisine, and exceptional service. See p. 92.

- **Royal** (Cancún; www.realresorts.com.mx): The Royal is a stunning all-inclusive, adults-only resort in which luxury abounds, from the sprawling infinity pools and gorgeous beach to the gourmet restaurants and sophisticated spa. The elegant marble lobby looks out one side to the Caribbean and the other to the lagoon, and the guest suites offer

every conceivable amenity, including two-person Jacuzzis. Guests in the top-category suites have access to BMW Mini Coopers. The all-inclusive package includes gourmet meals, premium drinks, and evening entertainment. See p. 97.

- **JW Marriott** (Cancún; www.jwmarriott cancun.com): This gorgeous resort affords elegance without pretense, combining classic and Caribbean styling with warm Mexican service. The inviting free-form infinity pool extends to the white-sand beach, and families feel just as comfortable here as romance-seeking couples. The hotel includes a spectacular 3,250-sq.-m (35,000-square-foot) spa. See p. 94.

- **Ritz-Carlton Cancún** (Cancún; www.ritzcarlton.com): For years, thick carpets, sparkling glass and brass, and rich mahogany have surrounded guests at this hotel, the standard-bearer of luxury in Cancún. The service is impeccable, leaving guests with an overall sense of pampered relaxation. Its restaurants are among the best in the city. See p. 96.

- **Presidente InterContinental Cozumel** (Cozumel; www.intercontinentalcozumel.com): Surrounded by shady palms, this hotel also has the best beach on the island, right in front of Paraíso Reef. Favorite rooms are the deluxe beachside units with spacious patios and direct access to the beach—you can even order romantic in-room dining on the patios, complete with a trio to serenade you. See p. 141.

- **The Tides Riviera Maya** (north of Playa del Carmen; www.tidesriviera maya.com): Small, secluded, and private, the Tides offers extraordinary personal service and spa treatments. Rooms are spread throughout the jungle, and there's a beautiful seaside pool and restaurant. See p. 151.

- **Maroma** (north of Playa del Carmen; www.maromahotel.com): You can't ask for a better setting for a resort than this beautiful stretch of Caribbean coast with palm trees and manicured gardens. You'll start to relax before you even take the first sip of your welcome cocktail. Service is very attentive, and the rooms are large and luxurious. See p. 151.

- **Hacienda Xcanatún** (outskirts of Mérida; www.xcanatun.com): With its large, boldly designed suites built with extravagance in mind, sprawling grounds, private spa, excellent restaurant, and ample staff, this hotel masters the difficult trick of being compact in size but expansive in offerings. See "Haciendas & Hotels" on p. 200.

- **Hacienda Puerta Campeche** (Campeche; www.luxurycollection.com): Not a hacienda at all, really, this gorgeous hotel was created out of several adjoining colonial houses. This makes for a large property (especially for having only 15 rooms), with an open area in back featuring a pool and tropical gardens under ancient crumbling walls. From any vantage point the hotel is beautiful—both in overall layout and design details. And the service is impeccable. See p. 234.

10 THE BEST INEXPENSIVE INNS

- **Rey del Caribe Hotel** (Cancún; www.reycaribe.com): An inexpensive retreat in downtown Cancún, this hotel has considered every detail in its quest for an organic and environmentally friendly atmosphere. Set in a tropical garden, the Rey del Caribe provides sunny rooms, warm service, yoga and meditation classes, and healthful dining—all a welcome respite from party-hearty Cancún. See p. 99.

- **Hotel Colonial** (Campeche; ⓒ **981/816-2222**): Okay, so it's not the most comfortable hotel in town, but it is by far the most endearing. It exudes character and a sense of timelessness that relaxes the spirit and transports guests to an uncomplicated era. And for $25, it's a steal. See p. 234.

- **Casa San Juan Bed & Breakfast** (Mérida; www.casasanjuan.com): This B&B, in a colonial house in Mérida's historic district, is the perfect combination of comfort and character at a great price. The guest rooms in the original building evoke an earlier time, while the modern rooms in back are quite large and border a lovely patio. See p. 203.

- **Hotel Real del Valle** (San Cristóbal; ☏ **967/678-0680**): In a city of inexpensive lodgings, this beats all the other bargain hotels for its combination of location, room size, and service. See p. 275.

11 THE BEST UNIQUE INNS

- **Casa de los Sueños** (Isla Mujeres; www.casadelossuenosresort.com): This B&B steeped in vibrant colors seems to descend into the cool Caribbean Sea. Its small, but well-appointed, spa "Zenter," which is also accessible to nonguests, offers yoga classes, massages, and holistic spa treatments, which take place either outdoors or in a tranquil indoor space. See p. 123.
- **Hotel Villa Rolandi Gourmet & Beach Club** (Isla Mujeres; www.villarolandi.com): In addition to being steps away from an exquisite private cove, a tranquil infinity pool, and Isla's finest restaurant, this intimate inn also pampers guests with every conceivable in-room amenity. Each unit even has a private Jacuzzi on the balcony and a shower that converts into a steam room. Guests are offered free transportation from Cancún via the hotel's private yacht. See p. 123.
- **Deseo Hotel + Lounge** (Playa del Carmen; www.hoteldeseo.com): Perhaps it should be Hotel = Lounge. That might be an overstatement, but the lounge is at the center of everything, making Deseo the perfect fit for outgoing types who are into an alternative lodging experience. Enjoy a cocktail at the bar or on one of the large daybeds and chill to the modern, er, lounge music. See p. 157.
- **Casa Mexilio** (Mérida; www.casamexilio.com): An imaginative arrangement of rooms around a courtyard features a pool surrounded by a riot of tropical vegetation. The rooms are divided among different levels for privacy and are connected by stairs and catwalks. Breakfast here provides an extra incentive for getting out of bed. See p. 202.
- **Casa Na-Bolom** (San Cristóbal de las Casas; www.nabolom.org): This unique house-museum is terrific for anthropology buffs. Built as a seminary in 1891, it was transformed into the headquarters of two anthropologists. The 12 guest rooms, named for surrounding villages, are decorated with local objects and textiles; all rooms have fireplaces and private bathrooms, and the room rate includes breakfast. See p. 269.

12 THE BEST RESTAURANTS

Best doesn't necessarily mean most luxurious. Although some of the restaurants listed here are fancy affairs, others are simple places to get fine, authentic Yucatecan cuisine.

- **Gustino** (Cancún; ☏ **998/848-9600**): The JW Marriott's signature restaurant is a gourmand's paradise, with fresh seafood, steaks, and homemade pastas prepared in the open kitchen using classic Italian ingredients. The beautiful dining room makes this one of the city's most romantic places to dine. See p. 102.
- **Labná** (Ciudad Cancún; ☏ **998/892-3056**): Steep yourself in traditional Yucatecan culture at this downtown eatery, which showcases Maya cuisine and music. The Labná Special samples four of the region's best dishes, including baked suckling pig with guacamole. See p. 105.

- **La Habichuela** (Ciudad Cancún; ☎ 998/884-3158): In Cancún's original downtown, this gourmet seafood restaurant is a romantic retreat off the beaten path. An expert waitstaff attends to the diners seated in the restaurant's lovely garden patio. See p. 104.
- **Thai** (Cancún; ☎ 998/144-0364): This enchanting Thai restaurant offers a handful of secluded tables in individual *palapas* over the lagoon. The waterfront setting provides a romantic backdrop to the classic and contemporary Thai cuisine. Plus, the restaurant's chill- out lounge makes for a perfect before or after dinner drink. See p. 103.
- **100% Natural for *Licuados:*** This casual eatery serves terrific breakfasts and healthy snacks throughout the day. Come for one of the *licuados,* drinks made from fresh fruit mixed with water or milk. The chain offers a wide selection, including innovative mixtures such as the Cozumel (spinach, pineapple, and orange) and the Caligula (orange, pineapple, beet, celery, parsley, carrot, and lime juices)—a healthy indulgence. Cancún has several branches. See p. 105.
- **Casa Rolandi** (Isla Mujeres; ☎ 998/877-0700): This exquisite restaurant attached to the Casa Rolandi boutique hotel serves the island's finest cuisine. The open-air establishment sits adjacent to the Caribbean and offers wonderful fresh fish, seafood, and pastas. See p. 126.
- **Cabaña del Pescador** (Cozumel; no phone): If you want an ideally seasoned, succulent lobster dinner, Cabaña del Pescador (Lobster House) is the place.

If you want anything else, you're out of luck—lobster dinner, expertly prepared, is all it serves. When you've achieved perfection, why bother with anything else? See p. 142.

- **Prima** (Cozumel; ☎ 987/872-4242): The Italian food here is fresh, fresh, fresh—from the hydroponically grown vegetables to the pasta and garlic bread. And it's all prepared after you walk in, most of it by owner Albert Domínguez, who concocts unforgettable shrimp fettuccine with pesto, crab ravioli with cream sauce, and crisp house salad in a chilled bowl. See p. 142.
- **Media Luna** (Playa del Carmen; ☎ 984/873-0526): The inviting atmosphere of this sidewalk cafe on Quinta Avenida is enough to lure you in. The expertly executed and innovative menu, together with great prices, makes it one of the top choices on the Caribbean coast. See p. 161.
- **Yaxché** (Playa del Carmen; ☎ 984/873-2502): No restaurant in the Yucatán explores the region's culinary traditions and use of local ingredients more than this one. Its menu presents several pleasant surprises and is a welcome relief from the standard offerings of most Yucatecan restaurants. See p. 160.
- **La Pigua** (Campeche; ☎ 981/811-3365): Campeche's regional specialty is seafood, and nowhere else will you find seafood like this. Mexican caviar, coconut-battered shrimp, and chiles stuffed with shark are just a few of the unique specialties. Thinking about La Pigua's pompano in a fine green herb sauce makes me want to start checking flight schedules. See p. 235.

The Yucatán, Tabasco & Chiapas in Depth

by Christine Delsol

Barely 35 years ago, the only people visiting the Yucatán were archaeologists headed to the ruins and scuba divers bound for Cozumel. Miles and miles of Caribbean coast sat ignored, except for the occasional fisherman. The changes wrought on the Yucatán Peninsula and even distant Chiapas by Cancún's creation and growth have transformed the region from a forgotten backwater to a major international destination within the span of a single generation.

Tourism, once an afterthought, is now the big enchilada. The change is most visible on the coast, where fishing villages and coconut plantations gave way to modern developments marching in lock step all the way south to Tulum and inching beyond. For the young Maya of the interior villages, growth means new work opportunities, an end to isolation, and their first close contact with the modern world—specifically the modern world in vacation mode. The shift from village society to vacation paradise is the very definition of culture shock, which the implacable Maya meet with equanimity.

Tourism also made its way inland, first to the splendid Yucatán capital of Mérida and the major ruins—Chichén Itzá, Uxmal, and Palenque—and then, over time, to the barely uncovered ancient cities of the deep interior. The ruins are wonders to behold, and it seems that every year brings new archeological discoveries. Some Maya ruins are just as newly discovered as some of the Caribbean resorts are newly built.

Curiously, all the excavation and renovation has left small town life little changed. Coastal natives not swept up in the tourism boom were relocated inland, where they continue their ancestors' ways. Families of workers in the tourist palaces remain in the tropical forest, living in round thatch houses with no electricity, indoor plumbing, or paved roads, gathering plants for food and medicine, cooling off in hidden cenotes, and appealing to the gods for successful crops. To explore an older world where the Mayan tongue's distinct intonations fill the air and traditions carry on as they have for untold centuries, you have only to drive inland from the Caribbean coast, venture to Campeche on the Gulf shore, or cross over into Chiapas.

The turquoise waters and tropical climate may beckon first, but what will ultimately draw you back, again and again, is the unique character of this land and its people. There is simply no other place like it.

1 THE YUCATÁN, TABASCO & CHIAPAS NOW

In the five states that make up the Yucatán and southeastern Mexico, great wealth lives alongside abject poverty. Paradoxically, the indexes of both wealth and poverty in this region are higher than the national average. A tremendous amount of money flows into the area—in the case of Yucatán and Quintana Roo, from tourism; in the case of Campeche, Tabasco, and Chiapas, from the oil industry. Most residents reap little benefit from the economic boom. These five states have a total population of almost 10 million—10% of Mexico's population—but account for only about 6% of the economic activity.

In some cases, development has increased demand for local products and services. For example, fishermen and *palaperos,* the native people who create the thatched roofs *(palapas)* that crown so many restaurants and hotels, are in high demand whenever a hurricane brushes the coast. At the same time, development has destroyed the livelihood of other locals. Coastal coconut growers were wiped out when Cancún developers brought turf from Florida to build a golf course, unwittingly introducing a disease that killed the original coconut palms; destruction of mangroves, crucial to the coastal food chain, has diminished fishermen's catches. A similar give-and-take is at play within the oil economies of Tabasco and Chiapas.

While residents' incomes have not improved, tourism and oil prosperity does have indirect benefits. Even without a coherent policy to combat social ills, the government has paved most of the peninsula's roads and fitted out even the most remote villages with electricity. Purified water is widely available. And with the increasing emphasis on ecotourism, some remote villages have formed partnerships with tour companies that allow them to profit from tourism while controlling the number and type of visitors.

TODAY'S MAYA CULTURE & PEOPLE

Yucatán state, Tabasco, and Chiapas often feel like a separate country. Their *jarana* music, sweetened by clarinets, and a cuisine redolent with capers, achiote, and saffron, exude Caribbean sensuality. And the region's proud, gentle people display little of the machismo or the relentless salesmanship that tries visitors' patience in northern and central Mexico.

The sense of "otherness" grows partly from geographical isolation but even more from the Maya's fierce, centuries-long resistance to being absorbed into the Spanish spoils; some Maya refuse to recognize Mexican sovereignty even today. All of which makes their warm, generous natures as much a wonder as their famous pyramid at Chichén Itzá.

In the Yucatán, especially, your simplest transaction with a local easily evolves into spirited conversation. In the Peninsula's interior, where some Maya Indians are uneasy speaking Spanish, you are more likely to encounter some initial reticence. Usually, it's quickly overcome with smiles and inventive gestures.

You don't need to leave Cancún to meet the Maya; thousands travel from the interior to jobs at hotels and restaurants, many shifting effortlessly between Spanish, English, and Yukatek, the local Mayan language. More than 350,000 Maya living in the peninsula's three states speak Yukatek, and most, especially men, also speak Spanish.

The estimated 1 million Tabascan and Chiapan Maya, who speak four Mayan languages with dozens of dialects, are more reserved. Highland Maya around San Cristóbal de las Casas generally remain aloof from outside cultures, preferring to live in mountain hamlets and meeting only for ceremonies and market days. In their chilly cloud-forest homeland they, too, live much as their ancestors did, but with beliefs distinct from their peninsular relatives.

Though they held fast to their language through the Spanish conquest, the Maya lost much of their living memory of pre-Hispanic life; what they retained is cloaked in myth and worked into elements of Catholicism. That process of syncretism, as anthropologists call it, continues today

In the Beginning

The animals showed them the road. And then grinding the yellow corn and the white corn, Xmucané made nine drinks…and with it they created the muscles and the strength of man… After that they began to talk about the creation and the making of our first mother and father; of yellow corn and of white corn they made their flesh; of corn meal dough they made the arms and the legs of man.

—Popol Vuh

in the many Maya communities that have native churches.

The question of their ancestors' rightful place among the world's ancient civilizations might be as much a mystery to today's Maya people as it is to scholars. But nearly every year, archaeological discoveries of the art and architecture of the ancients add to the growing picture of a complex urban culture that thrived where only sparsely populated jungle exists today.

THE WELL-LIVED LIFE

In the face of economic inequality, Mexican society remains tremendously resilient and cohesive—due in no small part to the way Mexicans live. They place paramount value on family and friends, social gatherings, and living in the present; worrying about the future takes a back seat. Mexicans always have time to meet with friends for a drink or a cup of coffee or attend a family get-together. The many spirited public celebrations Mexico is known for are simply another manifestation of this attitude.

You won't find more amiable people anywhere on earth, and you can invite the full force of their natural gregariousness by being mindful of some social norms. Here's a start:

Slow Down The stereotype of "*mañana* time" is mostly true. Life obeys slower rhythms, and "on time" is a flexible concept. Arriving 30 minutes to two hours late to a party in someone's home is acceptable—in fact, coming at the specified hour would be rude, for your hosts almost certainly will not be ready. Here's the "mostly" part: Dinner invitations are less flexible; arrive within 30 minutes of the appointed hour. And be on time for business appointments, public performances, weddings, and funerals.

Meet & Greet Don't short-circuit the hellos and goodbyes; Mexican culture places higher value on proper social form than on saving time. A Mexican must at least say "*¡Buenos días!*" even to total strangers. When meeting a group of people, an individual will greet each one separately, no matter how long it takes. Handshakes, *abrazos* (embraces), and, among women, kisses abound. Stick to handshakes until your host decides you rate a more intimate greeting. But don't back away from an embrace—that would amount to a rejection of friendship.

Have a Little Respect Mexicans are lavish with titles of respect. Dispense *señor, señora,* and *señorita* (Mr., Mrs., Miss) freely. Teachers, lawyers, architects, and other professionals have earned the right to a title: *licenciado* for lawyers (and some other professions requiring a college degree), *maestro* or *maestra* for elementary school teachers, *profesor* or *profesora* for secondary or college teachers, and so forth. Mexicans have two surnames, father's first and mother's second. Both appear on business cards (the mother's name might be abbreviated to an initial), but when addressing people, use just the first (paternal) surname.

Don't Get Huffy Mexicans are genuinely interested in foreigners. If they stare, it's friendly curiosity. They like to practice their English, and will ask about family, friends, money, and other intimate matters. If you are over 30 and have no children, they may express deep concern. Don't take it personally.

Show Some Culture Like most people, Mexicans quickly size up people they meet. Most divide the world into the well-raised and cultured *(bien educado)* and the poorly raised *(mal educado)*. Don't be shy about trying out your rudimentary Spanish; even the most elementary attempt is appreciated because it shows your interest in the culture. To be categorized as a foreigner is no big deal. What's important in Mexico is to be categorized as a cultured foreigner and not one of the barbarians.

2 A LOOK AT THE PAST

PRE-HISPANIC CIVILIZATIONS

The earliest "Mexicans" might have been Stone Age hunter-gatherers from the north, descendants of a race that had crossed the Bering Strait and reached North America around 12,000 B.C. A more recent theory points to an earlier crossing of peoples from Asia to the New World. What we do know is that Mexico was populated by 10,000 B.C. Sometime between 5200 and 1500 B.C., these early people began practicing agriculture and domesticating animals.

The Olmecs & Maya: The Pre-Classic Period (1500 B.C.–A.D. 300)

Agriculture eventually provided enough food to support large communities, with enough surplus to free some people from agricultural work. A civilization emerged that we call the **Olmec**—an enigmatic people who settled the lower Gulf Coast, today's Tabasco and Veracruz states. Anthropologists regard them as the mother culture of Mesoamerica because they established a pattern for later civilizations ranging from northern Mexico to Central America. The Olmec developed a basic calendar, established principles of urban layout and architecture, and originated the cult of the jaguar and the sacredness of

jade. They probably also bequeathed the sacred ball game common to all Meso-american culture.

A defining feature of the Olmec was its colossal carved stone heads, several of which reside today in the Parque Museo La Venta in Villahermosa, Tabasco. Their purpose and meaning remain a mystery, but they were immense projects, sculpted from basalt mined miles inland and transported to the coast, probably by river rafts. Their rounded, baby-faced look, marked by a peculiar, high-arched lip—a "jaguar mouth"—is an identifying mark of Olmec sculpture.

The **Maya** civilization began developing in the pre-Classic period, around 500 B.C. Understanding of this period is sketchy, but Olmec influences show up everywhere. The Maya perfected the Olmec calendar and developed their ornate system of hieroglyphic writing and the early architecture. The people of **Teoti-huacán,** north of present-day Mexico City, and the **Zapotec** of Monte Albán, in the valley of Oaxaca, also emerged around this time.

Teotihuacan, Monte Alban & Palenque: The Classic Period (A.D. 300–900)

The rise and fall of these three city-states are bookends to the Classic Period, the height of pre-Columbian Mesoamerican

It's All in the Game

The ancient Maya played a game with a solid rubber ball of such importance that ball courts appear in virtually every Maya city (Bonampak is a rare exception). They were laid out in an I shape with sloping walls in the center. Similar ball courts have been found as far south as Nicaragua and as far north as Arizona.

We know little about this sacred game or its rules. What we do know from ancient depictions of the game, early accounts by the Spanish, and the Maya "bible," the Popol Vuh, is that the ball was heavy and could inflict injury. Wearing thick padding and protective gear, players formed teams of 2 to 10 members, the object being to propel the ball through a stone ring or other goal using mainly the hips.

We also know the ball game was part sport and part religious ritual based on the Maya's cosmological belief system. It sometimes involved sacrifice, though we're not sure whether the winners, the losers, or perhaps prisoners of war were sacrificed. In the Popol Vuh, the hero twins, Hunahpu and Xbalanque, challenge the lords of the underworld to a ball game, playing part of the game with the head of one twin. Eventually the twins win and are allowed to return to the world of the living. Playing the ball game, then, might have been one way to cheat the underworld.

art and culture. Achievements include the pyramids and palaces of Teotihuacán; the ceremonial center of Monte Albán; and the stelae and temples of Palenque, Bonampak, and Calakmul. The Maya also made significant discoveries in science, including the concept of zero in mathematics and a complex calendar with which priests predicted eclipses and the movements of the stars.

Teotihuacán (100 B.C.–A.D. 700—near present-day Mexico City), a well-organized city built on a grid, is thought to have had 100,000 or more inhabitants at its zenith, led by an industrious, literate, and cosmopolitan ruling class. The city exerted tremendous influence as far away as Guatemala and the Yucatán Peninsula. Its feathered serpent god, Quetzalcóatl, joined the pantheon of many succeeding cultures, including the Toltecs, who brought the cult to the Yucatán. Teotihuacán's refined aesthetics, seen in its

beautiful, highly stylized sculpture and ceramics, show up in Maya and Zapotec objects. Around the 7th century, the city was abandoned for unknown reasons. Who these people were and where they went remains a mystery.

Toltecs & Aztec Invasions: The Post-Classic Period (A.D. 900–1521)

Warfare became more pervasive during this period, and these later civilizations were less sophisticated than those of the Classic period. The **Toltec** of central Mexico established their capital at Tula in the 10th century. Originally one of the barbarous hordes that periodically migrated from the north, they were influenced by remnants of Teotihuacán culture at some point and adopted the feathered-serpent god Quetzalcóatl. The Toltec maintained a large military class, and Tula spread its influence across Mesoamerica. But their

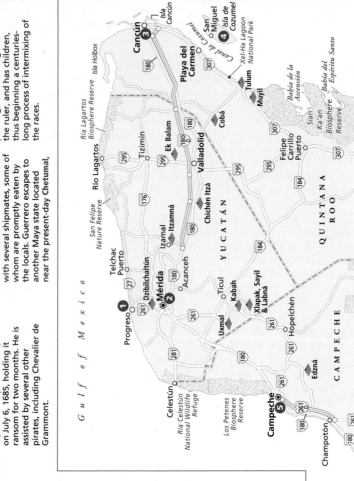

1 A large asteroid 1.6 to 8 km (1–5 miles) wide strikes the earth 65 million years ago, creating environmental havoc that leads to the extinction of the dinosaurs.

2 In 1845, the landowners of the Yucatán declare their independence from Mexico. They soon suffer terrible defeats during the Caste War, an armed revolt of Indians, and are forced to beg the Mexican government to send an army to rescue them.

3 In 1974 a government computer programmed to calculate all variables determining the creation of a new mega resort selects a deserted island on the northern Caribbean Coast and Cancún is born.

4 Gold found on Cozumel during an aborted Spanish expedition of the Yucatán Peninsula in 1516 arouses the interest of the Spanish governor in Cuba, who sends Juan de Grijalva on an expedition, followed by another, led by Hernán Cortez.

5 The famous Dutch pirate Laurens de Graaf, aka Lorencillo, captures the port of Campeche on July 6, 1685, holding it ransom for two months. He is assisted by several other pirates, including Chevalier de Grammont.

6 In 1511, Gonzalo Guerrero, a Spanish shipwreck survivor, washes ashore on the Yucatán with several shipmates, some of whom are promptly eaten by the locals. Guerrero escapes to another Maya state located near the present-day Chetumal, where he adopts Maya customs, including tattooing and piercing, weds a daughter of the ruler, and has children, thus beginning a centuries-long process of intermixing of the races.

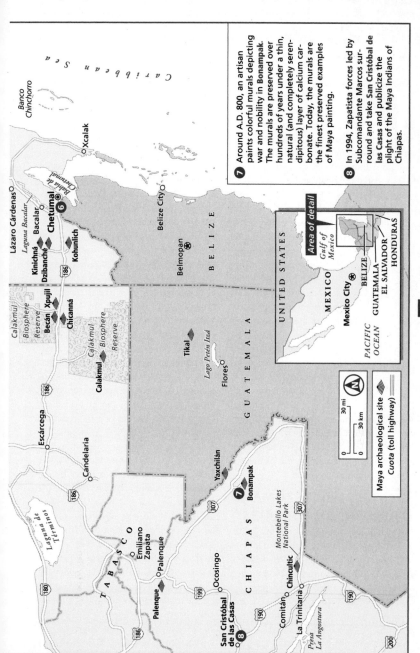

7 Around A.D. 800, an artisan paints colorful murals depicting war and nobility in Bonampak. The murals are preserved over hundreds of years under a thin, natural (and completely serendipitous) layer of calcium carbonate. Today, the murals are the finest preserved examples of Maya painting.

8 In 1994, Zapatista forces led by Subcomandante Marcos surround and take San Cristóbal de las Casas and publicize the plight of the Maya Indians of Chiapas.

might was played out by the 13th century, probably because of civil war and battles with invaders from the north.

The Maya of the Yucatán, especially the **Xiu** and **Itzáes,** might have departed from the norm with their broad trading networks and multiple influences from the outside world. They built beautiful cities in and around the Yucatán's Puuc hills, south of Mérida, their architecture characterized by elaborate exterior stonework above door frames and extending to the roofline. Impressive examples include the Codz Poop at Kabah and the palaces at Uxmal, Sayil, and Labná. Chichén Itzá, also ruled by Itzáes, was associated with the Puuc cities but shows strong Toltec influence in its architectural style and its cult of Quetzalcóatl, renamed Kukulkán.

The exact nature of the Toltec influence on the Maya is a subject of debate, but an intriguing myth in central Mexico tells how Quetzalcóatl quarrels with Tezcatlipoca and is tricked into leaving Tula. Quetzalcóatl heads east toward the morning star, vowing someday to return. In the language of myth, this could be a metaphor for a civil war between two factions in Tula, each led by the priesthood of a particular god. Could the losing faction have migrated to the Yucatán and later ruled Chichén Itzá? Perhaps. What we do know is that this myth of Quetzalcóatl's eventual return became, in the hands of the Spanish, a powerful weapon of conquest.

CORTEZ, MOCTEZUMA & THE SPANISH CONQUEST

In 1517, the first Spaniards arrived in Mexico and skirmished with Maya Indians off the coast of Campeche. A shipwreck left several Spaniards stranded as prisoners of the Maya. Another Spanish expedition, under **Hernán Cortez,** landed on Cozumel in February 1519. The coastal Maya were happy to tell Cortez about the gold and riches of the Aztec empire in central Mexico. Disobeying all orders from his

superior, the governor of Cuba, Cortez promptly sailed to the mainland and embarked on one of history's most bizarre culture clashes.

He sailed with his army to Tabasco, established a settlement in Veracruz, and worked his way up the Gulf Coast during the height of the Aztec empire's wealth and power. **Moctezuma II** ruled over the central and southern highlands and extracted tribute from lowland peoples; his greatest temples were literally plated with gold and encrusted with the blood of sacrificial captives. A fool, a mystic, and something of a coward, Moctezuma dithered in Tenochtitlán while Cortez blustered and negotiated his way into the highlands. Moctezuma, terrified, was convinced that Cortez was the returning Quetzalcóatl. By the time he arrived in the Aztec capital, Cortez had accumulated 6,000 indigenous allies who resented paying tribute to the Aztec. In November 1519, he took Moctezuma hostage in an effort to leverage control of the empire.

In the middle of Cortez's manipulations, another Spanish expedition arrived with orders to end Cortez's unauthorized mission. Cortez hastened to the coast, routed the rival force, and persuaded the vanquished to join him on his return to Tenochtitlán. The capital had erupted in his absence, and the Aztec chased his garrison out of the city. Moctezuma was killed during the attack, whether by the Aztec or the Spaniards is not clear. For the next year and a half, Cortez laid siege to Tenochtitlán, aided by rival Indians and a devastating smallpox epidemic. When the Aztec capital fell, all of central Mexico lay at the conquerors' feet, vastly expanding the Spanish empire. The king legitimized Cortez after his victory and ordered the forced conversion to Christianity of the new colony, to be called New Spain. By 1540, New Spain's territory included possessions from Vancouver to Panama. In the 2 centuries that followed, Franciscan and Augustinian friars converted millions of Indians to Christianity, and the Spanish lords built huge feudal estates on which Indian farmers served as serfs. The silver and gold that Cortez looted made Spain the richest country in Europe.

THE RISE OF MEXICO CITY & SPANISH COLONIALISM

Cortez set about building a new city upon the ruins of the Aztec capital, collecting tributes the Indians once paid to Moctezuma. Many paid in labor. This became the model for building the new colony.

Over the 3 centuries of the colonial period, Spain became rich from New World gold and silver chiseled out by Indian labor. The colonial elite built lavish homes filled with ornate furniture and draped themselves in imported velvets, satins, and jewels. Under the new class system, those born in Spain considered themselves superior to the *criollos* (Spaniards born in Mexico). People of other races and the *castas* (Spanish-Indian, Spanish-African, or Indian-African mixes) occupied the bottom rungs of society. Wealthy colonists lived extravagantly despite the Crown's insatiable demand for taxes and contributions.

Criollo discontent with Spanish rule following the 1767 expulsion of the Jesuits simmered for years. In 1808, **Napoleon** invaded Spain, deposed Charles IV and crowned his brother **Joseph Bonaparte.** To many in Mexico, allegiance to France was unthinkable. The next logical step was revolt.

HIDALGO, JUAREZ & MEXICO'S INDEPEN-DENCE

In 1810, **Father Miguel Hidalgo** set off the rebellion with his *grito,* the fabled cry for independence, in the town of Dolores, Guanajuato. With **Ignacio Allende** and a citizen army, Hidalgo marched toward Mexico City. Although he ultimately failed and was executed, Hidalgo is honored as "the Father of Mexican Independence." Another priest, José María Morelos, kept the revolt alive with several successful campaigns until 1815, when he, too, was captured and executed.

When the Spanish king who replaced Joseph Bonaparte decided to make social reforms in the colonies, conservative powers in Mexico decided they didn't need Spain after all. Royalist **Agustín de Iturbide** defected in 1821 and conspired with the rebels to declare independence from Spain, with himself as emperor. However, internal dissension soon brought Iturbide down, and Mexico was proclaimed a republic.

The young, politically unstable republic ran through 36 presidents in 22 years, in the midst of which it lost half its territory in the disastrous **Mexican-American War (1846-48).** The central figure, **Antonio López de Santa Anna,** assumed the presidency no fewer than 11 times and just might hold the record for frequency of exile. He was ousted for good in 1855 and finished his days in Venezuela.

Amid continuing political turmoil after ragtag Mexican troops defeated the well-equipped French force in a battle near Puebla in 1862 (now celebrated as Cinco de Mayo), conservatives hit upon the idea of bringing in a Habsburg to regain control. **Archduke Maximilian of Austria,** with the backing of the French, stepped in as emperor in 1864. After 3 years of civil war, the French finally abandoned the emperor's cause, and Maximilian was captured and executed in 1867. His adversary and successor as president was **Benito Juárez,** a Zapotec Indian lawyer and one of Mexico's greatest heroes. Juárez did his best to unify and strengthen his country before dying of a heart attack in 1872, and his plans and visions bore fruit for decades.

Of Henequén & Haciendas

Commercial production of *henequén,* the thorny agave that yields the rope fiber we know as sisal, began in 1830. Demand became almost insatiable during World War I and, with a virtual monopoly on the *oro verde* ("green gold"), Yucatán went from one of Mexico's poorest states to one of its richest. In addition to their baronial homes along Mérida's Paseo de Montejo, landowners built plantations to meet their every comfort when they traveled to the countryside. Their haciendas were small, self-contained cities supporting hundreds of workers, and each had its own school, infirmary, store, church, cemetery, and even a jail.

Invention of synthetic fibers during World War II devastated the henequén industry; abandoned haciendas became grand derelicts until a new generation of wealthy Mexicans began turning them into hotels in the early 1990s.

YUCATECAN INDEPENDENCE & THE CASTE WAR

In 1845, with Mexico unable to establish a stable government, the Yucatán's landed oligarchy decided to declare independence. They armed the populace—including Indians who had slaved their entire lives on the haciendas—to defend the territory from invasion. Resentful of their serfdom, the Indians realized it wasn't so important to them whether their oppressors lived in Mexico City or Mérida. They raised their arms against the landowners, igniting the War of the Castes. The slaughter would continue, off and on, for 60 years.

The peasants soon controlled most of the countryside, capturing several towns and the city of Valladolid. Mérida, too, was on the verge of surrender when planting season arrived. Rather than press their advantage and take the capital, the Maya inexplicably laid down their weapons to return to their corn fields. Yucatecan troops quickly regrouped, swore fealty to Mexico and called for a government army. Eventually the Maya rebels were driven back into what is now Quintana Roo, where they were largely left on their own, virtually a nation within a nation, until a

Mexican army with modern weaponry finally penetrated the region at the turn of the 20th century.

DIAZ, ZAPATA, PANCHO VILLA & THE MEXICAN REVOLUTION

A few years after Juárez's death, one of his generals, **Porfirio Díaz,** seized power in a coup. He ruled Mexico from 1877 to 1911, a period now called the "Porfiriato," maintaining power through repression and by courting the favor of powerful nations. With foreign investment came the concentration of great wealth in few hands, and discontent deepened.

In 1910, **Francisco Madero** led an armed rebellion that became the Mexican revolution ("La Revolución" in Mexico; the revolution against Spain is the "Guerra de Independencia"). Díaz was exiled and is buried in Paris. Madero became president, but **Victoriano Huerta,** in collusion with U.S. ambassador Henry Lane Wilson, betrayed and executed him in 1913. Those who had answered Madero's call rose up again—the great peasant hero **Emiliano Zapata** in the south, and the seemingly invincible **Pancho Villa** in the central north, flanked by **Alvaro Obregón** and **Venustiano Carranza.** They eventually put Huerta to flight and began hashing out a new constitution.

For the next few years, Carranza, Obregón, and Villa fought among themselves; Zapata did not seek national power, though he fought tenaciously for land for the peasants. Carranza, who was president at the time, betrayed and assassinated Zapata. Obregón finally consolidated power and probably had Carranza assassinated. He, in turn, was assassinated when he tried to break one of the tenets of the revolution—no re-election. Not until **Lázaro Cárdenas** was elected in 1934 did the Revolution appear to have a chance. He implemented massive land redistribution, nationalized the oil industry, instituted many reforms and gave shape to the ruling political party (precursor to today's Partido Revolucionario Institucional, or **PRI**). Cárdenas is practically canonized by most Mexicans.

MODERN MEXICO

The presidents who followed were noted more for graft than leadership, and the party's reform principles were abandoned. In 1968, the government quashed a democratic student demonstration in Mexico City, killing several hundred people. Though the PRI maintained its grip on power, it lost its image as a progressive party.

Economic progress, particularly in the form of large development projects, became the PRI's sole basis for legitimacy. In 1974 the government decided to build a new coastal megaresort. To determine the ideal location, data crunchers loaded all the variables into a computer. Out popped Cancún, and Mexico's economy was forever changed.

The government weathered several bouts of social unrest caused by periodic devaluations of the peso. But in 1985, the devastating Mexico City earthquake brought down many of its new, supposedly earthquake-proof buildings, exposing the widespread corruption that had fostered the shoddy construction, and triggering criticism of the government's relief efforts.

Meanwhile, opposition parties were gaining strength. The two largest were the **PRD** (Partido de la Revolución Democrática) on the left and the **PAN** (Partido Acción National) on the right. To ensure its candidate, Carlos Salinas de Gortari, would win the 1988 presidential election over the PRD's Cuauhtémoc Cárdenas (formerly of the PRI and son of former President Lázaro Cárdenas), the government simply unplugged election computers and declared a system failure.

Under pressure at home and abroad, the government moved to demonstrate a new commitment to democracy and even began to concede electoral defeats for state governorships and legislative seats. Power struggles between factions of reformists and hardliners within the party led to several political assassinations, most notably of the PRI's next candidate, Luis Colosio. After that assassination and the crippling economic crisis of 1994, his successor, Ernesto Zedillo, spent his 6 years in office trying to stabilize the economy and bring transparency to government.

In 2000 he shepherded the first true elections in 70 years of one-party rule. The winner was PAN candidate **Vicente Fox,** a former businessman who ran on a platform of economic liberalization and anticorruption. Many Mexicans voted for him to see if the PRI would relinquish power more than for any other reason. It did, but Fox didn't prove to be the master politician that the situation required. His efforts to build a coalition with segments of the PRI failed, and he accomplished little during his last 3 years in office.

The extremely close and bitterly disputed presidential election of 2006 tested Mexico's nascent pluralism. The ruling of the elections tribunal, declaring PAN's **Felipe Calderón** the winner while denying the PRD's request for a recount, was profoundly unpopular. Losing candidate **Andrés Manuel López Obrador** did not take defeat gracefully and provoked a constitutional crisis that only time has managed to heal. President Calderón, recognizing the PRD campaign's resonance with the poor, announced programs to boost employment, alleviate poverty, and stabilize the skyrocketing price of tortillas.

His biggest challenge, however, has proved to be the alarming escalation of drug-related violence—a conflagration widely attributed to his policy of cracking down on traffickers who ferry the contraband through Mexico on its way to the United States. The violence, directed at government and law enforcement officials, is concentrated along the U.S.-Mexico border and several specific areas of northern and central Mexico. It hasn't touched southern Mexico much, and the region's tourist areas are the safest places in Mexico, but the blaring headlines have scared travelers away in droves.

A Tale of Two Hurricanes

By 1988, when Hurricane Gilbert swept through, Cancún had more than 200,000 residents, with more than 12,000 hotel rooms and 11,000 more on the drawing boards. The storm's destruction barely slowed the explosive growth; existing resorts were promptly remodeled and reopened, followed by dozens of new ones. But the decision to slash hotel rates to lure tourists back, combined with the drinking age of 18, had the unintended effect of making Cancún the spring-break capital of North America. Images of binge-drinking college hordes replaced idyllic scenes of couples and families playing tag with impossibly turquoise waves.

Ironically, another—and far more destructive—hurricane was the occasion for turning this image around. On October 18, 2005, Hurricane Wilma parked on top of the region, battering it with 240kmph (150mph) winds. The bridges linking the Hotel Zone with the island collapsed, electricity and water were out for 10 days, and the world's most celebrated beaches were scoured down to rock. Tens of thousands of tourists were stranded in shelters for as much as a week by the most destructive natural disaster in Mexican history, surpassing even the 1985 Mexico City earthquake.

The government, insurance companies, and major resort hotel chains mobilized a massive recovery effort. Restoration of more than 11km (7 miles) of white-powder beach with sand pumped 35km (22 miles) from the ocean bottom grabbed all the attention, but a more important transformation was in the works. Within 3 months, 18,000 of the 22,000 hotel rooms were ready for guests. Crews built new roads, installed better street lamps, planted thousands of palms, and installed modern sculptures. In rebuilding, in some cases from the ground up, resorts took pains to distance themselves from the spring-break crowd, going bigger, better, and more luxurious than ever, with price hikes to match.

A Sticky Habit

Cigar smoking and gum chewing are two pleasures that we have the Maya to thank for, and, of the two, the latter is the more innocuous. Gum comes from the sap of a species of zapote tree that grows in the Yucatán and Guatemala. Chewing causes it to release natural sugars and a mild, agreeable taste. From the Maya, the habit of chewing gum spread to other cultures and eventually to the non-Indian population. In the second half of the 19th century, a Mexican (said to have been General Santa Anna) introduced gum to the American Thomas Adams, who realized that it could be sweetened further and given other flavors. He brought the idea to the U.S. and marketed chewing gum with great success. Chemists have since figured out how to synthesize the gum, but the sap is still collected in parts of the Yucatán and Guatemala for making natural chewing gum. *Chicle* is the Spanish word originally from the Nahuatl (Aztec) *tzictli,* and those who live in the forest and collect the sap are called *chicleros.* Because the tree takes so long to produce more sap, there is no way to cultivate the tree commercially, so it is still collected in the wild.

3 EATING & DRINKING

The tacos and burritos familiar north of the border are mere appetizers on Mexico's vast and varied menu. Though certain staples grace plates throughout the country, long distances and two formidable mountain ranges gave rise to distinct regional cuisines that evolved independently. It is not only possible but also one of life's greatest pleasures to eat your way through Mexico without downing a single taco or burrito.

When the Spanish arrived, they found Mexico's natives cooking with corn, beans, chiles, tomatoes, and squash, combined with turkey and other wild game. Local women promptly incorporated beef, pork and lamb, nuts, fruits, cheese, spices, and sugar cane (by way of the Caribbean) contributed by the conquistadors. To the dismay of the Spaniards—and the delight of travelers today—the result was not a simulation of European cuisine but new versions of native dishes.

Mexican cooking remains simple at its core; most of the *picante* flavor is added afterward with the chile and salsa found on every table. Regional variations range from the basic but nutritious dishes of the north to seafood specialties of the coastal regions to the complex variety of Mexico City and the central states to the earthy, piquant creations of the Maya in the south.

The national dish, *chiles en nogada,* was created in Puebla to honor Augustín de Iturbide for his role in winning independence from Spain and is the pride of menus throughout Mexico. Large, mild poblano chiles are stuffed with as many as 30 ingredients, including ground meat, fruit, nuts, and spices, and then covered with a silky sauce of cream, cheese, and walnuts. A garnish of pomegranate seeds completes the red, white, and green theme representing the nation's new flag. The first bite of this mysterious concoction is guaranteed to make your eyes roll back in your head.

A Debt of Gratitude

Lost among the laurels heaped upon the ancient Maya for their contributions to science, mathematics, architecture, astronomy, and writing is the wide array of foods they introduced. It's no exaggeration to say the Maya changed the world's eating habits in the 1500s. Just try to imagine life without:

Avocado From its origins in southern Mexico, where it was used as an aphrodisiac, the avocado spread to the Rio Grande and central Peru before the Europeans found out about it.

Black Beans Archaeological digs indicate the black bean originated in southern Mexico and Central America more than 7,000 years ago. Still the favorite in and around the Yucatán, it has spread widely throughout Latin America, the Caribbean, and the southern United States.

Chiles Chiles have been cultivated in the Americas for more than 6,000 years. Blame Christopher Columbus for calling them "peppers," but credit him for their worldwide reach. Southern Mexico's Capsicum annuum species, with its many cultivars, is crucial to nearly every fiery cuisine in the world.

Chocolate The Maya's "food of the gods," made from the toasted, fermented seeds of the cacao tree, is arguably the New World's greatest gift to civilization. Though Cortez learned of chocolate from the Aztecs, the Maya ate it many centuries earlier and used cacao beans as currency.

Corn The creation myth in *Popul Vuh*, the Maya "bible," attributes humankind's very existence to this domesticated strain of wild grass, easily the most important food in the Americas. Thousands of years after corn became a dietary staple, the Maya started cultivating it around 2500 B.C. and abandoned their nomadic ways to settle in villages surrounded by cornfields.

Papaya The large, woody, fast-growing herb—commonly referred to as a tree—was used to treat stomach ailments. After spreading from southern Mexico, it now grows in every tropical country.

Tomatoes Even the Italians had to make do without tomato sauce before Columbus set out for the New World. Precursors originated in Peru, but the tomato as we know it came from the Yucatán, where the Maya cultivated it long before the conquest.

Vanilla The elixir from the world's only known edible orchid originally flavored Maya chocolate drinks. Southern Mexico's jungle is still the only place the orchid grows wild, pollinated by native stingless bees that produce Maya honey. The prized Tahitian vanilla, which came from Mexican stock, must be hand-pollinated.

THE STAPLES

TORTILLAS The tortilla is Mexico's bread, and sometimes its fork and spoon, used to scoop up food. Corn is cooked in water and lime, ground into grainy *masa* dough, patted and pressed into thin cakes, and cooked on a *comal* (hot griddle). Even restaurants that serve bread always have tortillas available. The flour tortilla developed in northern Mexico and is less common in the south.

ENCHILADAS The most famous of numerous Mexican dishes based on the tortilla was originally called *tortilla enchilada,* meaning a tortilla dipped in a chile sauce; variations include *entomatada* (dipped in tomato sauce) and *enfrijolada* (in a bean sauce). The basic enchilada, still sold in food stands, is a tortilla dipped in hot oil and then into chile (usually ancho) sauce, then quickly folded or rolled on a plate and sprinkled with chopped onions and *queso cotija* (crumbly white cheese), often served with fried potatoes and carrots. Restaurants serve more elaborate enchiladas filled with cheese, chicken, pork, or seafood, and sometimes prepared as a casserole. Southern Mexico's, enchiladas are often bathed in a rich *mole* sauce.

TACOS Anything folded or rolled into a tortilla—sometimes two, either soft or fried—is a taco. *Flautas* and quesadillas (except in Mexico City, where they are a different animal) are species of tacos. This is the quintessential Mexican fast food, sold in *taquerías* everywhere.

FRIJOLES Beans are served daily in most Mexican households. Pinto beans are widely used in northern Mexico, but black beans are the Yucatán's legumes of choice. Mexicans add only a little onion and garlic and a pinch of herbs, as beans are meant to be a counterpoint to spicy foods. They also may be served at the end of a meal with a spoonful of sour cream.

Fried leftover beans often appear as *frijoles refritos,* a side dish often translated "refried beans." The beans are in fact fried only once; the prefix *re* means "well" (as in "thoroughly"), so a better translation would be "well-fried beans."

TAMALES The ultimate take-out meal, tamales (singular: *tamal*) developed in pre-Hispanic Mexico and became more elaborate after the Spanish introduced pork and other ingredients. To make a *tamal,* you mix corn *masa* with lard, beat the batter, add a filling, wrap it, and cook it. Every region has its own specialty. The most popular *rellenos* (fillings) are pork and cheese, but they might be anything from fish to iguana, augmented by pumpkin, pineapple, rice, or peanuts, and tucked into a blanket of yellow, black, or purple masa. Tamales are usually steamed but may be baked or grilled; the jackets are most often dried corn husks or fresh corn or banana leaves but are sometimes fashioned from palm, avocado, or *chaya* (a spinach-like vegetable) leaves.

Yucatecan tamales have a distinctly Maya flavor, filled with pork or chicken marinated in *achiote* (an earthy, mildly tangy paste made from the annatto seed) and cooked in an underground pit or oven that chars the banana leaf black. Tabasco makes liberal use of freshwater fish and seafood, rice, and a dizzying array of exotic produce. Chiapas' marvelous variety of tamales might be filled with *mole, chicharrón* (crispy, fried pork rind), or even flower buds; the best known are *tamales de bola,* with pork rib, a prune, and a small dried chili, all wrapped up in a corn husk tied on top to form a ball *(bola).*

Local Wisdom

The chile runs in our veins.
—Laura Esquivel, author of *Like Water For Chocolate* (1989) in introduction to
La Cocina del Chile (2003)

CHILES Hardly a traditional dish in all of Mexico lacks chiles. Appearing in wondrous variety throughout Mexico, they are bestowed different names depending on whether they are fresh or dried. Chiles range from blazing hot with little discernible taste to mild with a rich, complex flavor, and they can be pickled, smoked, stuffed, or stewed. Among the best-known are the *pimiento,* the large, harmless bell pepper familiar in the United States; the fist-sized poblano, ranging from mild to very hot; the short, torpedo-shaped *serrano;* the skinny and seriously fiery *chile de árbol;* the *jalapeño,* stubby and hot; the *chipotle,* a dried and smoked jalapeño usually served in *adobo* (a vinegar and garlic paste); and the tiny, five-alarm *pequín.*

If you suffer from misadventure by chile, a drink of milk, a bite of banana or cucumber, a spoonful of yogurt, or—if all else fails—a bottle of beer will help extinguish the fire.

DRINKS

Coca-Cola is nearly as entrenched in Mexico's drinking habits as tequila, having been a fixture since 1926. Pepsi is also sold in every city and town. These and other American *refrescos* outsell Mexican brands such as Manzana, a carbonated apple juice. If you like your soft drinks cold,

specify *frío,* or you may get them *clima* (room temperature).

Better yet, treat yourself to **licuados**— refreshing smoothies of fresh fruit or juice, milk, and ice, sold in bright, clean shops all over Mexico. **Aguas frescas** ("fresh waters") are lighter drinks made by adding a small amount of fresh fruit juice and sugar to water. Hibiscus, melon, tamarind, and lime are common, but rice, flowers, cactus fruit (called *tuna* in Spanish), and other exotic ingredients find their way into these refreshments. And inexpensive, fresh-squeezed juices from every fruit you can name—and a few you can't—are one of Mexico's greatest pleasures.

Coffee is one of Mexico's most important exports, and Chiapas grows some of the best. Tarted-up coffee isn't Mexico's style. Your basic choices are *café Americano,* the familiar gringo-style brew; espresso and sometimes cappuccino, served in cafes; and the widely popular *café con leche,* translated as "coffee with milk" but more accurately described as milk with coffee. Potent, delicious *café de olla,* traditionally brewed in a clay pot with raw sugar and cinnamon, is getting harder to find.

Hot chocolate is a traditional drink, usually made with cinnamon and often some crushed almonds. Another traditional hot drink is *atole,* made from cornmeal,

Tequila 101

Tequila is a variety of mescal produced from the *A. tequilana* agave species, or blue agave, in the Tequila area of Jalisco state. In the past 15 years, tequila's quality and the popularity have soared. Distillers—all but one still based in Jalisco—have formed an association to establish standards for labeling and denomination. The best tequilas are 100% agave, made with a set minimum of sugar to prime the fermentation process. These tequilas come in three categories based on how they were stored: *Blanco* is white tequila aged very little, usually in steel vats. *Reposado* (reposed) is aged in wooden casks for between 2 months and a year. The coveted *añejo* (aged) tequila is stored in oak barrels for a year or more.

Food Hygiene

The days when you had to carry water purification tablets to return from a trip to Mexico with your intestines intact are long gone. Nearly all restaurants that serve middle-class Mexicans use filtered water, disinfect their vegetables, and buy ice made from purified water. If in doubt, look for ice with a rough cylindrical shape and a hollow center, produced by the same kind of machinery across the country. Street vendors and market stalls are less consistent. I love street food, so I find clean, busy places and stick with cooked foods and unpeeled fruit.

milk, cinnamon, and pureed fresh fruit, often served for breakfast.

Mexican **beer** generally is light and well-carbonated, all the better to tame the chile burn. Brands such as Bohemia, Corona, Dos Equis, Pacifica, Tecate and Modelo are favorites around the world. Mérida's Cerveceria Yucateca, alas, was bought by Modelo in 1979 and closed in 2002, but its León Negra and Montejo beers are still produced in central Mexico.

Tequila's poorer cousins, **pulque** and **mescal,** originated with *octli,* an Aztec agave drink produced strictly for feasts. Mexicans drank *pulque,* made from juice straight from the plant, for more 5,000 years, but it has recently given way to more refined—and more palatable—spirits. The Spanish learned they could create serious fire power by roasting the agave hearts, then extracting, fermenting, and distilling the liquids. Thus were born tequila and *mescal. Mescal,* famous for the traditional worm at the bottom of the bottle, is more potent than *pulque* but easier to swallow. It's also available commercially; *pulque* is found mostly in central Mexico's *pulquerías.*

Tequila, once consigned to a stereotype in bad Westerns, has lately acquired a sophisticated aura. A growing coterie of connoisseurs has spotlighted high-quality varieties and is making inroads on the knock-back-a-shot mentality in favor of sipping and swirling as you would with fine Scotch or French cognac.

Don't overlook southern Mexico's **local spirits.** Kahlúa, the Arabica coffee-flavored liquor ubiquitous in U.S. bars, is the Yucatán's best-known product. Xtabentún, a honey-anisette liqueur based on the Maya's ceremonial liquor produced from the morning glory whose nectar fueled local honey production, is a popular after-dinner cordial. Its best-known maker, D'Aristi of Mérida, also makes Caribe rum and the lesser-known Kalani, a coconut liqueur made from trees grown in the Yucatán. Other after-dinner liqueurs are flavored with native flowers such as hibiscus *(jamaica)* or fruit such as bananas *(plátano)* and pomegranate *(granada).*

REGIONAL SPECIALTIES

The Yucatán evolved in isolation from the rest of the country until recent decades, and its cuisine is an amalgam of native, European, Caribbean, and even Middle Eastern flavors and techniques. Some of the most recognizable tastes are *achiote,* sour oranges, lime juice, pumpkin seeds, and pickled onions. Turkey *(pavo),* still the most common meat in Yucatecan homes, is prominent on most menus, though beef, pork, and chicken have become staples. Fish and seafood reign along the coast.

Achiote and sour orange came to the Yucatán by way of the Caribbean; Edam cheese through historical trade with the Dutch; and peas, likely from the English. A wave of Lebanese immigration around the turn of the 20th century also made its

Dining Service Tips

- The afternoon meal is the main meal of the day, and many restaurants offer a multicourse daily special called *comida corrida* or *menú del día*. This is the least expensive way to get a full dinner.
- In Mexico you need to ask for your check; it is considered rude to present a check to someone who hasn't requested it. If you're in a hurry, ask for the check when your food arrives.
- Tips are about the same as in the U.S. Restaurants sometimes include a 15% value-added tax, which shows up on the bill as "IVA." This is effectively the tip, which you may add to if you like, but make sure you're not tipping twice.
- To summon the waiter, wave or raise your hand, but don't motion with your index finger, which is a demeaning gesture. If you need your check, it's OK to summon any waiter and ask, "La Cuenta, por favor"—or simply catch someone's eye and pantomime a scribbling motion against the palm of your hand.

mark; the spit-broiled *tacos al pastor* is basically Mexican gyros, and you might come across *kibbeh* made of beef or potatoes instead of lamb or *dolmas* wrapped in chaya instead of grape leaves.

The Yucatán's trademark dishes are *pollo* or *cochinita* (chicken or pork) *pibil*, meat marinated in achiote, bitter orange and spices, wrapped in banana leaves and barbecued or baked in a pit; *poc chuc*, pork slices marinated in sour orange and garnished with pickled onions; and *sopa de lima* (lime soup), made of shredded, lime-marinated turkey or chicken and topped with sizzling tortilla strips.

Try starting your day with *huevos moluleños*—fried eggs over sliced plantains, beans, and fried tortillas, topped with a dusting of salty cheese, tomato sauce, and peas—but only if you're ravenous. *Cochinita pibil* is also served in the morning. The best place to have the former is in any reputable restaurant; the best place for the latter would be a market such as El Mercado de Santa Ana in Mérida.

Customary dishes for the afternoon meal include *relleno negro*, turkey cooked with a paste of charred chiles and vegetables with bits of hard-boiled eggs; *escabeche blanco*, chicken or turkey cooked in a vinegar-based sauce; or *queso relleno*, mild Edam cheese stuffed with seasoned ground beef. The unique *Tikinxic* (or some variant of this name) is grilled fish that has been lightly marinated in an *achiote* paste. All are served in restaurants for the afternoon meal; in Cancún and on the coast, they also appear on the evening menu. Traditional evening foods are based on turkey and include such finger foods as *salbutes* and *panuchos*, two dishes of tortillas or masa cakes layered with *frijoles*, or shredded turkey or chicken.

Campeche also has its own culinary traditions, a marriage of Spanish cuisine, recipes brought by pirates from all over the world, and local fruits and vegetables. The signature dish, *pan de cazón* (baby shark casserole)—a layered dish of tortillas, black beans, and shredded baby shark meat, smothered in tomato sauce—reaches its greatest heights at La Pigua. Lying on the Gulf Coast, Tabasco has more in common with the Caribbean flavors of Veracruz, which developed close ties to Cuba during colonial times. *Veracruzana,* a lightly spiced blend of tomato and onion, bathes fresh fish, meat, and seafood. The specialty is the fish *pejelagarto,* whose mild, nutty taste is enhanced by chile and lemon; La Jangada in Villahermosa is a favorite place to indulge. *Camarón* (shrimp), *ostión* (oyster), and *pulpo* (octopus) are ubiquitous, delicious, and cheap.

The Maya of Chiapas were great mathematicians and astronomers, like their kin throughout the Yucatán, but they also were particularly accomplished in agriculture. Though they depended above all on corn, native herbs such as *chipilin,* a fragrant, thin-leaved plant, and *hoja santa,* the large anise-scented leaves that characterize much of southern Mexico's cooking, flavor the many varieties of Chiapas' famous tamales, which are heavier and larger than central Mexican tamales. With the introduction of European cattle, Chiapans also became expert ranchers and, as a corollary, cheese makers. Similar to neighboring Guatemala, Chiapas' cooking uses a lot of beef, either grilled or in a stew.

Be sure to read the food glossary in "Appendix: Survival Spanish," to learn more about regional dishes.

4 ART & ARCHITECTURE

Mexico's art, architecture, politics, and religion were inextricable for more than 3,000 years. The Maya were perhaps the most gifted artists in the Americas, producing fantastically lifelike stone sculptures, soaring temples clad in colors we can only guess at today, and delicately painted pottery. The Spanish conquest in A.D. 1521 influenced the style and subject of Mexican art, yet failed to stamp out its roots.

PRE-HISPANIC FORMS

Nowhere is the interplay of religion and art more striking than in Mexico's renowned pyramids, which were temples crowning a truncated platform. Maya structures also served as navigation aids, administrative and ceremonial centers, tombs, astronomical outlooks, and artistic canvases.

Circular buildings such as Chichén Itzá's El Caracol and Palenque's observatory tower aided Maya priests' remarkably accurate astral calculations, used primarily for astrological divination but surprisingly accurate by modern astronomical standards. Chichén

Itzá's El Castillo itself is a massive and stunningly accurate calendar, with four staircases of 91 steps, equaling the 365 days of the solar year when the central platform is added. The 18 terraces on each face of the pyramid symbolize the number of months in the Maya calendar; the 52 panels on the terraces symbolize the 52-year cycle, when the solar and religious calendars converge. The architects aligned the temple to create the equinox phenomenon of the stairway's shadow slithering down a corner of the pyramid to the giant serpent's head at the bottom.

The ancient architecture shows a variety of influences, though the practice of building one pyramid on top of another was widespread. Chichén Itzá's strong Toltec influence, with its angular, stepped profiles, emphasizes war and human sacrifice; Uxmal's refined and more purely Maya geometry, including the beautifully sloped and rounded Temple of the Magician, incorporates the varied elevations of the Puuc hills.

The unjustly overlooked Edzná in Campeche state displays roof combs and corbeled arches resembling those of Palenque and giant stone masks similar to Guatemala's Petén style. The alternating vertical and sloping panels of Toltec and Aztec architecture surfaces in Dzibanché, a newly excavated site near Laguna de Bacalar in southern Quintana Roo.

The true arch was unknown in Mesoamerica, but the Maya devised the corbeled arch (or Maya arch) by stacking each successive stone to cantilever beyond the one below, until the two sides met at the top in an inverted V.

The Olmecs, who reigned over Tabasco's and Veracruz's Gulf coastal plains, are considered Mesoamerica's parent culture. Little survives of their pyramids, which were built of clay. We still have their enormous sculptural legacy, from small, intricately carved pieces of jade to the 40-ton carved basalt rock heads still found at La Venta, Tabasco (some of which are on view in the museum in Villahermosa).

Though later cities of stone are far more intact, an important aspect of ancient Maya art we do not see is their exuberant color. The stones originally were covered with a layer of painted stucco that gleamed red, blue, and yellow through the jungle foliage. Most of the fantastic murals that adorned their buildings are also lost to time, though surprisingly well-preserved fragments have been found at Bonampak and Ek Balam. Vestiges also remain at Mayapán, and Cobá.

Artisans also crafted marvelous stone murals and mosaics from thousands of pieces of fitted stone, adorning facades with figures of warriors, snakes, or geometric designs. Uxmal, in fact, evidently had not a single mural; all its artistry is in the intricate stonework.

Murals and stone carvings were more religious or historical than ornamental in purpose. Deciphering the hieroglyphs—rich, elegant symbols etched in stone or painted on pottery—allows scholars to identify rulers and untangle dynastic history. Michael Coe's

Breaking the Maya Code traces centuries-long efforts to decode Maya script and the recent breakthroughs that make it possible to decipher 90% of the glyphs. "Cracking the Maya Code," a "Nova" program based on Coe's book, is available for viewing on www.pbs. org or on DVD.

Good hieroglyphic examples appear in Palenque's site museum. Several stelae, the large, free-standing stone slabs where the Maya etched their history, are in place at Cobá. Calakmul is known for its many stelae, and good examples are displayed in Mexico City's Museum of Anthropology and the archaeology museum in Villahermosa.

SPANISH INFLUENCE

The Spaniards brought new forms of architecture to Mexico; in many cases they built Catholic churches, public buildings, and palaces with limestone from razed Maya cities. In the Yucatán, churches at Izamal, Tecoh, Santa Elena, and Muna rest atop former pyramids; numerous others rise from lesser buildings. Indian artisans, recruited to build the new structures, frequently implanted traditional symbolism, such as a plaster angel swaddled in feathers, reminiscent of the god Quetzalcoatl; they determined how many florets to carve around church doorways based on the ancient cosmos' 13 steps of heaven and nine levels of the underworld.

Spanish priests and architects altered their teaching and building methods in order to convert native populations. Church adornment became more explicit to combat the language barrier; frescoes of Biblical tales were splashed across church walls, and Christian symbols in stone supplanted pre-Hispanic figures.

Remnants of 16th century missions, convents, monasteries, and parish churches dot almost every Yucatán village. Examples well worth visiting include the Mission of San Bernardino de Sisal in Valladolid; the cathedral of Mérida; the vast atrium and church at Izamal; and the *retablos* (altarpieces), altars, and crucifixes in churches along the Convent Route, between the Puuc Hills and Mérida.

Porfirio Díaz's 35-year rule (1876–1911) brought a new infusion of European sensibility. Díaz commissioned imposing European-style public buildings and provided European scholarships to artists who later returned to paint Mexican subjects using techniques from abroad. Mérida is a veritable museum of opulent, European-style buildings built during the Díaz years; the most striking are the Palacio Cantón, now housing the Regional Anthropology Museum, and the Teatro Peón Contreras.

THE ADVENT OF MEXICAN MURALISM

The Mexican revolution that ripped the country apart between 1911 and 1917 ushered in a new social and cultural era. In 1923, as one way to reach the illiterate masses, Diego Rivera and several other budding artists were invited to paint Mexican history on the walls of the Ministry of Education building and the National Preparatory School in Mexico City. Thus was born Mexico's tradition of public murals.

The courtyard and History Room of the Governor's Palace in Mérida display 31 works of Castro Pacheco, the Yucatán's most prominent muralist. Though he painted on large panels rather than directly on the walls, he aligned with other great muralists in his affinity for strong colors and the belief that art is meant for public enjoyment, not just private collectors. Pacheco's murals are a chilling depiction of the bloody subjugation of the Yucatán, including the Popol Vuh legend, a jaguar with fierce warriors in headdresses, a Maya *henequén* worker's hands, and portraits of such heroes as Felipe Carrillo Puerto, the martyred Yucatecan governor who instituted agrarian reform.

5 RELIGION, MYTH & FOLKLORE

Nearly 90% of Mexicans embrace Roman Catholicism, but Catholicism in much of Mexico is laced with pre-Hispanic spiritual tradition. You need only to visit the *curandero* section of a Mexican market (where you can buy copal, an incense agreeable to the gods; rustic beeswax candles, a traditional offering; the native species of tobacco used to ward off evil; and other talismans), or watch pre-Hispanic dances performed at a village festival, to sense the supernatural beliefs running parallel with Christian ones.

Spanish Catholicism was disseminated by pragmatic Jesuit missionaries who grafted Christian tradition onto indigenous ritual to make it palatable to their flock. Nearly 500 years after the conquest, a large minority of Mexicans—devout Catholics every one—adhere to this hybrid religion, nowhere more so than in Chiapas and the Yucatán.

The padres' cause enjoyed a huge boost when a dark-skinned image of the Virgin Mary appeared to an Aztec potter near Mexico City in 1531. The Virgin of Guadalupe, fluent in the local language and acquainted with the indigenous gods, provided a crucial link between Catholic and native spiritual traditions. She remains Mexico's most beloved religious symbol, a comforting figure smiling from countless shrines, saloons, and kitchen walls. Millions of pilgrims walk and crawl to her Mexico City shrine on her December 12 feast day.

The equally pragmatic native people chose the path of least resistance, dressing their ancestral beliefs in Catholic garb. They gave their familiar gods the names of

The Maya Pantheon

Every ancient culture had its gods and goddesses, and their characteristics or purposes, if not their names, often crossed cultures. Chaac, the hook-nosed rain god of the Maya, was Tlaloc, the squat rain god of the Aztecs; Quetzalcóatl, the plumed-serpent man/god of the Toltecs, became Kukulkán of the Maya. Sorting out the ancient deities and beliefs can become a life's work, but here are some of the most important gods of the Maya world.

Itzamná   Often called the Supreme Diety; creator of mankind and inventor of corn, cacao, writing, and reading; patron of the arts and sciences.

Chaac   God of rain, striking the clouds with a lightning ax; sometimes depicted as four separate gods based in the four cardinal directions.

Kinich Ahau   Sun god, sometimes regarded as another manifestation of Itzamná; appeared in the shape of a firebird.

Kukulkán   Mortal who took on godly virtues, sometimes symbolized as Venus, the morning star.

Ixchel   Wife of Kinich Ahau; multitasking goddess of the moon, fertility and childbirth, water, medicine, and weaving.

Bacab   Generic name for four brothers who guarded the four points of the compass; closely associated with the four Chaacs.

Yumil Kaxob   God of maize, or corn, shown with a crown or headdress of corn and distinguished by his youth.

Balam   One of numerous jaguar spirits; symbol of power and protector of fields and crops.

Ixtab   Goddess of suicide; suicide was an honorable way to die, and Ixtab received their souls into heaven.

Christian saints and celebrated their old festivals on the nearest saint's day. Thus we find the Catholic feasts of All Saints' Day and All Souls' Day superimposed on the ancient Day of the Dead celebration, and the cult of the "Black Christ"—an amalgam of Jesus Christ and the cave-dwelling Maya god Ik'al—entrenched in the Yucatán, Chiapas, and Tabasco. In one of the most dramatic examples of this spiritual hybridization, the Tzotzil Maya of San Juan Chamúla in highland Chiapas carpet their church with pine needles, kneeling among candles and Coke bottles to pray in an archaic dialect under the painted eyes of helpful saints. They bring offerings of flower petals, eggs, feathers, or live chickens prescribed by local *curanderos* (medicine men) in an effort to dispel the demons of disease.

Common themes in the Catholic and Maya belief systems also made the Jesuits' task easier. The Catholics had the Bible, the Maya had the Popol Vuh. Both had long oral and written traditions (although Bishop Diego de Landa burned the Maya codices of Maní in the infamous *Auto de Fe* of 1562). Ceremonial processions with elaborate robes and incense were common to both religions, as were baptism by water and the symbol of the cross.

But the differences intrigue us most. The Maya's multitude of deities, 166 by some counts, is just the beginning. The Popol Vuh's creation myth, similar to Genesis in making man on the last day and striking down imperfect creations with an apocalyptic flood, departs from the Genesis plot in striking ways, not the least of which is fashioning man from corn (after failed tries with mud and wood). Maya mythology is a collection of convoluted tales, full of images placing nature on a level equal to man, that attempt to make sense of the universe, geography, and seasons.

The tall, straight *ceiba* tree was revered as a symbol of the cosmos. Its leaves and branches represented the 13 levels of heaven, the tree trunk the world of humans, and the roots the nine-level underworld—not hell but a cold, damp, dark place called *Xibalbá*. The manner of

death determined one's resting place: Men who died in battle or women who died in childbirth, for example, went straight to the sun. Everyone else had to journey first through the underworld.

Foremost among the Maya pantheon were those who influenced the growth of corn. The Maya worked hard to please their gods through prayer, offerings, and sacrifices, which could be anything from a priest giving his own blood to human sacrifice. They were obsessed with time, maintaining both a 260-day religious calendar and a 365-day solar calendar that guided crop planting and other practicalities. In fact, religion, art, and science were so entwined that the Maya might not even have perceived them as separate pursuits. So from a kernel of corn grew some of civilization's earliest and greatest accomplishments.

6 THE LAY OF THE LAND

The Yucatán Peninsula is truly a freak of nature—a flat, nearly 134,400 sq. km (51,892 sq. mi.) slab of limestone with almost 1,600km (1,000 miles) of shoreline but virtually devoid of surface water. The peninsula's geology, found nowhere else on Earth, was shaped by the same meteor thought to have extinguished the dinosaurs 65 million years ago. The impact sent shock waves through the brittle limestone, fracturing it into an immense network of fissures that drain all rainwater

away from the surface. You'll see no bridges, no rivers, lakes, or streams in the northern and central Yucatán, but fresh rainwater courses through a vast network of underground rivers stretching for hundreds of miles across the peninsula.

Breaches in the ceiling of this subterranean basin have created an estimated 3,000 cenotes—sinkholes that reveal the underground to the world above. The Maya called them *dzonots,* or sacred wells, and regarded them as gateways to the

---

(Finds **The Endemic Birds of the Yucatán**

The following 14 bird species are endemic to the Yucatán. See them while you're here, because you won't find them anywhere else on the planet: the black catbird, Cozumel emerald, Cozumel vireo, Cozumel thrasher, ocellated turkey, orange oriole, red-vented woodpecker, rose-throated tanager, yellow-lored (Yucatán) parrot, Yucatán poorwill, Yucatán nightjar, Yucatán flycatcher, Yucatán jay, and the Yucatán wren.

underworld. Precious stones, ceramics, and bones unearthed in cenotes suggest that they were ancient ceremonial sites.

Quiet, dark, and cool, cenotes offer respite from the bright, often steamy glare above. Some are underground, with only a small breach in a roof perforated by ropy tree roots seeking water. Some are open wells, and others open to the surface like a lake. Most tourists get their introduction to this subterranean world at Chichén Itzá, with its Grand Cenote, and Hidden Worlds Cenotes Park, with its system of underground caverns and waterways north of Tulum. But thousands more lie at the ends of narrow dirt roads throughout the peninsula, the greatest concentration being inland from the Playa del Carmen–Tulum corridor. The largest is the sea-like Cenote Azul, at the end of Laguna de Bacalar in southern Quintana Roo.

The thin layer of soil coating the Yucatán's limestone shelf gives rise to a surprisingly uniform terrain of dense, scrubby jungle full of wild ginger and orchids, jaguars, monkeys, and tropical birds. The only sense of height comes from the Puuc Hills, rising south of Chichén Itzá and extending into northwestern Campeche. Though they are less than 300m (984 ft.) high at their peak, their gently undulating roads can be unnerving after a few days on the Yucatán's arrow-straight highways. The geography changes abruptly when you reach Tabasco and Chiapas at the peninsula's isthmus.

Hot, marshy Tabasco is a low-lying state bordering the Gulf of Mexico at its southern extreme. With about 30% of Mexico's surface freshwater flowing through the state, Tabasco is said to have more water than land. Parts of the state are cloaked in thick rainforest, which extends through Chiapas. The capital, Villahermosa, lies in a shallow basin about an hour from the coast at the confluence of two rivers. Small lakes break up the landscape, especially in the modern parts of the city.

Chiapas, a much larger state of wildly varying elevations, extends from Tabasco all the way to the Pacific on one side and Guatemala on the other. It is washed by abundant lagoons, waterfalls, and rivers, including the Usumancinta, which forms the border with Guatemala. The high central plateau of a dramatic, pine-covered mountain range is the uncommonly chilly domain of San Cristóbal de las Casas, a small and ancient colonial city surrounded by Maya villages. Nearby Sumidero Canyon is a winding river gorge with some walls reaching 1,000m (3,281 ft.) into the sky. Palenque, one of Mexico's most exquisite ruins, sits where the northern highlands slide down to the Gulf coastal plain.

Southern Mexico is blessed with an astounding diversity of wildlife. North America's only two flamingo breeding grounds flank the northern Yucatán's Gulf Coast, and whale sharks convene off the peninsula's northeastern tip. Jaguars, howler monkeys, crocodiles, sea turtles, and hundreds of bird species populate the Sian Ka'an Biosphere Reserve south of the Riviera Maya.

Odd critters such as the paca (kind of a spotted guinea pig on steroids), the coati, and the kinkajou (tree-dwelling raccoon kin), might pop up as you roam ancient Maya cities or hike through mangrove thickets. Jaguars, ocelots, margays, and other smaller cats roam the region's tropical forests.

Most of Mexico's 1,000 species of colorful tropical birds inhabit southern Mexico. The resplendent quetzal, which inspired the "plumed serpent" god of Maya legend, is among the world's most spectacular feathered creatures, with its shimmering, 2-foot-long tail. Its numbers have dwindled, but it can still be found in Chiapas' highlands.

Tabasco's wetlands are a paradise for bird-watchers. Crocodiles are also common, and you might spot howler monkeys, large cats, and manatees. Coastal

The Lay of the Sea

Cozumel has been one of the world's top dive sites since Jacques Cousteau revealed its wonders to the world in a 1961 documentary film. The island is fringed by a coral reef system that grows into towering walls, peaks, valleys, arches, and tunnels inhabited by more than 4,000 species of fish and thousands of other plants and animals. Its colors and textures rival New England's fall foliage displays in the United States. This underwater mountain range, running for 32km (20 miles) along Cozumel's southwest coast, is part of the massive Great Meso-american Reef (also called the Great Mayan Reef) stretching from the Gulf of Mexico to Honduras—second in size only to Australia's Great Barrier Reef.

waters throughout the region teem with dolphins, rays, and sea turtles.

And those are just the animals you might have heard of. Others in this region include the Mexican caecilian, a primitive amphibian resembling a half-meter (2-foot) long earthworm; the striped basilisk, called the "Jesus Christ lizard" for its ability to skip across the water's surface; the roseate spoonbill, a flamingo burdened with an elongated duck's bill; and other strange and wondrous critters.

7 BOOKS, FILM & MUSIC

BOOKS

HISTORY & CULTURE   For an overview of pre-Hispanic cultures, pick up Michael D. Coe's *Mexico: From the Olmecs to the Aztecs* or Nigel Davies's *Ancient Kingdoms of Mexico.* Coe's *The Maya* is probably the best general account of the Maya. For a survey of Mexico's history through modern times, *A Short History of Mexico* by J. Patrick McHenry is both thorough and concise.

John L. Stephens's two-volume *Incidents of Travel in the Yucatán* is not only one of the great books of archaeological discovery but a travel classic. Before his expeditions, beginning in 1841, the world knew little about the region and nothing about the Maya. Stephens' account of 44 Maya sites is still the most authoritative.

Graham Greene's *The Lawless Roads,* covering the brutal religious oppression of the late 1930s, is a dyspeptic travelogue of Chiapas and Tabasco. This compelling look at what was then a remote region— flawed though it is by the author's distaste

for Mexico—also was the basis for his masterpiece, *The Power and the Glory.*

For contemporary culture, start with Octavio Paz's classic, *The Labyrinth of Solitude,* still controversial because of some of Paz' generalizations about Mexicans. *Our Word Is Our Weapon,* a recent collection of articulate and sometimes poetic writings by Zapatista leader Subcomandante Marcos, provides insight into Chiapas' armed revolt in the 1990s.

Lesley Byrd Simpson's *Many Mexicos* is a comprehensive cultural history; *Distant Neighbor* by Alan Riding is a classic of cultural insight.

ART & ARCHITECTURE   *Art and Time in Mexico: From the Conquest to the Revolution* by Elizabeth Wilder Weismann covers religious, public, and private architecture. *Maya Art and Architecture* by Mary Ellen Miller showcases and interprets the best of Maya artistic expression.

NATURE   *A Naturalist's Mexico* by Roland H. Wauer, is getting hard to find, but *A Hiker's Guide to Mexico's Natural History* by Jim Conrad is a good alternative. *Peterson Field Guides: Mexican Birds* by Roger Tory Peterson and Edward L. Chalif is predictably excellent. Les Beletsky's *Southern Mexico,* is a richly illustrated, engagingly written field guide and ecotourism manual in the Travellers' Wildlife Guides series.

LITERATURE   Jorge Ibargüengoitia, one of Mexico's most famous modern writers, died in 1983 but remains popular in Mexico and is available in translation. His novels *Estas ruinas que ves (These Ruins You See)* and *The Dead Girls* (a fictional account of a famous 1970s crime) display deft characterization and a sardonic view of Mexican life.

Novelist Carlos Fuentes is Mexico's pre-eminent living writer. His earlier novels, such as *The Death of Artemio Cruz,* are easier to read than more recent works, which are heavily post-structural and require a great deal of effort. Angeles Mastretta's *Arráncame la vida (Tear Up My Life),* a well-written novel about a young woman's life in postrevolutionary Puebla, is delightful. Laura Esquivel's *Like Water for Chocolate* (and the movie that followed) covers roughly the same period through a lens of magical realism and was instrumental in popularizing Mexican food abroad.

Hasta No Verte Jesús Mío by Elena Poniatowska, and anything by Pulitzer winner Luis Alberto Urrea, offer hard looks at third-world realities.

Guillermo Arriaga, screenwriter for *Amores Perros,* is a brilliant novelist, too. *El Bufalo de la Noche,* about a young man reeling from his best friend's suicide, is available in English. *Retorno 201,* a collection of stories set on the Mexico City street where Arriaga grew up, is rumored to be coming out in English soon.

MEXICAN CINEMA
Golden Age & Classics
During Mexico's "Golden Age of Cinema" in the 1940s, film studios stopped trying to mimic Hollywood and started producing black- and- white films that were Mexican to the core. Stars of the day are still cultural icons in Mexico. **Mario Moreno,** a.k.a. Cantinflas, was a comedic genius who personalized the *el pelado* archetype—a poor, picaresque, slightly naughty character trading on his wits alone getting nowhere. Mexican beauty **Dolores del Río** ended up in Hollywood, playing the steamy Latin babe. **Pedro Infante,** the singing cowboy, embodied the ideal of Mexican manhood.

Luis Buñuel's dark *Los Olvidados* (1950) was the Spanish surrealist's third Mexican film, exploring the life of young hoodlums in Mexico City's slums.

The New Cinema
The golden age was followed by a long fallow period, until a new generation of filmmakers came along in the 1990s. The first big *El Nuevo Cine Mexicano* (The New Cinema) hit outside of Mexico was *Like Water for Chocolate* (1992), directed by **Alfonso Arau,** then author Laura Esquivel's husband. He continues to make films, mainly in Mexico.

The second New Cinema film to emerge, *Sexo, Pudor y Lágrimas* (1999) by director **Antonio Serrano,** is an unflinching look at the battle of the sexes in Mexico City.

After **Alfonso Cuarón**'s debut film, the mordant social satire *Sólo con tu pareja* (1991), scored critical and commercial success in Mexico, he garnered international acclaim with his ironic *Y Tu Mamá También* (2001), which touches on class hypocrisy while following a pair of teenage boys on an impromptu road trip with a sexy older woman. Cuarón has since directed *Harry Potter and the Prisoner of Azkaban,* the science fiction thriller *Children of Men,* and other international productions.

In *Amores Perros* (2000), **Alejandro González Iñárritu** (director of *21 Grams* and *Babel*) presents a keen glimpse of contemporary Mexican society through three

Views from the Outside: Films Starring Mexico

Elia Kazan's 1952 classic, **Viva Zapata!**, written by John Steinbeck, stars Marlon Brando as revolutionary Emiliano Zapata. Orson Welles' 1958 film-noir **Touch of Evil** (preposterously billing Charlton Heston as a Mexican narcotics agent) looks at drugs and corruption in Tijuana—still compelling, even though it feels sanitized compared with today's screaming headlines.

HBO's 2003 flick, **And Starring Pancho Villa as Himself** with Antonio Banderas, is the true story of how revolutionaries allowed Hollywood to film Pancho Villa in battle. **Man on Fire** (2004), with Denzel Washington as a bodyguard hired to protect a little girl, is full of great Mexico City scenes, though the plot is depressing and all too real. Dylan Verrechia's **Tijuana Makes Me Happy** (2005), focusing on Tijuana's humanity rather than its perceived sins, has won awards in Latin America and at U.S. film festivals. For more on the border, Stephen Soderbergh's Academy Award–winning **Traffic** (2000), with Benicio del Toro, has powerful scenes focusing on Tijuana's drug war, while the documentary **Tijuana Remix** (2002) unveils the city's unique and idiosyncratic culture. Mel Gibson's controversial **Apocalypto** (2006) cast indigenous Maya in his depiction of the Maya empire's waning days; the rain forests of Veracruz state stand in for the lush jungles that must have covered the Yucatán centuries ago.

stories about different ways of life in Mexico City that converge at the scene of a horrific car accident. His Academy Award–nominated *Babel* (2006), another tour de force, features a Mexican border scene that is realistic, exhilarating, and frightening all at once.

Guillermo del Toro's debut, *Cronos* (1993), was a dark, atmospheric piece that garnered critical acclaim in Mexico. Moving into the international arena, he has directed similarly moody films such as *Hellboy* (2004) and Oscar winner *Pan's Labyrinth* (2006).

Julie Taymor's *Frida* (2002), with Mexican actress Salma Hayek producing and starring, is an enchanting biopic about Frida Kahlo's life and work, from her devastating accident to relationships with Diego Rivera and Leon Trotsky. The exquisite cinematography captures Mexico's inherent spirit of magic realism, evinced in Kahlo's work.

Director **Robert Rodriguez**'s breakout film, *El Mariachi* (1992), is set in a small central Mexican town. Made on a shoestring budget, the somewhat cheesy action flick is at least highly entertaining. His *Once Upon a Time in Mexico* (2003) isn't as great, but it's fun to see scenes of San Miguel Allende. Ditto for San Luis Potosí in *The Mexican* (2001) with Brad Pitt and Julia Roberts.

MUSIC
Marimba & Son

Marimba music flourishes in much of southern and central Mexico but is considered a traditional music only in Chiapas and the port city of Veracruz. Many bands travel from here to play in places like Oaxaca and Mexico City. You can hear marimba any night for free in Tuxtla Gutiérrez's Parque de las Marimba.

Son, a native art form from many parts of Mexico, employs a variety of stringed instruments. Ritchie Valens' "La Bamba" popularized one of the most famous forms, *son jarocho,* in the '50s. Often fast-paced, with lot of strumming and fancy string picking, it originated in southern Veracruz. *Jarana,* the Yucatán's principal dance music, is a form of *son jarocho* that adds woodwinds and a sensuous Caribbean beat. The dance was born as part of the annual *vaquerías,* or country fiestas, held on the haciendas and are still performed every week in Mérida's Plaza Mayor and many smaller parks.

Danzon & Bolero

These musical forms came from Cuba in the late 19th century and gained great popularity, especially in Veracruz and Mexico City. *Danzón* is orchestra music that combines Latin flavor with a stateliness uncommon in later Latin music.

The Yucatán had strong ties to Cuba, and its *son yucateca* probably influenced *bolero* and the closely related *trova,* or classical guitar trios. This soft, romantic, and often slightly melancholy music is a lynchpin of Yucatecan musical tradition, and singers sometimes use Mayan lyrics. Mérida's free nightly cultural events include *trova yucateca* in the Olimpo Cultural Center, and the city stages an annual trova festival.

Mariachi & Ranchera

Mariachis with their big sombreros, waist-length jackets and tight pants, exemplify Mexico's national spirit. The music originated from Jalisco state's *son,* arranged for guitars, violins, string bass, and trumpets. Now heard across Mexico and much of the American southwest, it is at its traditional best in Jalisco and its capital, Guadalajara. Though identified with central Mexico, *mariachi* is common in the Yucatán, especially in cantinas and during national celebrations. Yucatecan trova music even has *mariachi* adaptations.

The national pride, individualism, and sentimentality expressed in *mariachi's* kin, *ranchera,* earns it favored status as drinking music. Many Mexicans know the songs of famous composer **José Alfredo Jiménez** by heart.

Rock en Español

Mexican rock forged its identity in the 1980s and exploded during the 1990s with bands such as **Los Jaguares** and **Molotov** out of Mexico City and **Maná,** based in Guadalajara. Named for the 1920s cafe in the capital's Centro Histórico, **Café Tacvba** has been at it since 1989. Their music is influenced by indigenous Mexican music as much as folk, punk, bolero, and hip-hop. The fast-rising **Yucatán a Go Go**—hailing, despite the name, from central Mexico— fuses a bouncy pop beat to lyrics firmly rooted in cultural tradition.

Planning Your Trip to the Yucatán, Tabasco & Chiapas

by Shane Christensen

Unless you intend to stick to the well-serviced beaches of the Caribbean, a trip to Mexico's Yucatán Peninsula or the southern states of Tabasco and Chiapas will require planning, patience, and flexibility. Quintana Roo is by far the most advanced tourist state in this region, playing host to about half of all tourism to Mexico. It's easy to travel between Cancún and the beaches of the Riviera Maya, where tourist infrastructure is well developed. You can either plan on resort hopping along the Caribbean coast in a rental car, or taking buses to visit the Maya ruins in the Yucatán peninsula. Getting to and around Chiapas and Tabasco requires a little more ingenuity. Be prepared and willing to deal with everything.

Travelers to Mexico should be aware of security concerns in certain parts of the country and take precautions to maximize their safety. For the most part, Mexico is safe for travelers who steer clear of drugs and those who sell them, but visitors should still exercise caution in unfamiliar areas and remain aware of their surroundings at all times. See "Safety," below, for more details; and visit the U.S. State Department's website, www. state.gov, for up-to-date information on travel to Mexico.

For additional help in planning your trip and for more on-the-ground resources in the Yucatán peninsula, Tabasco, and Chiapas, please turn to "Fast Facts," on p. 283.

1 WHEN TO GO

High season in the Yucatán begins around December 20 and continues to Easter. This is the best time for calm, warm weather; snorkeling, diving, and fishing (the calmer weather means clearer and more predictable seas); and for visiting the ruins that dot the interior of the peninsula. Book well in advance if you plan to be in Cancún around the holidays.

Low season begins the day after Easter and continues to mid-December; during low season, prices may drop 20% to 50%. However, in Cancún and along the Riviera

Maya, demand by European visitors is creating a summer high season, with hotel rates approaching those charged in the winter months.

Generally speaking, Mexico's **dry season** runs from November to April, with the **rainy season** stretching from May to October. It isn't a problem if you're staying close to the beaches, but for those bent on road-tripping to Chichén Itzá, Uxmal, or other sites, temperatures and humidity in the interior can be downright stifling from May to July. Later in the rainy season, the frequency of **tropical storms** and **hurricanes** increases; such storms, of course, can put a crimp in your vacation. But they can lower temperatures, making climbing ruins more fun, accompanied by cool air and a slight wind. November is especially ideal for Yucatán travels. Cancún, Cozumel, and Isla Mujeres also have a rainy season from November to January, when

northern storms hit. This usually means diving visibility is diminished—and conditions may prevent boats from even going out.

Villahermosa is sultry and humid all the time. San Cristóbal de las Casas, at an elevation of 2,152m (7,059 ft.), is much cooler than the lowlands and is downright cold in winter.

Cancún's Average Temperatures

	Jan	Feb	Mar	Apr	May	June	July	Aug	Sept	Oct	Nov	Dec
Avg. High (°C)	27	27	28	29	31	31	32	32	31	30	28	27
Avg. High (°F)	81	82	84	85	88	89	90	90	89	87	84	82
Avg. Low (°C)	19	20	21	22	25	25	25	25	24	23	22	20
Avg. Low (°F)	67	68	71	73	77	78	78	77	76	74	72	69

CALENDAR OF EVENTS

Religious and secular festivals are a part of life in Mexico. Every town, city, and state holds its own specific festivals throughout the year commemorating religious and historic figures. Indeed, in certain parts of the country it sometimes feels like the festivities never die down, and the Yucatán, Tabasco, and Chiapas are no exception. For an exhaustive list of events beyond those listed here, check **http://events. frommers.com**, where you'll find a searchable, up-to-the-minute roster of what's happening in cities all over the world.

JANUARY

Año Nuevo (New Year's Day), nationwide. This national holiday is perhaps the quietest day in all of Mexico. Most people stay home or attend church. All businesses are closed. In traditional indigenous communities, new tribal leaders are inaugurated with colorful ceremonies rooted in the pre-Hispanic past. January 1.

Día de los Reyes (Three Kings' Day), nationwide. This day commemorates the Three Kings' presenting gifts to the Christ Child. On this day, children receive presents, much like they do at Christmas in the United States. Friends and families gather to share the *Rosca de Reyes*, a special cake. Inside the cake is a small doll representing the Christ Child; whoever receives the doll must

host a tamales-and-*atole* (a warm drink made of masa) party on February 2. January 6.

FEBRUARY

Día de la Candelaria (Candlemas), nationwide. Music, dances, processions, food, and other festivities lead up to a blessing of seed and candles in a ceremony that mixes pre-Hispanic and European traditions marking the end of winter. Those who attended the Three Kings celebration reunite to share *atole* and tamales at a party hosted by the recipient of the doll found in the Rosca. February 2.

Día de la Constitución (Constitution Day), nationwide. This national holiday is in honor of the current Mexican constitution, signed in 1917 as a result of the revolutionary war of 1910. It's celebrated through small parades. February 5.

Carnaval, nationwide. Carnaval takes place the 3 days preceding Ash Wednesday and the beginning of Lent. In Cozumel, the celebration resembles New Orleans's Mardi Gras, with a festive atmosphere and parades. In Chamula, the event harks back to pre-Hispanic times, with ritualistic running on flaming branches. Cancún also celebrates with parade floats and street parties.

Ash Wednesday, nationwide. The start of Lent and time of abstinence, this is a day of reverence nationwide; some towns honor it with folk dancing and fairs.

MARCH

Benito Juárez's Birthday, nationwide. This national holiday celebrating one of Mexico's most beloved leaders is observed through small hometown celebrations, especially in Juárez's birthplace, Guelatao, Oaxaca. March 21.

Spring Equinox, Chichén Itzá. On the first day of spring, the Temple of Kukulkán—Chichén Itzá's main pyramid—aligns with the sun, and the shadow of the plumed serpent moves slowly from the top of the building down. When the shadow reaches the bottom, the body joins the carved stone snake's head at the base of the pyramid. According to ancient legend, at the moment that the serpent is whole, the earth is fertilized. Visitors come from around the world to marvel at this sight, so advance arrangements are advisable. Elsewhere, equinox festivals and celebrations welcome spring, in the custom of the ancient Mexicans, with dances and prayers to the elements and the four cardinal points. It's customary to wear white with a red ribbon. March 21 (the shadow appears Mar 19–23).

APRIL

Semana Santa (Holy Week), nationwide. Mexico celebrates the last week in the life of Christ, from Palm Sunday to Easter Sunday, with somber religious processions, spoofing of Judas, and reenactments of biblical events, plus food and craft fairs. Some businesses close during this traditional week of Mexican national vacations, and almost all close on Maundy Thursday, Good Friday, Saturday, and Easter Sunday.

If you plan to travel to Mexico during Holy Week, make your reservations early. Airline seats into Cancún in particular will be reserved months in advance. Planes and buses to towns across the Yucatán and to almost anywhere else in Mexico will be full, so try arriving on the Wednesday or Thursday before Good Friday. Easter Sunday is quiet, and the week following is a traditional vacation period. Early April.

MAY

Labor Day, nationwide. Workers' parades countrywide; everything closes. May 1.

Cinco de Mayo, nationwide. This holiday celebrates the defeat of the French at the Battle of Puebla, although it (ironically) tends to be a bigger celebration in the United States than in Mexico. May 5.

Feast of San Isidro. The patron saint of farmers is honored with a blessing of seeds and work animals. May 15.

Cancún Jazz Festival. For dates and schedule information, check www.cancun.travel.

International Gay Festival. This 5-day event in Cancún kicks off with a welcome fiesta of food, drinks, and mariachi music. Additional festivities include a tequila party, tour of Cancún, sunset Caribbean cruise, bar and beach parties, and a final champagne breakfast. For schedule information, check www.cancun.eventguide.com.

JUNE

Navy Day (Día de la Marina). All coastal towns celebrate with naval parades and fireworks. June 1.

Corpus Christi, nationwide. The day honors the Body of Christ (the Eucharist) with religious processions, Masses, and food. Dates vary.

Día de San Pedro (St. Peter and St. Paul's Day), nationwide. Celebrated wherever St. Peter is the patron saint, this holiday honors anyone named Pedro or Peter. June 26.

AUGUST

Assumption of the Virgin Mary, nationwide. This is celebrated throughout the country with special Masses and in some places with processions. August 15 to August 17.

SEPTEMBER

Independence Day, nationwide. This day of parades, picnics, and family reunions throughout the country celebrates Mexico's independence from Spain. At 11pm on September 15, the president of Mexico gives the famous independence *grito* (shout) from the National Palace in Mexico City, and local mayors do the same in every town and municipality all over Mexico. On September 16, every city and town conducts a parade in which both government and civilians display their pride in being Mexican. For these celebrations, all important government buildings are draped in the national colors—red, green, and white—and the towns blaze with decorative lights. September 15 and 16; September 16 is a national holiday.

Fall Equinox, Chichén Itzá. The same shadow play that occurs during the spring equinox repeats at the fall equinox. September 21 to September 22.

OCTOBER

"Ethnicity Day" or Columbus Day (Día de la Raza), nationwide. This commemorates the fusion of the Spanish and Mexican peoples. October 12.

NOVEMBER

Day of the Dead (Día de los Muertos), nationwide. What's commonly called the Day of the Dead is actually 2 days: All Saints' Day, honoring saints and deceased children, and All Souls' Day, honoring deceased adults. Relatives gather at cemeteries countrywide, carrying candles and food to create an altar, and sometimes spend the night beside the graves of loved ones. Weeks before, bakers begin producing bread (called *pan de muerto*) formed in the shape of mummies or round loaves decorated with bread "bones." Decorated sugar skulls emblazoned with glittery names are sold everywhere. Many days ahead, homes and churches erect special altars laden with Day of the Dead bread, fruit, flowers, candles, favorite foods, and photographs of saints and of the deceased. On the 2 nights, children dress in costumes and masks, often carrying through the streets mock coffins and pumpkin lanterns, into which they expect money to be dropped. November 1 and 2; November 1 is a national holiday.

Revolution Day, nationwide. This commemorates the start of the Mexican Revolution in 1910 with parades, speeches, rodeos, and patriotic events. November 20.

Annual Yucatán Bird Festival (Festival de las Aves de Yucatán), Mérida, Yucatán. Bird-watching sessions, workshops, and exhibits are the highlights of this festival, designed to illustrate the special role birds play in our environment and in the Yucatán territory. Check out www.yucatanbirds.org.mx for details. Mid-November.

Feast of the Virgin of Guadalupe, nationwide. Throughout the country, religious processions, street fairs, dancing, fireworks, and Masses honor the patroness of Mexico. This is one of Mexico's most moving and beautiful displays of traditional culture. The Virgin of Guadalupe appeared to a young man, Juan Diego, in December 1531, on a hill near Mexico City. He convinced the bishop that he had seen the apparition by revealing his cloak, upon which the Virgin was emblazoned. It's customary for children to dress up as Juan Diego, wearing mustaches and red bandannas. One of the most famous and elaborate celebrations takes place at the Basílica of Guadalupe, north of Mexico City, where the Virgin appeared. Every village celebrates this day, though, often with processions of children carrying banners of the Virgin and with *charreadas* (rodeos), bicycle races, dancing, and fireworks. December 12.

Festival of San Cristóbal de las Casas, San Cristóbal de las Casas, Chiapas.

This 10-day festival in Chiapas includes a procession by the Tzotzil and Tzetzal Indians, *marimba* music, and a parade of horses. December 12 to December 21.

Christmas Posadas, nationwide. On each of the 9 nights before Christmas, it's customary to reenact the Holy Family's search for an inn, with door-to-door candlelit processions in cities and villages nationwide. These are also hosted by most businesses and community organizations, taking the place of the northern tradition of a Christmas party. December 15 to December 24.

Christmas. Mexicans extend this celebration and often leave their jobs beginning 2 weeks before Christmas all the way through New Year's Day. Many businesses close, and resorts and hotels fill up. Significant celebrations take place on December 24.

New Year's Eve. As in the rest of the world, New Year's Eve in Mexico is celebrated with parties, fireworks, and plenty of noise. December 31.

What's Biting When?

It's fishing season year-round along the Caribbean coast. Here's a general breakdown of what to look for during your trip.

- **Blue Marlin:** June, July, and August.
- **White Marlin:** April through June.
- **Sailfish:** March through July.
- **Grouper:** October through December.
- **Wahoo:** November through January, April through June.
- **Amberjack:** September through December.
- **Dolphin Fish, Blackfin Tuna:** April through May.
- **Bonita:** April through August.
- **Barracuda, Kingfish:** October through December.

PASSPORTS

All travelers to Mexico are required to present **photo identification** and **proof of citizenship,** such as a valid passport, naturalization papers, or an original birth certificate with a raised seal, along with a driver's license or official ID, such as a state or military-issued ID. Driver's licenses and permits, voter registration cards, affidavits, and similar documents are not sufficient to prove citizenship for readmission into the United States. If the last name on the birth certificate is different from your current name, bring a photo identification card *and* legal proof of the name change, such as the original marriage license or certificate. *Note:* Photocopies are *not* acceptable.

Virtually every air traveler **entering the U.S.** is required to show a passport. As of January 23, 2007, all U.S. and Canadian citizens traveling by **air** to Mexico are required to present a valid passport or other valid travel document to enter or reenter the United States. In addition, effective June 1, 2009, all travelers, including U.S. and Canadian citizens, attempting to enter the United States by **land** or **sea** must have a valid passport or other WHTI compliant document.

Other valid travel documents (known as WHTI-compliant documents; visit www.travel.state.gov for more information) include the new **Passport Card** and SENTRI, NEXUS, FAST, and the U.S. Coast Guard Mariner Document. Members of the U.S. Armed Forces on active duty traveling on orders are exempt from the passport requirement. U.S. citizens may apply for the new, limited-use, wallet-size **Passport Card.** The card is valid only for land and sea travel between the U.S. and Canada, Mexico, the Caribbean region, and Bermuda.

From our perspective, it's easiest just to travel with a valid passport. Safeguard your passport in an inconspicuous, inaccessible place, like a money belt, and keep a copy of the critical pages with your passport number in a separate place. If you lose your passport, visit the nearest consulate of your native country as soon as possible for a replacement.

VISAS

For detailed information regarding visas to Mexico, visit the **National Immigration Institute** at www.inm.gob.mx.

American and Canadian tourists are not required to have a visa or a tourist card for stays of 72 hours or less within the border zone (20–30km/12–19 miles from the U.S. border).

For travel to Mexico beyond the border zone, all travelers must be in possession of a tourist card, also called **Tourist Migration Form** (FMTTV: Migration Form for Tourists, Transmigrants, Visiting Businesspersons or Visiting Consultants). This document is provided by airlines or by immigration authorities at the country's points of entry. If you enter Mexico by land, it is your responsibility to stop at the immigration module located at the border.

Authorities can demand to see your tourist card at any time. You must therefore carry the original or a copy at all times and must surrender the original upon leaving Mexico. Failure to do so will result in a fine and/or expulsion.

In order to obtain a tourist card, travelers are required to present a valid passport or valid official photo identification (such as a passport or driver's license) and proof of citizenship (such as a passport, birth certificate or citizenship card).

Your tourist card is stamped on arrival. If traveling by bus or car, ensure you obtain such a card and have it stamped by immigration authorities at the border. If you do not receive a stamped tourist card at the border, ensure that, when you arrive at your destination within Mexico, you immediately go to the closest National Institute of Immigration office, present your bus ticket, and request a tourist card. Travelers who fail to have their tourist card stamped may be fined, detained, or expelled from the country.

An immigration official will determine the number of days you can remain in Mexico. Do not assume that you will be granted the full 180 days. An extension of your stay can be requested for a fee at the National Institute of Immigration of the Ministry of the Interior or its local offices.

If you plan to enter Mexico by car, please read the vehicle's importation requirements (p. 51).

Note on travel of minors: Mexican law requires that any non-Mexican citizen under the age of 18 departing Mexico without both parents must carry notarized written permission from the parent or guardian who is not traveling with the child to or from Mexico. This permission must include the name of the parent, the name of the child, the name of anyone traveling with the child, and the notarized signature(s) of the absent parent(s). The U.S. Department of State recommends that permission include travel dates, destinations, airlines, and a summary of the circumstances surrounding the travel. The child must be carrying the original letter (not a facsimile or scanned copy), and proof of the parent/child relationship (usually a birth certificate or court document) and an original custody decree, if applicable. Travelers should contact the Mexican Embassy or closest Mexican Consulate for current information.

CUSTOMS

Mexican Customs inspection has been streamlined. At most points of entry, tourists are requested to press a button in front of what looks like a traffic signal, which alternates on touch between red and green.

Green light and you go through without inspection; red light and your luggage or car may be inspected. If you have an unusual amount of luggage or an oversized piece, you may be subject to inspection anyway.

What You Can Bring into Mexico

When you enter Mexico, Customs officials will be tolerant if you are not carrying illegal drugs or firearms. Tourists are allowed to bring in their personal effects duty-free. A laptop computer, camera equipment, and sports equipment that could feasibly be used during your stay are also allowed. The underlying guideline is: Don't bring anything that looks as if it's meant to be resold in Mexico. **U.S. citizens** entering Mexico by the land border can bring in gifts worth up to $50 duty-free, except for alcohol and tobacco products. Those entering Mexico by air or sea can bring in gifts worth a value of up to $300 duty-free. The website for Mexican Customs (*Aduanas*) is **www.aduanas.gob. mx/aduana_mexico/2008/pasajeros/ 139_10134.html**.

What You Can Take Home from Mexico

For information on what you're allowed to bring home, contact one of the following agencies:

U.S. Citizens: U.S. Customs & Border Protection (CBP), 1300 Pennsylvania Ave., NW, Washington, DC 20229 (© **877/ 287-8667; www.cbp.gov**).

Canadian Citizens: Canada Border Services Agency (© **800/461-9999** in Canada, or 204/983-3500; **www.cbsa-asfc.gc.ca**).

U.K. Citizens: HM Customs & Excise at © **0845/010-9000** (from outside the U.K., 020/8929-0152), or consult their website at **www.hmce.gov.uk**.

Australian Citizens: Australian Customs Service at © **1300/363-263,** or log on to **www.customs.gov.au**.

New Zealand Citizens: New Zealand Customs, the Customhouse, 17–21 Whitmore St., Box 2218, Wellington (© **04/473-6099** or 0800/428-786; **www.customs.govt.nz**).

MEDICAL REQUIREMENTS

No special vaccinations are required for entry into Mexico. For other medical requirements and health-related recommendations, see "Health," p. 57.

3 GETTING THERE & GETTING AROUND

GETTING THERE

By Plane

Mexico has dozens of international and domestic airports. Among the airports in the Yucatán region are Cancún (CUN), Cozumel (CZM), and Mérida (MID). The major airport in Chiapas is in Tuxtla Gutierrez (NTR) and in Tabasco, Villahermosa (VSA). For a list of the major international airlines with service to Mexico, turn to "Fast Facts," p. 283.

Arriving at the Airport

Immigration and customs clearance at Mexican airports is generally efficient. Expect longer lines during peak seasons, but you can usually clear immigration and customs within an hour. For more on what to expect when passing through Mexican customs, see "Customs," p. 49.

By Car

Driving is not the cheapest way to get to Mexico, and it is definitely not the easiest way to get to the Yucatán peninsula. While driving is a convenient way to see the country, you may think twice about taking your own car south of the border once you've pondered the bureaucracy involved. One option is to rent a car once you arrive and tour around a specific region. The Yucatán peninsula is a great place to do this. Rental cars in Mexico generally are clean and well maintained, although they are often smaller than rentals in the U.S., may have manual rather than automatic transmission, and are comparatively expensive due to pricey mandatory insurance. Discounts are often available for rentals of a week or longer, especially when you make arrangements in advance online or from the United States. Be careful about estimated online rates, which often fail to include the price of the mandatory insurance. (See "Car Rentals," below, for more details.)

 Tips   Carrying Car Documents

You must carry your temporary car-importation permit, tourist permit (see "Entry Requirements," earlier in this chapter), and, if you purchased it, your proof of Mexican car insurance in the car at all times. The temporary car-importation permit papers are valid for 6 months to a year, while the tourist permit is usually issued for 30 days. It's a good idea to overestimate the time you'll spend in Mexico so if you have to (or want to) stay longer, you'll avoid the hassle of getting your papers extended. Whatever you do, don't overstay either permit. Doing so invites heavy fines, confiscation of your vehicle (which will not be returned), or both. Also remember that 6 months does not necessarily equal 180 days—be sure that you return before the earlier expiration date.

If, after reading the section that follows, you have additional questions or you want to confirm the current rules, call your nearest Mexican consulate or the Mexican Government Tourist Office. Although travel insurance companies generally are helpful, they may not have the most accurate information. To check on road conditions or to get help with any travel emergency while in Mexico, call ✆ **01-800/482-9832,** or 55/5089-7500 in Mexico City. English-speaking operators staff both numbers.

In addition, check with the **U.S. Department of State** (www.state.gov) for warnings about dangerous driving areas.

Car Documents

To drive your car into Mexico, you'll need a **temporary car-importation permit,** which is granted after you provide a required list of documents (see below). The permit can be obtained through Banco del Ejército (Banjercito) officials at the *aduana* (Mexican Customs) building after you cross the border into Mexico.

The following requirements for border crossing were accurate at press time:

- **A valid driver's license,** issued outside of Mexico.
- **Current, original car registration and a copy of the original car title.** If the registration or title is in more than one name and not all the named people are traveling with you, a notarized letter from the absent person(s) authorizing use of the vehicle for the trip is required; have it ready. The registration and your credit card (see below) must be in the same name.
- **Original immigration documentation.** This is either your tourist permit (FMT) or the original immigration booklet, FM2 or FM3, if you hold more permanent status.
- **Processing fee and posting of a bond.** With an international credit card, you are required to pay a $27 car-importation fee.

The credit card must be in the same name as the car registration. Mexican law also requires the posting of a bond at a Banjercito office to guarantee the export of the car from Mexico within a time period determined at the time of the application. For this purpose, American Express, Visa, or MasterCard credit card holders will be asked to provide credit card information; others will need to make a cash deposit of $200 to $400, depending on the make/model/year of the vehicle. In order to recover this bond or avoid credit card charges, travelers must go to any Mexican Customs office immediately before leaving Mexico.

If you receive your documentation at the border, Mexican officials will make two copies of everything and charge you for the copies. For up-to-the-minute information, a great source is the Customs office in Nuevo Laredo, or *Módulo de Importación Temporal de Automóviles, Aduana Nuevo Laredo* (✆ 867/712-2071).

Important reminder: Someone else may drive, but the person (or relative of the person) whose name appears on the car-importation permit must *always* be in the car. (If stopped by police, a nonregistered family member driving without the registered driver must be prepared to prove familial relationship to the registered driver—no joke.) Violation of this rule subjects the car to impoundment and the driver to imprisonment, a fine, or both. You can drive a car with foreign license plates only if you have a foreign (non-Mexican) driver's license.

Mexican Auto Insurance (*Seguros de Auto*)

Liability auto insurance is legally required in Mexico. U.S. insurance is invalid; to be insured in Mexico, you must purchase Mexican insurance. Any party involved in an accident who has no insurance may be sent to jail and have his or her car impounded until all claims are settled.

This is true even if you just drive across the border to spend the day. U.S. companies that broker Mexican insurance are commonly found at the border crossing, and several quote daily rates.

You can also buy car insurance through **Sanborn's Mexico Insurance,** P.O. Box 52840, 2009 S. 10th, McAllen, TX (© **800/ 222-0158;** fax 800/222-0158 or 956/686-0732; www.sanbornsinsurance.com). The company has offices at all U.S. border crossings. Its policies cost the same as the competition's do, but you get legal coverage (attorney and bail bonds if needed) and a detailed guide for your proposed route. Most of the Sanborn's border offices are open Monday through Friday; a few are staffed on Saturday and Sunday. **AAA** auto club (www.aaa.com) also sells insurance.

Returning to the U.S. with Your Car

You *must* return the car documents you obtained when you entered Mexico when you cross back with your car, or within 180 days of your return. (You can cross as many times as you wish within the 180 days.) If the documents aren't returned, heavy fines are imposed ($250 for each 15 days you're late), your car may be impounded and confiscated, or you may be jailed if you return to Mexico. You can only return the car documents to a Banjercito official on duty at the Mexican *aduana* building *before* you cross back into the United States. Some border cities have Banjercito officials on duty 24 hours a day, but others do not; some do not have Sunday hours.

By Ship

Numerous cruise lines serve Mexico. Some (such as Carnival and Royal Caribbean) cruise from Houston or Miami to the Caribbean (which often includes stops in Cancún, Playa del Carmen, and Cozumel). Several cruise-tour specialists sometimes offer last-minute discounts on unsold cabins. One such company is **CruisesOnly** (© **800/278-4737;** www. cruisesonly.com).

By Bus

Greyhound-Trailways (or its affiliates) offers service from around the United States to the Mexican border, where passengers disembark, cross the border, and buy a ticket for travel into Mexico. Many border crossings have scheduled buses from the U.S. bus station to the Mexican bus station.

More than likely, if you travel to the Yucatán by bus from the northern border you will pass through Mexico City, the country's capitol and main transportation hub. Expect a trip from the border to last several grueling days of all day (and/or all night) travel on roads of varying quality.

In each applicable section in this book, we've listed bus arrival information.

GETTING AROUND
By Air

Mexico has two large private national carriers: **Mexicana** (© **800/531-7921** in the U.S., or 01-800/801-2010 in Mexico; www.mexicana.com) and **AeroMéxico** (© **866/275-6419** in the U.S., or 01-800/021-4000 in Mexico; www.aero mexico.com), in addition to several up-and-coming low-cost carriers. Mexicana and AeroMéxico offer extensive connections to the United States as well as within Mexico.

Up-and-coming low-cost carriers include **Aviacsa** (www.aviacsa.com), **Click Mexicana** (www.click.com.mx), **InterJet** (www.interjet.com.mx), and **Volaris** (www.volaris.com.mx). In each applicable section of this book, we've mentioned regional carriers with all pertinent telephone numbers.

Because major airlines may book some regional carriers, check your ticket to see if your connecting flight is on a smaller carrier—they may use a different airport or a different counter.

AIRPORT TAXES Mexico charges an airport tax on all departures. Passengers leaving the country on international flights pay about $24 or the peso equivalent. It has become a common practice to include this departure tax in your ticket price. Taxes on each domestic departure within Mexico are around $17, unless you're on a connecting flight and have already paid at the start of the flight.

RECONFIRMING FLIGHTS Although Mexican airlines say it's not necessary to reconfirm a flight, it's still a good idea. To avoid getting bumped on popular, possibly overbooked flights, check in for an international flight 1½ hours in advance of travel.

By Car

Most Mexican roads are not up to U.S., Canadian, and European standards of smoothness, hardness, width of curve, grade of hill, or safety markings. Driving at night is dangerous—the roads are rarely lit; trucks, carts, pedestrians, and bicycles usually have no lights; and you can hit potholes, animals, rocks, dead ends, or uncrossable bridges without warning.

The spirited style of Mexican driving sometimes requires keen vision and reflexes. Be prepared for new customs, as when a truck driver flips on his left turn signal when there's not a crossroad for many kilometers. He's probably telling you the road's clear ahead for you to pass. Another custom that's very important to respect is turning left. Never turn left by stopping in the middle of a highway with your left-turn signal on. Instead, pull onto the right shoulder, wait for traffic to clear, and then proceed across the road.

GASOLINE There's one government-owned brand of gas and one gasoline station name throughout the country—**Pemex** (Petroleras Mexicanas). There are two types of gas in Mexico: *magna*, 87-octane unleaded gas, and *premio* 93 octane. In Mexico, fuel and oil are sold by the liter,

which is slightly more than a quart (1 gal. equals about 3.8L). Many franchise Pemex stations have bathroom facilities and convenience stores—a great improvement over the old ones. Gas stations accept both credit and debit cards for gas purchases.

TOLL ROADS Mexico charges some of the highest tolls in the world for its network of new toll roads, so they are rarely used. Generally, though, using toll roads cuts travel time. Older toll-free roads are generally in good condition, but travel times tend to be longer.

BREAKDOWNS If your car breaks down on the road, help might already be on the way. Radio-equipped green repair trucks, run by uniformed English-speaking officers, patrol major highways during daylight hours. These **"Green Angels/Angeles Verdes"** perform minor repairs and adjustments free, but you pay for parts and materials.

Your best guide to repair shops is the Yellow Pages. For repairs, look under *Automóviles y Camiones: Talleres de Reparación y Servicio;* auto-parts stores are under *Refacciones y Accesorios para Automóviles.* To find a mechanic on the road, look for the sign TALLER MECÁNICO.

Places called *vulcanizadora* or *llantera* repair flat tires, and it is common to find them open 24 hours a day on the most traveled highways.

MINOR ACCIDENTS When possible, many Mexicans drive away from minor accidents, or try to make an immediate settlement, to avoid involving the police. If the police arrive while the involved persons are still at the scene, the cars will likely be confiscated and both parties will likely have to appear in court. Both parties may also be taken into custody until liability is determined. Foreigners who don't speak fluent Spanish are at a distinct disadvantage when trying to explain their version of the event. Three steps may help the foreigner who doesn't wish to do as the

Mexicans do: If you were in your own car, notify your Mexican insurance company, whose job it is to intervene on your behalf. If you were in a rental car, notify the rental company immediately and ask how to contact the nearest adjuster. (You did buy insurance with the rental, right?) Finally, if all else fails, ask to contact the nearest Green Angel, who may be able to explain to officials that you are covered by insurance. See also "Mexican Auto Insurance," in "Getting There," earlier in this chapter.

CAR RENTALS You'll get the best price if you reserve a car at least a week in advance. For a list of car-rental firms operating in this region, turn to "Fast Facts: Airline, Hotel & Car Rental Websites," p. 287.

Cars are easy to rent if you are 25 or older and have a major credit card, valid driver's license, and passport with you. Without a credit card, you must leave a cash deposit, usually a big one. One-way rentals are usually simple to arrange, but they are more costly.

Car-rental costs are high in Mexico because cars are more expensive. The condition of rental cars has improved greatly over the years, and clean new cars are the norm. You will pay the least for a manual car without air-conditioning. Prices may be considerably higher if you rent around a major holiday. Also double-check charges for insurance—some companies will increase the insurance rate after several days. Always ask for detailed information about all charges you will be responsible for.

Car-rental companies usually write credit card charges in U.S. dollars.

DEDUCTIBLES Be careful—these vary greatly; some are as high as $2,500 which comes out of your pocket immediately in case of damage.

INSURANCE Insurance is offered in two parts: **Collision and damage** insurance covers your car and others if the accident is your fault, and **personal accident** insurance covers you and anyone in your car. Read the fine print on the back of your rental agreement and note that insurance may be invalid if you have an accident while driving on an unpaved road.

DAMAGE Inspect your car carefully and note every damaged or missing item, no matter how minute, on your rental agreement, or you may be charged.

By Taxi

Taxis are the preferred way to get around almost all of Mexico's resort areas, and around Mexico City. Fares for short trips within towns are generally preset by zone, and are quite reasonable compared with U.S. rates. For longer trips or excursions to nearby cities, taxis can generally be hired for around $15 to $20 per hour, or for a negotiated daily rate. A negotiated one-way price is usually much less than the cost of a rental car for a day, and a taxi travels much faster than a bus. For anyone who is uncomfortable driving in Mexico, this is a convenient, comfortable alternative. A bonus is that you have a Spanish-speaking person with you in case you run into trouble. Many taxi drivers speak at least some English. Your hotel can assist you with the arrangements.

⚠ Warning!   Bus Hijackings

The U.S. Department of State notes that bandits target long-distance buses traveling at night, but daylight robberies have occurred as well. First-class buses on toll *(cuota)* roads sustain a markedly lower crime rate than second-class and third-class buses that travel the less secure "free" *(libre)* highways.

By Bus

Mexican buses run frequently, are readily accessible, and can transport you almost anywhere you want to go. Taking the bus is common in Mexico, and the executive and first-class coaches can be as comfortable as business class on an airline. Buses are often the only way to get from large cities to other nearby cities and small villages. Don't hesitate to ask questions if you're confused about anything, but note that little English is spoken in bus stations.

Dozens of Mexican companies operate large, air-conditioned, Greyhound-type buses between most cities. Classes are *segunda* (second), *primera* (first), and *ejecutiva* (deluxe), which goes by a variety of names. Deluxe buses often have fewer seats than regular buses, show video movies, are air-conditioned, and make few stops. Many run express from point to point. They are well worth the few dollars more. In rural areas, buses are often of the school-bus variety, with lots of local color.

Whenever possible, it's best to buy your reserved-seat ticket, often using a computerized system, a day in advance on long-distance routes and especially before holidays.

For each relevant destination, we list bus arrival and contact information.

4 MONEY & COSTS

The Value of the Mexican Peso vs. Other Popular Currencies

Pesos	US$	Can$	UK£	Euro (€)	Aus$	NZ$
100	US$7.00	C$8.75	£4.90	€5.20	A$10.25	NZ$12.60

Frommer's lists exact prices in the local currency. The currency conversions quoted above were correct at press time. However, rates fluctuate, so before departing consult a currency exchange website such as **www.oanda.com/convert/classic** to check up-to-the-minute rates.

In general, the southern region of Mexico is considerably cheaper not just than most U.S. and European destinations, but also than many other parts of Mexico, although prices vary significantly depending on the specific location. The most expensive destinations are those with the largest number of foreign visitors, such as Cancún. The least expensive are those off the beaten path and in small rural villages, particularly in the poorer states of Tabasco and Chiapas. In the major cities, prices vary greatly depending on the neighborhood. As you might imagine, tourist zones tend to be much more expensive than local areas.

The currency in Mexico is the **peso.** Paper currency comes in denominations of 20, 50, 100, 200, and 500 pesos. Coins come in denominations of 1, 2, 5, 10, and 20 pesos, and 20 and 50 **centavos** (100 centavos = 1 peso). The current exchange rate for the U.S. dollar, and the one used in this book, is 13 pesos; at that rate, an item that costs 13 pesos would be equivalent to US$1.

Many establishments that deal with tourists, especially in coastal resort areas, quote prices in U.S. dollars. To avoid confusion, they use the abbreviations "Dlls." for dollars and "M.N." (*moneda nacional,* or national currency) for pesos. ***Note:*** Establishments that quote their prices primarily in U.S. dollars are listed in this guide with U.S. dollars.

Getting **change** is a problem. Small-denomination bills and coins are hard to come by, so start collecting them early in your trip. Shopkeepers and taxi drivers everywhere always seem to be out of change and small bills; that's doubly true in markets. There seems to be an expectation that the customer should provide appropriate change, rather than the other way around.

Don't forget to have enough pesos to carry you over a weekend or Mexican holiday, when banks are closed. In general, avoid carrying the U.S. $100 bill, the bill most commonly counterfeited in Mexico and therefore the most difficult to exchange, especially in smaller towns. Because small bills and coins in pesos are hard to come by in Mexico, the $1 bill is very useful for tipping. *Note:* A tip of U.S. coins, which cannot be exchanged into Mexican currency, is of no value to the service provider.

Casas de cambio (exchange houses) are generally more convenient than banks for money exchange because they have more locations and longer hours; the rate of exchange may be the same as at a bank or slightly lower. Before leaving a bank or exchange-house window, count your change in front of the teller before the next client steps up.

Large airports have currency-exchange counters that often stay open whenever flights are operating. Though convenient, they generally do not offer the most favorable rates.

A hotel's exchange desk commonly pays less favorable rates than banks; however, when the currency is in a state of flux, higher-priced hotels are known to pay higher rates than banks, in an effort to attract dollars. *Note:* In almost all cases, you receive a better rate by changing money first, then paying.

The bottom line on exchanging money: Ask first, and shop around. Banks generally pay the top rates.

Banks in Mexico have expanded and improved services. Except in the smallest towns, they tend to be open weekdays from 9am until 5pm, and often for at least a half day on Saturday. In larger resorts and cities, they can generally accommodate the exchange of dollars (which used to stop at noon) anytime during business hours. Some, but not all, banks charge a 1% fee to exchange traveler's checks. But you can pay for most purchases directly with traveler's checks at the establishment's stated exchange rate. Don't even bother with personal checks drawn on a U.S. bank—the bank will wait for your check to clear, which can take weeks, before giving you your money.

Travelers to Mexico can easily withdraw money from **ATMs** in most major cities and resort areas. The U.S. Department of State recommends caution when you're using ATMs in Mexico, stating that they should only be used during business hours and in large protected facilities, but this pertains primarily to Mexico City, where crime remains a significant problem. In most resorts in Mexico, the use of ATMs is perfectly safe—just use the same precautions you would at any ATM. The exchange rate is generally more favorable than at *casas de cambio.* Most machines offer Spanish/English menus and dispense pesos, but some offer the option of withdrawing dollars.

In Mexico, Visa, MasterCard, and American Express are the most accepted cards. You'll be able to charge most hotel, restaurant, and store purchases, as well as

Money Matters

The **universal currency sign ($)** is used to indicate pesos in Mexico. The use of this symbol in this book, however, denotes U.S. currency.

> ### ⓘ Tips   A Few Words About Prices
>
> Most hotels in Mexico—except places that receive little foreign tourism—quote prices in U.S. dollars. Thus, currency fluctuations are unlikely to affect the prices most hotels charge.
>
> Mexico has a **value-added tax** of 15% (*Impuesto de Valor Agregado,* or IVA; pronounced "*ee*-bah") on most everything, including restaurant meals, bus tickets, and souvenirs. (Exceptions are Cancún, Cozumel, and Los Cabos, where the IVA is 10%; as ports of entry, they receive a break on taxes.) Hotels charge the usual 15% IVA, plus a locally administered bed tax of 2% (in most areas), for a total of 17%. In Cancún, Los Cabos, and Cozumel, hotels charge the 10% IVA plus 2% room tax. The prices quoted by hotels and restaurants do not necessarily include IVA. You may find that upper-end properties (three or more stars) quote prices without IVA included, while lower-priced hotels include IVA. Ask to see a printed price sheet and ask if the tax is included.

almost all airline tickets, on your credit card. Pemex gas stations have begun to accept credit card purchases for gasoline, though this option may not be available everywhere and often not at night—check before you pump. You can get cash advances of several hundred dollars on your card, but there may be a wait of 20 minutes to 2 hours. Charges will be made in pesos, then converted into dollars by the bank issuing the credit card. Generally you receive the favorable bank rate when paying by credit card. However, be aware that some establishments in Mexico add a 5% to 7% surcharge when you pay with a credit card. This is especially true when using American Express. Many times, advertised discounts will not apply if you pay with a credit card.

5 HEALTH

As of June 12, 2009, the **World Health Organization** (WHO) had reported nearly 30,000 A(H1N1) ("swine flu") cases in 74 countries including 145 deaths, with Mexico among the most heavily affected countries. The number of cases continued to rise worldwide, and it was too early to tell how far or for how long the virus would spread. The WHO pandemic alert reached level 6 at press time, signaling pandemic, although with moderate severity. According to the **Centers for Disease Control and Prevention** (CDC), the symptoms of this contagious virus are similar to those of seasonal flu and include fever, cough, sore throat, runny or stuffy nose, body aches, headache, chills, and fatigue. Many people who have been infected with this virus also reported diarrhea and vomiting. Like seasonal flu, severe symptoms and death have occurred as a result of illness associated with this virus. It is important to note, however, that most cases of influenza are not the A(H1N1) virus. For the latest information regarding the risks of swine flu when traveling to Mexico, and what to do if you get sick, please consult the **U.S. State Department**'s website at www.travel.state.gov, the **CDC** website at www.cdc.gov, or the website of the **World Health Organization** at www.who.int.

GENERAL AVAILABILITY OF HEALTH CARE

In most of Mexico's resort destinations, you can usually find health care that meets U.S. standards. Care in more remote areas is limited. Standards of medical training, patient care, and business practices vary greatly among medical facilities in beach resorts throughout Mexico. Cancún has first-rate hospitals, for example, but other cities along the Caribbean coast do not. In recent years, some U.S. citizens have complained that certain health-care facilities in beach resorts have taken advantage of them by overcharging or providing unnecessary medical care. Only rudimentary health care is generally available in much of Chiapas, Tabasco, and the Yucatán.

Prescription medicine is broadly available at Mexico pharmacies; however, be aware that you may need a copy of your prescription or to obtain a prescription from a local doctor.

COMMON AILMENTS

SUN/ELEMENTS/EXTREME WEATHER EXPOSURE
Mexico is synonymous with sunshine; much of the country is bathed in intense sunshine for much of the year. Avoid excessive exposure, especially in the tropics where UV rays are more dangerous. The hottest months in Mexico's south are April and May, but the sun is intense most of the year.

DIETARY RED FLAGS
Travelers' diarrhea (locally known as *turista,* the Spanish word for "tourist")—persistent diarrhea, often accompanied by fever, nausea, and vomiting—used to attack many travelers to Mexico. (Some in the U.S. call this "Montezuma's revenge," but you won't hear it called that in Mexico.) Widespread improvements in infrastructure, sanitation, and education have greatly diminished this ailment, especially in well-developed resort areas. Most travelers make a habit of drinking only bottled water, which also helps to protect against

unfamiliar bacteria. In resort areas, and generally throughout Mexico, only purified ice is used. If you do come down with this ailment, nothing beats Pepto Bismol, readily available in Mexico. Imodium is also available in Mexico and is used by many travelers for a quick fix. A good high-potency (or "therapeutic") vitamin supplement and even extra vitamin C can help; yogurt is good for healthy digestion.

Since dehydration can quickly become life-threatening, be careful to replace fluids and electrolytes (potassium, sodium, and the like) during a bout of diarrhea. Drink Pedialyte, a rehydration solution available at most Mexican pharmacies, or natural fruit juice, such as guava or apple (stay away from orange juice, which has laxative properties), with a pinch of salt added.

The U.S. Public Health Service recommends the following measures for preventing travelers' diarrhea: **Drink only purified water** (boiled water, canned or bottled beverages, beer, or wine). **Choose food carefully.** In general, avoid salads (except in first-class restaurants), uncooked vegetables, undercooked protein, and unpasteurized milk or milk products, including cheese. Choose food that is freshly cooked and still hot. Avoid eating food prepared by street vendors. In addition, something as simple as **clean hands** can go a long way toward preventing *turista.*

HIGH-ALTITUDE HAZARDS
Travelers to certain regions of Mexico occasionally experience **elevation sickness,** which results from the relative lack of oxygen and the decrease in barometric pressure that characterizes high elevations (more than 1,500m/5,000 ft.). Symptoms include shortness of breath, fatigue, headache, insomnia, and even nausea. Mexico City is at 2,240m (7,349 ft.) above sea level, as are a number of other central and southern cities, such as San Cristóbal de las Casas (even higher than Mexico City). At high elevations, it takes about 10 days to acquire

Tips   **Over-the-Counter Drugs in Mexico**

Antibiotics and other drugs that you'd need a prescription to buy in the States are often available over the counter in Mexican pharmacies. Mexican pharmacies also carry a limited selection of common over-the-counter cold, sinus, and allergy remedies.

the extra red blood corpuscles you need to adjust to the scarcity of oxygen. To help your body acclimate, drink plenty of fluids, avoid alcohol, and don't overexert yourself during the first few days. If you have heart or lung trouble, consult your doctor before flying above 2,400m (7,872 ft.).

BUGS, BITES & OTHER WILDLIFE CONCERNS   **Mosquitoes** and **gnats** are prevalent along the coast and in the Yucatán lowlands. *Repelente contra insectos* (insect repellent) is a must, and it's not always available in Mexico. If you'll be in these areas and are prone to bites, bring along a repellent that contains the active ingredient DEET. Avon's Skin So Soft also works extremely well. Another good remedy to keep the mosquitoes away is to mix citronella essential oil with basil, clove, and lavender essential oils. If you're sensitive to bites, pick up some antihistamine cream from a drugstore at home.

Most readers won't ever see an *alacrán* (scorpion). But if one stings you, go immediately to a doctor. The one lethal scorpion found in some parts of Mexico is the *Centruroides*, part of the Buthidae family, characterized by a thin body, thick tail, and triangular-shaped sternum. Most deaths from these scorpions result within 24 hours of the sting as a result of respiratory or cardiovascular failure, with children and elderly people most at risk. Scorpions are not aggressive (they don't hunt for prey), but they may sting if touched, especially in their hiding places. In Mexico, you can buy scorpion toxin antidote at any drugstore. It is an injection, and it costs around $25.

This is a good idea if you plan to camp in a remote area, where medical assistance can be several hours away.

TROPICAL ILLNESSES   You shouldn't be overly concerned about tropical diseases if you stay on the normal tourist routes and don't eat street food. However, both dengue fever and cholera have appeared in Mexico in recent years. Talk to your doctor or to a medical specialist in tropical diseases about precautions you should take. You can protect yourself by taking some simple precautions: Watch what you eat and drink; don't swim in stagnant water (ponds, slow-moving rivers, or wells); and avoid mosquito bites by covering up, using repellent, and sleeping under netting. The most dangerous areas seem to be on Mexico's west coast, away from the big resorts.

On occasion, coastal waters from the Gulf of Mexico can become contaminated with rapid growth in algae (phytoplankton), leading to a phenomenon known as harmful algal bloom or a "red tide." The algal release of neurotoxins threatens marine life and can cause rashes and even flu-like symptoms in exposed humans. Although red tides happen infrequently, you should not enter the water if you notice a reddish-brown color or are told there is a red tide.

WHAT TO DO IF YOU GET SICK AWAY FROM HOME

Any English-speaking embassy or consulate staff in Mexico can provide a list of area doctors who speak English. If you get

Tips Smoke-Free Mexico?

In early 2008, the Mexican president signed into law a nationwide smoking ban in workplaces and public buildings, and on public transportation. Under this ground-breaking law, private businesses are only permitted to allow public smoking in enclosed ventilated areas. Hotels may maintain up to 25% of guest rooms for smokers. Violators face stiff fines, and smokers refusing to comply could receive up to 36-hour jail sentences. Despite some uncertainty over how thoroughly the legislation is being followed and enforced throughout different parts of the country, the law places Mexico—where a significant percentage of the population smokes—at the forefront of efforts to curb smoking and improve public health in Latin America. So before you light up, be sure to ask about the application of local laws in Mexican public places and businesses you visit.

sick in Mexico, consider asking your hotel concierge to recommend a local doctor— even his or her own. You can also try the emergency room at a local hospital or urgent care facility. Many hospitals also have walk-in clinics for emergency cases that are not life-threatening; you may not get immediate attention, but you won't pay emergency room prices.

For travel to Mexico, you may have to pay all medical costs upfront and be reimbursed later. Before leaving home, find out what medical services your health insurance covers. To protect yourself, consider buying medical travel insurance.

We list **emergency numbers** in "Fast Facts," p. 283.

6 SAFETY

Mexico is one of the world's great travel destinations and millions of visitors travel safely here each year. In most places, it's uncommon for foreign visitors to face anything worse than petty crime. Always use common sense and exercise caution when in unfamiliar areas. Leave valuables and irreplaceable items in a safe place, or don't bring them at all. Use hotel safes when available. Avoid driving alone, especially at night. You can generally trust a person whom you approach for help or directions, but be wary of anyone who approaches you offering the same. The more insistent a person is, the more cautious you should be. Stay away from areas where drug dealing and prostitution occur.

These tips should help make your trip even more enjoyable.

It is important to know that Mexico has experienced a serious escalation in drug-related and border violence in the past couple years, including cities that previously received significant tourism, including Tijuana, Ciudad Juarez, and Ciudad Chihuahua.

The U.S. and Mexico share a border more than 3,000km (nearly 2,000 miles) long and Americans comprise the vast majority of tourists to Mexico. Due to this close and historically intertwined relationship, we recommend that all travelers read the **U.S. Department of State travel advisories** for Mexico (**www.state.gov**).

One More Author Gives His Two Cents: Safety in Mexico

David Baird Stories of murder and mayhem are making all the headlines about Mexico these days. Stories of assassinations, kidnappings, and shootouts sell newspapers but are of no help evaluating the risk in traveling through the country. They are newsworthy in that they document the gravity of the problem Mexico faces in gaining control of its borders and ensuring public safety. The best way to understand the risk of traveling in Mexico is to read the U.S. State Department Travel Alert (www.state.gov).

The current situation has changed the way I travel in two ways beyond the usual precautions—such as not flashing a lot of money, not wearing an expensive watch, keeping aware of my surroundings, and not driving on the highway at night (for reasons that have more to do with practicalities than issues of crime). The changes I've made can be boiled down to two objectives: Avoid being in the wrong place at the wrong time, and avoid the possibility of mistaken identity. The **first** is largely met by not lingering in Mexico's northern border states (including Durango and the interior of Sinaloa). This is where the immense majority of the violence is occurring. The **second** is meant to minimize any risk of being held up or nabbed by kidnappers, and it is achieved by looking as much like a tourist as possible. Kidnappers in Mexico don't target tourists. They have targeted resident foreigners who have family in the country or business people who have associates. They do this because they need someone to demand the ransom from. The risk here is from small-time gangs who act opportunistically. (Serious kidnappers aren't a threat because they won't do anything without planning and surveillance.) In the last few years, small-time gangs have increased. The best way I know of to avoid this risk is not to carry a briefcase or satchel, which is a business symbol. What's more, by hauling around a backpack, you will automatically escape scrutiny because businesspersons in Mexico never use them. The backpack (*mochila*) in Mexico is a strong cultural identifier. It's associated with students and counterculture types, so much so that the word *mochilero* has come to describe hippies. For this very reason, I used to lug my computer around in a briefcase and now I always use a backpack.

The U.S. State Department encourages its citizens to use main roads during daylight hours, stay in well-known tourist destinations and tourist areas with better security, and provide an itinerary to a friend or family member not traveling with them. It can be useful to travel with a working cell phone, as well. This is good advice for all travelers to Mexico.

For emergency numbers, turn to p. 283.

CRIME IN RESORT TOWNS

There have been a number of rapes reported in Cancún and other resort areas, usually at night or in the early morning. Armed street crime is a serious problem in all the major cities. Some bars and nightclubs, especially in resort cities such as Cancún, can be havens for drug dealers and petty criminals.

It is also advised that you should not hike alone in backcountry areas nor walk alone on less-frequented beaches, ruins, or trails.

Highway Safety

Travelers should exercise caution while traveling Mexican highways, avoiding travel at night, and using toll *(cuota)* roads rather than the less secure free *(libre)* roads whenever possible. Cooperate with official checkpoints when traveling on Mexican highways.

Bus travel should take place during daylight hours on first-class conveyances. Although bus hijackings and robberies have occurred on toll roads, buses on toll roads have a markedly lower rate of incidents than second-class and third-class buses that travel the less secure "free" highways.

Bribes & Scams

As is the case around the world, there are the occasional bribes and scams in Mexico, targeted at people believed to be naive, such as telltale tourists. For years, Mexico was known as a place where bribes—called *mordidas* (bites)—were expected; however, the country is rapidly changing. Frequently, offering a bribe today, especially to a police officer, is considered an insult, and it can land you in deeper trouble.

When you are crossing the border, should the person who inspects your car ask for a tip, you can ignore this request—but understand that the official may suddenly decide that a complete search of your belongings is in order. If you sense you're being asked for a bribe, understand that although it may be common, offering a bribe to a public official to avoid a ticket or other penalty is officially a crime in Mexico.

Many tourists have the impression that everything works better in Mexico if you "tip"; however, in reality, this only perpetuates the *mordida* tradition. If you are pleased with a service, feel free to tip. But you shouldn't tip simply to attempt to get away with something illegal or inappropriate—whether it is evading a ticket that's deserved or a car inspection as you're crossing the border.

Whatever you do, **avoid impoliteness;** you won't do yourself any favors if you insult a Mexican official. Extreme politeness, even in the face of adversity, rules Mexico. In Mexico, *gringos* have a reputation for being loud and demanding. By adopting the local custom of excessive courtesy, you'll have greater success in negotiations of any kind. Stand your ground, but do it politely.

As you travel in Mexico, you may encounter several types of **scams,** which are typical throughout the world. One involves some kind of a **distraction** or feigned commotion. While your attention is diverted, for example, a pickpocket makes a grab for your wallet. In another common scam, an **unaccompanied child** pretends to be lost and frightened and takes your hand for safety. Meanwhile the child or an accomplice plunders your pockets. A third involves **confusing currency.** A shoeshine boy, street musician, guide, or other individual might offer you a service for a price that seems reasonable—in pesos. When it comes time to pay, he or she tells you the price is in dollars, not pesos. Be very clear on the price and currency when services are involved.

7 SPECIALIZED TRAVEL RESOURCES

In addition to the destination-specific resources listed below, please visit Frommers.com for additional specialized travel resources.

GAY & LESBIAN TRAVELERS

Mexico is a conservative country, with deeply rooted Catholic religious traditions.

Public displays of same-sex affection are rare and still considered shocking for men, especially outside of urban or resort areas. Women in Mexico frequently walk hand in hand, but anything more would cross the boundary of acceptability. However, gay and lesbian travelers are generally treated with respect and should not experience harassment, assuming they give the appropriate regard to local customs.

While much of Mexico is socially conservative, Cancún and Playa del Carmen are not. Popular with many gay travelers, both coastal resorts offer gay-friendly accommodations, bars, and activities. For more information, visit **MexGay Vacations** at www.mexgay.com. Information about gay-friendly accommodations in Mérida, Yucatán is available at www.gay places2stay.com.

TRAVELERS WITH DISABILITIES

Mexico may seem like one giant obstacle course to travelers in wheelchairs or on crutches. At airports, you may encounter steep stairs before finding a well-hidden elevator or escalator—if one exists. Airlines will often arrange wheelchair assistance to the baggage area. Porters are generally available to help with luggage at airports and large bus stations, once you've cleared baggage claim.

Mexican airports are upgrading their services, but it is not uncommon to board from a remote position, meaning you either descend stairs to a bus that ferries you to the plane, which you board by climbing stairs, or you walk across the tarmac to your plane and ascend the stairs. Deplaning presents the same problem in reverse.

Escalators (and there aren't many in the country) are often out of order. Stairs without handrails abound. Few restrooms are equipped for travelers with disabilities; when one is available, access to it may be through a narrow passage that won't accommodate a wheelchair or a person on crutches. Many deluxe hotels (the most expensive) now have rooms with bathrooms designed for people with disabilities. Those traveling on a budget should stick with one-story hotels or hotels with elevators. Even so, there will probably still be obstacles somewhere. Generally speaking, no matter where you are, someone will lend a hand, although you may have to ask for it.

FAMILY TRAVEL

If you have trouble getting your kids out of the house in the morning, dragging them to a faraway foreign country may seem like an insurmountable challenge. But family travel can be immensely rewarding, giving you new ways of seeing the world through the eyes of children.

Children are considered the national treasure of Mexico, and Mexicans will warmly welcome and cater to your children. Many parents were reluctant to bring young children into Mexico in the past, primarily due to health concerns, but I can't think of a better place to introduce children to the exciting adventure of exploring a different culture. One of the best destinations for kids is Cancún. Hotels can often arrange for a babysitter.

Before leaving, ask your doctor which medications to take along. Disposable diapers cost about the same in Mexico but are of poorer quality. You can get Huggies Supreme and Pampers identical to the ones sold in the United States, but at a higher price. Many stores sell Gerber's baby foods. Dry cereals, powdered formulas, baby bottles, and purified water are easily available in midsize and large cities or resorts.

Cribs may present a problem; only the largest and most luxurious hotels provide them. However, rollaway beds are often available. Child seats or high chairs at restaurants are common.

Consider bringing your own car seat; they are not readily available for rent in Mexico.

Every country's regulations differ, but in general children traveling abroad should have plenty of documentation on hand, particularly if they're traveling with someone other than their own parents (in which case a notarized form letter from a parent is often required). For details on entry requirements for children traveling abroad, turn to p. 49.

To locate accommodations, restaurants, and attractions that are particularly kid-friendly, refer to the "Kids" icon throughout this guide.

WOMEN TRAVELERS

Mexicans in general, and men in particular, are nosy about single travelers, especially women. If a taxi driver or anyone else with whom you don't want to become friendly asks about your marital status, family, and so forth, my advice is to make up a set of answers (regardless of the truth): "I'm married, traveling with friends, and I have three children." Saying you are single and traveling alone may send the wrong message. U.S. television—widely viewed now in Mexico—has given many Mexican men the image of American single women as being sexually promiscuous.

SENIOR TRAVEL

Mexico is a popular country for retirees. For decades, North Americans have been living indefinitely in Mexico by returning to the border and recrossing with a new tourist permit every 6 months. Mexican immigration officials have caught on, and now limit the maximum time in the country to 6 months within any year. This is to encourage even partial residents to acquire proper documentation.

AIM-Adventures in Mexico, Apartado Postal 31–70, 45050 Guadalajara, Jalisco, is a well-written, informative newsletter for prospective retirees. Subscriptions are $29 to the United States.

Sanborn Tours, 2015 S. 10th St., P.O. Drawer 519, McAllen, TX 78505-0519 (*©* **800/395-8482;** www.sanborns.com), offers a "Retire in Mexico" orientation tour.

STUDENT TRAVEL

Because Mexicans consider higher education a luxury rather than a birthright, there is no formal network of student discounts and programs. Most Mexican students travel with their families rather than with other students, so student discount cards are not commonly recognized.

However, more hostels have entered the student travel scene. **Hostels.com.mx** offers a list of hostels in Cancún, Mérida, Playa del Carmen, and San Cristobal Las Casas.

8 SUSTAINABLE TOURISM

Mexico's ecological diversity is among the broadest of any country in the world, with an abundance of ecosystems that ranges from the northern deserts to the central conifer forests, and the southern tropical rainforests. Mexico also supports a population of 108 million people and welcomes more than 11 million visitors each year. Tourism is one of the country's biggest and most lucrative industries, and while tourism

has brought jobs and growth to much of Mexico, it has also created and even accelerated many of Mexico's ecological problems. **Cancún** may be the most high-profile example: Rapidly developed from a rural outpost to an international resort destination, Cancún imported turf from Florida for its golf courses, inadvertently introducing a disease that wiped out the local coconut palms. The region's mangroves, a key habitat for native

> ## (Tips) Biodegradable Sunscreen
>
> Recent scientific studies have shown that the chemicals in commercial sunscreen can do long-term damage to coral reefs, collect in freshwater, and even build up in your own body system. The Riviera Maya receives more than 2.5 million visitors every year, many of them drawn to its rare marine environment—a unique combination of freshwater cenotes and the world's second-largest coral reef. A few ounces of sunscreen multiplied by 2.5 million is equal to a substantial amount of harmful chemicals suspended in the ocean and freshwater. That's why tours to the **Sian Ka'an Biosphere Reserve** and water parks **Xcaret** and **Xel-Ha** ask that you use only biodegradable sunscreen or wear none at all when swimming in their ocean or cenotes. You might just be inspired to use a biodegradable formula wherever you swim.
>
> The label of a biodegradable sunscreen should state that it is 100% biodegradable (and only 100% will do). Xcaret gives out packets of biodegradable formula, but Xel-Ha charges $16 for theirs. If you're curious, you can obtain a list of banned chemicals by contacting the parks directly. Buy a supply of biodegradable formula before you go from **www.mexitan.com** or **www.caribbeansol.com**.

species and vital to protecting the land from hurricanes and erosion, have also suffered.

However, tourism has also encouraged the development of ecological conservation. Mexico is home to seven of the world's eight species of sea turtle, and the entire sea turtle population was decimated on both coasts as a result of tourism growth and local overfishing. A recent success story comes from the **Riviera Maya,** where marine biologists are working with hotels to guard nesting turtles and their eggs.

Mexico's people are proud of their land and culture, and through your travels, especially in rural areas, you will likely encounter *ejidos,* and *cooperativos,* or local cooperatives, that offer small-scale tourism services—this may be as simple as a taking visitors on a boat ride through a lake or as visible as controlling access to archeological ruins. *Ejidos* will also run tours to popular eco-tourism destinations similar to those offered by large travel agencies. When you deal with *ejidos,* everyone you encounter will be from the community and you know that your money goes directly back to them. States with a strong network of cooperatives include Quintana Roo and Yucatán.

The Mexican Caribbean supports the Great Mesoamerican Barrier Reef, the second largest reef in the world, which extends down to Central America. This reef and other marine ecosystems face increasing pressure from sedimentation, pollution, over-fishing, and exploitative recreational activities, all newly associated with growing regional tourism. The **Coral Reef Alliance** (CORAL; www.coral.org) is an example of an organization that, by teaming up with the **World Wildlife Fund** (WWF; www.wwf.org) and **United Nations Environmental Program** (UNEP; www.unep.org), has been working to address threats to the Mesoamerican Barrier Reef and improve environmental sustainability throughout the region. CORAL partners with Mexican Amigos de Sian Ka'an, Conservation International, and the Cozumel Reefs National Park in an effort to build sustainability into mass tourism (such as cruise ships and hotels). CORAL assists marine tourism operators in implementing a voluntary code of conduct for best environmental practices. CORAL is soon to spread its influence to the Yum Balam region of the Yucatán Peninsula, where guidelines for whale shark interactions are greatly needed.

One of the best contributions a diver can make to support a healthy reef while diving is to avoid physical contact with the reef. Talk to your scuba outfitter about proper buoyancy control and body position to avoid damaging these fragile ecosystems.

Tabasco suffered severe flooding in 2007 that devastated much of the land and brought widespread suffering to the population, which is among Mexico's poorest. The floods also affected Chiapas, though to a lesser extent. Tabasco's sinking land, and the extraction of oil and gas, land erosion, and deforestation all contributed to the state's vulnerability to flooding.

Ecotourism and sustainable tourism opportunities abound in **Chiapas,** where a growing number of small, local tourism cooperatives have organized to take tourists on guided hikes, treks, and even kayak expeditions into the state's isolated jungles and nature reserves. The **Chiapas Tourism Secretariat** has information in Spanish about ecotourism at locations across the state (www.turismochiapas.gob.mx). Two private companies that run ecotours throughout Chiapas are **Ecochiapas** (Primero de Marzo 30, San Cristóbal de las Casas; ✆ **967/674-6660;** www.ecochiapas.com) and **Latitud 16** (Calle 28 de Agosto 4, San Cristóbal de las Casas; ✆ 967/674-6915).

The **Mesoamerican Ecotourism Alliance** (✆ **800/682-0584** in the US; www.travelwithmea.org) offers award-winning ecotours recognized by *National Geographic* to the Yucatán and Chiapas.

ANIMAL-RIGHTS ISSUES

The Yucatán presents many opportunities to **swim with dolphins.** The capture of wild dolphins was outlawed in Mexico in 2002. The only dolphins added to the country's dolphin swim programs since then were born in captivity. This law may have eased concerns about the death and implications of capturing wild dolphins, but the controversy is not over. Local organizations have been known to staple notes to Dolphin Discovery ads in magazines distributed in Cancún hotels. Marine biologists who run the dolphin swim programs say the mammals are thriving and that the programs provide a forum for research, conservation, education, and rescue operations. Animal rights advocates maintain that keeping these intelligent mammals in captivity is nothing more than exploitation. Their argument is that these private dolphin programs don't qualify as "public display" under the Marine Mammal Protection Act because the entry fees bar most of the public from participating.

Visit the website of the **Whale and Dolphin Conservation Society** at www.wdcs.org or the **American Cetacean Society,** www.acsonline.org, for further discussion on the topic.

Bullfighting is considered an important part of Latin culture, but you should know, before you attend a *correo,* that the bulls (at least four) will ultimately be killed in a gory spectacle. This is not the case in some countries, such as France and Portugal, but the Mexicans follow the Spanish model. That said, a bullfight is a portal into understanding Mexico's Spanish colonial past, although nowadays bullfights are more of a tourist attraction, especially in tourist laden Cancún. To read more about the implications of attending a bullfight, visit **www.peta.org**, the website of People for the Ethical Treatment of Animals (PETA) (or see specifically: www.peta.org/mc/factsheet_display.asp?ID=64).

PLANNING YOUR TRIP TO THE YUCATÁN, TABASCO & CHIAPAS

3

SPECIAL INTEREST TRIPS & ESCORTED GENERAL TOURS

General Resources for Green Travel

In addition to the resources for the Yucatán, Tabasco, and Chiapas listed above, the following websites provide valuable wide-ranging information on sustainable travel. For a list of even more sustainable resources, as well as tips and explanations on how to travel greener, visit www.frommers.com/planning.

- **Responsible Travel** (www.responsibletravel.com) is a great source of sustainable travel ideas; the site is run by a spokesperson for ethical tourism in the travel industry. **Sustainable Travel International** (www.sustainabletravel international.org) promotes ethical tourism practices, and manages an extensive directory of sustainable properties and tour operators around the world.
- In the U.K., **Tourism Concern** (www.tourismconcern.org.uk) works to reduce social and environmental problems connected to tourism. The **Association of Independent Tour Operators (AITO)** (www.aito.co.uk) is a group of specialist operators leading the field in making holidays sustainable.
- In Canada, **www.greenlivingonline.com** offers extensive content on how to travel sustainably, including a travel and transport section.
- In Australia, the national body which sets guidelines and standards for ecotourism is **Ecotourism Australia** (www.ecotourism.org.au). **The Green Directory** (www.thegreendirectory.com.au), **Green Pages** (www.thegreen pages.com.au), and **Eco Directory** (www.ecodirectory.com.au) offer sustainable travel tips and directories of green businesses.
- **Carbonfund** (www.carbonfund.org), **TerraPass** (www.terrapass.org), and **Carbon Neutral** (www.carbonneutral.org) provide info on "carbon offsetting," or offsetting the greenhouse gas emitted during flights.
- **Greenhotels** (www.greenhotels.com) recommends green-rated member hotels around the world that fulfill the company's stringent environmental requirements. **Environmentally Friendly Hotels** (www.environmentally friendlyhotels.com) offers more green accommodation ratings.
- For information on animal-friendly issues throughout the world, visit **Tread Lightly** (www.treadlightly.org).
- **Volunteer International** (www.volunteerinternational.org) has a list of questions to help you determine the intentions and the nature of a volunteer program. For general info on volunteer travel, visit **www.volunteer abroad.org** and **www.idealist.org**.

9 SPECIAL INTEREST TRIPS & ESCORTED GENERAL INTEREST TOURS

ACADEMIC TRIPS & LANGUAGE CLASSES

For Spanish-language instruction, **IMAC** (© **866/306-5040;** www.spanish-school. com.mx) offers programs in Guadalajara, Puerto Vallarta, and Playa del Carmen. The **Spanish Institute** (© **800/539-9710;** www.spanishtoday.com) is affiliated with intensive Spanish language schools in Puebla and Mérida.

To explore your inner Frida or Diego while in Mexico, look into **Mexico Art Tours,** 1233 E. Baker Dr., Tempe, AZ 85282 (© **888/783-1331** or 480/730-1764; www.mexicanarttours.com). Typically led by Jean Grimm, a specialist in the arts and cultures of Mexico, these unique tours feature compelling speakers who are themselves respected scholars and artists. Itineraries include visits to Chiapas, Guadalajara, Guanajuato, Puebla, Puerto Vallarta, Mexico City, San Miguel de Allende, and Veracruz—and other cities. Special tours involve archaeology, architecture, interior design, and culture—such as a Day of the Dead tour.

The **Archaeological Conservancy,** 5301 Central Ave. NE, Suite 402, Albuquerque, NM 87108 (© **505/266-1540;** www.americanarchaeology.com), presents various trips each year, led by an expert, usually an archaeologist. The trips change from year to year and space is limited; make reservations early.

ATC Tours and Travel, Av. 16 de Septiembre, 29200 San Cristóbal de las Casas, Chis. (© **967/678-2550,** -2557; fax 967/678-3145; www.atctours.com), a Mexico-based tour operator with an excellent reputation, offers specialist-led trips, primarily in southern Mexico. In addition to trips to the ruins of Palenque and Yaxchilán (extending into Belize and Guatemala by river, plane, and bus if desired), ATC runs horseback tours to Chamula or Zinacantán, and day trips to the ruins of Toniná around San Cristóbal de las Casas; birding in the rainforests of Chiapas and Guatemala (including in the El Triunfo Reserve of Chiapas); hikes to the shops and homes of textile artists of the Chiapas highlands; and walks from the Lagos de Montebello in the Montes Azules Biosphere Reserve, with camping and canoeing. The company can also prepare custom itineraries.

ADVENTURE TRIPS

AMTAVE (Asociación Mexicana de Turismo de Aventura y Ecoturismo, A.C.) is an active association of ecotourism and adventure tour operators. It publishes an annual catalog of participating firms and their offerings, all of which must meet certain criteria for security, quality, and training of the guides, as well as for sustainability of natural and cultural environments. For more information, contact **AMTAVE** (© **55/5688-3883;** www.amtave.org).

The California Native, 6701 W. 87th Place, Los Angeles, CA 90045 (© **800/926-1140** or 310/642-1140; www.calnative.com), offers small-group deluxe 7-, 8, 11-, and 14-day escorted tours through the Riviera Maya, the Yucatán, and Chiapas.

MexicoTravel.net, 300-3665 Kingsway, Vancouver, BC V5R 5W2 Canada (© **604/454-9044;** fax 604/454-9088; www.mexicotravel.net), runs adventure, cultural, and sports tours to Mexico City and surrounding areas, Baja, Veracruz, the Copper Canyon, the Mayan Route, and other destinations.

Trek America, 16/17 Grange Mills Weir Road, LONDON, SW12ONE, UK (© **800/873-5872** in the U.S.; 0845/313-2614 in the UK; www.trekamerica.com); organizes lengthy, active trips that combine trekking, hiking, van transportation, and camping along the Mayan Route and across the Yucatán.

FOOD & WINE TRIPS

If you're looking to eat your way through Mexico, sign up with **Culinary Adventures,** 6023 Reid Dr. NW, Gig Harbor, WA 98335 (© **253/851-7676;** fax 253/851-9532; www.marilyntausend.com). It runs a short but select list of cooking tours in Mexico. Culinary Adventures features well-known cooks, with travel to regions known for excellent cuisine. Destinations vary each year. The owner, Marilyn Tausend, is the author of *Cocinas de la Familia* (Family Kitchens), *Savoring Mexico,* and *Mexican,* and co-author of *Mexico the Beautiful Cookbook.*

10 STAYING CONNECTED

TELEPHONES

Mexico's telephone system is slowly but surely catching up with modern times. Most telephone numbers have 10 digits. Every city and town that has telephone access has a two-digit (Mexico City, Monterrey, and Guadalajara) or three-digit (everywhere else) area code. In Mexico City, Monterrey, and Guadalajara, local numbers have eight digits; elsewhere, local numbers have seven digits. To place a local call, you do not need to dial the area code. Many fax numbers are also regular phone numbers; ask whoever answers for the fax tone *("me da tono de fax, por favor").*

The **country code** for Mexico is **52.**

To call Mexico:

1. Dial the international access code: 011 from the U.S.; 00 from the U.K., Ireland, or New Zealand; or 0011 from Australia.
2. Dial the country code: 52.
3. Dial the two- or three-digit area code, then the eight- or seven-digit number. For example, if you wanted to call the U.S. consulate in Acapulco, the entire number would be 011-52-744-469-0556. If you wanted to dial the U.S. embassy in Mexico City, the entire number would be 011-52-55-5209-9100.

To make international calls: To make international calls from Mexico, dial 00, then the country code (U.S. or Canada 1, U.K. 44, Ireland 353, Australia 61, New Zealand 64). Next, dial the area code and number. For example, to call the British Embassy in Washington, you would dial 00-1-202-588-7800.

For directory assistance: Dial ℂ **040** if you're looking for a number inside Mexico. *Note:* Listings usually appear under the owner's name, not the name of the business, and your chances to find an English-speaking operator are slim.

For operator assistance: If you need operator assistance in making a call, dial ℂ **090** to make an international call, and ℂ **020** to call a number in Mexico.

Toll-free numbers: Numbers beginning with 800 within Mexico are toll-free, but calling a U.S. toll-free number from Mexico costs the same as an overseas call. To call an 800 number in the U.S., dial 001-880 and the last seven digits of the toll-free number. To call an 888 number in the U.S., dial 001-881 and the last seven digits of the toll-free number. For a number with an 887 prefix, dial 882; for 866, dial 883.

CELLPHONES

Telcel is Mexico's expensive, primary cellphone provider. It has upgraded its systems to GSM and offers good coverage in much of the country, including the major cities and resorts. Most Mexicans buy their cellphones without a specific coverage plan and then pay as they go or purchase prepaid cards with set amounts of air-time credit. These cellphone cards with scratch-off pin numbers can be purchased in Telcel stores as well as many newspaper stands and convenience stores.

Many U.S. and European cellphone companies offer networks with roaming coverage in Mexico. Rates can be very high, so check with your provider before committing to making calls this way. An increasing number of Mexicans, particularly among the younger generation, prefer the less expensive rates of **Nextel** (www.nextel. com.mx), which features push-to-talk service. **Cellular Abroad** (www.cellular abroad.com) offers cellphone rentals and purchases as well as SIM cards for travel abroad. Whether you rent or purchase the cellphone, you need to purchase a SIM card that is specific for Mexico.

To call a Mexican cellular number in the same area code, dial 044 and then the number. To dial the cellular phone from anywhere else in Mexico, first dial 01, and then the three-digit area code and the seven-digit number. To place an international call to a cellphone (e.g., from the U.S.), you now must add a 1 after the country code: for example, 011-52-1 + 10-digit number.

INTERNET & E-MAIL

Wireless Internet access is increasingly common in Mexico's major cities and resorts. Mexico's largest airports offer Wi-Fi access provided for a fee by Telcel's Prodigy Internet service. Most five-star hotels now offer Wi-Fi in the guest rooms, although you will need to check in advance whether this service is free or for a fee. Hotel lobbies often have Wi-Fi as well. To find public Wi-Fi hotspots in Mexico, go to **www.jiwire.com**; its Hotspot Finder holds the world's largest directory of public wireless hotspots.

Many large Mexican airports have **Internet kiosks,** and quality Mexican hotels usually have business centers with Internet access. You can also check out such copy stores as **FedEx Office** or **OfficeMax,** which offer computer stations with fully loaded software (as well as Wi-Fi).

11 TIPS ON ACCOMMODATIONS

MEXICO'S HOTEL RATING SYSTEM

The hotel rating system in Mexico is called "Stars and Diamonds." Hotels may qualify to earn one to five stars or diamonds. Many hotels that have excellent standards are not certified, but all rated hotels adhere to strict standards. The guidelines relate to service, facilities, and hygiene more than to prices.

Five-diamond hotels meet the highest requirements for rating: The beds are comfortable, bathrooms are in excellent working order, all facilities are renovated regularly, infrastructure is top-tier, and services and hygiene meet the highest international standards.

Five-star hotels usually offer similar quality, but with lower levels of service and detail in the rooms. For example, a five-star hotel may have less luxurious linens or, perhaps, room service during limited hours rather than 24 hours.

Four-star hotels are less expensive and more basic, but they still guarantee cleanliness and basic services such as hot water and purified drinking water. Three, two-, and one-star hotels are at least working to adhere to certain standards: Bathrooms are cleaned and linens are washed daily, and you can expect a minimum standard of service. Two- and one-star hotels generally provide bottled water rather than purified water.

The nonprofit organization Calidad Mexicana Certificada, A.C., known as **Calmecac** (www.calmecac.com.mx), is responsible for hotel ratings; visit their website for additional details about the rating system.

HOTEL CHAINS

In addition to the major international chains, you'll run across a number of less-familiar brands as you plan your trip to Mexico. They include:

- **Brisas Hotels & Resorts** (www.brisas. com.mx). These were the hotels that originally attracted jet-set travelers to Mexico. Spectacular in a retro way, these properties offer the laid-back luxury that makes a Mexican vacation so unique.
- **Fiesta Americana** and **Fiesta Inn** (www.posadas.com). Part of the Mexican-owned Grupo Posadas company,

(Finds) Boutique Lodgings

Mexico lends itself beautifully to the concept of small, private hotels in idyllic settings. They vary in style from grandiose estate to palm-thatched bungalow. **Mexico Boutique Hotels** (www.mexicoboutiquehotels.com) specializes in smaller places to stay with a high level of personal attention and service. Most options have less than 50 rooms, and the accommodations consist of entire villas, *casitas*, bungalows, or a combination. The Yucatán is especially noted for the luxury haciendas throughout the peninsula.

these hotels set the country's midrange standard for facilities and services. They generally offer comfortable, spacious rooms and traditional Mexican hospitality. Fiesta Americana hotels offer excellent beach-resort packages. Fiesta Inn hotels are usually more business-oriented. Grupo Posadas also owns the more luxurious Caesar Park hotels and the eco-oriented Explorean hotels.

- **Hoteles Camino Real** (www.camino real.com). Once known as the premier Mexican hotel chain, Camino Real still maintains a high standard of service at its properties, although the company was sold in 2005, and many of the hotels that once formed a part of it have been sold off or have become independent. Its beach hotels are traditionally located on the best beaches in the area. This chain also focuses on the business market. The hotels are famous for their vivid and contrasting colors.
- **NH Hoteles** (www.nh-hotels.com). The NH hotels are noted for their family-friendly facilities and quality standards. The beach properties' signature feature is a pool, framed by columns, overlooking the sea.
- **Quinta Real Grand Class Hotels and Resorts** (www.quintareal.com). These

hotels, owned by Summit Hotels and Resorts, are noted for architectural and cultural details that reflect their individual regions. At these luxury properties, attention to detail and excellent service are the rule. Quinta Real is the top-line Mexican hotel brand.

HOUSE RENTALS & SWAPS

House and villa rentals and swaps are becoming more common in Mexico, but no single recognized agency or business provides this service exclusively for Mexico. In the chapters that follow, we have provided information on independent services that we have found to be reputable.

You'll find the most extensive inventory of homes at **Vacation Rentals by Owner** (**VRBO;** www.vrbo.com). They have more than 33,000 homes and condominiums worldwide, including a large selection in Mexico. Another good option is **Vacation-Spot** (© **888/903-7768;** www.vacation spot.com), owned by Expedia and a part of its sister company Hotels.com. It has fewer choices, but the company's criteria for adding inventory is much more selective and often includes on-site inspections. They also offer toll-free phone support.

Suggested Yucatán Itineraries

by David Baird

The following itineraries assume you're flying in and out of Cancún, by far the most common port of entry for the Yucatán. The airport is south of town in the direction of the Riviera Maya, so if you rent a car to drive down the coast, you won't have to deal with city traffic.

For traveling around the Yucatán, rental cars work well. The roads are all easy to figure out, and there's not much traffic when you move inland. Finding your way around Mérida is a little tricky, but Cancún and the other cities of the peninsula are easy. You can take buses for long distances during your entire trip, but keep in mind that buses in the Riviera Maya do not run along the small roads that connect the highway to the beach. Your bus will drop you on the side of the highway at the junction with the road to your paradise, and you'll have to flag a taxi to take you the rest of the way. This is a fine method, but can be time- consuming.

These itineraries are merely suggestions; you should tweak them to your specific tastes and interests. Though I've included an itinerary that takes you south into Tabasco and Chiapas, interested travelers should consider taking a fully-dedicated trip to these states on their own. I recommend against being too ambitious with your vacation time. The heat and humidity bring about a lethargy that can be enjoyable if you're not preoccupied with a timetable. Keep in mind as well that it gets dark early here, and it's not a good idea to do much night driving.

1 THE REGIONS IN BRIEF

Travelers to the peninsula have an opportunity to see pre-Hispanic ruins—such as **Chichén Itzá, Uxmal,** and **Tulum**—and the living descendants of the cultures that built them, as well as the ultimate in resort Mexico: **Cancún.** The Yucatán peninsula borders the aquamarine Gulf of Mexico on the west and north, and the clear blue Caribbean Sea on the east. It covers almost 197,600 sq. km (76,294 sq. miles), with nearly 1,600km (1,000 miles) of shoreline. Underground rivers and natural wells, called cenotes, are a peculiar feature of this region.

Lovely rock-walled Maya villages and crumbling *henequén* haciendas dot the interior of the peninsula. The placid interior contrasts with the hubbub of the Caribbean coast. From Cancún south to **Chetumal,** the jungle coastline is spotted with all kinds of development, from posh to budget. This swath has been dubbed the **Riviera Maya,** and boasts an enormous array of wildlife, including hundreds of species of birds. The Gulf Coast beaches, while good enough, don't compare to those on the Caribbean. National parks near **Celestún** and **Río Lagartos** on the

Gulf Coast are home to amazing flocks of flamingos.

Of course, the primary allure of the Yucatán peninsula for tourists is its long Caribbean coast, stretching the entire coast of the state of **Quintana Roo.** The 25-year boom in tourism is rapidly transforming this state's economy away from agriculture and toward construction, transportation, and the service sector.

Things change, however, when you move inland, into the states of **Yucatán,** the northern portion of the peninsula, and **Campeche,** the western portion. Change here is measured on an entirely different scale, and everywhere you go the past is with you. Even the landscape seems infused with a sense of time, dotted by crumbling haciendas and the stark ruins of ancient cities. This is the world of the present-day Maya, where life moves slowly in simple villages bordered by rock walls and small cornfields. On narrow roads you happen upon wandering livestock or field workers going to and fro on bicycles. And in the cities and towns, such as **Mérida** and **Izamal** in Yucatán state, and **Campeche City** in Campeche state, you'll find traditional Yucatán, with its highly pronounced regional flavor, and a way of life that is informed by traditions that are centuries old.

To present the Maya world in its entirety, this book also covers the states of **Tabasco** and **Chiapas.** The Gulf Coast state of Tabasco was once home to the Olmec, the mother culture of Mesoamerica. At Villahermosa's Parque–Museo La Venta, you can see the impressive 40-ton carved rock heads that the Olmec left behind.

San Cristóbal de las Casas, in Chiapas, inhabits cooler, greener mountains, and is more in the mold of a provincial colonial town. Approaching San Cristóbal from any direction, you see small plots of corn tended by colorfully clad Maya. The surrounding villages are home to many craftspeople, from woodcarvers to potters to weavers. In the eastern lowland jungles of Chiapas lie the classic Maya ruins of **Palenque.** Deeper into the interior, for those willing to make the trek, are the ruins of **Yaxchilán** and **Bonampak.**

NATURAL LIFE & PROTECTED AREAS The Yucatán state's nature preserves include the 47,200-hectare (116,584-acre) **Río Lagartos Wildlife Refuge** north of Valladolid—where you'll find North America's largest flock of nesting flamingos—and the 5,600-plus-hectare (13,832-acre) **Celestún Wildlife Refuge,** which harbors most of the flamingos during non-nesting season. The state also has incorporated nature trails into the archaeological site of **Dzibilchaltún,** north of Mérida.

In 1989, Campeche state set aside 71,480 hectares (176,556 acres) in the **Calakmul Biosphere Reserve** that it shares with Guatemala. The area includes the ruins of Calakmul, as well as acres of thick jungle.

Quintana Roo's protected areas are some of the region's most wild and beautiful lands. In 1986, the state set aside the 520,000-hectare (1.3-million-acre) **Sian Ka'an Biosphere Reserve,** conserving a significant part of the coast in the face of development south of Tulum. **Isla Contoy,** also in Quintana Roo, off the coast of Isla Mujeres and Cancún, is a beautiful island refuge for hundreds of birds, turtles, plants, and other wildlife. Cozumel's Chankanaab Lagoon gives visitors an idea of the biological importance of Yucatán's lengthy shoreline: Four of Mexico's eight marine turtle species—loggerhead, green, hawksbill, and leatherback—nest on Quintana Roo's shores, and more than 600 species of birds, reptiles, and mammals have been counted.

Tabasco, though a small state, has set aside a vast preserve of wetlands called **Pantanos de Centla,** just northeast of Villahermosa. Three reserves in Chiapas

encompass jungles and lakes, and some of Mexico's most bio-diverse lands. The largest by far is the nature preserve called **Montes Azules,** the old homeland of the Lacandón Indians in the extreme eastern lowlands bordering Guatemala. Not far

from San Cristóbal de las Casas is also a small preserve of high cloud forest habitat called **Huitepec.** A good distance west of Tuxtla Gutiérrez, the state capital, is an extensive nature preserve containing upland forests called **Selva del Ocote.**

Tips ## If You Have Even Less Time . . .

Given Cancún and the Riviera Maya's proximity to the United States, the vast majority of visitors to this region are weekenders and snowbirds looking for a quick beach fix. Of course, that's what Cancún was made for and even if you have a mere 3 days, you can still experience a taste of what this fascinating region has to offer.

With a weekend trip, fly into Cancún and check into your hotel for an afternoon and evening by the beach and pool. On your full day, you can go on a tour to the Maya ruins of **Chichén Itzá** (p. 236), stopping for lunch and a stroll in colonial **Valladolid** (p. 243)—you'll be back on the beach by late afternoon. You could also easily take a day trip to **Isla Mujeres** (p. 115) for more beach time or **Isla Contoy** (p. 122) for bird-watching, though these trips will take up more of your time. You can easily take a day trip with **Alltournative** (www.alltournative.com; p. 149), which has offices in Cancún, to go zip-lining in the jungle or snorkeling in cenotes. Since Cancún's **nightlife** (p. 112) kicks into high-gear on the weekends, you're bound to find something to your liking in the hotel zone, for everything from mega-clubs to chic lounges, or in downtown, for nightlife with a Mexican flavor.

Take your last morning as an opportunity to meander along the beach and dip your toes in the Caribbean one last time . . . and plan your next trip back.

2 NORTHERN YUCATÁN IN A WEEK

You could extend this itinerary to 10 days, even 2 weeks—it all depends on how much time you want to spend on the beach. Once you've spent a little time in that clear blue water, it's hard to pull yourself away to move inland.

Days ❶ & ❷: Somewhere on the Caribbean Coast

Spend a few days relaxing on the beach. See chapter 7 for more details.

Day ❸: Chichén Itzá ★★★

Have a morning swim before driving to the ruins of **Ek Balam** (p. 246), which lie north of the colonial city of Valladolid. If you're coming from Cancún or the northern Riviera Maya, you can take the modern toll highway and save a lot of travel time, though the toll of $20 is a bit pricey.

If you're in Playa del Carmen or farther south, you're better off driving south to Tulum and taking the highway to Cobá. You can stop and see the ruins of **Cobá** (p. 175) if you allow enough time. When you get to Valladolid, head north on Highway 295 to the turnoff for Ek Balam. After climbing the main pyramid and inspecting the beautifully worked sacred doorway, head back to Valladolid for a late lunch. Drive to Chichén Itzá via the old highway. Shortly after leaving town, stop to enjoy **Cenote Dzitnup** (p. 245). Continue on to

Chichén Itzá (p. 236) and check into a hotel in the area. In the evening, see the sound-and-light show, and then visit the ruins the next morning.

Days ❹ & ❺: Mérida & Environs ★★

Drive to **Mérida** (p. 192) and enjoy an evening in this bustling tropical city. The next day, you can explore the town, or perhaps do some shopping. Or, as a third option, take a side trip during the day and enjoy Mérida in the evening. Choices include the **Celestún National Wildlife Refuge** (p. 215), where you can take a boat ride and see some pink flamingos, or **Dzibilchaltún** (p. 216), to see the ruins and site museum. You might also consider visiting **Progreso** and **Xcambó** (for details on both routes, see p. 217), for another good chance of seeing flamingos.

Day ❻: The Ruins of Uxmal ★★★

No matter whether you take the short way or the long way (for details on both routes, see p. 217), try to get to **Uxmal** by late afternoon, so that you can rest and cool off before seeing the sound-and-light show. Uxmal's **Pyramid of the Magician** is one of the most dramatic structures in the Maya world and it becomes even more intriguing when lit at night. The next morning, you can explore the ruins in more detail. See p. 221.

Day ❼: Cancún

This last day will necessarily include a good bit of driving. Take the short route back via Umán, then use the loop or *periférico* to avoid entering Mérida. After about 45 minutes, you'll see signs for the highway to Cancún. See chapter 5.

3 THE YUCATÁN IN 2 WEEKS

The Yucatán's good roads and fairly contained shape allow for a complete circuit of the peninsula within a 2-week time frame. By moving counterclockwise, you'll save the best beach time for the end of your trip. Plan on arriving in and departing from Cancún.

❶: Cancún

Spend your first day in **Cancún** and unwind after your flight with a swim in the Caribbean or in your hotel pool. See chapter 5.

Day ❷: Valladolid ★

Take your time in the morning, and drive to **Valladolid** (p. 243) in time for a late lunch. This small colonial-era city is compact and walkable, and its highlights include Spanish churches, a lively central plaza, and even a small collection of cenotes.

Day ❸: Ek Balam ★ & Chichén Itzá ★★★

The next day, drive north of Valladolid to visit the ruins of **Ek Balam** (p. 246). Then head to **Chichén Itzá** (p. 236) and check into one of the nearby hotels. In the evening, see the sound-and-light show, and then visit the ruins the next morning.

Day ❹: Mérida ★★

The capital of Yucatán state, **Mérida** (p. 192) is the region's center of culture and

history and well worth a few nights' stay. It also makes a good base for excursions into the countryside or to the beach.

If you are driving to Mérida from Chichén Itzá, consider a detour through **Izamal** (p. 215), another colonial town with Maya ruins right in the center.

Get an introduction to Mérida on one of two bus/trolley tours (p. 207). Stroll the main plaza surrounded by 500-year-old buildings, built from the stone of Mayan pyramids torn down by the Spanish Conquistadors.

Each evening, free cultural events (p. 196) take place in the historic district. Sunday is a big day for festivities that last all day.

Day ❺: Celestún

From Mérida, **Celestún** (p. 215) is an easy day trip where travelers can combine a day on the beach with a boat trip to see flocks of pink flamingos in the ecological biosphere.

Day ❻: Uxmal ★★★

Check out of your Mérida hotel and head south to see the Maya ruins of **Uxmal** (p. 220). If you're driving, choose from two different routes (p. 217) that take you past tiny Maya villages, crumbling Spanish haciendas, and more archeological finds. Check into a hotel near Uxmal and tour the ruins; return in the evening for the light show. Explore the ruins further the next morning, when the temperature is much cooler.

Day ❼: Campeche ★

Campeche (p. 229) is the best-preserved walled city in the Americas. The United Nations declared it a World Heritage Site in 2000, which secures protection for its narrow cobblestone streets and colonial-era buildings, painted in pastel colors. Check in and rest up: The next 2 days involve lots of road time.

Day ❽: Xpujil & the Río Bec Ruins

Leave Campeche early to visit **Edzná** (p. 228), about 50km (31 miles) southeast. Then it's a long drive through Escárcega to Xpujil (p. 184) and the ruins of the Río Bec area (p. 183). Easy-to-access local ruins are Xpujil, Chicanná, and Becán.

The ruins of **Calakmul** (p. 188) are perhaps the Yucatán's most mysterious and difficult to reach—a 90 minute drive off the highway. The best way to see these ruins is to overnight in Xpujil or nearby and set out at dawn. If you decide to go to Calakmul, devote an extra day.

Day ❾: Lago Bacalar ★

Xpujil marks the geographic halfway point; from here you're on your way back to Cancún. Head west to **Lago Bacalar** (p. 180), and stop on the way to see the stone masks in the **Kohunlich** ruins (p. 186), and then have a late lunch in **Chetumal** (p. 181). Spend the night 37km (23 miles) north of the city at **Rancho Encantado** (p. 181), a lovely hotel on the edge of Lago Bacalar.

Days ❿ & ⓫: Tulum ★★

After an hour and a half drive's north to **Tulum** (p. 170), you'll reach the crystalline blue waters of the Caribbean. Plan to spend 2 nights at a beach hotel, allowing you 2 days to swim, relax, and beachcomb. If you plan on visiting the **Tulum ruins** (p. 171), go early in the day before the crowds arrive. Consider a nature tour of the **Sian Ka'an Biosphere** (p. 175), just south of town, with one of the local collectives of guides.

Days ⓬ & ⓭: Playa del Carmen ★ & Cozumel

Take the drive up to **Playa del Carmen** (p. 154), which can serve as a base to explore cenotes or even the ruins of **Cobá** (p. 175). Playa is also a great town for strolling and dining, so be sure to allow yourself time to take in the cobblestone Quinta Avenida.

The next morning, you can take the ferry to **Cozumel** (p. 175) for a day trip of diving, snorkeling, swimming with dolphins, or simply enjoying the beach. Stay for an early dinner and return to Playa for the night.

Day ⓮: Puerto Morelos

Spend your last day in **Puerto Morelos** (p. 149) or the vicinity, at an indulgent spa resort, or in the quiet town. You're only 31km (20 miles) from Cancún.

4 AN ECO-ADVENTURE FOR THE ENTIRE FAMILY

If you've got your own mask and snorkel (and fins, too) bring them for this trip; you can always get rentals, but you're better off with gear that fits well.

Day ❶: Arrive at Cancún Airport

For this itinerary, it's best to stay in the lower Riviera Maya, at a hotel or condo in the **Xpu-Ha–Akumal–Tulum** area. That puts you close to most of the places you'll be visiting. The drive from the airport to this part of the coast is at most 2 hours. See p. 166, 167, and 170.

Day ❷: Xel-Ha & the Ruins of Tulum ★★★

Start by enjoying a nice swim at **Xel-Ha**'s lovely lagoon (p. 166), go snorkeling, or simply enjoy the parklands encircling the water. You can stay here the entire day or combine this with a trip to see the ruins in **Tulum** (which you should do in the morning, when the air is cooler). See p. 171.

Day ❸: Hidden Worlds ★★★ & Aktun Chen ★

Between Akumal and Tulum are two attractions, each interesting in its own way. At **Hidden Worlds** (p. 169), you can snorkel in a couple of different cenotes (sinkholes or wellsprings) and subterranean rivers for which the Yucatán is famous. The water is cold, but wet suits are provided, as well as snorkel gear if you

don't bring your own. **Aktun Chen** (p. 168) is a cavern that you can hike through and see lots of rock formations. The small zoo houses local species such as spider monkeys and tropical birds, including a toucan.

Day ❹: Alltournative

Consider spending today with **Alltournative,** an adventure tour agency based in Playa del Carmen. Its day trips combine adventure with nature and interactions with contemporary Maya in one of their own villages. The tour company will pick you up at almost any hotel in the Riviera Maya. You can fly out over the jungle on a zip line, try your hand at rappelling, and have a Maya-style meal all in the same day. See p. 149.

Day ❺: Sian Ka'an Biosphere Reserve ★

Explore the largest wildlife preserve in the Yucatán; snorkel down canals built by the Maya, visit the large, pristine lagoon at the center of the park, and observe various forms of wildlife as you get an up-close-and-personal view of the peninsula's natural habitat. Tour agencies do full-day tours. See p. 175.

Day ❻: Chichén Itzá ★★★

Go for a morning snorkel trip with one of the local dive shops, and then drive to **Chichén Itzá** in the afternoon. Check into a hotel, and in the evening you can enjoy the sound-and-light show at the ruins. Return the next morning to get a closer look in daylight. See p. 236.

Day ❼: Cenote Dzitnup ★, Ek Balam ★★★ & Río Lagartos Nature Reserve ★

After seeing the ruins, head east on the old federal highway until you get to **Cenote Dzitnup,** shortly before the town of Valladolid. You'll find a dark cenote with a beautiful pool of water illuminated by a column of sunlight that penetrates the roof. Nearby is a second cenote. After a quick dip, continue into **Valladolid** (p. 243) for lunch. After you're nourished,

head north on Highway 295 to the turnoff for the ruins of **Ek Balam** (p. 246), noted for a beautifully sculpted sacred doorway on the tallest pyramid in northern Yucatán. Continue north, past the town of Tizimín, until you get to the coastal village of **Río Lagartos.** Here you can get a room at one of the economical hotels fronting the water and arrange for an early-morning boat tour of the wildlife sanctuary. Not only will you see those eye-catching natural wonders—pink flamingos—but you'll see a host of other species as well, and enjoy a boat ride through mangrove and saltwater estuaries. See p. 246.

Day ❽: Cancún

After your visit with pink flamingos, it's time to get back to Cancún and civilization. See chapter 5.

---

5 LA RUTA MAYA

This route, which connects the major Maya sites in Mexico, could be done quickly in 2 weeks, or more slowly in a month or perhaps broken up into two trips. I've kept the trip to the minimum by avoiding the city of Mérida, but you may want to visit it. There's a risk of overdosing on ruins by seeing too many in too short a time. I give you the fast-track approach here, but that doesn't mean that I'm encouraging you to move through this area that quickly. The best mode of travel would be a rental car: The highways have little traffic and are, for the most part, in good shape.

Day ❶: Arrive in Cancún

After you arrive, enjoy the rest of the day with a swim in the Caribbean or an afternoon by the pool. See chapter 5.

Day ❷: Ek Balam ★★★ & Chichén Itzá ★★★

Get on the modern toll highway that heads toward Mérida and take the exit for Valladolid. Head north, away from the town, to visit the ruins of **Ek Balam** (p. 246). Then head back to the town of Valladolid for lunch before driving the short distance to **Chichén Itzá** (p. 236) on the old federal highway. Just outside of town, stop to see

the **cenotes** of **Dzitnup** and **Sammulá** (for both, see p. 245). Further on is the **Balankanché Cave** (p. 243). When you get to Chichén, check into your hotel, and then go to the **ruins** later in the evening for the sound-and-light show. See p. 237.

Day ❸: Continuing to Uxmal ★★★

Spend more time at the **ruins of Chichén Itzá** in the morning, then continue west on the toll highway toward Mérida, and turn off at Ticopó. Head south toward the town of **Acanceh** (p. 218) and Highway 18. Stop to see the small but interesting ruins in the middle of town, and then proceed down

Highway 18 to the ruins of **Mayapán** (p. 219). Afterward, continue through Ticul to Santa Elena and Uxmal. Experience the sound-and-light show. See p. 221.

Day ❹: Edzná

Visit **Uxmal** (p. 220) in the morning, then drive back toward Santa Elena and take Highway 261 south to Hopelchén and on to the impressive ruins of **Edzná** (p. 228). Nearby is a fancy hacienda-turned-hotel, called **Uayamón** (p. 201). Better still, stay at the sister property in old-town Campeche, **Hacienda Puerta Campeche** (p. 234; reservations for either can be made through Starwood hotels). Or you can choose from several more modest digs.

Days ❺ & ❻: Palenque ★★, Bonampak & Yaxchilán

Stay on Highway 261 to Escárcega, then head west on Highway 186 toward Villahermosa, then south on Highway 199 to the town of **Palenque** (p. 256) with its magnificent pyramids. The next day go to the ruins of **Bonampak** and **Yaxchilán** (p. 262), using one of the local tour operators.

Days ❼ & ❽: San Cristóbal de las Casas ★★

Keep south on Highway 199 toward **San Cristóbal** (p. 264). On the way, take a swimming break at **Misol Ha** (p. 263), and visit the ruins of **Toniná** outside of the town of Ocosingo. From San Cristóbal, go with one of the local guides to see the present-day Maya communities of **Chamula** and **Zinacantán** (p. 271). Spend some time enjoying the towns.

Day ❾: Calakmul ★★★

Retrace your steps to Escárcega and continue east on Highway 186. If you have time, visit the fascinating sculptures of **Balamkú** (p. 189). Spend the night at one of the hotels in the vicinity of the turnoff for **Calakmul,** one of the prime city-states of the Classic age of the Maya, and not often visited.

Day ❿: Calakmul & Becán ★★★

Get to **Calakmul** (p. 188) early. Keep your eyes open for wildlife as you drive along a narrow jungle road. All the area surrounding the city is a **wildlife preserve.** For most of the city's history, Calakmul was the main rival to the city of Tikal, which is present-day Guatemala. It eventually defeated Tikal and subjugated it for 100 years. Calakmul's **Structure 2** is the highest Maya pyramid in Mexico. Afterward, continue east on Highway 186 to see the ruins of **Becán,** a large ceremonial center with tall temples. Also in the vicinity are **Xpujil** and **Chicanná.** Spend the night on the shores of **Lake Bacalar,** where you can cool off in its blue waters. See p. 180.

Days ⓫ & ⓬: Tulum

Drive north on Highway 307 to **Tulum** and settle into one of the small beach hotels there. In the morning, walk through the ruins and enjoy the lovely view of the coast. See p. 170.

Day ⓭: Back to Cancún

Drive back to Cancún. Depending on your schedule, you can enjoy some more beach time, or head straight to the airport (25 min. south of Cancún) and depart. See chapter 5.

Cancún

by Shane Christensen

It may be commercialized and more American than Mexican in design, but Cancún remains one of the finest resort destinations in the world—with breathtaking beaches and enough pleasure-pursuits to make even the most unrelenting hedonists blush. And while Cancún may be a top travel destination for Americans and other Western travelers who flock here like sun-seeking swallows in winter and spring, it's also a favorite for Mexicans who come to holiday year-round.

Due to Cancún's ideal mix of elements—its transparent turquoise sea, powdery white sand, and immense potential for growth—a group of Mexican government computer analysts targeted the town for tourism development in 1974, transforming it from a deserted beach area to a five-star resort. Since then, Cancún has sustained the devastations of hurricanes and other powerful tropical storms, only to emerge stronger and more irresistible. In the wake of Hurricane Wilma, which tore through the Yucatán peninsula in 2005, wreckage rapidly gave way to exacting renovations, luxurious upgrades, and brand-new destinations. Today Cancún is better than ever.

The allure hasn't changed much over the years—it's still the spectacular Caribbean beach. Cancún (which means "golden snake" in Mayan) stretches from the downtown area known as Cancún City east to the Hotel Zone, also known as Isla Cancún, which is a narrow 24-km (15-mile) island that runs southwest and is framed on one side by the beautiful Caribbean Sea and on the other by the picturesque Nichupté lagoon.

Cancún is home to breathtaking resorts; an unrivaled range of shopping, dining, and nightlife; and endless outdoor activities. Air travel is easy, with major airlines flying here from destinations across Mexico, the United States, Canada, and Europe. And it's a gateway to the nearby ruins of Tulum, Chichén Itzá, and Cobá.

Cancún embodies Caribbean splendor and the exotic joys of Mexico, but even a Western traveler feeling apprehensive about visiting foreign soil will feel completely at ease here. English is spoken and dollars accepted; roads are well paved and lawns manicured. Some travelers are surprised to find that Cancún is more like a U.S. beach resort than a part of Mexico. Indeed, signs of Americanism are rampant. U.S. college students continue to descend in droves during Spring Break—which, depending on your perspective, may be reason to rush headlong into the party or stay far, far away during this season. One astonishing statistic suggests that more Americans travel to Cancún than to any other foreign destination in the world. Indeed, almost three million people visit annually—most of them on their first trip to Mexico.

You won't find much in the way of authentic Mexican charm in the Hotel Zone, although you can get a glimpse of this in Cancún City, where most of the local population lives. You'll find good value hotels, a number of outstanding traditional restaurants, and some excellent shopping here. Cancún is also a convenient distance from the more traditional Mexican resorts of Isla Mujeres and the coastal stretch known as the Riviera

Maya—extending down from Cancún, through Playa del Carmen to the Mayan ruins at Tulum—making for easy day trips.

You will likely run out of vacation days before you run out of things to do in Cancún. Snorkeling, dolphin swims, jungle tours, and visits to ancient Mayan ruins and modern ecological theme parks are among the most popular diversions. A dozen malls sell name-brand and duty-free goods (with European imports for less than in the U.S.). With tens of thousands of hotel rooms and more than 350 restaurants and nightclubs, there's something for every taste and budget.

A day here could easily combine time at the pool or beach with a nearby excursion.

After soaking up the sun, you might want to browse some of the shops or head for a sunset cocktail. Choose a restaurant for fresh Caribbean seafood or creative Mexican cuisine before heading to a tequila bar or chill lounge to get the night started. Then end up at a rocking bar or dance club filled with nighttime revelers who can't bear going to sleep until the dawn.

Cancún's luxury hotels have swimming pools so spectacular that you may find it tempting to turn into what I'd like to call a pool potato—but don't. Set aside some time to get yourself to the beach and wriggle your toes in the fine, brilliant white sand. It is, after all, what put Cancún on the map—and no tempest of nature has been able to sweep it away.

1 ORIENTATION

GETTING THERE

BY PLANE If this is not your first trip to Cancún, you'll notice that the **airport**'s (© **998/848-7200**) facilities and services continue to expand. All flights to and from the U.S. now go through the new Terminal 3, which has money-exchange services, duty-free shops, restaurants, medical services, and even an express spa. **AeroMéxico** (© **866/275-6419** in the U.S., or 01-800/021-4000 in Mexico; www.aeromexico.com) operates connecting service to Cancún through Mexico City. **Mexicana** (© **800/531-7921** in the U.S., 01-800/366-5400 in Mexico, or 998/881-9090; www.mexicana.com) runs connecting flights to Cancún through Miami or Mexico City. In addition to these carriers, many **charter** companies—such as Apple Vacations and Funjet—travel to Cancún; these package tours make up as much as half of arrivals by U.S. visitors (see "Packages for the Independent Traveler," in chapter 3).

Regional carrier **Click Mexicana,** a Mexicana affiliate (© **01-800/112-5425** in Mexico; www.click.com.mx), flies from Havana, Cuba, Chetumal, Cozumel, Mexico City, Mérida, and other points within Mexico. You'll want to confirm departure times for flights to the U.S. **Aviacsa** (© **01-800/711-6733** in Mexico; www.aviacsa.com), **Interjet** (© **01-800/01-12345** in Mexico; www.interjet.com.mx), and **Volaris** (© **01-800/7865-2747** in Mexico; www.volaris.com.mx) are three other regional carriers that fly to Cancún from Mexico City.

The following major international carriers serve Cancún: **Alaska** (© 800/426-0333; www.alaskaair.com), **American** (© 800/433-7300; www.aa.com), **Continental** (© 800/231-0856; www.continental.com), **Delta** (© 800/221-1212; www.delta.com), **Frontier** (© 800/432-1359; www.frontierairlines.com), **JetBlue** (© **800/538-2583**; www.jetblue.com), **Northwest** (© 800/225-2525; www.nwa.com), **United** (© 800/241-6522; www.ual.com), and **US Airways** (© 800/428-4322; www.usairways.com).

Most major car-rental firms have outlets at the airport, so if you're renting a car, consider picking it up and dropping it off at the airport, to save on airport-transportation costs. Another way to save money is to arrange for the rental before you leave home. If you wait until you arrive, the daily cost will be around $50 to $75 for a compact vehicle. Major agencies include **Alamo** (© 800/462-5266 in the U.S., or 998/886-0448; www.alamo. com), **Avis** (© 800/331-1212 in the U.S., or 998/886-0221; www.avis.com), **Budget** (© 800/527-0700 in the U.S., or 998/886-0417; fax 998/884-4812; www.budget.com), **Dollar** (© 800/800-3665 in the U.S., or 998/886-2300; www.dollar.com), **Hertz** (© 800/654-3131 in the U.S. and Canada, or 998/884-1326; www.hertz.com), **National** (© 800/227-7368 in the U.S., or 998/886-0153; www.nationalcar.com), and **Thrifty** (© 800/847-4389; www.thrifty.com). The Zona Hotelera (Hotel Zone) lies 10km (6¼ miles)—a 20-minute drive—from the airport along wide, well-paved roads.

The rate for a **private taxi** from the airport is $58 to Ciudad Cancún (downtown) or the Hotel Zone. The return trip with an airport taxi is discounted by 50%. Green Line and Gray Line **van shuttles** run from the airport into town approximately every 20 minutes. Buy tickets, which cost about $14, from the booth to the far right as you exit the airport terminal. These services accept U.S. dollars, though you'll get a more favorable rate if you pay in pesos. There's **local bus** transportation (45 pesos) from the airport to Ciudad Cancún. From there, you can take another bus for less than a dollar to Puerto Juárez, where passenger ferries leave to Isla Mujeres regularly. There is no shuttle service returning to the airport from Ciudad Cancún or the Hotel Zone, so you'll have to take a taxi, but the rate will be much less than for the trip from the airport. (Only federally chartered taxis may take fares *from* the airport, but any taxi may bring passengers *to* the airport.) Ask at your hotel what the fare should be, but expect to pay about half what you paid from the airport to your hotel.

 The Best Websites for Cancún

- **All About Cancún: www.cancunmx.com** This site is a good place to start planning. Their database, called "The Online Experts," answers many of the most common questions. It's slow but current, with input from lots of recent travelers to the region.
- **Cancún Convention & Visitors Bureau: www.cancun.travel** The official site of the Cancún Convention & Visitors Bureau lists excellent information on events and attractions. Its hotel guide is one of the most complete available, and it has an active message board of recent visitors to Cancún.
- **Cancún Online: www.cancun.com** This comprehensive guide has lots of information about things to do and see in Cancún, though most details come from paying advertisers. The site lets you reserve package trips, accommodations, activities, and tee times.
- **Cancún Travel Guide: www.go2cancun.com** These online information specialists are also an excellent resource for Cancún rentals, hotels, and attractions. Note that this site lists only paying advertisers, which means you'll find most of the major players here.

CANCÚN

5

ORIENTATION

BY CAR   From Mérida or Campeche, take **Highway 180** east to Cancún. This is mostly a winding, two-lane road that branches off into the express **toll road 180D** between Izamal and Nuevo Xcan. Nuevo Xcan is approximately 40km (25 miles) from Cancún. Mérida is about 320km (198 miles) away.

BY BUS   Cancún's **ADO bus terminal** (© **01-800/702-8000** in Mexico or 998/884-4352) is in downtown Ciudad Cancún at the intersection of avenidas Tulum and Uxmal. All out-of-town buses arrive here. Buses run to Playa del Carmen, Tulum, Chichén Itzá, other nearby beach and archaeological zones, and other points within Mexico.

VISITOR INFORMATION

The **Cancún Municipal Tourism Office** is downtown at the Palacio Municipal (City Hall), on Avenida Tulum between avenidas Uxmal and Cobá (© **998/887-3379**). It's open Monday through Friday from 9am to 7pm. The office lists hotels and their rates, as well as ferry schedules. For information prior to your arrival in Cancún, visit the Convention Bureau's website, **www.cancun.travel**. The state tourism website is in Spanish, at www.qroo.gob.mx.

Pick up copies of the free booklet *Cancún Tips* (www.cancuntips.com.mx), and a seasonal tabloid of the same name.

CITY LAYOUT

There are really two Cancúns: **Ciudad Cancún (Cancún City)** and **Isla Cancún (Cancún Island).** The former, on the mainland, is the original downtown area, where most of the local population lives. It's home to traditional restaurants, shops, and less expensive hotels, as well as pharmacies, dentists, automotive shops, banks, travel and airline agencies, and car-rental firms—all within an area about 9 square blocks. The city's main thoroughfare is **Avenida Tulum.** Heading south, Avenida Tulum becomes the highway to the airport and to Tulum and Chetumal; heading north, it intersects the highway to Mérida and the road to Puerto Juárez and the Isla Mujeres ferries.

Isla Cancún is a sandy strip 22km (14 miles) long, shaped like a 7. It's home to the famed **Zona Hotelera,** or Hotel Zone (also called the Zona Turística, or Tourist Zone), connected to the mainland by the Playa Linda Bridge at the north end and the Punta Nizuc Bridge at the southern end. Between the two areas lies Laguna Nichupté. Avenida Cobá from Cancún City becomes Bulevar Kukulkán, the island's main traffic artery. Cancún's international airport is just inland from the south end of the island.

FINDING AN ADDRESS   Cancún City's street-numbering system is a holdover from its early days. Addresses are still given by the number of the building lot and by the *manzana* (block) or *supermanzana* (group of blocks). The city is relatively compact, and the downtown commercial section is easy to cover on foot.

On the island, addresses are given by kilometer number on Bulevar Kukulkán or by reference to some well-known location. In Cancún, streets are named after famous Maya cities. Boulevards are named for nearby archaeological sites, Chichén Itzá, Tulum, and Uxmal.

GETTING AROUND

BY TAXI   Taxi prices in Cancún are clearly set by zone, although keeping track of what's in which zone can take some doing. The minimum fare within the Hotel Zone is $8 per ride, making it one of the most expensive taxi areas in Mexico. In addition, taxis operating in the Hotel Zone feel perfectly justified in having a discriminatory pricing structure:

Local residents pay about half of what tourists pay, and prices for guests at higher-priced hotels are about double those for budget hotel guests—these are all established by the taxi union. Rates should be posted outside your hotel; if you have a question, all drivers are required to have an official rate card in their taxis, though it's generally in Spanish. Taxi drivers will accept dollars, though at a less favorable rate than pesos.

Within the downtown area, the cost is about $3 per cab ride (not per person); within any other zone, it's $6. Traveling between two zones will also cost $6, and if you cross two zones, that'll cost $8. Settle on a price in advance, or check at your hotel. Trips to the airport from most zones cost about $30. Taxis can also be rented for $25 per hour for travel around the city and Hotel Zone, but this rate can generally be negotiated down to about $20. If you want to hire a taxi to take you to Chichén Itzá or along the Riviera Maya, expect to pay about $35 per hour—many taxi drivers feel that they are also providing guide services.

BY BUS   Bus travel within Cancún continues to improve and is increasingly popular. In town, almost everything lies within walking distance. **Ruta 1** and **Ruta 2** (HOTELES) city buses travel frequently from Puerto Juárez on the mainland to the beaches along Avenida Tulum (the main street) and all the way to Punta Nizuc at the far end of the Hotel Zone on Isla Cancún. **Ruta 8** buses go to Puerto Juárez/Punta Sam for ferries to Isla Mujeres. They stop on the east side of Avenida Tulum. All these city buses run between 6am and 10pm daily. Buses also go up and down the main strip of the Hotel Zone day and night. Public buses have the fare painted on the front; at press time, the fare was 6.50 pesos.

BY SCOOTER   Scooters are a convenient but dangerous way to cruise through the very congested traffic. Rentals start at about $30 for a day, not including insurance, and a credit card voucher is required as security. You should receive a crash helmet (it's the law) and instructions on how to lock the wheels when you park. Read the fine print on the back of the rental agreement regarding liability for repairs or replacement in case of accident, theft, or vandalism.

Fast Facts   Cancún

Area Code   The telephone area code is **998**.

Climate   It's hot but not overwhelmingly humid. The rainy season is May through October. August to November is hurricane season, which brings erratic weather. November through February is generally sunny but can also be cloudy, windy, somewhat rainy, and even cool.

Consulates   The **U.S. Consular Agent** is in the Plaza Caracol 2, Bulevar Kukulkán Km 8.5, 3rd level, 320–323 (© **998/883-0272**); open Monday through Friday from 9am to 2pm. The **Canadian Consulate** is in the Plaza Caracol, 3rd level, Loc. 330 (© **998/883-3360**); open Monday through Friday from 9am to 3:30pm. The **United Kingdom** has a consular office at the Royal Sands Hotel in Cancún (© **998/881-0100;** fax 998/848-8662; consular.mexico@fco.gov.uk); open Monday through Friday from 9am to 5pm. Irish, Australian, and New Zealand citizens should contact their embassies in Mexico City.

Crime Car break-ins are just about the only frequent crime here. They happen repeatedly, especially around the shopping centers in the Hotel Zone. Rapes have also been reported in Cancún. Most have taken place at night or in the early morning.

Currency Exchange Most banks sit downtown along Avenida Tulum and are usually open Monday through Friday from 9am to 3pm, although some are open later and even half the day on Saturday. Many have ATMs for after-hours cash withdrawals. In the Hotel Zone, you'll find an HSBC bank in Kukulcán Plaza that's open Monday through Saturday from 9am to 7pm. There are also many *casas de cambio* (exchange houses). Downtown merchants are eager to change cash dollars, but island stores don't offer very good exchange rates. Avoid changing money at the airport as you arrive, especially at the first exchange booth you see—its rates are less favorable than those of any in town or others farther inside the airport. Dollars are widely accepted throughout Cancún.

Drugstores Across the street from Señor Frog's in the Hotel Zone, at Bulevar Kukulkán Km 9.5, **Farmacías del Ahorro** (© **998/892-7291**) offers 24-hour service and free delivery. Plenty of drugstores are in the major shopping malls in the Hotel Zone and are open until 10pm. In downtown Cancún, **Farmacía Cancún** is located at Av. Tulum 17 (© **998/884-1283**). It's open Monday to Saturday from 9am to 10pm, and Sunday from 10am to 10pm. You can stock up on over-the-counter and many prescription drugs without a prescription.

Emergencies To report an emergency, dial © **060,** which is supposed to be similar to 911 emergency service in the United States. For first aid, the **Cruz Roja,** or Red Cross (© **065** or 998/884-1616), is open 24 hours on Avenida Yaxchilán between avenidas Xcaret and Labná, next to the Telmex building. **Galenia Hospital** is one of the city's most modern, offering full emergency and other services with excellent care, at Avenida Tulum, SM 12, at Nizuc (© **998/891-5200;** www.hospitalgalenia. com). **AMAT,** Av. Nader 13, SM 2, at Avenida Uxmal (© **998/887-4422**), is a small emergency hospital with some English-speaking doctors. It's open 24 hours. Desk staff may have limited command of English. **Air Ambulance** (Global Ambulance) service is available by calling © **800/631-6565** in the U.S., or 01-800/305-9400 in Mexico (www.airambulance.com).

Internet Access **Häagen-Dazs,** on the bottom floor of Kukulcán Plaza, Bulevar Kukulkán Km 13, is a free Wi-Fi hot spot. Most hotels now have Internet access, and five-star hotels have business centers.

Luggage Storage & Lockers Hotels will generally tag and store luggage while you travel elsewhere.

Newspapers & Magazines Most hotel gift shops and newsstands carry English-language magazines and English-language Mexican newspapers, such as the *Miami Herald. Cancún Tips* is an entertainment magazine that offers descriptions of local activities, maps, and tourist information.

Police Dial © **066** for the police in an emergency. Cancún also has a fleet of English-speaking tourist police to help travelers. Dial © **998/885-2277.** The **Procuraduría Federal del Consumidor ("Profeco," the consumer protection agency),** Av. Cobá 9–11 (© **998/884-2634**), is opposite the Social Security Hospital and upstairs from the Fenix drugstore. It's open Monday through Friday from 9am to 3pm.

Post Office The main *correo* lies at the intersection of avenidas Sunyaxchen and Xel-Ha (*©* **998/884-1418**). It's open Monday through Friday from 9am to 4pm, and Saturday from 9am to noon for the purchase of stamps only.

Seasons Technically, high season runs from December 15 to April; low season extends from May to December 15, when prices drop 10% to 30%. Some hotels are starting to charge high-season rates during June and July, when Mexican, European, and school-holiday visitors often travel, although rates may still be lower than in winter months.

2 WHERE TO STAY

Island hotels—almost all of them offering modern facilities and English-speaking staffs—line the beach like concrete dominoes. Extravagance is the byword in the newer hotels. Some hotels, while exclusive, affect a more relaxed attitude. The water on the upper end of the island facing Bahía de Mujeres is placid, while beaches lining the long side of the island facing the Caribbean are subject to choppier water and crashing waves on windy days. (For more information on swimming safety, see "Beaches, Watersports & Boat Tours," later in this chapter.) Be aware that the farther south you go on the island, the longer it takes (20–30 min. in traffic) to get back to the "action spots," which are primarily between the Plaza Flamingo and Punta Cancún on the island and along Avenida Tulum on the mainland.

Following Hurricane Wilma's devastation, the news item that received the most coverage was the destruction of Cancún's famed white-sand beaches. Immediately following the storm, literally all of the sand was washed away from the northern border of Isla Cancún, and from Punta Cancún. However, thanks to Mother Nature and a $20-million effort by Mexico's government to pump the dislocated sand back to the beach, this is no longer an issue. The southern beaches of Isla Cancún actually benefited from the storm, and now they have especially wide beachfronts.

Almost all major hotel chains have real estate on Cancún Island (the "Hotel Zone"). The reality is that Cancún is so popular as a **package destination** from the U.S. that prices and special deals are often the deciding factor for consumers rather than loyalty to any one hotel brand (see "Packages for the Independent Traveler," in chapter 3). Ciudad Cancún offers independently owned, smaller, less-expensive lodging, all a 5- to 10-minute cab ride from the beach; prices are lower here off season (May to early Dec). For condo, home, and villa rentals, check with **Cancún Hideaways** (*©* **817/522-4466;** www.cancun-hideaways.com), an American company specializing in luxury properties, downtown apartments, and condos—many at prices much lower than comparable hotel stays. Owner Maggie Rodriguez, a former resident of Cancún, has made this niche market her specialty.

The hotel listings in this chapter begin on Cancún Island and finish in Cancún City (the real downtown), where bargain lodgings are available. Unless otherwise indicated, parking is free at Cancún's hotels.

Very Expensive

Aqua ★★★ Resurrected after being destroyed by Hurricane Wilma in 2005, Aqua once again stands at the pinnacle of Cancún's hotel scene. The ultramodern resort—New Age music seems to be piped in from each corner, behind every palm tree, and around the eight tempting pools—attracts a chic clientele pampered by an exceptionally gracious staff. The spa is exceptional, with indoor and outdoor treatments that incorporate the best techniques from around the globe. All of the soothing guest rooms face the ocean and boast i-Home sound systems, aromatherapy menus, and Molton Brown bath amenities and artisan soaps. I don't remember the last time I slept in such a comfortable bed; Egyptian cotton sheets share company with a plush collection of form-fitting pillows. The only thing calling you out of bed is likely to be the clear blue skies, deep turquoise waters, and brilliant white sand outside your window. Some of Mexico's top chefs oversee the gourmet restaurants, including acclaimed chef Martha Ortiz, who created **Siete,** featuring floor-to-ceiling windows overlooking the Caribbean and the resort pools.

Bulevar Kukulkán Km 12.5, 77500 Cancún, Q. Roo. Ⓒ **800/343-7821** in the U.S., or 998/881-7600. Fax 998/881-7635. www.feel-aqua.com. 371 units. High season $370 and up double, $630 and up suite; low season $150–$311 double, $442 and up suite. AE, MC, V. **Amenities:** 3 gourmet restaurants; 3 bars; concierge w/multilingual staff; fitness center; 8 outdoor pools w/luxury cabañas for rent; room service; sauna; boutique spa; 2 tennis courts. In room: A/C, TV w/DVD, i-Home, aromatherapy and pillow menu, hair dryer, minibar, Wi-Fi (fee).

Fiesta Americana Grand Coral Beach ★★ (Kids) This grand coral-colored resort sits on Punta Cancún, offering relative seclusion despite lying within easy walking distance of the hotel zone's key entertainment. In front, the whitest sand beach glides into emerald waters, where the surf is calm and perfect for swimming. Yet you may feel tempted not to leave the beautiful multitiered pools with waterfalls, fountains, swim-up bars, and lush surroundings. The all-suites hotel includes junior suites with sunken sitting areas, whitewashed furniture, marble bathrooms, and soothing California colors. Guests staying in Grand Club suites enjoy access to a private rooftop lounge, exclusive check-in, continental breakfast, hors d'oeuvres, and beverages. Service throughout this luxury property is gracious and attentive, and the magnificent lobby is embellished with elegant dark-green granite and fresh flowers. The *Fiesta Kids Activities* include nonstop games, contests, and shows for the little ones, and there are daylong sports and social activities planned for adults as well (the pool concierge provides daily information). The resort's international clientele includes many European, Japanese, Mexican, and American visitors. An American Express travel agency is located here.

Bulevar Kukulkán Km 9.5, 77500 Cancún, Q. Roo. Ⓒ **800/343-7821** in the U.S., or 998/881-3200. Fax 998/881-3288. www.fiestamericanagrand.com. 602 units. High season $539 and up double, $679 and up club-floor double; low season $359 and up double, $509 and up club-floor double. Parking $10. AE, MC, V. **Amenities:** 5 restaurants; 4 bars; babysitting; kids' club; concierge w/multilingual staff; fitness center; outdoor pool w/swim-up bars; room service; sauna; boutique spa; watersports equipment/rentals. In room: A/C, TV, CD player, hair dryer, minibar, Wi-Fi.

Hilton Cancún Golf & Spa Resort ★★ (Kids) Full of energy, this is a grand resort in every sense of the word. The Hilton Cancún sits on 100 hectares (247 acres) of prime beachside property, which means every room has a sea view (some have both sea and lagoon views). And there's an 18-hole par-72 golf course across the street. Like the sprawling resort, guest rooms are spacious and decorated in minimalist style. The Beach

ACCOMMODATIONS ■

Aqua **10**
Bel Air Collection Hotel
 & Spa **22**
Dreams Cancún Resort
 & Spa **5**
Fiesta Americana Grand
 Coral Beach **4**
Flamingo Cancún **7**
Hilton Cancún Golf
 & Spa Resort **21**
JW Marriott **19**
Le Méridien Cancún Resort
 & Spa **18**
Marriott Casa Magna **20**
ME **9**
Ritz-Carlton Cancún **17**
Riu Palace Las Américas **3**
Royal **8**
Temptation Resort
 & Spa Cancún **1**

DINING ◆

Aioli **18**
Casa de las Margaritas **11**
Casa Rolandi **2**
Club Grill **17**
El Shrimp Bucket **16**
Gustino **19**
Harry's **14**
La Destilería **12**
Laguna Grill **15**
Lorenzillo's **6**
Paloma Bonita **5**
Puerto Madero **13**
Thai **11**

CANCÚN

5

WHERE TO STAY

(Tips)   Deciphering Hotel Prices

In all price categories, Cancún's hotels generally set their rates in dollars, so they are immune to variations in the peso. Travel agents and wholesalers always have air/hotel packages available. Cancún also has numerous all-inclusive properties, which allow you to take a fixed-cost vacation. Note that the price quoted when you call a hotel's reservation number may not include Cancún's 12% tax (a 10% federal tax and 2% state lodging tax). Prices can vary considerably throughout the year and have dropped considerably during the global financial crisis, so it pays to consult a travel agent or shop around.

Club villas are the largest and best-located rooms, and come with continental breakfast and an evening cocktail hour. This Hilton is a kid-friendly hotel, with one of the island's best children's activity programs, children's pool, and babysitting. The spectacular multi-section swimming pool stretches out to the gorgeous beach. The Hilton is especially appealing to golfers because it's one of only two in Cancún with an on-site course (the other is the Meliá). Greens fees for guests during high season are $79 for 9 holes, $159 for 18 holes (low season discounts offered), and come with use of a cart. The Wellness Spa includes oceanfront massage cabañas, yoga, and aromatherapy. This Hilton has a friendly vibe and boasts excellent service.

Bulevar Kukulkán Km 17, Retorno Lacandones, 77500 Cancún, Q. Roo. ℂ **800/228-3000** in the U.S., or 998/881-8000. Fax 998/881-8080. www.hiltoncancun.com. 426 units. High season $249 and up double, $309 and up villa room, $409 and up suite; low season $159 and up double, $199 and up villa room, $279 and up suite. AE, DC, MC, V. **Amenities:** 4 restaurants; 2 bars; babysitting; kids' club; concierge; golf course across the street; golf clinic; 10 interconnected outdoor pools w/swim-up bar; 2 whirlpools; room service; wellness spa and fully equipped gym; 2 lighted tennis courts; watersports center. *In room:* A/C, flatscreen TV, hair dryer, minibar, Wi-Fi.

JW Marriott ★★★   This is my favorite resort in Cancún, a refined oasis that offers exceptional service without pretense. Despite its many touches of elegance, the JW is friendly and even family friendly—although more families stay at the neighboring and less expensive **Marriott Casa Magna** (p. 97). From the beautifully decorated marble and flower-filled lobby to the luxurious oceanview guest rooms, the resort combines classic and Caribbean styling with warm Mexican service. Guest rooms feature exquisite marble bathrooms with separate tub and shower, private balconies, flatscreen TVs, bathrobes and slippers, and twice-daily maid service. The wonderful free-form infinity pool meanders through the property and overlooks the sea. A spectacular 3,252-sq.-m (35,004-sq.-ft.) spa includes an indoor pool and Jacuzzi, high-tech fitness center, and full range of massages, body scrubs and polishes, facials, and healing water treatments. **Gustino** (p. 102) is the hotel's outstanding Italian restaurant seated off the lobby.

Bulevar Kukulkán Km 14.5, 77500 Cancún, Q. Roo. ℂ **800/223-6388** in the U.S., or 998/848-9600. Fax 998/848-9601. www.jwmarriottcancun.com. 448 units. High season $449 and up double; low season $300 and up double. AE, DC, MC, V. Small pets allowed with prior reservation. **Amenities:** 3 restaurants; deli; lobby bar and pool bar; access to kids' club at Marriott Casa Magna; concierge; expansive outdoor pool; dive pool w/ waterfalls; indoor pool; 3 whirlpools; room service; sauna; full-service spa; steam room; club floor w/special amenities and complimentary cocktails. *In room:* A/C, flatscreen TV, hair dryer, minibar, Wi-Fi.

Le Méridien Cancún Resort & Spa ★★ Frequented by Europeans familiar with this fine chain of hotels, Le Méridien is among Cancún's most inviting luxury options. The small lobby is elegant but not overdone, creating a sense of intimacy that extends throughout the hotel. Guest rooms are generous in size, with small balconies overlooking the pool; due to the hotel's design, they do not have ocean views. Each has a large marble bathroom with a separate tub and glassed-in shower. The resort's **Spa del Mar** is one of Mexico's most complete European spa facilities, with more than 4,570 sq. m (49,191 sq. ft.) of services dedicated to your body and soul. It consists of an extensive fitness center, full-service salon, selection of treatment rooms, and men's and women's steam rooms, saunas, whirlpools, and cold plunge pools. **Aioli** (p. 101) is the splendid fine-dining restaurant connected to the lobby. The hotel staff offers calm, personalized service.

Retorno del Rey Km 14, Zona Hotelera, 77500, Cancún, Q. Roo. ☎ **800/543-4300** in the U.S., or 998/881-2200. Fax 998/881-2201. www.meridiencancun.com.mx. 213 units. High season $593 double, $680 suite; low season $430 double, $519 suite. Ask about special spa packages. AE, DC, MC, V. Small dogs accepted with prior reservation. **Amenities:** 2 restaurants; bar; babysitting; supervised children's program w/ clubhouse, play equipment, wading pool; concierge; 3 cascading outdoor pools; whirlpool; room service; spa; 2 lighted championship tennis courts; watersports equipment/rentals. In room: A/C, TV, CD player, hair dryer, minibar, Wi-Fi.

Ritz-Carlton Cancún ★★★ (Kids) The exclusive Ritz-Carlton fronts a 366m (1,200-ft.) white-sand beach, and all guest rooms overlook the ocean and pools. Rooms and public areas have the low-key elegance that's a hallmark of the Ritz chain—think plush carpets; chandeliers; fresh flowers; and rooms with marble baths, fluffy featherbeds, and 400-count bed linens. Several new features will enhance your stay, including a culinary center that schedules daily Mexican and Maya cooking classes, as well as wine and tequila tastings. A group of specially designed "Itzy Bitzy Ritz Kids" guest rooms offer baby-friendly amenities and conveniences. In addition to the daytime Kids Camp, the Ritz offers a "Kids' Night Out" program that allows parents to steal away for the evening. The beach-front Kayantá Spa bases many of its treatments on traditional Maya rituals and therapies. The resort's oceanfront restaurant, **Casitas,** is the only beachside dining spot in Cancún, where you can dine on steakhouse fare in candlelit cabañas. The hotel's primary restaurant, **Club Grill,** is reviewed in the "Where to Dine" section, below; the **Lobby Lounge** (p. 114) is a refined space for an evening out. The resort itself, as well as Club Grill and Fantino, another Ritz-Carlton restaurant, has received AAA five diamonds.

Retorno del Rey 36, off Bulevar Kukulkán Km 13.5, 77500 Cancún, Q. Roo. ☎ **800/241-3333** in the U.S. and Canada, or 998/881-0808. Fax 998/881-0815. www.ritzcarlton.com. 365 units. . May 1–Dec 21 $309–$409 double, $489 and up club floor and suites; Dec 21–Jan 3 $799–$1,099 double, $1,679 and up club floor and suites; Jan 4–Apr 30 $549–$629 double, $769 and up club floor and suites. Ask about golf, spa, and weekend packages. AE, MC, V. **Amenities:** 6 restaurants; lounge w/sushi bar; babysitting; Kids Camp; concierge; fully equipped fitness center; 2 outdoor pools (heated in winter); room service; spa; a Cliff Drysdale tennis center w/3 lighted tennis courts; club floors. In room: A/C, TV, CD player, hair dryer, minibar, Wi-Fi.

Riu Palace Las Américas ★ (Kids) The all-inclusive Riu Palace is part of a family of Riu resorts in Cancún known for their grand, opulent style. This one is the smallest of the three and the most over-the-top, steeped in pearl-white Greco architecture. It looks more like it belongs on the Las Vegas strip than next to the Caribbean Sea, but then again, no one ever said Cancún had a consistent style. The location is prime—near the central shopping, dining, and nightlife centers, and just a 5-minute walk to the Convention Center. All rooms are spacious junior suites with an ocean or lagoon view, separate seating area with sofa or sofa bed, and a balcony or terrace. Eight have Jacuzzis. The beautiful central pools overlook the ocean and a small stretch of beach. Riu Palace offers guests virtually 24 hours of all-inclusive snacks, meals, and beverages. Activities include watersports, daytime entertainment for adults and kids, live music and shows at night, and access to other Riu hotels in Cancún. The hotel's European opulence stands in contrast to the mostly informal North American guests.

Bulevar Kukulkán Km 8.5, Lote 4, 77500 Cancún, Q. Roo. © **888/666-8816** in the U.S., or 998/891-4300. Fax 998/891-4301. www.riu.com. 372 units. High season $412 and up double; low season $322 and up double. Rates are all-inclusive, and 2-night stay may be required. AE, MC, V. **Amenities:** 6 restaurants; 2 bars; access to golf and tennis; fitness center; 2 outdoor pools; room service; spa; nonmotorized watersports, including windsurfing, kayaking, snorkeling, and introductory scuba lessons. *In room:* A/C, TV, hair dryer.

Royal ★★   Opened in early 2007, this adults-only luxury hotel sits at the pinnacle of Cancún's all-inclusive establishments, offering a level of services and amenities unmatched almost anywhere. From the stunning infinity pools and gorgeous beach to the gourmet restaurants and sophisticated spa, the owners have spared no expense. The elegant marble lobby looks out one side to the Caribbean and the other to the lagoon, with sitdown check-in and a champagne welcome. All of the innovative suites feature flatscreen TVs with CD/DVD players, marble bathrooms with rain showers, two-person Jacuzzis, and oceanview balconies with hammocks. Swim-up master suites have semiprivate plunge pools facing the resort's pool and beach; guests in the top-category suites have access to BMW Mini Coopers. The Mayan-inspired oceanview spa includes a massage room, Jacuzzi, sauna, traditional *temazcal* steam bath, massage waterfall, and state-of-the-art fitness center. Actually, the range of services is almost hard to believe, except that you will be paying top dollar for it. The all-inclusive package includes gourmet meals, premium drinks, and evening entertainment.

Bulevar Kukulkán Km 11.5, 77500 Cancún, Q. Roo. © **800/543-7556** in the U.S., or 998/881-5600. www.realresorts.com.mx. 285 units. $444–$804 double suite. AE, DC, MC, V. No children younger than 16. **Amenities:** 6 restaurants; 8 bars; concierge; well-equipped fitness center; expansive outdoor pool; room service; sauna; full-service spa; steam room. *In room:* A/C, flatscreen TV, hair dryer, minibar, Wi-Fi.

Expensive

Dreams Cancún Resort & Spa ⟨Kids⟩   The all-inclusive Dreams Resort enjoys one of the island's most idyllic locations—29 hectares (72 acres) at the tip of Punta Cancún. The setting is casual, and the hotel welcomes children. Bright colors and strategic angles define the design, which now looks somewhat dated relative to Cancún's newer establishments. There are two sets of rooms to choose from: those in the 17-story club section with ocean views and extra services and amenities, and those in the pyramid overlooking the dolphin-filled lagoon. The all-inclusive concept here includes meals, 24-hour room service, and premium-brand drinks, as well as the use of all resort amenities, nonmotorized watersports, theme-night entertainment, and tips. Use of the spa costs extra. One of the resort's restaurants is **Paloma Bonita** (p. 103), for Mexican cuisine. Unfortunately, service at the resort is inconsistent, perhaps owing to the all-inclusive concept.

Bulevar Kukulkán, 77500 Punta Cancún (Apdo. Postal 14), Cancún, Q. Roo. © **866/237-3267** in the U.S., or 998/848-7000. Fax 998/848-7001. www.dreamsresorts.com. 376 units. High season $500 double; $560 club double; low season $370 double, $430 club double. AE, DC, MC, V. **Amenities:** 5 restaurants; 5 bars; babysitting (w/advance notice); bikes; kids' club; fitness center w/steam bath; 2 outdoor pools; private saltwater lagoon w/dolphins and tropical fish; lighted tennis court; watersports; kayaks; Catamarans; paddleboats. *In room:* A/C, TV w/DVD player, hair dryer, minibar.

Marriott Casa Magna ★★ ⟨Kids⟩   This picture-perfect Marriott resort is one of the most enticing family destinations in Cancún. Entering through a half-circle of Roman columns, you'll pass through a domed foyer to a wide, lavishly marbled lobby filled with plants and shallow pools. It looks out to the sparkling pool and enormous whirlpool at the edge of the beach. Guest rooms are decorated with Mexican-Caribbean furnishings and have balconies facing the sea or lagoon. The Marriott caters to family travelers (up to two children stay free with parent), and the supervised children's program is one of the best of any resort here. That said, the resort never feels overrun by kids, and young couples will also have a wonderful time. Among the many places to dine, my favorite is the *teppanyaki*-style (cook-at-your-table) Mikado Japanese restaurant. Service throughout the resort is excellent.

Bulevar Kukulkán Km 14.5, 77500 Cancún, Q. Roo ℂ **800/228-9290** in the U.S., or 998/881-2000. Fax 998/881-2085. www.marriott.com. 452 units. $249–$309 double; $454 and up suite. Ask about packages. AE, MC, V. **Amenities:** 5 restaurants; lobby bar w/live music; babysitting; concierge; health club w/sauna and aerobics; outdoor pool and whirlpool; room service; spa; 2 lighted tennis courts. *In room:* A/C, flatscreen TV, hair dryer, minibar.

ME ★   The Spanish ME hotel by Meliá brings to Cancún a new level of minimalist chic with an atmosphere befitting a trendy nightclub more than a beach resort. Bathed in hues of beige and mauve, with polished marble, onyx lamps, and modern artwork, the hotel creates its own fashion statement—and the hip clientele reflects it. The modern lobby feels a bit like an urban cocktail lounge, with designer bars, sensual artwork, onyx lamps, and chill-out music filling the space. Guest rooms have distinctive contemporary furnishings, plasma TVs, CD players, and marble bathrooms with rain showers and Aveda bath products; half look to the Caribbean Sea and the other half to the lagoon. The super-stylish Yhi Spa overlooks the ocean and offers body glows and exfoliations, aromatherapy massages, body masks, and wraps. The Beach House restaurant appears sunken into the main pool and joins the beach in front. One drawback: Service is not as consistent as you might expect from such an upscale resort.

Bulevar Kukulkán Km 12, 77500 Cancún, Q. Roo. ℂ **800/336-3542** in the U.S., or 998/881-2500. Fax 998/881-2501. www.mecancun.travel. 448 units. $239 and up double. AE, MC, V. **Amenities:** 3 restaurants; Internet cafe; 2 bars; concierge; fitness center; 3 outdoor pools; whirlpool; full-service luxury spa; beach club; concierge floor. *In room:* A/C, TV, Wi-Fi, hair dryer, minibar.

Moderate

Bel Air Collection Hotel & Spa ★ (Value)   This trendy boutique hotel attracts the young, hip, and hot—making this beachfront hotel into something you'd expect to find in Miami, standing in direct contrast to the nearby all-inclusive megaresorts. Of the hotel's 156 rooms, nearly half face the ocean; the rest face the lagoon, which offers splendid sunset views. Guest rooms are modern and spacious, with minimalist white and red decor. There is an asymmetrical infinity pool that seems to spill over onto the turquoise Caribbean Sea, with guests lazing around it on comfortable mattresses. The Collection Spa offers a variety of services, including a chocolate facial. *Note:* This hotel is a 15-minute ride from the center of the Hotel Zone, and young children are not allowed, so if you're looking for privacy and peace, this is the place for you.

Bulevar Kukulkán Km 20.5, 77500 Cancún, Q. Roo. ℂ **998/193-1770.** www.belaircollection.com. 156 units. $150 and up double. Meal plans available. AE, MC, V. No children 11 and under. **Amenities:** 3 restaurants; sushi bar; 3 bars; concierge; exercise room; Jacuzzi; free Wi-Fi; infinity pool; room service; spa. *In-room:* A/C, satellite TV/DVD, hair dryer, minibar.

Flamingo Cancún (Kids)   The all-inclusive Flamingo seems to have been inspired by the dramatic, slope-sided architecture of the Dreams Cancún, but the Flamingo is considerably smaller and less expensive (guests can opt out of the all-inclusive package, which includes three meals and domestic drinks). With two pools and a casual vibe, it's also a friendly, accommodating choice for families. The bright guest rooms—all with balconies—border a courtyard facing the interior swimming pool and *palapa* pool bar. Some, but not all, of the rooms have been remodeled in recent years. The Flamingo lies in the heart of the island hotel district, opposite the Flamingo Shopping Center and close to other hotels, shopping centers, and restaurants.

Bulevar Kukulkán Km 11, 77500 Cancún, Q. Roo. ℂ **998/848-8870.** Fax 998/883-1029. www.flamingo cancun.com. 260 units. High season $199 double; low season $126 double; all-inclusive plan high season $400 double, low season $210 double. AE, MC, V. **Amenities:** 2 restaurants; 2 bars; kids' club; fitness center; 2 pools; room service. *In room:* A/C, TV, hair dryer, minibar.

Temptation Resort & Spa Cancún ★   This adults-only (21 and over) getaway is a spirited, sexy, all-inclusive resort favored by those looking for significant social interaction. By day, pool time is all about flirting, seducing, and getting a little wacky with adult games such as teasing time and a dirty jokes contest. The main pools are top-optional. Note that tops are also optional on the beach in front, which has calm waters for swimming. Come night, theme dinners, shows, and other live entertainment keep the party going. The small, somewhat dated rooms are housed in two sections, with "sexy" red lighting and garden views. Surrounded by acres of tropical gardens, this moderate hotel is ideally located at the northern end of the Hotel Zone, close to the major shopping plazas, restaurants, and nightlife. It reminds me of a Carnival Cruise, but on land.

Bulevar Kukulkán Km 3.5, 77500 Cancún, Q. Roo. ℂ **877/485-8367** in the U.S., or 998/848-7900. Fax 998/848-7994. www.temptationresort.com. 384 units. High season $179 per person per night double occupancy; low season $139 per person per night double occupancy. Rates include food, beverages, and activities. AE, MC, V. Guests must be at least 21 years old. **Amenities:** 6 restaurants; 5 bars; exercise room w/daily classes; 3 outdoor pools; 7 whirlpools; limited room service; spa; nonmotorized watersports equipment; snorkeling and scuba lessons. *In room:* A/C, TV, hair dryer.

CIUDAD CANCUN
Moderate
Radisson Hacienda Cancún ★ (Value)   This is the top hotel in downtown Cancún, and one of the best values in the area. The Radisson offers all the expected comforts of a chain, yet in an atmosphere of Mexican hospitality. Resembling a hacienda, the business-friendly hotel has rooms surrounding a large rotunda-style lobby with a cool onyx bar, as well as lush gardens and an inviting pool area. All have brightly colored fabric accents; views of the garden, the pool, or the street; and a small sitting area and balcony. The hotel lies within walking distance of downtown Cancún dining and shopping.

Av. Nader 1, SM2, Centro, 77500 Cancún, Q. Roo. ℂ **800/333-3333** in the U.S., or 998/881-6500. Fax 998/884-7954. www.radissoncancun.com. 248 units. $150 and up double; $170 and up junior suite. AE, MC, V. **Amenities:** 2 restaurants; lively lobby bar; small gym; free Wi-Fi in lobby; outdoor pool w/adjoining bar and separate wading area for children; room service; sauna; lighted tennis courts. *In room:* A/C, TV, hair dryer.

Rey del Caribe Hotel ★★ (Finds)   This ecological hotel is a unique oasis where every detail works toward establishing harmony with the environment. You might easily forget you're in the midst of downtown Cancún in the tropical garden setting, with blooming orchids and other flowering plants. The lovely grounds include statues of Mayan deities, hammocks, and a tiled swimming pool. There's a regularly changing schedule of yoga, Tai Chi, and meditation sessions, as well as special classes on astrology, tarot, and other subjects. The on-site spa offers facial and body treatments. Rooms are large and sunny, with a kitchenette and your choice of one king-size or two full-size beds; some have a terrace. The extent of ecological sensitivity is impressive—ranging from the use of collected rainwater to waste composting. Recycling is encouraged, and solar power is used wherever possible.

Av. Uxmal SM 2A (corner of Nader), 77500 Cancún, Q. Roo. ℂ 998/884-2028. Fax 988/884-9857. www. reycaribe.com. 31 units. High season $85 double; low season $65 double. Rates include breakfast. MC, V. **Amenities:** Outdoor pool; spa. *In room:* A/C, TV, kitchenette.

Inexpensive

Sol y Luna ⟨Value⟩   This simple but cheerful hotel next to the Parque Las Palapas has 11 individually decorated rooms with small balconies, and mosaic-trimmed baths with showers only. A tiny bridge crosses the small pool at the entrance. Come here if you want to explore the downtown and experience Cancún's more local flavor, but don't expect much in the way of service or amenities.

Calle Alcatraces 33, 77500 Cancún, Q. Roo. ℂ 998/887-5579. www.solylunahotel.com. 11 units. $50–$70 double. AE, MC, V. Street parking. **Amenities:** Outdoor pool. *In room:* A/C, TV, fridge.

Xbalamqué   Creatively designed to resemble a Maya temple, this downtown hotel features a full-service spa, a lovely pool and waterfall, and an authentic Mexican cantina. Live music plays evenings in the bookstore/cafe adjacent to the lobby. Guest rooms and 10 junior suites have rustic furnishings with regional touches, colorful tilework, and small bathrooms with showers. Ask for a room overlooking the ivy-filled courtyard. A tour desk is available to help you plan your vacation activities, and the spa offers some of the best rates of any hotel in Cancún. A small *tamaleria* serving delicious regional tamales is adjacent to the lobby.

Av. Yaxchilán 31, Sm. 22, Mza. 18, 77500 Cancún, Q. Roo. ℂ 998/884-9690. Fax 998/884-9690. www. xbalamque.com. 99 units. $75 double, $85 suite. AE, MC, V. **Amenities:** Restaurant; cafe; Internet cafe; cantina; lobby bar; outdoor pool; spa. *In room:* A/C, TV.

3 WHERE TO DINE

More than 300 restaurants spanning North American, European, and Asian cuisines have opened across Cancún. They have come to supplement the many U.S.-based franchise chains that have long dominated the Cancún restaurant scene. These include Hard Rock Cafe, Rainforest Cafe, Tony Roma's, T.G.I. Friday's, Ruth's Chris Steak House, and the gamut of fast-food burger places. The establishments listed here are typically locally owned, one-of-a-kind restaurants or exceptional selections at area hotels. Many schedule live music. Unless otherwise indicated, parking is free.

One unique way to combine dinner with sightseeing is aboard the **Lobster Dinner Cruise** (ℂ 998/849-4748; www.thelobsterdinner.com). Cruising around the tranquil, turquoise waters of the lagoon, passengers feast on lobster dinners accompanied by wine. Cost is $79 per person for the surf-and-turf menu and $89 for the lobster-only menu. There are two daily departures from the Aquatours Marina (Bulevar Kukulkán km 6.5). A sunset cruise leaves at 5pm during the winter and 5:30pm during the summer; a moonlight cruise leaves at 8pm winter, 8:30pm summer. Another—albeit livelier—lobster dinner option is the **Captain Hook Lobster Dinner Cruise** (ℂ 998/849-4451; www. pirateshipcancun.com), which is similar, but with the added attraction of a pirate show involving two 28m (93-ft.) replicas of 18th-century Spanish galleons, making this a fun choice for families. It costs $86 per person, departs at 7pm from El Embarcadero at Playa Linda, and returns at 10:30pm.

ISLA CANCUN

Very Expensive

Aioli ★★ FRENCH   The quality and originality of the cuisine and excellence of service make this a top choice for fine dining in Cancún. The Provençal—but definitely not provincial—Aioli offers exquisite French and Mediterranean gourmet specialties in a warm and cozy country French setting. Though it serves perhaps the best breakfast buffet in Cancún (for $26), most diners from outside the hotel come here in the evening, when low lighting and superb service promise a romantic experience. Delectable starters include foie gras medallions and caramelized grapes with a pinot noir coulis; among the best main courses are pan-seared jumbo shrimp in lobster sauce, lamb rack with polenta sauce, and breast of duck. Desserts are decadent, especially the signature "Fifth Element" with chocolate and a rich berry sauce.

In Le Méridien Cancún Resort & Spa (p. 96), Retorno del Rey Km 14. ℂ **998/881-2200.** Reservations recommended. No sandals or tennis shoes; men must wear long pants. Main courses $27–$45. AE, MC, V. Daily 6:30am–11pm.

Club Grill ★★★ INTERNATIONAL   The five-diamond Club Grill is the place for that special night out. Cancún's most acclaimed dining room is also among its most delicious. Even rival restaurateurs give it an envious thumbs-up. The gracious service starts as you enter the anteroom, with its elegant seating and superb selection of cocktails and wines. It continues in the candlelit dining room, with shimmering silver and crystal. Sophisticated plates of prime cuts, escargot, seared scallops, foie gras, truffles, and roasted duck arrive at a leisurely pace. The restaurant is exclusively smoke-free, and service is impeccable. A band plays romantic jazz for dancing from 7:30pm on.

In the Ritz-Carlton Cancún (p. 96), Retorno del Rey, 36 Bulevar Kukulkán Km 13.5. ℂ **998/881-0808.** Reservations required. No sandals or tennis shoes; men must wear long pants and collared shirts. Main courses $30–$46. AE, DC, MC, V. Tues–Sun 7–11pm.

Lorenzillo's ★★ **Kids** SEAFOOD   This longtime Cancún favorite hasn't changed much over the years. Lobster remains the star, and part of the appeal is selecting your dinner out of the giant lobster tank set in the lagoon (Lorenzillo's sits right on the lagoon under a giant *palapa* roof). A dock leads down to the main dining area, and when that's packed, a wharf-side bar handles the overflow. You'll find a large captain's wheel at the entrance to this nautical-themed restaurant. To start, I recommend *El Botin,* which consists of two soft- shell crabs breaded and fried to perfection. Good bets for the entree include lobster (which comes prepared in any of 20 different ways), shrimp stuffed with cheese and wrapped in bacon, the *Pescador* (Caribbean grouper prepared to taste), and steak and seafood combinations. Desserts include the tempting crepes suzette, prepared tableside. Lorenzillo's is as popular with families as it is with couples looking for lagoon-side romance. It's connected by a walkway to Limoncello, the waterfront Italian restaurant next door.

Bulevar Kukulkán Km 10.5. ℂ **998/883-1254.** www.lorenzillos.com.mx. Reservations recommended. Main courses $22–$49. AE, MC, V. Daily 1pm–12:30am.

Expensive

Casa de las Margaritas ★ MEXICAN   La Casa de las Margaritas is a celebration of the flavors and ¡fiesta! spirit of Mexico. With a decor as vibrant as a piñata, waiters dressed in regional costumes, and a soundtrack of background music that ranges from mariachi to marimba, the experience here is a crash course in the buoyant spirit of this colorful country. On the menu, best bets include the Margarita shrimp, flambéed in brandy, white wine, and chipotle chili sauce; chicken breast served with homemade mole; or traditional chicken enchiladas topped with tomato-and-sun-dried-pepper sauce with lettuce, avocado slices, and white cheese from Oaxaca. Inside La Isla shopping center, Casa de las Margaritas also serves a spectacular Sunday brunch buffet. Live traditional music is offered nightly from 7 to 8pm, including folkloric dance on Saturday and Sunday.

Paseo Kukulkán Km 12.5, La Isla Shopping Mall, Loc. E-17. ⓒ 998/883-3222, -3054. www.lacasadelas margaritas.com. Reservations recommended. Main courses $16–$45; Sun brunch $19. AE, MC, V. Mon–Sat 1–10pm; Sun brunch noon–5pm.

Casa Rolandi ★★★ SWISS/ITALIAN   Like its sister location on Isla Mujeres, Casa Rolandi blends sophisticated Swiss–Italian cuisine with fresh Caribbean fish and Mexican produce. Famous personalities, from international actors to Mexican presidents, have dined here. The casually elegant restaurant offers white linen tables with roses and candles at night, yet welcomes informal dress. Among the sophisticated selections are homemade ravioli stuffed with wild mushrooms over a creamy Alba truffle sauce; tagliolini with sautéed shrimp and ginger doused with sparkling wine; fresh fish (usually snapper or sea bass) baked in salt and accompanied by fresh vegetables and seasoned mashed potatoes; and grilled 18-ounce rib-eye served sizzling. Finish with the sublime tiramisu served with chocolate and rum cream. Service is personalized and friendly, and a cigar and wine bar has been added upstairs (p. 114).

Bulevar Kukulkán Km 8.5, in Plaza Caracol. ⓒ **998/883-2557.** www.rolandi.com. Reservations recommended. Main courses $17–$38. AE, MC, V. Daily 1–11:30pm.

Gustino ★★★ ITALIAN   JW Marriott's signature restaurant Gustino offers romantic Italian dining unsurpassed in Cancún. The exquisite dining room includes a gorgeous centerpiece candle display, floor-to-ceiling windows looking out to a lazy man-made lagoon and the beach beyond, and live saxophone. For an *antipasto*, I recommend the unusual pear carpaccio with parmesan nuggets and caramelized grapes, or the sautéed shrimp in a white wine sauce with capers and roasted celery crouton. The warm tossed spinach salad is one of the best I've ever tasted, topped with pancetta, mushrooms, sun-dried tomatoes, and walnuts. Expertly prepared main dishes include open lasagna with lobster and black olives, and seafood linguine tossed in a garlic white wine sauce. The menu, which changes seasonally, features other homemade pastas and succulent steak and seafood selections. Gustino boasts an open kitchen and wine cellar with an excellent variety of international grapes. Service is impeccable.

In the JW Marriott (p. 94), Bulevar Kukulkán Km 14.5. ⓒ **998/848-9600.** Reservations required. Main courses $15–$34. AE, DC, MC, V. Daily 6–11pm.

Harry's ★★ STEAK   Situated adjacent to the Nichupté Lagoon, this prime steakhouse and raw bar is the hottest new addition to Cancún's dining scene. The dining room and waterfront terrace combine local stone and wood with burned orange marble and large expanses of glass to create a sense of California chic. The attentive waitstaff brings to your table a tempting selection of different cuts of beef, as well as a presentation from the raw bar. The New York strips, rib-eyes, and other cuts of beef are broiled in a 1,000°C (1,700°F) oven, while the fish and seafood are grilled on a *parilla*. Dishes are served a la carte, and the food is prepared with careful attention to detail. Don't expect a kids' menu here: Even the Kobe beef burger is so big it could feed a family. An excellent selection of international and Mexican boutique wines accompanies the menu.

Laguna Grill ★★ FUSION Laguna Grill offers diners a contemporary culinary experience in a picturesque setting overlooking the lagoon. A tropical garden welcomes you at the entrance, while a small creek traverses the *palapa*-covered dining room set with tables made from the trunks of tropical trees. As magical as the decor is, the real star here is the kitchen, with its selection of Pacific Rim cuisine fused with regional flavors. Starters include martini *gyoza* (steamed dumplings), filled with shrimp and vegetables, or tuna tartare with soy and ginger. Fish and seafood dominate the menu, in preparations that combine Asian and Mexican flavors such as ginger, cilantro, garlic, and hoisin sauce. Grilled shrimp are marinated in rum, mint, and lime; surf-and-turf fusion dishes may include grilled lobster, beef, and shrimp skewers. For beef-lovers, the rib-eye served with mashed potatoes and black olives is excellent. For dessert, I recommend the crème brûlée served with a touch of Bailey's. If you're an early diner, request a table on the outside deck for a spectacular sunset view. An impressive selection of wines is available.

Bulevar Kukulkán Km 16.5. ℰ **998/885-0320**. www.lagunagrill.com.mx. Reservations recommended. Main courses $11–$37. AE, MC, V. Daily 4pm–midnight.

Paloma Bonita ★ (Kids) REGIONAL In a stylish setting overlooking the water, Paloma Bonita captures the essence of Mexico through its music and food. Since Paloma Bonita lies in a hotel (Dreams Cancún), prices are higher than at traditional Mexican restaurants in Ciudad Cancún, but this is a good choice for authentic food in the Hotel Zone. There are three sections: La Cantina Jalisco, with an open kitchen and tequila bar; the Salón Michoacán, which features that state's cuisine; and the Patio Oaxaca, which has oceanview seating. Mariachis serenade you while you dine in any of these areas. The menu encompasses the best of Mexico's other cuisines, with a few international dishes. A traditional starter is the *nopalitos* (cactus) salad with a vinaigrette dressing. For a main course, I recommend the stuffed chile La Doña—a mildly hot poblano pepper filled with lobster and *huitlacoche* (a type of mushroom that grows on corn) in a cream sauce. Live traditional music plays Tuesday through Sunday nights.

In the Dreams Cancún (p. 97), Punta Cancún (enter from the street). ℰ **998/848-7082**. Reservations recommended. Main courses $11–$52. AE, DC, MC, V. Daily 6–11:30pm.

Puerto Madero ★★ ARGENTINE/STEAKS/SEAFOOD As a tribute to the famed Puerto Madero of Buenos Aires, this trendy restaurant has quickly earned a reputation for its outstanding steaks and buzzing atmosphere. Overlooking the Nichupté Lagoon, the decor re-creates a 20th-century dock warehouse similar to what you'd find in the real Puerto Madero, with dark woods, exposed brick, and visible pipes. This steakhouse offers an extensive selection of prime-quality beef cuts, pastas, grilled fish, and shellfish, meticulously prepared with Argentine gusto. In addition to the classic carpaccio, the tuna tartar and halibut steak are favorites, but the real standouts here are the tender grilled steaks (particularly the rib-eye), served in ample portions. Enjoy a cocktail or glass of wine from the extensive selection, while viewing the sunset from the lagoonside deck. Service is excellent.

Marina Barracuda, Bulevar Kukulkán Km 14. ℰ 998/885-2829, -2830. www.puertomaderorestaurantes. com. Reservations recommended. Main courses $18–$59. AE, MC, V. Daily 1pm–1am.

Thai ★★★ (Moments) THAI This sensual restaurant and lounge feels like it should be in Southeast Asia rather than the edge of a Mexican shopping plaza. The stunning outdoor setting includes thick foliage and bamboo, with private *palapas* (open-air huts, each with its own table, sofa, and flickering candles) constructed like tiny islands over the expansive lagoon. Unobtrusive service, soft red and blue lighting, and Asian chill and lounge music contribute to the Buddha Bar–like ambience. Classic Thai specialties such as spicy shrimp soup with lemon grass and mushrooms, glass noodle salad, chicken satay, and chicken and shrimp curries and stir-fries are served alongside exotic cocktails to the beautiful crowd. A DJ works the stylish lounge on weekends. Thai opens at sunset.

La Isla Shopping Center, Loc. B-4. ✆ 998/144-0364. Reservations recommended during high season. Main courses $13–$31. AE, MC, V. Daily 6pm–1am.

Moderate

El Shrimp Bucket (Kids) SEAFOOD   This festive, family-friendly restaurant on the lagoon is all about "meaty, magnificent, and tender" shrimp cooked to your liking—peel-and-eat, breaded, beerbattered, coconut, grilled, and even bacon-barbecued. The kitchen serves only wild-caught shrimp from the Pacific coast of Mexico, which are extremely rich in flavor. The menu offers other fish and seafood selections, including ceviches, fish tacos, seafood pastas, and fish sandwiches. The casual eatery features a fun kids' playground that advises the children to "keep an eye on your parents." The indoor and outdoor seating is decorated with fish nets, shrimp buckets, and other nautical knickknacks. Salsa music plays in the background, and the servers are as cheerful as the atmosphere.

Bulevar Kukulkán Km 15. ✆ 998/840-6466. www.shrimpbucket.com. Main courses $8–$27. AE, MC, V. Daily noon–midnight.

La Destilería MEXICAN   To experience Mexico's favorite export on an enticing terrace overlooking the lagoon, this is your place (keep an eye out for Tequila, the lagoon crocodile who often comes to visit). La Destilería is more than a tequila-inspired restaurant; it's a minimuseum honoring the "spirit" of Mexico. It serves over 150 brands of tequila, including some treasures that never find their way across the country's northern border. A tequila tour is offered daily at 4:30pm, and patrons can always order tequila "samplers" at their tables. No surprise, the margaritas are also among the island's best. When you decide to order food with your tequila, you'll find a creative Mexican menu, with everything from quesadillas with zucchini flower, cheese, and poblano pepper to *arrachera* beef fajitas served in a hot pot with roasted *nopales* (cactus), Mexican sausage, and avocado.

Bulevar Kukulkán Km 12.65, across from Kukulcán Plaza. ✆ 998/885-1086, -1087. www.ladestileria.com. Main courses $15–$47. Tequila tour $8.50. AE, MC, V. Daily 1pm–midnight.

CIUDAD CANCUN

Expensive

La Habichuela ★★★ (Moments) SEAFOOD   What an enchanting restaurant. In a musically accented garden setting with flowering white-lit hibiscus trees, this downtown Caribbean seafood restaurant oozes romance. For an unforgettable culinary adventure, order crème of *habichuela* (string bean) soup; giant shrimp in any number of sauces, including Jamaican tamarind, tequila, or ginger and mushroom; and exotic Mayan coffee prepared tableside with Xtabentun (a strong, sweet, anise-based liqueur). Grilled seafood and steaks are excellent, and the menu includes luscious ceviches, Caribbean lobsters, an inventive seafood "parade," and shish kabob flambé with shrimp and lobster or beef. For something divine, try *cocobichuela,* lobster and shrimp in sweet curry served in a coconut shell and topped with fruit. Top it off with one of the boozy butterscotch crepes. Service here is fabulous.

Périco's ★★ (Kids) MEXICAN/SEAFOOD/STEAKS   Périco's is a joyous parade of performance, play, and brightly colored tourist hilarity. The unique restaurant and cantina features entertaining waiters dressed in a variety of festive costumes, murals that seem to dance off the walls, a bar area with saddles for barstools, and leather tables and chairs. Its extensive menu offers well-prepared steak, seafood, and traditional Mexican dishes for reasonable rates (except for lobster and surf-and-turf). This is a place not only to eat and drink, but also to let loose and join in the fun, so don't be surprised if diners drop their forks and don sombreros to shimmy and shake in a conga line around the dining room. The entertainment kicks off at 7:30pm, and there's an extensive kids' menu.

Yaxchilán 61. ℂ **998/884-3152.** www.pericos.com.mx. Reservations recommended. Main courses $14–$41. AE, MC, V. Daily noon–1am.

Moderate

Labná ★★ YUCATECAN   Coming for a meal at Labná is like a very special trip to a Yucatecan home, a place that serves delicious Mayan food and treats you like a friend. Specialties include a sublime lime soup, *poc chuc* (marinated, barbecue-style pork), chicken or pork *pibil* (sweet and spicy barbecue sauce served over shredded meat wrapped in banana leaves), and appetizers such as *papadzules* (tortillas stuffed with boiled eggs in a pumpkin-seed sauce). The Labná Special is a sampler of four typically Yucatecan main courses, including *poc chuc,* while another specialty of the house is baked suckling pig, served with guacamole. The refreshing Yucatecan beverage, *agua de chaya*—a blend of sweetened water and the leaf of the *chaya* plant, abundant in the area, to which sweet Xtabentun liquor (a type of anise) can be added for an extra kick—is also served here. The vaulted ceiling dining room is decorated with a mural of a pre-Hispanic Yucatacan scene, as well as with black-and-white photographs of Mérida, the capital of the Yucatán, dating from the 1900s. A local trio plays weekend afternoons.

Margaritas 29, next to Cristo Rey church and the Habichuela restaurant. ℂ **998/892-3056.** www.labna. com. Main courses $7–$20. AE, MC, V. Daily noon–10pm.

Inexpensive

100% Natural ★ BREAKFAST/HEALTH FOOD   If you want a healthy reprieve from an overindulgent night—or just like your meals as fresh and natural as possible—this is your oasis. No matter what your dining preference, you owe it to yourself to try a Mexican tradition, the fresh-fruit *licuado*. These smoothie-like drinks combine fresh fruit, ice, and water or milk. More creative combinations may mix in yogurt, granola, or other goodies. 100% Natural serves more than just quality drinks—there's a bountiful selection of healthy Mexican plates and terrific sandwiches served on whole-grain bread, with options for vegetarians. Breakfast is delightful, and there's an attached bakery featuring all-natural baked goods such as chocolate croissants and apple-cinnamon muffins. There are several 100% Natural locations in town, including branches at Playa Chac-Mool, in front of Señor Frog's, and downtown.

Av. Sunyaxchen 63. ℂ **998/884-0102.** www.100natural.com.mx. Reservations not accepted. Main courses $5–$16. AE, MC, V. Daily 7am–11pm.

Pizza Rolandi ★ (Kids) ITALIAN   At this shaded patio restaurant known for dependably tasty Italian delights, you can choose from an enticing selection of spaghetti, calzones, and Italian-style chicken and beef, as well as from almost two dozen delicious, if greasy, wood-oven pizzas (individual size). Why not try the deliciously spicy "Fiesta Mexicana" pizza with tomato, cheese, Mexican pepperoni, and jalapeños? A Cancún institution here since 1979, Pizza Rolandi has a duplicate branch on Isla Mujeres (see chapter 6). It's as popular with locals as with tourists.

Cobá 12. ℂ **998/884-4047.** Fax 998/884-4047. www.rolandi.com. Pasta $9–$12; pizza and main courses $7–$14. AE, MC, V. Daily 12:30pm–12:30am.

Roots INTERNATIONAL   This popular hangout for local residents is also a fun spot for visitors to Cancún. Located in the heart of downtown, this dimly lit restaurant and jazz club offers a smooth cosmopolitan ambience. The Caribbean-themed menu offers a range of casual dining choices, including soups, sandwiches, and fresh fish and steaks grilled on the *parilla*. It's accompanied by live music, including flamenco, jazz, and fusion. Decking the walls are original works of art by local painters. The music starts at 10:30pm, and Roots seldom fills up before 9:30pm.

Tulipanes 26, SM 22. ℂ **998/884-2437.** Main courses $6–$17. MC, V. Tues–Sat 6pm–1am.

4 BEACHES, WATERSPORTS & BOAT TOURS

THE BEACHES   Big hotels dominate the best stretches of beach. All of Mexico's beaches are public property, so you can use the beach of any hotel by walking through the lobby or directly onto the sand. Be especially careful on the east-facing beaches fronting the open Caribbean, where the undertow can be quite strong. By contrast, the waters of **Bahía de Mujeres** (Mujeres Bay), at the north end of the island, are usually calm and ideal for swimming. Get to know Cancún's water-safety pennant system, and make sure to check the flag at any beach or hotel before entering the water. Here's how it goes:

White	Excellent
Green	Normal conditions (safe)
Yellow	Changeable, uncertain (use caution)
Black or **red**	Unsafe—use the swimming pool instead!

In the Caribbean, storms can arrive and conditions can change from safe to unsafe in a matter of minutes, so be alert: If you see dark clouds heading your way, make for the shore and wait until the storm passes.

Playa Tortuga (Turtle Beach), Playa Langosta (Lobster Beach), Playa Linda (Pretty Beach), and Playa Las Perlas (Beach of the Pearls) are some of the public beaches. At most beaches, you can rent a sailboard and take lessons, ride a parasail, or partake in a variety of watersports. There's a small but beautiful portion of public beach on **Playa Caracol,** by the Xcaret Terminal. It faces the calm waters of Bahía de Mujeres and, for that reason, is preferable to those facing the Caribbean.

WATERSPORTS   Many beachside hotels offer watersports concessions that rent rubber rafts, kayaks, and snorkeling equipment. On the calm Nichupté lagoon are outlets for renting **sailboats, jet skis, sailboards,** and **water skis.** Prices vary and are often negotiable, so check around.

DEEP-SEA FISHING   You can arrange a shared or private deep-sea fishing charter at one of the numerous piers or travel agencies. Prices fluctuate widely depending on the length of the excursion (there's usually a 4-hr. minimum), number of people, and quality of the boat. Marinas will sometimes assist in putting together a group. Charters include a captain, a first mate, bait, gear, and beverages. Rates are lower if you depart from Isla Mujeres or from Cozumel—and, frankly, the fishing is better closer to those departure points. **Lagoonview Marina & Fishing Club** (© **998/845-0749**), located at Bulevar Kukulkán Km 13.5, rents 9.6m (32-ft.) Welcraft boats (maximum 6 people) that rent for $450 for 4 hours, $675 for 6 hours, and $795 for 8 hours.

SCUBA & SNORKELING   Known for its shallow reefs, dazzling color, and diversity of life, Cancún is one of the best places in the world for beginning scuba diving. Punta Nizuc is the northern tip of the **Gran Arrecife Maya (Great Mesoamerican Reef),** the largest reef in the Western Hemisphere and one of the largest in the world. In addition to the sea life along this reef system, several sunken boats add a variety of dive options. Inland, a series of caverns and cenotes (wellsprings) are fascinating venues for the more experienced diver. Drift diving is the norm here, with popular dives going to the reefs at **El Garrafón** and the **Cave of the Sleeping Sharks**—although be aware that the famed "sleeping sharks" have departed, driven off by too many people watching them snooze.

A variety of hotels offer resort courses that teach the basics of diving—enough to make shallow dives and slowly ease your way into this underwater world of unimaginable beauty. One preferred dive operator is **Scuba Cancún,** Bulevar Kukulkán Km 5 (© **998/ 849-4736;** www.scubacancun.com.mx), on the lagoon side. Full open-water PADI certification takes 3 days and costs $410. A half-day resort course for beginners with theory, pool practice, and a one-tank dive at a reef costs $88. Scuba Cancún is open daily from 7am to 8pm. For certified divers, Scuba Cancún also offers PADI specialty courses and diving trips in good weather to 18 nearby reefs, as well as to cenotes (9m/30 ft.) and Cozumel. The average dive is around 11m (36 ft.), while advanced divers descend farther (up to 18m/59 ft). Two-tank dives to reefs around Cancún cost $68, and one-tank dives cost $54; those to farther destinations cost $140. Discounts apply if you bring your own gear. Dives usually start around 9:30am and return by 1:30pm. Snorkeling trips cost $29 and leave daily at 1:30pm and 4pm for shallow reefs about a 20-minute boat ride away.

The largest dive operator is **Aquaworld,** across from the Meliá Cancún at Bulevar Kukulkán Km 15.2 (© **998/848-8300;** www.aquaworld.com.mx). It offers resort courses and diving at a reef barrier, as well as snorkeling, parasailing, jet-ski "jungle tours," fishing, day trips to Isla Mujeres and Cozumel, and other watersports activities. Single-tank dives cost $66; two-tank dives $72. Aquaworld has the **Sub See Explorer,** a boat with picture windows beneath the surface. The boat doesn't submerge—it's an updated version of a glass-bottom boat—but it does provide nondivers with a worthwhile peek at life beneath the sea.

Another interesting option is **BOB Submarines** (© **998/849-7284**), located at El Embarcadero next to Playa Linda, which rents propelled breathing observation bubbles (BOBs). These personal minisubs let you discover the Caribbean with a big air bubble over your head and operate much like a scooter would. The tours include instruction, soft drinks, and a 30-minute assisted dive. The cost is $80 per person and the minimum age is 12, with departures at 9am, 11:30am, and 2pm.

Besides snorkeling at **El Garrafón Natural Park** (see "Boating Excursions," below), travel agencies offer an all-day excursion to the natural wildlife habitat of **Isla Contoy,** which usually includes time for snorkeling. The island, 90 minutes past Isla Mujeres, is a major nesting area for birds and a treat for nature lovers. You can call any travel agent or see any hotel tour desk to get a selection of boat tours to Isla Contoy. Prices range from $50 to $80, depending on the length of the trip, and generally include drinks and snorkeling equipment.

The Great Mesoamerican Reef also offers exceptional snorkeling opportunities. In Puerto Morelos, 37km (23 miles; p. 151) south of Cancún, the reef hugs the coastline for 15km (9¼ miles). The reef is so close to the shore (about 460m/1,509 ft.) that it forms a natural barrier for the village and keeps the waters calm on the inside of the reef. The water here is shallow, from 1.5 to 9m (5–30 ft.), resulting in ideal conditions for snorkeling. Stringent environmental regulations implemented by the local community have kept the reef here unspoiled. Only a select few companies are allowed to offer snorkel trips, and they must adhere to guidelines that will ensure the reef's preservation. **Cancún Mermaid** (© **998/843-6517;** www.cancunmermaid.com), in Puerto Morelos, is considered the best—it's a family-run ecotour company that has operated in the area since the 1970s. It's known for highly personalized service. The tour typically takes snorkelers to two sections of the reef, spending about an hour in each area. When conditions allow, the boat drops off snorkelers and then follows them along with the current—an activity known as "drift snorkeling," which enables snorkelers to see as much of the reef as possible. The trip costs $50 for adults, $35 for children, and includes boat, snorkeling gear, life jackets, a light lunch, bottled water, sodas, and beer, plus round-trip transportation to and from Puerto Morelos from Cancún hotels. Departures are Monday through Saturday at 9am. For snorkelers who just can't get enough, a combo tour for $30 more adds a bicycle tour to additional snorkeling destinations. Reservations are required at least 1 day in advance; MasterCard and Visa are accepted.

JET-SKI/FAST BOAT TOURS   Several companies offer the thrilling **Jungle Cruise,** in which you drive your own small speed boat (called a *lancha*) or WaveRunner rapidly through Cancún's lagoon and mangrove estuaries out into the Caribbean Sea and a shallow reef. The excursion lasts about 2½ hours and costs $60 to $70, including snorkeling equipment. Many people prefer the companies offering two-person boats rather than WaveRunners, since they can sit side by side rather than one behind the other.

Jungle cruise operators and names offering excursions change often. To find out what's available, check with a local travel agent or hotel tour desk. The popular **Aquaworld,** Bulevar Kukulkán Km 15.2 (© **998/848-8300**), calls its trip the Jungle Tour and charges $66 for the 2½-hour excursion, which includes 30 minutes of snorkeling time. It even gives you a free snorkel and has the WaveRuner-style one-behind-the-other seating configuration. Departures are daily at 9am, noon, and 2:30pm. If you'd prefer a side-by-side boat so that you and your partner can talk or at least look at each other, try **Blue Ray,** Bulevar Kukulkán Km 13.5, next to Mambo Café (© **998/885-1108**), which charges $55, with departures every hour between 9am and 3pm. Expect to get wet, and wear plenty of sunscreen.

BOATING EXCURSIONS

ISLA MUJERES   The island of **Isla Mujeres,** just 13km (8 miles) offshore, is one of the most pleasant day trips from Cancún. At one end is **El Garrafón Natural Park,** which is good for snorkeling. At the other end is a captivating village with small shops, restaurants, and hotels, and **Playa Norte,** the island's best beach. If you're looking for relaxation and can spare the time, it's worth several days. For complete information about the island, see chapter 6.

There are four ways to get there: **public ferry** from Puerto Juárez, which takes between 15 and 20 minutes; **shuttle boat** from Playa Linda or Playa Tortuga, an hour-long ride, with irregular service; **water taxi** (more expensive, but faster), next to the Xcaret Terminal; and daylong **pleasure-boat cruises,** most of which leave from the Playa Linda pier.

The inexpensive but fast Puerto Juárez **public ferries** ★ lie just a few kilometers from downtown Cancún. From Cancún City, take the Ruta 8 bus on Avenida Tulum to Puerto Juárez. The air-conditioned *Ultramar* (© 998/881-5890; www.granpuerto.com.mx) boats cost $7 per person round-trip and take 15 to 20 minutes. Departures are every half-hour from 5am to 8:30pm and then at 9:30pm, 10:30pm, and 11:30pm. The slower *Caribbean Savage* (45–60 min.) costs about $4. It departs every 2 hours, or less frequently, depending on demand. Upon arrival, the ferry docks in downtown Isla Mujeres near all the shops, restaurants, hotels, and Norte beach. You'll need a taxi to get to El Garrafón park at the other end of the island. You can stay as long as you like on the island and return by ferry, but be sure to confirm the time of the last returning ferry.

Pleasure-boat cruises to Isla Mujeres are a favorite pastime. Modern motor yachts, sailboats (including the "Sea Passion" catamaran), and even old-time sloops—more than 25 boats a day—take swimmers, sun lovers, snorkelers, and shoppers out on the translucent waters. Some tours include a snorkeling stop at El Garrafón, lunch on the beach, and a short time for shopping in downtown Isla Mujeres. Most leave at 9:30 or 10am, last about 5 or 6 hours, and include continental breakfast, lunch, and rental of snorkel gear. Others, particularly sunset and night cruises, go to beaches away from town for pseudo-pirate shows and include a lobster dinner or Mexican buffet (p. 101). If you want to actually see Isla Mujeres, go on a morning cruise, or travel on your own using the public ferry from Puerto Juárez. Prices for the day cruises run around $80 per person. Reservations aren't necessary.

An all-inclusive entrance fee of $69, $50 for children to **Garrafón Natural Reef Park** ★★ (© 998/849-4748; www.garrafon.com), includes transportation from Playa Langosta in Cancún; meals; open bar with domestic drinks; access to the reef; and use of snorkel gear, kayaks, inner tubes, life vests, the pool, hammocks, and public facilities and showers (but not towels, so bring your own). There are also nature trails and several on-site restaurants.

Other excursions go to the **reefs** in glass-bottom boats, so you can have a near-scuba-diving experience and see many colorful fish. However, the reefs are some distance from the shore and are impossible to reach on windy days with choppy seas. They've also suffered from overvisitation, and their condition is far from pristine. Nautibus's **Atlantis Submarine** (© 987/872-5671; www.atlantisadventures.com) takes you close to the aquatic action. Departures vary, depending on weather conditions. Prices are $79 for adults, $45 for children ages 4 to 12. The submarine descends to a depth of 30m (98 ft.). Atlantis Submarine departs daily at 9am, 11am, and noon; the tour lasts about 40 minutes. The submarine departs from Cozumel, so you need to either take a ferry to get there or purchase a package that includes round-trip transportation from your hotel in Cancún ($103 adults, $76 children 4–12). Reservations are recommended.

5 OUTDOOR ACTIVITIES & ATTRACTIONS

OUTDOOR ACTIVITIES

DOLPHIN SWIMS On Isla Mujeres, you have the opportunity to swim with dolphins at **Dolphin Discovery** ★★ (© 998/877-0207 or 849-4757; www.dolphindiscovery. com). Groups of eight people swim with two dolphins and one trainer. Swimmers view an educational video and spend time in the water with the trainer and the dolphins before enjoying 15 minutes of free swimming time with them. Reservations are recommended (you can book online), and you must arrive an hour before your assigned swimming time, at 10:30am, noon, 2pm, or 3:30pm. The cost is $149 per person for the Dolphin Royal Swim. There are less expensive programs that allow you to learn about, touch, and hold the dolphins (but not swim with them) starting at $69. Ferry transfers from Playa Langosta in Cancún are available.

La Isla Shopping Center, Bulevar Kukulkán Km 12.5, has an impressive **Interactive Aquarium** (© 998/883-0411, -0436, -0413; www.aquariumcancun.com.mx), with dolphin swims and shows and the chance to feed a shark while immersed in the water in an acrylic cage. Guides inside the main tank use underwater microphones to point out the sea life, and even answer your questions. Open exhibition tanks enable visitors to touch a variety of marine life, including sea stars and manta rays. The educational dolphin program costs $65, while the dolphin swim is $135 and the shark-feeding experience runs $71. The entrance fee to the aquarium is $14 for adults, $9 for children under 11, and it's open daily from 9am to 6pm.

GOLF & TENNIS The 18-hole **Cancún Golf Club at Pok-Ta-Pok** (© 998/883-0871; www.cancungolfclub.com), located at Bulevar Kukulkán Km. 7.5, is a Robert Trent Jones II design on the northern leg of the island. Greens fees run $145 for 18 holes, including breakfast or lunch and golf cart (discounted fees after 2pm), with clubs renting for $45. A caddy costs $20 plus tip. The club is open daily from 6:30am to 5pm and accepts American Express, MasterCard, and Visa.

The **Hilton Cancún Golf & Spa Resort** (© 998-881-8016; www.hiltongolfclub. com/golf) has a championship 18-hole, par-72 course around the Ruinas Del Rey. Greens fees during high season for the public are typically $199 for 18 holes and $125 for 9 holes; Hilton Cancún guests pay discounted rates of $159 for 18 holes, or $79 for 9 holes, which includes a golf cart. Low-season and twilight discounts are available. Golf clubs and shoes are available for rent. The club is open daily from 6am to 6pm and accepts American Express, MasterCard, and Visa. The **Gran Meliá Cancún** (© 998/881-1100) has a 9-hole executive course; the fee is $30. The club is open daily from 7am to 3pm and accepts American Express, MasterCard, and Visa.

The first Jack Nicklaus Signature Golf Course in the Cancún area has opened at the **Moon Palace Spa & Golf Club** (© 998-881-6000; www.palaceresorts.com), along the Riviera Maya. The $260 greens fee includes cart, snacks, and drinks.

HORSEBACK RIDING **Cancún Mermaid** (© 998/843-6517; www.cancunmermaid. com), about 30 minutes south of town at the Rancho Loma Bonita, is a popular option for horseback riding. Five-hour packages include 2 hours of riding through the mangrove swamp to the beach, where you have time to swim and relax. The tour costs $66 for adults and $60 for children under 13. The ranch also offers a four-wheel ATV ride on the same route as the horseback tour. It costs $66 if you want to ride on your own, and $49 per person if you double up. Prices for both tours include transportation to the ranch, riding, soft drinks, and lunch, plus a guide and insurance. Only cash or traveler's checks are accepted.

---

6 SHOPPING

Aside from the surrounding natural splendor, Cancún is known throughout Mexico for its diverse shops and festive malls catering to international tourists. Visitors from the United States may find apparel more expensive in Cancún, but the selection is much broader than at other Mexican resorts. Numerous duty-free shops offer excellent value on European goods. The largest is **Ultrafemme,** Avenida Tulum, Supermanzana 25 ((C) **998/ 884-1402**), specializing in imported cosmetics, perfumes, and fine jewelry and watches. The downtown Cancún location offers slightly lower prices than branches in Plaza Caracol, La Isla, and Kukulcán Plaza. It's open Monday to Saturday from 9:30am to 9pm and Sunday from 2 to 9pm.

Handicrafts are more limited and more expensive in Cancún than in other regions of Mexico because they are not produced here. They are available, though; the best **open-air crafts market** is Mercado 28 in Cancún City. A less enticing open-air market in the hotel zone is **Coral Negro,** Bulevar Kukulkán Km 9.5, next to Plaza Dady'O, open daily from 7am to 11pm. **Plaza La Fiesta,** next to the Cancún Center ((C) **998/883-4519**), is a large Mexican outlet store selling handicrafts, jewelry, tequila, leather, and accessories. It's open daily from 7am to midnight.

Cancún's main venues are the **malls**—not quite as grand as their U.S. counterparts, but close. All are air-conditioned, sleek, and sophisticated. Most are on Bulevar Kukulkán between Km 7 and Km 12. They offer everything from fine crystal and silver to designer clothing and decorative objects, along with numerous restaurants and clubs. Stores are generally open daily from 10am to 10pm.

The **Kukulcán Plaza** ((C) **998/885-2200;** www.kukulcanplaza.com) houses more than 300 shops, restaurants, and entertainment. There's a bank, a bowling alley, several crafts stores, a Play City with gambling machines, a liquor and tobacco store, several bathing-suit specialty stores, music stores, a leather-goods shop (including shoes and sandals), and a store specializing in silver from Taxco. U.S. franchise eateries include Häagen-Dazs and Ruth's Chris Steak House. The adjacent Luxury Avenue complex features designer labels such as Cartier, Louis Vuitton, Pineda Covalin, Salvatore Ferragamo, and Ultrafemme. The mall is open daily from 10am to 10pm, until 11pm during high season. Assistance for those with disabilities is available upon request, and wheelchairs, strollers, and lockers are available at the information desk.

The long-standing **Plaza Caracol** ((C) **998/883-1038;** www.caracolplaza.com) is one of Cancún's less glamorous malls and holds, among other things, Señor Frog's clothing, Samsonite luggage, and Casa Rolandi (p. 102) restaurant. It's just before you reach the convention center as you come from downtown Cancún, and is open daily from 10am to 10pm.

The entertainment-oriented **Forum by the Sea,** Bulevar Kukulkán Km 9 ((C) **998/ 883-4425;** www.forumbythesea.com.mx), received a complete face-lift after Hurricane

Most people come here for the food and fun, choosing from Hard Rock Cafe, Carlos 'n' Charlie's, Rainforest Cafe, and CoCo Bongo, plus an extensive food court. Shops include Diesel, Harley-Davidson, Señor Frog's, Sunglass Island, and Zingara Beachwear and Swimwear. The mall is open daily from 10am to midnight (bars remain open later).

One of Mexico's most appealing malls is the **La Isla Shopping Village,** Bulevar Kukulkán Km 12.5 (© **998/883-5025;** www.laislacancun.com.mx), a wonderful open-air complex that borders the lagoon. Walkways lined with quality shops and restaurants cross little canals (boat rides are even offered through the canals), and there's a boardwalk along the lagoon itself, as well as an interactive aquarium and dolphin swim facility (p. 110). Shops include Bulgari, Diesel, Guess, Nautica, Nine West, Puma, Tommy Hilfiger, Ultrafemme, and Zara, as well as a large Mexican handicrafts store called Casa Bonita. Among the dining choices are Johnny Rockets, Chili's, Italianni's, Planet Hollywood, the fun-filled Mexican restaurant **La Casa de las Margaritas** (p. 101), and the romantic **Thai** restaurant (p. 103). You will also find a movie theater, video arcade, and several bars, including **La Madonna** (p. 113).

7 CANCÚN AFTER DARK

One of Cancún's main draws is its active nightlife. While the partying often begins by day at the beach, the cool crowd heads at happy hour to the many bars located along the Hotel Zone, which often serve two-for-one drinks at sunset. Hotels play in the happy hour scene, with special drink prices to entice visitors and guests from other resorts. Come night, the hottest centers of action are also along Kukulkán, and include **Plaza Dady'O, Forum by the Sea,** and **La Isla Shopping Village.** These places transform into spring break madness for most of March and April.

THE CLUB & MUSIC SCENE

Clubbing in Cancún is a favorite part of the vacation experience and can go on each night until the sun rises over that incredibly blue sea. Several big hotels have nightclubs or schedule live music in their lobby bars. At the clubs, expect to stand in long lines on weekends; pay a cover charge of about $40 with open bar, or $15 to $25 without open bar; and then pay $8 to $10 for a drink. Some of the higher-priced clubs include live entertainment. The places listed in this section are air-conditioned and accept American Express, MasterCard, and Visa.

A great idea to get you started is the **Bar Hopper Tour** ★★, with tickets available at Señor Frog's, most hotels, or various travel agencies around town. For $65, it takes you by bus to the Congo Bar, Señor Frog's, and CoCo Bongo, where you bypass any lines and spend about an hour at each establishment. The price includes entry to the bars, one welcome drink at each, and transportation by air-conditioned bus, allowing you to get a great sampling of the best of Cancún's nightlife. The tour runs from 8pm into the wee hours, with the meeting point at the Congo Bar.

Numerous restaurants, such as **Carlos 'n' Charlie's, Hard Rock Cafe, Señor Frog's,** and **T.G.I. Friday's,** double as nighttime party spots, offering wildish fun at a fraction of the price of more costly clubs.

If you have been drinking when you're ready go back to your accommodations, take public transportation or have someone with you rather than drive or get in a taxi alone.

Bling ★★★ This is one of the coolest nightspots in Cancún, featuring a chic outdoor terrace overlooking the lagoon. A fashionable 30-something crowd congregates amid sofas under the stars, a killer sound system, and flowing cocktails. A sushi and sashimi bar and some Mediterranean dishes are also offered. This upscale lounge is considerably more sophisticated than Cancún's typical frat-style bars, and it's open daily from 6pm to 4am. Bulevar Kukulkán Km 13.5. ⓒ 998/840-6014. www.blingcancun.com.

The City ★★ One of Cancún's hottest and largest nightclubs, The City features progressive electronic music spun by visiting DJs from New York, L.A., and Mexico City (the DJ station looks like an airport control tower). This is where celebrities come to party when they're in town. You actually need never leave, as The City is a day-and-night club. The City Beach Club opens at 10am and features beach cabañas, a pool, and food and bar service. The Terrace Bar, overlooking the action on Bulevar Kukulkán, serves food and drinks all day long. For a relaxing evening vibe, the Lounge features comfy couches, chill music, and an extensive menu of martinis, snacks, and desserts. Open from 10:30pm to 4am, the 2,500-sq.-m (26,910-sq.-ft.) nightclub features nine bars, stunning light shows, and several VIP areas. Bulevar Kukulkán Km 9.5. ⓒ 998/848-8380. www.thecity cancun.com. Cover $25; $45 with open bar.

CoCo Bongo ★★★ Continuing its reputation as the hottest party venue in town, CoCo Bongo combines an enormous dance club with extravagant theme shows. It has no formal dance floor, so you can dance anywhere—and that includes on the tables, on the bar, or even on the stage with the occasional live band. This place regularly packs in as many as 3,000 people—you have to experience it to believe it. Despite its capacity, lines are long on weekends and in high season. The music alternates between Caribbean, salsa, house, hip-hop, techno, and classics from the 1970s, '80s, and '90s. Open from 10:30pm to 3:30am, CoCo Bongo draws a hip young crowd. Forum by the Sea, Bulevar Kukulkán Km 9.5. ⓒ 998/883-5061. www.cocobongo.com.mx. Weekend cover $60 with open bar, $50 weekdays with open bar.

Dady'O This is a popular rave among the young and brave, with frequent long lines. MTV, Playboy, Fashion TV, and E Entertainment have all hosted events here. It opens nightly at 10pm and has a giant dance floor and awesome light system. Bulevar Kukulkán Km 9.5. ⓒ 998/883-3333. www.dadyo.com. Cover $20; $45 with open bar that also allows entry to Dady Rock (below).

Dady Rock Bar and Club The offspring of Dady'O, Dady Rock opens at 8pm and goes as long as any other nightspot, offering a combination of live rock bands and DJs spinning grooves, along with an open bar, full meals, a buffet, and dancing. Bulevar Kukulkán Km 9.5. ⓒ 998/883-1626. www.dadyo.com. Cover $20; $45 with open bar that also allows entry to Dady'O, above.

La Madonna This architecturally dazzling martini bar and restaurant emerges unexpectedly from La Isla shopping center like an Italian Renaissance showroom along the canal. With more than 150 creative martini selections accompanied by relaxing lounge music, La Madonna also offers authentic Italian and Swiss cuisine, including fondues. Enjoy your red mandarin, lychee, or green apple martini or flavored *caipirinha* elbow to elbow with Cancún's beautiful people on the outdoor patio. Inside, the dining room resembles one of the mystical Buddha Bars, with an enormous replica of the Mona Lisa looking over the dazzled clientele. It's open daily from noon to 1am. La Isla Shopping Village, Bulevar Kukulkán Km 12.5. ⓒ 998/883-2222.

The Lobby Lounge ★   This is the most refined of Cancún's nightly gathering spots, with a terrace overlooking the lagoon, a special martini collection, and a list of more than 80 premium tequilas for tasting or sipping. There's also a sushi and seafood bar, as well as a humidor collection of Cuban cigars. It's open daily from 5pm to 12am, with live music Wednesday through Saturday. Ritz-Carlton Cancún (p. 96), Retorno del Rey 36, off Bulevar Kukulkán Km 13.5. ⓒ 998/881-0808.

Ver y Wine ★   This new wine bar sits on the upper level of Casa Rolandi (p. 102), a relaxed place to come for a predinner drink or a nightcap. The gourmet bar has a fine wine and liquor selection, and also offers cigars. This is a refined alternative to Cancún's more raucous bars and clubs. It's open from 7pm until the last customer leaves. Bulevar Kukulkán Km 8.5, in Plaza Caracol. ⓒ 998/883-2557.

THE PERFORMING ARTS

Several hotels host **Mexican fiesta nights,** including a buffet dinner and a folkloric dance show; admission, including dinner, ranges from $35 to $50, unless you're at an all-inclusive resort that includes this as part of the package. Check out the **Fiesta Americana Coral Beach**'s (ⓒ 998/881-3200) a la carte dining show four times a week, or the nightly show at **Hacienda Sisal** (ⓒ 998/848-8220), located next to the Royal Sands at Blvd. Kukulkán Km 13.5.

Isla Mujeres & Cozumel

by David Baird

Mexico's two Caribbean islands are easy jaunts from Cancún and the Riviera Maya. During the winter high season, both receive a lot of day-trippers and cruise-ship visitors, but if you stay on to the evening, the relaxed pace of island life is yours to enjoy. Neither Isla Mujeres nor Cozumel is particularly large, and they still have that island feel—with small roads that don't go very far, lots of mopeds, few (if any) trucks, and a sense of remoteness from the rest of the world. Both offer a variety of lodging options, ample outdoor activities, and a laid-back atmosphere that contrasts with much of the mainland experience.

Fish-shaped **Isla Mujeres** is 13km (8 miles) northeast of Cancún, a quick boat ride away. Hotels range from rustic to regal. Passenger ferries travel to Isla Mujeres from Puerto Juárez, and car ferries leave from Punta Sam, both near Cancún. More expensive passenger ferries, with fewer departures, leave from the Playa Linda pier on Cancún Island.

Larger than Isla Mujeres and farther from the mainland (19km/12 miles off the coast from Playa del Carmen), **Cozumel** has its own international airport. Life here revolves around two major activities: scuba diving and cruise ships making a port of call. Cozumel is far and away the most popular destination along this coast for both activities.

Despite the cruise-ship traffic and all the stores spawned by it, life on Cozumel moves at a relaxed pace. There is just one town, San Miguel de Cozumel; to the north and south are resorts. The rest of the shore is deserted and predominantly rocky, with a scattering of small sandy coves that you can have all to yourself.

1 ISLA MUJERES ★★★

13km (8 miles) N of Cancún

Isla Mujeres (Island of Women) is a casual, laid-back refuge from the heady tempo of Cancún. It lies not far off the coast and is visible from the resort. As Caribbean islands go, Isla is a bargain and a good fit for anyone who prefers simplicity and ease over variety and action. The island's only town is right next to North Beach, the best beach on the island. With beach towel in hand, you can leisurely stroll to the beach from any hotel in town; there's no need for transportation. Don't think that Isla is an escape from commercialism—it isn't. But commercialism is writ small here, which is in character with the destination. The island is small, the town is small, the hotels (with a couple of exceptions) are small, the restaurants, the bars, the excursion boats—small, small, small. There are several inexpensive hotels, mostly in town, and a smattering of luxury boutique hotels spread out to other parts of the island.

The scale of the island heightens the contrast between high season and low season, making the crowds and bustle much more noticeable at peak travel times. At midday, suntanned visitors from the Cancún tour boats hang out in open-air cafes and stroll the pedestrian streets lined with zealous souvenir vendors calling attention to their wares. The scene takes on a carnivalesque hue during the hours when the tour-boat traffic is at its peak. Then, later in the afternoon, things settle down.

Trips to the Isla Contoy bird sanctuary are popular, as are the diving, snorkeling, and fishing jaunts. In 1998, the island's coral coast became part of Mexico's Marine National Park system. The reef suffered substantial hurricane damage in 2005, but it's rebounding. The water clarity illuminates the wonderful array of coral and tropical fish living here. The underwater life you are likely to see includes French angelfish, longspine squirrelfish, trumpet fish, four-eye butterfly fish, green angelfish, stoplight parrotfish, southern stingrays, sharp-nose puffer fish, blue tang, and great barracuda.

The island and several of its hotels attract regular gatherings of yoga practitioners. In the evening, most people find the slow, casual pace one of the island's biggest draws. The cool night breeze is a perfect accompaniment to casual open-air dining and drinking in small street-side restaurants.

ESSENTIALS

GETTING THERE & DEPARTING   Puerto Juárez, just north of Cancún, is the **dock** (© 998/877-0382) for passenger ferries to Isla Mujeres. *Ultramar* (© 998/843-2011; www.granpuerto.com.mx) has fast boats leaving every half-hour from "Gran Puerto" in Puerto Juárez, making the trip in 15 minutes. There is storage space for luggage and the fare is about 45 pesos each way. These boats operate daily, starting at 6am and usually ending at 10:30pm (check beforehand for latest schedules). They might leave early if they're full, so arrive ahead of schedule. Pay at the ticket office or on board if the ferry is about to leave.

Note: Upon arrival by taxi or bus in Puerto Juárez, be wary of pirate "guides" who tell you either that the ferry is canceled or that it's several hours until the next ferry. They'll offer the services of a private *lancha* (small boat) for about 450 pesos—and it's nothing but a scam. Small boats are available and, on a co-op basis, charge 200 to 350 pesos oneway, based on the number of passengers. They take about 50 minutes and are not recommended on days with rough seas. Check with the ticket office—the only accurate source for information.

On your return to Puerto Juárez, you'll see taxi fares posted by the street where the taxis park, so be sure to check the rate before agreeing to a taxi for the ride back to Cancún. Rates generally run 120 to 150 pesos, depending upon your destination. Moped and bicycle rentals are also readily available as you depart the ferry. This small complex also has public bathrooms, luggage storage, a snack bar, and souvenir shops.

Isla Mujeres is so small that a vehicle isn't necessary, but if you're taking one to the island, you'll use the **Punta Sam** port a little beyond Puerto Juárez. The 40-minute car ferry (© 998/877-0065) runs five or six times daily between 8am and 8pm, year-round except in bad weather. Times are generally as follows: Cancún to Isla 8 and 11am and 2:45, 5:30, and 8:15pm; Isla to Cancún 6:30 and 9:30am and 12:45, 4:15, and 7:15pm. Always check with the tourist office in Cancún to verify this schedule. Cars should arrive an hour before the ferry departure to register for a place in line and pay the posted fee, which varies depending on the weight and type of vehicle. A gas pump is at Avenida Rueda Medina and Calle Abasolo, northwest of the ferry docks.

Ferries to Isla Mujeres also depart from **Playa Linda,** known as the Embarcadero pier in Cancún, but they're less frequent and more expensive than those from Puerto Juárez. There are four to six scheduled departures per day to Isla Mujeres, depending upon the season. Adult fares are 150 pesos round-trip; kids ages 3 to 12 pay 75 pesos; children

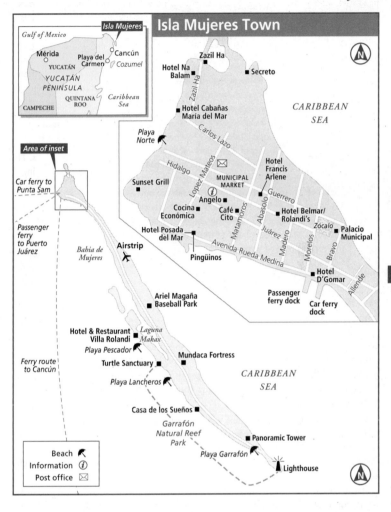

Isla Mujeres Town

Gulf of Mexico

Mérida

YUCATÁN

YUCATÁN PENINSULA

CAMPECHE

QUINTANA ROO

Playa del Carmen

Cancún

Cozumel

Caribbean Sea

Area of inset

Car ferry to Punta Sam

Passenger ferry to Puerto Juárez

Bahía de Mujeres

Airstrip

Ferry route to Cancún

Zazil Ha

Hotel Na Balam

Secreto

Hotel Cabañas María del Mar

CARIBBEAN SEA

Carlos Lazo

Playa Norte

Hidalgo

Lopez Mateos

Sunset Grill

MUNICIPAL MARKET

Hotel Francis Arlene

Guerrero

Angelo

Cocina Económica

Café Cito

Hotel Belmar/ Rolandi's

Abasolo

Matamoros

Juárez

Madero

Zócalo

Palacio Municipal

Hotel Posada del Mar

Avenida Rueda Medina

Pingüinos

Morelos

Bravo

Allende

Hotel D'Gomar

Passenger ferry dock

Car ferry dock

Ariel Magaña Baseball Park

Hotel & Restaurant Villa Rolandi

Laguna Makax

Playa Pescador

Turtle Sanctuary

Mundaca Fortress

CARIBBEAN SEA

Playa Lancheros

Casa de los Sueños

Garrafón Natural Reef Park

Panoramic Tower

Playa Garrafón

Lighthouse

Beach

Information

Post office

younger than 3 ride free. A **Water Taxi** (② **998/886-4270,** -4847; asterix@cablered.net.mx) to Isla Mujeres operates from **Playa Caracol,** between the Fiesta Americana Coral Beach Hotel and the Xcaret terminal on Cancún island; prices are about the same as those from Playa Linda.

To get to Puerto Juárez or Punta Sam from **Cancún,** take any Ruta 8 city bus from Avenida Tulum. From the Cancún airport, take the shuttle bus to the pier (160 pesos).

VISITOR INFORMATION The **City Tourist Office** (②/fax **998/877-0767,** -0307) is at Av. Rueda Medina 130, just across the street from the pier. It's open Monday through Friday from 9am to 4pm, closed on Saturday and Sunday. *Islander* is a free publication with local information, advertisements, and event listings.

(Tips) **The Best Websites for Isla Mujeres & Cozumel**

- **Isla Mujeres Tourist Information: www.isla-mujeres.net** The official site of the Isla Mujeres Tourism Board provides complete information on Isla, from getting there to where to stay.
- **My Isla Mujeres: www.myislamujeres.com** Get a local's view of the island; the active message boards are especially good.
- **Cozumel.net: www.cozumel.net** This site is a cut above the typical dining/lodging/activities sites. Click on "About Cozumel" to find schedules for ferries and island-hop flights, and to check the latest news. There's also a comprehensive listing of B&Bs and vacation-home rentals.
- **Cozumel Travel Planner: www.go2cozumel.com** This is a well-done guide to area businesses and attractions, by an online Mexico specialist.
- **Cozumel Hotel Association: www.islacozumel.com.mx** Operated by the tourism-promotion arm of the hotel association, this site gives more than just listings of the member hotels. There's info on packages and specials, plus brief descriptions of most of the island's attractions, restaurants, and recreational activities.

ISLAND LAYOUT   Isla Mujeres is about 8km (5 miles) long and 4km (2^1/$_2$ miles) wide, with the town at the northern tip. "Downtown" is a compact 4 blocks by 6 blocks, so it's very easy to get around. The **passenger ferry docks** are at the center of town, within walking distance of most hotels, restaurants, and shops. The street running along the waterfront and in front of the ferry docks is **Avenida Rueda Medina,** commonly called the *malecón* (**boardwalk**). The **Mercado Municipal (town market)** is by the post office on **Calle Guerrero,** an inland street at the north edge of town, which, like most streets in the town, is unmarked.

GETTING AROUND   A popular form of transportation on Isla Mujeres is the electric **golf cart,** available for rent at many hotels or rental shops for 150 pesos per hour or 450 pesos per day. Prices are set the same at all rental locations. **El Sol Golf Cart Rental,** Av. Benito Juárez Mza 3 #20 (corner of Matamoros; © **998/877-0791**), is one good option in the town center. The golf carts don't go more than 30kmph (19 mph), but they're fun. Anyway, you aren't on Isla Mujeres to hurry. Many people enjoy touring the island by *moto* (**motorized bike or scooter**). Fully automatic versions are available for around 450 pesos per day or 100 pesos per hour. They come with helmets and seats for two people. There's only one main road with a couple of offshoots, so you won't get lost. Be aware that the rental price does not include insurance, and any injury to yourself or the vehicle will come out of your pocket. **Bicycles** are also available for rent at some hotels for 35 pesos an hour or 120 pesos per day, usually including a basket and a lock.

Tricycle taxis are the least expensive and easiest way to get to your hotel if it's in town. From the ferry pier to any of the downtown hotels will cost about 20 to 30 pesos. If you ask the guys, they'll say "Oh, whatever you care to give." I will let them haul my bags and lead the way while I walk.

If you prefer to use a taxi, rates are about 25 pesos for trips within the downtown area, or 50 pesos for a trip to the southern end of Isla. You can also hire them for about 100 pesos per hour. Regular taxis are always lined up in a parking lot to the right of the pier, with their rates posted. The number to call for taxis is ℂ **998/877-0066.**

(*Fast Facts*)   Isla Mujeres

Area Code The telephone area code is **998.**

Consumer Protection You can reach the local branch of **Profeco** consumer protection agency at ℂ **998/887-3960.**

Currency Exchange Isla Mujeres has numerous *casas de cambio,* or currency exchanges, along the main streets. Most of the hotels listed here change money for their guests, although often at less favorable rates than the commercial enterprises. There is only one bank in Isla, **HSBC Bank** (ℂ **998/877-0005**), across from the ferry docks. It's open Monday through Friday from 8:30am to 6pm, and Saturday from 9am to 2pm. It has ATM machines.

Drugstore **Isla Mujeres Farmacía** (ℂ **998/877-0178**) has the best selection of prescription and over-the-counter medicines.

Emergencies To report an emergency, dial ℂ **060** anywhere in Mexico. Dial ℂ **065** for the Red Cross.

Hospital The **Hospital de la Armada** is on Avenida Rueda Medina at Ojón P. Blanco (ℂ **998/877-0001**). It's less than a kilometer (a half-mile) south of the town center. It will treat you only in an emergency. Otherwise, you're referred to the **Centro de Salud,** on Avenida Guerrero, a block before the beginning of the *malecón* (ℂ **998/877-0117**).

Internet Access Owned by a lifelong resident of Isla, **Cyber Isla Mujeres.com,** Av. Francisco y Madero 17, between calles Hidalgo and Juárez (ℂ **998/877-0272**), offers Internet access for 15 pesos per hour, daily 7am to 10pm, and serves complimentary Veracruzano coffee all day.

Post Office The *correo* is at Calle Guerrero 12 (ℂ **998/877-0085**), at the corner of López Mateos, near the market. It's open Monday through Friday from 9am to 4pm.

Taxis To call for a taxi, dial ℂ **998/877-0066.**

Telephone Ladatel phones accepting coins and prepaid phone cards are at the plaza and throughout town.

Tourist Seasons Isla Mujeres's tourist season (when hotel rates are higher) is a bit different from that of other places in Mexico. High season runs December through May, a month longer than in Cancún. Some hotels raise their rates in August, and some raise their rates beginning in mid-November. Low season is from June to mid-November.

BEACHES & OUTDOOR ACTIVITIES

BEACHES & SWIMMING   The most popular beach in town, and the best for swimming, is **Playa Norte** ★. It's a long stretch of beach extending around the northern tip of the island. This is perhaps the world's best municipal beach—a wide swath of fine white sand and calm, translucent, turquoise-blue water. The beach is easily reached on foot from the ferry and from all downtown hotels. Watersports equipment, beach umbrellas, and lounge chairs are available for rent. Areas in front of restaurants usually cost nothing if you use the restaurant as your headquarters for drinks and food, and the best of them have hammocks and swings from which to sip your piña coladas.

Garrafón Natural Reef Park ★★ (p. 121) is best known as a snorkeling area, but there is a nice stretch of beach on either side of the park. **Playa Lancheros** is on the Caribbean side of Laguna Makax and is probably the second-best for swimming. Local buses go to Lancheros and then turn inland and return downtown. The beach at Playa Lancheros is nice, with a variety of casual restaurants.

There are no lifeguards on duty on Isla Mujeres, which does not use the system of water-safety flags employed in Cancún and Cozumel. The bay between Cancún and Isla Mujeres is calm, with warm, transparent waters ideal for swimming, snorkeling, and diving. The east side of the island facing the open Caribbean Sea is typically rougher, with much stronger currents.

FISHING   To arrange a day of fishing, ask at the **Sociedad Cooperativa Turística** (the boatmen's cooperative), on Avenida Rueda Medina (*©* **998/877-1363**), next to Mexico Divers and Las Brisas restaurant, or the travel agency mentioned in "Isla Contoy," p. 122. Four to six others can share the cost, which includes lunch and drinks. Capt. Tony Martínez (*©* **998/877-0274**) also arranges fishing trips aboard the *Marinonis,* with advanced reservations recommended. Year-round you'll find bonito, mackerel, kingfish, and amberjack. Sailfish and sharks (hammerhead, bull, nurse, lemon, and tiger) are in good supply in April and May. In winter, larger grouper and jewfish are prevalent. Four hours of fishing close to shore costs around $125; 8 hours farther out goes for $250. The cooperative is open Monday through Saturday from 8am to 1pm and 5 to 8pm, and Sunday from 7:30 to 10am and 6 to 8pm.

SCUBA DIVING   Most of the dive shops on the island offer the same trips for the same prices: one-tank dives cost about $50, two-tank dives about $70. **Bahía Dive Shop,** Rueda Medina 166, across from the car-ferry dock (*©* **998/877-0340**), is a full-service shop that offers dive equipment for sale or rent. The shop is open daily from 10am to 7pm. Another respected dive shop is **Coral Scuba Center,** at Matamoros 13A and Rueda Medina (*©* **998/877-0061**, -0763). It's open daily from 8am to 12:30pm and 4 to 10pm. Both offer 2-hour snorkeling trips for about $20.

Cuevas de los Tiburones (Caves of the Sleeping Sharks) is Isla's most renowned dive site—but the name is slightly misleading, as shark sightings are rare these days. Two sites where you could traditionally see the sleeping shark are the Cuevas de Tiburones and **La Punta,** but the sharks have mostly been driven off, and a storm collapsed the arch featured in a Jacques Cousteau film showing them, but the caves survive. Other dive sites include a **wreck** 15km (9¼ miles) offshore; **Banderas** reef, between Isla Mujeres and Cancún, where there's always a strong current; **Tabos** reef on the eastern shore; and **Manchones** reef, 1km (a half-mile) off the southeastern tip of the island, where the water is 4.5 to 11m (15–36 ft.) deep. **The Cross of the Bay** is close to Manchones reef. A bronze cross, weighing 1 ton and standing 12m (39 ft.) high, was placed in the water between Manchones and Isla in 1994, as a memorial to those who have lost their lives at sea.

SNORKELING   One of the most popular places to snorkel is **Garrafón Natural Reef Park ★★** (p. 121). **Manchones Reef,** off the southeastern coast, is also good. It's just offshore and accessible by boat. You can snorkel around *el faro* (the lighthouse) in the

Bahía de Mujeres at the southern tip of the island. The water is about 2m (6¹/₂ ft.) deep. Boatmen will take you for around 250 pesos per person if you have your own snorkeling equipment or 300 pesos if you use theirs.

YOGA   Increasingly, Isla is becoming popular among yoga enthusiasts. The trend began at **Hotel Na Balam** ★★ (p. 124; © 998/877-0279, -0058; www.nabalam.com), which offers yoga classes under its large poolside *palapa,* complete with yoga mats and props. The hotel also offers yoga instruction vacations featuring respected teachers and a more extensive practice schedule; the current schedule of yoga retreats is posted on their website. Another yoga center that has sprung up and is drawing together a community is **Elements of the Island** (www.elementsoftheisland.com). It's located at Juárez 64, between López Mateos and Matamoros. And there's **Casa de los Sueños Resort and Zenter** (© 998/877-0651; www.casadelossuenosresort.com), which regularly holds yoga classes, as well as chi gong and Pilates.

MORE ATTRACTIONS

DOLPHIN DISCOVERY ★★   You can swim with dolphins (© **998/849-4748** or 849-4757; fax 998/849-4751; www.dolphindiscovery.com) in an enclosure at Treasure Island, on the side of Isla Mujeres that faces Cancún. Groups of eight people swim with two dolphins and one trainer. Swimmers view an educational video and spend time in the water with the trainer and the dolphins before enjoying 15 minutes of free swimming time with them. Reservations are necessary, and you must arrive an hour before your assigned swimming time, at 10:30am, noon, 2 or 3:30pm. The cost is $139 per person for the Dolphin Royal Swim. There are less expensive programs that allow you to learn about, touch, and hold the dolphins (but not swim with them), starting at $79.

TURTLE SANCTUARY ★★   Years ago, fishermen converged on the island nightly from May to September to capture turtles when they would come ashore to lay eggs. Then a concerned fisherman, Gonzalo Chale Maldonado, began convincing others to spare the eggs, which he protected. It was a start. Following his lead, the fishing ministry founded the **Centro de Investigaciones Pesqueras** to find ways to protect the species and increase the turtle populations. Although the local government provides some assistance, most of the funding comes from private-sector donations. Since the center opened, tens of thousands of young turtles have been released, and local schoolchildren have participated, helping to educate a new generation of islanders for the cause. Releases are scheduled from May to October, and visitors are invited to take part. Inquire at the center.

Three species of sea turtles nest on Isla Mujeres. An adult green turtle, the most abundant species, is 1 to 1.5m (3¹/₄–5 ft.) long and can weigh 204kg (450 lb.). At the center, visitors walk through the indoor and outdoor turtle pool areas, where the creatures paddle around. Turtles are separated by age, from newly hatched up to 1 year. People who come here usually end up staying at least an hour, especially if they opt for the guided tour, which I recommend. They also have a small gift shop and snack bar. The sanctuary is on a spit of land jutting out from the island's west coast. The address is Carr. Sac Bajo #5; you'll need a taxi to get there. Admission is 24 pesos; the shelter is open daily from 9am to 5pm. For more information, call © **998/877-0595.**

GARRAFÓN NATIONAL PARK & PUNTA SUR ★★   El Garrafón (© **998/849-4748;** www.garrafon.com) is at the southern end of the island. The pricey but well-equipped park has two restaurant/bars, beach chairs, a swimming pool, kayaks, changing rooms, rental lockers, showers, a gift shop, and snack bars. Once a public national underwater park, Garrafón is now operated by Dolphin Discovery. Public facilities have improved, with the addition of new attractions and facilities each year. Activities include snorkeling and Snuba (a tankless version of scuba diving, when you descend while breathing through a long air tube); "Sea Trek," which allows you to explore the Caribbean seabed wearing a helmet with compressed air; crystal-clear canoes for viewing underwater life; and a zip line that takes you over the water. On land are tanning decks, shaded hammocks, a 12m (39-ft.) climbing tower, and—of course—a souvenir superstore. A new panoramic tower had yet to open as of my last trip. At 50m (164-ft.) high, it will afford visitors a bird's-eye view of the entire island. Several restaurants and snack bars are available. Basic admission is $36; the all-inclusive package is $50 (American Express, MasterCard, and Visa are accepted). More expensive packages include transportation and/or swims with dolphins at Dolphin Discovery (see above). The park is open daily in high season from 9am to 5pm. In low season, it closes for 2 or 3 days per week.

Next to the panoramic tower, you'll find **Sculptured Spaces,** an impressive and extensive garden of large sculptures donated to Isla Mujeres by internationally renowned sculptors as part of the 2001 First International Sculpture Exhibition. Among Mexican sculptors represented by works are José Luis Cuevas and Vladimir Cora.

Nearby is the **Caribbean Village,** with narrow lanes of colorful clapboard buildings that house cafes and shops displaying folk art. You can have lunch or a snack here at the kiosk and stroll around before heading on to the lighthouse and Maya ruins.

Also at this southern point of the island, and part of the ruins, is **Cliff of the Dawn,** the southeasternmost point of Mexico. Services are available from 9am to 5pm, but you can enter at any time; if you make it there early enough to see the sunrise, you can claim you were the first person in Mexico that day to be touched by the sun!

ISLA CONTOY ★   Try to visit this pristine uninhabited island, 30km (19 miles) by boat from Isla Mujeres. It became a national wildlife reserve in 1981. Lush vegetation covers the oddly shaped island, which is 6km (3¾ miles) long and harbors 70 species of birds, as well as a host of marine and animal life. Bird species that nest on the island include pelicans, brown boobies, frigates, egrets, terns, and cormorants. Flocks of flamingos arrive in April. Most excursions troll for fish (which will be your lunch), anchor en route for a snorkeling expedition, skirt the island at a leisurely pace for close viewing of the birds without disturbing the habitat, and then pull ashore. While the captain prepares lunch, visitors can swim, sun, follow the nature trails, and visit the fine nature museum, which has bathroom facilities. The trip from Isla Mujeres takes about 45 minutes each way and can be longer if the waves are choppy. Because of the tight-knit boatmen's cooperative, prices for this excursion are the same everywhere: 550 pesos for adults, 280 pesos for children (cash only). You can buy a ticket at the **Sociedad Cooperativa,** on Avenida Rueda Medina, next to Mexico Divers and Las Brisas restaurant (© **998/877-1363**). Trips leave at 9am and return around 4:30pm. Boat captains should respect the cooperative's regulations regarding ecological sensitivity and boat safety, including the availability of life jackets for everyone on board. If you're not given a life jacket, ask for one. Snorkeling equipment is usually included in the price, but double-check before heading out.

A MAYA RUIN ★★   Just beyond the lighthouse, at the southern end of the island, are the remains of a small Maya temple. Archaeologists believe it was dedicated to the moon and fertility goddess Ixchel. The location, on a lofty bluff overlooking the sea, is worth seeing and makes a great place for photos. It is believed that Maya women traveled here on annual pilgrimages to seek Ixchel's blessings of fertility.

A PIRATE'S FORTRESS   Almost in the middle of the island is a large building purported to have been a pirate fortress. A slave trader who arrived here in the early 19th

century claimed to have been the pirate Mundaca Marecheaga. He set up a business selling slaves to Cuba and Belize, and prospered here. According to island lore, a charming
local girl captivated him, only to spurn him in favor of a local. Admission is 20 pesos;
the fortress is open daily from 10am to 6pm.

SHOPPING

Shopping is a casual activity here. Several shops, especially concentrated on Avenida
Hidalgo, sell Saltillo rugs, onyx, silver, Guatemalan clothing, blown glassware, masks,
folk art, beach paraphernalia, and T-shirts in abundance. Prices are lower than in Cancún
or Cozumel.

WHERE TO STAY

You'll find plenty of hotels in all price ranges on Isla Mujeres. The rates listed below
include the 12% room tax. They do not necessarily apply to the brief Christmas/New
Years season, when many hotels charge extra. High season runs from December through
May and sometimes includes August. Low season is the rest of the year.

Elizabeth Wenger of **Yucatan Peninsula Travel** in Montello, Wisconsin (*C* **800/552-
4550** in the U.S.), specializes in Mexico travel and books a lot of hotels in Isla Mujeres.
Her service is helpful in the high season. Those interested in private home rentals or
longer-term stays can contact **Mundaca Travel and Real Estate** in Isla Mujeres (*C* **998/
877-0025;** fax 998/877-0076; www.mundaca.com.mx), or book online with **Isla Beckons** property rental service (www.islabeckons.com).

Very Expensive

Casa de los Sueños Resort & Spa Zenter ★★★ Originally built as a private
residence and later converted into an adults-only boutique hotel in 1998, this property
has 10 guest rooms loaded with plush amenities and thoughtful comforts, and each
comes with a balcony or terrace overlooking the water. There's an open breezeway,
tropical gardens, a sunken living area (with Wi-Fi access), and an infinity pool that melts
into the cool Caribbean waters. One master suite has an extra-large bathroom area with
whirlpool and steam room/shower. The Zenter has an extensive menu of massages and
holistic spa treatments, and yoga classes, held either outdoors or in a serene indoor space.
The property is on the west side of the southern end of the island.

Carretera Garrafón Lote 9, Fracc. Mar Turquesa, 77400 Isla Mujeres, Q. Roo. *C* **998/877-0651,** -0369. Fax
998/877-0708. www.casadelossuenosresort.com. 10 units. High season $350–$500 double; low season
$300–$500 double. Rates include continental breakfast and taxes. AE, MC, V. No guests under 21. **Amenities:** Restaurant; bar; yoga center; infinity pool; room service; smoke-free rooms; spa; watersports equipment. *In room:* A/C, hair dryer, minibar.

Hotel Villa Rolandi Gourmet & Beach Club ★★★ (Moments) Villa Rolandi is a
romantic escape on a little sheltered cove with a pristine white-sand beach. Each of the
luxurious suites holds a separate sitting area and large terrace or balcony with private whirlpool overlooking the sea. All rooms feature in-room sound systems, subtle lighting, and
marble surfaces. The bathrooms have Bulgari products and enticing showers with multiple
showerheads that convert into steam baths. In-room breakfast is delivered through a small
portal. The hotel spa also offers an outdoor Thalasso therapy whirlpool and beachside massages. The owner is a Swiss-born restaurateur who made a name for himself with his restaurants on Isla Mujeres and in Cancún. You can eat well without having to go off property.

Fracc. Lagunamar, SM 7, Mza. 75, Locs. 15 and 16, 77400 Isla Mujeres, Q. Roo. *C* **998/877-0700.** Fax
998/877-0100. www.villarolandi.com. 35 units. High season $518 double, $586 junior suite; low season

$374–$490 double, $412–$530 junior suite. Rates include continental breakfast and a la carte lunch or dinner in the on-site restaurant. AE, MC, V. **Amenities:** Restaurant (see "Where to Dine," below); airport transfer via van and catamaran; concierge; small fitness room; infinity pool w/waterfall; room service; smoke-free rooms; spa. *In room:* TV, hair dryer, minibar.

Expensive

Hotel Na Balam ★★ ⓕ Finds   This popular two-story hotel on Playa Norte has simple, comfortable rooms and well-tended beach grounds. Rooms are in three sections; some face the beach, and others are across the street in a garden setting with a swimming pool. The large rooms contain a king-size or two double beds, a seating area, folk-art decorations, and a terrace or balcony with hammocks. Master suites have additional amenities, including small pools with hydromassage. The older section is well kept and surrounds a peaceful, palm-filled, sandy inner yard and Playa Norte. The hotel gets a lot of yoga practitioners and offers classes on a regular basis. The restaurant, **Zazil Ha,** is one of the island's most popular (see "Where to Dine," below). A beachside bar serves a selection of natural juices and is one of the most popular spots for sunset-watching.

Zazil Ha 118, 77400 Isla Mujeres, Q. Roo. ⓒ **998/877-0279.** Fax 998/877-0446. www.nabalam.com. 33 units. High season $242–$266 standard, $396–$425 suite; low season $180–$204 standard, $335–$360 suite. Ask about weekly and monthly rates. AE, MC, V. **Amenities:** Restaurant; snack bar; bar; babysitting; mopeds and golf carts for rent; yoga classes; Wi-Fi; spa; diving and snorkeling trips available. *In room:* A/C, hair dryer, minibar, no phone.

Secreto ★★ ⓕ Finds   This boutique hotel has a chic Mediterranean feel. Nine suites overlook an infinity pool and the open sea. Located on the northern end of the island, Secreto lies within walking distance of town, yet feels removed enough to make for an idyllic retreat. Tropical gardens surround the pool, and an outdoor living area offers large couches and small dining areas. Guest rooms are contemporary, featuring lots of space, simple and bold design lines, and lots of amenities. Each includes a veranda with private cabaña ideal for ocean-gazing beyond Halfmoon Beach. Three suites include king-size beds draped in mosquito netting, while the remaining six have two double beds. Secreto is distinguished by its style and service.

Sección Rocas, Lote 1, 77400 Isla Mujeres, Q. Roo. ⓒ **998/877-1039.** Fax 998/877-1048. www.hotel secreto.com. 9 units. $252–$336 double. Extra person $25. 1 child younger than 5 stays free in parent's room. Rates include continental breakfast. AE, MC, V. **Amenities:** Bar; coffee service; outdoor pool; dinner delivery from Rolandi's restaurant available; smoke-free rooms; diving and snorkeling. *In room:* A/C, TV/ DVD, CD player, fridge, hair dryer, minibar.

Moderate

Hotel Cabañas María del Mar ★   A good choice for simple beach accommodations, the Cabañas María del Mar is on the popular Playa Norte. The older two-story section behind the reception area and beyond the garden offers nicely outfitted rooms facing the beach. All have two single or double beds, refrigerators, and oceanview balconies strung with hammocks. Eleven single-story cabañas closer to the reception area are decorated in a rustic Mexican style. The third section, **El Castillo,** is located across the street, over and beside Buho's restaurant. All rooms are "deluxe," though some are larger than others. The five rooms on the ground floor have large patios. Upstairs rooms have small balconies. Most have ocean views. The central courtyard contains a small pool.

Av. Arq. Carlos Lazo 1 (on Playa Norte, a half-block from the Hotel Na Balam), 77400 Isla Mujeres, Q. Roo. ⓒ **800/223-5695** in the U.S. and Canada, or 998/877-0179. Fax 998/877-0213. www.cabanasdelmar. com. 73 units. High season 1,200–1,600 pesos double; low season 750–1,000 pesos double. MC, V. **Amenities:** Golf cart and *moto* rentals; pool; smoke-free rooms. *In room:* A/C, fridge (in some).

Hotel Belmar ★★   In the center of Isla's entertainment district, this charming three-story hotel (no elevator) sits above Rolandi's restaurant. The simple, attractive rooms come with tile floors, nicely finished bathrooms, and either a king bed or two twins or two doubles. The rooms are well maintained and have good, quiet air-conditioning. It's one of the few island hotels that offer televisions with U.S. channels. One large suite has a sitting area, large patio, and whirlpool. The rooms have double-glazed windows. Though I had no trouble with noise from the restaurant in my third-floor room, light sleepers might want to look elsewhere.

Av. Hidalgo 110 (btw. Madero and Abasolo, 3¹/₂ blocks from the passenger-ferry pier), 77400 Isla Mujeres, Q. Roo. ℂ **998/877-0430.** Fax 998/877-0429. www.rolandi.com. 11 units. High season 650–780 pesos double, 1,230 pesos suite; low season 440–500 pesos double, 1,230 pesos suite. AE, MC, V. **Amenities:** Restaurant/bar (see "Where to Dine," below); room service. In room: A/C, fan, TV.

Hotel D'Gomar Ⓥ**alue**   This hotel is at the bottom of the inexpensive range, while still being comfortable. The basic accommodations are regularly updated. Rooms have two double beds and a wall of windows affording breezes and views. The higher prices are for air-conditioned rooms with refrigerators. The hotel is four stories with no elevator, but it's conveniently located cater-corner from the ferry pier (look right). The name of the hotel is the most visible sign on the "skyline."

Rueda Medina 150, 77400 Isla Mujeres, Q. Roo. ℂ/fax **998/877-0541.** www.hoteldgomar-islamujeres. com. 20 units. High season 550–650 pesos double; low season 450–560 pesos double. MC, V. In room: A/C (in some), fan, fridge (in some), no phone.

Hotel Francis Arlene ★   The Magaña family operates this neat little two-story inn built around a shady courtyard. It's bright, cheerful, and well managed, and has attractive common spaces. For these reasons, it gets a lot of return guests; it's especially popular with families and seniors. Some rooms have ocean views, and all are remodeled or updated each year. They are comfortable, with tile floors, tiled bathrooms, and a very homey feel. Normal rooms have a coffeemaker and a refrigerator; top-floor rooms come with kitchenettes and have an ocean view. Most rooms have either a balcony or a patio. Ten rooms have only a ceiling fan and are the lowest-priced doubles.

Guerrero 7 (5¹/₂ blocks inland from the ferry pier, btw. Abasolo and Matamoros), 77400 Isla Mujeres, Q. Roo. ℂ/fax **998/877-0310,** -0861. www.francisarlene.com. 24 units. High season 680–760 pesos double, 900 pesos top-floor double; low season 450–560 pesos double, 730 pesos top-floor double. MC, V. In room: A/C (in some), fridge, kitchenette (in some), no phone.

Hotel Posada del Mar Ⓚⓘⓓⓢ   Simply furnished, quiet, and comfortable, this long-established hotel faces the water 3 blocks north of the ferry pier. This is probably the best choice in Isla for families. For the spaciousness of the rooms (half of which have ocean views) and the location, it's also among the island's best values. A wide, appealing, but seldom-used stretch of Playa Norte lies across the street, where watersports equipment is available for rent. A casual *palapa* bar and a lovely pool are on the back lawn, along with hammocks, and the restaurant **Pingüinos** (see "Where to Dine," below) is by the side-walk at the front of the property and also provides room service to hotel guests.

Av. Rueda Medina 15 A, 77400 Isla Mujeres, Q. Roo. ℂ **800/544-3005** in the U.S. and Canada, or 998/877-0044. Fax 998/877-0266. www.posadadelmar.com. 52 units. High season $115 double; low season $70 double. Children 11 and under stay free in parent's room. AE, MC, V. **Amenities:** Restaurant/bar; outdoor pool. In room: A/C, fan, TV.

At the **Municipal Market,** next to the telegraph office and post office on Avenida Guerrero, obliging, hardworking women operate several little food stands. At the **Panadería La Reyna** (no phone), at Madero and Juárez, you can pick up inexpensive sweet bread, muffins, cookies, and yogurt. It's open Monday through Saturday from 7am to 9:30pm. For a frozen treat, check out **Cool** ice cream store (no phone), on Avenida Madero between Hidalgo and Juárez. It serves some wonderful flavors. The German and Peruvian owners might be opening another store on north Juárez.

Expensive

Casa Rolandi ★★ ITALIAN/SEAFOOD A gourmet restaurant outside of town in the Villa Rolandi hotel, this place offers a beautiful setting with windows over the island's western shore and an open-air terrace. The menu here is more sophisticated than Rolandi's downtown, including some original creations not offered by the other locale. But there are several dishes common to both, including one of the signature dishes, *pescado a la sal* (fish baked in a cocoon of salt and egg whites). Both restaurants make good use of wood-burning stoves to produce some great baked fish dishes. And take care with the wood-oven-baked bread; it arrives looking like a puffer fish, and it's so divine you're apt to fill up on it. This is a great place to enjoy the sunset. They stock a selection of fine international wines and more than 80 premium tequilas. Service is personalized and attentive.

On the pier of Villa Rolandi (p. 123), Lagunamar SM 7. © **998/877-0700.** Reservations necessary. Main courses $13–$35. AE, MC, V. Daily 7–10:30pm.

Sunset Grill ★★ SEAFOOD/STEAKS This outdoor venue approaches the ideal for a beach restaurant, with its comfortable tables and chairs by the water, under a shady *palapa.* When the sun goes down, the restaurant sets up tables on the beach, and, weather permitting, there's no better ambience. The breakfasts are good, lunch includes a variety of sandwiches and burgers, and for dinner they serve such specialties as fish seared in a light *achiote* sauce, fish and chips, and a variety of steaks. To get to this restaurant, you have to walk through the parking lot of the Nautibeach Condominiums, which you access via a sand road that is the continuation of Rueda Medina.

Nautibeach Condominiums, North Beach. © **998/877-0785.** Reservations recommended. Main courses 150–260 pesos; sandwiches and breakfasts 60–95 pesos. AE, MC, V. Daily 8am–9pm.

Moderate

Angelo ★ ITALIAN An Italian restaurant in the town center, Angelo offers a selection of antipasti, pasta, grilled seafood, and wood-oven-baked pizzas. The Sardinian-born owner instills his menu with the flavors of his homeland, including a rich tomato sauce. Consider starting with a bowl of seafood soup or black mussels au gratin and continuing with the grilled shrimp kabobs or seafood pasta in an olive oil and white-wine sauce. The open-air restaurant includes an inviting sidewalk terrace and lies across the street from a casual Cuban restaurant also owned by Angelo.

Av. Hidalgo 14 (btw. Lopez Mateos and Matamoros). © **998/877-1273.** Main courses 150–200 pesos. MC, V. Daily 4pm–midnight.

Pingüinos MEXICAN/SEAFOOD Seafood grilled Mexican style is the specialty of this open-air restaurant and bar facing the ocean. Late in the evening, it's sometimes a place to party. Dishes include fresh lobster—you'll get a large, beautifully presented lobster tail with a choice of butter, garlic, and secret sauces. The grilled seafood platter, seafood casserole, and fajitas are also standouts. Breakfasts include fresh fruit, yogurt, and granola, or sizable platters of eggs, served with homemade wheat bread.

In front of the Hotel Posada del Mar (3 blocks west of the ferry pier), Av. Rueda Medina 15-A. ✆ **998/877-0044,** ext. 157. Breakfast 50–80 pesos; main courses 70–140 pesos; lobster 230–450 pesos. AE, MC, V. Daily 7am–11pm; bar closes at midnight.

Rolandi's ★ ITALIAN/SEAFOOD   This restaurant is an Isla institution. The plate-size pizzas and calzones feature exotic ingredients—including lobster, black mushrooms, pineapple, and Roquefort cheese—as well as more traditional tomatoes, olives, basil, and salami. A wood-burning oven imparts the signature flavor of the pizzas, as well as baked chicken, roast beef, and mixed seafood casserole with lobster. The extensive menu offers a selection of salads and appetizers, plus an ample array of homemade pasta dishes, steaks, fish, and desserts. The setting is the open courtyard of the Hotel Belmar (p. 125), with a porch overlooking the action on Avenida Hidalgo.

Av. Hidalgo 10 (3¹/₂ blocks inland from the pier, btw. Madero and Abasolo). ✆ **998/877-0430,** ext. 18. Main courses 80–160 pesos. AE, MC, V. Daily 11am–11pm.

Zazil Ha ★★ CARIBBEAN/INTERNATIONAL   Here you can enjoy some of the island's best food while sitting at tables on the sand among palms and gardens. Come night, candlelit tables sparkle underneath the open-air *palapa*. Specialties include Maya chicken stuffed with corn mushroom and goat cheese, black pasta with calamari and pesto sauce, and fish of the day with *achiote* sauce draped in a banana leaf. A selection of fresh juices complements the vegetarian options, and there's even a special menu for those participating in yoga retreats. The delicious breads are baked in-house. Between the set meal times, you can order all sorts of enticing food, such as tacos and sandwiches, ceviche, terrific nachos, and vegetable and fruit drinks.

At the Hotel Na Balam (at the end of Playa Norte, almost at the end of Calle Zazil Ha; p. 124). ✆ **998/877-0279.** Fax 998/877-0446. Breakfast 40–100 pesos; main courses 80–220 pesos. AE, MC, V. Daily 7:30am–10:30pm.

Inexpensive

Café Cito CAFE   Brisa and Luis Rivera own this adorable, Caribbean-blue corner restaurant where you can begin the day with flavorful coffee and a croissant and cream cheese (this is the only place in town where you can have breakfast until 2pm). Terrific crepes come with yogurt, ice cream, fresh fruit, or *dulce de leche* (caramel sauce made from goat's milk), as well as ham and cheese.

Calle Matamoros 42, at Juárez. ✆ **998/877-1470.** Crepes 30–60 pesos; breakfast 40–60 pesos; sandwiches 35–45 pesos. No credit cards. Daily 7am–2pm.

ISLA MUJERES AFTER DARK

Those in a party mood by day's end may want to start out at the beach bar of the **Na Balam** hotel on Playa Norte, which usually hosts a crowd until around midnight. On Saturday and Sunday, live music plays between 4 and 7pm. **Jax Bar & Grill,** on Avenida Rueda Medina, close to Hotel Posada del Mar, is a Texas-style sports bar offering live music nightly. **Las Palapas Chimbo's** restaurant on the beach becomes a jammin' dance joint with a live band from 9pm until whenever. Farther along the same stretch of beach, **Buho's,** the restaurant/ beach bar of the Cabañas María del Mar, has its moments as a popular, low-key hangout, complete with swinging seats over the sand. **Pingüinos** (p. 126), in the Hotel Posada del Mar, offers a convivial late-night hangout, where a band plays nightly during high season from 9pm to midnight. If you want to sample one of nearly 100 tequila brands on a relaxing sidewalk terrace, stop by **La Adelita,** located at Av. Hidalgo 12 and open nightly from 5:30pm to 2:30am. Near Matamoros and Hidalgo, **KoKo Nuts** caters to a younger crowd, with international music for late-night dancing. **Om Bar and Chill Lounge,** on Calle Matamoros, serves cocktails in an atmosphere that includes jazzy Latino music, open from 6pm to 2am. For a late-night dance club, **Club Nitrox,** on Avenida Guerrero, is open Wednesday to Sunday from 9pm to 3am. In general, the crowds hitting these bars are in their 20s.

2 COZUMEL ★★★

70km (43 miles) S of Cancún; 19km (12 miles) SE of Playa del Carmen

Cozumel consistently ranks among the top five dive destinations in the world. Tall reefs line the southwest coast, creating towering walls that offer divers a fairy-tale landscape to explore. For nondivers, Cozumel has the beautiful water of the Caribbean with all the accompanying watersports and seaside activities. The island gets a lot more visitors from North America than Europe for reasons that probably have to do with the limited flights. It is in many ways more cozy and mellow than the mainland—no big highways, no big construction projects. It's dependable. And one of my favorite things about this island is that the water on the protected side (western shore) is as calm as an aquarium, unless a front is blowing through. The island is 45km (28 miles) long and 18km (11 miles) wide, and lies 19km (12 miles) from the mainland. Most of the terrain is flat and clothed in a low tropical forest.

The only town on the island is San Miguel, which, despite the growth of the last 20 years, can't be called anything more than a small town. It's not a stunningly beautiful town, but it and its inhabitants are agreeable—life moves along at a slow pace, and every Sunday evening, residents congregate around the plaza to enjoy live music and see their friends. Staying in town can be fun and convenient. You get a choice of a number of restaurants and nightspots.

Because Cozumel enjoys such popularity with the cruise ships, the waterfront section of town holds wall-to-wall jewelry stores, duty-free, and souvenir shops. This and the area around the town's main square are about as far as most cruise-ship passengers venture into town.

Should you come down with a case of island fever, **Playa del Carmen** and the mainland are a 40-minute ferry ride away. Some travel agencies on the island can set you up with a tour of the major ruins on the mainland, such as **Tulum** or **Chichén Itzá,** or a visit to a nature park such as **Xel-Ha** or **Xcaret** (see "Trips to the Mainland," later in this chapter).

During pre-Hispanic times, Maya women would cross over to the island to make offerings to the goddess of fertility, Ixchel. More than 40 sites containing shrines remain around the island, and archaeologists still uncover the small dolls that were customarily part of those offerings. Though the island has its own ruins, they cannot compare with the major sites of the mainland.

ESSENTIALS
Getting There & Departing
BY PLANE During high season, several more international commercial flights fly in and out of Cozumel's airport (CZM) than in low season, including a few flights from

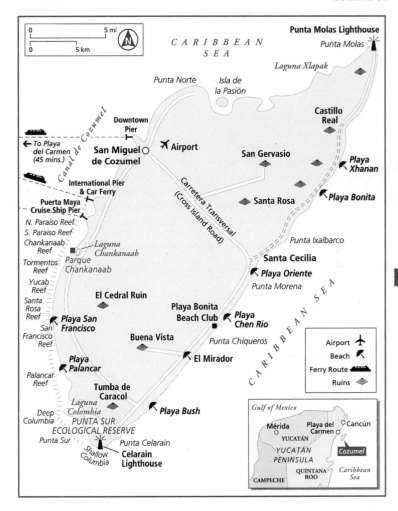

northern U.S. cities. You might also inquire about buying a ticket on one of the charter flights. Some packagers, such as **Fun Jet** (www.funjet.com), will sell you just a ticket. But look into packages, too. Several of the island's independent hotels work with packagers.

BY FERRY   Passenger ferries run to and from Playa del Carmen. **Barcos México** (© 987/872-1508, -1588) and **Ultramar** (© 987/869-2775) offer departures almost every hour in the morning and about every 2 hours in the afternoon. The schedules change according to seasons. The trip takes 30 to 45 minutes, depending on conditions, and costs $14 one-way. The boats are air-conditioned. In Playa del Carmen, the ferry dock is 1¹/₂ blocks from the main square. In Cozumel, the ferries use Muelle Fiscal, the town pier, a block from the main square. Luggage storage at the Cozumel dock costs 20 pesos per day.

The car ferry that used to operate from Puerto Morelos now uses the Calica pier just south of Playa del Carmen. The fare for a standard car is $80. **Marítima Chankanaab** (© **987/872-7671**, -7504) has four departures daily from Calica at 4am, 8am, 1:30pm,

An All-Inclusive Vacation in Cozumel

Booking a room at an all-inclusive should be done through a vacation packager. Booking lodging directly through the hotel usually doesn't make sense, even with frequent-flier mileage to burn, because the discounts offered by most packagers are so deep. I include websites for you to find out more info about the properties, but don't expect to find clear info on rates. The game of setting rates with these hotels is complicated and always in flux.

Two all-inclusives are north of town: **El Cozumeleño** (www.elcozumeleno.com) and the **Meliá Cozumel** (www.meliacozumel.com). Both occupy multistory modern buildings. Both have attractive rooms. El Cozumeleño is the larger of the two resorts and has the nicest hotel pool on the island. It's best suited for active types. The Meliá is quieter and offers golf discounts for the nearby golf course. The Cozumeleño's small beach has to be replenished with sand periodically. The Meliá's beach is long and narrow and pretty, but occasionally seaweed washes up, which doesn't happen on the rest of the island's coast. The advantages of staying in these two are the proximity to town, with its restaurants, clubs, movie theaters, and so on, and the fact that most rooms at these hotels come with views of the ocean.

The **Cozumel Palace** (www.palaceresorts.com) is right on the water on the southern fringes of town, occupying the property that used to be Plaza las Glorias. Despite the location, it doesn't have a beach. But that's not so bad. The water is usually so calm on Cozumel's west shore that swimming here is like swimming in the pool, and you can snorkel right out of the hotel.

Of the all-inclusives to the south, my favorites are the **Occidental** resort (**Grand Cozumel;** www.occidentalhotels.com) and the **Iberostar Cozumel** (www.iberostar.com). These are "village" style resorts with two- and three-story buildings, often with thatched roofs, spread over a large area at the center of which is the pool and activities area. Rooms at the Grand Cozumel are larger and more attractive than the all-inclusives in the south. Like the Occidental chain, Iberostar has several properties in the Mexican Caribbean. This one is the smallest. I like its food and service and the beauty of the grounds. The rooms are attractive and well maintained. The advantage to staying in these places is that you're close to a lot of dive sites; the disadvantage is that you're somewhat isolated from town, and you don't have many rooms with ocean views.

Other all-inclusives include the **Wyndham Cozumel Resort** (www.wyndham. com), which used to be the Reef Club, and the **Holiday Village White Sands**, which used to be the Allegro Cozumel but is now a First Choice property (www.firstchoice.co.uk). It probably has one of the nicest beaches on the island. And finally, there's the **Hotel Cozumel & Resort** (formerly the Costa Club; www.hotelcozumel.com.mx), which is on the inland side of the road in a crowded section of the island.

and 6pm. Arrive 1 hour before departure. The schedule is subject to change, so double-check it. The ferry docks in Cozumel at the **Muelle Internacional** (the **International Pier,** which is south of town near La Ceiba Hotel).

BY BUS   If you plan to travel on the mainland by bus, there is a ticket office for **ADO buses** called **Ticket Bus** where you can purchase tickets in advance. One is located on the municipal pier and is open while the ferries are running. Another is on Calle 2 Norte and Avenida 10 (© **987/872-1706**). Hours are from 8am to 9pm daily.

Orientation

ARRIVING   Cozumel's **airport** is inland from downtown. **Transportes Terrestres** provides hotel transportation in air-conditioned Suburbans. Buy your ticket as you exit the terminal. To hotels downtown, the fare is $7 per person; to hotels along the north shore, $10; and to hotels along the south shore, $11 to $15. Passenger ferries arrive at the Muelle Fiscal, the municipal pier, by the town's main square. Cruise ships dock at the **Punta Langosta** pier, several blocks south of the Muelle Fiscal, and at the **International Pier,** which is at Km 4 of the southern coastal road. A third cruise-ship pier, the **Puerta Maya,** near the International Pier, is finally operational after severe damage caused by hurricanes in 2006.

VISITOR INFORMATION   The **Municipal Tourism Office** (©/fax **987/869-0212**) has an information booth at the municipal ferry pier, on the main square. It's open 8am to 8pm Monday to Saturday. There are other information booths at each of the cruise-ship piers and at the airport.

CITY LAYOUT   San Miguel's main waterfront street is **Avenida Rafael Melgar.** Running parallel to Rafael Melgar are *avenidas* numbered in multiples of five—5, 10, 15. **Avenida Juárez** runs perpendicular to these, heading inland from the ferry dock. Avenida Juárez divides the town into northern and southern halves. The *calles* (streets) that parallel Juárez to the north have even numbers. The ones to the south have odd numbers, except for Calle Rosado Salas, which runs between calles 1 and 3.

ISLAND LAYOUT   One road runs along the western coast of the island, which faces the Yucatán mainland. It has different names. North of town, it's **Santa Pilar** or **San Juan;** in the city, it is **Avenida Rafael Melgar;** south of town, it's **Costera Sur.** Hotels stretch along this road north and south of town. The road runs to the southern tip of the island (Punta Sur), passing **Chankanaab National Park. Avenida Juárez** (and its extension, the **Carretera Transversal**) runs east from the town across the island. It passes the airport and the turnoff to the ruins of San Gervasio before reaching the undeveloped ocean side of the island. It then turns south and follows the coast to the southern tip, where it meets the Costera Sur.

GETTING AROUND   You can walk to most destinations in town. Getting to outlying hotels and beaches requires a taxi, rental car, or moped.

   Car rentals are roughly the same price as on the mainland, depending on demand. **Avis** (© **987/872-0099**) and **Executive** (© **987/872-1308**) have counters in the airport. Other major rental companies have offices in town. Rentals are easy to arrange through your hotel or at any of the many local rental offices.

 Tips   **Be Streetwise**

North–south streets—the *avenidas*—have the right of way, and traffic doesn't slow down or stop.

Moped rentals are readily available and cost 250 to 500 pesos for 24 hours, depending upon the season. If you rent a moped, be careful. Riding a moped made a lot more sense when Cozumel had less traffic; now it involves a certain amount of risk as taxi drivers and other motorists have become more numerous and pushier. Moped accidents easily rank as the greatest cause of injury in Cozumel. Before renting one, inspect it carefully to see that all the gizmos—horn, light, starter, seat, mirror—are in good shape. I've been offered mopeds with unbalanced wheels, which made them unsteady at higher speeds, but the renter quickly exchanged them upon my request. You are required to stay on paved roads. It's illegal to ride a moped without a helmet outside of town (subject to a 300 peso fine).

Cozumel has lots of **taxis** and a strong drivers' union. Fares have been standardized—there's no bargaining. Here are a few sample fares for two people (there is an additional charge for extra passengers to most destinations): island tour, 500 pesos; town to southern hotel zone, 110 to 180 pesos; town to northern hotels, 50 to 70 pesos; town to Chankanaab, 100 pesos for up to four people; in and around town, 30 to 40 pesos.

(Fast Facts Cozumel

Area Code The telephone area code is **987.**

Climate From October to December, there can be strong winds all over the Yucatán, as well as some rain. June through October is the rainy season.

Clinics **Médica San Miguel** (© **987/872-0103**) works for most things and includes intensive-care facilities. It's on Calle 6 Norte between avenidas 5 and 10. **Centro Médico Cozumel** (© **987/872-3545**) is an alternative. It's at the intersection of Calle 1 Sur and Avenida 50.

Currency Exchange The island has several banks and *casas de cambio,* as well as ATMs. Most places accept dollars, but you usually get a better deal paying in pesos.

Diving Bring proof of your diver's certification and your log. Underwater currents can be strong, and many of the reef drops are quite steep, so dive operators want to make sure divers are experienced.

Emergencies To report an emergency, dial © **060,** which is similar to 911 emergency service in the United States. Dial © **065** for the Red Cross.

Internet Access Several cybercafes are in and about the main square. If you go just a bit off Avenida Rafael Melgar and the main square, prices drop. **Modutel,** Av. Juárez 15 (at Av. 10), offers good rates. Hours are Monday through Saturday from 10am to 8pm.

Post Office The *correo* is on Avenida Rafael Melgar at Calle 7 Sur (© **987/872-0106**), at the southern edge of town. It's open Monday through Friday from 9am to 3pm, Saturday from 9am to noon.

Recompression Chamber There are four *cámaras de recompresión.* The best are **Buceo Médico Mexicano,** staffed 24 hours, at Calle 5 Sur 21-B, between Avenida Rafael Melgar and Avenida 5 Sur (© **987/872-2387,** -1430); and the **Hyperbaric Center of Cozumel** (© **987/872-3070**), at Calle 6 Norte, between avenidas 5 and 10.

Seasons High season is from Christmas to Easter and August.

For **diving** and **snorkeling,** there are plenty of dive shops to choose from, including those recommended below. For **island tours, ruins tours** on and off the island, **evening cruises,** and other activities, go to a travel agency, such as **InterMar Cozumel Viajes,** Calle 2 Norte 101-B, between avenidas 5 and 10 (© **987/872-1535,** -2022; fax 987/ 872-0895; cozumel@travel2mexico.com). Office hours are Monday through Saturday from 8am to 8pm, Sunday from 9am to 5pm.

Watersports

SCUBA DIVING Cozumel is the number-one dive destination in the Western Hemisphere. Don't forget your dive card and dive log. Dive shops will rent you scuba gear but won't take you out on a boat until you show some documentation. If you have a medical condition, bring a letter signed by a doctor stating that you've been cleared to dive. A two-tank morning dive costs from $65 to $90; some shops offer an additional afternoon one-tank dive for $35 for those who took the morning dives. A lot of divers save some money by buying a dive package with a hotel. These usually include two dives a day.

Diving in Cozumel is drift diving, which can be a little disconcerting for novices. The current that sweeps along Cozumel's reefs, pulling nutrients into them and making them as large as they are, also dictates how you dive here. The problem is that it pulls at different speeds at different depths and in different places. When it's pulling strong, it can quickly scatter a dive group. The role of the dive master becomes more important, especially with choosing the dive location. Cozumel has a lot of dive locations. To mention but a few: the famous **Palancar Reef,** with its caves and canyons, plentiful fish, and sea coral; the monstrous **Santa Rosa Wall,** famous for its depth, sea life, coral, and sponges; the **San Francisco Reef,** with a shallower drop-off wall and fascinating sea life; and the **Yucab Reef,** with its beautiful coral.

Finding a dive shop in town is even easier than finding a jewelry store. Cozumel has more than 50 dive operators. I know and can recommend Bill Horn's **Aqua Safari,** which has a location on Avenida Rafael Melgar at Calle 5 (© **987/872-0101;** fax 987/872-0661; www.aquasafari.com). I also know Roberto Castillo at **Liquid Blue Divers** (© **987/869-2812;** www.liquidbluedivers.com), on Avenida 5 between Rosado Salas and Calle 3 Sur. He does a good tour, has a fast boat, and keeps the number of divers to 12 or fewer. His wife, Michelle, handles the Internet inquiries and reservations and is quick to respond to questions.

A popular activity in the Yucatán is cenote diving. The peninsula's underground **cenotes** (seh-*noh*-tehs)—sinkholes or wellsprings—lead to a vast system of underground caverns. The gently flowing water is so clear that divers seem to float on air through caves complete with stalactites and stalagmites. If you want to try this but didn't plan a trip to the mainland, contact **Yucatech Expeditions,** Avenida 5, on the corner of Calle 3 Sur (©/fax **987/872-5659;** www.yucatech.net), which offers a trip five times a week.

(**Moments** **Carnaval**

Carnaval (similar to Mardi Gras) is Cozumel's most colorful fiesta. It begins the Thursday before Ash Wednesday, with daytime street dancing and nighttime parades on Thursday, Saturday, and Monday (the best).

Cenotes are 30 to 45 minutes from Playa del Carmen, and a dive in each cenote lasts around 45 minutes. Dives are within the daylight zone, about 40m (131 ft.) into the caverns, and no more than 18m (59 ft.) deep. Company owner Germán Yañez Mendoza inspects diving credentials carefully, and divers must meet his list of requirements before cave diving is permitted. For information and prices, call or drop by the office.

SNORKELING Anyone who can swim can snorkel. When contracting for a snorkel tour, stay away from the companies that cater to the cruise ships. Those tours are crowded and not very fun. For a good snorkeling tour, contact **Victor Casanova** (© 987/872-1028; wildcatcozumel@hotmail.com). He speaks English, owns a couple of boats, and does a good 5-hour tour. He takes his time and doesn't rush through the trip. You can also try the **Kuzamil Snorkeling Center,** 50 Av. bis 565 Int. 1, between 5 Sur and Hidalgo, Colonia Adolfo López Mateos (© 987/872-4637, -0539). Even though you won't see a lot of the more delicate structures, such as fan coral, you will still see plenty of sea creatures and enjoy the clear, calm water of Cozumel's protected west side.

BOAT TRIPS Travel agencies and hotels can arrange boat trips, a popular pastime on Cozumel. Choose from evening cruises, cocktail cruises, glass-bottom boat cruises, and other options. One novel boat ride is offered by **Atlantis Submarines** (© 987/872-5671; www.atlantisadventures.com). The sub can hold 48 people. It operates almost 3km (1³/₄ miles) south of town in front of the Casa del Mar hotel and costs $84 per adult, $48 for kids ages 4 to 12. This is a superior experience to the **Sub See Explorer** offered by **Aqua World,** which is really just a glorified glass-bottom boat. You can make reservations online and get a bit of a discount.

FISHING The best months for fishing are March through June, when the catch includes blue and white marlin, sailfish, tarpon, and swordfish. The least expensive option would be to contact a boat owner directly. Try Victor Casanova, listed above under "Snorkeling." Or try an agency such as **Aquarius Travel Fishing,** Calle 3 Sur 2 between Avenida Rafael Melgar and Avenida 5 (© 987/872-1092; gabdiaz@yahoo.com).

Anatomy of the Coral Reef

Corals are polyps, tiny animals with hollow, cylindrical bodies that attach by the thousands to hard surfaces of the sea floor. The polyps extract calcium carbonate from the seawater to create hard, cup-shaped skeletons that assume an endless variety of shapes and sizes. These massive limestone structures shelter nearly one-fourth of all marine life. The soft, delicate polyps retreat into their skeletons during the day, but their protruding tentacles can be seen when they feed at night.

Two distinct types of coral formations dominate Cozumel's waters. Bases of the less developed platform reefs, such as Colombia Shallows, Paradise, and Yucab, are rarely more than 9 to 15m (30–50 ft.) in depth. Edge reefs are more complex structures built up over many millennia, and their layered structures peak high above the edge of the drop-off, extending as much as 55m (180 ft.) below the surface. These are found mostly in the south; examples include Palancar, Colombia Deep, Punta Sur, and Maracaibo.

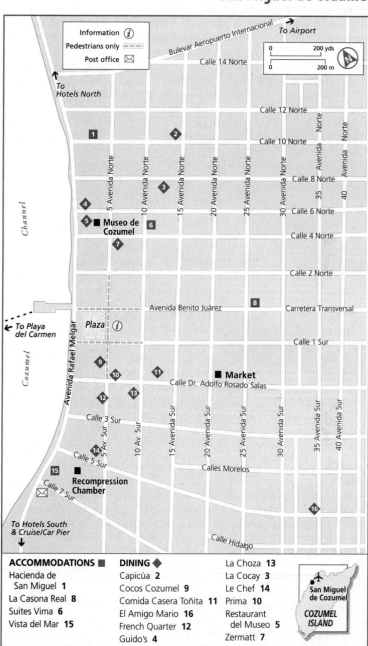

ISLA MUJERES & COZUMEL

6

COZUMEL

Information ⓘ
Pedestrians only ▭▭▭
Post office ⊠

Bulevar Aeropuerto Internacional → To Airport

Calle 14 Norte

0   200 yds
0   200 m

To Hotels North

Channel

Cozumel

Calle 12 Norte

Calle 10 Norte

Calle 8 Norte

Calle 6 Norte

Calle 4 Norte

Calle 2 Norte

35 Avenida Norte
40 Avenida Norte

5 Avenida Norte
10 Avenida Norte
15 Avenida Norte
20 Avenida Norte
25 Avenida Norte
30 Avenida Norte

1
2
3
4
5 ■ Museo de Cozumel
6
7

Avenida Benito Juárez

8

Carretera Transversal

Calle 1 Sur

← To Playa del Carmen

Plaza ⓘ

Avenida Rafael Melgar

9
10
11
■ Market
Calle Dr. Adolfo Rosado Salas

12
13

Calle 3 Sur

5 Av. Sur
10 Av. Sur
15 Avenida Sur
20 Avenida Sur
25 Avenida Sur
30 Avenida Sur
35 Avenida Sur
40 Avenida Sur

14
Calle 5 Sur

15
Calle 7 Sur ⊠
■ Recompression Chamber

Calles Morelos

16

To Hotels South & Cruise/Car Pier ↓

Calle Hidalgo

ACCOMMODATIONS ■
Hacienda de San Miguel **1**
La Casona Real **8**
Suites Vima **6**
Vista del Mar **15**

DINING ◆
Capicúa **2**
Cocos Cozumel **9**
Comida Casera Toñita **11**
El Amigo Mario **16**
French Quarter **12**
Guido's **4**

La Choza **13**
La Cocay **3**
Le Chef **14**
Prima **10**
Restaurant del Museo **5**
Zermatt **7**

San Miguel de Cozumel

COZUMEL ISLAND

Chankanaab National Park ★ is the pride of many islanders. In Mayan, Chankanaab means "little sea," which refers to a beautiful land-locked pool connected to the sea through an underwater tunnel—a sort of miniature ocean. Snorkeling in this natural aquarium is not permitted, but the park itself has a beach for sunbathing and snorkeling. Arrive before 9am to stake out a chair and *palapa* before the cruise-ship crowd arrives. The snorkeling is also best before noon. There are bathrooms, lockers, a gift shop, several snack huts, a restaurant, and a *palapa* for renting snorkeling gear.

You can also swim with dolphins. **Dolphin Discovery** (© 800/293-9698; www.dolphindiscovery.com) has several programs for experiencing these sea creatures. These are popular, so plan ahead—you should make reservations well in advance. The surest way is through the website—make sure to pick the Cozumel location, as there are a couple of others on this coast. There are three different programs for swimming with dolphins. The one of longest duration costs $149 and features close interaction with the beautiful swimmers. There are also swim-and-snorkel programs for $70 and $100 that get you in the water with these creatures.

Surrounding the land-locked dolphin pool is a botanical garden that suffered greatly from Hurricane Wilma and still hasn't returned to its former shape. Admission to the park is expensive, costing 170 pesos for adults, 80 pesos for children 9 to 12. I think the authorities are trying to recoup some of the money spent restoring the park, and it is being marketed to the cruise-ship crowd. The park is open daily from 8am to 5pm. It's south of town, just past the Fiesta Americana Hotel. Taxis run constantly between the park, the hotels, and town (100 pesos from town for up to four people).

Faro Celerain Ecological Reserve (admission 100 pesos), once called Punta Sur, is a large area at the southern tip of the island that includes the Columbia Lagoon. The only practical way of going there is to rent a car or scooter; there is no taxi stand and, usually, few people. This is an ecological reserve, not a park, so don't expect much infrastructure. The reserve has an information center, several observation towers, and a snack bar. Punta Sur has some interesting snorkeling (bring your own gear), and lovely beaches that are kept as natural as possible and are usually unpopulated. Regular hours are daily 9am to 5pm. If you have a rental car, getting here is no problem, and this is usually a great place to get away from the crowds and have a lot of beach to yourself. Occasionally, boat tours of the lagoon are offered. Ask at the information office.

Beaches

Along both the west and east sides of the island you'll see signs advertising beach clubs. A "beach club" in Cozumel can mean just a *palapa* hut that's open to the public and serves soft drinks, beer, and fried fish. It can also mean a recreational beach with the full gamut of offerings, from banana boats to parasailing. They also usually have locker rooms, a pool, and food. The two biggest of these are **Mr. Sancho's** (© 987/879-0021; www.mrsanchos.com) and **Playa Mía** (© 987/872-9030; www.playamia.com). They get a lot of business from the cruise ships. Mr. Sancho's is free, while Playa Mía charges between $12 for simple admission to $42 for the full all-inclusive package. Quieter versions of beach clubs are **Playa San Francisco** (no phone), **Paradise Beach** (no phone, next to Playa San Francisco), and **Playa Palancar** (no phone). All of these beaches are south of Chankanaab Park and easily visible from the road. Several have swimming pools with beach furniture, a restaurant, and snorkel rental. Most of these beaches cost around **137** 50 pesos.

Once you get to the end of the island, the beach clubs become simple places where you can eat, drink, and lay out on the beach for free. **Paradise Cafe** is on the southern tip of the island across from Punta Sur Nature Park, and as you go up the eastern side of the island you pass **Playa Bonita, Chen Río,** and **Punta Morena** (not yet back in business on my last visit). Except on Sunday, when the locals head for the beaches, these places are practically deserted. Most of the east coast is unsafe for swimming because of the surf. The beaches tend to be small and occupy gaps in the rocky coast.

Island Tours

Travel agencies can arrange a variety of tours, including horseback, Jeep, and ATV tours. Taxi drivers charge 550 pesos for a 4-hour tour of the island, which most people would consider only mildly amusing, depending on the driver's personality. The best horseback tours are offered at **Rancho Palmitas** (no phone), on the Costera Sur highway, across from the Occidental Cozumel resort. Unless you're staying in a resort on the south end, talk to the owners of **Cocos Cozumel** restaurant to arrange a tour (see the listing later in this chapter, making sure to note the limited hours). Rides can be from 1 to 2¹/₂ hours long and cost 200 to 300 pesos.

Other Attractions

MAYA RUINS A popular island excursion is to **San Gervasio** (100 B.C.–A.D. 1600). Follow the paved transversal road, and you'll see the well-marked turnoff about halfway between town and the eastern coast. For what you see, it's a bit overpriced. You have to pay a 60 pesos fee to enter plus an additional 30 pesos fee charged by the state agency; camera permits cost an additional 50 pesos. A small tourist center at the entrance sells cold drinks and snacks. The ruins are open from 7am to 4pm.

When it comes to Cozumel's Maya ruins, getting there is most of the fun—do it for the mystique and for the trip, not for the size or scale of the ruins. The buildings, though preserved, are crudely made and would not be much of a tourist attraction if they were not the island's principal ruins. More significant than beautiful, this site was once an important ceremonial center where the Maya gathered, coming even from the mainland. The important deity was Ixchel, the goddess of weaving, women, childbirth, pilgrims, the moon, and medicine. Although you won't see any representations of Ixchel at San Gervasio today, Bruce Hunter, in his *Guide to Ancient Maya Ruins,* writes that priests hid behind a large pottery statue of her and became the voice of the goddess, speaking to pilgrims and answering their petitions. Ixchel was the wife of Itzamná, the sun god.

Guides charge 200 pesos for a tour for one to six people. A better option is to find a copy of the green booklet *San Gervasio,* sold at local checkout counters and bookstores, and tour the site on your own. Seeing it takes 30 minutes. Taxi drivers offer transportation for about 330 pesos, which includes the driver waiting for you outside the ruins.

A HISTORY MUSEUM The **Museo de la Isla de Cozumel** ★, Avenida Rafael Melgar between calles 4 and 6 Norte (✆ **987/872-1475**), is more than just a nice place to spend a rainy hour. On the first floor, an exhibit illustrates endangered species, the origin of the island, and its present-day topography and plant and animal life, including an explanation of coral formation. The second-floor galleries feature the history of the town, artifacts from the island's pre-Hispanic sites, and Colonial-Era cannons, swords, and ship paraphernalia. It's open daily from 9am to 5pm (but closes at 4pm on Sun). Admission

ISLA MUJERES & COZUMEL

is $3. A rooftop restaurant serves breakfast and lunch (and you don't need to pay admission to eat there.

GOLF   Cozumel has an 18-hole course designed by Jack Nicklaus. It's at the **Cozumel Country Club** (© 987/872-9570), north of San Miguel. Greens fees are $170 for a morning tee time, including cart rental and tax. Afternoon tee times cost $105. Tee times can be reserved 3 days in advance. A few hotels have special memberships with discounts for guests and advance tee times; guests at Playa Azul Golf and Beach Club pay no greens fees, but the cart costs $25.

TRIPS TO THE MAINLAND

CHICHÉN ITZÁ, TULUM & COBÁ   Travel agencies can arrange day trips to the ruins of **Chichén Itzá** ★★★ by air or bus. The ruins of **Tulum** ★, overlooking the Caribbean, and **Cobá** ★, in a dense jungle setting, are closer and cost less to visit. These latter two cities are quite a contrast to Chichén Itzá. Cobá is a large, mostly unrestored city beside a lake in a remote jungle setting, while Tulum is smaller, more compact, and right on the beach. It's more intact than Cobá. A trip to both Cobá and Tulum begins at 8am and returns around 6pm. A shorter, more relaxing excursion goes to Tulum and the nearby nature park of Xel-Ha.

PLAYA DEL CARMEN & XCARET   Going on your own to the nearby seaside town of **Playa del Carmen** and the **Xcaret** nature park is as easy as a quick ferry ride from Cozumel (for ferry information, see "Getting There & Departing," earlier in this chapter). For information on Playa and Xcaret, see chapter 7. Cozumel travel agencies offer an Xcaret tour that includes the ferry ride, transportation to the park, and the admission fee. The price is $100 for adults, $55 for kids. The tour is available Monday through Saturday.

SHOPPING

If you're looking for silver jewelry or souvenirs, go no farther than the town's coastal avenue, Rafael Melgar. Along this road, you find one store after another—jewelry, souvenirs, and duty-free merchandise. But if you're looking for something original, seek out a gallery and store called **Inspiración** (© 987/869-8293), on Avenida 5 between Rosado Salas and Calle 3. Owner Dianne Hartwig displays the creations of some of the best-known folk artists in the Yucatán—objects that are very hard to come by if you don't actually go the villages where many of these artists live. She also represents some talented contemporary local artists. Stores carrying Mexican handicrafts include **Los Cinco Soles** (© 987/872-2040), **Indigo** (© 987/872-1076), and **Viva México** (© 987/872-5466). All of these are on Avenida Rafael Melgar. There are also some import/export stores in the Punta Langosta Shopping Center in the southern part of town in front of the cruise-ship pier. Prices for serapes, T-shirts, and the like are lower on the side streets off Avenida Melgar.

WHERE TO STAY

I've grouped Cozumel's hotels by location—**north** of town, **in town,** and **south** of town. The prices quoted are public rates and include the 12% tax. High season is from December to Easter. Expect rates from Christmas to New Year's to be still higher than the regular high-season rates quoted here. Low season is the rest of the year, though a few hotels raise their rates in August, when Mexican families go on vacation.

All of the beach hotels in Cozumel, even the small ones, have deals with vacation packagers. Keep in mind that some packagers will offer last-minute deals to Cozumel with hefty discounts; if you're the flexible sort, keep an eye open for these.

Most hotels have an arrangement with a dive shop and offer dive packages. These can be good deals, but if you don't buy a dive package, it's quite okay to stay at one hotel and dive with a third-party operator—any dive boat can pull up to any hotel pier to pick up customers. Most dive shops won't pick up from the hotels north of town.

As an alternative to a hotel, you can try **Cozumel Vacation Villas and Condos,** Av. Rafael Melgar 685 (btw. calles 3 and 5 Sur; ℂ **800/224-5551** in the U.S., or 987/872-0729; www.cvvmexico.com), which offers accommodations by the week.

North of Town

Carretera Santa Pilar, or San Juan, is the name of Avenida Rafael Melgar's northern extension. All the hotels lie close to each other on the beach side of the road a short distance from town and the airport.

Very Expensive

Playa Azul Golf-Scuba-Spa ★★★ This quiet hotel is perhaps the most relaxing of the island's properties. It's smaller than the others, and service is personal. It's an excellent choice for golfers; guests pay no greens fees, only cart rental. The hotel's small beach with shade *palapas* has a quiet little beach bar. Almost all the rooms have balconies and ocean views. The units in the original section are all suites—very large, with oversize bathrooms with showers. The new wing has mostly standard rooms that are comfortable and large. The corner rooms are master suites and have large balconies with Jacuzzis overlooking the sea. If you prefer lots of space over having a Jacuzzi, opt for a suite in the original building. Rooms contain a king-size bed or two double beds; some suites offer two convertible single sofas in the separate living room. The hotel also offers deep-sea-and fly-fishing trips.

Carretera San Juan Km 4, 77600 Cozumel, Q. Roo. ℂ **987/869-5160,** -5165. Fax 987/869-5173. www. playa-azul.com. 50 units. High season $275 double, $330–$380 suite; low season $210–$225 double, $252–$342 suite. Rates include unlimited golf and full breakfast. Internet specials available. AE, MC, V. Free guarded parking. **Amenities:** Restaurant; 2 bars; babysitting; unlimited golf privileges at Cozumel Country Club; medium-size outdoor pool; room service; smoke-free rooms; spa; watersports gear rental; dive shop. *In room:* A/C, TV, fridge, hair dryer, Wi-Fi.

Expensive

Condumel Condobeach Apartments (Value) If you want some distance from the crowds, consider lodging here. It's not a full-service hotel, but in some ways, it's more convenient. The one-bedroom apartments are designed and furnished in practical fashion—airy, with sliding glass doors that face the sea and allow for good cross-ventilation (especially in the upper units). They also have ceiling fans, air-conditioning, and two twin beds or one king-size. Each apartment has a separate living room and a full kitchen with a partially stocked fridge, so you don't have to run to the store on the first day. There's a small, well-tended beach area (with shade *palapas* and a grill for guests' use) that leads to a low, rocky fall-off into the sea.

Carretera Hotelera Norte s/n, 77600 Cozumel, Q. Roo. ℂ **987/872-0892.** Fax 987/872-0661. www. condumel.com. 10 units. High season $160 double; low season $134 double. Dive packages available. No credit cards. *In room:* A/C, kitchen, no phone.

In Town

Staying in town is not like staying in Playa del Carmen, where you can walk to the beach. The oceanfront in town is too busy for swimming, and there's no beach, only the *malecón.* Prices are considerably lower, but you'll have to drive or take a cab to the beach; it's pretty easy. English is spoken in almost all of the hotels.

Hacienda San Miguel ★ ⟨Value⟩   This is a peaceful hotel built in Mexican colonial style around a large garden courtyard. The property is well maintained and the service is good. It's located a half-block from the shoreline on the town's north side. Rooms are large and attractive, and come with equipped kitchens, including full-size refrigerators. Most of the studios have a queen-size bed or two doubles. The junior suites have more living area and come with a queen-size and a twin bed. The two-bedroom suite comes with four double beds. For this hotel, high season is from January to August; low season is from September to December, excluding the holiday season.

Calle 10 Norte 500 (btw. Rafael Melgar and Av. 5), 77600 Cozumel, Q. Roo. ☎ **866/712-6387** in the U.S., or 987/872-1986. Fax 987/872-7036. www.haciendasanmiguel.com. 11 units. High season 1,050 pesos studio, 1,200 pesos junior suite, 1,730 pesos 2-bedroom suite; low season 920 pesos studio, 1,050 pesos junior suite, 1,730 pesos 2-bedroom suite. Rates include continental breakfast and free entrance to Mr. Sancho's beach club. MC, V. Guarded parking on street. *In room:* A/C, TV, hair dryer, kitchen, no phone.

Vista del Mar ★   This hotel is located on the town's shoreline boulevard. All the rooms in front have ocean views. The balconies are large enough to be enjoyable and are furnished with a couple of chairs. Rooms are a little larger than standard, with better lighting than you find in most of the hotels in town. They are simply furnished and decorated, but come with several amenities. Bathrooms are medium size or a little smaller and have showers. The rooms in back go for 100 pesos less than the oceanview rooms and look out over a small pool and large Jacuzzi. This hotel is run by the same people who run Hacienda San Miguel, and it has the same high season/low season split, with higher rates for Carnaval and Christmas time.

Av. Rafael Melgar 45 (btw. calles 5 and 7 Sur), 77600 Cozumel, Q. Roo. ☎ **888/309-9988** in the U.S., or 987/872-0545. Fax 987/872-7036. www.hotelvistadelmar.com. 20 units. High season 900–1,000 pesos double; low season 800–900 pesos. Discounts sometimes available. AE, MC, V. Limited street parking. **Amenities:** Bar; Jacuzzi; outdoor pool. *In room:* A/C, TV, fridge, hair dryer.

Inexpensive

La Casona Real ⟨Value⟩   Five blocks from the waterfront, this two-story hotel is a bargain for those wanting a hotel with a pool. The rooms are small to medium in size, but modern and attractive, and come with good air-conditioning. Rooms are attractive and come with two comfortable double beds or one king-size (costing 100 pesos less). Bathrooms are medium in size. A courtyard with an oval pool is on the west side of the building. This is not the quietest of properties. Next door is a club that opens on weekends, and on the other side of the hotel is a fairly busy street.

Av. Juárez 501, 77600 Cozumel, Q. Roo. ☎ **987/872-5471.** 14 units. 450–550 pesos double. Discounts sometimes available in low season. No credit cards. Limited street parking. **Amenities:** Medium-size outdoor pool. *In room:* A/C, TV, no phone.

Suites Vima ⟨Value⟩   This three-story hotel is 4 blocks from the main square. It offers large, plainly furnished rooms for a good price. The lighting is okay, the showers are good, and every room comes with its own fridge, which for island visitors can be a handy feature. The rooms are fairly quiet. Choose between two doubles or one king bed. There is no restaurant, but there is a pool and lounge area. As is the case with other small hotels on the island, the staff at the front desk doesn't speak English. Reservations through e-mail can be made in English. This is one of the few hotels in town that doesn't use high season/low season rates.

Av. 10 Norte btw. Calles 4 and 6, 77600 Cozumel, Q. Roo. ☎ **987/872-5118.** suitesvima@hotmail.com. 12 units. 560 pesos double. No credit cards. Limited street parking. **Amenities:** Pool. *In room:* A/C, fridge.

The hotels in this area tend to be more spread out and farther from town than hotels to the north. Some are on the inland side of the road; some are on the beach side, which means a difference in price. Those farthest from town are all-inclusive properties. The beaches tend to be slightly better than those to the north, but all the hotels have swimming pools and piers from which you can snorkel, and all of them accommodate divers. Head south on Avenida Rafael Melgar, which becomes the coastal road **Costera Sur** (also called Carretera a Chankanaab).

Very Expensive

Presidente InterContinental Cozumel ★★★   Palatial in scale and modern in style, the Presidente spreads out across a long stretch of coast with only distant hotels for neighbors. Rooms come in three categories—pool view, ocean view, and beach front. A terrace or a balcony offers the indoor/outdoor mix that's so enjoyable in a beach hotel. Downstairs rooms are beach front, ocean suites, and reef rooms (larger and practically right up to the water), upstairs are ocean view. Rooms are oversize and have large, beautifully finished bathrooms. A long stretch of sandy beach, dotted with *palapas* and palm trees, fronts the entire hotel. This property is now a member of Leading Hotels of the World.

Costera Sur Km 6.5, 77600 Cozumel, Q. Roo. ℭ **800/327-0200** in the U.S., or 987/872-9500. Fax 987/872-9528. www.intercontinentalcozumel.com. 220 units. High season $330 pool view, $398 ocean view, $582 and up for beach fronts and suites; low season $257–$291 pool view, $302–$358 ocean view, $370–$504 and up for beach fronts and suites. Internet specials sometimes available. AE, MC, V. Free valet parking. **Amenities:** 3 restaurants; 4 bars; babysitting; 24-hr. butler service in reef section; children's club; concierge; access to golf club; fully equipped fitness center; 2 outdoor pools; wading pool; room service; smoke-free rooms; spa; 2 lighted tennis courts; watersports equipment rental; dive shop. *In room:* A/C, TV w/pay movies, hair dryer, minibar, Wi-Fi.

Expensive

El Cantil Condominiums ★★   This condo property on the south side of town rents out 30 (of the 45 total) units by the night or the week. El Cantil is worth consideration because it's an attractive property with large rooms and convenient location. The shore here is rocky, but there's a sandy area for guests and a beautiful seaside pool and Jacuzzi, as well as a boat dock and easy entry into the sea. Extras include free long-distance calls to the U.S.

Av. Rafael Melgar, btw. calles 13 and 15. 77600 Cozumel, Q. Roo. ℭ **954/323-8491** in the U.S., or 987/869-1517. Fax 987/869-2053. www.elcantilcondos.com. 30 units. High season $200 studio, $200–$310 1-bedroom, $252–$615 2-bedroom; low season $170 studio, $170–$250 1-bedroom, $200–$330 2-bedroom. AE, DISC, MC, V. Free sheltered parking. **Amenities:** Restaurant (see "Where to Dine," below); bar; concierge; saltwater Jacuzzi; heated outdoor pool; room service; smoke-free rooms; watersports equipment rental. *In room:* A/C, TV, hair dryer, kitchen (in all but studio units), Wi-Fi or high-speed Internet.

WHERE TO DINE

The island offers a number of good restaurants. Taxi drivers will often steer you toward restaurants that pay them commissions; don't heed their advice.

Zermatt (ℭ **987/872-1384**), a nice little bakery, is on Avenida 5 at Calle 4 Norte. **Le Chef** (ℭ **987/876-3437**), at Avenida 5 and Calle 5 Sur, is a deli/gourmet food store. It has a daily menu of salads, pizzas, and prepared foods, as well as cold meats, cheeses, baguettes, and other makings for a picnic. For inexpensive local fare during the day, I like **Comida Casera Toñita** (ℭ **987/872-0401**), at Calle Rosado Salas 265 between avenidas 10 and 15. It closes at 6pm. For morning tacos of *cochinita pibil* (traditionally a breakfast item), go to **El Amigo Mario** (ℭ **987/872-0742**), on Calle 5 Sur, between Francisco Mújica and Avenida 35. The doors close at 12:30pm.

Finally, there's a restaurant on the top floor of El Cantil condos called **The Wynston** (☎ **987/869-1517**) with panoramic views of the ocean. The owner also owns Prima (see review below), which has a similar menu of mostly steaks and seafood; main courses run from 180 to 400 pesos. Definitely make reservations in high season.

Very Expensive

Cabaña del Pescador (Lobster House) ★★ LOBSTER   Lobster is the main attraction here. You select a lobster tail, and brothers Fernando or Enrique will weigh it, boil it with a hint of spices, and serve it with melted butter, accompanied by sides of rice, vegetables, and bread. Does lobster require anything more? This is the only thing on the menu on Fernando's side of the restaurant, but Enrique will cook up steaks, shrimp, or fish if you don't feel like lobster. The setting is quite tropical—a pair of thatched bungalows bordering a pond with lily pads and reeds, traversed by a small footbridge. The rooms are softly lit with the glow of candles and furnished with rustic tables and chairs. The restaurant rambles around quite a bit, so explore until you find the spot most to your taste.

Carretera Santa Pilar Km 4 (across from Playa Azul Hotel). No phone. Reservations not accepted. Lobster (by weight) 250–400 pesos. No credit cards. Daily 6–10:30pm.

Expensive

French Quarter ★★ SOUTHERN   You can dine very well here in a comfortable upstairs open-air setting. The owners are from Louisiana and care a great deal about food. You can order Southern and Creole classics, such as jambalaya and étouffée, or you can order the daily catch stuffed or blackened, or choose a steak of imported Black Angus beef. They serve a filet mignon with red-onion marmalade that's delicious. The downstairs bar is a popular hangout for many locals.

Av. 5 Sur 18. ☎ **987/872-6321.** Reservations recommended during Carnaval. Main courses 120–300 pesos. AE, MC, V. Wed–Mon 5–11pm.

Guido's ★★ MEDITERRANEAN   The inviting interior, with director's chairs and rustic wood tables, makes this a restful place in daytime and a romantic spot at night. The specialty is oven-baked pizzas. Also keep an eye out for the daily specials, which may include an appetizer of sea bass carpaccio, a couple of meat dishes, and usually a fish dish, depending on what the daily catch is. The other thing that people love here is the *pan de ajo*—a house creation of bread made with olive oil, garlic, and rosemary. There's a good wine list.

Av. Rafael Melgar, btw. calles 6 and 8 Norte. ☎ **987/872-0946.** Reservations accepted. Main courses 130–210 pesos; pizzas 120–130 pesos. AE, MC, V. Mon–Sat 11am–11pm.

La Cocay ★★★ SEAFOOD/MEDITERRANEAN   This kitchen serves the most original cooking on the island. The dining room and outdoor courtyard, modern in style and softly lit, make for a comfortable ambience. I tried a few *tapas* for appetizers, and they were beautifully seasoned concoctions of garbanzos, chorizo, bell peppers, panela cheese, and sun-dried tomatoes on small slices of bread. For a main course, try the subtle and tender grilled fish in lavender sauce. The choice of meat dishes is usually good. And give special consideration to the daily specials and the wonderful chocolate torte. It takes a little extra time to prepare, so order it early.

Calle 8 Norte 208 (btw. avs. 10 and 15). ☎ **987/872-5533.** Reservations recommended. Main courses 120–300 pesos. AE, MC, V. Mon–Sat 1:30–11pm.

Prima ★★★ ITALIAN   Everything at this ever-popular hangout is fresh—pastas, vegetables, and seafood. The menu changes daily and concentrates on seafood. It might

include shrimp scampi, fettuccine with pesto, and lobster and crab ravioli with cream **143**
sauce. The fettuccine Alfredo is wonderful, the salads crisp, and the steaks are Black
Angus beef. Pizzas are cooked in a wood-burning oven. Desserts include Key lime pie and
tiramisu. The food and the service are consistently good here. Dining is upstairs on an
open-air terrace.

Calle Rosado Salas 109A (corner of Av. 5) ℂ **987/872-4242.** Reservations recommended during high
season. Pizzas and pastas 70–140 pesos; seafood 120–200 pesos; steaks 150–200 pesos. AE, MC, V. Daily
4:30–10pm.

Moderate
Capicúa TAPAS/SEAFOOD   A new restaurant for the island, Capicúa looks to attract
customers tired of the usual run of the island's restaurants with some original cooking.
The selection of *tapas* varies but usually includes such things as smoked duck or abalone.
And for those wanting something closer to comfort food, there are barbecued chicken
wings or shrimp *al ajillo* (with garlic and strips of toasted *guajillo* chile). I enjoyed the
mahimahi encrusted with white and black sesame seeds, which was cooked just right.
Salads can be had, too. There is an okay selection of wines and a full bar. The house in
which the restaurant is located is decorated with a sense of humor; choose between a
dining room with one of those beautiful, old tile floors and an old patio sheltered by a
large tamarind tree.

Calle 10 Norte 299 (corner of Av. 15). ℂ **987/869-8265.** Reservations accepted. Tapas 40–100 pesos;
main courses 100–150 pesos. MC, V. Tues–Sun 5pm–midnight.

El Moro ★ ⟨**Value**⟩ REGIONAL   El Moro is an out-of-the-way place that has been
around for a long time and has always been popular with the locals, who come for the
food, the service, and the prices—but not the decor, which is orange, orange, orange, and
Formica. Get there by taxi, which will cost a couple of bucks. Portions are generous. Any
of the shrimp dishes use the real jumbo variety when available. For something different,
try the *pollo Ticuleño,* a specialty from the town of Ticul, a layered dish of tomato sauce,
mashed potatoes, crispy baked corn tortillas, and fried chicken breast, topped with shredded cheese and green peas. Other specialties include enchiladas and seafood prepared
many ways, plus grilled steaks and sandwiches.

75 bis Norte 124 (btw. calles 2 and 4 Norte). ℂ **987/872-3029.** Reservations not accepted. Main courses
50–150 pesos. MC, V. Fri–Wed 1–11pm.

La Choza ★ YUCATECAN/MEXICAN   For Mexican food, I like this place, and so
do a lot of locals. Platters of poblano chiles stuffed with shrimp, grilled *brochetas*
(kebobs), and *pollo en relleno negro* (chicken in a sauce of blackened chiles) are among the
specialties. The table sauces and guacamole are great, and the daily specials can be good,
too. This is an open-air restaurant with well-spaced tables under a tall thatched roof.
Breakfasts are good as well.

Rosado Salas 198 (at Av. 10 Sur). ℂ **987/872-0958.** Reservations accepted for groups of 6 or more.
Breakfast 45 pesos; main courses 100–160 pesos. AE, MC, V. Daily 7am–10pm.

Inexpensive
Cocos Cozumel MEXICAN/AMERICAN   Cocos offers the largest breakfast menu
on the island, including all the American and Mexican classics, from *huevos divorciados*
(fried eggs on corn tortillas) to ham and eggs. Indulge in such stateside favorites as hash
browns, corn flakes and bananas, gigantic blueberry muffins, cinnamon rolls, and bagels,
or go for something with tropical ingredients, such as a blended fruit drink. The service

and the food are excellent. The American and Mexican owners, Terri and Daniel Ocejo, are good folk and can set you up with a horseback ride or a fishing or snorkeling trip.

Av. 5 Sur 180 (1 block south of the main plaza). © **987/872-0241.** Breakfast 40–60 pesos. No credit cards. Tues–Sun 6am–noon. Closed Sept–Oct.

Restaurant del Museo BREAKFAST/MEXICAN   The most pleasant place in San Miguel for breakfast or lunch (weather permitting) is at this rooftop cafe above the island's museum. It offers a serene view of the water, removed from the traffic noise below and sheltered from the sun above. Choices are limited to American and Mexican breakfast staples, and lunch dishes such as sandwiches and enchiladas.

Av. Rafael Melgar (corner of Calle 6 Norte). © **987/872-0838.** Reservations not accepted. Breakfast 40–50 pesos; lunch main courses 50–100 pesos. No credit cards. Daily 7am–2pm.

COZUMEL AFTER DARK

Most of the music and dance venues are along Avenida Rafael Melgar. **Carlos 'n' Charlie's** (© **987/869-1648,** -1646), which is in the Punta Langosta shopping center, is practically next to **Señor Frog's** (© **987/869-1650**). Punta Langosta is just south of Calle 7 Sur. The **Hard Rock Cafe** (© **987/872-5271**) is also on Avenida Rafael Melgar, at #2, just north of the municipal pier.

In town, there are a few Latin music clubs. These open and close with every high season. They do well when people have cash in their pockets, but then they have to close down when the flow of tourism stops bringing in money. There's a sports bar at the corner of Avenida 5 and Calle 2 Norte called **All Sports Bar** (© **987/869-2246**), which operates as a salsa club Thursday to Saturday from 10pm to 3am. So go for sports, stay for salsa. Also, there's a working-class nightclub on Avenida Juárez, between avenidas 25 and 30, called **Los Delfines** (no phone), which puts on drag shows from Thursday to Sunday. These start around 11pm.

On Sunday evenings, the place to be is the main square, which usually has a free concert and lots of people strolling about and visiting with friends.

The town of San Miguel has three **movie theaters.** Your best option is **Cinépolis,** the modern multicinema in the Chedraui Plaza Shopping Center at the south end of town. It mainly shows Hollywood movies. Most of these are in English with Spanish subtitles *(película subtitulada);* before buying your tickets, make sure the movie hasn't been dubbed *(doblada).*

The Caribbean Coast: The Riviera Maya

by David Baird

I could go on and on about how the Riviera Maya has "endless stretches of pristine beaches of soft white sand gently caressed by the turquoise-blue waters of the Caribbean," yadda, yadda, yadda . . . but my bet is that you've already heard it. You've seen the ads, the brochures, and the articles in the Sunday travel section. So I'll spare you the purple prose and go right to the things you'll need to know.

The Yucatán's Caribbean coast is 380km (236 miles) long, stretching from Cancún all the way to Chetumal, at the border with Belize. The northern half of the coast has been dubbed the Riviera Maya; the southern half, the Costa Maya. In between is the large Sian Ka'an Biosphere Reserve.

A long reef system, the second-longest in the world, protects most of the shore. Where there are gaps in the reef—Playa del Carmen, Xpu-Ha, and Tulum—you find good beaches. The action of the surf washes away silt and sea grass and erodes rocks, leaving a sandy bottom. Where the reef is prominent, you get good snorkeling and diving with lots of fish and other sea creatures. Here mangrove often occupies the shoreline; the beaches are usually sandy up to the water's edge, but shallow, with a silty or rocky floor.

Inland you'll find jungle, caverns, the famous cenotes (natural wells leading to underwater rivers), and the even more famous ruins of the Maya. Activities abound.

So do lodging options. On this coast, you can stay in a variety of communities or distance yourself from all of them. There's just about every choice you can think of: rustic cabins, secluded spa resorts, boutique hotels, B&Bs, all-inclusive megaresorts, whatever you want. With so many options, you need to make some decisions. I hope what follows will help.

EXPLORING MEXICO'S CARIBBEAN COAST

A single road, Hwy. 307, runs down the coast from Cancún to Chetumal. The section between Cancún's airport and Playa del Carmen (51km/32 miles) is a four-lane divided highway with speed limits up to 110kmph (68 mph). There are a couple of traffic lights and several reduced-speed zones around the major turnoffs. From Playa to Tulum (80km/50 miles), the road has recently been widened to four lanes. It still takes about 1¹/₂ hours to drive from the Cancún airport to Tulum.

From Tulum, the highway turns inland to skirt the edges of Sian Ka'an. The roadway is two lanes, without shoulders, and in some areas the forest crowds in on both sides. The speed limit is mostly 80kmph (50 mph), but you'll need to slow down where the road passes through villages, and keep an eye out for *topes* (speed bumps). After the town of Limones, new road construction has widened and smoothed the highway. To drive from Tulum to Chetumal takes 3 hours.

PUERTO MORELOS   This town between Cancún and Playa remains a little village affectionately known by the locals as Muerto Morelos (*muerto* means "dead"), for its phenomenally quiet low season. It has a few small hotels and rental houses, and nearby are a few secluded spa resorts. The coast is sandy and well protected by an offshore reef, which means good snorkeling and diving nearby, but the lack of surf means sea grass and shallow water. If you're looking for good swimming, head farther down the coast. If you're looking for a relaxing seaside retreat with a clean beach in an easy-going community, this will work for you.

PLAYA DEL CARMEN   Playa, as it is called, is the most happening place on the coast—a delightful beach (especially when the wind and currents are flowing in the right direction), hotels for every budget, a good choice of restaurants, and an active nightlife, most of which is on or around Quinta Avenida (Fifth Avenue), Playa's well-known promenade. In the last few years, the town has grown quickly, and local residents and the tourism board are working to keep it from becoming a smaller version of Cancún.

PUERTO AVENTURAS   The first major town south of Playa is a modern condomarina development with a 9-hole golf course, several restaurants, and a few hotels. I don't think it's a fun place to stay, but you might come here to go deep-sea fishing or swim with dolphins.

AKUMAL   A bit farther south are Akumal and Half Moon Bay. The community is relatively old for this shore, which means that it's already built up and doesn't have the boomtown feel of Playa and Tulum. Akumal has a strong ecological orientation and is a prominent scuba and snorkeling center. The locals are a mix of Americans and Mexicans who enjoy the unhurried lifestyle of the tropics, making this a good place to relax and work on your hammock technique. There are a few hotels; most of the lodging is rental houses and condos. Consequently, the town is a favorite with families who enjoy the calmness of the place and can save money by buying groceries and cooking for themselves.

TULUM   The town of Tulum (near the ruins of the same name) has a hotel district of about 30 *palapa* (palm-leaf roofed) hotels, which stretch down the coast of the Punta Allen peninsula. A few years ago, it was mainly a destination for backpacker types, but with some of the most beautiful beaches on this coast and many improvements in hotel amenities, it now attracts people with big budgets. Here you can enjoy the beach in relative solitude and quiet (unless your hotel is busy building additional rooms). The downside of this is that Tulum doesn't have the variety of restaurants that Playa and Cancún do, but you can still eat well.

COSTA MAYA   South of Tulum lies the large Sian Ka'an Biosphere Reserve and, beyond that, what is known as the Costa Maya, which designates the rest of the coast all the way down to Belize. The Costa Maya is a relaxing getaway. Most of the coast is along the Majahual Peninsula, which has a lot of sandy beaches with silt bottoms. It's attractive to scuba divers, snorkelers, fly fishermen, and people who want to get away from the crowds. Farther south is Lake Bacalar, a large, clear freshwater lake. Inland from here are the impressive Maya ruins of the Río Bec area.

THINGS TO DO ALONG THE RIVIERA MAYA

If you need a break from lounging on the beach, you can find plenty of activities up and down this coast. The following is a brief list to help you consider your options.

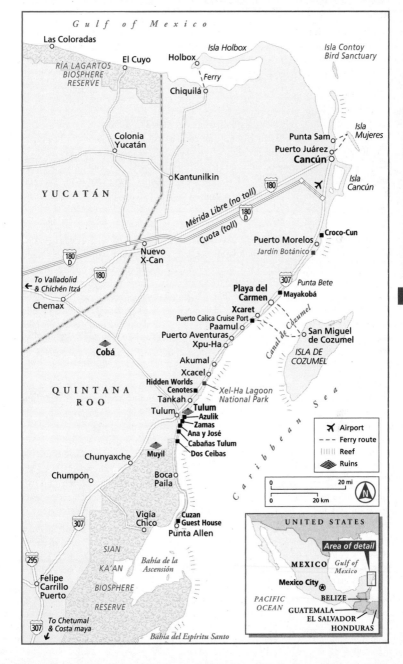

THE CARIBBEAN COAST: THE RIVIERA MAYA

DAY SPA To relax after all that exertion, try **Spa Itzá.** It's in downtown Playa between calles 12 and 14 in a retail area called Calle Corazón. The phone number is ✆ **984/803-2588.**

DEEP-SEA FISHING The largest marina on the coast is at **Puerto Aventuras,** not far south of Playa. Here's where you'll find most of your options for boating and fishing. See p. 165.

FLY FISHING The **Boca Paila Fishing Lodge** (www.bocapaila.com) specializes in fly-fishing, with weeklong all-inclusive fishing packages. It is in Sian Ka'an, between Tulum and Punta Allen.

GOLF & TENNIS The Playacar Golf Club (✆ **984/873-4990;** www.palace-resorts. com/playacar-golf-club) has an 18-hole **golf course** designed by Robert von Hagge. It's run by the Palace Resorts hotel chain, which offers golf packages. Greens fees are $180 in the morning (including tax and cart) and $120 after 2pm; club rental costs $30. The club also has two **tennis** courts, which cost $10 per hour. If you stay at the Fairmont Mayakoba hotel, you'll have access to a course designed by Greg Norman, which hosts a PGA tour event. See Mayakobá, below, in the section "South of Puerto Morelos."

HORSEBACK RIDING A few places along the highway offer horseback rides. The best of these, **Rancho Punta Venado,** is just south of Playa, past the Calica Pier. This ranch is less touristy than the others, and the owner takes good care of his horses. It has a nice stretch of coast with a sheltered bay and offers kayaking and snorkeling outings. It's best to make arrangements in advance and tell them you're a Frommer's reader so that they can schedule you on a day when they have fewer customers. E-mail (ptavenado@yahoo. com) is the best way to reach them; sometimes they don't answer their office number ✆ **984/803-5224.** Another option is to call the ranch's cellphone from Mexico (✆ **044-984/116-3213**); there is a charge for the call. Talk to Gabriela or Francisco; both speak English. Or try dropping by. The turnoff for the ranch is 2km (1¼ miles) south of the Calica overpass near Km 279.

MAYA RUINS Four cities are within easy reach of Playa and most of the coast. The easiest to access is **Tulum** (see "Tulum, Punta Allen & Sian Ka'an," below). A half-hour inland from Tulum on a pock-marked road is **Cobá** (see "Cobá" below), rising up from a jungle setting. This city has not been reconstructed to the same degree as the other three and doesn't have the rich imagery or clearly delineated architecture. The other two cites, **Chichén Itzá** and **Ek Balam,** are 2½ hours distant in the interior of the peninsula. My favorite way to see them is to rent a car and drive to Chichén in the afternoon, check into a hotel (perhaps one with a pool), see the sound-and-light show that evening, and then tour the ruins in the cool of the morning before the big bus tours arrive. Then drive back via Valladolid and Ek Balam. See chapter 8 for a description of these places.

SCUBA & SNORKELING There are dive shops up and down this coast. In Playa, **Tank-Ha Dive Center** (✆ **984/873-0302;** www.tankha.com) arranges reef and cavern diving. Snorkeling trips cost around $40 per person. Two-tank dive trips are $70; resort courses with SSI and PADI instructors cost $110. The area around Akumal has a number of underwater caverns and cenotes that are popular scuba and snorkeling destinations. The **Akumal Dive Shop** specializes in cavern diving and offers a variety of dives. But the easiest way to try cavern diving or snorkeling is through **Hidden Worlds Cenotes,** which is right on the highway, 15km (9¼ miles) south of Akumal. They provide everything, including wet suit. See "South of Playa del Carmen," later in this chapter.

SWIMMING WITH DOLPHINS   In the two nature parks south of Playa, Xcaret and Xel-Ha, you can interact with these intelligent creatures. Also, there's an outfit in Puerto Aventuras called **Dolphin Discovery** that is quite good. See "South of Playa del Carmen," later in this chapter, and "Xcaret: A Park Celebrating the Yucatán" p. 164.

TOURS   Tours to all of the ruins mentioned below run from Playa and the rest of the coast. The tour buses usually stop at a few places along the way for refreshments and souvenirs, which is why I prefer the small tours. Some combine the ruins of Tulum with a visit to a nature park. A tour agency in Playa called **Alltournative** (© 800/507-1902 in the U.S. and Canada, or 984/803-9999; www.alltournative.com) offers small tours that combine a little of everything: culture (visiting a contemporary Maya village), adventure (kayaking, rappelling, snorkeling, cenote diving), natural history, and ruins. It offers these tours daily using vans for transportation. The tours are fun. You can call the agency directly or arrange a tour through your hotel; they pick up at most of the large resorts along the coast. There is a smaller tour service called **Edventure Tours** (© 984/871-2209 or 875-4151; www.edventuretours.com.mx), based in Tulum, that does something similar but concentrates on snorkeling in cenotes and in the ocean, along the shore between Akumal and Tulum. It's a family business run by Eduardo and Bonnie Romano. They offer personal service and have a basic tour program. Group sizes usually run between 6 and 10 people. The best way to get in touch is through their web page. They also have a shop, which is in the row of shops outside the entrance to the Tulum ruins.

Selvática (© 866/552-8825 in the U.S., or 998/898-4312; www.selvatica.com.mx), operating out of offices in Cancún, offers guests a little adventure tourism in the jungle, with 2.5km (1 1/2 miles) of zip lines strung up in the forest canopy. The tour also includes biking and swimming in cenotes. In high season, you should make your reservation a month before your trip. The cost ($80–$90) includes transportation, activities, a light lunch, locker, and all equipment. Another interesting option is an ecological tour of the **Sian Ka'an Biosphere Reserve.** To do this, however, you have to get to Tulum. See the Tulum section, later in this chapter.

XCARET & XEL-HA NATURE PARKS These parks make full-day excursions, offering opportunities for swimming, snorkeling, and other seaside activities, and educational tours about the region's natural history and local Maya culture and entertainment. They are completely self-contained and offer food, drink, watersports equipment, and various kinds of merchandise. Xcaret is just south of Playa, while Xel-Ha is farther south, almost to Tulum. (See section 3, later in this chapter.)

> **Biodegradable Sunscreen**
>
> Don't forget to bring your biodegradable sunscreen to Xcaret, Xel-Ha, and any cenotes.
>
> For more information on biodegradable sunscreen, see p. 65.

1 PUERTO MORELOS & VICINITY

BETWEEN CANCUN & PLAYA DEL CARMEN

The coast directly south of the Cancún airport has several roadside attractions, all-inclusive hotels, small cabaña hotels, and some spa resorts. Much of the latest development is targeting the well-heeled traveler—small luxury hotels with or without a marina and with or without a golf course. This stretch of coast between the airport and Playa del Carmen is only 51km (32 miles) long. Midway is Puerto Morelos.

ROADSIDE ATTRACTIONS Near the Puerto Morelos turnoff is **Rancho Loma Bonita,** which has all the markings of a tourist trap and offers horseback riding and ATV tours. For this sort of activity, I prefer Rancho Punta Venado, just south of Playa (see "Things to Do Along the Riviera Maya" earlier in this chapter). You'll also come across **Jardín Botánico Dr. Alfredo Barrera** (no phone). Opened in 1990 and named after a biologist who studied tropical forests, the botanical garden is open Monday to Saturday from 9am to 5pm. Admission is 70 pesos. This place is disappointing because it's not maintained well. It will be of most interest to gardeners and plant enthusiasts, but it will probably bore children. But occasionally monkeys are spotted there, and it's good place to spot birds. Kids are much more likely to enjoy the interactive zoo, **CrocoCun** (© **998/ 850-3719;** www.crococunzoo.com), a zoological park a mile north of Puerto Morelos. It raises crocodiles from eggs and keeps several species of animals native to the Yucatán Peninsula. A visit to the reptile house is fascinating, though it may make you wary of venturing into the jungle. The rattlesnakes and boa constrictors are particularly intimidating, and the tarantulas are downright enormous. The guided tour lasts $1^{1}/_{2}$ hours. The guides have great enthusiasm, and the spider monkeys and wild pigs draw special attention from the kids. Wear plenty of bug repellent. The on-site restaurant, CrocoCun, is open daily from 8:30am to 5:30pm. Entrance fees are high, as are most of the roadside attractions on this coast: $20 adults, $12 children 6 to 12, free for children younger than 6.

SPA RESORTS ★★★ In the area around Puerto Morelos, four spa resorts provide variations on the hedonistic resort experience. Only 20 to 30 minutes from the Cancún airport, they are well situated for a quick weekend escape from the daily grind. You can jet down to Cancún, get whisked away by the hotel car, and be on the beach with a cocktail in hand before you can figure out whether you crossed a time zone. All four resorts pride themselves on their service, amenities, and spa and salon treatments. Being in the Yucatán, they add the healing practices of the Maya, especially the use of *temazcal,* the native steam bath. Rates quoted below include taxes but not the 5% to 10% service charge.

Ceiba del Mar This resort consists of seven three-story buildings set on a landscape of ponds and pools. Rooms are large, with a terrace or balcony. Bathrooms are large, with a shower and tub and stone counters. Service is attentive and unobtrusive—exemplified by the morning coffee and juice delivery, accomplished without disturbing the guests through the use of a blind pass-through. The spa area is ample, quite attractive, and well designed.

Av. Niños Héroes s/n, 77580 Puerto Morelos, Q. Roo. © **877/545-6221** in the U.S., or 998/872-8060. Fax 998/872-8061. www.ceibadelmar.com. 88 units. High season $380–$428 deluxe and junior suite, from $606 suite; low season $320–$360 deluxe and junior suite, from $550 suite. Rates include continental breakfast. Spa packages available. AE, MC, V. Free parking. **Amenities:** 2 restaurants; 2 bars; babysitting; bikes; concierge; complete state-of-the-art gym w/sauna, steam room, whirlpool, and Swiss showers; 2 outdoor pools (1 heated); room service; smoke-free rooms; spa offering a wide variety of treatments; dive shop w/watersports equipment. *In room:* A/C, TV/VCR, CD player, hair dryer, minibar, Wi-Fi.

Maroma ★ This resort has been around the longest, owns a large parcel of land inland that it protects from development, and has a gorgeous beach and beautifully manicured grounds. Two- and three-story buildings house the large guest rooms; most have king-size beds. The grounds are lovely, and the beach is fine white sand. The hotel has also spent a lot of effort and money on upgrades to the rooms. Nine new suites are outrageous examples of extravagance. There is a new beach bar that makes for an enjoyable place to pass the evening hours; it's a little more glitzy than the old one, but still comfy. As at Tides Riviera Maya (see below), but to a lesser degree, the smaller size makes for more personal service and a deeper sense of escape.

Carretera 307 Km 51, 77710 Q. Roo. ℭ **866/454-9351** in the U.S., or 998/872-8200. Fax 998/872-8220. www.maromahotel.com. 65 units. $610 garden-view double; $997 ocean view; from $1,366 suite. Rates include ground transfer, full breakfast, and snorkeling tour. AE, MC, V. Free valet parking. No children 15 and under. **Amenities:** Restaurant; 3 bars; concierge; fitness center; Jacuzzi; 3 outdoor spring-fed pools; room service; spa; steam bath; watersports equipment rental. *In room:* A/C, hair dryer.

Zoetry Paraíso de la Bonita   This resort has the most elaborate spa of all. I'm not a spa-goer and cannot discuss the relative merits of different treatments, but my work takes me to plenty of spas, and this one, which operates under the French system of thalassotherapy, is beyond anything I've seen. It uses seawater, sea salts, and sea algae in its treatments. The pool and common areas of the spa are uncommonly attractive. The rooms occupy some unremarkable three-story buildings. They are, in decor and furnishings, more impressive than the rooms of the three other resorts reviewed in this section. The ground-floor rooms have a plunge pool; upstairs rooms come with a balcony.

Carretera Cancún–Chetumal Km 328, Bahía Petempich, 77710 Q. Roo. ℭ **866/751-9175** in the U.S., or 998/872-8300. Fax 998/872-8301. www.paraisodelabonita.com. 90 units. High season from $1,000 suite; low season from $800 suite. Rates include ground transfer. AE, MC, V. Free valet parking. No children 11 and under. **Amenities:** 2 restaurants; 2 bars; concierge; 2 Jacuzzis; 4 outdoor pools; room service; smoke-free rooms; spa; lighted tennis court; watersports equipment rental. *In room:* A/C, TV/DVD, hair dryer, minibar.

The Tides Riviera Maya (formerly Ikal del Mar)   The smallest of the four resorts in this section, this property is all about privacy and tranquillity. Thirty well-separated bungalows—each with its own piece of jungle, a little pool, and an outdoor shower—are connected by lit pathways through the vegetation. The bungalows are large, filled with amenities, and decorated in a modern, spare style. The bathrooms have only a shower. Service here is the most personal of the four—you never have to leave your bungalow. The bar and restaurant, overlooking an inviting pool, make for an attractive common area. And, of course, there's the spa.

Playa Xcalacoco, Carretera Cancún–Tulum, 77710 Q. Roo. ℭ **800/578-0281** in the U.S. and Canada, or 984/877-3000. Fax 713/528-3697. www.tidesrivieramaya.com. 30 units. High season from $784 villa; low season from $655 villa. Rates include full breakfast. AE, MC, V. Free secure parking. No children 17 and under. **Amenities:** Restaurant; 2 bars; courtesy shuttle to Playa; concierge; 2 Jacuzzis; large outdoor pool; room service; spa; steam bath; watersports equipment. *In room:* A/C, TV/DVD, fridge, hair dryer.

PUERTO MORELOS

Puerto Morelos remains a quiet place—perfect for lying on the white-sand beach and reading, with the occasional foray into watersports, especially snorkeling, diving, kite-surfing, windsurfing, and kayaking. A prominent reef offshore was declared a national park for its protection. It's shallow and easy to snorkel, and it protects the coast from storm surges. The beaches are great, maintained by the local government. The water is shallow, calm, and clear, with sea grass growing on the bottom. The town is small, and the inhabitants are laid-back. There is a large English-language bookstore that sells new and used titles. The car ferry that used to depart from here for Cozumel has moved down the coast to the Calica pier just south of Playa del Carmen.

GETTING THERE **By Car** At Km 31, there's a traffic light at the intersection and a large sign pointing to Puerto Morelos.

By Bus Buses from Cancún to Tulum and Playa del Carmen usually stop here, but be sure to ask in Cancún if your bus makes the Puerto Morelos stop.

Exploring in & Around Puerto Morelos

Puerto Morelos attracts visitors who seek seaside relaxation without crowds and high prices. The town has a few hotels and a few restaurants. For outdoor recreation, there are two dive shops and plenty of recreational boats for fishing or snorkeling. Try **Dive In Puerto Morelos** (www.diveinpuertomorelos.com), at Av. Rojo Gómez 14. On the main square, **Alma Libre** (© 998/871-0713; www.almalibrebooks.com) sells more English-language books than any other bookstore in the Yucatán. The owners, a couple of Canadians named Joanne and Rob Birce, stock everything from volumes on Maya culture to English classics, to maps of the region. The store is open October through the first week in June, Tuesday to Sunday from 10am to 3pm and 6 to 9pm.

The reef directly offshore is very shallow and protected by law. Snorkelers are required to wear life vests to prevent them from diving down to the reef. I'm unaccustomed to snorkeling in a vest and found it bothersome, but it didn't prevent me from getting a close look at the reef, which is quite shallow—3m ($9^3/_4$ ft.) at its deepest, rising to within a foot of the surface. In a short time, I spotted four different eels and sea snakes, lots of fish, and a ray. **Cancún Mermaid** (p. 108; © 998/843-6517; www.cancunmermaid. com) is the preferred snorkeling outfitter in town.

On Wednesday and Friday, anyone in Puerto Morelos can get a good massage or a spa treatment at the **Jungle Spa** (© 998/208-9148). This is a cooperative endeavor by Maya women in the area who have been trained in spa techniques. The spa is located a short distance on the other side of the highway (in the jungle). The rates are a lot less expensive than at the spa hotels in the area, and your money goes directly to support some of the local people. There is also a Sunday Jungle Market where you can buy handcrafts.

Where to Stay

For condo rentals, check out the website of Alma Libre books (see above).

Amar Inn Simple rooms on the beach, in a home-style setting, make this small inn a good place for those wanting a quiet seaside retreat. The hostess, Ana Luisa Aguilar, is the daughter of Luis Aguilar, a Mexican singer and movie star of the 1940s and 1950s. She keeps busy promoting environmental and equitable-development causes. She can line up snorkeling and fishing trips and jungle tours for guests with local operators. There are three cabañas in back, opposite the main house, and six upstairs rooms with views of the beach. The most expensive rooms are the third-story "penthouse" rooms with a view of the ocean. The cabañas get less of a cross-breeze than the rooms in the main house. Bedding choices include one or two doubles, one king-size, or five twin beds. A full Mexican breakfast is served in the garden.

Av. Javier Rojo Gómez (at Lázaro Cárdenas), 77580 Puerto Morelos, Q. Roo. © 998/871-0026. amar_inn@ hotmail.com. 10 units. High season 550–850 pesos double; low season 400–750 pesos double. Rates include full breakfast. No credit cards. Limited free parking. *In room:* Fan, fridge, no phone.

Posada El Moro This hotel offers nicer rooms for about the same amount of money as Amar Inn, but it's not on the water. All but the least expensive rooms come with air-conditioning. Suites come with kitchenettes. The hotel is just off the square, on the town's principal street.

Av. Rojo Gómez SM2, M 5, Lote 17, 77580 Puerto Morelos, Q. Roo. (©) **998/871-0159**. www.posadael moro.com. 31 units. High season $60–$80 double, $90 suite; low season $50–$70 double, $80 suite. Rates include continental breakfast. MC, V. Limited free parking. **Amenities:** Small outdoor pool. *In room:* A/C (in some), TV (in some), no phone.

Where to Dine

Most of Puerto Morelos's restaurants are on or around the main square. These include **Los Pelícanos** for seafood, **Bodo's** (just south of the square on Rojo Gómez, the main road) for good lunch specials and a few German dishes, **David Lau's** for Asian food, **El Pirata** if you have kids (for its large menu), and **Le Café d'Amancia** for coffee and pastries. The most expensive is **John Gray's,** a couple blocks north of the plaza and 3 blocks inland. It's open for dinner except on Sunday. The owner is a former chef for the Ritz-Carlton. **La Suegra** (owned and operated by a Mexican woman who happens to be John Gray's mother-in-law) is a new casual restaurant, just north of the square on the beach, near the lighthouse. It serves well-prepared typical beach food, including things like burgers, and has a full bar.

SOUTH OF PUERTO MORELOS

Petit Lafitte Hotel ★★   One kilometer (a half-mile) south of the original Posada Lafitte, this new property has the same easy-going attitude that characterized the old property. In relative isolation, you still get all the amenities of a relaxing vacation. The three-story building has 30 rooms. Surrounding it are 13 bungalows. Rooms are spacious and attractive. They are larger than the rooms at the original hotel, but like those others, they have the simplicity of an attractive beach hotel. The staff is the same from the old property, so service is still personal and attentive.

Carretera Cancún–Tulum Km 63 (Xcalacoco), 77710 Playa del Carmen, Q. Roo. (©) **800/538-6802** in the U.S. and Canada, or 934/803-4371. www.petitlafitte.com. 43 units. High season $250–$275 double, $270–$350 bungalow; low season $180–$200 double, $200–$270 bungalow. Minimum 2–4 nights. Rates include breakfast and dinner. MC, V. Free guarded parking. **Amenities:** Restaurant; bar; outdoor pool. *In room:* A/C (in some), TV, minibar, Wi-Fi.

MAYAKOBA RESIDENTIAL GOLF & SPA RESORT

Basically, **Mayakobá** (www.mayakoba.com) is a large upscale residential resort community with a 400-room **Fairmont** hotel attached ((©) **800/540-6088** in the U.S. and Canada, or 984/206-3000; www.fairmont.com/mayakoba). It's built around a golf course designed by Greg Norman and some serious landscaping, which has created a network of freshwater canals and lagoons, bordered by natural areas of mangrove and jungle.

Mayakobá shares the same concept as other developments, such as Playacar, just to the south of Playa del Carmen, but it's unmatched by anything else on this coast. Aside from the Fairmont, there are three other resorts taking part in building this community: Rosewood (already opened), Banyan Tree (timeshares opening in 2009), and Viceroy (opening in 2010). The resorts are designed to be a connected endeavor—residents of one resort can sample the amenities of the other three, including restaurants and spas.

For the last couple of years, Mayakobá has been hosting the only PGA tour event in Mexico, usually scheduled for late February/early March. The resort attracts lots of golfers. If you're interested in golf and luxury (and beauty), you should consider this place. Standard rooms at the Fairmont run from $225 to $500 a night, depending on the season. People more focused on being on the beach should probably look elsewhere. The resort is about 10km (6¼ miles) north of Playa del Carmen.

Beach Cabañas

Five kilometers (3 miles) north of Playa are some economical lodgings on a mostly rocky beach. A sign that says PUNTA BETE marks the access road to Xcalacoco; in a short time, you reach the water. Before you do, the road forks off in a few places and you'll see signs for different cabañas. The word may conjure up visions of idyllic dwellings with thatched roofs, but on the Yucatecan coast, it usually means simple lodging. This is mostly the case here; rates run 700 to 800 pesos a night for two people. Of the four groupings of cabañas in Xcalacoco, the best is **Coco's Cabañas** (www.travel-center.com). It's a handful of rooms with electricity and ceiling fans, a good little budget restaurant, and a small pool. Two of the rooms have air-conditioning. Next door is the spa resort Tides Riviera Maya (see "Spa Resorts," above).

2 PLAYA DEL CARMEN ★★★

32km (20 miles) S of Puerto Morelos; 70km (43 miles) S of Cancún; 10km (6½ miles) N of Xcaret; 13km (8 miles) N of Puerto Calica

Though it no longer has the feel of a village, Playa still provides that rare combination of simplicity (at its core, still primarily a beach town) and variety (many unique hotels, restaurants, and stores). There is a comfortable feel to the town. The local architecture has adopted elements of native building—rustic clapboard walls, stucco, thatched roofs, rough-hewn wood, and a ramshackle, unplanned look to many structures. Cheap-looking commercial architecture has intruded, with chain restaurants and stores, detracting from Playa's individuality, but Playa still retains the feel of a cosmopolitan getaway with a counterculture ethos.

A strong European influence has made topless sunbathing (nominally against the law in Mexico) a nonchalantly accepted practice anywhere there's a beach. The beach grows and shrinks, from broad and sandy to narrower with rocks, depending on the currents and wind. When this happens, head to the beaches in north Playa.

From Playa, it's easy to shoot out to Cozumel on the ferry, drive south to the nature parks and the ruins at Tulum and Cobá, or drive north to Cancún. Directly south of town is the Playacar development, which has a golf course, several large all-inclusive resorts, and a residential development.

ESSENTIALS
Getting There & Departing
BY AIR You can fly into Cancún and take a bus directly from the airport (see "By Bus," below), or fly into Cozumel and take the passenger ferry.

BY CAR Hwy. 307 is the only highway that passes through Playa. As you approach Playa from Cancún, the highway divides. Keep to the inside lanes to permit turning left at any of the traffic lights. The two main arteries into Playa are Avenida Constituyentes, which works well for destinations in northern Playa, and Avenida Juárez, which leads to the town's main square. If you stay in the outside lanes, you will need to continue past Playa until you get to the turnaround, then double- back, staying to your right.

ACCOMMODATIONS ■
Acanto Hotel and Suites **1**
Deseo Hotel + Lounge **3**
Jardín de Marieta **8**
Los Itzaes **7**
Hotel Lab Nah **10**
Hotel Lunata **6**
Playa Maya **11**

DINING ◆
Casa Mediterranea **9**
Los Carboncitos **12**
La Casa del Agua **13**
La Parrilla **5**
Media Luna **2**
La Tarraya Restaurant/Bar **14**
Yaxché **4**

New Bus Station ■

Calle 14
Calle 12
Calle 10
Calle 8
Calle 6
Calle 4
Calle 2
Calle 1

Av. 20
Av. 15
Av. 10
Av. 25
5A Av.
1st N.

Caribbean Sea

Post office ✉
Pedestrians Only
← To Highway 307
Avenida Juárez
Riviera Bus Station ■
Plaza

0   200 yds
0   200 m

Gulf of Mexico
Playa del Carmen
Mérida
YUCATÁN
○ Cancún
Cozumel
YUCATÁN PENINSULA
QUINTANA ROO
CAMPECHE
Caribbean Sea
✈ Airport

Ferry Pier to Cozumel (Muelle)

BY FERRY Air-conditioned passenger ferries to Cozumel leave from the town's pier 1 block from the main square. There is also a car ferry to Cozumel from the Calica pier just south of the Playacar development. The schedule for the passenger ferries has been in flux. Lately, ferries have been departing every hour in the mornings and every 2 hours in the afternoons. For more information about both ferries, see "Getting There & Departing" in the Cozumel section of chapter 6.

BY TAXI Taxi fares from the Cancún airport are about 650 to 750 pesos one-way.

BY BUS **Autobuses Riviera** offers service from the Cancún airport about 12 times a day. Cost is 80 pesos one-way. You'll see a ticket counter in the corridor leading out of the airport. From the Cancún bus station, there are frequent departures—almost every 30 minutes.

Orientation
ARRIVING Playa has two **bus** stations. Buses coming from Cancún and places along the coast, such as Tulum, arrive at the Riviera bus station, at the corner of Juárez and Quinta Avenida, by the town square. Buses coming from destinations in the interior of the peninsula arrive at the new ADO station, on Avenida 20 between calles 12 and 14.

A word of caution: Approach any timeshare salesperson as you would a wounded rhino. And remember that whatever free trinket is offered for simply viewing apartments, it either won't materialize or won't be worth the time you invest in your dealings with these people. You have been warned.

CITY LAYOUT   The main street, **Avenida Juárez,** leads to the town square from Hwy. 307. As it does so, it crosses several numbered avenues that run parallel to the beach, all of which are multiples of 5. **Quinta Avenida (Fifth Avenue)** is closest to the beach; it's closed to traffic from the *zócalo* to Calle 6 (and some blocks beyond, in the evening). On this avenue are many hotels, restaurants, and shops. Almost the entire town is north and west of the square. To the south is "Playacar," a golf-course development of private residences and a dozen resort hotels.

(Fast Facts   Playa del Carmen

Area Code The telephone area code is **984.**

Currency Exchange Playa has several banks and ATMs. Many currency-exchange houses are close to the pier or along Quinta Avenida at Calle 8.

Doctor For serious medical attention, go to **Hospitén** in Cancún (© **998/881-3700**). In Playa, **Dr. G. Ambriz** speaks English and was trained in the U.S. and Europe. His office is at the corner of Avenida 30 and Calle 14 (© **984/109-1245**).

Drugstore The **Farmacía del Carmen,** Avenida Juárez between avenidas 5 and 10 (© **984/873-2330**), is open 24 hours.

Internet Access Internet cafes are all over town; most have fast connections.

Parking Most parking in Playa is on the street. Spots can be hard to come by. The most accessible parking lot is the Estacionamiento México, at avenidas Juárez and 10 (where the entrance is located). It's open daily 24 hours and charges 15 pesos per hour, 100 pesos per day. There's also a 24-hour lot a block from the pier, where you can leave your car while you visit Cozumel.

Post Office The *correo,* on Avenida Juárez, 3 blocks from the plaza, is on the right past the Hotel Playa del Carmen and the launderette.

Seasons The main high season is from mid-December to Easter. There is a mini high season in August. Low season is all other months.

WHERE TO STAY

Playa has a lot of small hotels with affordable prices that give you a better feel for the town than staying in one of the resorts in Playacar. Don't hesitate to book a place that's not on the beach. Town life here is much of the fun, and staying on the beach in Playa has its disadvantages—in particular, the noise from a couple of beach bars. Beaches are public property in Mexico, and you can lay out your towel anywhere you like. There are some beach clubs in north Playa where, for a small sum, you can have the use of lounge chairs, towels, and food and drink.

> **Tips** **Driving the Riviera Maya**
>
> Driving along this coast isn't difficult. There's only one highway, so you can't get lost. Speed limits are clearly posted, but lots of cars ignore them, *except around Playa,* where police are known to ticket drivers. Watch your speed when you're passing through town. Maximum speed for the center lanes is 60kmph (37 mph); for the outside lanes, it's 40kmph (25 mph).
>
> South of Playa, the highway is four lanes as far as Tulum. You're not allowed to stop on the highway to make a left turn. You're supposed to pull over to the right and wait for traffic in both directions to clear before crossing the road. There are several more gas stations in the Riviera Maya now, so you shouldn't have a problem getting gas. But make sure the attendant gives you back the right amount of money—I've had people try to short-change me.

High season is mid-December to Easter. August is also high season for some hotels but not others. At other times of the year, you can come to Playa and score walk-in offers. The rates listed below include the 12% hotel tax. I don't include the rates for Christmas to New Year's, which are still higher than the standard high-season rates.

Expensive

Acanto Hotel & Suites ★★ (Finds) In my view, this property is (dare I say it) the most romantic in Playa. There is intimacy and flair and even a sense of isolation. Seven stylish suites endowed with color and texture encircle a pool and softly lit courtyard. Figures of Buddha and Asian decoration add an exotic feel and draw a division between this small enclave and the world outside the hotel's door. The suites come with kitchens so you can, should you choose, limit your comings and goings. The rooms are large and comfortable and come with a queen bed and small sitting area. The location is great, just around the corner from Quinta Avenida, on a secluded street. The owner is building more units next door.

Calle 16 Bis (btw. avs. 5th and 1st), 77710 Playa del Carmen, Q. Roo. ✆ **631/882-1986** in the U.S., or 984/873-1252. www.acantohotels.com. 7 units. $170–$297 suite. 3-night minimum stay for holidays. AE, MC, V. Street parking. **Amenities:** Small outdoor pool; smoke-free rooms. *In room:* A/C, TV, CD player, hair dryer, no phone.

Deseo Hotel + Lounge ★★★ This hotel is designed to foster social interaction. The lounge plays the central role, appropriating the functions of lobby, restaurant, bar, and pool area at once. It's a raised open-air platform with bar, pool, self-serve kitchen, and daybeds for sunning or sipping an evening drink when the bar is in full swing. The clientele is predominantly 25- to 45-year-olds. This hotel is one of the few in town that has weekday (lower) and weekend (higher) rates.

The guest rooms are comfortable, original, and striking but don't tempt one to stay indoors—no TV, no cushy armchair. Their simplicity gives them an almost Asian feel, heightened by nice touches such as sliding doors of wood and frosted glass. All rooms have king-size beds with deep mattresses. From the bottom of each bed, a little drawer slides out with a night kit containing incense, earplugs, and condoms.

And in case Deseo doesn't work for you, the owners have opened another archly styled hotel 2 blocks down called **Hotel Básico** (✆ **984/879-4448;** www.hotelbasico.com). It's a fun mix of industrial and '50s styles, built with materials that have found a lot of favor with architects these days: concrete, plywood, and plastics. Along with all this you get a cushy bed and a forceful shower. As with Deseo, the common areas are not wasted space.

Av. 5 (at Calle 12), 77710 Playa del Carmen, Q. Roo. ✆ **984/879-3620.** Fax 984/879-3621. www. hoteldeseo.com. 15 units. $199–$233 lounge view; $222–$255 balcony; $278–$311 suite. Rates include continental breakfast. AE, MC, V. No parking. No children 17 and under. **Amenities:** Bar; Jacuzzi; small rooftop pool; room service. *In room:* A/C, hair dryer (on request), minibar.

Shangri-La Caribe ★★★   This hotel—a loose grouping of cabañas on one of the best beaches in Playa—is hard to beat for sheer fun and leisure. And it's far enough from the center of town to be quiet. The older, south side of the hotel (the Caribe section) consists of one- and two-story cabañas. The north side (Playa section) has a few larger buildings, holding four to six rooms. A preference for one or the other section is a matter of taste; the units in both are similar in amenities, privacy, and price. All rooms have a patio or porch complete with hammock. Most come with two double beds, but a few have a king-size bed. Windows are screened, and ceiling fans circulate the breeze. All rooms come with air-conditioning. The real difference in price depends on the proximity to the water—oceanfront, ocean view, or garden view. Garden view is the best bargain, being only a few steps farther from the water; most of these are in the Pueblito section, which is a third section farthest from the water. On the property are two restaurants (breakfast and dinner are included in the rates).

In the last year, the hotel changed owners. The property was slated for condo development, but that project fell through, so it's still functioning as a *palapa* beach hotel. The name might change in 2009, but the phone numbers won't. The web page will change, but the management can't tell me yet what the new address will be. You might need to do a search.

Calle 38 (Apdo. Postal 253), 77710 Playa del Carmen, Q. Roo. ✆ **800/538-6802** in the U.S. and Canada, or 984/873-0611. Fax 984/873-0500. www.shangrilacaribe.net. 107 units. High season $240–$275 garden view, $295 ocean view, $345 oceanfront; low season $180–$220 garden view, $240–$290 ocean view, $300 oceanfront. Rates include breakfast and dinner. AE, MC, V. Free guarded parking. From Hwy. 307 from Cancún, U-turn at the light for Av. Constituyentes, making sure to get into the far-right lane. Backtrack to the Volkswagen dealership, turn right, and head for the beach. This will be Calle 38. **Amenities:** 2 restaurants; poolside grill; 3 bars; airport transfer; babysitting; 2 large pools; whirlpool; watersports equipment; dive shop. *In room:* Hair dryer, no phone.

Moderate

Hotel Lunata ★★   In the middle of Playa, there isn't a more comfortable or more attractive place to stay than this small hotel on Quinta Avenida. The rooms offer character, good looks, and polish. There are a few standard rooms, which are midsize and come with a queen-size or a double bed. Deluxe rooms are large and come with a king-size bed and small fridge. Junior suites come with two doubles. Bathrooms are well designed and have good showers. Light sleepers should opt for a room facing the garden. On my last stay, I took a room facing the street with double-glazed glass doors that opened to a balcony. I enjoyed looking out over Quinta Avenida and, with the doors shut, the noise was not bothersome.

Av. 5 (btw. calles 6 and 8), 77710 Playa del Carmen, Q. Roo. ✆ **984/873-0884.** Fax 984/873-1240. www. lunata.com. 10 units. High season $139 standard, $179–$189 deluxe and junior suite; low season $125 standard, $145–$165 deluxe and junior suite. Rates include continental breakfast. Promotional rates

available. AE, MC, V. Secure parking $5. No children 12 and under. **Amenities:** Free use of bike and water- **159**
sports equipment; smoke-free rooms. *In room:* A/C, TV, fridge (in some), hair dryer (on request), no
phone.

Los Itzaes ★   This small hotel in the middle of Playa accommodates business people,
making it something of a refuge from tourists. The rooms are attractive and comfortable,
with good air-conditioning and double-glazed windows. The mattresses are comfortable.
Rates include membership at one of the local beach clubs. Rooms with a king bed cost a
little less than rooms with two doubles. Junior suites have two doubles and a sofa bed.
There is no pool, but there is an enjoyable rooftop whirlpool tub.

Av. 10 btw. calles 6 and 8, 77710 Playa del Carmen, Q. Roo. ✆ **984/873-2397,** -2398. www.itzaes.com. 16
units. High season $145–$170 standard, $225 junior suite; low season $135–$157 standard, $202 junior
suite. Rates include continental breakfast and beach club membership. 5-night minimum stay during
holidays. AE, MC, V. Secure parking $13. Small pets accepted. **Amenities:** Restaurant; bar; airport transfer;
small outdoor Jacuzzi; smoke-free rooms. *In room:* A/C, TV, hair dryer, minibar, Wi-Fi.

Playa Maya ★ (Value)   Of the beach hotels in downtown Playa, this one would be my
first choice. There are a lot of reasons to like it (good location, good price, comfortable
rooms, and friendly and helpful management), but one thing that really strikes my fancy
is that you enter this hotel from the beach. This little, seemingly inconsequential detail
shouldn't be any reason for picking a hotel, but it just sets the mood and creates a little
separation from the busy street scene. What's more, the design and location make it a
quiet hotel; it's a couple of blocks from the nearest live-music venue and sheltered by the
neighboring hotels. The pool and sunning terrace are attractive and nicely set apart.
Rooms are large, with midsize bathrooms; a couple of them have private garden terraces
with Jacuzzis, while others have balconies that face the beach. High-season rates at Playa
Maya extend from Christmas through August.

Zona FMT (btw. calles 6 and 8 Norte), 77710 Playa del Carmen, Q. Roo. ✆ **984/803-2022.** www.playa-
maya.com. 20 units. High season $150–$207 double; low season $112–$180 double. Rates include continental breakfast. MC, V. Limited street parking. **Amenities:** Restaurant; bar; Jacuzzi; outdoor pool; room
service. *In room:* A/C, TV, fridge, hair dryer, Wi-Fi.

Inexpensive
Hotel Lab Nah (Value)   Good rooms in a central location for a good price are the main
attraction at this economy hotel in the heart of Playa. The cheapest rooms have windows
facing Quinta Avenida. There was some noise—mostly late-night bar hoppers. It didn't
bother me much. Nevertheless, I think it's worth the money to get one of the partial-
oceanview standards with balcony on the third floor because they are quieter and larger.
The garden-view rooms are directly below the ocean view, are just as large and quiet, but
are not quite as fixed up. And the difference in price is little. A rooftop *palapa* is the
largest room available, good for three or four people.

Calle 6 (and Av. 5), 77710 Playa del Carmen, Q. Roo. ✆ **984/873-2099.** www.labnah.com. 33 units. High
season 550–750 pesos double, 1,050 pesos rooftop *palapa;* low season 490–650 pesos double, 860 pesos
rooftop *palapa.* Rates include continental breakfast. MC, V. Limited street parking. **Amenities:** Small
outdoor pool. *In room:* A/C, hair dryers (in some), no phone.

Jardín de Marieta (Value) (Finds)   Besides the economical rates, I like this place for its
central, yet half-hidden location in a small interior property without any street frontage
on La Quinta. Rooms vary a good bit, but most are large, bright, and cheerful. And the
location is quiet. Four rooms have kitchenettes, which can work for some simple meals.

Most of the rooms encircle a tree-shaded patio with a few shops and a restaurant. The place has a pleasant, quirky feel.

Av. 5 Norte 173 (btw. calles 6 and 8), 77710 Playa del Carmen, Q. Roo. (✆ **984/873-0224.** www.jardinde marieta.com. 10 units. High season 600–1,000 pesos double; low season 500–900 pesos double. No credit cards. Limited street parking. **Amenities:** Restaurant. *In room:* A/C, TV, fridge, kitchenette (in 4 units), no phone, Wi-Fi.

WHERE TO DINE

Aside from the restaurants listed below, I would point you in the direction of a few that don't need a full review. For a delicious Veracruz-style breakfast in pleasant, breezy surroundings, try the upstairs terrace restaurant of the **Hotel Básico,** at Quinta Avenida and Calle 10 Norte. For fish tacos and inexpensive seafood, try **El Oasis,** on Calle 12, between avenidas 5 and 10 (no phone). For *arrachera* (fajita) tacos, the place to go is **Super Carnes H C de Monterrey** (✆ **984/803-0488**), on Calle 1 Sur between avenidas 20 and 25.

Expensive

La Casa del Agua ★★ EUROPEAN/MEXICAN   Excellent food in inviting surroundings. Instead of obtrusive background music, you hear the sound of falling water. The German owners work at presenting what they like best about the old and new worlds. They do a good job with seafood—try the grilled seafood for two. For a mild dish, try chicken in a scented sauce of fine herbs accompanied by fettuccine; for something heartier, there's the tortilla soup listed as "Mexican soup." The restaurant offers a number of cool and light dishes that would be appetizing for lunch or an afternoon meal, such as an avocado stuffed with shrimp and flavored with a subtle horseradish sauce on a bed of alfalfa sprouts and julienne carrots—a good mix of tastes and textures. For dessert, try the chocolate mousse. This is an upstairs restaurant under a large and airy *palapa* roof.

Av. 5 (at Calle 2). (✆ **984/803-0232.** Reservations recommended in high season. Main courses 165–280 pesos. MC, V. Daily 10am–midnight.

La Parrilla MEXICAN/GRILL   Still a fun place, but it's having problems handling its success. Prices have gone up, and service is slower. But the fajitas remain good, as do many of the Mexican standards, such as tortilla soup, enchiladas, and quesadillas. Mariachis show up around 8pm; plan accordingly.

Av. 5 (at Calle 8). (✆ **984/873-0687.** Reservations recommended in high season. Main courses 100–250 pesos. AE, MC, V. Daily noon–1am.

Yaxché ★★★ YUCATECAN   The menu here makes use of many native foods and spices, to present a more elaborate regional cooking than the usual offerings at Yucatecan restaurants—and it was about time for someone to show a little creativity with such an interesting palette of tastes. Excellent examples are a cream of *chaya* (a native leafy vegetable) and an *xcatic* chili stuffed with *cochinita pibil.* I also like the classic Mexican-style fruit salad with lime juice and dried powdered chili. There are several seafood dishes; the ones I had were fresh and well prepared.

Calle 8 (btw. avs. 5 and 10). (✆ **984/873-2502.** Reservations recommended in high season. Main courses 100–260 pesos. AE, MC, V. Daily noon–midnight.

Moderate

Casa Mediterránea ★★★ ITALIAN   Tucked away on a quiet little patio off Quinta Avenida, this small, homey restaurant serves excellent food. Maurizio Gabrielli and Mary

Michelon are usually there to greet customers and make recommendations. Maurizio came to Mexico to enjoy the simple life, and this inclination shows in the restaurant's welcoming, unhurried atmosphere. The menu is mostly northern Italian, with several dishes from other parts of Italy. There are daily specials, too. Pastas (except penne and spaghetti) are made in-house, and none are precooked. Try fish and shrimp ravioli or penne alla Veneta. The lobster is prepared beautifully. There are several wines, mostly Italian, to choose from. The salads are good and carefully prepared—dig in without hesitation.

Av. 5 (btw. calles 6 and 8; look for a sign for Hotel Marieta). ✆ **984/876-3926.** Reservations recommended in high season. Main courses 120–220 pesos. No credit cards. Wed–Mon 2–11pm.

El Asador de Manolo ★★ STEAKS/ARGENTINE   If I want a steak in Playa, this is where I go. (You might want to call ahead to make sure the restaurant is at its present location. For the last couple of years, there has been talk about a move to Calle 28.) The owner is an Argentine who has been living in Mexico so long, he's gone Mexican. But the food is faithful to his native land: steaks, good empanadas, and southern-style pastas, and you can't go wrong with any of the soups. When ordering a steak, see the appendix for the proper terminology. For dessert, there are crepes and flan.

Av. 10 (btw. calles 24 and 26). ✆ **984/803-0632.** Reservations recommended in high season. Main courses 70–220 pesos; steaks 200–400 pesos. MC, V. Mon–Fri 1–11pm; Sat–Sun 4pm–midnight.

La Cueva del Chango ★ HIPPIE MEXICAN   Good food in original surroundings with a relaxed "mañana" attitude. True to its name (The Monkey's Cave), the place suggests a cave and has little waterways meandering through it, and there are two spider monkeys that hang about in the back of the place. But take away the water and the monkeys, and, oddly enough, it brings to mind the Flintstones. You'll enjoy great juices, blended fruit drinks, salads, soups, Mexican specialties with a natural twist, and handmade tortillas. The fish is fresh and delicious. Mosquitoes can sometimes be a problem at night, but the management has bug spray for the guests.

Calle 38 (btw. Av. 5 and the beach). ✆ **984/116-3179.** Main courses 80–140 pesos. No credit cards. Mon–Sat 8am–11pm; Sun 8am–2pm.

La Vagabunda ITALIAN/MEXICAN   This place is old-style Playa in its simple charm. A large *palapa* shelters several simple wood tables sitting on a gravel floor. It's low key and quiet—a good place for breakfast, with many options, including delicious blended fruit drinks, waffles, and omelets. The specials are a good value. In the afternoon and evening, they serve light fare such as panini, pastas, and ceviche.

Av. 5 (btw. calles 24 and 26). ✆ **984/873-3753.** Breakfast 40–60 pesos; main courses 70–120 pesos. MC, V. High season daily 7am–11:30pm; low season daily 7am–3:30pm.

Media Luna ★★ FUSION   This restaurant has an inventive menu that favors grilled seafood, sautés, and pasta dishes. Everything is fresh and prepared beautifully. Try the very tasty pan-fried fish cakes with mango and honeyed hoisin sauce. Another choice is the black pepper–crusted fish. Be sure to eye the daily specials. For lunch, you can get sandwiches and salads, as well as black-bean quesadillas and crepes. The decor is primitive tropical chic.

Av. 5 (btw. calles 12 and 14). ✆ **984/873-0526.** Breakfast 40–60 pesos; sandwich with salad 50–70 pesos; main courses 80–150 pesos. No credit cards. Daily 8am–11:30pm.

Inexpensive

La Tarraya Restaurant/Bar (Value) SEAFOOD/YUCATECAN   THE RESTAURANT THAT WAS BORN WITH THE TOWN, proclaims the sign. It's right on the beach, where the

Choosing an All-Inclusive in the Riviera Maya

More than 40 all-inclusive resorts line this coast. Most people are familiar with the concept—large hotels that work with economies of scale to offer lodging, food, and drink all for a single low rate. All-inclusives offer convenience and economy, especially for families with many mouths to feed. Because they are enclosed areas, they make it easy for parents to watch their children.

A certain sameness pervades these hotels so that a lot can be said that applies to all. They're usually built around a large pool with activities and an activities organizer. There is often a quiet pool, too. One large buffet restaurant and a snack bar serve the needs of most guests, but there will be a couple of specialty restaurants at no extra charge but that require reservations. Colored bracelets serve to identify guests. In the evenings, a show is presented at the hotel's theater.

These resorts work best for those who are looking for a relaxing beach vacation and to get away from the cold weather. They don't work for those who aim to get away from crowds—these hotels are large and operate with a high occupancy rate. Yes, staying at these all-inclusives is convenient and hassle-free. They make everything easy, including taking tours and day trips—all the organizing is done for you. On the downside, you don't often get the spontaneity or the sense of adventure that comes with other styles of travel. The question you have to ask yourself is "What kind of vacation am I looking for?"

The best way to get a room at an all-inclusive is through a vacation packager or one of its travel agents. You get a better deal than by contacting the hotel directly. Even if you have frequent-flier miles to burn, you will still find it difficult to match the rates of a full package offered by one of the biggies like Funjet.

Of the many all-inclusives in the Riviera Maya, there are a few that are my favorites and might bear looking into.

Of the several all-inclusives that are in Playa del Carmen/Playacar, I like **Iberostar Quetzal** or **Tucán** (two names for different halves of the same hotel; www. iberostar.com). The food is better than at most, and the central part of the hotel is made of raised walkways and terraces over the natural mangrove habitat. Other resorts in Playacar that bear investigation are the **Sandos Playacar** and any of the hotels in the southern half. Those in the northern half are losing beach.

The **Hotel Copacabana,** in Xpu-Ha (www.hotelcopacabana.com), has raised walkways, preserving much of the flora and making it visually interesting. And Xpu-Ha is blessed with a stunning beach.

Aventura Spa Palace (www.palaceresorts.com) is another hotel in the Palace chain—this one is just for grownups. It has a large spa and gym, and attractive common areas and guest rooms. There is a large pool but no beach; guests can take a shuttle to the Xpu-Ha property if they want.

Freedom Paradise (www.freedomparadise.com) is billed as the first size-friendly vacation resort. The management has worked hard to create an environment that large people will find comfortable. I like it because it doesn't have all the froufrou of so many other resorts—it's friendly and unpretentious.

water practically laps at the foundation. Because the owners are fishermen, the fish is so fresh it's still practically wiggling. The wood hut doesn't look like much, but they also have tables right on the beach. You can have your fish prepared in several ways. If you haven't tried the Yucatecan specialty *tik-n-xic*—fish with *achiote* and bitter-orange sauce, cooked in a banana leaf—this is a good place to do so. I can also recommend the ceviche and the beer.

Calle 2 Norte. ☎ **984/873-2040.** Main courses 50–100 pesos; whole fish 100 pesos per kilo (2.2 lb.). No credit cards. Daily noon–9pm.

Los Carboncitos ★ MEXICAN   The menu is simple, but there's hardly anything to steer clear of. One of the main things to order are the tacos, which are mainly grilled meat, such as the fajitas (*arrachera*) or *al pastor*. These are served with a great collection of salsas. I can also recommend the soups, which are well made, especially the Mexican-style chicken soup (*caldo xochitl*) and the traditional *pozole*. For the seafood, you can try the shrimp al chipotle or the shrimp kebobs. Also try the good sides, commonly served in Mexico City taco places, such as the fried crispy cheese (*chicharrón de queso*) and the guacamole.

Calle 4 (btw. avs. 5 and 10). ☎ **984/873-1382.** Main courses 60–110 pesos; order of tacos 40–60 pesos. No credit cards. Daily 9am–1am.

PLAYA DEL CARMEN AFTER DARK

It seems as if everyone in town is out strolling along La Quinta until midnight; there's pleasant browsing, dining, and drinking available at the many establishments on the street. Here's a quick rundown of the bars that you won't find on Quinta Avenida. The beach bar that is an institution in Playa is the **Blue Parrot** (☎ **984/873-0083**). It gets live acts, mostly rock, and attracts a mixed crowd. It's between calles 12 and 14. Just to the south is **Om** (no phone), which gets a younger crowd with louder musical acts.

Alux (☎ **984/110-5050**) is a one-of-a-kind club occupying a large cave with two dramatically lit chambers and several nooks and sitting areas. It's worth going to, if only for the novelty. The local conservancy group approved all the work, and great care was taken not to contaminate the water, which is part of a larger underground river system. The club books a variety of music acts, usually with no cover. Often there's belly dancing, which is quite in keeping with the surroundings, and I couldn't help but think that I had stepped into a scene from a James Bond film. The bar is cash only and is open Tuesday to Sunday from 7pm to 2am. Take Avenida Juárez across to the other side of the highway—2 blocks down on your left.

For movie going, **Cine Hollywood,** Avenida 10 and Calle 8, in the Plaza Pelícanos shopping center, shows a lot of films in English with Spanish subtitles. Before you buy your ticket, make sure the film is subtitled (*subtitulada*) and not dubbed (*doblada*).

3 SOUTH OF PLAYA DEL CARMEN

South of Playa del Carmen, you'll find a succession of small communities and resorts and two nature parks. From north to south, this section covers them in the following order: Xcaret, Paamul, Puerto Aventuras, Xpu-Ha, Akumal, Xel-Ha, Punta Solimán, and Tankah. This section spans about 56km (35 miles).

Renting a car is the best way to move around down here. Southbound buses depart regularly from Playa, but the best they might do is get you close to your destination. And from the highway, it can be a hot walk to the coast. Another option is to hire a car and driver.

Beyond Paamul, you'll see signs for this or that cenote or cave. There are thousands of cenotes in the Yucatán, and each is slightly different. These turnoffs are less visited than the major attractions and can make for a pleasant visit. Two major attractions bear specific mention: **Hidden Worlds,** offering remarkable snorkeling and diving tours of a couple of cenotes, and **Aktun Chen** cavern with a small nature park. Both are south of Akumal and described later in this chapter.

XCARET: A PARK CELEBRATING THE YUCATAN

A billboard in the airport of faraway Guadalajara reads in Spanish "And when visiting Xcaret, don't forget to enjoy the pleasures of the Riviera Maya, too." An exaggeration, but its point is well taken: Xcaret (pronounced "eesh-ca-*ret*") is the biggest attraction in these parts and is practically a destination unto itself. It even has its own resort. If you're coming to these shores to avoid crowds, avoid this place. If you're here for entertainment and activities, you should consider visiting Xcaret. What Xcaret does, it does very well, and that is to present in one package a little bit of everything that the Yucatán (and the rest of Mexico, for that matter) has to offer.

Think of the activities that people come to the Yucatán for: hanging out on the beach, engaging in scuba diving and snorkeling, going cavern diving, visiting ruins, taking a siesta in a hammock under a grove of palm trees, hiking through tropical forest, meeting native Maya peoples—Xcaret has all that plus handicraft exhibitions; a bat cave; a butterfly pavilion; mushroom and orchid nurseries; and lots of wildlife on display, including native jaguars, manatees, sea turtles, monkeys, macaws, flamingos, and a petting aquarium. Children love it. What probably receives most of the comments is the underground river (a natural feature of the park and common in much of the Yucatán) that's been opened in places to allow snorkelers to paddle along with the current. What else? A number of tours and shows, including *charros* (Mexican cowboys) from the state of Jalisco, and the Totonac Indian *voladores* ("flyers" who do a daring pole dance high above the ground) from the state of Veracruz.

The park is famous for its evening spectacle that is a celebration of the Mexican nation. I've seen it and have to say that it's some show, with a large cast and lots of props. It starts with the Maya and an interpretation of how they may have played the pre-Hispanic ball game/ritual known as *pok-ta-pok,* and then to another version of a ball game still practiced in the western state of Michoacán. From there, it moves on to the arrival of the Spanish and eventually to the forging of the new nation, its customs, its dress, and its music and dance.

Xcaret is 10km (6¼ miles) south of Playa del Carmen (you'll know when you get to the turnoff). It's open daily from 8:30am to 9pm. Admission prices are $69 for adults, $35 for children 5 to 12. Some activities cost extra: horseback ride $30, Snuba/sea trek/ snorkel tour $50, scuba $60 to $85, swimming with dolphins $120. Other costs: lockers $2 per day, snorkel equipment $10 per day, food and drink variable. The park is an all-day affair; it's best to arrive early and register for tours and activities right away. Note that Xcaret allows use of only biodegradable sunblock (p. 65). For more info, call ℂ **998/ 883-3143** or visit www.xcaret.net.

Tips **Avoiding the Cruise-Ship Crowds**

Fewer ships arrive on weekends than on weekdays, which makes the weekend a good time for visiting the major attractions on this coast.

Four kilometers (2¹/₂ miles) south of the entrance to Xcaret is the turnoff for **Puerto Calica,** the cruise-ship pier. Passengers disembark here for tours of Playa, Xcaret, the ruins, and other attractions on the coast.

PAAMUL: SEASIDE GETAWAY

About 15km (9¹/₄ miles) beyond Xcaret and 25km (16 miles) from Playa del Carmen is Paamul, which in Mayan means "a destroyed ruin." The exit is clearly marked. At Paamul (also written Pamul), you can enjoy the Caribbean with relative quiet; the water at the out-of-the-way beach is wonderful, but the shoreline is rocky. There are four rooms for rent, a restaurant, and many trailer and RV lots with hookups.

There's also a dive shop. **Scuba-Mex** (© **984/875-1066;** fax 984/874-1729; www.scubamex.com) is a fully equipped PADI- and SSI-certified dive shop next to the cabañas. Using two boats, the staff takes guests on dives 8km (5 miles) in either direction. If it's too choppy, the reefs in front of the hotel are also good. The cost for a two-tank dive is $60, plus $25 to rent gear. Snorkeling is also excellent in this protected bay and the one next to it. The shop offers a great 3-hour snorkeling trip ($30).

Where to Stay & Dine

Cabañas Paamul ★   Mostly Paamul works with the trailer crowd renting spaces by the day or month. But there are also 12 modern units called "junior suites" on or near the water's edge that are comfortable and spacious. These units are large and come with a kitchenette and two queen beds. Slightly cheaper, but more limited in size and amenities, are the "eco-cabañas." Trailer guests have access to 12 showers and separate bathrooms for men and women. Laundry service is available nearby. The large, breezy *palapa* restaurant is a Brazilian-style grill under the management of Kalú da Silva, a retired Brazilian soccer player who closed his restaurant in León, Guanajuato, to live on the coast. Restaurant customers are welcome to use the beach, which is rocky along this stretch of the coast. Prices vary according to season.

Carretera Cancún–Tulum Km 85. © 984/875-1051. www.paamul.com. 22 units; 190 trailer spaces (all with full hookups). $100–$150 junior suite; $80–$120 cabaña. RV space with hookups $30 per day, $600 per month. No credit cards. Ask about discounts for stays longer than 1 week. Free parking. **Amenities:** Restaurant; bar; pool; dive shop. *In room:* A/C, TV, kitchenette.

PUERTO AVENTURAS: A RESORT COMMUNITY

Five kilometers (3 miles) south of Paamul and 104km (64 miles) from Cancún is the glitzy development of Puerto Aventuras, on Chakalal Bay. It's a condo/marina community with a 9-hole golf course. At the center of the development is a collection of restaurants bordering a dolphin pool. They offer a variety of food—Mexican, Italian, steaks, even a popular pub. The major attraction is the dolphins. To swim with them in a highly interactive program, you must make reservations by contacting **Dolphin Discovery**

> ## (Tips) In Case of Emergency
>
> The Riviera Maya, south of Puerto Aventuras, is susceptible to power failures that can last for hours. Gas pumps and cash machines shut down when this happens, and once the power returns, they attract long lines. It's a good idea to keep a reserve of gas and cash.

(© **998/849-4757**; www.dolphindiscovery.com). Make reservations well in advance—the surest way is through the website.

This is also the place to come for boating and deep-sea fishing. I can recommend **Capt. Rick's Sportfishing Center** (© **984/873-5195**, -5387; www.fishyucatan.com). The best fishing on this coast is from March to August. The captain will be happy to combine a fishing trip with some snorkeling, which makes for a leisurely day.

I don't find Puerto Aventuras to be an interesting place for lodging and prefer to stay elsewhere on the coast. It's like a mini- Cancún, but lacking Cancún's vibrancy. There are a couple of fancy hotels. The main one is the **Omni Puerto Aventuras** (© **800/843-6664** in the U.S., or 984/873-5101). It looks larger than its 30 rooms would indicate and was probably intended to be bigger but didn't get the expected traffic.

XPU-HA: BEAUTIFUL BEACH

Three kilometers (1³/₄ miles) beyond Puerto Aventuras is **Xpu-Ha** (eesh-poo-*hah*) ★★★, a wide bay lined by a broad, beautiful sandy beach. Much of the bay is taken up by private houses and condos. There are a few all-inclusive resorts. One is **Xpu-Ha Palace** and another is the **Copacabana.** These suffered a lot of damage with Hurricane Emily but are open and back in business. Only a part of Xpu-Ha Palace is open, as the other half awaits repair. The beach is big enough to accommodate the hotel guests, residents, and day-trippers without feeling crowded.

Besides the establishments reviewed here, a few hotels offer basic lodging—a couple of beds, cement floors, small private bathroom, and minimal decoration. These rent on a first-come, first-served basis. Rates vary from 500 to 800 pesos a night, depending upon how busy they are. Lodging options are better in nearby Akumal, and if you're renting a car, you can come for the day to enjoy the beach.

Al Cielo ★ (Moments)   This is a good choice if you want a small hotel on the beach where you can go native. The four rooms (two upstairs, two down) occupy a large thatched building right on the beach. The restaurant is popular, but the rooms are rustic and simple, which sometimes works to draw guests into the beach experience as an escape from the modern world. If you're looking for more amenities, this won't be for you.

Carretera Cancún-Tulum Km. 118, 77710 Xpu-Ha, Q. Roo. No phone. www.alcielohotel.com. 4 units. $212–$258 double. MC, V. No children accepted. Rates include full breakfast. Free secure parking. **Amenities:** Restaurant; bar; room service; Hobie cat. *In room:* Fan, hair dryer, no phone, Wi-Fi.

Esencia ★★★   There's not a property on this entire coast that epitomizes leisure and escape more than this one. Lots of space, lots of beauty, lots of privacy, and an air of serenity pervade the entire complex. And, of course, the beach is magnificent. Service is personal and understated (a service fee is added to the room rate). If the spa were any more relaxing, it would lead to an out-of-body experience. Also, the hotel offers 2 hours of complimentary babysitting per day for when the guests are at the spa or dining at the **167** restaurant.

Predio Rústico Xpu-Ha, Fracc. 16 y 18, L. 18, 19 (exit Xpu-Ha-2), 77710 Xpu-Ha, Q. Roo. ℰ **877/528-3490** in the U.S. or Canada, or 984/873-4830. www.hotelesencia.com. 29 units. High season $665 and up for room or suite; low season $580 and up for room or suite. Rates include full breakfast. Internet specials sometimes available. AE, MC, V. Free valet parking. **Amenities:** Restaurant; 2 bars; babysitting; concierge; Jacuzzi; 2 pools; room service; smoke-free rooms; spa. *In room:* A/C, TV/DVD, hair dryer, high-speed Internet access, minibar.

AKUMAL: BEAUTIFUL BAYS & CAVERN DIVING

Continuing south on Hwy. 307 for 2km (1¼ miles), you'll come to the turnoff for Akumal, marked by a traffic light. This is a small, ecologically oriented community built on the shores of two beautiful bays. Akumal has been around long enough that it feels more relaxed than booming places such as Playa and Tulum, and hotel rooms tend to go for less here. Akumal draws a lot of families, who can save money by renting a condo with a kitchen to fix meals. Less than 1km (a half-mile) down the road is a white arch. Just before it are a couple of grocery stores (the one named Super Chomak has an ATM) and a laundry service. Just after it (to the right) is the Hotel Akumal Caribe. If you follow the road to the left and keep to the left, you'll reach Half Moon Bay, lined with two- and three-story condos, and eventually Yal-ku Lagoon, which is a snorkeling park. For renting a condo, contact **Info-Akumal** (ℰ **800/381-7048** in the U.S.; www.info-akumal. com), **Akumal Vacations** (ℰ **800/448-7137** in the U.S.; www.akumalvacations.com), or **Loco Gringo** (www.locogringo.com).

Both bays have sandy beaches with rocky or silt bottoms. This is a popular diving spot. There are three dive shops in town and at least 30 dive sites offshore. The **Akumal Dive Shop** (ℰ **984/875-9032;** www.akumal.com), one of the oldest and best dive shops on the coast, offers courses in technical diving and cavern-diving trips. It and **Akumal Dive Adventures** (ℰ **984/875-9157**), at the Vista del Mar hotel on Half Moon Bay, offer resort courses as well as complete certification.

Yal-ku Lagoon snorkeling park is like a miniature and more primitive Xel-Ha. It's open daily from 8am to 5:30pm. Admission is 70 pesos for adults, 40 pesos for children 3 to 14. The lagoon is about 700m (2,296 ft.) long and about 200m (656 ft.) at its widest. You can paddle around comfortably in sheltered water with little current and see fish and a few other creatures. It makes for a relaxing outing, but for sheer variety, I prefer snorkeling along the reefs.

Where to Stay

Rates below are for two people and include taxes. Most hotels and condo rentals charge higher rates than those listed here for the holidays.

Hotel Akumal Caribe ★★ **(Kids)**   The hotel rooms and garden bungalows of this hotel sit along Akumal Bay. Both are large and comfortable, with tile floors and good-size bathrooms. The 40 bungalows are simply and comfortably furnished, with kitchenettes. The 21 rooms in the three-story beachside hotel are more elaborately furnished, with refrigerators. They have a king-size bed or two queen-size beds, tile floors, and Mexican accents. There is a large pool on the grounds. Other rooms belonging to the hotel are condos and the lovely **Villas Flamingo** on Half Moon Bay. The villas have two or three bedrooms and large living, dining, and kitchen areas, as well as lovely furnished patios just steps from the beach. The four villas share a pool.

Carretera Cancún–Tulum (Hwy. 307) Km 104. ✆ 984/206-3500. www.hotelakumalcaribe.com. (Reservations: P.O. Box 13326, El Paso, TX 79913; ✆ **800/351-1622** in the U.S., 800/343-1440 in Canada, or 915/584-3552.) 70 units. High season $123 bungalow, $156 hotel room, $190–$360 villa or condo; low season $100 bungalow, $122 hotel room, $130–$212 villa or condo. Reservations with prepayment by check only. AE, MC, V. Free parking. Low-season packages available. **Amenities:** 2 restaurants; bar; babysitting; children's activities (seasonal); large outdoor pool; dive shop. *In room:* A/C, fridge, kitchenette (in some), no phone.

Vista del Mar Hotel and Condos ★ (Value)   This beachside property is a great place to stay, for several reasons. It offers hotel rooms at good prices and large, fully equipped condos that you don't have to rent by the week. The lovely, well-tended beach in front of the hotel has chairs and umbrellas. There's an on-site dive shop, which eliminates the hassle of organizing dive trips. Hotel rooms are small and contain either a queen-size bed or a double and a twin bed. They consist of a well-equipped kitchen, a living area, two or three bedrooms, and one to three bathrooms. All have balconies or terraces facing the sea and are furnished with hammocks. Several rooms come with whirlpool tubs.

Half Moon Bay, 77760 Akumal, Q Roo. ✆ **877/425-8625** in the U.S. Fax 505/988-3882. www.akumalinfo.com. 27 units. High season $102 double, $207–$325 condo; low season $84 double, $124–$196 condo. MC, V. Limited free parking. **Amenities:** Restaurant; bar; small outdoor pool; watersports equipment rental; dive shop. *In room:* A/C, TV, CD player, fridge, kitchenette, no phone.

Where to Dine

There are about 10 places to eat in Akumal, and there's a convenient grocery store, **Super Chomak,** by the archway. The **Turtle Bay Café and Bakery** is good (not open for supper in low season), as is **La Buena Vida,** on Half Moon Bay.

XEL-HA: SNORKELING & SWIMMING ★★

Before you get to Xel-Ha (shell-*hah*) nature park, you'll pass the turnoff for **Aktun Chen ★** cavern (a bit beyond Akumal). Of the several caverns that I've toured in the Yucatán, this is one of the best—it has lots of geological features, good lighting, several underground pools, and large chambers, all carefully preserved. The tour takes about an hour and requires a good amount of walking, but the footing is good. You exit not far from where you enter. There is also a zoo with specimens of the local fauna. Some of the critters are allowed to run about freely. In my opinion, the cost of admission is high—170 pesos for adults, 90 pesos for children—but this is true of several attractions on this coast. The cavern is open 9am to 5pm daily. The turnoff is to the right, and the cave is about 4km (2¹/₂ miles) from the road.

Thirteen kilometers (8 miles) south of Akumal is **Xel-Ha** (✆ **998/884-9422** in Cancún, 984/873-3588 in Playa, or 984/875-6000 at the park; www.xelha.com.mx). The centerpiece of Xel-Ha is a large, beautiful lagoon where freshwater and saltwater meet. You can swim, float, and snorkel in beautifully clear water surrounded by jungle. A small train takes guests upriver to a drop-off point. There you can store all your clothes and gear in a locked sack that is taken down to the locker rooms in the main part of the building. The water moves calmly toward the sea, and you can float along with it. Snorkeling here is more comfortable than on the open sea—there are no waves and currents to pull you about, but there are several species of fish, including rays.

Inside the park, you can rent snorkeling equipment and an underwater camera. Platforms allow nonsnorkelers to view the fish. Another way to view fish is to use the park's Snuba gear—a contraption that allows you to breathe air through 6m (20-ft.) tubes connected to scuba tanks floating on the surface. It frees you of the cumbersome tank while allowing you to stay down without having to hold your breath. Rental costs $50 for about an hour. Like Snuba but more involved is sea-trek, a device consisting of an elaborate plastic helmet with air hoses. It allows you to walk around on the bottom, breathing normally, and perhaps participate in feeding the stingrays.

The park has completely remodeled and enlarged the dolphin area. This has improved the experience of swimming with these intelligent, powerful creatures. A 1-hour swim costs $134 plus park admission; a shorter program costs $100. You can also participate in a program that includes transportation from most hotels in the Riviera Maya and takes you to the dolphin area. It includes locker and equipment, too, all for $135. Make reservations at least 24 hours in advance by calling (© **998/887-6840**) or going on the Internet.

Other attractions include a plant nursery; an apiary for the local, stingerless Maya bees; and a lovely path through the tropical forest bordering the lagoon. Xel-Ha is open daily from 8:30am to 5pm. Parking is free. Admission is $40 adults and $30 children ages 5 to 11; children younger than 5 enter free. Admission includes use of inner tubes, life vest, and shuttle train to the river, and the use of changing rooms and showers. (Though not listed on the website, the park often has discount admission during the weekend.) An all-inclusive option includes snorkeling equipment rental, locker rental, towels, food, and beverages: adults for $70, and children for $45. These prices are not discounted on the weekend. The park has five restaurants, two ice-cream shops, and a store. It accepts American Express, MasterCard, and Visa, and it has an ATM. Bring your biodegradable sunblock (p. 65).

Signs clearly mark the turnoff to Xel-Ha, close to the ruins of Tulum. A popular day tour from Cancún or Playa combines the two. If you're traveling on your own, the best time to enjoy Xel-Ha without the crowds is during the weekend from 9am to 2pm.

About 2km (1¼ miles) south of Xel-Ha is **Hidden Worlds Cenotes** ★★★ (© **984/877-8535;** www.hiddenworlds.com.mx), which offers an excellent opportunity to snorkel or dive in a couple of nearby caverns. The caverns are part of a vast network that makes up a single underground river system. The water is crystalline (and cold), and the rock formations impressive. These caverns were filmed for the IMAX production *Journey into Amazing Caves.* The snorkel tour costs $40 and takes you to two different caverns (a half-tour costs $25. The main form of transportation is "jungle mobile," with a guide who throws in information and lore about the jungle plant life that you see. You'll be walking some, so take shoes or sandals. I've toured several caverns, but floating through one gave me an entirely different perspective. For divers, a one-tank dive is $50, a two-tank experience is $90. The owners have also installed a 180m (590-ft.) zip line on the property.

PUNTA SOLIMAN & TANKAH BAYS

The next couple of turnoffs lead to Punta Solimán and Tankah bays. On Punta Solimán Bay is a beach restaurant called **Oscar y Lalo's.** Here you can rent kayaks and snorkel equipment, and paddle out to the reefs for some snorkeling. Three kilometers (1¾ miles) farther is the turnoff for Tankah Bay, which has a handful of lodgings and some rental houses. The most interesting hotel is **Casa Cenote** (© **998/874-5170;** www.casacenote. com). It has an underground river that surfaces at a cenote in the back of the property, then goes underground and bubbles up into the sea just a few feet offshore. Casa Cenote has seven rooms, all on the beach. The double rate runs from $150 to $200, depending upon the season, including breakfast. The American owner provides kayaks and snorkeling gear and can arrange dives, fishing trips, and sailing charters.

A beach road connects the two bays. I found the snorkeling in Tankah better than in Punta Solimán. Snorkeling in the latter was both interesting and frustrating. I've never before experienced so many thermoclines, which are produced by freshwater seeping from the floors of the bay and coming in contact with the warmer saltwater. Light passing through the water is refracted in funny ways. At first I found the effect interesting—it lent an ethereal shininess to everything I was seeing—but then it just got annoying as it cut down sharply on visibility. At one point, I was floating through some of the worst of it, trying not to stir up the water, when a giant silvery barracuda came ghostlike through the shimmering water and crossed my field of vision about 2m (6¹/₂ ft.) away. As he passed slowly by me, I was astonished by how beautiful and luminescent he looked. Still, I will take clear water over shimmering water every time.

4 TULUM ★★★, PUNTA ALLEN & SIAN KA'AN

Tulum *pueblo* (130km/80 miles from Cancún) is a small town on Hwy. 307 where it intersects the road to Cobá. Nearby is an incredible beach, which has become the Tulum hotel zone—a collection of about 30 *palapa* hotels stretching from the Tulum ruins southward, along the Punta Allen Peninsula, all the way to the entrance to the Sian Ka'an Biosphere Reserve. All must generate their own electricity, but recently, someone politically connected managed to build a larger property—a small all-inclusive—and connect it to the town's electrical grid. It has been the object of several legal challenges. I don't know what will come of all this, but it may well represent the end of an era for the Tulum hotel zone.

The Tulum ruins are a walled Maya city of the post-Classic age perched on a rocky cliff overlooking the Caribbean. Tulum beach used to be a destination for backpackers, but the *palapa* hotels have gone upscale, and the beach now attracts a well-heeled crowd that seeks to get away from the bustle of the big hotels and resorts. The town of Tulum has several modest hotels, more than a dozen restaurants, several stores and pharmacies, three cybercafes, a few dive shops, a bank, two ATMs, and a new bus station.

For those who really want to leave the modern world behind, there's the Punta Allen Peninsula. Getting to the end of the peninsula from Tulum can take 1¹/₂ to 3 hours, depending on the condition of the road, which can be downright ugly. It's a quiet, out-of-the-way place; the generator (if there is one) shuts down at 10pm. For most people, Tulum will be far enough away from the crowds. But in Punta Allen, you'll find great fishing and snorkeling, the natural riches of the Sian Ka'an Biosphere Reserve, and a chance to rest up at what truly feels like the end of the road. A few beach cabañas offer reliable power, telephones, and hot showers.

ORIENTATION To visit the Tulum area, get a rental car; it will make everything much easier. From the north, you'll pass the entrance to the ruins before you enter the town. After the ruins, you'll come to a highway intersection with a traffic light. To the right is the highway leading to the ruins of Cobá (see "Cobá Ruins," later in this chapter); to the left is the Tulum hotel zone, which begins about 2km (1¹/₄ miles) away. The road sign reads BOCA PAILA. Take this road and you'll come to a T junction. There are hotels in both directions. If you turn left (north), you'll be heading toward the ruins. If you take a right, you'll pass a long line of more *palapa* hotels until you get to an entrance to Sian Ka'an. As I mentioned earlier, the road from here to the end of the Punta Allen peninsula can be really ugly and slow going.

Tips **Getting to the Beach**

If you're staying elsewhere but want some beach time in Tulum, the easiest thing to do is drive to El Paraíso Beach Club. It's about 1km (a half-mile) south of the ruins (take a left at the T junction). This is a great place—there's a long, broad beach that is pure sand, and access is free. The owners make money by selling food and drink, so they ask you not to bring your own. If you want isolation, drive down the dirt road toward Punta Allen. After you pass the last of the beach hotels, there are a couple of places where the beach comes into view. You can pull over and spread out your beach towel.

The town of Tulum is growing quickly. It now extends for 3 or 4 blocks in either direction from the highway. The highway widens here and is called Avenida Tulum. It is lined with stores, restaurants, and what seems like a drug store on every corner. One place that I find handy is a travel agency/communications/package center called **Savana** (© 984/871-2081), on the east side of Avenida Tulum between calles Orion and Beta. Most of the staff speaks English and can answer questions about tours and calling home. There's also a good bicycle rental store: **Iguana Bike** (© 984/871-2357; hugo_bike@ hotmail.com), on Calle Satélite Sur near the corner of Calle Andrómeda. The owner, Hugo Herrera, maintains his bikes well and organizes tours.

EXPLORING THE TULUM ARCHEOLOGICAL SITE

Thirteen kilometers (8 miles) south of Xel-Ha are the ruins of Tulum, a Maya fortress-city on a cliff above the sea. The ruins are open to visitors daily from 7am to 5pm in the winter, 8am to 6pm in the summer. It's always best to go early, before the crowds start showing up (around 9:30am). The entrance to the ruins is about a 5-minute walk from the archeological site. There are artisans' stands, a bookstore, a museum, a restaurant, several large bathrooms, and a ticket booth. Admission fee to the ruins is 48 pesos. If you want to ride the shuttle from the visitor center to the ruins, it's another 15 pesos. Parking is 30 pesos. A video camera permit costs 45 pesos. Licensed guides have a stand next to the path to the ruins and charge 200 pesos for a 45-minute tour in English, French, or Spanish for up to four persons. In some ways, they are like performers and will tailor their presentation to the responses they receive from you. Some will try to draw connections between the Maya and Western theology, and they will point out architectural details that you might otherwise miss.

By A.D. 900, the end of the Classic period, Maya civilization had begun its decline, and the large cities to the south were abandoned. Tulum is one of the small city-states that rose to fill the void. It came to prominence in the 13th century as a seaport, controlling maritime commerce along this section of the coast, and remained inhabited well after the arrival of the Spanish. The primary god here was the diving god, depicted on several buildings as an upside-down figure above doorways. Seen at the Palace at Sayil and Cobá, this curious, almost comical figure is also known as the bee god.

The most imposing building in Tulum is a large stone structure above the cliff called the **Castillo** (castle). Actually a temple as well as a fortress, it was once covered with stucco and painted. In front of the Castillo are several unrestored palacelike buildings partially covered with stucco. On the **beach** below, where the Maya once came ashore, tourists swim and sunbathe, combining a visit to the ruins with a dip in the Caribbean.

The **Temple of the Frescoes,** directly in front of the Castillo, contains interesting 13th-century wall paintings, though entrance is no longer permitted. Distinctly Maya, they represent the rain god Chaac and Ixchel, the goddess of weaving, women, the moon, and medicine. On the cornice of this temple is a relief of the head of the rain god. If you pause a slight distance from the building, you'll see the eyes, nose, mouth, and chin. Notice the remains of the red-painted stucco—at one time all the buildings at Tulum were painted bright red.

Much of what we know of Tulum at the time of the Spanish Conquest comes from the writings of Diego de Landa, third bishop of the Yucatán. He wrote that Tulum was a small city inhabited by about 600 people who lived in platform dwellings along a street and supervised the trade traffic from Honduras to the Yucatán. Though it was a walled city, most of the inhabitants probably lived outside the walls, leaving the interior for the residences of governors and priests and ceremonial structures. Tulum survived about 70 years after the conquest, when it was finally abandoned. Because of the great number of visitors this site receives, it is no longer possible to climb all of the ruins. In many cases, visitors are asked to remain behind roped-off areas to view them.

WHERE TO STAY

If you can afford staying at one of the small beach hotels in Tulum, do so. The experience is enjoyable and relaxing. But most are on the expensive side. Demand is high, supply is limited, and the hotels have to generate their own electricity (bring a flashlight). If you're on a budget, you will be better off staying in Akumal or in one of the modest hotels in town and be a day-tripper to the beach.

Take the Boca Paila road from Hwy. 307. Three kilometers (1¾ miles) ahead, you come to a T-junction. To the south are most of the *palapa* hotels; to the north are several, too. The rates listed below don't include the week of Christmas and New Year, when prices go above regular high-season rates.

Very Expensive

Ana y José ★★ This *palapa* hotel has gone "boutique," with a spa, suites, and serious remodeling of rooms. It's a far cry now from what it used to be—a simple collection of cabins and a restaurant on the beach. Now there are marble countertops and marble tile floors. Rooms are large and comfortable. There's air-conditioning in all the lower rooms that don't catch the sea breeze. The beach here is excellent. Ana y José is 6.5km (4 miles) south of the Tulum ruins.

Carretera Punta Allen Km 7 (Apdo. Postal 15), 77780 Tulum, Q. Roo. ☎ **998/880-5629.** Fax 998/880-6021. www.anayjose.com. 22 units. $232–$256 garden and pool view; $304–$370 beachfront and ocean view. AE, MC, V. Free parking. **Amenities:** Restaurant; outdoor pool; spa. *In room:* A/C (in some rooms), no phone.

Azulik ★★ Azulik is all about slowing down, leaving civilization behind (except for such niceties as indoor plumbing and room service), and enjoying the simple life (with or without clothes). I enjoyed the simple life during a brief stay here and appreciated the design and positioning of the individual cabañas. Most sit on a stone ledge above the sea. The ledge is just high enough to provide privacy while you sit out on the semishaded wood deck in front of your cabaña enjoying either the sun or the stars. For that purpose, they come with chairs, hammocks, and a wooden tub for soaking. (There is a larger wooden tub indoors for bathing.) Each cabaña is constructed entirely of wood and glass

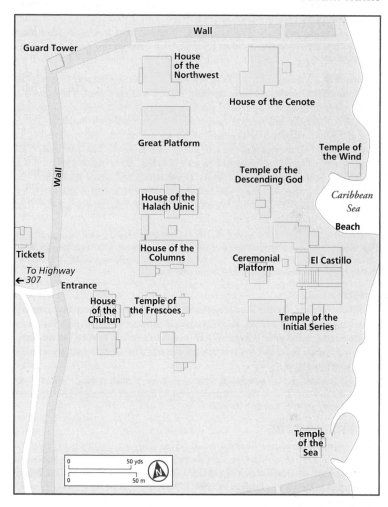

and thatch. There is no electricity, only candles. Each has a king-size bed with mosquito netting and a queen-size bed, suspended on ropes, for lounging during the day.

Carretera Boca Paila Km 5.5, 77780 Tulum, Q. Roo. © **877/532-6737** in the U.S. and Canada. www.azulik. com. 15 units. High season $325–$350 double; low season $255–$285 double. MC, V. Limited free parking. No children 17 and under. **Amenities:** Restaurant; bar; room service; spa. *In room:* No phone.

Moderate

Posada Dos Ceibas ★ Of all the places along this coast, this one reminds me the most of the way hotels in Tulum used to be: simple, quiet, and ecological without being pretentious. This is a good choice for a no-fuss beach vacation. The one- and two-story cottages are spread out through the vegetation. Rooms are simply furnished and come with ceiling fans, and almost all have private patios or porches. Price varies according to the size of the rooms. The grounds are well tended. The electricity is solar generated and comes on at 6pm. There is a pure sand beach.

Carretera Tulum-Boca Paila Km 10, 77780 Tulum, Q. Roo. ☎ **984/877-6024.** www.dosceibas.com. 8 units. High season $110–$200 double; low season $90–$170. MC, V. **Amenities:** Restaurant; yoga classes. *In room:* No phone.

Zamas ★★　A couple from San Francisco has made this rustic getaway most enjoyable by concentrating on the essentials: comfort, privacy, and good food. The cabañas are simple, attractive, and well situated for catching the breeze. Most rooms are in individual structures; the suites and oversize rooms are in modest two-story buildings. For the money, I like the garden *palapas*, which are attractive, spacious, and comfortable, and come with a queen-size bed and a twin or a king- and queen-size bed. Two small beachfront cabañas with one queen-size bed go for a little less. The most expensive rooms are the upstairs oceanview units, which enjoy a large terrace and lots of sea breezes. They come with a king-size and a queen-size bed or two queen-size beds. The restaurant serves the freshest seafood—I've seen the owner flag down passing fishermen to buy their catch. A white-sand beach stretches between rocky areas.

Carretera Punta Allen Km 5, 77780 Tulum, Q. Roo. ☎ **415/387-9806** in the U.S. www.zamas.com. 20 units. High season $120–$160 beachfront double, $130–$160 garden double, $200 oceanview double; low season $90–$125 beachfront double, $95–$125 garden double, $145 oceanview double. No credit cards. Limited free parking. **Amenities:** Restaurant. *In room:* No phone.

Inexpensive

Cabañas Tulum　Next to Ana y José is a row of cinderblock bungalows facing the same beautiful ocean and beach. Rooms are simple and poorly lit, with basic bathrooms. All rooms have two double beds (most with new mattresses), screens on the windows, a table, one electric light, and a porch facing the beach. Electricity is available from 7 to 11am and 5 to 11pm.

Carretera Punta Allen Km 7 (Apdo. Postal 63), 77780 Tulum, Q. Roo. ☎ **984/115-9912.** Fax 984/802-5326. www.hotelstulum.com. 32 units. 700–1,100 pesos double. No credit cards. Limited free parking. **Amenities:** Restaurant; game room. *In room:* No phone.

WHERE TO DINE

There are several restaurants in the town of Tulum. They are reasonably priced and do an okay job. On the main street are **Charlie's** (☎ 984/871-2136), my favorite for Mexican food, and **Don Cafeto's** (☎ 984/871-2207). **La Nave** (☎ 984/871-2592) is a good Italian restaurant. At **Azafrán** (☎ 984/129-6130), you can get surprisingly sophisticated cooking served in a small, rustic dining room. Also in town are a couple of roadside places that grill chicken and serve it with rice and beans. And there's a local people's restaurant at the southern end of town called **Doña Tina.** Meals on the coast are going to be more expensive but more varied. Many of the hotels have restaurants—I've eaten well at **Copal,** north of the T-junction, and **Zamas,** which is south.

EXPLORING THE PUNTA ALLEN PENINSULA

If you've been captured by an adventurous spirit and have an excessively sanguine opinion of your rental car's off-road capabilities, you might want to take a trip down the Punta Allen Peninsula, especially if your interests lie in fly-fishing, birding, or simply exploring new country. The far end of the peninsula is only 50km (31 miles) away, but it can be a very slow and bouncy trip (up to 3 hr., depending on the condition of the

Halfway down the peninsula, at a small bridge, is the **Boca Paila Fishing Lodge**
(www.bocapaila.com). Not for the general traveler, it specializes in hosting fly-fishers,
with weeklong all-inclusive fishing packages. At this point, the peninsula is quite narrow.
You can see the Boca Paila lagoon on one side and the sea on the other. Another 25km
(16 miles) gets you to the village of Punta Allen. Before the town is a little hotel called
Rancho Sol Caribe. It has only four rooms and a lovely beach all to itself. Punta Allen
is a lobstering and fishing village on a palm-studded beach. Isolated and rustic, it's very
much the laid-back end of the line. It has a lobster cooperative, a few streets with modest
homes, and a lighthouse. The **Cuzan Guesthouse** (www.flyfishmx.com) is a collection
of 12 cabins and 1 restaurant on a nice sandy beach. Its main clientele is fly-fishers, and
it offers all-inclusive fishing packages. But co-owner Sonia Litvak, a Californian, will rent
to anyone curious enough to want to go down there. She also offers snorkeling trips and
boat tours.

THE SIAN KA'AN BIOSPHERE RESERVE   Down the peninsula a few miles south of
the Tulum ruins, you'll pass the guardhouse of the Sian Ka'an Biosphere Reserve. The
reserve is a tract of 500,000 hectares (1.2 million acres) set aside in 1986 to preserve tropical forests, savannas, mangroves, coastal and marine habitats, and 110km (68 miles) of
coastal reefs. The area is home to jaguars; pumas; ocelots; margays; jaguarundis; spider and
howler monkeys; tapirs; white-lipped and collared peccaries; manatees; brocket and white-
tailed deer; crocodiles; and green, loggerhead, hawksbill, and leatherback sea turtles. It also
protects 366 species of birds—you might glimpse an ocellated turkey, a great curassow, a
brilliantly colored parrot, a toucan or trogon, a white ibis, a roseate spoonbill, a jabiru (or
wood stork), a flamingo, or one of 15 species of herons, egrets, and bitterns.

The park has three parts: a "core zone" restricted to research; a "buffer zone," to which
visitors and families already living there have restricted use; and a "cooperation zone,"
which is outside the reserve but vital to its preservation. There are two principal entrances
to the biosphere reserve: one is from the community of Muyil, which is off Hwy. 307,
south of Tulum (you take a boat down canals built by the Maya that connect to the Boca
Paila lagoon); the other is from the community of Punta Allen (by Jeep down the peninsula, which separates the Boca Paila Lagoon from the sea).

Visitors can arrange day trips in Tulum from **Centro Ecológico de Sian Ka'an**
(© 984/871-2499; www.cesiak.org). Its office is at Av. Tulum 68. This is a nonprofit for
the support of Sian Ka'an. **Community Tours Sian Ka'an** (Av. Tulum between Centauro
and Ori'on; © 984/114-0750; www.siankaantours.com) is a cooperative of local guides
that runs snorkeling, birding, and adventure tours into the biosphere.

---

5 COBÁ RUINS

168km (104 miles) SW of Cancún

Older than most of Chichén Itzá and much larger than Tulum, Cobá was the dominant
city of the eastern Yucatán before A.D. 1000. The site is large and spread out, with thick
forest growing between the temple groups. Rising high above the forest canopy are tall
and steep pyramids of the Classic Maya style. Of the major sites, this one is the least
reconstructed and so disappoints those who expect another Chichén Itzá. The stone
sculpture here has worn off and has become impossible to make out. But the structures

themselves and the surrounding jungle and twin lakes make the experience enjoyable. This is not a cenote area, and the water has nowhere to go but stay on the surface. The forest canopy is also higher than in the northern part of the peninsula.

ESSENTIALS

GETTING THERE & DEPARTING   By Car   The road to Cobá begins in Tulum and continues for 65km (40 miles). Watch out for both *topes* (speed bumps) and potholes. The road was widened and repaved last year and should be in good condition. Close to the village of Cobá, you will come to a triangle offering you three choices: Nuevo Xcan, Valladolid, and Cobá. Make sure not to get on the other two roads. The entrance to the ruins is a short distance down the road past some small restaurants and the large lake.

By Bus   Several buses a day leave Tulum and Playa del Carmen for Cobá. Several companies offer bus tours.

EXPLORING THE COBA RUINS

The Maya built many intriguing cities in the Yucatán, but few grander than Cobá ("water stirred by wind"). Much of the 67-sq.-km (26-sq.-mile) site remains unexcavated. A 100km (62-mile) *sacbé* (a pre-Hispanic raised road) through the jungle linked Cobá to Yaxuná, once an important Maya center 50km (31 miles) south of Chichén Itzá. It's the Maya's longest-known *sacbé,* and at least 50 shorter ones lead from here. An important city-state, Cobá flourished from A.D. 632 (the oldest carved date found here) until after the rise of Chichén Itzá, around 800. Then Cobá faded in importance and population until it was finally abandoned. Scholars believe Cobá was an important trade link between the Yucatán Caribbean coast and inland cities.

Once at the site, keep your bearings—you can get turned around in the maze of dirt roads in the jungle. And bring bug spray. As spread out as this city is, renting a bike (which you can do at the entrance for 30 pesos) is a good option. Branching off from every labeled path, you'll notice unofficial narrow paths into the jungle, used by locals as shortcuts through the ruins. These are good for birding, but be careful to remember the way back.

The **Grupo Cobá** holds an impressive pyramid, **La Iglesia (the Church).** Take the path bearing right after the entrance. The urge to climb the temple is great, but the view is better from El Castillo in the Nohoch Mul group farther back.

From here, return to the main path and turn right. You'll pass a sign pointing right to the ruined *juego de pelota* **(ball court),** but the path is obscure.

Continuing straight ahead on this path for 5 to 10 minutes, you'll come to a fork in the road. To the left and right, you'll notice jungle-covered, unexcavated pyramids, and at one point you'll see a raised portion crossing the pathway—this is the visible remains of the *sacbé* to Yaxuná. Throughout the area, carved stelae stand by pathways or lie forlornly in the jungle underbrush. Although protected by crude thatched roofs, most are weatherworn enough that they're indiscernible.

The left fork leads to the **Nohoch Mul Group,** which contains **El Castillo.** With the exception of Structure 2 in Calakmul, this is the tallest pyramid in the Yucatán (even higher than El Castillo at Chichén Itzá and the Pyramid of the Magician at Uxmal). Visitors can climb to the top. From this lofty perch, you can see unexcavated jungle-covered pyramidal structures poking up through the forest canopy all around.

The right fork (more or less straight on) goes to the **Conjunto Las Pinturas.** Here the main attraction is the **Pyramid of the Painted Lintel,** a small structure with traces of its original bright colors above the door. You can climb up for a close look. Though maps **177** of Cobá show ruins around two lakes, there are really only two excavated groups.

Admission is 35 pesos, free for children younger than age 12. Parking is 12 pesos. A video camera permit costs 35 pesos. The site is open daily from 8am to 5pm, sometimes longer. *Note:* Visit Cobá in the morning or after the heat of the day has passed. Mosquito repellent, drinking water, and comfortable shoes are imperative.

WHERE TO STAY & DINE

If nightfall catches you in Cobá, you have limited lodging choices. There is one tourist hotel called **Villas Arqueológicas Cobá,** which fronts the lake. Though smaller than its sister hotels in Uxmal and Chichén Itzá, it's the same in style—modern rooms that are attractive and functional, so long as you're not too tall. It has a restaurant that serves all three meals and a swimming pool. The hotel could be empty or full, given that most of its business comes from bus tours. To make reservations, call © **987/872-9300,** ext. 8101. There's also a cheap hotel in town called **El Bocadito** (no phone), with simple rooms for 220 pesos per night. It has a small restaurant; there are a couple more eateries in the town as well.

EN ROUTE TO THE LOWER CARIBBEAN COAST: FELIPE CARRILLO PUERTO

Mexico's lower Caribbean coast is officially called the Costa Maya. This area attracts fishermen, divers, archeology enthusiasts, birders, and travelers looking to get away from the crowds. For divers, there is some great diving along the coastal reefs and at the Chinchorro Reef, which lies about 30km (20 miles) offshore (see below). You'll find sandy beaches good for sunbathing, but not for swimming because of the prominent coastal reef. But if you want to snorkel or dive among less-visited reefs, kayak in calm turquoise water, or perhaps do some fly-fishing away from the crowds, this area is a great option. And there's fine swimming in Lake Bacalar.

You also might enjoy the astounding Maya ruins in the Río Bec area, west of Bacalar. Here, too, you'll find a richer ecosystem than in the northern part of the peninsula. The forest canopy is higher and the wildlife is more abundant. If you're interested in exploring this territory, see "Side Trips to Maya Ruins from Chetumal," later in this chapter.

Continue south on Hwy. 307 from Tulum. The road narrows, the speed limit drops, and you begin to see *topes.* Down the road some 25km (16 miles), a sign points to the small but interesting ruins of **Muyil.** Take bug spray. The principal ruins are a small group of buildings and a plaza dominated by the Castillo, a pyramid of medium height but unusual construction. From here, a canal dug by the Maya enters what is now the Sian Ka'an Biosphere Reserve and empties into a lake, with other canals going from there to the saltwater estuary of Boca Paila. The local community offers a boat ride through these canals and lakes. The 3$^{1}/_{2}$-hour tour includes snorkeling the canal and letting the current carry you along. Soft drinks are also included. This is much the same Sian Ka'an tour offered by travel agencies in Tulum, but without some of the infrastructure. The agencies charge more but provide transportation, better interpretation, and lunches.

Felipe Carrillo Puerto (pop. 60,000) is the first large town you pass on the road to Ciudad Chetumal. It has two gas stations, a market, a bus terminal, and a few modest hotels and restaurants. Next to the gas station in the center of town is a bank with an ATM. Hwy. 184 goes from here into the interior of the peninsula, leading eventually to Mérida, which makes Carrillo Puerto a turning point for those making the "short circuit" of the Yucatán Peninsula.

THE CARIBBEAN COAST: THE RIVIERA MAYA

7

COBÁ RUINS

The town is of interest for having been a rebel stronghold during the War of the Castes and the center of the intriguing millenarian cult of the "Talking Cross." The town is still home to a strong community of believers in the cult who practice their own brand of religion and are respected by the entire town. Every month, a synod of sorts is held here for the church leaders of 12 neighboring towns.

6 MAJAHUAL, XCALAK & THE CHINCHORRO REEF

South of Felipe Carrillo Puerto, the speed bumps begin in earnest. In 45 minutes, you reach the turnoff for Majahual and Xcalak, which is after the town of Limones. From here, the highway has been widened and repaved. The roadwork was done to facilitate bus tours from the cruise-ship pier in **Majahual** (mah-hah-*wahl*) to some of the Maya ruins close by. Many passengers elect to enjoy some beach time in Majahual instead. The best option is to keep your distance from the pier and stay either in the lower Majahual area or at the bottom of the peninsula near Xcalak. You'll come to the turnoff for Xcalak before you get to Majahual. Xcalak has a decent dive shop. From Majahual to Xcalak takes a little less than an hour.

Xcalak (eesh-kah-*lahk*) is a depopulated, weather-beaten fishing village with a few comfortable places to stay and a couple of restaurants. It once had a population as large as 1,200 before the 1958 hurricane washed most of the town away; now it has only 300 permanent residents. It's charming in a run-down way, and you'll certainly feel miles away from the crush of the crowds. From here you work your way back up the coast to get to one of the several small inns just beyond the town.

ORIENTATION

ARRIVING   Driving south from Felipe Carrillo Puerto, you'll come to the clearly marked turnoff onto Hwy. 10, 2.5km (1¹/₂ miles) after Limones, at a place called Cafetal (before the turnoff, there's a gas station). From there it's a 50km (31-mile) drive to the coast and Majahual. The pier is north of the road; Balamkú Inn on the Beach, which I like, is to the south. If you're going to Xcalak, the turnoff will be 2km (1¹/₄ miles) before Majahual, at a military checkpoint. The road is paved, but usually with some potholes. It's 55km (34 miles) long.

DIVING THE CHINCHORRO REEF

The **Chinchorro Reef Underwater National Park** is 38km (24 miles) long and 13km (8 miles) wide. The oval reef is as shallow as 1m (3¹/₄ ft.) at its interior and as deep as 900m (2,952 ft.) at its exterior. It lies some 30km (20 miles) offshore. Locals claim it's the last virgin reef system in the Caribbean. It's invisible from the ocean side; hence, one of its diving attractions is the **shipwrecks**—at least 30—that decorate the underwater landscape. One is on top of the reef. Divers have counted 40 cannons at one wreck site. On the west side are walls and coral gardens.

Aventuras XTC (© **983/839-8865;** www.xtcdivecenter.com) is a fully equipped dive shop in Xcalak (technical diving, Nitrox, snorkeling, and fishing trips). You can arrange dives to the local reefs, San Pedro in Belize, and to the Chinchorro Reef.

WHERE TO STAY & DINE

Balamkú Inn on the Beach ★★   This is a comfortable and friendly place to stay in south Majahual. Rooms are in one- and two-story thatched bungalows distributed across 110m (361 ft.) of beautiful white beach. They are large and breezy, with large attractive bathrooms and comfortable mattresses. All have terraces facing the beach. This hotel is very ecological. All the energy is produced by wind and sun. To run this kind of operation takes a rare combination of skill and talent, which these owners have in ample supply.

Carretera Costera Km 5.7, Majahual, Q. Roo. ⓒ **983/839-5332.** www.balamku.com. 10 units. $75–$85 double. Rates include full breakfast. AE, MC, V for deposits only; no credit cards at hotel. Free guarded parking. **Amenities:** Airport transportation arranged; smoke-free rooms; watersports equipment. *In room:* No phone, Wi-Fi.

Costa de Cocos Dive & Fly-Fishing Resort ★★   Several freestanding cabañas sit around a large, attractive sandy beach graced with coconut palms. The cabañas are comfortable and have a lot of cross-ventilation, ceiling fans, hot water, and comfortable beds. They also come with 24-hour electricity using wind and solar power and purified tap water. One is a two-bedroom unit with two bathrooms. Activities include kayaking, snorkeling, scuba diving, and fly-fishing. The resort has experienced English-speaking fishing guides and a dive instructor. It has a large dive boat capable of taking divers to the Chinchorro Reef. The casual restaurant/bar offers good home-style cooking.

Carretera Majahual–Xcalak Km 52, Q. Roo. No phone. www.costadecocos.com. 16 cabañas. High season $90 double; low season $85 double. Dive and fly-fishing packages available by e-mail request. Rates include breakfast buffet. AE, MC, V. Free parking. **Amenities:** Restaurant; bar; watersports equipment; dive shop. *In room:* No phone.

Hotel Tierra Maya ★   This is a comfortable, modern-style hotel on the beach. Rooms in the two-story building are spacious and designed to have good cross-ventilation. They come with ceiling fans. Each has a private balcony or terrace that looks out to the sea, hammocks, and bottled purified water. Solar generators provide electricity. Bathrooms are large, and beds are either twins or queen size. The owners arrange diving, fishing, and snorkeling trips for guests. Guests have Internet access and the use of kayaks and bikes.

Carretera Majahual–Xcalak Km 54, Q. Roo. No phone. www.tierramaya.net. 7 units. High season $85–$150 double; low season $75–$135 double. Rates include continental breakfast. MC, V for advance payments. Limited free parking. **Amenities:** Restaurant; bar; bikes; Internet access; kayaks. *In room:* No phone.

---

7 LAGO BACALAR ★★★

104km (64 miles) SW of Felipe Carrillo Puerto; 37km (23 miles) NW of Chetumal

Bacalar Lake is an elaborate trick played upon the senses. I remember once standing on a pier on the lake and gazing down into perfectly clear water. As I lifted my eyes, I could see the blue tint of the Caribbean. Beyond lay a dense tropical forest. A breeze blowing in from the sea smelled of salt air, and though I knew it to be untrue, I couldn't help but believe that the water I was gazing on was, in fact, an inlet of the sea and not a lake at all—perhaps a well-sheltered lagoon like Xel-Ha. Lakes in tropical lowlands, especially those surrounded by tropical jungle, are turbid and muddy. How could this one be so clear? It's because Bacalar is fed not by surface runoff, but by several cenotes that lie beneath its surface. Only in the Yucatán is such a thing possible.

This is the perfect spot for being bone idle. But there's plenty to do, too. You can explore the jungle, visit some particularly elegant Maya ruins in the nearby Río Bec area, or take in a wonderful museum about the Maya in Chetumal. The town of Bacalar is quiet and quaint. There are a few stores and a couple of restaurants. An 18th-century fort with a moat and stout bastions is by the lake. Inside the fort is a small museum (admission is 8 pesos) that has several artifacts on display. All text is in Spanish.

ORIENTATION   Driving south on Hwy. 307, the town of Bacalar is 1¹/₂ hours beyond Felipe Carrillo Puerto, clearly marked by signs. If you're driving north from Chetumal, it takes about a half-hour. Buses going south from Cancún and Playa del Carmen stop here, and there are frequent buses from Chetumal. There are now a couple of gas stations on the highway here.

WHERE TO STAY

Hotel Laguna   The Laguna overlooks the lake from a lovely vantage point. All the rooms share the view and have little terraces that make enjoyable sitting areas. The midsize rooms have ceiling fans, and most come with two double beds. The mattresses in the bungalows aren't good. The bathrooms are simple but have no problem delivering hot water.

A restaurant that shares the same view is open from 7am to 9pm. The bar makes a credible margarita. The highest occupancy rates are from July to August and December to January, when you should make a reservation. The hotel is hard to spot from the road; look for the sign about 1km (half a mile) after you pass through the town of Bacalar.

Bulevar Costera de Bacalar 479, 77010 Lago Bacalar, Q. Roo. © **983/834-2206.** Fax 983/834-2205. 34 units. 550 pesos double; 930–1,160 pesos bungalow for 5–8 persons. MC, V. Free parking. **Amenities:** Restaurant; bar; small outdoor pool; boat rides on the lake. *In room:* No phone.

Rancho Encantado Cottage Resort ★★   This serene lakeside retreat consists of 13 white-stucco cottages scattered over a shady lawn beside the smooth Lago Bacalar. Each is large and has louvered windows, a red-tile floor, a dining table and chairs, a living room or sitting area, a porch with chairs, and hammocks strung between trees. Some rooms have cedar ceilings and red-tiled roofs, and others have thatched roofs. Four cottages are waterfront (nos. 9–12). Beds come in different combinations of doubles and twins. The Laguna Suite is a one-bedroom townhouse with study, air-conditioning, and private dock; it rents by the week. Orange, lime, mango, sapote, Ceiba, banana, palm, and oak trees; wild orchids; and bromeliads on the grounds make great bird shelters, attracting flocks of chattering parrots, turquoise-browed motmots, toucans, and many more species. The hotel offers almost a dozen excursions.

Carretera Bacalar–Felipe Carrillo Puerto Km 3, 77930 Chetumal, Q. Roo. ©/fax **983/101-3358.** www. encantado.com. (Reservations: P.O. Box 1256, Taos, NM 87571. © **800/505-6292** in the U.S., or ©/fax 505/894-7074.) 13 units. High season $160–$190 double; low season $120–$150 double. Rates include continental breakfast and dinner. MC, V. Free parking. **Amenities:** Restaurant; bar; large outdoor whirlpool; spa; watersports equipment. *In room:* Fridge.

WHERE TO DINE

Besides the restaurants at the hotels discussed above, you may enjoy the **Restaurante Cenote Azul** (© **983/834-2460;** www.cenoteazul.com.mx), a comfortable open-air thatched-roof restaurant on the edge of the beautiful Cenote Azul. Main courses cost 50 to 160 pesos. To get to Restaurant Cenote Azul, follow the highway to the south edge of town and turn left at the restaurant's sign; follow the road around to the restaurant. At the restaurant, you can take a dip in placid Cenote Azul, as long as you don't have creams or lotions on your skin.

8 CHETUMAL

251km (156 miles) S of Tulum; 37km (23 miles) S of Lago Bacalar

Capital of the state, and the second-largest city (after Cancún), Chetumal (pop. 210,000) is not a tourist destination. The old part of town, down by the river (Río Hondo), has a Caribbean feel, but the rest is unremarkable. Chetumal is the gateway to Belize, Tikal (Guatemala), and the Río Bec ruins. If you're going to spend the night here, visit the **Museo de la Cultura Maya** (© **983/832-6838**), especially if you plan to follow the Río Bec ruin route (see "Side Trips to Maya Ruins from Chetumal," below).

ESSENTIALS
Getting There & Departing
BY PLANE   Aviacsa (© 983/872-7698) and **Click** (© 983/832-6675) have a direct flight to and from Mexico City. The airport is west of town, just north of the entrance from the highway.

BY CAR Chetumal is a little more than 3 hours from Tulum. If you're heading to Belize, you won't be able to take your rental car because the rental companies won't allow it. To get to the ruins of Tikal in Guatemala, you must go through Belize to the border crossing at Ciudad Melchor de Mencos. To drive into Chetumal, there's a flyover now where the road splits off for Belize.

BY BUS The main bus station (✆ 983/832-5110) is 20 blocks from the town center on Insurgentes at Niños Héroes. Buses go to Cancún, Tulum, Playa del Carmen, Puerto Morelos, Mérida, Campeche, Villahermosa, and Tikal, Guatemala.

To Belize: Buses depart from the Lázaro Cárdenas market (most often called *el mercado nuevo*). Ask for **Autobuses Novelo.** The company has local service every 45 minutes (140 pesos) and four express buses per day (185 pesos).

Visitor Information

The **State Tourism Office** (✆ 983/835-0860, ext. 1811) is at Calzada del Centenario 622, between Comonfort and Ciricote. It's open Monday to Friday from 9am to 6pm.

Orientation

The telephone **area code** is **983.**

Traffic enters the city from the west and feeds onto Avenida Obregón into town. Stay on Obregón and don't take the exit for Avenida Insurgentes. Eventually, you'll cross Avenida Héroes, which is the main north–south street.

A MUSEUM NOT TO MISS

Museo de la Cultura Maya ★★★ This modern museum unlocks the complex world of the Maya through interactive exhibits and genuine artifacts. Push a button, and an illustrated description appears, explaining the medicinal and domestic uses of plants with their Mayan and scientific names; another exhibit describes the social classes of the Maya by their manners of dress. One of the most fascinating exhibits describes the Maya's ideal of personal beauty and the subsequent need to deform craniums, scar the face and body, and induce cross-eyed vision. An enormous screen flashes images taken from an airplane flying over more than a dozen Maya sites from Mexico to Honduras. Another large television shows the architectural variety of Maya pyramids and how they were probably built. Then a walk on a glass floor takes you over representative ruins in the Maya world. In the center of the museum is the three-story, stylized, sacred Ceiba tree, which the Maya believed connected Xibalba (the underworld), Earth, and the heavens. If you can arrange it, see the museum before you tour the Río Bec ruins.

Av. Héroes s/n. ✆ **983/832-6838.** Admission 66 pesos. Tues–Thurs 9am–7pm; Fri–Sat 9am–8pm. Btw. Colón and Gandhi, 8 blocks from Av. Obregón, just past the Holiday Inn.

WHERE TO STAY

Hotel Holiday Inn Puerta Maya This modern hotel (formerly the Hotel Continental) has the best air-conditioning in town and is only a block from the Museo de la Cultura Maya. Most rooms are midsize and come with two double beds or one king-size bed. Bathrooms are roomy and well lit.

Av. Héroes 171, 77000 Chetumal, Q. Roo. ✆ **800/465-4329** in the U.S., or 983/835-0400. Fax 983/832-1676. 85 units. 1,250 pesos double. AE, MC, V. Free secure parking. From Av. Obregón, turn left on Av. Héroes, go 6 blocks, and look for the hotel on the right. **Amenities:** Restaurant; bar; fitness room; midsize outdoor pool; room service. *In room:* A/C, TV, Wi-Fi.

Hotel Nachancán   One block from *el mercado nuevo* (the new market), this hotel offers plain rooms, with one or two double beds. Bathrooms are small, with no counter space, but they offer plenty of hot water.

Calzada Veracruz 379, 77000 Chetumal, Q. Roo. (✆ **983/832-3232.** 20 units. 310 pesos double; 500 pesos suite. No credit cards. Drive the length of Av. Obregón to where it stops at Calzada Veracruz, turn left, and drive 2km (1¼ miles); the hotel will be on the right. Off-street parking. **Amenities:** Restaurant; bar. *In room:* A/C, TV, no phone.

WHERE TO DINE

For an economical meal with some local atmosphere, try **Restaurante Pantoja,** on the corner of calles Ghandi and 16 de Septiembre (✆ 983/832-3957), 2 blocks east of the Museum of Maya Culture. It offers a cheap daily special, good green enchiladas, and such local specialties as *poc chuc* (grilled marinated pork). It's open Monday to Saturday from 7am to 7pm. To sample excellent *antojitos,* the local supper food, go to **El Buen Gusto,** on Calzada Veracruz across from the market (no phone). A Chetumal institution, it serves excellent *salbutes* and *panuchos* (both dishes are similar to *gorditas*), tacos, and sandwiches. It's open in the morning until 2pm and then opens again around 7pm and closes at midnight. If for some reason it's closed, go next door to **La Ideal,** which many locals hold to be the better of the two supper joints. It has delicious *tacos de pierna* (soft tacos with thinly sliced pork shoulder) and *agua de horchata* (water flavored with rice, vanilla, and toasted pumpkin seed).

ONWARD FROM CHETUMAL

From Chetumal you have several choices. The Maya ruins of Lamanai, in Belize, are an easy day trip if you have transportation (not a rental car). You can explore the Río Bec ruin route directly west of the city (see below) by taking Hwy. 186. If you want a guided tour of any of the ruins, contact **Luis Téllez** (✆ 983/832-3496; www.mayaruinsand birds.com). He lives in Chetumal, knows the region and its wildlife, and stays up-to-date with the archeological excavations. He speaks English and is a good driver.

9 SIDE TRIPS TO MAYA RUINS FROM CHETUMAL

A few miles west of Bacalar and Chetumal begins an area of Maya settlement known to archaeologists as the Río Bec region. A number of ruins stretch from close to Bacalar well into the state of Campeche. These ruins are numerous, intriguing, and dramatic. Their architecture is heavily stylized, with lots of decoration. In recent years, excavation has led to many discoveries. With excavation has come restoration, but the ruins here have not been rebuilt to the same degree as those at Uxmal and Chichén Itzá. Often, though, buildings were in such great shape that reconstruction was unnecessary.

Nor have these sites been cleared of jungle growth in the same manner as the marquee ruins mentioned above. Trees and vines grow in profusion around the buildings, giving the sites the feel of lost cities. In visiting them, you can imagine what John Lloyd Stephens and Frederick Catherwood must have felt when they traipsed through the Yucatán in the 19th century. And watch for wildlife; on my last visit I saw several denizens of the tropical forest. The fauna along the entire route is especially rich. You might see a toucan, a grand curassow, or a macaw hanging about the ruins, and orioles, egrets, and several birds of prey are extremely common. Gray fox, wild turkey, *tesquintle* (a bushy-tailed, plant-eating rodent), the raccoon relative coatimundi (with its long tapered snout and tail), and armadillos inhabit the area in abundance. At Calakmul, and in the surrounding jungle, circulate two bands of spider monkeys and four bands of howler monkeys.

THE ROUTE'S STARTING POINT Halfway between Bacalar and Chetumal is the turnoff for Highway 186 to Escárcega (about 20km/12 miles from either town). A major highway, it's well marked. This is the same road that leads to Campeche, Palenque, and Villahermosa. A couple of

> ## Opening Hours
>
> The archaeological sites along the Río Bec are open daily, 8am to 5pm.

gas stations are en route; one is at the town of Xpujil. Keep plenty of cash with you as credit cards are little used in the area. The Río Bec sites are at varying distances off this highway. You pass through a guard station at the border with Campeche State. The guards might ask you to present your travel papers, or they might just wave you on. You can divide your sightseeing into several day trips from Bacalar or Chetumal, or you can spend the night in this area and see more the next day. If you get an early start, you can easily visit a few of the sites mentioned here in a day.

Evidence shows that these ruins, especially Becán, were part of the **trade route** linking the Caribbean coast at Cobá to Edzná and the Gulf coast, and to Lamanai in Belize and beyond. At one time, a great number of cities thrived in this region, and much of the land was dedicated to the intensive cultivation of maize. Today everything lies hidden under a dense jungle, which blankets the land from horizon to horizon.

I've listed the following sites in east-to-west order, the way you would see them driving from the Caribbean coast. If you decide to tour these ruins, take the time to visit the Museo de la Cultura Maya (p. 182) in Chetumal first. It will lend context to what you see. If you want a guide to show you the area, contact **Luis Téllez** (© **983/832-3496;** www.mayaruinsandbirds.com), who lives in Chetumal. The best way to reach him is through the e-mail link on his website. Luis is the best guide for this region; he's knowledgeable, speaks English, and drives safely and well. He's acquainted with most of the archaeologists excavating these ruins and stays current with their discoveries. He also knows and can identify the local wildlife and guides many tours for birders.

Entry to each site is 30 to 60 pesos. Informational signs at each building are in Mayan, Spanish, and English. Few if any refreshments are available at the ruins, so bring your own water and food. All the principal sites have toilets.

FOOD & LODGING Your lodging choices are growing. On the upscale side are the Explorean hotel (see below) near Kohunlich and the eco-village in Chicanná. Food and lodging of the no-frills sort can be found in the town of Xpujil and near Calakmul.

The **Explorean** (© **888/679-3748** in the U.S.; www.theexplorean.com) is an eco-lodge for adventure travelers who like their comfort. It sits all alone on the crest of a small hill not far from the ruins of Kohunlich. It has a small pool and spa and lovely rooms, and offers guide services and adventure tours (mountain biking, rappelling, kayaking) as part of an all-inclusive package. The cost is over $500 for two people and, in addition to the tours, includes food and drink. The hotel is a member of the Fiesta Americana chain.

The **Chicanná Eco Village,** Carretera Escárcega Km 296 (© **981/811-9191** for reservations; www.hoteldelmar.com.mx), is just beyond the town of Xpujil. It offers 42 nicely furnished rooms distributed among several two-story thatched bungalows. The comfortable rooms have two doubles or a king-size bed, ceiling fans, a large bathroom, and screened windows. The manicured lawns and flower beds are lovely, with pathways linking the bungalows to each other and to the restaurant and swimming pool. Double rooms go for $116.

In the village of Xpujil (just before the ruins of Xpujil) are three modest hotels and a couple of restaurants. The best food and lodging are at **Restaurant y Hotel Calakmul** (℅ **983/871-6029**), run by Doña María Cabrera. The hotel has 27 rooms that go for $48. They have tile floors, private bathrooms with hot water, and good beds. The restaurant is open daily from 6am to midnight. Main courses cost 45 to 120 pesos. The chicken cooked in herbs is worth ordering. Between Xpujil and Calakmul are three hotels. Two are simple, comfortable, and attractive; one is large and was made with bus tours in mind.

Rio Bec Dreams (℅ **983/871-6057;** www.riobecdreams.com) is a good choice because the owners live on the premises and keep maintenance and service sharp. It's 11km (7 miles) west of Xpujil. You can choose between a private or shared bathroom. The rooms are attractive and well spaced across a nice tract of tropical forest. Each has a little terrace, plenty of screened windows, and lots of cross-ventilation. The hotel restaurant is better than anything else in the area. Another choice is **Puerta Calakmul** (www.puertacalakmul.com.mx), at the turnoff for the ruins of Calakmul.

DZIBANCHE & KINICHNA

The turnoff for this site is 37km (23 miles) from the highway intersection and is well marked. From the turnoff, it's another 23km (14 miles) to the ruins. You should ask about the condition of the road before going. These unpaved roads can go from good to bad pretty quickly, but this is such an important site that road repair is generally kept up. Dzibanché (or Tzibanché) means "place where they write on wood"—obviously not the original name, which remains unknown. Exploration began here in 1993, and the site opened to the public in late 1994. Scattered over 42 sq. km (16 sq. miles) are several groupings of buildings and plazas; only a small portion is excavated. It dates from the Classic period (A.D. 300–900) and was occupied for around 700 years.

TEMPLES & PLAZAS   Two large adjoining plazas have been cleared. The most important structure yet excavated is called the Temple of the Owl, which is in the main plaza, Plaza Xibalba. Archaeologists found a stairway that descends from the top of the structure deep into the pyramid, ending in a burial chamber. It's closed to visitors. But there

---

> ⓘ **Tips**   **Recommended Reading**
>
> For a bit of background reading to help you make the most of your visit, try *A Forest of Kings: The Untold Story of the Ancient Maya,* by Linda Schele and David Freidel; *The Blood of Kings: Dynasty and Ritual in Maya Art,* by Linda Schele and Mary Ellen Miller; and *The Maya Cosmos,* by David Freidel and Linda Schele. *Arqueología Mexicana* magazine devoted its July/August 1995 issue to the Quintana Roo portion of the Río Bec ruin route. The best companion book to have is Joyce Kelly's *An Archaeological Guide to Mexico's Yucatán Peninsula,* despite the fact that it lacks historical and cultural information, and many sites have expanded since it was written.

they uncovered a number of beautiful polychromatic lidded vessels, one of which has an owl painted on the top handle with its wings spreading onto the lid. White owls were messengers of the gods of the underworld in the Maya religion. Also found here were the remains of a sacrificial victim and what appear to be the remains of a Maya queen, which is unique in the archaeology of the Maya.

Opposite the Temple of the Owl is the **Temple of the Cormorant,** named after a polychromed drinking vessel found here depicting the bird. Here, too, archaeologists have found evidence of an interior tomb similar to the one in the Temple of the Owl, but excavations of it have not yet begun. Other magnificently preserved pottery pieces found during excavations include an incense burner with an almost three-dimensional figure of the diving god attached to the outside, and another incense burner with an elaborately dressed representation of the god Itzamná attached.

Situated all by itself is **Structure 6,** a miniature rendition of Teotihuacán's style of *tablero* and *talud* architecture. Each step of the pyramid is made of a *talud* (sloping surface) crowned by a *tablero* (vertical stone facing). Teotihuacán was near present-day Mexico City, but its influence stretched as far as Guatemala. At the top of the pyramid is a doorway with a wooden lintel still intact after centuries of weathering. This detail gave the site its name. Carved into the wood are date glyphs for the year A.D. 733.

Near the site is another city, **Kinichná** (Kee-neech-*nah*). About 2.5km (1¹/₂ miles) north, it is reachable by a road that becomes questionable during the rainy season. An Olmec-style jade figure was found there. It has a large acropolis with five buildings on three levels, which have been restored and are in good condition, with fragments of the remaining stucco still visible.

KOHUNLICH ★

Kohunlich (Koh-*hoon*-leech), 42km (26 miles) from the turnoff for Highway 186, dates from around A.D. 100 to 900. Turn left off the road, and the entrance is 9km (5¹/₂ miles) ahead. From the parking area, you enter the grand, parklike site, crossing a large and shady ceremonial area flanked by four large, conserved pyramidal edifices. Continue walking, and just beyond this grouping you'll come to Kohunlich's famous **Pyramid of the Masks** under a thatched covering. The masks, actually enormous plaster faces from around A.D. 500, are on the facade. Each mask has an elongated face and wears a headdress with a mask on its crest and a mask on the chin piece, essentially masks within masks. The top one is thought to represent the astral world, while the lower one represents the underworld, suggesting that the wearer of this headdress is among the living and not in either of the other worlds. Note the carving on the pupils, which suggests a solar connection, possibly with the night sun that illuminated the underworld. This may mean that the person had shamanic vision.

It's speculated that masks covered much of the facade of this building, built in the Río Bec style, with rounded corners, a false stairway, and a false temple on the top. At least one theory holds that the masks are a composite of several rulers at Kohunlich. In the buildings immediately to the left after you enter, recent excavations uncovered two intact pre-Hispanic skeletons and five decapitated heads that were probably used in a ceremonial ritual. To the right after you enter (follow a shady path through the jungle) is another recently excavated plaza. It's thought to have housed priests or rulers, due to the high quality of pottery found there and the fine architecture of the rooms. Scholars believe that overpopulation led to the decline of Kohunlich.

XPUJIL

Xpujil (Eesh-poo-*heel;* also spelled Xpuhil), meaning either "cattail" or "forest of kapok trees," flourished between A.D. 400 and 900. This is a small site that's easy to get to. Look for a blue sign on the highway pointing to the right. The entrance is just off the highway. After buying a ticket, you have to walk 180m (590 ft.) to the main structure. Along the path are some *chechén* trees. Don't touch; they are poisonous and a stick from one will provoke blisters. You can recognize them by their blotchy bark. On the right, you'll see a platform supporting a restored two-story building with a central staircase on the eastern side. Decorating the first floor are the remnants of a decorative molding and two galleries connected by a doorway. About 90m (295 ft.) farther you come to the site's main structure—a rectangular ceremonial platform 2m (6¹/₂ ft.) high and 50m (164 ft.) long supporting the palace, decorated with three tall towers shaped like miniature versions of the pyramids in Tikal, Guatemala. These towers are purely decorative, with false stairways and temples that are too small to serve as such. The effect is beautiful. The main body of the building holds 12 rooms, which are now in ruins.

BECÁN ★★★

Becán (Beh-*kahn*) is about 7km (4¹/₂ miles) beyond Xpujil and is visible on the right side of the highway. Becán means "moat filled by water," and, in fact, it was protected by a moat spanned by seven bridges. The extensive site dates from the early Classic to the late post-Classic (600 B.C.–A.D. 1200) period. Although it was abandoned by A.D. 850, ceramic remains indicate that there may have been a population resurgence between 900 and 1000, and it was still used as a ceremonial site as late as 1200. Becán was an administrative and ceremonial center with political sway over at least seven other cities in the area, including Chicanná, Hormiguero, and Payán.

The first plaza group you see after you enter was the center for grand ceremonies. From the highway, you can see the back of a pyramid (Structure 1) with two temples on top. Beyond and in between the two temples you can see the Temple atop Structure 4, which is opposite Temple 1. When the high priest appeared exiting the mouth of the earth monster in the center of this temple (which he reached by way of a hidden side stairway that's now partially exposed), he would have been visible from well beyond the immediate plaza. It's thought that commoners had to watch ceremonies from outside the plaza—thus the site's position was for good viewing purposes. The back of Structure 4 is believed to have been a civic plaza where rulers sat on stone benches while pronouncing judgments. The second plaza group dates from around A.D. 850 and has perfect twin towers on top, where there's a big platform. Under the platform are 10 rooms that are thought to be related to Xibalba (Shee-*bahl*-bah), the underworld. Hurricane Isidore damaged them, and they are still closed. Earth monster faces probably covered this building (and appeared on other buildings as well). Remains of at least one ball court have been unearthed. Next to the ball court is a well-preserved figure in an elaborate headdress behind glass. He was excavated not far from where he is now displayed. The markings are well defined, displaying a host of details.

CHICANNA

Slightly over 1.5km (1 mile) beyond Becán, on the left side of the highway, is Chicanná, which means "house of the mouth of snakes." Trees loaded with bromeliads shade the central square surrounded by five buildings. The most outstanding edifice features a monster-mouth doorway and an ornate stone facade with more superimposed masks. As you enter the mouth of the earth monster, note that you are walking on a platform configured as the open jaw of the monster with stone teeth on both sides. Again you find a lovely example of an elongated building with ornamental miniature pyramids on each end.

CALAKMUL ★★★

This area is both a massive Maya archaeological zone, with at least 60 sites, and a 70,000-hectare (172,900-acre) rainforest designated in 1989 as the Calakmul Biosphere Reserve, including territory in both Mexico and Guatemala. The best way to see Calakmul is to spend the night at Xpujil or Chicanná and leave early in the morning for Calakmul. If you're the first one to drive down the narrow access road to the ruins (1¹/₂ hr. from the highway), you'll probably see plenty of wildlife. On my last trip to the ruins, I saw two groups of spider monkeys swinging through the trees on the outskirts of the city and a group of howler monkeys sleeping in the trees in front of Structure 2. I also saw a couple of animals that I couldn't identify, and heard the growl of a jungle cat that I wasn't able to see.

THE ARCHAEOLOGICAL ZONE   Since 1982, archaeologists have been excavating the ruins of Calakmul, which date from 100 B.C. to A.D. 900. It's the largest of the area's 60 known sites. Nearly 7,000 buildings have been discovered and mapped. At its zenith, at least 60,000 people may have lived around the site, but by the time of the Spanish Conquest in 1519, there were fewer than 1,000 inhabitants. Visitors arrive at a large plaza filled with a forest of trees. You immediately see several stelae; Calakmul contains more of these than any other site, but they are much more weathered and indistinguishable than the stelae of Palenque or Copán in Honduras. On one of them you can see the work of looters who carefully used some sort of stone-cutting saw to slice off the face of the monument. By Structure 13 is a stele of a woman that dates from A.D. 652. She is thought to have been a ruler.

Several structures here are worth checking out; some are built in the Petén style, some in the Río Bec style. Structure 3 must have been the residence of a noble family. Its design is unique and quite lovely; it managed to retain its original form and was never remodeled. Offerings of shells, beads, and polychromed tripod pottery were found inside. Structure 2 is the tallest pyramid in the Yucatán, at 54m (177 ft.). From the top of it you can see the outline of the ruins of El Mirador, 50km (31 miles) across the forest in Guatemala. Notice the two stairways that ascend along the sides of the principal face of the pyramid in the upper levels, and how the masks break up the space of the front face.

Temple 4 charts the line of the sun from June 21, when it falls on the left (north) corner; to September 21 and March 21, when it lines up in the east behind the middle temple on the top of the building; to December 21, when it falls on the right (south) corner. Numerous jade pieces, including spectacular masks, were uncovered here, most of which are on display in the Museo Regional in Campeche. Temple 7 is largely unexcavated except for the top, where, in 1984, the most outstanding jade mask yet to be found at Calakmul was uncovered. In their book *A Forest of Kings,* Linda Schele and David Freidel tell of wars among the Calakmul, Tikal, and Naranjo (the latter two in Guatemala), and how Ah-Cacaw, king of Tikal (120km/74 miles south of Calakmul), captured King Jaguar-Paw in A.D. 695 and later Lord Ox-Ha-Te Ixil Ahau, both of Calakmul. The site is open Tuesday to Sunday from 7am to 5pm, but it gets so wet during the rainy season from June to October that it's best not to go during that time.

high forest, a rainforest that annually records as much as 5m (16 ft.) of rain. Notice that the canopy of the trees is higher here than in the forest of Quintana Roo. It lies very close to the border with Guatemala, but, of course, there is no way to get there. Among the plants are cactus, epiphytes, and orchids. Endangered animals include the white-lipped peccary, jaguar, and puma. So far, more than 250 species of birds have been recorded. At present, no overnight stay or camping is permitted. If you want a tour of a small part of the forest and you speak Spanish, you can inquire for a guide at one of the two nearby *ejidos* (cooperatives). Some old local *chicleros* (the men who tap sapodilla trees for their gum) have expert knowledge of flora and fauna and can take you on a couple of trails.

> **A Driving Caution**
>
> Numerous curves in the road obscure oncoming traffic (what little there is).

The turnoff on the left for Calakmul is located 53km (33 miles) from Xpujil, just before the village of Conhuas. There's a guard station there where you pay 50 pesos per car. From the turnoff, it's an hour drive on a paved one-lane-road. Admission to the site is 40 pesos.

It's advisable to take with you some food and drink and, of course, bug spray.

BALAMKU ★★

Balamkú (Bah-lahm-*koo*) is easy to reach and worth the visit. A couple of buildings in the complex were so well preserved that they required almost no reconstruction. Inside one you will find three impressive figures of men sitting in the gaping maws of crocodiles and toads as they descend into the underworld. The concept behind this building, with its molded stucco facade, is life and death. On the head of each stucco figure are the eyes, nose, and mouth of a jaguar figure, followed by the full face of the human figure, then a neck formed by the eyes and nose of another jaguar, and an Olmec-like face on the stomach, with its neck ringed by a necklace. These figures were saved from looters who managed to get away with a fourth one. Now they're under the protection of a caretaker, who keeps the room under lock and key. If you speak Spanish, you can get the caretaker to explain something of the figures and their complex symbolism. A beautiful courtyard and another set of buildings are adjacent to the main group.

Mérida, Chichén Itzá & the Maya Interior

by David Baird

Ask most people about the Yucatán, and they think of Cancún, the Caribbean coast, and Chichén Itzá. With a little exploring, though, you'll find a world beyond the region's tourist magnets. One day, you might spend the morning scrambling over Maya ruins and in the afternoon take a dip in the cool, clear water of a cenote (a natural underground pool). On the next day, you might be strolling along a lonely beach or riding in a skiff through mangroves to visit a colony of pink flamingos. By the evening, you could be dancing in the streets of **Mérida** (the largest city in the region). This chapter covers the interior of the Yucatán peninsula, including the famous Maya ruins at **Chichén Itzá** and **Uxmal,** the flamingo sanctuaries at **Celestún** and **Río Lagartos,** as well as many other spots that might find special favor with you.

EXPLORING THE YUCATAN'S MAYA HEARTLAND

The best way to see the Yucatán is by car. The terrain is flat, there is little traffic once you get away from the cities, and the main highways are in good shape. If you drive at all around this area, you will add at least one new word to your Spanish vocabulary—*topes* (*toh*-pehs), meaning speed bumps. And along with *topes* you might learn a few new curse words. *Topes* come in varying shapes and sizes and with varying degrees of warning. Don't let them surprise you.

Off the main highways, the roads are narrow and rough, but hey—you'll be driving a rental car. Rentals are, in fact, a little pricey (due perhaps to wear and tear?), but some promotional deals are available, especially in low season. For more on renting a car, see "Getting Around: By Car," in "Mérida: Gateway to the Maya Heartland," below.

Plenty of buses ply the roads between the major towns and ruins. And plenty of tour buses circulate, too. But buses to the smaller towns and ruins and the haciendas are infrequent. One bus company, Autobuses del Oriente (ADO), controls most of the first-class bus service and does a good job with the major destinations. Second-class buses go to some out-of-the-way places, but they can be slow, stop a lot, and usually aren't air-conditioned. I use them to cover short distances. If you don't want to rent a car, a few tour operators transport small groups to more remote attractions such as ruins, cenotes, and villages.

The Yucatán is *tierra caliente* (the hot lands). Don't travel in this region without a hat, sun block, mosquito repellent, and water. The coolest weather is from November to February; the hottest is from April to June. From July to October, thundershowers moderate temperatures. More tourists come to the interior during the winter months, but not to the same extent as on the Caribbean coast. The high season/low season distinction is less pronounced here.

Should you decide to travel into this part of the world, don't miss **Mérida.** It is, and has been for centuries, the cultural and commercial center of the Yucatán. You won't find a more vibrant tropical city anywhere. Every time I visit, there is some festival or celebration to attend, on top of the nightly performances that the city offers its citizens and visitors. It's also the Yucatán's shopping center, where you can buy the area's specialty items, such as hammocks, Panama hats, and the embroidered native blouses known as *huipiles.*

Aside from Mérida, here are some other places to consider.

CHICHÉN ITZÁ & VALLADOLID These destinations are almost midway between Mérida and Cancún. From Mérida, it's 2¹/₂ hours by car to Chichén on the new *autopista* (toll road). You can spend a day at the ruins and then stay at one of the nearby hotels— or drive 40km (25 miles) to Valladolid, a quiet, charming colonial town with a pleasant central square. Valladolid features two eerie cenotes. The spectacular ruins at **Ek Balam** are only 40km (25 miles) to the north. Also in the area is the **Río Lagartos Nature Reserve,** teeming with flamingos and other native birds.

CELESTÚN NATIONAL WILDLIFE REFUGE These flamingo-sanctuary wetlands along the Gulf coast contain a unique shallow-water estuary where freshwater from cenotes mixes with saltwater, creating the perfect feeding ground for flamingos. Touring this area by launch is relaxing and rewarding. Only 1¹/₂ hours from Mérida, Celestún makes for an easy day trip.

DZIBILCHALTÚN This Maya site, now a national park, is 14km (8³/₄ miles) north of Mérida along the road to Progreso. Here you'll find pre-Hispanic ruins, nature trails, a cenote, and the Museum of the Maya. You can make this the first stop in a day trip to Progreso and other attractions north of Mérida.

PROGRESO A port city and Gulf Coast beach escape 34km (21 miles) north of Mérida, Progreso has a wide beach and oceanfront drive that's popular on the weekends and during the summer. The recent arrival of cruise ships might make Progreso even more popular, but with so much beach, you'll easily have a place to yourself. From Progreso, you can drive down the coast to **Uaymitún** to see some flamingos and visit the recently excavated ruins of **Xcambó.**

(Tips) **The Best Websites for Mérida, Chichén Itzá & the Maya Interior**

- **Maya: Portraits of a People: www.nationalgeographic.com/explorer/maya/more.html** A fascinating collection of articles from *National Geographic* and other sources.
- **Yucatán Travel Guide: www.mayayucatan.com** Yucatán's Ministry of Tourism maintains this site. It has an update section and good general info on different destinations in the state.
- **Mexico's Yucatán Directory: www.mexonline.com/yucatan.htm** A nice roundup of vacation rentals, tour operators, and information on the Maya sites. For more information on Mexico's indigenous history, see the links on the pre-Columbian page (www.mexonline.com/precolum.htm).

UXMAL   Smaller than Chichén, but architecturally more striking and mysterious, Uxmal is about 80km (50 miles) south of Mérida. You can see it in a day, though it's a good idea to extend that somewhat to see the sound-and-light show and spend the night at one of the hotels by the ruins. Several other nearby sites make up the Puuc route and can be explored the following day. It's also possible, though a bit rushed, to see Uxmal and the other ruins on a 1-day trip by special excursion bus from Mérida.

CAMPECHE   This beautiful, walled colonial city has been so meticulously restored that it's a delight just to stroll down the streets. Campeche is about 3 hours southwest of Mérida in the direction of Palenque. A full day should give you enough time to see its highlights and museums, but there is something about Campeche that makes you want to linger.

1 MÉRIDA: GATEWAY TO THE MAYA HEARTLAND ★★

1,440km (893 miles) E of Mexico City; 320km (198 miles) W of Cancún

Mérida is the capital of the state of Yucatán and has been the dominant city in the region since the Spanish Conquest. It is a busy city and suffers from the same problems that plague other colonial cities in Mexico—traffic and noise. Still, it's a fun city and has many admirers. I get comments from people all the time about how much they enjoyed Mérida. People there know how to have a good time, and they seem driven to organize concerts, theater productions, art exhibitions, and such. In recent years, the city has been in the midst of a cultural explosion.

ESSENTIALS
Getting There & Departing
BY PLANE   AeroMéxico (② 01-800/021-4000 in Mexico, or 999/927-9277; www. aeromexico.com) flies nonstop to and from Miami and Mexico City. **Mexicana** (② 01-800/502-2000 in Mexico, or 999/924-6633; www.mexicana.com.mx) has nonstop service to and from Mexico City. **Continental** (② 999/946-1888, -1900; www.continental. com) has nonstop service to and from Houston. **Click,** a Mexican budget airline and part of Mexicana (www.click.com.mx), provides nonstop service to and from Mexico City and Veracruz. **Aviacsa** (② 01-800/006-2000 in Mexico; www.aviacsa.com) provides nonstop service to and from Villahermosa and Mexico City. **Aerolitoral** (② 01-800/800-2674 in Mexico; www.aerolitoral.com) flies to and from Mexico City and Villahermosa. **Volaris** (② 01-800/786-5274 in Mexico; www.volaris.com.mx) is a discount domestic air carrier that flies to and from Toluca.

BY CAR   Hwy. 180 is the old *carretera federal* (federal highway) between Mérida and Cancún. The trip takes 6 hours, and the road is in good shape; you will pass through many Maya villages. A four-lane divided *cuota,* or *autopista* (toll road) parallels Hwy. 180 and begins at the town of Kantunil, 56km (35 miles) east of Mérida. By avoiding the tiny villages and their not-so-tiny speed bumps, the *autopista* cuts 2 hours from the journey between Mérida and Cancún; one-way tolls cost 320 pesos. Coming from the direction of Cancún, Hwy. 180 enters Mérida by feeding into Calle 65, which passes 1 block south of the main square.

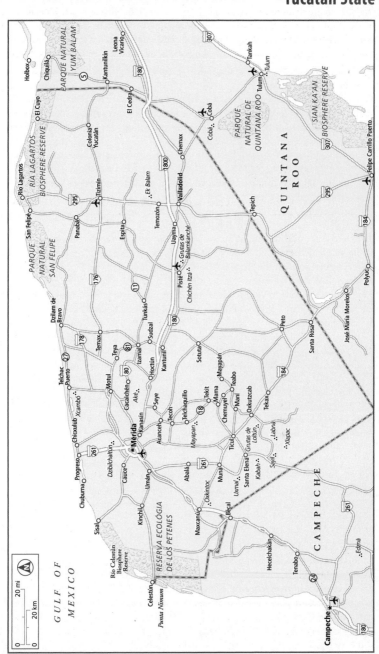

8

Coming from the south (Campeche or Uxmal), you will enter the city on Avenida Itzáes. To get to the town center, turn right on Calle 59 (the first street after the zoo).

A *periférico* (loop road) encircles Mérida, making it possible to skirt the city. Directional signs into the city are generally good, but going around the city on the loop requires vigilance.

BY BUS   There are five bus stations in Mérida, two of which offer first-class buses; the other three provide local service to nearby destinations. The larger of the first-class stations, **CAME,** is on Calle 70, between calles 69 and 71 (see "City Layout," below). The ADO bus line and its affiliates operate the station. When you get there, you'll see a row of ticket windows; all but the last couple to the right sell first-class tickets. The last two windows sell tickets for ADO's deluxe services, ADO-GL and UNO. The former is only slightly better than first class; the latter has superwide, roomy seats. Unless it's a long trip, I generally choose the bus that has the most convenient departure time. Tickets can be purchased in advance; just ask the ticket agent for the different options and departure times for the route you need.

The other first-class station is the small **Maya K'iin** used by the bus company **Elite.** It's at Calle 65 no. 548, between calles 68 and 70.

To and from Cancún: You can pick up a bus at the CAME (almost every hour) or through Elite (five per day). Both bus lines also pick up passengers at the Fiesta Americana Hotel, across from the Hyatt (12 per day). You can buy a ticket in the hotel's shopping arcade at the **Ticket Bus** agency or at the Elite ticket agency. Cancún is 4 hours away; a few buses stop in **Valladolid.** If you're downtown, you can purchase tickets from the agency in Pasaje Picheta, on the main square a couple of doors down from the Palacio de Gobierno.

To and from Chichén Itzá: Three buses per day (2¹/₂-hr. trip) depart from the CAME. Also check out tours operating from the hotels in Mérida if you want to visit for the day.

To and from Playa del Carmen, Tulum, and Chetumal: From the CAME, there are 10 departures per day for Playa del Carmen (5-hr. trip), six for Tulum (6-hr. trip), and eight for Chetumal (7-hr. trip). From Maya K'iin, there are three per day to Playa, which stop at the Fiesta Americana.

To and from Campeche: From the CAME station, there are 36 departures per day. Elite has four departures per day. It's a 2¹/₂-hour trip.

To and from Palenque and San Cristóbal de las Casas: There is service to San Cristóbal twice daily from the CAME, and once daily on Elite. To Palenque there are three and one, respectively. There have been reports of minor theft on buses to Palenque. You should do three things: Don't take second-class buses to this destination; check your luggage so that it's stowed in the cargo bay; and put your carry-on in the overhead rack, not on the floor.

The main **second-class bus station** is around the corner from the CAME on Calle 69, between calles 68 and 70.

To and from Uxmal: There are four buses per day. (You can also hook up with a tour to Uxmal through most hotels or any travel agent or tour operator in town.) One bus per day combines Uxmal with the other sites to the south (Kabah, Sayil, Labná, and Xlapak—known as the Puuc route) and does the whole round-trip in a day. It stops for 2 hours at Uxmal and 30 minutes at each of the other sites.

To and from Progreso and Dzibilchaltún: Transportes AutoProgreso offers service to and from its station at Calle 62 no. 524, between calles 65 and 67. The trip to Progreso takes an hour by second-class bus.

To and from Celestún: The Celestún station is at Calle 50 between calles 65 and 67. The trip takes 1¹/₂ to 2 hours, depending on how often the bus stops. There are 10 buses per day.

To and from Izamal: The bus station is at the corner of Calle 65 and Calle 48. Departures are every half-hour. The trip takes 1¹/₂ hours.

Orientation

ARRIVING BY PLANE Mérida's airport is 13km (8 miles) from the city center on the southwestern outskirts of town, near the entrance to Hwy. 180. The airport has desks for rental cars, hotel reservations, and tourist information. Taxi tickets to town (16 pesos) are sold outside the airport doors, under the covered walkway.

VISITOR INFORMATION The city tourism offices and state tourism offices have different resources; if you can't get the information you're looking for at one, go to the other. I have better luck with the city's **visitor information office** (© **999/942-0000,** ext. 80119), which is on the ground floor of the Ayuntamiento building, facing the main square on Calle 62. Look for a glass door under the arcade. Hours are Monday to Saturday from 8am to 8pm, and Sunday from 8am to 2pm. Monday through Saturday, at 9:30am, the staff offers visitors a free tour of the area around the main square. The state operates two downtown tourism offices: One is in the **Teatro Peón Contreras,** facing Parque de la Madre (© **999/924-9290**), and the other is on the main plaza, in the **Palacio de Gobierno,** immediately to the left as you enter. These offices are open daily from 8am to 9pm. There are also information booths at the airport and the CAME bus station.

Also keep your eye out for the free monthly magazine *Yucatán Today;* it's a good source of information for Mérida and the rest of the region.

CITY LAYOUT Downtown Mérida has the standard layout of towns in the Yucatán: Streets running north–south are even numbers; those running east–west are odd numbers. The numbering begins on the north and the east sides of town, so if you're walking on an odd-numbered street and the even numbers of the cross-streets are increasing, then you are heading west; likewise, if you are on an even-numbered street and the odd numbers of the cross-streets are increasing, you are going south.

Address numbers don't tell you anything about what cross-street to look for. This is why addresses almost always list cross-streets, usually like this: "Calle 60 no. 549 × 71 y 73." The "×" is a multiplication sign—shorthand for the word *por* (meaning "by")—and *y* means "and." So this place would be on Calle 60 between calles 71 and 73. Outside of the downtown area, the numbering of streets gets a little crazy, so it's important to know the name of the neighborhood *(colonia)* where you're going. This is the first thing taxi drivers will ask you.

The town's main square is the busy **Plaza Mayor,** known as **El Centro.** It's bordered by calles 60, 62, 61, and 63. Calle 60, which runs in front of the cathedral, is an important street to remember; it connects the main square with several smaller plazas, some theaters and churches, and the University of Yucatán, just to the north. Here you'll find a concentration of handicraft shops, restaurants, and hotels. Around Plaza Mayor are the cathedral, the Palacio de Gobierno (state government building), the Ayuntamiento (town hall), and the Palacio Montejo. The plaza always has a crowd, and it's full on Sunday, when it holds a large street fair. (See "Daily Festivals & Special Events in Mérida," below.) Within a few blocks are several smaller plazas and the bustling market district.

(Moments) Daily Festivals & Special Events in Mérida

Many Mexican cities offer weekend concerts in the park and such, but Mérida surpasses them all by offering performances every day of the week. Unless otherwise indicated, admission to the following is free.

Sunday Each Sunday from 9am to 9pm, there's a fair called *Mérida en Domingo* (Mérida on Sunday). The main plaza and a section of Calle 60 from El Centro to Parque Santa Lucía close to traffic. Parents come with their children to stroll around and take in the scene. There are booths selling food and drink, along with a lively little flea market and used-book fair, children's art classes, and educational booths. At 11am in front of the Palacio del Gobierno, musicians play everything from jazz to classical and folk music. Also at 11am, the police orchestra performs Yucatecan tunes at the Santa Lucía park. At 11:30am, you'll find bawdy comedy acts at the Parque Hidalgo, on Calle 60 at Calle 59. There's a lull in the midafternoon, and then the plaza fills up again as people walk around and visit with friends. Around 7pm in front of the Ayuntamiento, a large band starts playing mambos, rumbas, and cha-chas with great enthusiasm; you may see 1,000 people dancing in the street. Afterward, folk ballet dancers reenact a typical Yucatecan wedding inside.

Monday Every Monday at 9pm in front of the *Palacio Municipal,* performers play *Vaquería regional,* traditional music and dancing to celebrate the Vaquerías feast, which was associated originally with the branding of cattle on Yucatecan haciendas. Among the featured performers are dancers with trays of bottles or filled glasses balanced on their heads—a sight to see.

Tuesday At 9pm in Parque Santiago, Calle 59 at Calle 72, the Municipal Orchestra plays Latin and American big-band music from the 1940s.

Wednesday At 9pm in the Teatro Peón Contreras, Calle 60 at Calle 57, the University of Yucatán Ballet Folklórico presents *Yucatán and Its Roots.* Admission is 50 pesos.

Thursday Yucatecan *trova* music (boleros, baladas) and dance are presented at the Serenata in Parque Santa Lucía at 9pm.

Friday At 9pm in the courtyard of the University of Yucatán, Calle 60 at Calle 57, the University of Yucatán Ballet Folklórico performs typical regional dances from the Yucatán.

Saturday Noche Mexicana, at the park at the beginning of Paseo de Montejo, begins at 9pm and features several performances of traditional Mexican music and dance. Some of the performers are amateurs who acquit themselves reasonably well; others are professionals who thoroughly know their craft. Food stands sell good *antojitos* (finger foods), as well as drinks and ice cream.

Mérida's most fashionable district is the broad, tree-lined boulevard **Paseo de Montejo** and its surrounding neighborhood. The Paseo de Montejo parallels Calle 60 and begins 7 blocks north and a little east of the main square. There are a number of trendy restaurants,

modern hotels, offices of various banks and airlines, and a few clubs here, but the boulevard
is mostly known for its stately mansions built during the boom times of the *henequén*
industry. Near where the Paseo intersects Avenida Colón, you'll find the Hyatt and the
Fiesta Americana hotels.

GETTING AROUND **By Car** In general, reserve your car in advance from home to
get the best weekly rates during high season (Nov–Feb); in low season, I usually do better
renting a car once I get to Mérida. The local rental companies are competitive and have
promotional deals that you can get only if you are there. When comparing, make sure
that it's apples to apples; ask if the price quote includes the IVA tax and insurance coverage. Practically everybody offers free mileage. For tips on saving money on car rentals, see
"Getting There & Getting Around," in chapter 3. Rental cars are generally a little more
expensive (unless you find a promotional rate) than similar rentals in the U.S. By renting
for only a day or two, you can avoid the high cost of parking lots in Mérida. These *esta-
cionamentos* charge one price for the night and double that if you leave your car for the
following day. Many hotels offer free parking, but make sure they include daytime parking in the price.

By Taxi Taxis are easy to come by and much cheaper than in Cancún.

By Bus City buses are a little tricky to figure out but aren't needed very often because
almost everything of interest is within walking distance of the main plaza. Still, it's a bit of
a walk from the plaza to the Paseo de Montejo, and you can save yourself some work by
taking a bus, minibus, or *colectivo* (Volkswagen minivan) that is heading north on Calle 60.
Most of these will take you within a couple of blocks of the Paseo de Montejo. The *colectivos* or *combis* (usually painted white) run out in several directions from the main plaza along
simple routes. They usually line up along the side streets next to the plaza.

(Fast Facts) Mérida

Area Code The telephone area code is **999.**

Bookstore The English-language bookstore **Amate Books** (© 999/924-2222) is
at Calle 60 453-A, by Calle 51. It stocks a large selection of books on many subjects
and is open Tuesday through Sunday from 10:30am to 8:30pm. **The Librería
Dante,** Calle 59 between calles 60 and 62 (© 999/928-3674), has a small selection of English-language cultural-history books on Mexico.

Business Hours Generally, businesses are open Monday to Saturday from 10am
to 2pm and 4 to 8pm.

Climate From November to February, the weather can be pleasantly cool and
windy. In other months, it's just hot, especially during the day. Rain can occur
any time of year, especially during the rainy season (July–Oct), and usually comes
in the form of afternoon tropical showers.

Consulates The **American Consulate** is at Calle 60 no. 338-K, 1 block north of
the Hyatt hotel (Col. Alcalá Martín). The phone number is © **999/942-5700.** Office
hours are Monday to Friday from 9am to 1pm.

Currency Exchange I prefer *casas de cambio* (currency exchange offices) over
banks. There are many of these; one called **Cambios Portales,** Calle 61 no. 500

(© **999/923-8709**), is on the north side of the main plaza in the middle of the block. It's open daily from 8:30am to 8:30pm. There are also many ATMs; one is on the south side of the same plaza.

Drugstore **Farmacía Yza,** Calle 63 no. 502, between calles 60 and 62 (© **999/924-9510**), on the south side of the plaza, is open 24 hours.

Hospitals The best hospital is **Centro Médico de las Américas,** Calle 54 no. 365 between 33-A and Avenida Pérez Ponce. The main phone number is © **999/926-2619;** for emergencies, call © **999/927-3199.** You can also call the **Cruz Roja (Red Cross)** at © **999/924-9813.**

Internet Access There are so many Internet access providers in town that you hardly have to walk more than a couple of blocks to find one.

Police Mérida has a special body of police to assist tourists. They patrol the downtown area and the Paseo de Montejo. They wear white shirts bearing the words POLICIA TURISTICA. Their phone number is © **999/925-2555.**

Post Office The *correo* moved recently. It's now on Calle 53 between calles 52 and 54. It's open Monday to Friday from 8am to 4:30pm, Saturday from 9am to 1pm.

Seasons There are two high seasons for tourism, but they aren't as pronounced as on the coast. One is in July and August, when Mexicans take their vacations, and the other is between November 15 and Easter Sunday, when Canadians and Americans flock to the Yucatán to escape winter weather.

WHERE TO STAY

Mérida is easier on the budget than the resort cities. The stream of visitors is steadier than on the coast, so most hotels no longer use a high season/low season rate structure. Still, you are more likely to find promotional rates during low season. Mérida has a convention center, which attracts large trade shows that can fill the city's hotels, so it's a good idea to make reservations. The rates quoted here include the 17% tax. When inquiring about prices, always ask if the price quoted includes tax. Most hotels in Mérida offer at least a few air-conditioned rooms, and some also have pools. But many inexpensive hotels haven't figured out how to provide a comfortable bed. Either the mattresses are poor quality or the bottom sheet is too small to tuck in properly. Some hotels here would offer a good deal if only they would improve their beds. One last thing to note: Without exception, every hotel in Mérida that doesn't have its own parking has an arrangement with a nearby parking garage, where you can park your car for a fee. Or you can park on the street, where, for the most part, cars are safe from vandalism. In Mérida, free parking is a relative concept—for many hotels, free parking means only at night; during the day, there may be a charge.

Very Expensive

Fiesta Americana Mérida ★★   This six-story hotel on the Paseo de Montejo is built in the grand *fin-de-siècle* style of the old mansions along the Paseo. Guest rooms are off the cavernous lobby, so all face outward and have views of one or another of the avenues. The rooms are comfortable and large, with furnishings and decorations striving for, and achieving, innocuousness in light, tropical colors. The floors are tile and the

ACCOMMODATIONS ■

Casa Mexilio Guest House **6**

Casa San Juan **20**

Fiesta Americana Mérida **1**

Hotel Caribe **18**

Hotel Dolores Alba **19**

Hotel Maison Lafitte **12**

Hotel Marionetas **4**

Hotel MedioMundo **5**

Hotel Mucuy **14**

Hyatt Regency Mérida **2**

DINING ◆

Alberto's Continental **9**

Amaro **11**

Café Alameda **13**

Casa de Frida **8**

Eladio's **16**

El Templo **17**

La Flor de Santiago **7**

Restaurante Kantún **3**

Restaurant Los Almendros **15**

Vito Corleone **10**

Haciendas & Hotels

Haciendas in the Yucatán have had a bumpy history. During the colonial period, they were isolated, self-sufficient fiefdoms—not terribly efficient, but they didn't have to be. Mostly they produced foodstuffs—enough for the needs of the owners and peasants, plus a little extra that the owners could sell for a small sum in the city. The owners, though politically powerful, especially within the confines of their large estates, were never rich.

This changed in the 19th century, when the expanding world market created high demand for *henequén,* the natural fiber of the sisal plant, which was used to bale hay. In a few years, all of the haciendas shifted to mass production of this commodity. Prices and profits kept climbing through the end of the century and into the 20th. Hacienda owners now had lots of cash to spend on their estates and on heavy machinery to process the *henequén* fiber more efficiently. Then came the bust. Throughout the 1920s, prices and demand fell, and no other commodity could replace sisal. The haciendas entered a long decline, but by then, the cultivation and processing of sisal had become part of local culture.

To see and understand what things were like during the golden age, you can visit a couple of haciendas. One, by the name of **Sotuta de Peón,** has recently been refurbished and runs much like in the old days—a living museum involving an entire community (see "Side Trips from Mérida," later in this chapter). At the other one, **Yaxcopoil** (see "En Route to Uxmal," later in this chapter), you can wander about the shell of a once-bustling estate and look at faded splendor.

Today another boom of sorts has brought haciendas back, this time as retreats, country residences, and hotels. The hotels convey an air of the past— elegant gateways, thick walls, open arches, and high ceilings—you get the feel of an era gone by. Indeed, there are a few features that make a guest feel like lord and master, especially the extravagant suites and personal service. But what strikes me the most when I visit these haciendas is the contrast between them and the world outside. They are like little islands of order and tranquillity in the sea of chaos that is the Yucatán.

There are five luxury hacienda hotels. The most opulent of these is **La Hacienda Xcanatún** (✆ **888/883-3633** in the U.S.; www.xcanatun.com). It's on the

bathrooms large and well equipped. Service is very attentive, better than at the Hyatt. There is a shopping center on the ground floor, below the lobby.

Av. Colón 451, corner of Paseo Montejo, 92127 Mérida, Yuc. ✆ **800/343-7821** in the U.S. and Canada, or 999/942-1111. Fax 999/942-1112. www.fiestaamericana.com.mx. 350 units. $220 double; $260 executive level; $280 junior suite. AE, DC, MC, V. Free secure parking. **Amenities:** 2 restaurants; bar; babysitting; children's programs; concierge; health club w/saunas, men's steam room, and unisex whirlpool; midsize outdoor pool; room service; tennis court; executive-level rooms. *In room:* A/C, TV w/pay movies, hair dryer, high-speed Internet, minibar.

Hyatt Regency Mérida ★★   This Hyatt is much like Hyatts elsewhere, wherein lies this hotel's chief asset. The rooms are dependably comfortable and quiet, the quietest in a noisy city. They're carpeted and well furnished, with great bathrooms. In decoration outskirts of Mérida, off the highway to Progreso. The suites are large and have extravagant bathrooms. The decor is in muted colors with rich materials and modern pieces that evoke the simplicity of an earlier age. It has the best restaurant in the Mérida area and a complete spa. The owners personally manage their hotel and keep the service sharp.

The other four luxury hotels are all owned by Roberto Hernández, one of the richest men in Mexico. The hospitality and reservation system is handled by **Starwood Hotels** (© **800/325-3589** in the U.S. and Canada; www.luxury collection.com). The owner has taken great pains to restore all four haciendas to original condition, and all are beautiful. **Temozón** (p. 204), off the highway to Uxmal, is the most magnificent. **Uayamón,** located between the ruins of Edzná and the colonial city of Campeche, is perhaps the most romantic. **Hacienda San José Cholul** ★, located east of Mérida toward Izamal, is a personal favorite, and picturesque **Santa Rosa** lies southwest of Mérida, near the town of Maxcanú. Packages are available for staying at two or more of these haciendas. All offer personal service, activities, and spas.

Two haciendas offer economical lodging. On the western outskirts of Mérida by the highway to Chichén Itzá and Cancún is **Hacienda San Pedro Nohpat** (© **999/988-0542;** www.haciendaholidays.com). It retains only the land that immediately surrounds the residence, but it offers a great bargain in lodging—large, comfortable rooms and an attractive garden area and pool. The other is **Hacienda Blanca Flor** (© **999/925-8042;** www.blancaflor.com.mx), which lies between Mérida and Campeche just off the highway. It's the only hacienda hotel that actually operates like one, producing most of the food served there. The owners work with bus tours but also welcome couples and individuals. Rooms are in a modern building and are large and simply furnished.

Two other haciendas can be leased by small groups for retreats and group vacations: **Hacienda Petac** (© **800/225-4255** in the U.S.; www.haciendapetac. com) and **Hacienda San Antonio** (© **999/910-6144;** www.haciendasan antonio.com.mx). Both have beautiful rooms, common areas, and grounds.

and comfort, I find them superior to those of the Fiesta Americana, but they certainly don't have any local flavor. The Hyatt's facilities, especially its tennis courts and health club, also rank above the Fiesta Americana's. The pool is more attractive and larger, but its location keeps it in the shade for most of the day, and the water never gets a chance to heat up. Rising 17 stories, the Hyatt is not hard to find in Mérida's skyline; it's near the Paseo de Montejo and across Avenida Colón from the Fiesta Americana.

Calle 60 no. 344 (at Av. Colón), 97000 Mérida, Yuc. © **800/223-1234** in the U.S. and Canada, or 999/942-1234. Fax 999/925-7002. www.mérida.regency.hyatt.com. 299 units. $200 standard double; $220 Regency Club double. Ask about promotional rates. AE, DC, MC, V. Free guarded parking. **Amenities:** 2 restaurants; 2 bars (1 swim-up, open seasonally); babysitting; children's activities (seasonal); concierge; state-of-the-art health club w/men's and women's whirlpool, sauna, and steam rooms; large outdoor pool; room service; smoke-free rooms; 2 lighted tennis courts; executive-level rooms. *In room:* A/C, TV, hair dryer, minibar.

Hotel Marionetas ★   This quiet and attractive B&B, 6 blocks north of the main square, has a comforting feel to it. Even though I've heard the story, I'm still not clear on how the hosts, Sofi (Macedonian) and Daniel (Argentinean), ended up in Mérida. But they are engaging, interesting people and attentive innkeepers. They have created a lovely space with common areas in front, rooms in back, and a lush garden/pool area in between. It's the kind of place that tempts you to lounge about.

Calle 49 no. 516 (btw. calles 62 and 64), 97000 Mérida, Yuc. ☎ **999/928-3377.** www.hotelmarionetas. com. 8 units. $110 double. Rates include full breakfast. 2-night minimum stay. MC, V. Free secure parking for compact cars. No children 11 and under. **Amenities:** Small outdoor pool; smoke-free rooms. *In room:* A/C, fridge, hair dryer, Wi-Fi.

Moderate

Casa Mexilio Guest House ★ (**Moments**)   This bed-and-breakfast is unlike any other I know. The owners are geniuses at playing with space in an unexpected and delightful manner. Rooms are at different levels, creating private spaces joined to each other and to rooftop terraces by stairs and catwalks. Most are spacious and airy, furnished and decorated in an engaging mix of new and old, polished and primitive. Five come with air-conditioning. A small pool with a whirlpool and profuse tropical vegetation takes up most of the central patio. Breakfasts are great. It's 4 blocks west of the plaza. A small bar serves drinks during happy hour, and, weather permitting, you can have your cocktail on one of the rooftop terraces.

Calle 68 no. 495 (btw. calles 57 and 59), 97000 Mérida, Yuc. ☎ **877/639-4546** in the U.S. and Canada, or 999/928-2505. www.casamexilio.com. 9 units. $50–$85 double; $120 penthouse. Rates include full breakfast. MC, V. Limited street parking. **Amenities:** Bar; small outdoor pool; whirlpool; smoke-free rooms. *In room:* A/C (in some), no phone.

Hotel Caribe   This three-story colonial-style hotel (no elevator) is great for a couple of reasons: Its location at the back of Plaza Hidalgo is both central and quiet, and it has a nice little pool and sun deck on the rooftop with a view of the cathedral. The rooms are moderately comfortable, though they aren't well lit and have only small windows facing the central courtyard. Thirteen *clase económica* rooms don't have air-conditioning, but standard rooms do; superior rooms (on the top floor) have been remodeled and have safes, hair dryers, larger windows, and quieter air-conditioning. Avoid the rooms on the ground floor. The hotel offers a lot of variety in bedding arrangements, mostly combinations of twins and doubles. Mattresses are often softer than standard. Nearby parking is free at night but costs extra during the day beginning at 7am. The restaurant serves good Mexican food.

Calle 59 no. 500 (at Calle 60), 97000 Mérida, Yuc. ☎ **888/822-6431** in the U.S. and Canada, or 999/924-9022. Fax 999/924-8733. www.hotelcaribe.com.mx. 53 units. 490 pesos *clase económica* double; 660–780 pesos standard or superior double. AE, MC, V. Free nearby night parking. **Amenities:** Restaurant; bar; small outdoor pool; room service. *In room:* A/C (in some), TV, hair dryer (in some).

Hotel Maison Lafitte ★   This three-story hotel has modern, attractive rooms with good air-conditioning, as well as tropical touches such as wooden louvers over the windows and light furniture with caned backs and seats. Rooms are medium to large, with midsize bathrooms that have great showers and good lighting. Most rooms come with either two doubles or a king-size bed. Rooms are quiet and overlook a pretty little garden with a fountain. A few rooms don't have windows. The location is excellent.

Calle 60 no. 472 (btw. calles 53 and 55), 97000 Mérida, Yuc. ☎ **800/538-6802** in the U.S. and Canada, or 999/928-1243. Fax 999/923-9159. www.maisonlafitte.com.mx. 30 units. 790 pesos double. Rates include

full breakfast. AE, MC, V. Free limited secure parking for compact cars. **Amenities:** Restaurant; bar; small
outdoor pool; room service. *In room:* A/C, TV, hair dryer, minibar, Wi-Fi.

Hotel MedioMundo ★ (Finds)   This is a quiet courtyard hotel with beautiful rooms
and a good location 3 blocks north of the main plaza. The English-speaking owners,
Nicole and Nelson, have been in the hotel business for years and have invested their
money in the right places, going for high-quality mattresses, good lighting, quiet air-
conditioning, lots of space, and good bathrooms with strong showers. What they didn't
invest in were TVs, which adds to the serenity. Higher prices are for the eight rooms with
air-conditioning, but all units have windows with good screens and get ample ventila-
tion. Breakfast is served in one of the two attractive courtyards.

Calle 55 no. 533 (btw. calles 64 and 66), 97000 Mérida, Yuc. ℂ/fax **999/924-5472.** www.hotelmedio
mundo.com. 12 units. $70–$90 double. MC, V. Limited street parking. **Amenities:** Small outdoor pool;
smoke-free rooms. *In room:* A/C (in some), no phone.

Inexpensive

Casa San Juan (Value)   This B&B, in a colonial house, is loaded with character and
provides a good glimpse of the old Mérida that lies behind the colonial facades in the
historic district. Guest rooms are beautifully decorated, large, and comfortable. Those in
the original house have been modernized but maintain a colonial feel, with 7m (23-ft.)
ceilings and 45cm-thick (18-inch) walls. The modern rooms in back look out over the
rear patio. The lower rate is for the rooms without air-conditioning (they have ceiling
and floor fans). Choice of beds includes one queen-size, one double, or two twins, all
with good mattresses and sheets. Breakfast includes fruit or juice, coffee, bread, and
homemade preserves. Casa San Juan is 4 blocks south of the main square.

Calle 62 no. 545a (btw. calles 69 and 71), 97000 Mérida, Yuc. ℂ/fax **999/986-2937.** www.casasanjuan.
com. 8 units (7 with private bathroom). $30–$60 double. Rates include continental breakfast. No credit
cards. Parking nearby $2. *In room:* A/C (in some), no phone.

Hotel Dolores Alba (Value)   The Dolores Alba offers attractive, comfortable rooms,
an inviting swimming pool, good air-conditioning, and free parking, all for a great price.
The three-story section (with elevator) surrounding the courtyard offers large rooms with
good-size bathrooms. Beds (either two doubles or one double and one twin) have sup-
portive foam-core mattresses, usually in a combination of one medium-firm and one
medium-soft. All rooms have windows or balconies looking out over the pool. An old
mango tree shades the front courtyard. The older rooms in this section are decorated with
local crafts and have small bathrooms. The family that owns the Hotel Dolores Alba
outside Chichén Itzá manages this hotel; you can make reservations at one hotel for the
other. This hotel is 3½ blocks from the main square.

Calle 63 no. 464 (btw. calles 52 and 54), 97000 Mérida, Yuc. ℂ **999/928-5650.** Fax 999/928-3163. www.
doloresalba.com. 100 units. 440 pesos double. Internet specials available. MC, V (with 8% surcharge). Free
guarded parking. **Amenities:** Restaurant; outdoor pool; room service. *In room:* A/C, TV.

Hotel Mucuy (Value)   The Mucuy is a simple, quiet, pleasant hotel in a great location.
The gracious owners strive to make guests feel welcome, with conveniences such as a
communal refrigerator in the lobby and, for a small extra charge, the use of a washer and
dryer. Guest rooms are basic; most contain two twin beds or a queen (with comfortable
mattresses) and some simple furniture. A neat garden patio with comfortable chairs is the
perfect place for sitting and reading. The Mucuy is named for a small dove said to bring
good luck to places where it alights. The hotel has a few rooms with air-conditioning,
which cost 50 pesos more. English is spoken.

Calle 57 no. 481 (btw. calles 56 and 58), 97000 Mérida, Yuc. ℂ **999/928-5193.** Fax 999/923-7801. www. mucuy.com. 21 units. 220 pesos double. No credit cards. Limited street parking. **Amenities:** Small outdoor pool. *In room:* A/C (in some), no phone.

WHERE TO STAY OUTSIDE OF MÉRIDA

Hacienda Temozón ★★★   This magnificent 17-century estancia presides over 37 hectares (91 acres) of subtropical gardens and cenotes, 39km (24 miles) from Mérida. Built in 1655 by Don Diego de Mendoza, Temozón was the region's most productive livestock estancia in the early 18th century, then the region's top producer of sisal in the late 1800s. Meticulously restored in 1997, it's now a Starwood property committed to employing local workers and using organic produce from nearby farms in the restaurant. Spacious Spanish colonial–style rooms have 5.5m (18-ft.) ceilings with exposed rafters, fans, and thick whitewashed walls; Spanish-tile floors and baths; hammocks positioned to catch natural breezes; dark, tropical hardwood furniture; and large, plush beds with white linens adorned daily with fresh flowers. Superior rooms have showers, and three have tubs. Suites have tubs, private terraces, and plunge pools. The Casa del Patrón suite has accommodated many global heads of state.

KM 182 Carretera Mérida-Uxmal, 97825 Temozon Sur, Yuc. ℂ **888-625-5144** or 999/923-8089. www. haciendasmexico.com/temozon/overview.php. 28 units. $405 double; $485 junior suite; $545 deluxe suite; $1,155 presidential suite. AE, MC, V. **Amenities:** Restaurant; free airport transfers; bikes; horseback riding; concierge; health club; outdoor pool; room service; smoke-free rooms; spa; outdoor tennis court. *In room:* AC, fan, CD and MP3, high-speed Internet, safe.

WHERE TO DINE

The people of Mérida have strong ideas and traditions about food. Certain dishes are always associated with a particular day of the week. In households across the city, Sunday would feel incomplete without *puchero* (a kind of stew). On Monday, at any restaurant that caters to locals, you are sure to find *frijol con puerco* (pork and beans). Likewise, you'll find *potaje* (potage) on Thursday; fish, of course, on Friday; and *chocolomo* (a beef dish) on Saturday. These dishes are heavy and slow to digest; they are for the midday meal and not suitable for supper. What's more, Meridanos don't believe that seafood is a healthy supper food. All seafood restaurants in Mérida close by 6pm unless they cater to tourists. The preferred supper food is turkey (which, by the way, is said to be high in tryptophan, a soporific), and it's best served in the traditional *antojitos*—*salbutes* (small, thin rounds of *masa* fried and topped with turkey, pork, or chicken, and onions, tomatoes, and lettuce) and *panuchos* (sliced open and lightly stuffed with bean paste, before having toppings added)—and turkey soup.

Another thing you may notice about Mérida is the surprising number of Middle Eastern restaurants. The city received a large influx of Lebanese immigrants around 1900. This population has had a strong influence on local society, to the point where Meridanos think of kibbe the way Americans think of pizza. Speaking of pizza, if you want to get some to take back to your hotel room, try **Vito Corleone,** on Calle 59 between calles 60 and 62. Its pizzas have a thin crust with a slightly smoky taste from the wood-burning oven.

It's becoming more difficult to recommend good restaurants for fine dining in the downtown area. Most of the best places are in the outlying districts, near the upper-class neighborhoods and shopping plazas. They are a little difficult to get to. If you want something special, I would recommend dining at the Hacienda Xcanatún on the outskirts of town, off the Progreso road. (See "Haciendas & Hotels," above.)

Expensive

Alberto's Continental LEBANESE/YUCATECAN   There's nothing quite like dining here at night in a softly lit room or on the wonderful old patio framed in Moorish arches. Nothing glitzy—just elegant *mudejar*-patterned tile floors, simple furniture, decoration that's just so, and the gurgling of a fountain creating a romantic mood. I find the prices on the expensive side. For supper, you can choose a sampler plate of four Lebanese favorites, or traditional Yucatecan specialties, such as *pollo pibil* or fish Celestún (bass stuffed with shrimp). You can finish with Turkish coffee.

Calle 64 no. 482 (at Calle 57). (*C*) **999/928-5367.** Reservations recommended. Main courses 80–220 pesos. AE, MC, V. Daily 1–11pm.

Casa de Frida ★★ MEXICAN   If you're longing for some classic Mexican food from the central highlands, try this place. It serves some of the dishes Mexico is best known for, such as *mole poblano* and *sopa azteca*. The *mole* was good when I was last there, as was an interesting *flan de berenjena* (a kind of eggplant timbale). This is a comfortable, nononsense sort of place decorated a la Mexicana. The menu has enough breadth to satisfy any appetite.

Calle 61 no. 526 (at Calle 66). (*C*) **999/928-2311.** Reservations recommended. Main courses 100–130 pesos. No credit cards. Mon–Sat 6–10pm.

Moderate

Amaro REGIONAL/VEGETARIAN   The menu at this courtyard restaurant lists some interesting vegetarian dishes, such as *crema de calabacitas* (cream of squash soup), apple salad, and avocado pizza. There is also a limited menu of fish and chicken dishes; you might want to try the Yucatecan chicken. The *agua de chaya* (chaya is a leafy vegetable prominent in the Maya diet) is refreshing on a hot afternoon. All desserts are made in-house. The restaurant is a little north of Plaza Mayor.

Calle 59 no. 507 Interior 6 (btw. calles 60 and 62). (*C*) **999/928-2451.** Main courses 50–90 pesos. MC, V. Mon–Sat 11am–2am.

El Príncipe Tutul Xiú ★★ (Finds) REGIONAL   Yucatecan specialties from a limited menu. The original is in the town of Maní—the owner opened this restaurant because he got tired of hearing Meridanos asking him why he didn't open one in the capital. It's a short taxi ride from downtown, and to return you can pick up a local bus that passes by the restaurant. This is a great place to try the famous *sopa de lima*, and one of the six typical main courses, served with great handmade tortillas. And you can order, with confidence, one of the flavored waters such as *horchata* or *tamarindo*.

Calle 123 no. 216 (btw. calles 46 and 46b), Colonia Serapio Rendón. (*C*) **999/929-7721.** Reservations not accepted. Main courses 58 pesos. MC, V. Daily 11am–6pm.

El Templo ★★ MEXICAN NUEVA COCINA   The odd layout of the place and the decor, which plays loosely with Mexican popular culture and iconography, are amusing. And the triptych menu, divided into Yucatecan, Mexican, and original, holds a lot of uncommon choices, plus a couple of daily specials. Sample dishes include the Cornish game hen in a guava-lime glaze and a salmon in a tamarind and black sesame sauce. Good stuff. When the restaurant first opened, I was hesitant to put it in the guidebook because I feared that it might not survive, given the conservative tastes of most Meridanos, but I was happily proven wrong.

Calle 59 no. 438 (btw. calles 50 and 52). (*C*) **999/930-9303.** Reservations accepted. Main courses 70–100 pesos. MC, V. Mon–Sat 6pm–1am.

Restaurante Kantún ★★ ⓥalue SEAFOOD   This modest restaurant serves up the freshest seafood for incredibly low prices. The owner-chef is always on the premises taking care of details. The menu includes excellent ceviche and seafood cocktails, and fish cooked in a number of ways. I had the *especial Kantún,* which was lightly battered and stuffed with lobster, crab, and shrimp. The dining room is air-conditioned, the furniture comfortable, and the service attentive.

Calle 45 no. 525-G (btw. calles 64 and 66). ℭ 999/923-4493. Reservations recommended. Main courses 60–120 pesos. MC, V. Daily noon–8pm (occasionally closes Mon).

Restaurant Los Almendros ⓞverrated YUCATECAN   Ask where to eat Yucatecan food, and locals will inevitably suggest this place, mostly because it was the first place to offer tourists such Yucatecan specialties as *salbutes, panuchos* and *papadzules, cochinita pibil,* and *poc chuc.* The menu even comes with color photographs to facilitate acquaintance with these strange-sounding dishes. The food is okay and not much of a risk, but you can find better elsewhere. The service is slow. Still, it's a safe place to try Yucatecan food for the first time, and it's such a fixture that the idea of a guidebook that doesn't mention this restaurant is unthinkable. It's 5 blocks east of Calle 60, facing the Parque de la Mejorada.

Calle 50A no. 493. ℭ 999/928-5459. Main courses 60–100 pesos. AE, MC, V. Daily 10am–11pm.

Inexpensive

Café Alameda MIDDLE EASTERN/VEGETARIAN   The trappings here are simple and informal (metal tables, plastic chairs), and it's a good place for catching a light meal. The trick is figuring out the Spanish names for popular Middle Eastern dishes. Kibbe is *quebbe bola* (not *quebbe cruda*), hummus is *garbanza,* and shish kabob is *alambre.* I leave it to you to figure out what a spinach pie is called (and it's excellent). Café Alameda is a treat for vegetarians, and the umbrella-shaded tables on the patio are perfect for morning coffee and *mamules* (walnut-filled pastries).

Calle 58 no. 474 (btw. calles 55 and 57). ℭ 999/928-3635. Main courses 22–58 pesos. No credit cards. Daily 8am–5pm.

Eladio's ★ YUCATECAN   This is where locals come to relax in their off hours, drink very cold beer, and snack on Yucatecan specialties. There are 4 or 5 of these restaurants scattered about the city; this is the closest to the center of downtown. You have two choices: order a beer and enjoy *una botana* (a small portion that accompanies a drink—in this case, usually a Yucatecan dish), or order from the menu. *Cochinita, poc chuc,* and *relleno negro* (turkey flavored with burnt chiles) are all good. Or try the *panuchos* or *salbutes.* Often there is live music in this open-air restaurant, which is 3 blocks east of Parque de la Mejorada.

Calle 59 (at Calle 44). ℭ 999/923-1087. Main courses 40–85 pesos. AE, MC, V. Daily noon–9pm.

La Flor de Santiago REGIONAL   This is a curious place with classic ambience and classically slow service. I like it best in the morning for breakfast. The dining area is very typical of Mérida, with its high ceiling, plain furniture, and local clientele. A wood-fired stove produces baked goods, and there's a sampling of Yucatecan specialties on the menu. Often it can be annoying because the cooks run out of food.

Calle 70 no. 478 (btw. calles 57 and 59). ℭ 999/928-5591. *Comida corrida* 40 pesos; main courses 50–65 pesos. No credit cards. Daily 7am–11pm.

Most of Mérida's attractions are within walking distance from the downtown area. To see a larger area of the city, take a popular **bus tour** by **Transportadora Carnaval.** The owner bought a few buses, painted them bright colors, pulled out the windows, raised the roof several inches, and installed wooden benches; the overall effect will remind you of the folksy buses of coastal Latin America, known as *chivas* in Colombia and Venezuela or as *guaguas* in other places. You can find these buses on the corner of calles 60 and 55 (next to the church of Santa Lucía) at 10am and 1, 4, and 7pm. The tour costs 70 pesos per person and lasts 2 hours. A national company, called Turibus, operates another city tour in large, modern, bright-red, double-decker buses. You can pick them up in front of the cathedral every half-hour. The tour costs 88 pesos. Another option for seeing the city is a **horse-drawn carriage.** A 45-minute ride around central Mérida costs 250 pesos. You can usually find the carriages beside the cathedral on Calle 61.

PLAZA MAYOR Downtown Mérida is a great example of a lowland colonial city. The town has a casual, relaxed feel. Buildings lack the severe baroque and neoclassical features that characterize central Mexico; most are finished in stucco and painted light colors. Mérida's gardens add to this relaxed, tropical atmosphere. Gardeners don't strive for control over nature. Here natural exuberance is the ideal; plants grow in a wild profusion that disguises human intervention. Mérida's plazas are a slightly different version of this aesthetic: Unlike the highland plazas, with their carefully sculpted trees, Mérida's squares are typically built around large trees that are left to grow as tall as possible. Hurricane Isidore blew down several of these in 2002 and has changed the appearance of these plazas as well as the Paseo de Montejo.

Plaza Mayor has been relandscaped after the hurricane and is now the exception to the rule. It still remains a comfortable and informal place to meet up with friends. Even when there's no orchestrated event in progress, the park is full of people sitting on the benches, talking, or taking a casual stroll. A plaza like this is a great advantage for a big city such as Mérida, giving it a personal feel and a sense of community. Notice the beautiful scale and composition of the major buildings surrounding it. The most prominent of these is the cathedral.

The oldest **cathedral** on the continent, it was built between 1561 and 1598. Much of the stone in the cathedral's walls came from the ruined buildings of Tihó, the former Maya city. The original finish was stucco, and you can see some remnants still clinging to the bare rock. However, people like the way the unfinished walls show the cathedral's age. Notice how the two top levels of the bell towers are built off-center from their bases, marking them as later additions. Inside, decoration is sparse, with altars draped in fabric colorfully embroidered like a Maya woman's shift. The most notable item is a picture of Ah Kukum Tutul Xiú, chief of the Xiú people, visiting the Montejo camp to make peace; it's hanging over the side door on the right.

To the left of the main altar is a small shrine with a curious figure of Christ that is a replica of one recovered from a burned-out church in the town of Ichmul. In the 1500s a local artist carved the original figure from a miraculous tree that was hit by lightning and burst into flames—but did not char. The statue later became blistered in the church fire at Ichmul, but it survived. In 1645, it was moved to the cathedral in Mérida, where the locals attached great powers to the figure, naming it *Cristo de las Ampollas* (Christ of the Blisters). It did not, however, survive the sacking of the cathedral in 1915 by revolutionary forces, so another figure, modeled after the original, was made. Take a look in the side chapel (daily 8–11am and 4:30–7pm), which contains a life-size diorama of the Last Supper. The Mexican Jesus is covered with prayer crosses brought by supplicants asking for intercession.

Next door to the cathedral is the old bishop's palace, now converted into the city's contemporary art museum, **Museo de Arte Contemporáneo Ateneo de Yucatán** (© **999/928-3236**). The palace was confiscated and rebuilt during the Mexican Revolution in 1915. The museum's entrance faces the cathedral from the recently constructed walkway between the two buildings called the Pasaje de la Revolución. The 17 exhibition rooms display work by contemporary artists, mostly from the Yucatán. (The best known are Fernando García Ponce and Fernando Castro Pacheco, whose works also hang in the government palace described below.) Nine of the rooms hold the museum's permanent collection; the rest are for temporary exhibits. It's open Wednesday to Monday from 10am to 6pm. Admission is free.

As you move clockwise around the plaza, the **Palacio Montejo** is on the south side. Its facade, with heavy decoration around the doorway and windows, is a good example of the Spanish architectural style known as plateresque. But the content of the decoration is very much a New World creation. Conquering the Yucatán was the Montejo family business, begun by the original Francisco Montejo and continued by his son and nephew, both named Francisco Montejo. Construction of the house started in 1542 under the son, Francisco Montejo El Mozo ("The Younger"). Bordering the entrance are politically incorrect figures of conquistadors standing on the heads of vanquished Indians—borrowed, perhaps, from the pre-Hispanic custom of portraying victorious Maya kings treading on their defeated foes. The posture of the conquistadors and their facial expression of wide-eyed dismay make them less imposing than the Montejos might have wished. A bank now occupies the building, but you can enter the courtyard, view the garden, and see for yourself what a charming residence it must have been for the descendants of the Montejos, who lived here as recently as the 1970s. (Curiously enough, Mérida society keeps track of who is descended from the Montejos, as well as who is descended from the last Maya king, Tutul Xiú.)

In stark contrast to the severity of the cathedral and Casa Montejo is the light, unimposing **Ayuntamiento** or **Palacio Municipal (town hall).** The exterior dates from the mid–19th century, an era when a tropical aesthetic tinged with romanticism began asserting itself across coastal Latin America. On the second floor, you can see the meeting hall of the city council and enjoy a view of the plaza from the balcony. Next door to the Ayuntamiento is a recently completed building called **El Nuevo Olimpo (The New Olympus).** It took the place of the old Olimpo, which a misguided town council demolished in the 1970s, to the regret of many older Meridanos. The new building tries to incorporate elements of the original while presenting something new. It holds concert and gallery space, a bookstore, and a lovely courtyard. There is a comfortable cafe under the arches, and a bulletin board at the entrance to the courtyard with postings of upcoming performances.

Cater-corner from the Nuevo Olimpo is the old **Casa del Alguacil (Magistrate's House).** Under its arcades is something of an institution in Mérida: the **Dulcería y Sorbetería Colón,** an ice cream and sweet shop that will appeal to those who prefer less-rich ice creams. A spectacular side doorway on Calle 62 bears viewing, and across the street is the **Cine Mérida,** with two movie screens showing art films and one stage for live performances. Returning to the main plaza, down a bit from the ice cream store, is a **shopping center** of boutiques and convenience food vendors called **Pasaje Picheta.**

8

Casa del Alguacil **7**

Cathedral **2**

El Nuevo Olimpo **6**

Iglesia de Jesús **10**

Iglesia de Santa Lucía **13**

Museo de Arte Contemporáneo **3**

Museo de la Ciudad **9**

Palacio Cantón/Museo Regional
 de Antropología **14**

Palacio de Gobierno **8**

Palacio Montejo **4**

Palacio Municipal **5**

Plaza Mayor **1**

Teatro Ayala **8**

Teatro Peón Contreras **11**

Universidad de Yucatán **12**

At the end of the arcade is the **Palacio de Gobierno (state government building),** dating from 1892. Large murals by the Yucatecan artist Fernando Castro Pacheco, completed between 1971 and 1973, decorate the walls of the courtyard. Scenes from Maya and Mexican history abound, and the painting over the stairway depicts the Maya spirit with ears of sacred corn, the "sunbeams of the gods." Nearby is a painting of mustachioed Lázaro Cárdenas, who, as president, in 1938, expropriated 17 foreign oil companies and was hailed as a Mexican liberator. Upstairs is a long, wide gallery with more of Pacheco's paintings, which achieve their effect by localizing color and imitating the photographic technique of double exposure. The palace is open Monday to Saturday from 8am to 8pm, Sunday from 9am to 5pm. There is a small tourism office to the left as you enter.

A few blocks from Plaza Mayor is the **Museo de la Ciudad (City Museum),** on Calle 56 between 65 and 65A. It now occupies the former Post Office building. An exhibit outlining the history of Mérida will be of interest to those curious about the city; there is explanatory text in English. Hours are Tuesday to Friday from 9am to 8pm, Saturday and Sunday from 9am to 2pm. Admission is free.

CALLE 60 Heading north from Plaza Mayor up Calle 60, you'll see many of Mérida's old churches and squares. Several stores along Calle 60 sell gold-filigree jewelry, pottery, clothing, and folk art. A stroll along this street leads to the Parque Santa Ana and continues to the fashionable boulevard Paseo de Montejo and its **Museo Regional de Antropología (Anthropology Museum).**

The first place of interest is the **Teatro Daniel de Ayala,** only because it sometimes schedules interesting performances. On the right side of Calle 60 will be a small park called **Parque Cepeda Peraza** (or Parque Hidalgo). Named for 19th-century Gen. Manuel Cepeda Peraza, the *parque* was part of Montejo's original city plan. Small outdoor restaurants front hotels on the park, making it a popular stopping place at any time of day. Across Calle 59 is the **Iglesia de Jesús,** or El Tercer Orden (the Third Order). Built by the Jesuit order in 1618, it has the richest interior of any church in Mérida, making it a favorite spot for weddings. The entire block on which the church stands belonged to the Jesuits, who are known for being great educators. The school they left behind after their expulsion became the Universidad de Yucatán.

On the other side of the church is the **Parque de la Madre.** The park contains a modern statue of the *Madonna and Child,* a copy of the work by Renoir. Beyond the Parque de la Madre and across the pedestrian-only street is the **Teatro Peón Contreras,** an opulent theater designed by Italian architect Enrico Deserti a century ago. The theater is noted for its Carrara marble staircase and frescoed dome. Try to peek inside, and check the schedule to see if any performances will take place during your stay. National and international performers appear here often. In the southwest corner of the theater, facing the Parque de la Madre, is a **tourist information office.** Across Calle 60 is the main building of the **Universidad de Yucatán.** Inside is a flagstone courtyard where the *ballet folklórico* performs on Friday nights.

A block farther north is **Parque Santa Lucía.** Bordered by an arcade on the north and west sides, this park was where visitors first alighted from the stagecoach. On Sunday, Parque Santa Lucía holds a used-book market, and several evenings a week it hosts popular entertainment. On Thursday nights, performers present Yucatecan songs and poems. Facing the park is the **Iglesia de Santa Lucía** (1575).

Four blocks farther up Calle 60 is **Parque Santa Ana;** if you turn right, you'll come to the beginning of the Paseo de Montejo in 2 blocks.

Spanish Classes

Maya scholars, Spanish teachers, and archaeologists from the United States are among the students at the **Centro de Idiomas del Sureste,** Calle 14 no. 106 at Calle 25, Col. México, 97000 Mérida, Yuc. (© **999/926-1155;** fax 999/926-9020). The school has two locations: in the Colonia México, a northern residential district, and on Calle 66 at Calle 57, downtown. Students live with local families or in hotels; sessions running 2 weeks or longer are available for all levels of proficiency and areas of interest. For brochures and applications, contact the director, Chloe Conaway de Pacheco.

PASEO DE MONTEJO The Paseo de Montejo is a broad, tree-lined boulevard that runs north–south starting at Calle 47, 7 blocks north and 2 blocks east of the main square. In the late 19th century, stalwarts of Mérida's upper crust (mostly plantation owners) decided that the city needed something grander than its traditional narrow streets lined by wall-to-wall town houses. They built this monumentally proportioned boulevard and lined it with mansions. Things went sour when the *henequén* industry went bust, but several mansions survive—some in private hands, others as offices, restaurants, or consulates. Today this is the fashionable part of town, with many restaurants, trendy dance clubs, and expensive hotels.

Of the surviving mansions, the most notable is the Palacio Cantón, which houses the **Museo Regional de Antropología (Anthropology Museum)** ★★ (© **999/923-0557**). Designed and built by Enrico Deserti, the architect of the Teatro Peón Contreras, it was constructed between 1909 and 1911, during the last years of the Porfiriato. It was the residence of Gen. Francisco Cantón Rosado, who enjoyed his palace for only 6 years before dying in 1917. For a time, the mansion served as the official residence of the state's governor. Viewing the museum affords you an opportunity to see some of the surviving interior architecture.

The museum's main focus is the pre-Columbian cultures of the peninsula, especially the Maya. Topics include cosmology, history, and culture. Starting with fossil mastodon teeth, the exhibits take you through the Yucatán's history, paying special attention to the daily life of its inhabitants.

Exhibits illustrate such strange Maya customs as tying boards to babies' heads to create the oblong shape that they considered beautiful, and filing teeth or perforating them to inset jewels. Enlarged photos of several archaeological sites and drawings illustrate the various styles of Maya dwellings. Captions for the permanent displays are mostly in Spanish, but even if you barely know Spanish, this is a worthwhile stop, providing background for explorations of Maya sites. The museum is open Tuesday to Saturday from 8am to 8pm, Sunday from 8am to 2pm. Admission is 44 pesos.

ECOTOURS & ADVENTURE TRIPS

The Yucatán Peninsula has seen a recent explosion of companies that organize nature and adventure tours. One well-established outfit with a great track record is **Ecoturismo Yucatán,** Calle 3 no. 235, Col. Pensiones, 97219 Mérida (© **999/920-2772;** fax 999/925-9047; www.ecoyuc.com). Alfonso and Roberta Escobedo create itineraries to meet just about any special or general interest you may have for going to the Yucatán or southern Mexico. Alfonso has been creating adventure and nature tours for more than a dozen years. Specialties include archaeology, birding, natural history, and kayaking. The company also offers day trips that explore contemporary Maya culture and life in villages in the Yucatán. Package and customized tours are available.

SHOPPING

Mérida is known for hammocks, *guayaberas* (lightweight men's shirts worn untucked), and Panama hats. Baskets and pottery made in the Yucatán are for sale in the central market. Mérida is also the place to pick up prepared *adobo,* a pastelike mixture of ground *achiote* seeds (annatto), oregano, garlic, and other spices used as a marinade for making dishes such as *cochinita pibil* (pit-baked pork). Simply mix the paste with sour orange to a soupy consistency before applying to the meat. Try it on chicken for *pollo pibil.* It can be purchased in a bottle, too.

Mérida's bustling **market district** is a few blocks southeast of the Plaza Mayor. The market and surrounding few blocks make up the commercial center of the city. Hordes of people come here to shop and work. It is by far the most crowded part of town, and the city government is refurbishing the whole area to relieve the traffic congestion. Behind the post office (at calles 65 and 56) is the oldest part of the market, the **Portal de Granos (Grains Arcade),** a row of maroon arches where the grain merchants used to sell their goods. Just east, between calles 56 and 54, is the market building, Mercado Lucas de Gálvez. The city has built a new municipal market building on the south side of this building, but it was having difficulty persuading the market venders to move. When this happens the city's plan is to tear down the Lucas de Gálvez and replace it with a plaza. Inside, chaos seems to reign, but after a short while, a certain order emerges. Here you can find anything from fresh fish to flowers, to leather goods. In and around the market, you can find more locally manufactured goods; a secondary market is on Calle 56, labeled **Bazaar de Artesanías (crafts market)** in big letters. Another crafts market, **Bazaar García Rejón,** lies a block west of the market on Calle 65 between calles 58 and 60.

Crafts

Casa de las Artesanías ★   This store occupies the front rooms of a restored monastery. Here you can find a wide selection of crafts, 90% of which come from the Yucatán. For the most part, the quality of work is higher than elsewhere, but so are the prices. The monastery's back courtyard is used as a gallery, with rotating exhibits on folk and fine arts. It's open Monday to Saturday from 9am to 8pm, Sunday from 9am to 1pm. Calle 63 no. 513 (btw. calles 64 and 66). ✆ **999/928-6676.**

Miniaturas   This fun little store is packed to the rafters with miniatures, a traditional Mexican folk art form that has been evolving in a number of directions, including social and political satire, pop art, and bawdy humor. Alicia Rivero, the owner, collects them from several parts of Mexico and offers plenty of variety, from traditional miniatures, such as dollhouse furniture, to popular cartoon characters and celebrities. The store also sells other forms of folk art, such as masks, games, and traditional crafts. Hours are Monday to Saturday from 10am to 8pm. Calle 59 no. 507A-4 (btw. calles 60 and 62). ✆ **999/928-6503.**

Guayaberas

Business suits are hot and uncomfortable in Mérida's tropical climate, so businessmen, bankers, and bus drivers alike wear the *guayabera,* a loose-fitting shirt decorated with narrow tucks, pockets, and sometimes embroidery, worn over the pants rather than tucked in. Mérida is famous as the best place to buy *guayaberas,* which can go for less than 150 pesos at the market or for more than 650 pesos custom made. A *guayabera* made of linen can cost about 800 pesos. Most are made of cotton, although other materials are available. The traditional color is white.

Most shops display ready-to-wear shirts in several price ranges. *Guayabera* makers pride themselves on being innovators. I have yet to enter a shirt-maker's shop in Mérida that did not present its own updated version of the *guayabera.* When looking at *guayaberas,* here are a few things to keep in mind: When Yucatecans say *seda,* they mean polyester; *lino* is linen or a linen/polyester combination. Take a close look at the stitching and such details as the way the tucks line up over the pockets; with *guayaberas,* the details are everything.

Guayaberas Jack The craftsmanship here is good, the place has a reputation to maintain, and some of the salespeople speak English. Prices are as marked. This will give you a good basis of comparison if you want to hunt for a bargain elsewhere. If the staff does not have the style and color of shirt you want, they will make it for you in about 3 hours. This shop also sells regular shirts and women's blouses. Hours are Monday to Saturday from 10am to 8pm, Sunday from 10am to 2pm. Calle 59 no. 507A (btw. calles 60 and 62). ℂ **999/928-6002.**

Hammocks

Natives across tropical America used hammocks long before the Europeans arrived in the New World. The word comes from the Spanish *hamaca,* which is a borrowing from Taíno, a Caribbean Indian language. Hammocks are still in use throughout Latin America and come in a wide variety of forms, but none is so comfortable as the Yucatecan hammock, which is woven with cotton string in a fine mesh. For most of us, of course, the hammock is lawn furniture, something to relax in for an hour or so on a lazy afternoon. But for the vast majority of Yucatecans, hammocks are the equivalent of beds, and they greatly prefer hammocks to mattresses. I know a hotel owner who has 150 beds in his establishment but won't sleep on any of them. When he does, he complains of waking up unrested and sore. Many well-to-do énos keep a bed just for show. In hotels that cater to Yucatecans, you will always find hammock hooks in the walls because many Yucatecans travel with their own hammock.

My advice to the hammock buyer: The woven part should be cotton, it should be made with fine string, and the strings should be so numerous that when you get in it and stretch out diagonally (the way you're supposed to sleep in these hammocks), the gaps between the strings remain small. Don't pay attention to the words used to describe the size of a hammock; they have become practically meaningless. Good hammocks don't cost a lot of money (250–350 pesos). If you want a superior hammock, ask for one made with fine crochet thread, *hilo de crochet* (the word *crochet* is also overused, but you can readily see the difference). This could run as high as 1,200 pesos.

Nothing beats a tryout; the shops mentioned here will gladly hang a hammock for you to test-drive. When it's up, look to see that there are no untied strings. You can also see what street vendors are offering, but you have to know what to look for, or they are likely to take advantage of you.

Hamacas El Aguacate El Aguacate sells hammocks wholesale and retail. It has the greatest variety and is the place to go for a really fancy or extra-large hammock. A good hammock is the no. 6 in cotton; it runs around 340 pesos. The store is open Monday to Friday from 8:30am to 7:30pm, Saturday from 8am to 5pm. It's 6 blocks south of the main square. Calle 58 no. 604 (at Calle 73). (Ⓒ **999/928-6429.**

Tejidos y Cordeles Nacionales   This place near the municipal market sells only cotton hammocks, priced by weight—a pretty good practice because hammock lengths are fairly standardized. The prices are better than at El Aguacate, but quality control isn't as good. My idea of a good hammock is one that weighs about 1½ kg (3½ lb.) and runs about 270 pesos. Calle 56 no. 516-B (btw. calles 63 and 65). (Ⓒ **999/928-5561.**

Panama Hats

Another useful and popular item is this soft, pliable hat made from the fibers of the jipijapa palm in several towns south of Mérida along Hwy. 180, especially Becal, in the neighboring state of Campeche. The hat makers in these towns work inside caves so that the moist air keeps the palm fibers pliant.

Jipi hats come in various grades determined by the quality (pliability, softness, and fineness) of the fibers and closeness of the weave. The difference in weave is easy to see, as a fine weave improves the shape of a hat. It has more body and retains its shape better. You'll find Panama hats for sale in several places, but often without much selection. One of the market buildings has a hat store: Walk south down Calle 56 past the post office; right before the street ends in the marketplace, turn left into a passage with hardware stores at the entrance. The fourth or fifth shop is **Casa de los Jipis.**

MÉRIDA AFTER DARK

For nighttime entertainment, see the box, "Daily Festivals & Special Events in Mérida," p. 196, or check out the theaters noted here.

Teatro Peón Contreras, Calle 60 at Calle 57, and **Teatro Ayala,** Calle 60 at Calle 61, feature a wide range of performing artists from Mexico and around the world. **El Nuevo Olimpo,** on the main square, schedules frequent concerts; and **Cine Mérida,** a half-block north of the Nuevo Olimpo, has two screens for showing classic and art films, and one live stage.

Mérida's club scene offers everything from ubiquitous rock/dance to some one-of-a-kind spots that are nothing like what you find back home. Most of the dance clubs are in the big hotels or on Paseo de Montejo. For dancing, a small cluster of clubs on Calle 60, around the corner from Santa Lucía, offer live rock and Latin music. For salsa, go to **Mambo Café** in the Plaza las Américas shopping center.

2 SIDE TRIPS FROM MÉRIDA

SOTUTA DE PEÓN

What started out as one man's hobby—to restore an old hacienda for a weekend getaway and perhaps see what it takes to plant a few acres of *henequén*—spiraled out of control until it grew into one of the best living-museums you'll see anywhere. And it has engrossed the imagination of an entire rural community.

You can arrange transportation from any of Mérida's hotels by calling **Hacienda Sotuta de Peón** at (Ⓒ **999/941-8639.** You can also take your own car, but it's a bit tricky. The hacienda is open from Monday to Saturday. The giant fiber-extracting machine is now in operation every day, whereas before it was running only a few days per week. The tour starts with a visit to the *henequén* fields via mule-drawn carts, the same as are used to transport the leaves of the plant to the hacienda's headquarters. You get to see it being harvested and, later, processed at the *casa de máquinas,* and even used in the manufacturing of twine and such. Along the way, you get a glimpse into the local culture surrounding *henequén* production. You visit a house of one of the workers, as well as the house of the *hacendado* (the owner). Make sure to bring your bathing suit; there's a cenote on the property. You can also try some of the regional cooking—a restaurant on the premises turns out some good food. Admission costs 300 pesos per adult, 150 pesos per child. Transportation is extra. Packages are available that combine entrance fee, transportation from Mérida, and food. There are two tours per day, at 10am and 1pm. For more information, see **www.haciendatour.com.**

IZAMAL

Izamal is a sleepy town some 80km (50 miles) east of Mérida, an easy day trip by car. You can visit the famous Franciscan convent of **San Antonio de Padua** and the ruins of four large pyramids that overlook the center of town. One pyramid is partially reconstructed. Visit the **Centro Cultural y Artesanal** (30 pesos) across the square from the convent for an introduction to the many handicrafts produced in Izamal. You can also pick up a map of the town showing where you can visit craftsmen in their workshops and homes. Life in Izamal is easygoing in the extreme, as evidenced by the *victorias,* the horse-drawn buggies that serve as taxis here. Even if you come by car, you should make a point of touring the town in one of these. There is also a sound-and-light show in the old convent. The half-hour show costs 48 pesos and is held on Tuesday, Thursday, Friday, and Saturday at 8:30pm. It's in Spanish, but you can rent headphones in other languages for 30 pesos.

CELESTÚN NATIONAL WILDLIFE REFUGE: FLAMINGOS & OTHER WATERFOWL

On the coast, west of Mérida, is a large wetlands area that has been declared a biopreserve. It is a long, shallow estuary where freshwater mixes with Gulf saltwater, creating a habitat perfect for flamingos and many other species of waterfowl. This *ría* (estuary), unlike others that are fed by rivers or streams, receives fresh water through about 80 cenotes, most of which are underwater. It is very shallow (.3–1m/1–3¹/₄ ft. deep) and thickly grown with mangrove, with an open channel .5km (a quarter-mile) wide and 50km (31 miles) long, sheltered from the open sea by a narrow strip of land. In this narrow estuary, you can ride a launch to see flamingos as they dredge the bottom of the shallows for a species of small crustacean and a particular insect that make up the bulk of their diet.

You can get here by car or bus; it's an easy 90-minute drive. (For information on buses, see "Getting There & Departing: By Bus," earlier in this chapter.) To drive, leave downtown Mérida on Calle 57. Shortly after Santiago Church, Calle 57 ends and there's a dogleg onto Calle 59-A. This crosses Avenida Itzáes, and its name changes to Jacinto Canek; continue until you see signs for Celestún Hwy. 178. This will take you through Hunucmá, where the road joins Hwy. 281, which takes you to Celestún. You'll know you have arrived when you get to the bridge.

In the last few years, the state agency cultur has come into Celestún and established order where once there was chaos. Immediately to your left after the bridge, you'll find modern facilities with a snack bar, clean bathrooms, and a ticket window. Prices for tours are fixed. A 75-minute tour costs about $50 and can accommodate up to six people. You can join others or hire a boat by yourself. On the tour, you'll definitely see some flamingos; you'll also get to see some mangrove close up, and one of the many underwater springs. Please do not urge the boatmen to get any closer to the flamingos than they are allowed to; if pestered too much, the birds will abandon the area for another, less fitting habitat. The ride is quite pleasant—the water is calm, and cultur has supplied the boatmen with wide, flat-bottom skiffs that have canopies for shade.

In addition to flamingos, you will see frigate birds, pelicans, spoonbills, egrets, sandpipers, and other waterfowl feeding on shallow sandbars at any time of year. At least 15 duck species have been counted, and there are several species of birds of prey. Of the 175 bird species that are here, some 99 are permanent residents. Nonbreeding flamingos remain here year-round; the larger group of breeding flamingos takes off around April to nest on the upper Yucatán Peninsula east of Río Lagartos, returning to Celestún in October.

Hotel Eco Paraíso Xixim ★★   Eco Paraíso is meant to be a refuge from the modern world. It sits on a deserted 4km (2¹/₂-mile) stretch of beach that was once part of a coconut plantation. It attracts much the same clientele as the former-haciendas-turned-luxury-hotels, but in some ways it has more going for it (like the beach). Some guests come here for a week of idleness; others use this as a base of operations for visiting the biopreserve and making trips to the Maya ruins in the interior. The hotel offers its own tours to various places. Rooms are quite private; each is a separate bungalow with *palapa* roof. Each comes with two comfortable queen-size beds, a sitting area, ceiling fans, and a private porch with hammocks. On my last visit, the food was very good, and the service was great. The hotel composts waste, and treats and uses wastewater.

Antigua Carretera a Sisal Km 10, 97367 Celestún, Yuc. (C) **988/916-2100.** Fax 988/916-2111. www.eco paraiso.com. 15 units. High season $240 double; low season $200 double. Rates include 2 meals per person. AE, MC, V. Free parking. **Amenities:** Restaurant; bar; midsize outdoor pool. *In room:* Hair dryer.

DZIBILCHALTÚN: MAYA RUINS & MUSEUM

This destination makes for a quick morning trip that will get you back to Mérida in time for a siesta, or it could be part of a longer trip to Progreso, Uaymitún, and Xcambó. It's located 14km (8³/₄ miles) north of Mérida along the Progreso road and 4km (2¹/₂ miles) east of the highway. To get there, take Calle 60 all the way out of town and follow signs for Progreso and Hwy. 261. Look for the sign for Dzibilchaltún, which also reads UNIVERSIDAD DEL MAYAB; it will point you right. After a few miles, you'll see a sign for the entrance to the ruins and the museum. If you don't want to drive, take one of the *colectivos* that line up along Parque San Juan.

Dzibilchaltún was founded about 500 B.C., flourished around A.D. 750, and was in decline long before the coming of the conquistadors. Since the ruins were discovered in 1941, more than 8,000 buildings have been mapped. The site covers an area of almost 15 sq. km (5³/₄ sq. miles), with a central core of almost 25 hectares (62 acres), but the area of prime interest is limited to the buildings surrounding two plazas next to the cenote, and another building, the Temple of the Seven Dolls, connected to these by a *sacbé* (causeway). Dzibilchaltún means "place of the stone writing," and at least 25 stelae have been found.

Start at the **Museo del Pueblo Maya,** which is worth seeing. It's open Tuesday to Sunday from 8am to 4pm. Admission is 48 pesos. The museum's collection includes artifacts from various sites in the Yucatán. Explanations are printed in bilingual format and are fairly thorough. Objects include a beautiful example of a plumed serpent from Chichén Itzá and a finely designed incense vessel from Palenque. From this general view of the Maya civilization, the museum moves on to exhibit specific artifacts found at the site of Dzibilchaltún, including the rather curious dolls that have given one structure its name. Then there's an exhibit on Maya culture in historical and present times, including a collection of *huipiles*, the woven blouses that Indian women wear. From here, a door leads out to the site.

The first thing you come to is the *sacbé* that connects the two areas of interest. To the left is the **Temple of the Seven Dolls**. The temple's doorways and the *sacbé* line up with the rising sun at the spring and autumnal equinoxes. To the right are the buildings grouped around the Cenote Xlacah, the sacred well, and a complex of buildings around **Structure 38**, the **Central Group** of temples. The Yucatán State Department of Ecology has added nature trails and published a booklet (in Spanish) of birds and plants seen along the mapped trail.

PROGRESO, UAYMITÚN & XCAMBÓ: GULF COAST CITY, FLAMINGO LOOKOUT & MORE MAYA RUINS

For a beach escape, go to the port of Progreso, Mérida's weekend beach resort. This is where Meridanos have their vacation houses and where they come in large numbers in July and August. It is also the part-time home of some Americans and Canadians escaping northern winters. Except for July and August, it is a quiet place where you can enjoy the Gulf waters in peace. Along the *malecón,* the wide oceanfront drive that extends the length of a sandy beach, you can pull over and enjoy a swim anywhere you like. The water here isn't the blue of the Caribbean, but it's clean. A long pier extends several kilometers into the gulf to load and unload large ships. Cruise ships dock here twice a week. Along or near the *malecón* are several hotels and a number of restaurants where you can get good fresh seafood.

From Mérida, buses to **Progreso** leave from the bus station at Calle 62 no. 524, between calles 65 and 67, every 15 minutes, starting at 5am. The trip takes almost an hour and costs 35 pesos.

If you have a car, you might want to drive down the coastal road east toward Telchac Puerto. After about 20 minutes, on the right you'll see a large, solid-looking wooden observation tower for viewing flamingos. A sign reads UAYMITUN. The state agency cultur constructed the tower, operates it, and provides binoculars free of charge. A few years ago, flamingos from Celestún migrated here and established a colony. Your chances of spotting them are good, and you don't have to pay for a boat.

Twenty minutes farther down this road, there's a turnoff for the road to Dzemul. On my last trip, I didn't see any flamingos at Uaymitún, but just after turning here, I found a flock of 500, only 30m (98 ft.) from the highway. After a few minutes, you'll see a sign for **Xcambó** that points to the right. This Maya city is thought to have prospered as a production center for salt. Archaeologists have reconstructed the small ceremonial center, which has several platforms and temples. Admission is free. After viewing these ruins, you can continue on the same road through the small towns of Dzemul and Baca. At Baca, take Hwy. 176 back to Mérida.

EN ROUTE TO UXMAL

Two routes go to Uxmal, about 80km (50 miles) south of Mérida. The most direct is Hwy. 261, via Umán and Muna. On the way, you can stop to see Hacienda Yaxcopoil, which is 30km (19 miles) from Mérida. If you have the time and want a more scenic route, try the meandering State Hwy. 18. It's sometimes called the Convent Route, but all tourism hype aside, it makes for a pleasant drive with several interesting stops. One thing you might do is make your trip to Uxmal into a loop by going one way and coming back the other with an overnight stay at Uxmal. You could plan on arriving in Uxmal in the late afternoon, attend the sound-and-light show in the evening, and see the ruins the next morning while it is cool and uncrowded.

While traveling in this area, you'll pass through small villages without directional signs, so get used to poking your head out the window and saying, *"Buenos días. ¿Dónde está el camino para . . . ?"* which translates as "Good day. Where is the road to . . . ?" I end up asking more than one person. The streets in these villages are full of children, bicycles, and livestock, so drive carefully and, as always, keep an eye out for unmarked *topes*.

The attractions on these routes all have the same hours: Churches are open daily from 10am to 1pm and 4 to 6pm; ruins are open daily from 8am to 5pm.

HWY. 261: YAXCOPOIL & MUNA

From downtown Mérida, take Calle 65 or 69 to Avenida Itzáes and turn left; this feeds onto the highway. You can save some time by looping around the busy market town of Umán. To do so, take the exit for Hwy. 180 Cancún and Campeche, and then follow signs toward Campeche. You'll be on Hwy. 180 headed south; take it for a few miles to where it intersects with Hwy. 261; take the exit labeled UXMAL. Very shortly, you'll come to the town and **Hacienda Yaxcopoil** (yash-koh-*poyl;* ✆ 999/900-1193; www.yaxcopoil.com), a ruined hacienda in plain sight on the right side of the road. In the front courtyard—now a parking lot—is a giant Indian laurel tree. You can take a half-hour tour of the place, including the manor, and the *henequén* factory. It's open Monday to Saturday from 8am to 5pm, and Sunday 9am to 1pm. Admission is 50 pesos. It's a little overpriced because the owners have not put much effort into making it a special attraction, but the grounds are attractive, and there are some things of interest.

After Yaxcopoil comes the little market town of **Muna** (65km/40 miles from Mérida). Here you can find excellent **reproductions of Maya ceramics.** An artisan named Rodrigo Martín Morales has worked 25 years perfecting the style and methods of the ancient Maya. He and his family have two workshops in town. They do painstaking work and sell a lot of their production to archeologists and museum stores. The first store is on the right at the junction of a bypass for Muna. Look for a typical Maya dwelling and a small store. The main store is 3km (1³/₄ miles) farther on, just as you enter Muna. Keep an eye out for two large Ceiba trees growing on the right side of the road. Under the trees, a small plaza with stalls sell handcrafts or food. Make a right turn and go down 45m (148 ft.). On your left will be a store. It's not well marked, but it will be obvious. The name of the place is **Taller de Artesanía Los Ceibos** (✆ 997/971-0036). The family will be working in the back. Only Spanish is spoken. The store is open from 9am to 6pm daily. In addition to ceramics, Rodrigo works in stone, wood, and jade. Uxmal is 15km (9¹/₄ miles) beyond Muna.

HWY. 18 (THE CONVENT ROUTE): KANASÍN & ACANCEH

From downtown Mérida, take Calle 63 east to Circuito Colonias and turn right; look for a traffic circle with a small fountain and turn left. This feeds onto Hwy. 18 to Kanasín (kah-nah-*seen*) and then Acanceh (ah-kahn-*keh*). In **Kanasín,** the highway divides into two roads, and a sign will tell you that you can't go straight; instead, you go to the right, which will curve around and flow into the next parallel street. Go past the market, church, and the main square on your left, and then stay to the right when you get to a fork.

Shortly after Kanasín, the highway has been upgraded and now bypasses a lot of villages. After a few of these turnoffs, you'll see a sign pointing left to **Acanceh.** Across the street from and overlooking Acanceh's church is a restored pyramid. On top of this pyramid, under a makeshift roof, are some large stucco figures of Maya deities. The caretaker, Mario Uicab, will guide you up to see the figures and give you a little explanation (in Spanish). Admission is 25 pesos. There are some other ruins a couple of blocks away called **El Palacio de los Estucos.** In 1908, a stucco mural was found here in mint condition. It was left exposed and has deteriorated somewhat. Now it is sheltered, and you can still easily distinguish the painted figures in their original colors. To leave Acanceh, head back to the highway on the street that passes between the church and the plaza.

The next turnoff will be for **Tecoh,** on the right side. Tecoh's parish church sits on a massive pre-Columbian raised platform—the remains of a ceremonial complex that was sacrificed to build the church. With its rough stone and simple twin towers that are crumbling around the edges, the church looks ancient. Inside are three carved *retablos* (altarpieces) covered in gold leaf and unmistakably Indian in style. In 1998, they were refurbished and are well worth seeing.

Also in Tecoh are some caverns, shown by a local. The bad news is that the owner doesn't have a very good flashlight, and I found myself groping around in the dark. You'll find them as you leave town heading back to the highway. Then it's on to the ruins of Mayapán.

Mayapán ★

Founded, according to Maya lore, by the man-god Kukulkán (Quetzalcoatl in central Mexico) in about A.D. 1007, Mayapán quickly established itself as the most important city in northern Yucatán. For almost 2 centuries, it was the capital of a Maya confederation of city-states that included Chichén Itzá and Uxmal. But before 1200, the rulers of Mayapán ended the confederation by attacking and subjugating the other two cities. Eventually, a successful revolt by the other cities brought down Mayapán, which was abandoned during the mid-1400s.

The city extended out at least 4 sq. km (1¹/₂ sq. miles), but the ceremonial center is quite compact. In the last few years, archaeologists have been busy excavating and rebuilding it, and work continues. Several buildings bordering the principal plaza have been reconstructed, including one that is similar to El Castillo in Chichén Itzá. The excavations have uncovered murals and stucco figures that provide more grist for the mill of conjecture: atlantes (columns in the form of a human figure supporting the structure), skeletal soldiers, macaws, entwined snakes, and a stucco jaguar. This place is definitely worth a stop.

The site is open daily from 8am to 5pm. Admission is 35 pesos. Use of a personal video camera is 45 pesos.

FROM MAYAPÁN TO TICUL   About 20km (12 miles) after Mayapán, you'll see the highway for **Mama** on your right. This will put you on a narrow road that quickly enters the town. For some reason, I really like this village; some parts of it are quite pretty. It's often called Mamita by the locals, using the affectionate diminutive suffix. The main attraction is the church and former convent. Inside are several fascinating *retablos* sculpted in a native form of baroque. During the restoration of these buildings, colonial-age murals and designs were uncovered and restored. Be sure to get a peek at them in the sacristy. From Mama, continue on for about 20km (12 miles) to Ticul, a large (for this area) market town with a couple of simple hotels.

Best known for the cottage industry of *huipil* (native blouse) embroidery and for the manufacture of women's dress shoes, Ticul isn't the most exciting stop on the Puuc route, but it's a convenient place to wash up and spend the night. It's also a center for large-scale pottery production—most of the widely sold sienna-colored pottery painted with Maya designs comes from here. If it's a cloudy, humid day, the potters may not be working (part of the process requires sun drying), but they still welcome visitors to purchase finished pieces.

Ticul is only 20km (12 miles) northeast of Uxmal, so thrifty tourists stay either here or in Santa Elena instead of the more expensive hotels at the ruins. On the main square is the **Hotel Plaza,** Calle 23 no. 202, near the intersection with Calle 26 (© **997/972-0484**). It's a modest but comfortable hotel. A double room with air-conditioning costs 350 pesos; without air-conditioning, 250 pesos. In both cases, there's a 5% charge if you want to pay with a credit card (MasterCard and Visa accepted). Get an interior room if you're looking for quiet, because Ticul has quite a lively plaza. From Ticul, you can do one of two things: head straight for Uxmal via Santa Elena, or loop around the Puuc Route, the long way to Santa Elena. For information on the Puuc route, see "The Puuc Maya Route & Village of Oxkutzcab," below.

FROM TICUL TO UXMAL   Follow the main street (Calle 23) west through town. Turn left on Calle 34. It's 15km (9¹⁄₄ miles) to Santa Elena, and from there another 15km (9¹⁄₄ miles) to Uxmal. In Santa Elena, by the side of Hwy. 261, is a clean restaurant with good food, **El Chaac Mool,** and on the opposite side of the road is the **Flycatcher Inn B&B** (see listing, below).

---

3 THE RUINS OF UXMAL ★★★

80km (50 miles) SW of Mérida; 19km (12 miles) W of Ticul; 19km (12 miles) S of Muna

The ceremonial complex of Uxmal (pronounced "oosh-*mahl*") is one of the masterworks of Maya civilization. It is strikingly different from all other cities of the Maya for its expansive and intricate facades of carved stone. Unlike other sites in northern Yucatán, such as Chichén Itzá and Mayapán, Uxmal isn't built on a flat plane. The builders worked into the composition of the ceremonial center an interplay of elevations that adds complexity. And then there is the strange and beautiful oval-shaped Pyramid of the Magician, which is unique among the Maya. The great building period took place between A.D. 700 and 1000, when the population probably reached 25,000. After 1000, Uxmal fell under the sway of the Xiú princes (who may have come from central Mexico). In the 1440s, the Xiú conquered Mayapán, and not long afterward, the age of the Maya ended with the arrival of the Spanish conquistadors.

Close to Uxmal, four smaller sites—**Sayil, Kabah, Xlapak,** and **Labná**—can be visited in quick succession. With Uxmal, these ruins are collectively known as the **Puuc route.** See "Seeing Puuc Maya Sites," below, if you want to explore these sites.

ESSENTIALS

GETTING THERE & DEPARTING   **By Car**   Two routes to Uxmal from Mérida, Hwy. 261 and State Hwy. 18, are described in "En Route to Uxmal," above. *Note:* There's no gasoline at Uxmal.

By Bus   See "Getting There & Departing" in "Mérida: Gateway to the Maya Heartland," earlier in this chapter, for information about bus service between Mérida and Uxmal. To return, wait for the bus on the highway at the entrance to the ruins. To see the sound-and-light show, don't bother with regular buses; sign up with a tour operator in Mérida.

ORIENTATION   Entrance to the ruins is through the visitor center where you buy your tickets (two per person, hold on to both). It has a restaurant; toilets; a first-aid station; shops selling soft drinks, ice cream, film, batteries, and books; a state-run Casa de Artesanía (crafts house); and a small museum, which isn't very informative. The site is open daily from 8am to 5pm. Admission to the archaeological site is around 111 pesos, which includes admission to the nightly sound-and-light show. Bringing in a video camera costs 45 pesos. Parking costs 10 pesos. If you're staying the night in Uxmal, it is possible (and I think preferable) to get to the site late in the day and buy a ticket that allows you to see the sound-and-light show that evening and lets you enter the ruins the next morning to explore them before it gets hot. Just make sure that the ticket vendor knows what you intend to do, and keep the ticket.

Guides at the entrance of Uxmal give tours in a variety of languages and charge $40 for a single person or a group. The guides frown on unrelated individuals joining a group. They'd rather charge you as a solo visitor, but you can ask other English speakers if they'd like to join you in a tour and split the cost. As at other sites, the guides vary in quality but will point out areas and architectural details that you might otherwise miss. You should think of these guided tours as performances—the guides try to be as entertaining as possible and adjust their presentations according to the interests of the visitors.

Included in the price of admission is a 45-minute **sound-and-light show** each evening at 7pm. It's in Spanish, but headsets are available for rent (25 pesos) for listening to the program in several languages. The narrative is part Hollywood, part high school, but the lighting of the buildings is worth making the effort to see it. After the show, the chant *"Chaaac, Chaaac"* will echo in your mind for weeks.

A TOUR OF THE RUINS

THE PYRAMID OF THE MAGICIAN   As you enter the ruins, note a *chultún,* or cistern, where Uxmal stored its water. Unlike most of the major Maya sites, Uxmal has no cenote to supply fresh water. The city's inhabitants were much more dependent on rainwater, and consequently venerated the rain god Chaac with unusual devotion.

Rising in front of you is the Pirámide del Adivino. The name comes from a myth told to John Lloyd Stephens on his visit in the 19th century. It tells the story of a magician-dwarf who reached adulthood in a single day after being hatched from an egg and built this pyramid in 1 night. Beneath it are five earlier structures. The pyramid has an oval base and rounded sides. You are looking at the east side. The main face is on the west side. Walk around the left, or south, side to see the front. The pyramid was designed so that the east side rises less steeply than the west side, which shifts the crowning temples to the west of the central axis of the building, causing them to loom above the plaza below. The temple doorway is heavily ornamented, characteristic of the Chenes style, with 12 stylized masks representing Chaac.

THE NUNNERY QUADRANGLE   From the plaza you're standing in, you want to go to the large Nunnery Quadrangle. Walk out the way you walked into the plaza, turn right, and follow the wall of this long stone building until you get to the building's main door—a corbelled arch that leads into the quadrangle. You'll find yourself in a plaza bordered on each side by stone buildings with elaborate facades. The 16th-century Spanish historian Fray Diego López de Cogullado gave the quadrangle its name when he decided that its layout resembled a Spanish convent.

The quadrangle does have a lot of small rooms, about the size of a nun's cell. You might poke your head into one to see the shape and size of it, but don't bother trying to explore them all. These rooms were long ago abandoned to the swallows that fly above the city. No interior murals or stucco work have been found here—at least, not yet. No, the richness of Uxmal lies in the stonework on its exterior walls.

The Nunnery is a great example of this. The first building your eye latches onto when you enter the plaza is the north building in front of you. It is the tallest, and the view from the top includes all the major buildings of the city, making it useful for the sound-and-light show. The central stairway is bordered by a common element in Puuc architecture, doorways supported by rounded columns. The remnants of the facade on the second level show elements used in the other three buildings and elsewhere throughout the city. There's a crosshatch pattern and a pattern of square curlicues, called a step-and-fret design, and the long-nosed god mask repeated vertically, used often to decorate the corners of buildings in what I call a Chaac stack. Though the facades of these buildings share these common elements and others, their composition varies. On the west building, you'll see long, feathered serpents intertwined at head and tail. A human head stares out from a serpent's open mouth. I've heard and read a number of interpretations of this motif, repeated elsewhere in Maya art, but they all leave me somewhat in doubt. And that's the trouble with symbols: They are usually the condensed expression of multiple meanings, so any one interpretation could be true, but only partially true.

THE BALL COURT   Leaving the Nunnery by the same way you entered, you will see a ball court straight ahead. What would a Maya city be without a ball court? And this one is a particularly good representative of the hundreds found elsewhere in the Maya world. Someone has even installed a replica of one of the stone rings that were the targets for the players, who would make use of their knees, hips, and maybe their arms to strike a solid rubber ball (yes, the Maya knew about natural rubber and extracted latex from a couple of species of rubber trees). The inclined planes on both sides of the court were in play and obviously not an area for spectators, who are thought to have observed the game from atop the two structures.

THE GOVERNOR'S PALACE   Continuing in the same direction (south), you come to the large raised plaza on top of which sits the Governor's Palace, running in a north–south direction. The surface area of the raised plaza measures 140m x170m (459 ft.x558 ft.), and it is raised about 10m (33 ft.) above the ground—quite a bit of earth moving. Most of this surface is used as a ceremonial space facing the front (east side) of the palace. In the center is a double-headed jaguar throne, which is seen elsewhere in the Maya world. From here, you get the best view of the building's remarkable facade. Like the rest of the palaces here, the first level is smooth and the second is ornate. Moving diagonally across a crosshatch pattern is a series of Chaac masks. Crowning the building is an elegant cornice projecting slightly outward from above a double border, which could be an architectural reference to the original crested thatched roofs of the Maya. Human figures adorned the main doors, though only the headdress survives of the central figure.

THE GREAT PYRAMID   Behind the palace, the platform descends in terraces to another plaza with a large pyramid on its south side. This is known as the Great Pyramid.

On top is the Temple of the Macaws, for the repeated representation of macaws on the face of the temple, and the ruins of three other temples. The view from the top is wonderful.

THE DOVECOTE   This building is remarkable, in that roof combs weren't a common feature of temples in the Puuc hills, although you'll see one (of a very different style) on El Mirador at Sayil.

WHERE TO STAY

Flycatcher Inn B&B ⏥ **Value**   This pleasant little bed-and-breakfast is in the village of Santa Elena, just off Hwy. 261. The rooms are quiet, attractive, and spacious, and come with comfortable beds and decorative ironwork made by one of the owners, Santiago Domínguez. The other owner is Kristine Ellingson, an American from the Northwest who has lived in Santa Elena for years and is happy to aid her guests in their travels. The rooms are comfortable, and the grounds are large and attractive. A hiking trail explores some of the property.

Carretera Uxmal–Kabah, 97840 Santa Elena, Yuc. No phone. www.flycatcherinn.com. 7 units. $55–$75 double ($10 extra for A/C). Rates include breakfast. No credit cards. Free secure parking. *In room:* A/C in 6 units.

Hacienda Uxmal and The Lodge at Uxmal ★★★   The Hacienda is the oldest hotel in Uxmal. Located just up the road from the ruins, it was built for the archaeology staff. Rooms are large and airy, exuding a feel of days gone by, with patterned tile floors, heavy furniture, and louvered windows. Room nos. 202 through 214 and 302 through 305 are the nicest of the superiors. Corner rooms are labeled A through F and are even larger and come with Jacuzzi tubs. A handsome garden courtyard with towering royal palms, a bar, and a pool adds to the air of tranquillity. A guitar trio usually plays on the open patio in the evenings.

The Lodge is right at the entrance to the ruins. It's made up of several two-story thatched buildings ("bungalows") situated around two pools and surrounded by landscaped grounds. Each building has a large, open breezeway with ceiling fans and rocking chairs. Rooms are extra large and attractively finished with details such as carved headboards. Bathrooms are large and come with stone countertops and either a bathtub or a Jacuzzi tub. Upstairs rooms have thatched roofs.

Highest rates are for Christmas/New Years, the spring equinox (Mar 19–23), and the month of November. A secondary high season extends from January to April. Low season includes May to October and the first three weeks of December.

Carretera Mérida–Uxmal Km 80, 97844 Uxmal, Yuc. ⏥ **997/976-2011.** www.mayaland.com. (Reservations: Mayaland Resorts, Robalo 30 SM3, 77500 Cancún, Q. Roo; ⏥ 800/235-4079 in the U.S., or 998/887-2450; fax 998/887-4510.) 113 units. Hacienda: High season $173–$222 double, $255–$280 superior; low season $115 double, $145 superior. Lodge: High season $438–$460 bungalow; low season $292 bungalow. AE, MC, V. Free guarded parking. **Amenities:** 2 restaurants; bar; 4 outdoor pools; smoke-free rooms. *In room:* A/C, TV, hair dryer (upon request), minibar.

Villas Arqueológicas Uxmal ★   This hotel and its sister properties were sold to a Mexican resort group called Islander Collection, but it's still business as usual, much as it was when the place was part of Club Med. A two-story layout surrounds a garden patio and a pool. At guests' disposal are a tennis court, a library, and an audiovisual show on the ruins in English, French, and Spanish. Each of the modern, medium-size rooms has a double and a twin bed that fit into spaces that are walled on three sides. Very tall people should stay elsewhere. You can also ask for rates that include half- or full board.

Ruinas Uxmal, 97844 Uxmal, Yuc. ℂ **987/872-9300,** ext. 8101. www.islandercollection.com. 48 units. $130 double. Rates include continental breakfast. Half-board (breakfast plus lunch or dinner) $20 per person; full board (3 meals) $40 per person. AE, MC, V. Free guarded parking. **Amenities:** Restaurant; bar; outdoor pool; tennis court. *In room:* A/C, hair dryer.

WHERE TO DINE

I've eaten well at the hotel restaurant of the Lodge at Uxmal, ordering the Yucatecan specialties, which were fresh and well prepared. I've also eaten well at the hotel restaurant at the Villas Arqueológicas, but again, keeping it simple. There are some *palapa* restaurants by the highway as you approach the ruins from Mérida. I've had good and bad experiences at these. They do a lot of business with bus tours, so the best time to try them is early afternoon.

4 THE PUUC MAYA ROUTE & VILLAGE OF OXKUTZCAB

South and east of Uxmal are several other Maya cities worth visiting. Though smaller in scale than Uxmal or Chichén Itzá, each contains gems of Maya architecture. The Palace of Masks at **Kabah,** the palace at **Sayil,** and the fantastic caverns of **Loltún** are well worth viewing.

Kabah is 28km (17 miles) southeast of Uxmal via Hwy. 261 through Santa Elena. From there it's only a couple kilometers to Sayil. Xlapak is almost walking distance (through the jungle) from Sayil, and Labná is just a bit farther east. A short drive beyond Labná brings you to the caves of Loltún. Oxkutzcab is at the road's intersection with Hwy. 184, which you can follow west to Ticul or east all the way to Felipe Carrillo Puerto. If you aren't driving, a daily bus from Mérida goes to all these sites, with the exception of Loltún. (See "By Bus" in "Getting There & Departing," earlier in this chapter.)

PUUC MAYA SITES

KABAH ★   To reach Kabah from Uxmal, head southwest on Hwy. 261 to Santa Elena (1km/¹/₂ mile), then south to Kabah (13km/8 miles). The ancient city lies along both sides of the highway. Turn right into the parking lot.

(Tips)   Seeing Puuc Maya Sites

All of these sites are currently undergoing excavation and reconstruction, and some buildings may be roped off when you visit. The sites are open daily from 8am to 5pm. Admission is 20 to 30 pesos for each site, and 48 pesos for Loltún. Loltún has specific hours for tours—9:30 and 11am, and 12:30, 2, 3, and 4pm. Even if you're the only person at the cave at one of these times, the guide must give you a tour, and he can't try to charge you more money as if you were contracting his services for an individual tour. Sometimes the guides try to do this. Use of a video camera at any time costs 45 pesos; if you're visiting Uxmal in the same day, you pay only once for video permission and present your receipt as proof at each ruin.

The most outstanding building at Kabah is the **Palace of Masks,** or Codz Poop ("rolled-up mat"), named for its decorative motif. You'll notice it to the right as you enter. Its outstanding feature is the Chenes-style facade, completely covered in a repeated pattern of 250 masks of Chaac, each one with curling remnants of Chaac's elephant trunk–like nose. There's nothing else like this facade in all of Maya architecture. For years, parts of this building lay lined up in the weeds like pieces of a puzzle awaiting the master puzzle-solver to put them into place. Sculptures from this building are in the anthropology museums in Mérida and Mexico City.

Just behind and to the left of the Codz Poop is the **Palace Group** (also called the East Group), with a fine Puuc-style colonnaded facade. Originally, it had 32 rooms. On the front are seven doors, two divided by columns, a common feature of Puuc architecture. Across the highway is what was once the **Great Temple.** Past it is a **great arch,** which was much wider at one time and may have been a monumental gate into the city. A *sacbé* linked this arch to a point at Uxmal. Compare this corbelled arch to the one at Labná (see below), which is in much better shape.

SAYIL   About 4km (2¹/₂ miles) south of Kabah is the turnoff (left, or east) to Sayil, Xlapak, Labná, Loltún, and Oxkutzcab. The ruins of **Sayil** ("place of the ants") are 4km (2¹/₂ miles) along this road.

Sayil is famous for **El Palacio ★★**. This palace of more than 90 rooms is impressive for its size alone. At present it is roped off. Climbing is not permitted. But this is unimportant because what makes it a masterpiece of Maya architecture is the facade, which is best appreciated from the ground. It stretches across three terraced levels, and its rows of columns give it a Minoan appearance. On the second level, notice the upside-down stone figure known to archaeologists as the Diving God, or Descending God, over the doorway; the same motif was used at Tulum a couple of centuries later. The large circular basin on the ground below the palace is an artificial catch basin for a *chultún* (cistern); this region has no natural cenotes (wells) to use to irrigate crops.

In the jungle beyond El Palacio is **El Mirador,** a small temple with an oddly slotted roof comb. Beyond El Mirador, a crude stele (tall, carved stone) has a phallic idol carved on it in exaggerated proportions. Another building group, the Southern Group, is a short distance down a trail that branches off from the one heading to El Mirador.

XLAPAK   Xlapak (*shla*-pahk) is a small site with one building; it's 5.5 km (3¹/₂ miles) down the road from Sayil. The Palace at Xlapak bears the masks of the rain god Chaac. You won't miss much if you skip this place.

LABNÁ   Labná, which dates from between A.D. 600 and 900, is 30km (19 miles) from Uxmal and only 3km (1³/₄ miles) past Xlapak. Descriptive placards fronting the main buildings are in Spanish, English, and German. The first thing you see on the left as you enter is **El Palacio,** a magnificent Puuc-style building much like the one at Sayil, but in poorer condition. Over a doorway is a large, well-conserved mask of Chaac with eyes, a huge snout nose, and jagged teeth around a small mouth that seems on the verge of speaking. Jutting out on one corner is a highly stylized serpent's mouth from which pops a human head with an unexpectedly serene expression. From the front, you can gaze out to the enormous grassy interior grounds flanked by vestiges of unrestored buildings and jungle.

From El Palacio, you can walk across the interior grounds on a reconstructed *sacbé* leading to Labná's **corbelled arch.** At one time, there were probably several such arches spread through the region. This one has been extensively restored, although only remnants of the roof comb can be seen. It was once part of a more elaborate structure that is completely gone. Chaac's face is on the corners of one facade, and stylized Maya huts are fashioned in stone above the two small doorways.

You pass through the arch to **El Mirador,** or El Castillo. Towering above a large pile of rubble is a singular room crowned with a roof comb etched against the sky.

There's a snack stand with toilets at the entrance.

LOLTÚN   The caverns of Loltún are 31km (19 miles) past Labná on the way to Oxkutzcab, on the left side of the road. These fascinating caves, home of ancient Maya, were also used as a refuge during the War of the Castes (1847–1901). Inside are statuary, wall carvings and paintings, *chultunes* (cisterns), and other signs of Maya habitation. Guides will explain much of what you see. When I was there, the guide spoke English but was a little difficult to understand.

The admission price includes a 90-minute **tour;** tours begin daily at 9:30 and 11am, and 12:30, 2, 3, and 4pm. The floor of the cavern can be slippery in places; if you have a flashlight, take it with you. Admission is 48 pesos. I've heard reports of guides canceling the regularly scheduled tour so that they can charge for a private tour. Don't agree to such a thing.

To return to Mérida from Loltún, drive the 7km (4¹/₄ miles) to Oxkutzcab. From there, you have a couple of options for returning to Mérida: The slow route is through Maní and Teabo, which will allow you to see some convents and return by Hwy. 18, known as the "Convent Route" (see "En Route to Uxmal," earlier in this chapter). Alternately, you can head toward Muna to hook up with Hwy. 261 (also described earlier).

OXKUTZCAB

Oxkutzcab (ohsh-kootz-*kahb*), 11km (6³/₄ miles) from Loltún, is the center of the Yucatán's fruit-growing region. Oranges abound. The tidy village of 21,000 centers on a beautiful 16th-century church and the market. **Su Cabaña Suiza** (no phone) is a dependable restaurant in town. The last week of October and first week of November is the **Orange Festival,** when the village turns exuberant, with a carnival and orange displays in and around the central plaza.

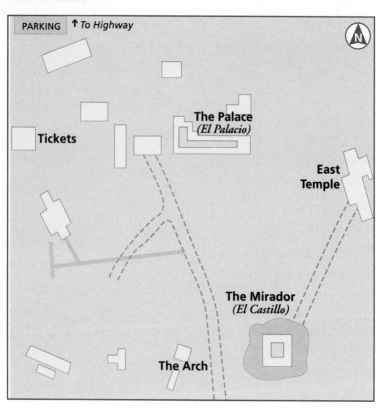

EN ROUTE TO CAMPECHE

From Oxkutzcab, head back 43km (27 miles) to Sayil, and then drive south on Hwy. 261 to Campeche (126km/78 miles). After crossing the state line, you'll pass through the towns of Bolonchén and Hopelchén. The drive is pleasant, and there's little traffic. Both towns have gas stations. When going through the towns, watch carefully for directional traffic signs so that you stay on the highway. From Hopelchén, Hwy. 261 heads west. After 42km (26 miles), you'll find yourself at Cayal and the well-marked turnoff for the ruins of the city of Edzná, 18km (11 miles) farther south.

EDZNÁ ★   This city is interesting for several reasons. The area was populated as early as 600 B.C., with urban formation by 300 B.C. From that point on, Edzná grew impressively in a way that evinces considerable urban-planning skills. An ambitious and elaborate canal system was dug, which must have taken decades to complete but would have allowed for a great expansion in agricultural production and, hence, concentration of population. This made Edzná the preeminent city for a wide territory.

Another boom in construction began around A.D. 500, amid the Classic period. This was when the city's most prominent feature, the **Great Acropolis,** was started.

Sitting on top of this raised platform are five main pyramids, the largest being the much-photographed **Pyramid of Five Stories.** It combines the features of temple platform and palace. In Maya architecture, you have palace buildings with many vaulted chambers and you have solid pyramidal platforms with a couple of interior temples or burial passages. These are two mutually exclusive categories—but not here. Such a mix is found only in the Puuc and Río Bec areas and only in a few examples, and none similar to this, which makes this pyramid a bold architectural statement. The four lesser pyramids on the Acropolis are each constructed in a different style, and each is a pure example of that style. It's as if the rulers of this city were flaunting their cosmopolitanism, showing that they could build in any style they chose but preferred creating their own, superior architecture.

West of the Acropolis, across a large open plaza, is a long, raised building whose purpose isn't quite clear. But its size, as well as that of the plaza, makes you wonder just how many people this city actually held to necessitate such a large public space.

The site takes an hour to see and is open daily from 8am to 5pm. Admission is 45 pesos, plus the same amount to use your video camera.

5 CAMPECHE ★★

251km (156 miles) SW of Mérida; 376km (233 miles) NE of Villahermosa

Campeche, the capital of the state of the same name, is a beautifully restored colonial city. The facades of all the houses in the historic center of town have been repaired and painted, all electrical and telephone cables have been routed underground, and the streets have been paved to look cobbled. Several Mexican movie companies have taken advantage of the restoration to shoot period films here.

Despite its beauty, not many tourists come to Campeche. Those who do, tend to be either on their way to the ruins at Palenque (see chapter 9) or the Río Bec region (see chapter 7), or the kind of travelers who are accidental wanderers. A couple of things do need to be said: Campeche is not geared to foreign tourism the way Mérida is, so expect less in the way of English translations and such at museums and other sights. Also, expect less in the way of nightlife, except on weekend nights when they block off the main square for a street party.

If you're interested in seeing the ruins along the Río Bec route, see the section "Side Trips to Maya Ruins from Chetumal," in chapter 7. **Calakmul ★★★** (p. 188) is a large and important site, with the tallest pyramid in the Yucatán peninsula, and if you're going that far, you should stop at Balamkú and perhaps a few other ruins in the area. From the Campeche side, you can get information and contract a tour with one of several tour operators. You can also rent a car. Calakmul is too far away for a day trip. There are a few small hotels in the area. Hotel Del Mar in Campeche has two: **Chicanná Eco-village** and **Puerta Calakmul.**

From the Calakmul area, it's easy to cross over the peninsula to Yucatán's southern Caribbean coast. Then you can head up the coast and complete a loop of the peninsula.

Campeche has an interesting history. The conquistadors arrived in 1517, when Francisco de Córdoba landed here while exploring the coast and stayed just long enough to celebrate Mass. Attempts to settle here were unsuccessful because of native resistance until Montejo The Younger was able to secure a settlement in 1540.

In the 17th and 18th centuries, pirates repeatedly harassed the city. The list of Campeche's attackers reads like a who's who of pirating. On one occasion, several outfits banded together under the famous Dutch pirate Peg Leg (who most likely was the inspiration for the many fictional one-legged sailors) and managed to capture the city. The Campechanos grew tired of hosting pirate parties and erected walls around the city. The walls had a number of *baluartes* (bastions) at critical locations. For added security, they constructed two forts, complete with moats and drawbridges, on the hills flanking the city. There were four gates to the city, and the two main ones are still intact: the Puerta de Mar (Sea Gate) and the Puerta de Tierra (Land Gate). The pirates never cared to return, but in Mexico's stormy political history, the city did withstand a couple of sieges by different armies. Eventually, in the early 1900s, the wall around the city was razed, but the bastions and main gates were left intact, as were the two hilltop fortresses. Most of the bastions and both forts now house museums.

ESSENTIALS

GETTING THERE & DEPARTING **By Plane** AeroMéxico (ⓒ 981/816-6656; www. aeromexico.com.mx) flies once daily to and from Mexico City. The **airport** is several kilometers northeast of the town center, and you'll have to take a taxi into town (about 65 pesos).

By Car Hwy. 180 goes south from Mérida, passing near the basket-making village of Halacho and near Becal, known for its Panama-hat weavers. The trip takes 2¹/₂ hours. At Tenabo, take the shortcut (right, Hwy. 24) to Campeche rather than going farther to the crossroads near Chencoyí. The longer way from Mérida is along Hwy. 261 past Uxmal.

When returning to Mérida via Hwy. 180, go north on Avenida Ruiz Cortines, bearing left to follow the water (this becomes Av. Pedro Sainz de Baranda, but there's no sign). Follow the road as it turns inland to Hwy. 180, where you turn left (there's a gas station at the intersection).

If you're leaving Campeche for Edzná and Uxmal, go north on either Ruiz Cortines or Gobernadores, and turn right on Madero, which feeds onto **Hwy. 281.** To go south to Villahermosa, take Ruiz Cortines south.

By Bus ADO (ⓒ 981/816-2802) offers a first-class *de paso* (passing through) bus to Palenque (6 hr.; 178 pesos) four times a day and buses to Mérida (2¹/₂ hr.; 89 pesos) every hour from 5:30am to midnight. The ADO **bus station** is on Avenida Patricio Trueba, a kilometer (a half-mile) from the Puerta de Tierra.

INFORMATION The **State of Campeche Office of Tourism** (ⓒ/fax 981/127-3300; http://campeche.travel) is in Plaza Moch-Couoh, Avenida Ruiz Cortines s/n, 24000 Campeche. This is in one of the state buildings between the historic center and the shore. There are also information offices in the bastions of Santa Rosa, San Carlos, and Santiago. It's open Monday to Friday from 9am to 2pm and 4 to 7pm.

CITY LAYOUT The most interesting part of the city is the restored old part, most of which once lay within the walls. Originally, the seaward wall was at the water's edge, but now land has been gained from the sea between the old walls and the coastline. This is where you'll find most of the state government buildings, which were built in a glaringly modernist style around **Plaza Moch-Couoh:** buildings such as the office tower **Edificio de los Poderes (Judicial Building)** or **Palacio de Gobierno (headquarters for the state of Campeche),** and the futuristic **Cámara de Diputados (Chamber of Deputies),** which looks like a cubist clam.

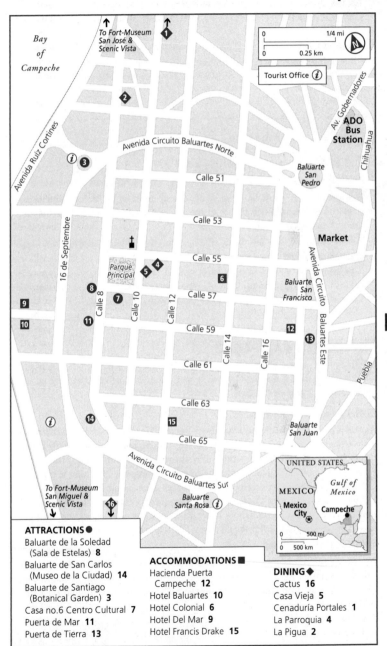

Bay
of
Campeche

To Fort-Museum
San José &
Scenic Vista

1

2

Tourist Office (i)

Avenida Ruiz Cortines

(i) 3

Avenida Circuito Baluartes Norte

Calle 51

Av Gobernadores

Chihuahua

ADO
Bus
Station

Baluarte
San
Pedro

Calle 53

16 de Septiembre

Calle 55

Market

Parque
Principal

5 4

6

Avenida Circuito

Baluarte
San
Francisco

8

7

Calle 8

Calle 10

Calle 57

9

10

11

Calle 12

Calle 59

12

13

Baluartes Este

Calle 14

Calle 16

Calle 61

Puebla

Calle 63

(i)

14

15

Calle 65

Baluarte
San Juan

To Fort-Museum
San Miguel &
Scenic Vista

16

Avenida Circuito Baluartes Sur

Baluarte
Santa Rosa (i)

UNITED STATES

MEXICO

Gulf of
Mexico

Mexico
City

Campeche

0   500 mi

0   500 km

ATTRACTIONS ●
Baluarte de la Soledad
  (Sala de Estelas) **8**
Baluarte de San Carlos
  (Museo de la Ciudad) **14**
Baluarte de Santiago
  (Botanical Garden) **3**
Casa no.6 Centro Cultural **7**
Puerta de Mar **11**
Puerta de Tierra **13**

ACCOMMODATIONS ■
Hacienda Puerta
  Campeche **12**
Hotel Baluartes **10**
Hotel Colonial **6**
Hotel Del Mar **9**
Hotel Francis Drake **15**

DINING ◆
Cactus **16**
Casa Vieja **5**
Cenaduría Portales **1**
La Parroquia **4**
La Pigua **2**

Campeche's system of street numbering is much like that of other cities in the Yucatán, except that the numbers of the north–south streets increase as you go east instead of the reverse. (See "City Layout" in "Mérida: Gateway to the Maya Heartland," earlier in this chapter.)

GETTING AROUND Most of the recommended sights, restaurants, and hotels are within walking distance of the old city, except for the two fort-museums. Campeche isn't easy to negotiate by bus, so take taxis for anything beyond walking distance—they are inexpensive.

Fast Facts   Campeche

Area Code The telephone area code is **981.**

ATMs There are more than 10 cash machines around the downtown area.

Emergencies To report an emergency, dial ℭ **060,** which is supposed to be similar to 911 emergency service in the United States. Dial ℭ **065** for the Red Cross.

Internet Access There are plenty of places to check e-mail—just look for signs with the words INTERNET or CYBERCAFE.

Post Office The *correo* is in the Edificio Federal, at Avenida 16 de Septiembre and Calle 53 (ℭ **981/816-2134**), near the Baluarte de Santiago; it's open Monday to Saturday from 7:30am to 8pm. The telegraph office is also here.

EXPLORING CAMPECHE

With beautiful surroundings, friendly people, and an easy pace of life, Campeche is worthy of at least a day on your itinerary. It has some interesting museums, one outstanding restaurant, and plenty to do.

Inside the City Walls

A good place to begin is the pretty *zócalo*, or **Parque Principal**, bounded by calles 55 and 57 running east and west, and calles 8 and 10 running north and south. On Saturday nights and Sundays, the city closes the main square to traffic and contracts bands to play. People set up tables in the streets, and the entire scene becomes a fun kind of block party. Construction of the church on the north side of the square began in 1650 and was finally completed 150 years later. A pleasant way to see the city is to take the *tranvía* (trolley) tour that leaves three or four times a day from the main plaza; check with one of the tourist information offices for the schedule. The cost is 60 pesos for a 45-minute tour.

Baluarte de la Soledad This bastion next to the sea gate houses Maya stelae recovered from around the state. Many are badly worn, but the line drawings beside the stones allow you to appreciate their former design.

Calle 57 and Calle 8, opposite Plaza Principal. No phone. Admission 25 pesos. Tues–Sat 9am–8pm; Sun 9am–1pm.

Baluarte de San Carlos/Museo de la Ciudad The city museum deals primarily with the design and construction of the fortifications. A model of the city shows how it

looked in its glory days and provides a good overview for touring within the city walls. **233**
There are several excellent ship models as well. All text is in Spanish.

Circuito Baluartes and Av. Justo Sierra. No phone. Admission 25 pesos. Tues–Sat 9am–8pm; Sun 9am–1pm.

Baluarte de Santiago The Jardín Botánico Xmuch'haltun is a jumble of exotic and common plants within the stone walls of this bastion. More than 250 species of plants and trees share a small courtyard.

Av. 16 de Septiembre and Calle 49. No phone. Free admission. Mon–Fri 9am–8pm; Sat–Sun 9am–1pm.

Casa no. 6 Centro Cultural In this remodeled colonial house, you'll see some rooms decorated with period furniture and accessories. The patio of mixtilinear arches supported by simple Doric columns is striking. Exhibited in the patio are photos of the city's fine colonial architecture. Several of the photographed buildings have recently been renovated. There is also a small bookstore in back, as well as temporary exhibition space.

Calle 57 no. 6. No phone. Free admission. Daily 9am–9pm.

Puerta de Tierra At the Land Gate is a small museum displaying portraits of pirates and the city founders. The 1732 French 5-ton cannon in the entryway was found in 1990. On Tuesday, Friday, and Saturday at 8pm, there's a light-and-sound show, as long as 15 or more people have bought tickets. Some shows are in English and some are in Spanish; it depends on the audience. The show is amusing.

Calle 59 at Circuito Baluartes/Av. Gobernadores. No phone. Free admission to museum; show $3 adults, $1 children younger than 11. Daily 9am–9pm.

Outside the Walls: Scenic Vistas

Fuerte–Museo San José el Alto This fort is higher and has a more sweeping view of Campeche and the coastline than Fuerte San Miguel, but it houses only a small exhibit of 16th- and 17th-century weapons and scale miniatures of sailing vessels. It's a nice place for a picnic. Take a cab. En route, you will pass an impressive statue of Juárez.

Av. Morazán s/n. No phone. Admission 25 pesos. Tues–Sun 8am–8pm.

Fuerte–Museo San Miguel ★★ For a good view of the city and a great little museum, take a cab up to Fuerte–Museo San Miguel. San Miguel is a small fort with a moat and a drawbridge. Built in 1771, it was the most important of the city's defenses. General Santa Anna captured it when he attacked the city in 1842. The museum of the Maya world was renovated in 2000 and is worth seeing. It groups the artifacts around central issues in Maya culture. In a room devoted to Maya concepts of the afterlife, there's a great burial scene with jade masks and jewelry from Maya tombs at Calakmul. Another room explains Maya cosmology, another depicts war, and another explains the gods. There are also exhibits on the history of the fort.

Ruta Escénica s/n. No phone. Admission 30 pesos. Tues–Sat 9am–8pm; Sun 8am–noon.

SHOPPING

Casa de Artesanías Tukulná This store, run by dif (a government family-assistance agency), occupies a restored mansion. There is an elaborate display of regional arts and crafts in the back. The wares in the showrooms represent everything that is produced in the state. There are quality textiles, clothing, and locally made furniture. Open Monday to Saturday from 9am to 8pm. Calle 10 no. 333 (btw. calles 59 and 61). © **981/816-9088.**

MÉRIDA, CHICHÉN ITZÁ & THE MAYA INTERIOR

8

CAMPECHE

Rates quoted include the 17% tax.

Very Expensive

Hacienda Puerta Campeche ★★★   This hotel was created from several adjoining colonial townhouses. It's a beautiful and original property just inside the Puerta de Tierra in Campeche's colonial center. There is a tropical garden in the center and a pool that runs through the ruined walls of one of the houses. It's quite picturesque. Rooms are colonial with flare—large with old tile floors, distinctive colors, and beamed ceilings. "Hacienda" is in the name to make it apparent that this is one of the properties connected to the four haciendas managed by Starwood hotels. (See "Haciendas & Hotels" in the Mérida section, earlier in this chapter).

Calle 59 71, 24000 Campeche, Camp. ✆ **800/325-3589** in the U.S. or Canada, or 981/816-7508. www. luxurycollection.com. 15 units. $362–$435 superior; $500 and up suite. AE, MC, V. Free guarded parking. **Amenities:** Restaurant; 2 bars; airport transportation; babysitting; concierge; outdoor pool; room service; spa. *In room:* A/C, TV, fridge, hair dryer, high-speed Internet, minibar.

Expensive

Hotel Del Mar ★   Rooms in this four-story hotel are large, bright, and comfortably furnished. All have balconies that face the Gulf of Mexico. The beds (two doubles or one king-size) are comfortable. The Del Mar is on the main oceanfront boulevard, between the coast and the city walls. It offers more services than the Baluartes and is a little more expensive. You can make a reservation here to stay in the Río Bec area, or you can buy a package that includes guide and transportation. The hotel also offers a tour to Edzná.

Av. Ruiz Cortines 51, 24000 Campeche, Camp. ✆ **981/811-9192**, -9193. Fax 981/811-1618. www.delmar hotel.com.mx. 146 units. 1,330 pesos double; 1,690 pesos executive-level double. AE, MC, V. Free parking. **Amenities:** 2 restaurants; bar; babysitting; gym w/sauna; large outdoor pool; room service; smoke-free rooms; executive-level rooms. *In room:* A/C, TV.

Moderate

Hotel Baluartes ★   Between the Sea Gate and the Gulf of Mexico, this was the city's original luxury hotel. All the rooms have been completely refurbished, with new tile floors, new furniture, and new mattresses—one king-size bed or two doubles. They are cheerful and have good lighting, but the bathrooms are small.

Av. 16 de Septiembre no. 128, 24000 Campeche, Camp. ✆ **981/816-3911.** Fax 981/816-2410. www. baluartes.com.mx. 128 units. 1,100 pesos double; 1,550 pesos suite. Rates include breakfast buffet. AE, MC, V. Free guarded parking. **Amenities:** 2 restaurants; bar; large outdoor pool; room service; smoke-free rooms. *In room:* A/C, TV, hair dryer.

Hotel Francis Drake ★ (Value)   A three-story hotel in the *centro histórico* (historical district) with comfortable, attractive rooms at good prices. Rooms are midsize and come with tile floors and one king-size bed, two doubles, or two twins. The bathrooms are modern, with large showers. Suites are larger and better furnished. The location is excellent, inside the original walls, in the southeast quadrant.

Calle 12 no. 207 (btw. calles 63 and 65), 24000 Campeche, Camp. ✆ **981/811-5626**, -5627. www.hotel francisdrake.com. 24 units. 650 pesos double; 850 pesos junior suite; 900 pesos suite. AE, MC, V. Limited free parking. **Amenities:** Restaurant; room service. *In room:* A/C, TV, hair dryer, minibar.

Inexpensive

Hotel Colonial (Moments)   What, you ask, in a cheap hotel could possibly qualify for a Frommer's Mexican Moment? Well, first of all, the hotel hasn't changed in 50 years; it exudes an air of a past long since disappeared with the coming of globalization. The rooms have the original tiles—once made in Mérida, but alas, no longer—beautiful things with lovely colors in swirls and geometrics; each room has a different pattern. And then there's the plumbing, which, in my room, was so bodacious in design and execution that to hide it within the walls would have been pure Philistinism. Remarkable, too, are the bathroom fixtures, the four-color paint job, and the '40s-style furniture. Sure, you have to make sacrifices for such character—the rooms and bathrooms are small, and the mattresses aren't the best—but even character aside, this hotel is cleaner and more cheerful than any in its class.

Calle 14 no. 122, 24000 Campeche, Camp. ✆ **981/816-2222.** 30 units. 240 pesos double; 330 pesos double with A/C. No credit cards. *In room:* A/C (some units), no phone.

WHERE TO EAT

Campeche is a fishing town, so seafood predominates. The outstanding restaurant is **La Pigua.** For breakfast, you have your hotel restaurant or one of the traditional eateries such as **La Parroquia.** For a light supper, either get some *antojitos* (small dishes) in the old *barrio* of San Francisco or have supper above the main plaza at **La Casa Vieja.** If you want a steak, your best bet is **Cactus.**

Moderate

Cactus STEAKS/MEXICAN If seafood isn't to your taste, try this steakhouse; it's a favorite with the locals. The rib-eyes are good, as is everything but the *arrachera,* which is the same cut of meat used for fajitas and is very tough.

Av. Malecón Justo Sierra. ✆ **981/811-1453.** Main courses 120–250 pesos. No credit cards. Daily 7am–2am.

Casa Vieja MEXICAN/INTERNATIONAL I'm afraid that Casa Vieja has gotten a little old. There's been a drop in effort here, but it still has the prettiest dining space in the city—an upstairs arcade overlooking the main square. Your best option is to order something simple. If you're lucky, they'll be on the upswing in that mysterious cycle of quality through which so many restaurants operate.

Calle 10 no. 319. ✆ **981/811-1311.** Reservations not accepted. Main courses 60–160 pesos. No credit cards. Tues–Sun 9am–2am; Mon 5:30pm–2am.

La Pigua ★★★ SEAFOOD The dining area is an air-conditioned version of a traditional Yucatecan cabin, but with walls of glass looking out on green vegetation. The owner has recently remodeled and enlarged his restaurant so that there's less trouble getting a table these days. He also is now opening in the evenings to accommodate tourists. Sure to be on the menu is fish stuffed with shellfish, which I wholeheartedly recommend. If you're lucky, you might find pompano in a green-herb sauce seasoned with a peppery herb known as *hierba santa.* Other dishes that are sure to please are coconut-battered shrimp with applesauce and *chiles rellenos* with shark. Service is excellent, and the accommodating owner can have your favorite seafood prepared in any style you want.

Av. Miguel Alemán no. 179A. ✆ **981/811-3365.** Reservations recommended. Main courses 120–260 pesos. AE, MC, V. Daily noon–8pm. From Plaza Principal, walk north on Calle 8 for 3 blocks; cross Av. Circuito by the botanical garden where Calle 8 becomes Miguel Alemán; the restaurant is 1¹⁄₂ blocks farther up, on the right side of the street.

Inexpensive

Cenaduría Portales ★ ANTOJITOS This is the most traditional of supper places for Campechanos. It's a small restaurant under the stone arches that face the Plaza San

Francisco in the *barrio* (neighborhood) of San Francisco. This is the oldest part of town, but it lies outside the walls just to the north. Don't leave without ordering the *horchata* (a sweet milky-white drink made of a variety of things—in this case, coconut). For food, try the turkey soup, which is wonderful, and the *sincronizadas* (tostadas) and *panuchos*.

Calle 10 no. 86, Portales San Francisco. ℭ **981/811-1491.** *Antojitos* 4–15 pesos. No credit cards. Daily 6pm–midnight.

La Parroquia MEXICAN   This local hangout offers good, inexpensive fare. It's best for breakfasts and the afternoon *comida corrida*. Selections on the *comida corrida* might include pot roast, meatballs, pork, or fish, with rice or squash, beans, tortillas, and fresh fruit–flavored water.

Calle 55 no. 9. ℭ **981/816-8086.** Breakfast 45 pesos; main courses 50–120 pesos; *comida corrida* (served noon–3pm) 40–55 pesos. MC, V. Daily 24 hr.

6 THE RUINS OF CHICHÉN ITZÁ ★★★

179km (111 miles) W of Cancún; 120km (74 miles) E of Mérida; 138km (86 miles) NW of Tulum

The ruins of Chichén Itzá (no, it doesn't rhyme with "chicken pizza"; the accents are on the last syllables: chee-*chen* eet-*zah*) are the Yucatán's best-known ancient monuments. They are plenty hyped but don't disappoint. Walking among these stone temples, pyramids, and ball courts gives the viewer an appreciation for this civilization that books simply cannot convey and allows for a sense of scale of this ancient city. The ceremonial center is indeed large. To fill the plazas during one of the mass rituals that occurred here a millennium ago would have required an enormous number of celebrants. Even today, with the massive flow of tourists through these plazas, the ruins can feel empty.

When visiting the ruins, keep in mind that much of what is said about the Maya (especially by tour guides, who speak in tones of utter certainty) is merely educated guessing. This much we do know: The area was settled by farmers as far back as the 4th century A.D. The first signs of an urban society appear in the 7th century in the construction of stone temples and palaces in the traditional Puuc Maya style. These buildings can be found in the "Old Chichén" section of the city. Construction continued for a couple hundred years. In the 10th century (the post-Classic Era), the city came under the rule of the Itzáes, who arrived from central Mexico by way of the Gulf Coast. They may have been a mix of highland Toltec Indians (the people who built the city of Tula in central Mexico) and lowland Putún Maya, who were a commercial people thriving on trade between the different regions of the area. In the following centuries, the city saw its greatest growth. Most of the grand architecture was built during this age in a style that is clearly Toltec influenced. The new rulers may have been refugees from Tula. There is a myth told in pre-Columbian central Mexico about a fight that occurred between the gods Quetzalcoatl and Tezcatlipoca, which resulted in Quetzalcoatl being forced to leave his homeland and venture east. Mythic accounts tell of a civil war in Tula, different religious factions, with the losers fleeing to the Yucatán, where they were welcomed by the local Maya. Over time, the Itzáes adopted more and more the ways of the Maya. Sometime at the end of the 12th century, the city was captured by its rival, Mayapán.

Though it's possible to make a day trip from Cancún or Mérida, it's preferable to overnight here or in nearby Valladolid. It makes for a more relaxing trip. You can see the light show in the evening and return to see the ruins early the next morning when it is cool and before the tour buses start arriving.

ESSENTIALS

GETTING THERE & DEPARTING   By Plane   Travel agents in the United States, Cancún, and Cozumel can arrange day trips from Cancún and Cozumel.

By Car   Chichén Itzá is on old Hwy. 180 between Mérida and Cancún. The fastest way to get there from either city is to take the *autopista* (or *cuota*). The toll is 120 pesos from Mérida, 200 pesos from Cancún. Once you have exited the *autopista,* you will turn onto the road leading to the village of Pisté. Once in the village, you'll reach a T junction at Hwy. 180 and turn left to get to the ruins. The entrance to the ruins is well marked. If you stay on the highway for a few kilometers more, you'll come to the exit for the hotel zone at Km 121 (before you reach the turnoff, you'll pass the eastern entrance to the ruins, which is usually closed). Chichén is 1½ hours from Mérida and 2½ hours from Cancún. From Tulum, take the highway that leads to Cobá and Chemax. It connects to Hwy. 180 a bit east of Valladolid.

By Bus   From Mérida, there are four first-class ADO buses per day. There are also a few first-class buses to Cancún and Playa that stop here. Otherwise, you can buy a second-class bus ticket to Valladolid and a first-class from there. If you want to take a day trip from Mérida or Cancún, go with a tour company.

AREA LAYOUT   The village of **Pisté,** where most of the budget hotels and restaurants are located, is about 2.5km (1½ miles) to the west of the ruins. Public buses can drop you off here. And located on the old highway 2.5km (1½ miles) east from the ruins is another budget hotel, the Dolores Alba (see "Where to Stay," below). Situated at the ruins of Chichén Itzá are three luxury hotels.

EXPLORING THE RUINS

The site occupies 6.5 sq. km (2½ sq. miles), and it takes most of a day to see all the ruins, which are open daily from 8am to 5pm. Service areas are open from 8am to 10pm. Admission is 111 pesos, free for children 11 and younger. A video camera permit costs 45 pesos. Parking is extra. *You can use your ticket to re-enter on the same day.* The cost of admission includes the **sound-and-light show,** which is worth seeing since you're being charged for it anyway. The show, held at 7 or 8pm depending on the season, is in Spanish, but headsets are available for rent in several languages. The narrative is okay, but the real reason for seeing the show is the lights, which show off the beautiful geometry of the city.

The large, modern visitor center, at the main entrance where you pay admission, is beside the parking lot. It consists of a museum, an auditorium, a restaurant, a bookstore, and bathrooms. You can see the site on your own or with a licensed guide who speaks English or Spanish. Guides usually wait at the entrance and charge around 450 pesos for one to six people. Although the guides frown on it, there's nothing wrong with approaching a group of people who speak the same language and asking if they want to share a guide. These guides can point out architectural details you might miss on your own. Chichén Itzá has two parts: the central (new) zone, which shows distinct Toltec influence, and the southern (old) zone, with mostly Puuc architecture.

EL CASTILLO   As you enter from the tourist center, the magnificent 25m (82-ft.) El Castillo pyramid (also called the Pyramid of Kukulkán) will be straight ahead across a large open area. It was built with the Maya calendar in mind. The four stairways leading up to the central platform each have 91 steps, making a total of 364, which when you add the central platform equals the 365 days of the solar year. On either side of each stairway are 9 terraces, which makes 18 on each face of the pyramid, equaling the number of months in the Maya religious calendar. On the facing of these terraces are 52 panels (we don't know how they were decorated), which represent the 52-year cycle when both the solar and religious calendars would become realigned. The pyramid's alignment is such that on the **spring** or **fall equinox** (Mar 21 or Sept 21), a curious event occurs. The setting sun casts the shadow of the terraces onto the ramp of the northern stairway. A diamond pattern is formed, suggestive of the geometric designs on snakes. Slowly it descends into the earth. The effect is more conceptual than visual, and to view it requires being with a large crowd. It's much better to see the ruins on other days when it's less crowded.

El Castillo was built over an earlier structure. A narrow stairway at the western edge of the north staircase leads inside that structure, where there is a sacrificial altar-throne—a red jaguar encrusted with jade. The stairway is open from 11am to 3pm and is cramped, usually crowded, humid, and uncomfortable. A visit early in the day is best. Photos of the jaguar figure are not allowed.

JUEGO DE PELOTA (MAIN BALL COURT)   Northwest of El Castillo is Chichén's main ball court, the largest and best preserved anywhere, and only one of nine ball courts built in this city. Carved on both walls of the ball court are scenes showing Maya figures dressed as ball players and decked out in heavy protective padding. The carved scene also shows a headless player kneeling with blood shooting from his neck; another player holding the head looks on.

Players on two teams tried to knock a hard rubber ball through one of the two stone rings placed high on either wall, using only their elbows, knees, and hips. According to legend, the losing players paid for defeat with their lives. However, some experts say the victors were the only appropriate sacrifices for the gods. One can only guess what the incentive for winning might be in that case. Either way, the game must have been riveting, heightened by the wonderful acoustics of the ball court.

THE NORTH TEMPLE   Temples are at both ends of the ball court. The North Temple has sculptured pillars and more sculptures inside, as well as badly ruined murals. The acoustics of the ball court are so good that from the North Temple, a person speaking can be heard clearly at the opposite end, about 135m (443 ft.) away.

TEMPLE OF JAGUARS   Near the southeastern corner of the main ball court is a small temple with serpent columns and carved panels showing warriors and jaguars. Up the steps and inside the temple, a mural chronicles a battle in a Maya village.

TZOMPANTLI (TEMPLE OF THE SKULLS)   To the right of the ball court is the Temple of the Skulls, an obvious borrowing from the post-Classic cities of central Mexico. Notice the rows of skulls carved into the stone platform. When a sacrificial victim's head was cut off, it was impaled on a pole and displayed in a tidy row with others. Also carved into the stone are pictures of eagles tearing hearts from human victims. The word *Tzompantli* is not Mayan, but comes from central Mexico. Reconstruction using scattered fragments may add a level to this platform and change the look of this structure by the time you visit.

PLATFORM OF THE EAGLES   Next to the Tzompantli, this small platform has reliefs showing eagles and jaguars clutching human hearts in their talons and claws, as well as a human head emerging from the mouth of a serpent.

PLATFORM OF VENUS   East of the Tzompantli and north of El Castillo, near the road to the Sacred Cenote, is the Platform of Venus. In Maya and Toltec lore, a feathered monster or a feathered serpent with a human head in its mouth represented Venus. This is also called the tomb of Chaac-Mool because a Chaac-Mool figure was discovered "buried" within the structure.

SACRED CENOTE   Follow the dirt road (actually an ancient *sacbé*, or causeway) that heads north from the Platform of Venus; after 5 minutes, you'll come to the great natural well that may have given Chichén Itzá (the Well of the Itzáes) its name. This well was used for ceremonial purposes. Sacrificial victims were thrown in. Anatomical research done early in the 20th century by Ernest A. Hooten showed that bones of both children and adults were found in the well.

Edward Thompson, who was the American consul in Mérida and a Harvard professor, purchased the ruins of Chichén early in the 20th century and explored the cenote with dredges and divers. His explorations exposed a fortune in gold and jade. Most of the riches wound up in Harvard's Peabody Museum of Archaeology and Ethnology—a matter that continues to disconcert Mexican classicists today. Excavations in the 1960s unearthed more treasure, and studies of the recovered objects detail offerings from throughout the Yucatán and even farther away.

TEMPLO DE LOS GUERREROS (TEMPLE OF THE WARRIORS)

Due east of El Castillo is one of the most impressive structures at Chichén: the Temple of the Warriors, named for the carvings of warriors marching along its walls. It's also called the Group of the Thousand Columns for the rows of broken pillars that flank it. During the recent restoration, hundreds more of the columns were rescued from the rubble and put in place, setting off the temple more magnificently than ever. A figure of Chaac-Mool sits at the top of the temple, surrounded by impressive columns carved in relief to look like enormous feathered serpents. South of the temple was a square building that archaeologists call **El Mercado (The Market);** a colonnade surrounds its central court. Beyond the temple and the market in the jungle are mounds of rubble, parts of which are being reconstructed.

The main Mérida–Cancún highway once ran straight through the ruins of Chichén, and though it has been diverted, you can still see the great swath it cut. South and west of the old highway's path are more impressive ruined buildings.

TUMBA DEL GRAN SACERDOTE (TOMB OF THE HIGH PRIEST)

Past the refreshment stand to the right of the path is the Tomb of the High Priest, which stood atop a natural limestone cave in which skeletons and offerings were found, giving the temple its name.

CASA DE LOS METATES (TEMPLE OF THE GRINDING STONES)

This building, the next one on your right, is named after the concave corn-grinding stones the Maya used.

TEMPLO DEL VENADO (TEMPLE OF THE DEER)

Past Casa de los Metates is this fairly tall, though ruined, building. The relief of a stag that gave the temple its name is long gone.

CHICHANCHOB (LITTLE HOLES)

This next temple has a roof comb with little holes, three masks of the rain god Chaac, three rooms, and a good view of the surrounding structures. It's one of the oldest buildings at Chichén, built in the Puuc style during the late Classic period.

EL CARACOL (OBSERVATORY)

Construction of the Observatory, a complex building with a circular tower, was carried out over centuries; the additions and modifications reflected the Maya's careful observation of celestial movements and their need for increasingly exact measurements. Through slits in the tower's walls, astronomers could observe the cardinal directions and the approach of the all-important spring and autumn equinoxes, as well as the summer solstice. The temple's name, which means "snail," comes from a spiral staircase within the structure.

On the east side of El Caracol, a path leads north into the bush to the **Cenote Xtoloc,** a natural limestone well that provided the city's daily water supply. If you see lizards sunning there, they may well be *xtoloc,* the species for which this cenote is named.

TEMPLE DE LOS TABLEROS (TEMPLE OF PANELS)

Just south of El Caracol are the ruins of a *temazcalli* (a steam bath) and the Temple of Panels, named for the carved panels on top. This temple was once covered by a much larger structure, only traces of which remain.

EDIFICIO DE LAS MONJAS (EDIFICE OF THE NUNS)

If you've visited the Puuc sites of Kabah, Sayil, Labná, or Xlapak, the enormous nunnery here will remind you of the palaces at those sites. Built in the late Classic period, the new edifice was constructed over an older one. Suspecting that this was so, Le Plongeon, an archaeologist working early in the 20th century, put dynamite between the two and blew away part of the

exterior, revealing the older structures within. You can still see the results of Le Plongeon's **241**
indelicate exploratory methods.

On the east side of the Edifice of the Nuns is **Anexo Este (annex),** constructed in highly ornate Chenes style with Chaac masks and serpents.

LA IGLESIA (THE CHURCH)   Next to the annex is one of the oldest buildings at Chichén, the Church. Masks of Chaac decorate two upper stories. Look closely, and you'll see other pagan symbols among the crowd of Chaacs: an armadillo, a crab, a snail, and a tortoise. These represent the Maya gods, called *bacah,* whose job it was to hold up the sky.

AKAB DZIB (TEMPLE OF OBSCURE WRITING)   Beloved of travel writers, this temple lies east of the Edifice of the Nuns. Above a door in one of the rooms are some Mayan glyphs, which gave the temple its name because the writings are hard to make out. In other rooms, traces of red handprints are still visible. Reconstructed and expanded over the centuries, Akab Dzib may be the oldest building at Chichén.

CHICHEN VIEJO (OLD CHICHEN)   For a look at more of Chichén's oldest buildings, constructed well before the time of Toltec influence, follow signs from the Edifice of the Nuns southwest into the bush to Old Chichén, about 1km (a half-mile) away. Be prepared for this trek with long trousers, insect repellent, and a local guide. The attractions here are the **Templo de los Inscripciones Iniciales (Temple of the First Inscriptions),** with the oldest inscriptions discovered at Chichén, and the restored **Templo de los Dinteles (Temple of the Lintels),** a fine Puuc building. Some of these buildings have recently undergone restoration.

WHERE TO STAY

The expensive hotels in Chichén all occupy beautiful grounds, are close to the ruins, and serve decent food. All have toll-free reservations numbers. These hotels do a lot of business with tour operators—they can be empty one day and full the next. From these hotels, you can easily walk to the back entrance of the ruins, next to the Hotel Mayaland. There are several inexpensive hotels in the village of Pisté, just to the west of the ruins. There is no advantage to staying in Pisté other than the proximity to Chichén Itzá. It is an unattractive village with little to recommend it. Another option is to stay in the colonial town of Valladolid (p. 243), 40 minutes away.

Expensive

Hacienda Chichén Resort ★★   This is the smallest and most private of the hotels at the ruins, also the quietest. This former hacienda served as the headquarters for the Carnegie Institute's excavations in 1923. Several bungalows scattered about the property were built to house the institute's staff. Each one houses one or two units. Rooms come with a dehumidifier, a ceiling fan, and good air-conditioning. The floors are ceramic tile, the ceilings are stucco with wood beams, and the walls are decorated with carved stone trim. Trees and tropical plants fill the manicured gardens. You can enjoy these from your room's porch or from the terrace restaurant, which occupies part of the original main house. Standard rooms come with a queen-size, two twin, or two double beds. Suites come with king-size beds.

Zona Arqueológica, 97751 Chichén Itzá, Yuc. ⓒ/fax **985/851-0045.** www.haciendachichen.com. (Reservations office in Mérida: 877/631-4005 in the U.S., or 999/920-8407.) 28 units. High season $188 double, $199–$264 suite; low season $140 double, $152–$193 suite. AE, MC, V. Free guarded parking. **Amenities:** Restaurant; 2 bars; large outdoor pool; smoke-free rooms; spa. *In room:* A/C, hair dryer, minibar, no phone.

MÉRIDA, CHICHÉN ITZÁ & THE MAYA INTERIOR

THE RUINS OF CHICHÉN ITZÁ

Hotel & Bungalows Mayaland, The Lodge at Chichén Itzá ★★★ The main doorway frames El Caracol (the Observatory) in a stunning view—that's how close these hotels are to the ruins. There is an entrance right by the hotel. The long main building is three stories high. The rooms are large, with comfortable beds and large tiled bathrooms. Bungalows, scattered about the rest of the grounds, are built native style, with thatched roofs and stucco walls; they're a good deal larger than the rooms. The grounds are gorgeous, with huge trees and lush foliage—the hotel has had 75 years to get them in shape. The suites are on the top floor of the main building and come with terraces and two-person Jacuzzis. The Lodge consists of two groupings of larger bungalows in the back of the property surrounded by a lovely garden and pool area. High season is January to April (higher still for the Mar equinox, Christmas, and month of November). Low season includes May to October and the first three weeks of December.

Zona Arqueológica, 97751 Chichén Itzá, Yuc. ✆ 985/851-0100. www.mayaland.com. (Reservations: Mayaland Resorts, Robalo 30 SM3, 77500 Cancún, Q. Roo; ✆ 800/235-4079 in the U.S., or 998/887-2495; fax 998/887-4510.) 97 units. Hotel: High season $192–$230 superior, $278–$340 suites and bungalows; low season $129 superior, $168–$230 suites and bungalows. Lodge: High season bungalows from $438–$460; low season bungalows from $293. AE, MC, V. Free guarded parking. **Amenities:** 2 restaurants; bar; babysitting; 3 outdoor pools; room service. *In room:* A/C, TV, minibar.

Moderate

Villas Arqueológicas Chichén Itzá ★ This hotel is built around a courtyard and pool. Two massive royal Poinciana trees tower above the grounds, and bougainvillea drapes the walls. This chain has similar hotels at Cobá and Uxmal. The rooms are modern and comfortable, unless you're 1.9m (6 ft., 2 in.) or taller—each bed is in a niche, with walls at the head and foot. Most rooms have one double bed and a twin bed. You can book a half- or full-board plan or just the room.

Zona Arqueológica, 97751 Chichén Itzá, Yuc. ✆ 987/872-9300, ext. 8101 or 985/851-0034 or 856-2830. www.islandercollection.com. 40 units. $130 double. Rates include continental breakfast. Half-board (breakfast plus lunch or dinner) $20 per person; full board (3 meals) $35 per person. AE, MC, V. Free parking. **Amenities:** Restaurant; bar; large outdoor pool; tennis court. *In room:* A/C, hair dryer.

Inexpensive

Hotel Dolores Alba (Value) This place is of the motel variety, perfect if you come by car. It is a bargain for what you get: two pools (one really special), *palapas* and hammocks around the place, and large, comfortable rooms. The restaurant serves good meals at moderate prices. There is free transportation to the ruins and the Caves of Balankanché during visiting hours, though you will have to take a taxi back. The hotel is on the highway 2.5km (1½ miles) east of the ruins (toward Valladolid). Rooms come with two double beds.

Carretera Mérida–Valladolid Km 122, Yuc. ✆ 985/858-1555. www.doloresalba.com. (Reservations: Hotel Dolores Alba, Calle 63 no. 464, 97000 Mérida, Yuc.; ✆ 999/928-5650; fax 999/928-3163.) 40 units. 470 pesos double. MC, V (8% service charge). Free parking. **Amenities:** Restaurant; bar; 2 outdoor pools; room service. *In room:* A/C, TV, no phone.

WHERE TO DINE

Although there's no great food in this area, there is plenty of decent food. The best idea is to stick to simple choices. The restaurant at the visitor center at the ruins serves decent snack food. The hotel restaurants mostly do a fair job, and, if you're in the village of Pisté, you can try one of the restaurants along the highway there that cater to the bus tours, such as **Fiesta** (✆ 985/851-0111). The best time to go is early lunch or regular supper hours, when the buses are gone.

Ik-Kil is a large cenote on the highway just across from the Hotel Dolores Alba, 2.5km (1^1/$_2$ miles) east of the main entrance to the ruins. And it's deep, with lots of steps leading down to the water's edge. Unlike Dzitnup, these steps are easy to manage. The view from both the top and the bottom is dramatic, with lots of tropical vegetation and curtains of hanging tree roots stretching all the way to the water's surface. Take your swimsuit and enjoy the cold water. The best swimming is before 11:30am, at which time bus tours start arriving from the coast. These bus tours are the main business of Ik-Kil, which also has a restaurant and souvenir shops. Ik-Kil is open from 8am to 5pm daily. Admission is 60 pesos per adult, 30 pesos per child 7 to 12 years old.

The **Cave of Balankanché** is 5.5km (3^1/$_2$ miles) from Chichén Itzá on the road to Valladolid and Cancún. Taxis will make the trip and wait. The entire excursion takes about a half-hour, but the walk inside is hot and humid. Of the cave tours in the Yucatán, this is the tamest; it has good footing and requires the least amount of walking and climbing. It includes a cheesy and uninformative recorded tour. The highlight is a round chamber with a central column that gives the impression of being a large tree. You exit the same way you enter. The cave became a hideout during the War of the Castes. You can still see traces of carving and incense burning, as well as an underground stream that supplied water to the refugees. Outside, take time to meander through the botanical gardens, where most of the plants and trees are labeled with their common and botanical names.

Admission is 48 pesos, free for children 6 to 12. Children younger than age 6 are not admitted. Use of a video camera costs 45 pesos, or it's free if you've already bought a video permit in Chichén the same day. Tours in English are at 11am and 1 and 3pm, and, in Spanish, at 9am, noon, and 2 and 4pm. Double-check these hours at the main entrance to the Chichén ruins.

7 VALLADOLID

40km (25 miles) E of Chichén Itzá; 160km (99 miles) SW of Cancún; 98km (61 miles) NW of Tulum

Valladolid (pronounced "bah-yah-doh-*leed*") is a small, pleasant, colonial city halfway between Mérida and Cancún. The people are friendly and informal, and, except for the heat, life is easy. The city's economy is based on commerce and small-scale manufacturing. There is a large cenote in the center of town and a couple more 4km (2^1/$_2$ miles) down the road to Chichén. Not far away are the intriguing ruins of Ek Balam, the flamingo-infested waters of Río Lagartos, and the sandy beaches of Holbox (see "Side Trips from Valladolid," below).

ESSENTIALS
GETTING THERE & DEPARTING   By Car   From Mérida or Cancún, you have two choices: the *cuota* (toll road) or Hwy. 180. The toll from Cancún is 220 pesos, from Mérida 110 pesos. The *cuota* passes 2km (1^1/$_4$ miles) north of the city; the exit is at the crossing of Hwy. 295 to Tizimín. **Hwy. 180** takes significantly longer because it passes through a number of villages (with their requisite speed bumps). Both 180 and 295 lead directly to downtown. Leaving is just as easy: From the main square, Calle 41 turns into 180 East to Cancún; Calle 39 heads to 180 West to Chichén Itzá and Mérida. To take the *cuota* to Mérida or Cancún, take Calle 40 (see "City Layout," below).

By Bus There are several direct buses to Mérida (13 per day) or Cancún (5 per day). Each runs 125 pesos. You can also get direct buses for Playa (five per day) and Tulum (four per day). Buses to Playa take the toll road and cost 155 pesos; buses to Tulum take the shortcut via Chemax and cost 70 pesos. To get to Chichén Itzá, take a second-class bus, which leaves every hour and sometimes on the half-hour. The recently remodeled bus station is at the corner of calles 39 and 46.

VISITOR INFORMATION The small **tourism office** is in the Palacio Municipal. It's open Monday to Friday from 8am to 9pm, Saturday and Sunday from 9am to 9pm.

CITY LAYOUT Valladolid has the standard layout for towns in the Yucatán: Streets running north–south are even numbers; those running east–west are odd numbers. The main plaza is bordered by Calle 39 on the north, 41 on the south, 40 on the east, and 42 on the west. The plaza is named Parque Francisco Cantón Rosado, but everyone calls it **El Centro.** Taxis are easy to come by.

EXPLORING VALLADOLID

Before it became Valladolid, the city was a Maya settlement called Zací (zah-*kee*), which means "white hawk." There is one cenote in town: **Cenote Zací,** at the intersection of calles 39 and 36, in a small park. A trail leads down close to the water. Caves, stalactites, and hanging vines contribute to a wild, prehistoric feel. The park has a large *palapa* restaurant. Admission is 12 pesos.

Ten blocks to the southwest of the main square is the Franciscan monastery of **San Bernardino de Siena** (1552). Most of the compound was built in the early 1600s; a large underground river is believed to pass under the convent and surrounding neighborhood, which is called Barrio Sisal. "Sisal," in this case, is a corruption of the Mayan phrase *sis-ha,* meaning "cold water." The *barrio* underwent extensive restoration and is a delight to behold.

Valladolid's main square is the social center of town and a thriving market for Yucatecan dresses. On its south side is the principal church, **La Parroquia de San Servacio.** Vallesoletanos, as the locals are known, believe that almost all cathedrals in Mexico point east, and they cherish a local legend to explain why theirs points north—but don't believe a word of it. On the east side of the plaza is the municipal building, **El Ayuntamiento.** Get a look at the dramatic paintings outlining the peninsula's history. My favorite depicts a horrified Maya priest foreseeing the arrival of Spanish galleons. On Sunday nights, beneath the stone arches of the Ayuntamiento, the municipal band plays *jaranas* and other traditional music of the region.

SHOPPING

The **Mercado de Artesanías de Valladolid (crafts market),** at the corner of calles 39 and 44, gives you a good idea of the local merchandise. Perhaps the main handicraft of the town is embroidered Maya dresses, which can be purchased here or from women around the main square. The area around Valladolid is cattle country; locally made leather goods such as *huaraches* (sandals) and bags are inexpensive and plentiful. On the main plaza is a small shop above the municipal bazaar. A good sandal maker has a shop called **Elios,** Calle 37 no. 202, between calles 42 and 44 (no phone). An Indian named **Juan Mac** makes *alpargatas,* the traditional sandals of the Maya, in his shop on Calle 39, near the intersection with Calle 38, 1 block from the main plaza. It's almost on the corner, across from the Bar La Joya. There's no sign, but the door jamb is painted yellow. Juan Mac can be found there most mornings. Most of his output is for locals, but he's happy to knock out a pair for visitors. He also makes a dress *alpargata,* but I like the standard ones better.

WHERE TO STAY

Aside from the hotels listed below, you can stay in town at **Hotel Zací,** Calle 44 between calles 37 and 39 (© **985/856-2167**), for about 400 pesos per night, or at María de la Luz, on the main square, for about 450 pesos. The Zací has nicer beds.

For something a bit different, you can stay in a small ecohotel in the nearby village of Ek Balam, close to the ruins: **Genesis Retreat Ek Balam** (© **985/858-9375;** www. genesisretreat.com). It is owned and operated by a Canadian woman, Lee Christie. She takes guests on tours of the village showing what daily life is like among the contemporary Maya. There are other activities, too. She rents some simple cabañas (with shared or private bathrooms) that surround a lovely pool and a restaurant.

Casa Quetzal ★   The landlady, Judith Fernández, is a gracious Mexican woman who moved to Valladolid to slow down. She has created an airy and attractive lodging space in the refurbished Barrio Sisal, which is within easy walking distance of the main square. Emphasis is on comfort and service—good linens and mattresses, quiet air-conditioning, and a large and inviting central courtyard. There is a full line of spa treatments and therapies. English is spoken, and Sra. Fernández has lined up a good guide you can contract to take you to outlying areas.

Calle 51 no. 218, Barrio Sisal, 97780 Valladolid, Yuc. ©/fax **985/856-4796.** www.casa-quetzal.com. 7 units. $65–$75 double. Rates include full breakfast. 2-night minimum stay. No credit cards. Free secure parking. **Amenities:** Babysitting; small outdoor pool; room service; spa. *In room:* A/C, TV, no phone, Wi-Fi.

El Mesón del Marqués ★   This was originally a small colonial hotel that has grown large and modern. The first courtyard surrounds a fountain and abounds with hanging plants and bougainvillea. This was the original house, now occupied mostly by the restaurant (see "Where to Dine," below). In back are the new construction and the pool. Rooms are medium to large and are attractive. Most come with two double beds. The hotel is on the north side of El Centro, opposite the church.

Calle 39 no. 203, 97780 Valladolid, Yuc. © **985/856-3042,** -2073. Fax 985/856-2280. www.mesondel marques.com. 90 units. 620 pesos double; 730 pesos superior; 1,150 pesos junior suite. AE. Free secure parking. **Amenities:** Restaurant; bar; outdoor pool; room service. *In room:* A/C, TV.

WHERE TO DINE

Valladolid is not a center for haute cuisine, but you can try some of the regional specialties. Some of the best food I had was at **El Mesón del Marqués,** right on the main square. There is another restaurant on the main square called **Las Campanas,** which is okay. Locals like to eat at one of the stalls in the **Bazar Municipal,** next door to the Mesón del Marqués. They also frequent the **taco stands** that set up around the main square during the morning hours.

SIDE TRIPS FROM VALLADOLID

Cenotes Dzitnup & Sammula

The **Cenote Dzitnup** ★ (also known as Cenote Xkekén) is 4km (2½ miles) west of Valladolid off Hwy. 180 in the direction of Chichén Itzá. It's worth a side trip, especially if you have time for a dip. You can take the bike trail there. Antonio Aguilar, who owns a sporting goods store at Calle 41 no. 225, between calles 48 and 50, rents bikes. Once you get there, you descend a short flight of rather perilous stone steps, and at the bottom, inside a beautiful cavern, is a natural pool of water so clear and blue that it seems plucked from a dream. If you decide to swim, be sure that you don't have creams or other chemicals on your skin—they damage the habitat of the small fish and other organisms living there. Also, no alcohol, food, or smoking is allowed in the cavern. Admission is 25 pesos. The cenote is open daily from 7am to 7pm. If it's crowded, about 90m (295 ft.) down the road on the opposite side is another cenote, **Sammulá,** where you can swim.

Ek Balam: Dark Jaguar ★★★

About 18km (11 miles) north of Valladolid, off the highway to Río Lagartos, are the spectacular ruins of **Ek Balam,** which, owing to a certain ambiguity in Mayan, means either "dark jaguar" or "star jaguar." Relatively unvisited by tourists, the Ek Balam ruins are about to hit it big. A new road now runs from the highway to the ruins.

Take Calle 40 north out of Valladolid to Hwy. 295; go 20km (12 miles) to a large marked turnoff. Ek Balam is 13km (8 miles) from the highway; admission is 35 pesos, 45 pesos for each video camera. The site is open daily from 8am to 5pm.

In the last few years, a team of archeologists has been doing extensive excavation and renovation. What they have found has the world of Mayan scholars all aquiver. Built between 100 B.C. and A.D. 1200, the smaller buildings are architecturally unique—especially the large, perfectly restored **Caracol.** Flanked by two smaller pyramids, the imposing central pyramid is about 160m (525 ft.) long and 60m (197 ft.) wide. At more than 30m (98 ft.) high, it is easily taller than El Castillo in Chichén Itzá. On the left side of the main stairway, archaeologists have uncovered a large ceremonial doorway of perfectly preserved stucco work. It is an astonishingly elaborate representation of the gaping mouth of the underworld god. Around it are several beautifully detailed human figures. Excavation inside revealed a long chamber filled with Mayan hieroglyphic writing. From the style, it appears that the scribes probably came from Guatemala. So far, this chamber is closed to the public. From this script, an epigrapher, Alfonso Lacadena, has found the name of one of the principal kings of the city—Ukit Kan Le'k Tok'. If you climb to the top of the pyramid, in the middle distance you can see untouched ruins looming to the north. To the southeast, you can spot the tallest structures at **Cobá,** 50km (31 miles) away.

Also visible are the **raised causeways** of the Maya—the *sacbé* appear as raised lines in the forest. More than any of the better-known sites, Ek Balam inspires a sense of mystery and awe at the scale of Maya civilization and the utter ruin to which it fell.

Río Lagartos Nature Reserve ★

Some 80km (50 miles) north of Valladolid (40km/25 miles north of Tizimín) on Hwy. 295 is Río Lagartos, a 50,000-hectare (123,500-acre) refuge established in 1979 to protect the largest nesting population of flamingos in North America. The nesting area is off-limits, but you can see plenty of flamingos, as well as many other species of fowl, and take an enjoyable boat ride around the estuary here.

To get to Río Lagartos, you pass through Tizimín, which is about 30 minutes away. If you need to spend the night there, try **Hotel 49,** Calle 49 373-A (© **986/863-2136**), by the main square. There is not much to do in Tizimín unless you are there during the first 2 weeks of January, when it holds the largest fair in the Yucatán. The prime fiesta day is January 6.

Río Lagartos is a small fishing village of around 3,000 people who make their living from the sea and from the occasional tourist who shows up to see the flamingos. Colorfully painted houses face the *malecón* (the oceanfront street), and brightly painted boats dock here and there.

(Tips)   Visiting the Whale Sharks of Isla Holbox

In 2002, Mexico's whale sharks were designated an endangered species. As a result, the government, along with environmental groups, closely monitors their activity and the tours that visit them off Isla Holbox. Several restrictions apply to how tours are run, and all tour operators must abide by them. To learn more about the whale sharks and the measures being taken to protect them, go to www.domino.conanp.gob.mx/rules.htm.

Tours to visit the sharks are kept small, since only two people at a time are allowed to snorkel with the sharks. Tours typically cost around $90 per person and last 4 to 6 hours. Many of the hotels or outfitters on the island can arrange a tour for you.

When you drive into town, keep going straight until you get to the shore. Look for where Calle 10 intersects with the *malecón;* it's near a modern church. There, in a little kiosk, is where the guides can be found (no phone). The sign reads PARADOR TURISTICO NAHOCHIN. There you can make arrangements for a 2-hour tour, which will cost 500 to 600 pesos for two to three people. The best time to go is in the early morning, so it's best to overnight here at one of the cheap hotels along the *malecón.* I looked at a few and liked **Posada Lucy** (no phone; 250 pesos for two).

I had a pleasant ride the next morning, and saw several species of ducks, hawks, cranes, cormorants, an osprey, and lots of flamingos. The guide also wanted to show me how easy it was to float in some evaporation pools used by the local salt producer at Las Coloradas (a good source of employment for the locals until it was mechanized) and a place where freshwater bubbles out from below the saltwater estuary.

Isla Holbox ★

A sandy strip of an island off the northeastern corner of the Yucatán Peninsula, Holbox (pronounced "hohl-*bosh*") was a remote corner of the world with only a half-deserted fishing village, until tourists started showing up for the beach. Now it's a semiprosperous little community that gets its livelihood from tourist services, employment at the beach hotels, and tours. It's most popular with visitors from May to September, when over a hundred **whale sharks** congregate in nearby waters (precisely why they come here is not known). These gentle giants swim slowly along the surface of the water and don't seem to mind the boat tours and snorkelers that come to experience what it's like to be in the wild with these creatures. Whale sharks don't fit the common picture of a shark; they are much larger, attaining a length of up to 18m (59 ft.), and they are filter feeders, for the most part, dining on plankton and other small organisms. That said, they can do some mischief if you annoy them.

The beach here is broad and sandy (with fine-textured sand). It is also shallow. Instead of the amazing blue color of the Caribbean, it's more of a dull green. There are several beach hotels just beyond town. **Villas Flamingos** (② **800/538-6802** in the U.S. and Canada) and **Villas Delfines,** which has an office in Cancún (② **998/884-8606** or 984/875-2197; www.holbox.com), are two good options. The latter is a personal favorite. Rates run between 1,000 and 1,500 pesos for a large free-standing beach bungalow with a large porch, a thatched roof, mosquito netting, and plenty of cross-ventilation. This is very much an ecohotel, with composting toilets and solar water heaters. There is a pool, a good restaurant, and lovely grounds. If you want air-conditioning, try **Casa Sandra** (© 984/875-2171).

From Valladolid, take Hwy. 180 east for about 90km (56 miles) toward Cancún; turn north after Nuevo Xcan at the tiny crossroads of El Ideal. Drive nearly 100km (62 miles) north on a state highway to the tiny port of Chiquilá, where you can park your car in a secure parking lot; walk 180m (590 ft.) to the pier, and catch the ferry to the island. It runs 10 times per day. When you get off in the village, you can contract with one of the golf cart taxis for a ride to your hotel.

Tabasco & Chiapas

by David Baird

Even though these two states aren't part of the Yucatán, we've included them so that we can present Mexico's entire **Maya region.** Many travelers who go to the Yucatán to see Chichén Itzá and Uxmal also take a side trip to Chiapas to see the famous ruins of Palenque. Some go even farther, all the way to San Cristóbal, to visit the highland Maya.

If you have the time, you might even want to make this part of Mexico the object of a separate trip. First, there's a lot to see and do; second, much of it is best appreciated at a leisurely pace; and third, transportation in, out, and through the area is a bit problematic—not the kind of challenge you want to take on with a tight schedule.

Tabasco and Chiapas feel different from the Yucatán. The lowland jungle of most of Tabasco and eastern Chiapas is thicker, with a taller canopy. It rains a lot more here, and the rivers, some of the largest in Mexico, are wide and flowing. The mountainous central highlands of Chiapas are cool and wet, and the mountain air feels refreshing after you've experienced the heat and humidity of the lowlands. This part of Chiapas has striking mountain vistas, deep canyons, and isolated cloud forests.

Tabasco is a small, oil-rich state along the Gulf coast. The capital, **Villahermosa,** has a definite boomtown feel, but it also has a past. People have inhabited this coastal jungle for millennia. It is the homeland of the Olmec, the mother-culture of Mesoamerica. The Olmec were the first to develop a large-scale civilization in Mexico. At the Parque–Museo La Venta, in Villahermosa, you can see some artifacts that they left to posterity, including the famous megalithic heads.

Chiapas has much that is interesting, but perhaps the most important areas to visit are the eastern lowland jungles and the central highlands. In the former lie the famous ruins of **Palenque,** a city that dates from the Classic age of Maya civilization. The ruins look unspeakably old, and the surrounding jungle seems poised to reclaim them, should their caretakers ever falter in their duties. Deeper into the interior are the sites of **Yaxchilán** and **Bonampak.** The central highlands are just as dramatic but easier to enjoy. Of particular interest is the colonial city of **San Cristóbal de las Casas,** with its surrounding Indian villages. The Indians here cling so tenaciously to their beliefs and traditions that for awhile this area was more popular with anthropologists than tourists.

Fifteen years ago, Chiapas made international news when the Zapatista Liberation Army launched an armed rebellion and captured San Cristóbal. This forced the Mexican government to recognize the existence of social and economic disparities in Chiapas. Negotiations achieved minor results, and then stalled. Political violence erupted again in the winter of 1997 and 1998. But no foreigners were attacked, and no restrictions were ever placed on travel to Palenque or the San Cristóbal region. Since then, especially in the last couple of years, the Zapatista movement has dropped the talk about armed insurrection in an effort to broaden its base as a political movement.

1 VILLAHERMOSA

142km (88 miles) NW of Palenque; 469km (291 miles) SW of Campeche; 160km (99 miles) N of San Cristóbal de las Casas

Villahermosa (pop. 550,000) is the capital of and the largest city in the state of Tabasco. It lies in a shallow depression about an hour's drive from the Gulf coast, at the confluence of two rivers: the Grijalva and the Carrizal. The land is marshy, with shallow lakes scattered here and there. For most of the year it's hot and humid.

Oil has brought money to this town and raised prices. Villahermosa is one of the most expensive cities in the country and contrasts sharply with inexpensive Chiapas. Though there's a lot of money, it's all being pulled to the modern western sections surrounding a development called Tabasco 2000. This area, especially the neighborhoods around the **Parque–Museo La Venta,** is the most attractive part of town, surrounded by small lakes. The historic center has been left to decay. It's gritty, crowded, and unpleasant. The main reason to be downtown is for the cheap hotels.

Two names that you will likely see and hear are Carlos Pellicer Cámara and Tomás Garrido Canabal; both were interesting people. The first was a mid-20th-century Tabascan poet and intellectual. The best known of Mexico's *modernista* poets, he was a fiercely independent thinker. Garrido Canabal, socialist governor of Tabasco in the 1920s and 1930s, was even more fiercely independent. He wanted to turn the conservative, backwater state of Tabasco into a model of socialism and fought for many socialist causes. But his enmity for Mexico's Catholic church is what he is most remembered for today. He went so far as to name his son Lucifer and his farm animals Jesus and the Virgin Mary.

ESSENTIALS
Getting There & Departing

BY PLANE   Villahermosa (airport code: VSA) is served by the following carriers. **Continental ExpressJet** (© 800/525-0280 in the U.S., or 01-800/900-5000 in Mexico; www.continental.com) has direct service to/from Houston on a regional jet. **Mexicana** (© 800/531-7921 in the U.S., or 01-800/502-2000 in Mexico; www.mexicana.com) and **AeroMéxico** (© 800/237-6639 in the U.S., or 01-800/021-4000 in Mexico; www.aeromexico.com) both have flights to and from Mexico City. **Aviación de Chiapas (Aviacsa;** © 01-800/006-2200 in Mexico or 993/316-5700; www.aviacsa.com) flies to and from Mexico City. The regional airline **Aerolitoral,** a subsidiary of AeroMéxico (© 800/237-6639 in the U.S., or 993/312-6991), goes through Mexico City with a connection to Tampico, Monterrey, and Houston. It also has a direct flight to Veracruz and Mérida. **Click** (© 01-800/122-5425 in Mexico; www.clickmx.com), a subsidiary for Mexicana, provides nonstop service to and from Mexico City.

BY CAR   Highway 180 connects Villahermosa to Campeche (6 hr.). Highway 186, which passes by the airport, joins Highway 199 to Palenque and San Cristóbal de las Casas. The road to Palenque is a good one, and the drive takes 2 hours. Between Palenque and San Cristóbal, the road enters the mountains and takes 4 to 5 hours. On any of the mountain roads, conditions are apt to get worse during the rainy season from May to October.

BY BUS   The **bus station** is at Mina and Merino (© 993/312-8900; www.ticketbus.com.mx), three blocks off Highway 180. There are eight nonstop buses per day to/from

ACCOMMODATIONS ■
Best Western Hotel
Maya Tabasco **5**
Hotel Plaza
Independencia **3**
Hotel Provincia Express **4**
Hyatt Villahermosa **7**

DINING ◆
Jangada **8**
Los Tulipanes **2**

ATTRACTIONS ●
Museo Regional de
Antropología Carlos
Pellicer Cámara **1**
Parque-Museo La Venta **6**

Palenque (2½ hr.). There are seven nonstop buses per day to Mexico City (10 hr.), six deluxe services on **ADO-GL,** and two superdeluxe on **UNO.** To Campeche, there are eight buses nonstop per day (7 hr.); some of these go on to Mérida.

Orientation

ARRIVING   Villahermosa's **airport** is 16km (8 miles) east of town. The trip takes between 20 and 30 minutes. Once you cross the bridge over the Río Grijalva, turn left to reach downtown. Taxis to the downtown area cost 170 pesos.

Parking downtown can be difficult; it's best to find a parking lot. Use one that's guarded round-the-clock.

VISITOR INFORMATION   The **State Tourism Office** (© 993/316-5122, ext. 229) has two information booths: The one at the **airport** is staffed daily from 10am to 5pm; the one at **Parque–Museo La Venta** (next to the ticket counter for the park) is staffed Tuesday to Sunday from 10am to 5pm.

CITY LAYOUT   The downtown area, including the pedestrian-only **Zona Luz,** is on the west bank of the Grijalva River. About 1.5km (1 mile) upstream (south) is **CICOM,** an academic organization with the large archaeology museum named for the poet Carlos Pellicer Cámara. The **airport** is on the east side of the river. Highway 180 passes the airport and crosses the river just north of downtown, becoming **Bulevar Ruiz Cortines.** To get to the downtown area, turn left onto **Madero** or **Pino Suárez.** By staying on Ruiz Cortines you can reach the city's biggest attraction, the Parque–Museo la Venta. It's well marked. Just beyond that is the intersection with **Paseo Tabasco,** the heart of the modern hotel and shopping district.

GETTING AROUND   **Taxis** are your best way to get around town. Villahermosa is rare for being a Mexican city without a capable public transportation system.

FAST FACTS   The telephone **area code** is **993.** There aren't a lot of *casas de cambio,* but you can exchange money at the airport, the hotels, and downtown banks on calles Juárez and Madero. ATMs are plentiful.

EXPLORING VILLAHERMOSA

Major sights include the **Parque–Museo La Venta** and the **Museo Regional de Antropología Carlos Pellicer Cámara.** You can hit them both in a day. There is also an ecological park called **Yumká** (see below), which is 16km (10 miles) out of town in the direction of the airport.

Stroll about the pedestrian-only Zona Luz, and you'll see signs that investment might be returning to the old downtown area. Outside the Zona Luz, things get more unpleasant, with lots of traffic and crowds of pedestrians. But, as unpleasant as it is, there are things of interest for those who like to explore Mexican society and culture. You can walk south along the banks of the Grijalva until you come to a pedestrian bridge with an observation tower. That's the highlight. You won't miss much by keeping away.

Museo Regional de Antropología Carlos Pellicer Cámara ★★   This museum on the west bank of the river about 1.5km (1 mile) south of the town center is closed owing to flooding in the fall of 2007. It should open by the summer of 2009. It normally has a well-organized collection of pre-Hispanic artifacts, not only from the local region (Totonac, Zapotec, and Olmec), but from other parts of Mexico and Central America, as well.

The second floor is devoted to the Olmec. The third floor features artifacts from central Mexico, including the Tlatilco and Teotihuacán cultures; the Huasteca culture of

Veracruz, San Luis Potosí, and Tampico states; and the cultures of Nayarit State, on the **253**
west coast. Photographs and diagrams provide vivid images, but the explanatory signs are
mostly in Spanish. Look especially for the figurines that were found in this area and for
the colorful Codex (an early book of pictographs). Allow 1 to 2 hours.

CICOM Center, Av. Carlos Pellicer Cámara 511. ℂ **993/312-6344**. Admission 35 pesos. Tues–Sun 9am–5pm.

Parque–Museo La Venta ★★ The Olmec created the first civilization in Mexico
and developed several cultural traits that later spread to all subsequent civilizations
throughout Mesoamerica. In addition to their monumental works, they carved small
exquisite figurines in jade and serpentine, which can be seen in the Museo Regional de
Antropología (see above). This *parque-museo* occupies a portion of a larger park named
after Tomás Garrido Canabal, which includes a serene lake, a zoo, a natural history
museum, and a lot of green space with several walkways frequented by joggers. Once
inside the *parque-museo*, a trail leads you from one sculpture to the next. Most of the
pieces are massive heads or altars. These can be as tall as 2m (6¹/₂ ft.) and weigh as much
as 40 tons. The faces seem to be half adult, half infant. They have highly stylized mouths
with thick fleshy lips that turn down (known as the "jaguar mouth," this is one of the
identifying characteristics of Olmec art). At least 17 heads have been found: 4 at La
Venta, 10 at San Lorenzo, and 3 at Tres Zapotes—all Olmec cities on Mexico's east coast.
The pieces in this park were taken from La Venta, a major city during the pre-Classic
period (2000 B.C.–A.D. 300). Most were sculpted around 1000 B.C. without the use of
metal chisels. The basalt rock used for these heads and altars was transported to La Venta
from more than 113km (70 miles) away. It is thought that the rock was brought most of
the way by raft. Most of these pieces were first discovered in 1938. Now all that remains
at La Venta are some grass-covered mounds that were once earthen pyramids. An exhibition area at the entrance to the park does a good job of illustrating how La Venta was laid
out and what archaeologists think the Olmec were like.

As you stroll along, you will see labels identifying many species of local trees, including
a grand ceiba tree of special significance to the Olmec and, later, the Maya. A few varieties of local critters scurry about, seemingly unconcerned with the presence of humans or
with escaping from the park. Allow at least 2 hours for wandering through the jungly
sanctuary and examining the 3,000-year-old sculpture. *Note:* Don't forget the mosquito
repellent.

Bulevar Ruiz Cortines s/n. ℂ **993/314-1652**. Admission 45 pesos. Tues–Sun 8am–4pm.

Yumká Half safari park, half ecological reserve, Yumká contains native and not-so-
native wildlife. A good choice for kids, the park offers visitors a guided tour of the
indigenous tropical forest, a boat tour of the wetlands (20 pesos extra for the ride), and
a small train ride through grasslands populated with various species of African wildlife.
This is a large park; allow at least 2 hours. There's a restaurant on the premises. Yumká
is 16km (10 miles) from downtown, toward the airport. A minibus provides transportation (ask at your hotel or at a travel agency), or you can take a cab (190 pesos).

Camino Yumká s/n, 86200 Ejido Dos Montes, Tab. ℂ **993/356-0107**. Admission 100 pesos adults, 70
pesos children 12 and under. Daily 9am–5pm.

WHERE TO STAY

Hotel rooms in Villahermosa are a little pricier than in other Mexican cities. Rates listed
below include the 17% tax. Rates can go up during conventions, but there is no high-
season/low-season split. Several of the inexpensive downtown hotels have figured out that

TABASCO & CHIAPAS

9

VILLAHERMOSA

to survive they must offer nightly entertainment to their mostly businessmen clientele. It's unfortunate that they aren't really set up to do this and provide quiet guest rooms at the same time. The only inexpensive hotel I could find that didn't have a bar is listed below, as well as some nicer, albeit more expensive, accommodations.

Very Expensive

Hyatt Villahermosa ★★   A slightly simpler version of the usual Hyatt, this hotel still has the services and amenities you'd expect. I like it better than the Camino Real (which is the other top hotel in the city), for its great location and service. A short walk away is the Parque–Museo La Venta. The rooms are large, quiet, and comfortable. The restaurant caters to international tastes. The majority of clients are business travelers.

Av. Juárez 106, 86000 Villahermosa, Tab. ℂ 800/233-1234 in the U.S., or 993/310-1234. Fax 993/315-1963. www.villahermosa.regency.hyatt.com. 206 units. $227–$289 double; $265–$335 Regency Club room; $330–$375 junior suite. AE, DC, MC, V. Free guarded parking. **Amenities:** 2 restaurants; 3 bars (1 w/ live music; 1 sports bar); large pool, wading pool; 2 lighted tennis courts; small exercise room; concierge; nonsmoking floor; concierge level. *In room:* A/C, TV, high-speed Internet, minibar, hair dryer.

Expensive

Best Western Hotel Maya Tabasco   This hotel is centrally located between the downtown area and the modern western section. It's close to the Parque–Museo La Venta, the bus station, and the city's principal restaurant district. The rooms are large, and most are carpeted and have midsize bathrooms. They don't offer any surprises. An attractive pool area separates the hotel from the hotel's bar, which gets fairly good live talent—Latin music and comedy acts. Another bar, inside the main building, offers soft piano or guitar music.

Bulevar Ruiz Cortines 907, 86000 Villahermosa, Tab. ℂ 800/528-1234 in the U.S. and Canada, or 993/358-1111, ext. 822. Fax 993/312-1097. www.bestwestern.com. 151 units. $99–$127 double; $125–$144 junior suite. AE, MC, V. Rates include full breakfast. Free guarded parking. **Amenities:** Restaurant; 2 bars; large pool; free shuttle service to airport and downtown; nonsmoking rooms. *In room:* A/C, TV, minibar, coffeemaker, hair dryer.

Moderate

Hotel Plaza Independencia (Value)   The Plaza Independencia is the only hotel in this price range with a pool and enclosed parking. Get a room on one of the first three floors, which have been remodeled. End rooms, which end in 01, 02, 14, and 15, have balconies and are generally preferable. It's 2 blocks south of the Plaza de Armas.

Independencia 123, 86000 Villahermosa, Tab. ℂ 993/312-1299, -7541. Fax 993/314-4724. www.hoteles plaza.com.mx. 90 units. 800 pesos double. AE, MC, V. Free secure parking. **Amenities:** Restaurant; bar; small pool. *In room:* A/C, TV, minibar, hair dryer.

Inexpensive

Hotel Provincia Express (Value)   For an inexpensive hotel without a loud bar, this place is your best option. Located downtown in the Zona Luz pedestrian-only section of town, rooms are simple, quiet, and medium-size, with good air-conditioning. Management is capable and doesn't complicate things by offering services and options that its clientele doesn't want.

Lerdo de Tejada 303, 86000 Villahermosa, Tab. ℂ 993/314-5376, or 01-800/715-3968 in Mexico. Fax 993/314-5442. willaop@prodigy.net.mx. 25 units. 550–600 pesos double. MC, V. **Amenities:** Restaurant. *In room:* A/C, TV.

Like other Mexican cities, Villahermosa has seen the arrival of U.S. franchise restaurants, but as these things go, I prefer the Mexican variety: **Sanborn's,** Av. Ruiz Cortines 1310, near Parque–Museo La Venta (© **993/316-8722**), and **VIPS,** Av. Fco. I. Madero 402, downtown (© **993/312-3237**). Both usually do a good job with traditional dishes such as enchiladas or *antojitos.*

Jangada ★★ SEAFOOD   My favorite restaurant in the city is an all-you-can-eat seafood buffet. Before you get to the line, you are served a small glass of delicious seafood broth and an appetizing empanada of *pejelagarto,* a freshwater fish for which Tabasco is famous (it is also, in fact, the political moniker of Andrés Manuel López Obrador, the former mayor of Mexico City and former presidential candidate, who hails from Tabasco). From here, move on to the salad and cold seafood bar, which offers a seafood salad made with freshwater lobster, different kinds of ceviche, and an area where you can get a seafood cocktail made to order. There's a variety of seafood soups—don't leave without trying the shrimp-and-*yuca* chowder, a dish I remember fondly. And then, of course, there are the main dishes, including a well-made paella, charcoal-grilled *pejelagarto* (mild taste—light and almost nutty), and fish kabobs. Jangada is in the fancy western part of town in La Choca neighborhood. It closes early, but next door is a good Brazilian-style steakhouse (Rodizio) that stays open until 9pm.

Paseo de la Choca 126, Fracc. La Choca. © **993/317-6050.** Reservations not accepted. 270 pesos per person, excluding drinks and dessert. AE, DC, MC, V. Daily 12:30–7pm.

Los Tulipanes SEAFOOD/STEAKS/REGIONAL   Los Tulipanes offers good food and has excellent service. The staff tends to a full house with ease, and, on busy days, a guitar trio strolls and serenades. Because the restaurant is on the Río Grijalva near the Pellicer Museum of Anthropology, you can combine a visit to the museum with lunch here. The staff may bring you a plate of *tostones de plátano*—mashed banana chips. In addition to seafood and steaks, Los Tulipanes serves such Mexican specialties as chiles rellenos, tacos, and enchiladas. It has a popular buffet on Sunday.

CICOM Center, Periférico Carlos Pellicer Cámara 511. © **993/312-9209,** -9217. Main courses 100–175 pesos; Sun buffet 180 pesos. AE, MC, V. Daily 1–9pm.

A SIDE TRIP TO CHOCOLATE PLANTATIONS & THE RUINS OF COMALCALCO

Eighty kilometers (50 miles) from Villahermosa is **Comalcalco,** the only pyramid site in Mexico made of kilned brick. This site will be of interest to the hard-core Maya freaks, but it isn't as stunning as Palenque or the picturesque ruins of the Río Bec region. If you have a car, you can get there in an hour, but be prepared for a lack of good directional signs. You'll have to ask directions when you get to the town of Comalcalco. If you don't have a car, you can take a taxi, which will run 600 to 700 pesos to get you there and back with time to see the place. Or you can take a bus to the town of Comalcalco, and a taxi from there. ADO runs first-class buses twice daily. From the town of Comalcalco, the ruins are 3km (2 miles) away. This part of Tabasco is cacao-growing country, where you can visit plantations and factories to see the cacao from the pod on the tree to the finished chocolate bars.

The fastest route from Villahermosa is Highway 180 west to a new (and, as far as I could tell, unnumbered) highway that leads to Cunduacán. The turnoff is clearly marked, but if you miss it, you can continue to Cárdenas and take Highway 187 north.

Comalcalco is a busy agricultural center and market town. The **ruins of Comalcalco** are about 3km (2 miles) on the same highway past the town; watch for signs to the turnoff on the right. Park in the lot and pay admission at the visitor center by the museum. The museum, with many pre-Hispanic artifacts, is small but interesting and worth the 20 minutes or so it takes to see it. Unfortunately, all the descriptions are in Spanish. It presents a history of the people who lived here, the Putún/Chontal Maya. They were traders, spoke Mayan dialect, and were believed to have founded, or at least greatly influenced, Chichén Itzá.

This city had an extension of 7 sq. km (2³/₄ sq. miles), but the site contains only the ceremonial center, comprising an expansive plaza bordered by pyramidal structures and an acropolis with the remains of a palace and some ceremonial structures, probably funerary temples. This city reached its height during the Classic period, A.D. 300 to 900. Of the pyramids around the plaza, one has been fully excavated. A carpet of grass grows over others, with partial excavation here and there. These pyramids were made of compacted earth with brick facing, in some places covered in stucco. To the south of the plaza and above it is the acropolis, a complex of temples and palace rooms that sits well above the plaza. There you will find a couple of structures with carvings and molded stucco with scenes of Maya royalty. There are only a few. Workers had cordoned off a couple of the structures in this complex when I was last there, and I'm not sure whether they will be open soon. Because of the fragile nature of these ruins, there are many NO SUBIR ("no climbing") signs warning visitors against scaling particular structures. But there is one path with arrows that leads you up to the **palace** where you have a good view of the whole site. You can make out the remains of a double vault and a colonnaded chamber that were the principal chambers of this palace. Seeing the ruins takes an hour or so. Admission is 35 pesos, and the site is open daily from 8am to 5pm.

2 PALENQUE ★★

142km (88 miles) SE of Villahermosa; 229km (142 miles) NE of San Cristóbal de las Casas

The ruins of Palenque look out over the jungle from a tall ridge that juts out from the base of steep, thickly forested mountains. It is a dramatic sight colored by the mysterious feel of the ruins themselves. The temples here are in the Classic style, with high-pitched roofs crowned with elaborate combs. Inside many are representations in stone and plaster of the rulers and their gods, which give evidence of a cosmology that is—and perhaps will remain—impenetrable to our understanding. This is one of the grand archaeological sites of Mexico.

Eight kilometers (5 miles) from the ruins is the town of Palenque. There you can find lodging and food, as well as make travel arrangements. Transportation between the town and ruins is cheap and convenient.

ESSENTIALS
Getting There & Departing
BY PLANE   There is no regular commercial air service to Palenque.

BY CAR   The 230km (143-mile) trip from San Cristóbal to Palenque takes 5 hours and passes through lush jungle and mountain scenery. Take it easy, though, and watch out for potholes and other hindrances. **Hwy. 186** from Villahermosa should take about 2 hours. You may encounter military roadblocks that involve a cursory inspection of your travel credentials and perhaps your vehicle.

BY BUS   The two first-class bus stations are 2 blocks apart. Both are on Palenque's main street between the main square and the turnoff for the ruins. The smaller company, **Transportes Rodolfo Figueroa** (© 916/345-1322), offers first-class service four times a day to and from San Cristóbal (5 hr.) and Tuxtla (6¹/₂ hr.). **ADO/Cristóbal Colón** (© 916/345-1344) runs to those destinations and Campeche (six per day, 5 hr.), Villahermosa (nine per day, 2 hr.), and Mérida (two per day, 9 hr.).

Orientation

VISITOR INFORMATION   The downtown tourism office is a block from the main square at the corner of Avenida Juárez and Abasolo. It's open Monday to Saturday from 9am to 9pm, Sunday from 9am to 1pm. There's no phone at the downtown office. To get info over the phone, call the tourism office's business office (© 916/345-0356).

CITY LAYOUT   **Avenida Juárez** is Palenque's main street. At one end is the **main plaza;** at the other is the oversized sculpture of the famous Maya head that was discovered here. To the right of the statue is the entrance to La Cañada; to the left is the road to the ruins, and straight ahead past the statue are the airport and the highway to Villahermosa. The distance between the town's main square and the monument is about 1.5km (1 mile).

La Cañada is a restaurant and hotel zone tucked away in the forest. Aside from the main plaza area, this is the best location for travelers without cars, because the town is within a few blocks, and the buses that run to the ruins pass right by.

GETTING AROUND   The cheapest way to get back and forth from the ruins is on the white **VW buses** *(colectivos)* that run down Juárez every 10 minutes from 6am to 6pm. The buses pass La Cañada and hotels along the road to the ruins, and can be flagged down at any point, but they may not stop if they're full. The cost is 10 pesos per person.

FAST FACTS   The telephone **area code** is **916.** As for the **climate,** Palenque's high humidity is downright oppressive in the summer, especially after rain showers. During the winter, the damp air can occasionally be chilly in the evening. Rain gear is handy at any time of year. **Internet service** and **ATMs** are easily available.

EXPLORING PALENQUE

The reason to come here is the ruins; although you can tour them in a morning, many people savor Palenque for days. There are no must-see sights in town.

Parque Nacional Palenque ★★★

A **museum and visitor center** sits not far from the entrance to the ruins. Though it's not large, the museum is worth the time it takes to see; it's open Tuesday to Sunday from 10am to 5pm and is included in the price of admission. It contains well-chosen and artistically displayed exhibits, including jade from recently excavated tombs. Explanatory text in Spanish and English explains the life and times of this magnificent city. New pieces are sometimes added as they are uncovered in ongoing excavations.

The **main entrance,** about 1km (¹/₂ mile) beyond the museum, is at the end of the paved highway. There you'll find a large parking lot, a refreshment stand, a ticket booth, and several shops. Among the vendors selling souvenirs are often some Lacandón Indians wearing white tunics and hawking bows and arrows.

Admission to the ruins is 85 pesos. The fee for using a video camera is 50 pesos. Parking at the main entrance and at the visitor center is free. The site and visitor center shops are open daily from 8am to 4:45pm. A map of the site is in the color section at the front of this book.

TOURING THE RUINS   Pottery shards found during the excavations show that people lived in this area as early as 300 B.C. By the Classic period (A.D. 300–900), Palenque was an important ceremonial center. It peaked around A.D. 600 to 700.

When John Stephens visited the site in the 1840s, the ruins that you see today were buried under centuries of accumulated earth and a thick canopy of jungle. The dense jungle surrounding the cleared portion still covers unexcavated temples, which are easily discernible in the forest even to the untrained eye. But be careful not to drift too far from the main path—there have been a few incidents where tourists venturing alone into the rainforest were assaulted.

Of all Mexico's ruins, this is the most haunting, because of its majesty; its history, recovered by epigraphers; and its mysterious setting. Scholars have identified the rulers and constructed their family histories, putting visitors on a first-name basis with these ancient people etched in stone. You can read about it in *A Forest of Kings,* by Linda Schele and David Freidel.

As you enter the ruins, the building on your right is the **Temple of the Inscriptions,** named for the great stone hieroglyphic panels found inside. (Most of the panels, which portray the family tree of King Pacal, are in the National Anthropological Museum in Mexico City.) This temple is famous for the crypt of King Pacal deep inside the pyramid, but the crypt is closed to the public. The archaeologist Alberto Ruz Lhuillier discovered the tomb in the depths of the temple in 1952—an accomplishment many scholars consider one of the great discoveries of the Maya world. In exploratory excavations, Ruz Lhuillier found a stairway leading from the temple floor deep into the base of the pyramid. The original builders had carefully concealed the entrance by filling the stairway with stone. After several months of excavation, Ruz Lhuillier finally reached King Pacal's crypt, which contained several fascinating objects, including a magnificent carved stone sarcophagus. Ruz Lhuillier's own gravesite is opposite the Temple of the Inscriptions, on the left as you enter the park.

Just to your right as you face the Temple of the Inscriptions is **Temple 13,** which is receiving considerable attention from archaeologists. They recently discovered the burial of another richly adorned personage, accompanied in death by an adult female and an adolescent. Some of the artifacts found there are on display in the museum.

Back on the main pathway, the building directly in front of you is the **Palace,** with its unique tower. The explorer John Stephens camped in the Palace when it was completely covered in vegetation, spending sleepless nights fighting off mosquitoes. A pathway between the Palace and the Temple of the Inscriptions leads to the **Temple of the Sun,** the **Temple of the Foliated Cross,** the **Temple of the Cross,** and **Temple 14.** This group of temples, now cleared and in various stages of reconstruction, was built by Pacal's son, Chan-Bahlum, who is usually shown on inscriptions with six toes. Chan-Bahlum's plaster mask was found in Temple 14 next to the Temple of the Sun. Archaeologists have begun probing the Temple of the Sun for Chan-Bahlum's tomb. Little remains of this temple's exterior carving. Inside, however, behind a fence, a carving of Chan-Bahlum shows him ascending the throne in A.D. 690. The panels depict Chan-Bahlum's version of his historic link to the throne.

To the left of the Palace is the North Group, also undergoing restoration. Included in this area are the **Ball Court** and the **Temple of the Count.** At least three tombs, complete with offerings for the underworld journey, have been found here, and the lineage of at least 12 kings has been deciphered from inscriptions left at this site.

Just past the North Group is a small building (once a museum) now used for storing the artifacts found during restorations. It is closed to the public. To the right of the building, a stone bridge crosses the river, leading to a pathway down the hillside to the new museum. The rock-lined path descends along a cascading stream, on the banks of which grow giant ceiba trees. Benches are placed along the way as rest areas, and some small temples have been reconstructed near the base of the trail. In the early morning and evening, you may hear monkeys crashing through the thick foliage by the path; if you keep noise to a minimum, you may spot wild parrots as well. Walking downhill (by far the best way to go), it will take you about 20 minutes to reach the main highway. The path ends at the paved road across from the museum. The *colectivos* (minibuses) going back to the village will stop here if you wave them down.

WHERE TO STAY

English is spoken in all the more expensive hotels and about half of the inexpensive ones. The quoted rates include the 17% tax. High season in Palenque is limited to Easter week, July to August, and December.

Expensive

Chan-Kah Resort Village ★   This hotel is a grouping of comfortable, roomy bungalows that offer privacy and quiet in the surroundings of a tropical forest. The hotel is on the road between the ruins and the town, but because the town of Palenque isn't particularly worth exploring, you don't miss much by staying here. The grounds are beautifully tended, and there is an inviting pool that resembles a lagoon. A broad stream runs through the property. Some of the bungalows can have a musty smell. Christmas prices will be higher than those quoted here, and you may be quoted a higher price if you reserve a room in advance from outside the country. The outdoor restaurant and bar serves only passable Mexican food. Room service is pricey.

Carretera Las Ruinas Km 3, 29960 Palenque, Chi. ℭ **916/345-1100.** Fax 916/345-0820. www.chan-kah.com.mx. 73 units. 1,850 pesos casita; 2,740 pesos master suite. MC, V. Free guarded parking. **Amenities:** Restaurant; bar; 3 outdoor pools (1 large w/natural spring); room service. *In room:* A/C, hair dryer.

Misión Palenque ★★   This hotel has returned to being among the most comfortable in the city after a total remodeling that includes new air-conditioning and other amenities. Rooms are medium-size and attractively furnished with light, modern furniture. Bathrooms are spacious, with ample counters. The hotel has extensive grounds and is very quiet. In one corner of the property, a natural spring flows through an attractive bit of jungle, where the hotel has installed the spa. Part of the spa is a *temazcal,* or Native American steam bath. There's also a mud bath along with the more common elements. The hotel is a few blocks east of the town's main square.

Periférico Oriente d/c, 29960 Palenque, Chi. ℭ **916/345-0241,** or 01/800-900-3800 in Mexico. Fax 916/345-0300. www.hotelesmision.com.mx. 156 units. 1,100 pesos double; 2,925 pesos junior suite. AE, MC, V. Free guarded parking that includes vehicle checkup. **Amenities:** Restaurant; bar; courtesy trips to ruins; babysitting; fitness room; Jacuzzi; 2 outdoor pools; room service; spa; 2 tennis courts. *In room:* A/C, TV, hair dryer (on request).

Hotel Ciudad Real   Though not really fancy, this hotel does the important things right—the rooms are ample, quiet, and well lit, and are comfortably, if plainly, furnished. Suites have a sitting room with sleeping sofa. Most units hold two double beds; a few have king-size beds. All rooms have a small balcony, which, in the best case, overlooks an attractive garden. When making a reservation, specify the hotel in Palenque (there's also a Ciudad Real in San Cristóbal). It's at the edge of town in the direction of the airport.

Carretera a Pakal-Na Km 1.5, 29960 Palenque, Chi. ℂ **916/345-1343** (reservations: ℂ 967/678-4400). www.ciudadreal.com.mx. 72 units. High season 1,330 pesos double, 1,695 pesos junior suite. Low season 900 pesos double, 1,150 pesos junior suite. AE, MC, V. Free secured parking. Internet discounts sometimes available. **Amenities:** Restaurant; bar; outdoor pool; baby pool; room service; smoke-free rooms. *In room:* A/C, TV, hair dryer.

Hotel Maya Tucán   Book a room in back, and you will have a view of the hotel's natural pond. The cheerfully decorated rooms are adequate in size; they have double beds and large bathrooms. Suites are larger and have king-size beds. The grounds are well tended and lush; scarlet macaws kept by the hotel fly about the parking lot. The Maya Tucán is on the highway to the airport. Bathrooms are larger and better lit, but done with less polish than at Ciudad Real. Beds have rubber mattress covers.

Carretera-Palenque Km 0.5, 29960 Palenque, Chi. ℂ **916/345-0443.** Fax 916/345-0337. mayatucan@ palenque.com.mx. 56 units. 1,150 pesos double; 1,550 pesos suite. MC, V. Free secured parking. **Amenities:** Restaurant; bar; outdoor pool; room service. *In room:* A/C, TV, hair dryer, no phone.

Hotel Maya Tulipanes   This is an attractive hotel tucked away in the Cañada. I like it for its location and the close attention paid by the management. Service and upkeep are both good. Rooms are medium to large and come with a queen-size, a king-size, or two double beds. Tropical vegetation adorns the grounds, along with some reproductions of famous Mayan architecture. The Maya Tulipanes has an arrangement with a sister hotel at the ruins of Tikal, in Guatemala. The travel agency operates daily tours to Bonampak and other attractions.

Calle Cañada 6, 29960 Palenque, Chi. ℂ **916/345-0201,** -0258. Fax 916/345-1004. www.mayatulipanes. com.mx. 72 units. High season 1,190 pesos standard; low season 785–1,000 pesos standard. Internet packages available. AE, MC, V. Free secured parking. **Amenities:** Restaurant; bar; ground transportation to/from Villahermosa airport; outdoor pool; room service; smoke-free rooms. *In room:* A/C, TV, hair dryer, no phone, Wi-Fi.

Inexpensive

Hotel Xibalba   This modern small two-story hotel is inspired by Maya architecture. The medium-to-small rooms are clean and cheerful. The upstairs units are a little smaller than the downstairs units. Most of the beds have firm mattresses. You can arrange a trip to Bonampak or Misol Ha with the hotel management, which owns a travel agency, Viajes Shivalva (pronounced like Xibalba: "shee-*bahl*-bah").

Calle Merle Green 9, Col. La Cañada, 29960 Palenque, Chi. ℂ **916/345-0392.** Fax 916/345-0411. www. palenquemx.com/shivalva. 15 units. 480–700 pesos double. MC, V. No parking. **Amenities:** Restaurant; bar. *In room:* A/C, TV, no phone.

WHERE TO DINE

Palenque and, for that matter, the rest of backwater Chiapas, is not for gourmets. Who'd a thunk? I had an easy time eliminating a number of restaurants that didn't even seem to be keeping up the appearance of serving food. But the situation has been improving, and you can at least get some decent Mexican food.

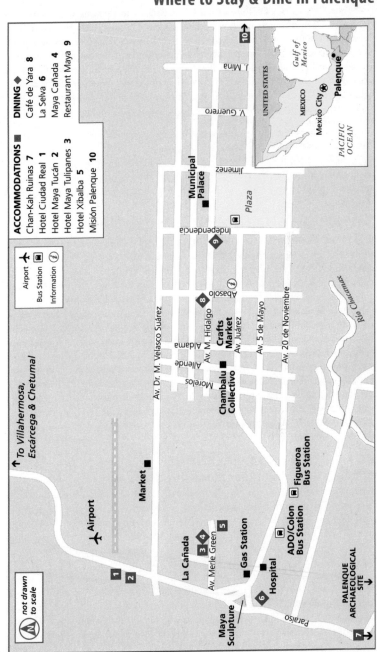

TABASCO & CHIAPAS

9

PALENQUE

ACCOMMODATIONS ■
Chan-Kah Ruinas **7**
Hotel Ciudad Real **1**
Hotel Maya Tucán **2**
Hotel Maya Tulipanes **3**
Hotel Xibalba **5**
Misión Palenque **10**

DINING ◆
Café de Yara **8**
La Selva **6**
Maya Cañada **4**
Restaurant Maya **9**

Airport ✈
Bus Station ■
Information ⓘ

not drawn to scale

To Villahermosa, Escárcega & Chetumal

Airport
Market
La Cañada
Gas Station
Hospital
Maya Sculpture
ADO/Colon Bus Station
Figueroa Bus Station
PALENQUE ARCHAEOLOGICAL SITE

Av. Dr. M. Velasco Suárez
Av. Merle Green
Paraíso
Rio Chacamax

Chambalu Collectivo
Crafts Market
Municipal Palace
Plaza

Morelos
Allende
Aldama
Av. M. Hidalgo
Abasolo
Av. Juárez
Av. 5 de Mayo
Av. 20 de Noviembre
Independencia
Jimenez
V. Guerrero
J. Mina

UNITED STATES
Gulf of Mexico
MEXICO
Mexico City
Palenque
PACIFIC OCEAN

La Selva MEXICAN/INTERNATIONAL   At La Selva (the jungle), you dine under a large, attractive thatched roof beside well-tended gardens. The menu includes seafood, freshwater fish, steaks, and Mexican specialties. The most expensive thing on the menu is *pigua,* freshwater lobster caught in the large rivers of southeast Mexico. These can grow quite large— the size of small saltwater lobsters. This and the finer cuts of meat have been frozen, but you wouldn't want otherwise in Palenque. I liked the fish stuffed with shrimp, and the *mole* enchiladas. La Selva is on the highway to the ruins, near the statue of the Maya head.

Carretera Palenque Ruinas Km 0.5. (✆ **916/345-0363.** Main courses 105–200 pesos. MC, V. Daily 11:30am–11:30pm.

Inexpensive

Café de Yara MEXICAN   A small, modern cafe and restaurant with a comforting, not overly ambitious menu. The cafe's strong suit is healthy salads (with disinfected greens) and home-style Mexican entrees, such as the beef or chicken *milanesa* or chicken cooked in a *chile pasilla* sauce.

Av. Hidalgo 66 (at Abasolo). (✆ **916/345-0269.** Main courses 40–95 pesos. MC, V. Daily 7am–11pm.

Restaurant Maya and Maya Cañada ★ MEXICAN   These two are the most consistently good restaurants in Palenque. One faces the main plaza from the corner of Independencia and Hidalgo, the other is in La Cañada (✆ **916/345-0216**). Menus are somewhat different, but much is the same. Both do a good job with the basics—good strong, locally grown coffee and soft, pliant tortillas. The menu offers a nice combination of Mexican standards and regional specialties. If you're in an exploratory mood, try one of the regional specialties such as the *mole chiapaneco* (dark red, like *mole poblano,* but less sweet) or any of the dishes based on *chaya* or *chipilin* (mild-flavored local greens), such as the soup with *chipilin* and *bolitas de masa* (corn dumplings). If you want something more comforting, go for the chicken and rice vegetable soup, or the *sopa azteca.* The plantains stuffed with cheese and fried Mexican style are wonderful. Waiters sometimes offer specials not on the menu, and these are often the thing to get. You can also try *tascalate,* a pre-Hispanic drink made of water, *masa,* chocolate, and *achiote,* and served room temperature or cold.

Av. Independencia s/n. (✆ **916/345-0042.** Breakfast 40–60 pesos; main courses 65–140 pesos. AE, MC, V. Daily 7am–11pm.

ROAD TRIPS FROM PALENQUE
Bonampak & Yaxchilán: Murals in the Jungle

Intrepid travelers may want to consider the day trip to the Maya ruins of Bonampak and Yaxchilán. The **ruins of Bonampak,** southeast of Palenque on the Guatemalan border, were discovered in 1946. The site is important for the vivid **murals** of the Maya on the interior walls of one temple. Particularly striking is an impressive battle scene, perhaps the most important painting of pre-Hispanic Mexico. Reproductions of these murals are on view in the Regional Archaeology Museum in Villahermosa.

Several tour companies offer a day trip. The drive to Bonampak is 3 hours. From there you continue by boat to the **ruins of Yaxchilán,** famous for its highly ornamented buildings. Bring rain gear, boots, a flashlight, and bug repellent. All tours include meals and cost about 900 pesos. No matter what agency you sign up with, the hours of departure and return are the same because the vans of the different agencies caravan down and back for safety. You leave at 6am and return at 7pm.

Try **Viajes Na Chan Kan** (© **916/345-2154**), at the corner of avenidas Hidalgo and Jiménez, across from the main square, or **Viajes Shivalva,** Calle Merle Green 1 (© **916/ 345-0411;** fax 916/345-0392). A branch of Viajes Shivalva (© **916/345-0822**) is a block from the *zócalo* (main plaza) at the corner of Juárez and Abasolo, across the hall from the State Tourism Office. It's open Monday to Saturday from 9am to 9pm.

Waterfalls at Misol Ha & Agua Azul

A popular excursion from Palenque is a day trip to the Misol Ha waterfall and Agua Azul. **Misol Ha** is 20km (12 miles) from Palenque, in the direction of Ocosingo. It takes about 30 minutes to get there, depending on the traffic. The turn-off is clearly marked; you'll turn right and drive another 1.5 km (1 mile). The place is absolutely beautiful. Water pours from a rocky cliff into a broad pool of green water bordered by thick tropical vegetation. There's a small restaurant and some rustic cabins for rent for 350 to 450 pesos per night, depending on the size of the cabin. The place is run by the *ejido* cooperative that owns the site, and it does a good job of maintaining the place. To inquire about the cabins, call © **916/345-1506.** Admission for the day is 10 pesos.

Approximately 44km (27 miles) beyond Misol Ha are the **Agua Azul waterfalls**—270m (886 ft.) of tumbling falls with lots of water. There are cabins for rent here, too, but I would rather stay at Misol Ha. You can swim either above or below the falls, but make sure you don't get pulled by the current. You can see both places in the same day or stop to see them on your way to Ocosingo and San Cristóbal. Agua Azul is prettiest after 3 or 4 consecutive dry days; heavy rains can make the water murky. Check with guides or other travelers about the water quality before you decide to go. The cost to enter is 25 pesos per person. Trips to both of these places can be arranged through just about any hotel.

Ocosingo & the Ruins of Toniná

By the time you get to Agua Azul, you're halfway to Ocosingo, which lies halfway between Palenque and San Cristóbal. So instead of returning for the night to Palenque, you can go on to Ocosingo. It's higher up and more comfortable than Palenque. It's a nice little town, not touristy, not a lot to do other than see the ruins of Toniná. But it is a nice place to spend the night so that you can see the ruins early before moving on to San Cristóbal. There are about a half-dozen small hotels in town; the largest is not the most desirable. I would stay at the **Hospedaje Esmeralda** (© **919/673-0014**) or the **Hotel Central** (© **919/673-0024**), on the main square. Both of these are small and simple, but welcoming. The restaurant in front of Hotel Central has good cooking.

Ruins of Toniná ★★

The ruins of Toniná (the name translates as "house of rocks") are 14km (8³/₄ miles) east of Ocosingo. You can take a cab there and catch a *colectivo* to return. The city dates from the Classic period and covered a large area, but the excavated and restored part is all on one hillside that faces out toward a broad valley. This site is not really set up for lots of tourists. There's a lot of up and down, and some of it is a little precarious. It's not a good place to take kids. Admission is 35 pesos.

This complex of courtyards, rooms, and stairways is built on multiple levels that are irregular and asymmetrical. The overall effect is that of a ceremonial area with multiple foci instead of a clearly discernable center.

As early as A.D. 350, Toniná emerged as a dynastic center. In the 7th and 8th centuries, it was locked in a struggle with rival Palenque and, to a lesser degree, with faraway Calakmul. This has led some scholars to see Toniná as more militaristic than its neighbors—a sort of Sparta of the classic Maya. Toniná's greatest victory came in 711, when, under the rule of Kan B'alam, it attacked Palenque and captured its king, K'an Joy Chitam, depicted on a stone frieze twisted, his arms bound with rope.

But the single most important artifact yet found at Toniná, is up around the fifth level of the acropolis—a large stucco frieze divided into panels by a feathered framework adorned with the heads of sacrificial victims (displayed upside down) and some rather horrid creatures. The largest figure is a skeletal image holding a decapitated head—very vivid and very puzzling. There is actually a stylistic parallel with some murals of the Teotihuacán culture of central Mexico. The other special thing about Toniná is that it holds the distinction of having the last ever date recorded in the long count (A.D. 909), which marks the end of the Classic period.

3 SAN CRISTÓBAL DE LAS CASAS ★★★

229km (142 miles) SW of Palenque; 80km (50 miles) E of Tuxtla Gutiérrez; 74km (46 miles) NW of Comitán; 166km (103 miles) NW of Cuauhtémoc; 451km (280 miles) E of Oaxaca

San Cristóbal is a colonial town of white stucco walls and red-tile roofs, of cobblestone streets and narrow sidewalks, of graceful arcades and open plazas. It lies in a green valley 2,120m (6,954 ft.) high. The city owes part of its name to the 16th-century cleric Fray Bartolomé de las Casas, who was the town's first bishop and spent the rest of his life waging a political campaign to protect the indigenous peoples of the Americas.

Surrounding the city are many villages of Mayan-speaking Indians who display great variety in their language, dress, and customs, making this area one of the most fascinating in Mexico. San Cristóbal is the principal market town for these Indians, and their point of contact with the outside world. Most of them trek down from the surrounding mountains to sell goods and run errands

Several Indian villages lie within reach of San Cristóbal by road: **Chamula,** with its weavers and unorthodox church; **Zinacantán,** whose residents practice their own syncretic religion; **Tenejapa, San Andrés,** and **Magdalena,** known for brocaded textiles; **Amatenango del Valle,** a town of potters; and **Aguacatenango,** known for embroidery. Most of these "villages" consist of little more than a church and the municipal government building, with homes scattered for miles around and a general gathering only for church and market days (usually Sun).

Many Indians now live on the outskirts of town because they've been expelled from their villages over religious differences. They are known as *los expulsados.* No longer involved in farming, they make their living in commerce and handicrafts. Most still wear traditional dress, but they've adopted Protestant religious beliefs that prevent them from partaking in many of their community's civic and religious celebrations.

The influx of outsiders hasn't created in most Indians a desire to adopt mainstream customs and dress. It's interesting to note that the communities closest to San Cristóbal are the most resistant to change. The greatest threat to the cultures in this area comes not from tourism, but from the action of large market forces, population pressures, environmental damage, and poverty. The Indians aren't interested in acting or looking like the foreigners they see. They may steal glances or even stare at tourists, but mainly they pay little attention to outsiders, except as potential buyers for handicrafts.

You may see or hear the word *Jovel,* San Cristóbal's Indian name, incorporated often in the names of businesses. You'll hear the word *coleto,* used in reference to someone or

TABASCO & CHIAPAS

9

SAN CRISTÓBAL DE LAS CASAS

Sna Jolobil

Museo Templo y Convento Santo Domingo

Chiapa de Corzo

Chiapa de Corzo

Comitán

Comitán

Escuadrón 201

Dr. Navarro

Tapachula

Tapachula

28 de Agosto

Ejército Nacional

Ejército Nacional

Primero de Marzo

Paniagua

5 de Febrero

Ma. Adelina Flores

Nicolás Ruelz

Plaza de la Iglesia (PARKING)

Catedral

Real de Guadalupe

Real de Guadalupe

Guadalupe Victoria

To Museo del Ambar

Main Plaza

Francisco I. Madero

Diego de Mazariegos

Cuauhtémoc

Felipe Flores

UNITED STATES

Gulf of Mexico

MEXICO

Mexico City

PACIFIC OCEAN

San Cristóbal de las Casas

Niños Héroes

Francisco León

Casa de Artesanías Amanecer

Hnos. Domínguez

Callejón Libertad

Palacio de las Bellas Artes

Julio M. Corzo

Alvaro Obregón

Ramón

Corona

Pedro Moreno

Sostenes Esponda

Hnos. Pineda

Pan American Highway

Cristóbal Colón Bus Station

ACCOMMODATIONS ■

Casa Felipe Flores **6**

Casa Na-Bolom **1**

Hotel Casa Mexicana **16**

Hotel Casavieja **3**

Hotel Don Quijote **4**

Hotel El Paraíso **15**

Hotel Palacio de Moctezuma **10**

Hotel Real del Valle **7**

Mansión de los Ángeles **8**

DINING ◆

El Edén **15**

Emiliano's Moustache **14**

La Casa del Pan Papalotl **5**

La Paloma **13**

Madre Tierra **11**

Normita's **9**

Pierre **2**

Restaurant Tuluc **12**

✝ Church
ⓘ Information
▣ Pedestrian Only
✉ Post Office

something from San Cristóbal. You'll see signs for *tamales coletos, pan coleto,* and *desayuno coleto* (Cristóbal breakfast).

ESSENTIALS
Getting There & Departing
BY PLANE Flights from Mexico City have been canceled. The closest airport is in Tuxtla Gutiérrez (p. 278).

BY CAR From Tuxtla Gutiérrez, the 1¹/₂-hour trip winds through beautiful mountain country. From Palenque, the road is just as beautiful (if longer—5 hr.), and it provides jungle scenery, but portions of it may be heavily potholed or obstructed during rainy season. Check with the local state tourism office before driving.

BY TAXI Taxis from Tuxtla Gutiérrez to San Cristóbal cost around 550 pesos. Another way to travel to and from Tuxtla is by *combi.* The Volkswagen vans, which can get extremely crowded, make the run every 15 to 30 minutes. They can be found just off the highway by the bus station. You'll have to ask someone to point them out to you because there isn't a sign.

BY BUS The two bus stations in town are directly across the Pan American Highway from each other. The smaller one belongs to **Transportes Rodolfo Figueroa,** which provides first-class service to and from Tuxtla (every 40 min.) and Palenque (four buses per day, with a stop in Ocosingo—cheaper than the competition). For other destinations, go to the large station run by **ADO** and its affiliates, Altos, Cristóbal Colón, and Maya de Oro. This company offers service to and from Tuxtla (12 buses per day), Palenque (almost every hour), and several other destinations: Mérida (two buses per day), Villahermosa (two buses per day), Oaxaca (two buses per day), and Puerto Escondido (two buses per day). To buy a bus ticket without going down to the station, go to the **Ticket Bus** agency, Real de Guadalupe 5 (© **967/678-8503**). Hours are Monday to Saturday from 7am to 11pm, Sunday from 9am to 5pm.

Orientation
ARRIVING To get to the main plaza from the highway, turn on to **Avenida Insurgentes** (at the traffic light). From the bus station, the main plaza is 9 blocks north up Avenida Insurgentes (a 10-min. walk, slightly uphill). Cabs are cheap and plentiful.

The Zapatista Movement & Chiapas

In January 1994, Indians from this area rebelled against the Mexican government over health care, education, land distribution, and representative government. Their organization, the **Zapatista Liberation Army,** known as EZLN (Ejército Zapatista de Liberación Nacional), and its leader, Subcomandante Marcos, have become emblematic of the problems Mexico has with social justice. In the last couple of years, the rhetoric of armed revolt has ended, and the Zapatistas are talking about building a broad leftist coalition—but not a political party. What this means for Mexican politics is not clear, but for travelers it means not having to worry about political unrest.

The **State Tourism Office** is better than the municipal
office. It's just half a block south of the main plaza, at Av. Hidalgo 1-B (© **967/678-6570**);
it's open Monday to Friday from 10am to 8pm, Saturday from 10am to 6pm, and Sunday
from 10am to 2pm. The **Municipal Tourism Office** (©/fax **967/678-0665**) is in the town
hall, west of the main square. Hours are Monday to Saturday from 9am to 8pm. Check the
bulletin board here for apartments, shared rides, cultural events, and local tours. Both
offices are helpful, but the state office is open an hour later and is better staffed.

CITY LAYOUT San Cristóbal is laid out on a grid; the main north–south axis is **Insur-
gentes/Utrilla,** and the east–west axis is **Mazariegos/Madero.** All streets change names
when they cross either of these streets. The *zócalo* (main plaza) lies where they intersect.
An important street to know is **Real de Guadalupe,** which runs from the plaza eastward
to the church of Guadalupe; located on it are many hotels and restaurants. The market
is 7 blocks north of the *zócalo* along Utrilla.

Take note that this town has at least three streets named Domínguez and two streets
named Flores. There are Hermanos Domínguez, Belisario Domínguez, and Pantaleón
Domínguez; and María Adelina Flores and Dr. Felipe Flores.

GETTING AROUND Most of the sights and shopping in San Cristóbal are within
walking distance of the plaza.

Urbano **buses** (minibuses) take passengers between town and the residential neighborhoods. All buses pass by the market and central plaza on their way through town.
Utrilla and Avenida 16 de Septiembre are the two main arteries; all buses use the market
area as the last stop. Any bus on Utrilla will take you to the market.

Colectivos to outlying villages depart from the public market at Avenida Utrilla. Buses
late in the day are usually very crowded. Always check to see when the last or next-to-last
bus returns from wherever you're going, and then take the one before that—those last
buses sometimes don't materialize, and you might be stranded. I speak from experience!

Rental cars come in handy for trips to the outlying villages and may be worth the
expense when shared by a group, but keep in mind that insurance is invalid on unpaved
roads. Try **Optima Car Rental,** Av. Mazariegos 39 (© **967/674-5409**). Office hours are
daily from 9am to 1pm and 5 to 8pm. You'll save money by arranging the rental from
your home country; otherwise, a day's rental with insurance will cost around 700 pesos
for a VW Beetle with manual transmission, the cheapest car available.

Scooters can be rented from Darren and Natasha, two easygoing Australians who tell
me that they've found the best way to enjoy the city and surrounding countryside. Look
for **Croozy Scooters** (© **967/631-4329**), at Belisario Domínguez 7-A.

Bikes are another option for getting around the city; a day's rental is about 120 pesos. **Los
Pingüinos,** Av. Ecuador 4-B (© **967/678-0202;** pinguinosmex@yahoo.com), offers bike
tours to a few out-of-town locations. Tours in the valley around San Cristóbal last 4 to 6 hours
and cost 300 to 400 pesos. It's open daily from 10am to 2:30pm and 4 to 7pm.

⌒Fast Facts   San Cristóbal de las Casas

Area Code The telephone area code is **967.**

Books The People of the Bat: Mayan Tales and Dreams from Zinacantán, by
Robert M. Laughlin, is a priceless collection of beliefs from that village near San
Cristóbal. Another good book with a completely different view of today's Maya

is *The Heart of the Sky,* by Peter Canby, who traveled among the Maya to chronicle their struggles (and wrote his book before the Zapatista uprising).

Bookstore For the best selection of new and used books and reading material in English, go to **La Pared,** Av. Hidalgo 2 (© **967/678-6367**). The owner, Dana Gay Burton, keeps a great collection of books on the Maya, and Mexico in general, both fiction and nonfiction.

Bulletin Boards San Cristóbal is a cultural crossroads for travelers, and several places maintain bulletin boards with information on Spanish classes, local specialty tours, rooms or houses to rent, rides needed, and so on. These include boards at the **Tourism Office, Café El Puente, Madre Tierra,** and **Casa Na-Bolom.**

Climate San Cristóbal can be chilly when the sun isn't out, especially during the winter. It's 2,120m (6,954 ft.) above sea level. Most hotels are not heated, although some have fireplaces. There is always a possibility of rain, but I would avoid going to San Cristóbal from late August to late October, during the height of the rainy season.

Currency Exchange There are at least five *casas de cambio* on Real de Guadalupe, near the main square, and a couple under the colonnade facing the square. Most are open until 8pm, and some are open Sunday. There are also a number of ATMs.

Doctor Try **Dr. Roberto Lobato,** Av. Belisario Domínguez 17, at Calle Flavio A. Paniagua (© **967/678-7777**). Don't be unsettled by the fact that his office is next door to Funerales Canober.

Internet Access There are Internet cafes everywhere.

Parking If your hotel does not have parking, use the *estacionamiento* (underground public lot) in front of the cathedral, just off the main square on 16 de Septiembre. Entry is from Calle 5 de Febrero.

Post Office The *correo* is at Crescencio Rosas and Cuauhtémoc, a block south and west of the main square. It's open Monday to Friday from 8am to 7pm, Saturday from 9am to 1pm.

Spanish Classes The **Instituto Jovel,** María Adelina Flores 21 (©/fax **967/678-4069**), gets higher marks for its Spanish courses than the competition. It also offers classes in weaving and cooking. The **Centro Bilingüe,** at the Centro Cultural El Puente, Real de Guadalupe 55 (© **800/303-4983** in the U.S., or ©/fax 967/678-3723), offers classes in Spanish. Both schools can arrange home stays for their students.

Telephone The best price for long-distance telephone calls and faxing is at **La Pared** bookstore (see "Bookstore," above), at Av. Hidalgo 2, across the street from the State Tourism Office.

EXPLORING SAN CRISTOBAL

San Cristóbal is a lovely town in a lovely region. A lot of people come for the beauty, but the main thing that draws most visitors here is the highland Maya. They can be seen anywhere in San Cristóbal, but most travelers take at least one trip to the outlying villages to get a close-up of Maya life.

Casa Na-Bolom ★★ If you're interested in the anthropology of the region, you'll want to visit this house museum. Stay here, if you can. The house, built as a seminary in 1891, became the headquarters of anthropologists Frans and Trudy Blom in 1951, and the gathering place of outsiders interested in studying the region. Frans Blom led many early archaeological studies in Mexico, and Trudy was noted for her photographs of the Lacandón Indians and her efforts to save them and their forest homeland. A room at Na-Bolom contains a selection of her Lacandón photographs, and postcards of the photographs are on sale in the gift shop (daily 9am–2pm and 4–7pm). A tour of the home covers the displays of pre-Hispanic artifacts collected by Frans Blom; the cozy library, with its numerous volumes about the region and the Maya (weekdays 10am–2pm); and the gardens Trudy Blom started for the ongoing reforestation of the Lacandón jungle. The tour ends with a showing of *La Reina de la Selva,* an excellent 50-minute film on the Bloms, the Lacandón, and Na-Bolom. Trudy Blom died in 1993, but Na-Bolom continues to operate as a nonprofit public trust.

The 12 guest rooms, named for surrounding villages, are decorated with local objects and textiles. All rooms have fireplaces and private bathrooms. Prices (including breakfast and admission to the museum) are 750 pesos for a single, 950 pesos for a double.

Even if you're not a guest here, you can come for a meal, usually an assortment of vegetarian and other dishes. Just be sure to make a reservation at least 2¹/₂ hours in advance, and be on time. The colorful dining room has one large table, and the eclectic mix of travelers sometimes makes for interesting conversation. Breakfast costs 60 to 70 pesos; lunch and dinner cost 150 pesos each. Dinner is served at 7pm. Following breakfast (8–10am), a guide not affiliated with the house offers tours to San Juan Chamula and Zinacantán (see "The Nearby Maya Villages & Countryside," below).

Av. Vicente Guerrero 3, 29200 San Cristóbal de las Casas, Chi. ⓒ **967/678-1418.** Fax 967/678-5586. Group tour and film 50 pesos. Tours daily 11:30am (Spanish only) and 4:30pm. Leave the square on Real de Guadalupe, walk 4 blocks to Av. Vicente Guerrero, and turn left; Na-Bolom is 5¹/₂ blocks up Guerrero.

Catedral San Cristóbal's main cathedral was built in the 1500s. It has little of interest inside besides a lovely, uncommon beam ceiling and a carved wooden pulpit.

Calle 20 de Noviembre at Guadalupe Victoria. No phone. Free admission. Daily 7am–6pm.

El Mercado Once you've visited Santo Domingo (see listing below), meander through the San Cristóbal town market and the surrounding area. Every time I do, I see something different to elicit my curiosity.

By Santo Domingo church. No phone. Mon–Sat 8am–7pm.

Museo del Ambar If you've been in this town any time at all, you know what a big deal amber is here. Chiapas is the third-largest producer of amber in the world, and many experts prefer its amber for its colors and clarity. A couple of stores tried calling themselves museums, but they didn't fool anybody. Now a real museum moves methodically through all the issues surrounding amber—mining, shaping, and identifying it, as well as the different varieties found in other parts of the world. It's interesting, it's cheap, and you get to see the restored area of the old convent it occupies. There are a couple of beautiful pieces of worked amber that are on permanent loan—make sure you see them. In mid-August, the museum holds a contest for local artisans who work amber; they do remarkable work.

Exconvento de la Merced, Diego de Mazariegos s/n. ⓒ **967/678-9716.** Admission 20 pesos. Tues–Sun 10am–2pm and 4–7pm.

Museo Templo y Convento Santo Domingo　　Inside the front door of the carved-stone plateresque facade, there's a beautiful gilded wooden altarpiece built in 1560, walls with saints, and gilt-framed paintings. Attached to the church is the former Convent of Santo Domingo, which houses a small museum about San Cristóbal and Chiapas. The museum has changing exhibits and often shows cultural films. It's 5 blocks north of the *zócalo,* in the market area.

Av. 20 de Noviembre. ℂ **967/678-1609.** Free admission to church; museum 20 pesos. Museum Tues–Sun 10am–5pm; church daily 10am–2pm and 5–8pm.

Palacio de las Bellas Artes　　Bellas Artes periodically hosts dance events, art shows, and other performances. The schedule of events is usually posted on the door if the Bellas Artes is not open. There's a public library next door. Around the corner, the Centro Cultural holds concerts and other performances; check the posters on the door to see what's scheduled.

Av. Hidalgo, 4 blocks south of the plaza. No phone.

Templo de San Cristóbal　　For the best view of San Cristóbal, climb the seemingly endless steps to this church and *mirador* (lookout point). A visit here requires stamina. There are 22 more churches in town, some of which also demand strenuous climbs.

At the very end of Calle Hermanos Domínguez.

Horseback Riding

The **Casa de Huéspedes Margarita,** Real de Guadalupe 34, and **Hotel Real del Valle** (see "Where to Stay," below) can arrange horseback rides for around 150 pesos, including a guide. Reserve your steed at least a day in advance. A horseback-riding excursion might go to San Juan Chamula, to nearby caves, or up into the hills.

The Nearby Maya Villages & Countryside

The Indian communities around San Cristóbal are fascinating worlds unto themselves. If you are unfamiliar with these indigenous cultures, you will understand and appreciate more of what you see by visiting them with a guide, at least for your first foray out into the villages. Guides are acquainted with members of the communities and are viewed with less suspicion than newcomers. These communities have their own laws and customs—and visitors' ignorance is no excuse. Entering these communities is tantamount to leaving Mexico, and if something happens, the state and federal authorities will not intervene except in case of a serious crime.

The best guided trips are the locally grown ones. Three operators go to the neighboring villages in small groups. They all charge the same price (120 pesos per person), use minivans for transportation, and speak English. They do, however, have their own interpretations and focus.

Pepe leaves from **Casa Na-Bolom** (see "Attractions in Town," above) for daily trips to San Juan Chamula and Zinacantán at 10am, returning to San Cristóbal between 2 and 3pm. Pepe looks at cultural continuities, community relationships, and religion.

Alex and Raúl can be found in front of the cathedral between 9:15 and 9:30am. They are quite personable and get along well with the Indians in the communities. They focus on cultural values and their expression in social behavior, which provides a glimpse of the details and the texture of life in these communities (and, of course, they talk about religion). Their tour is very good. They can be reached at ℂ **967/678-3741** or chamul@hotmail.com.

For excursions farther afield, see "Road Trips from San Cristóbal," later in this chapter. **271**
Also, Alex and Raúl can be contracted for trips to other communities besides Chamula and Zinacantán; talk to them.

CHAMULA & ZINACANTÁN   A side trip to the village of San Juan Chamula will get you into the spirit of life around San Cristóbal. Sunday, when the market is in full swing, is the best day to go for shopping; other days, when you'll be less impeded by eager children selling their crafts, are better for seeing the village and church.

The village, 8km (5 miles) northeast of San Cristóbal, has a large church, a plaza, and a municipal building. Each year, a new group of citizens is chosen to live in the municipal center as caretakers of the saints, settlers of disputes, and enforcers of village rules. As in other nearby villages, on Sunday local leaders wear their leadership costumes, including beautifully woven straw hats loaded with colorful ribbons befitting their high position. They solemnly sit together in a long line somewhere around the central square. Chamula is typical of other villages, in that men are often away working in the "hot lands," harvesting coffee or cacao, while women stay home to tend the sheep, the children, the cornfields, and the fires.

Don't leave Chamula without seeing the **church interior.** As you step from bright sunlight into the candlelit interior, you feel as if you've been transported to another country. Pine needles scattered amid a sea of lighted candles cover the tile floor. Saints line the walls, and before them people are often kneeling and praying aloud while passing around bottles of Pepsi-Cola. Shamans are often on hand, passing eggs over sick people or using live or dead chickens in a curing ritual. The statues of saints are similar to those you might see in any Mexican Catholic church, but beyond sharing the same name, they mean something completely different to the Chamulas. Visitors can walk carefully through the church to see the saints or stand quietly in the background.

In Zinacantán, a wealthier village than Chamula, you must sign a strict form promising *not to take any photographs* before you see the two side-by-side **sanctuaries.** Once permission is granted and you have paid a small fee, an escort will usually show you the church, or you may be allowed to see it on your own. Floors may be covered in pine needles here, too, and the rooms are brightly sunlit. The experience is an altogether different one from that of Chamula.

AMATENANGO DEL VALLE   About an hour's ride south of San Cristóbal is Amatenango, a town known mostly for its **women potters.** You'll see their work in San Cristóbal—small animals, jars, and large water jugs—but in the village, you can visit the potters in their homes. Just walk down the dirt streets. Villagers will lean over the walls of family compounds and invite you in to select from their inventory. You may even see them firing the pieces under piles of wood in the open courtyard or painting them with color derived from rusty iron water. The women wear beautiful red-and-yellow *huipiles,* but if you want to take a photograph, you'll have to pay. To get here, take a *colectivo* from the market in San Cristóbal. Before it lets you off, be sure to ask about the return-trip schedule.

AGUACATENANGO   This village, 16km (10 miles) south of Amatenango, is known for its **embroidery.** If you've visited San Cristóbal's shops, you'll recognize the white-on-white and black-on-black floral patterns on dresses and blouses for sale. The locals' own regional blouses, however, are quite different.

TENEJAPA   The **weavers** of Tenejapa, 28km (17 miles) from San Cristóbal, make some of the most beautiful and expensive work you'll see in the region. The best time to

TABASCO & CHIAPAS

9

SAN CRISTÓBAL DE LAS CASAS

visit is on market day (Sun and Thurs, though Sun is better). The weavers of Tenejapa taught the weavers of San Andrés and Magdalena—which accounts for the similarity in their designs and colors. To get to Tenejapa, try to find a *colectivo* in the very last row by the market, or hire a taxi. On Tenejapa's main street, several stores sell locally woven regional clothing, and you can bargain for the price.

THE HUITEPEC CLOUD FOREST **Pronatura,** Av. Benito Juárez 11-B (✆ **967/678-5000**), a private, nonprofit, ecological organization, offers environmentally sensitive tours of the cloud forest. The forest is a haven for **migratory birds,** and more than 100 bird species and 600 plant species have been discovered here. Guided tours run from 9am to noon Tuesday to Sunday. They cost 250 pesos per group of up to eight people. Make reservations a day in advance. To reach the reserve on your own, drive on the road to Chamula; the turnoff is at Km 3.5. The reserve is open Tuesday to Sunday from 9am to 4pm.

SHOPPING

Many Indian villages near San Cristóbal are noted for **weaving, embroidery, brocade work, leather,** and **pottery,** making the area one of the best in the country for shopping. You'll see beautiful woolen shawls, indigo-dyed skirts, colorful native shirts, and magnificently woven *huipiles,* all of which often come in vivid geometric patterns. A good place to find textiles as well as other handicrafts, besides what's mentioned below, is in and around Santo Domingo and the market. There are a lot of stalls and small shops in that neighborhood that make for interesting shopping. Working in leather, the craftspeople are artisans of the highest caliber. Tie-dyed *jaspe* from Guatemala comes in bolts and is made into clothing. The town is also known for **amber,** sold in several shops; one of the best is mentioned below.

Crafts

Casa de Artesanías Amanecer   The showroom has examples of every craft practiced in the state. It is run by the government in support of Indian crafts. You should take a look, if only to survey what crafts the region practices. It's open Monday to Friday from 9am to 9pm, Saturday 10am to 9pm, and Sunday 10am to 3pm. Niños Héroes at Hidalgo. ✆ **967/678-1180.**

El Encuentro   Noted for having reasonable prices, this shop carries many ritual items, such as new and used men's ceremonial hats, false saints, and iron rooftop adornments, plus many *huipiles* and other textiles. It's open Monday to Saturday from 9am to 8pm. Calle Real de Guadalupe 63-A (btw. Diego Dujelay and Vicente Guerrero). ✆ **967/678-3698.**

La Galería   This art gallery beneath a cafe shows the work of national and international painters. Also for sale are paintings and greeting cards by Kiki, the owner, a German artist who has found her niche in San Cristóbal. There are some Oaxacan rugs and pottery, plus unusual silver jewelry. It's open daily from 10am to 9pm. Hidalgo 3. ✆ **967/678-1547.**

Lágrimas de la Selva   "Tears of the Jungle" deals in amber and jewelry, and no other amber shop in town that I know of has the variety, quality, or artistic flair of this one. It's not a bargain hunter's turf, but a great place for the curious to go. Often you can watch the jewelers in action. Open daily from 10am to 8pm. Hidalgo 1-C (half-block south of the main square). ✆ **967/674-6348.**

Textiles

Plaza de Santo Domingo   The plazas around this church and the nearby Templo de Caridad fill with women in native garb selling their wares. Here you'll find women from Chamula weaving belts or embroidering, surrounded by piles of loomed woolen textiles from their village. Their inventory includes Guatemalan shawls, belts, and bags. There are also some excellent buys on Chiapanecan-made wool vests, jackets, rugs, and shawls, similar to those at Sna Jolobil (described below), if you take the time to look and bargain. Vendors arrive between 9 and 10am and begin to leave around 3pm. Av. Utrilla. No phone.

Sna Jolobil Meaning "weaver's house" in Mayan, this place is in the former convent (monastery) of Santo Domingo, next to the Templo de Santo Domingo. Groups of Tzotzil and Tzeltal craftspeople operate the cooperative store, which has about 3,000 members who contribute products, help run the store, and share in the moderate profits. Their works are simply beautiful; prices are high, as is the quality. It's open Monday to Saturday from 9am to 2pm and 4 to 6pm; credit cards are accepted. Calzada Lázaro Cárdenas 42 (Plaza Santo Domingo, btw. Navarro and Nicaragua). ℂ 967/678-2646.

Unión Regional de Artesanías de los Altos Also known as J'pas Joloviletic, this cooperative of weavers is smaller than Sna Jolobil (described above) and not as sophisticated in its approach to potential shoppers. It sells blouses, textiles, pillow covers, vests, sashes, napkins, baskets, and purses. It's near the market and worth looking around. Open Monday to Saturday from 9am to 2pm and 4 to 7pm, Sunday from 9am to 1pm. Av. Utrilla 43. ℂ 967/678-2848.

WHERE TO STAY

Among the most interesting places to stay in town is the seminary-turned-hotel-and-museum **Casa Na-Bolom;** see "Attractions in Town," earlier in this chapter.

Hotels in San Cristóbal are inexpensive. You can do tolerably well for $50 to $70 per night per double. Rates listed here include taxes. High season is Easter week, July, August, and December.

Moderate

Casa Felipe Flores ★★ This beautifully restored colonial house is the perfect setting for getting a feel for San Cristóbal. The patios and common rooms are relaxing and comfortable, and their architectural details are so very *coleto*. The guest rooms are nicely furnished and full of character. And they are warm in winter. The owners, Nancy and David Orr, are gracious people who enjoy sharing their appreciation and knowledge of Chiapas and the Maya. Their cook serves up righteous breakfasts.

Calle Dr. Felipe Flores 36, 29230 San Cristóbal de las Casas, Chi. ℂ/fax **967/678-3996.** www.felipeflores. com. 5 units. $95–$125 double. Rates include full breakfast. 10% service charge. No credit cards. Limited street parking. **Amenities:** Library. *In room:* No phone.

Hotel Casa Mexicana ★★ Created from a large mansion, this beautiful hotel with a colonial-style courtyard offers comfortable lodging. Rooms, courtyards, the restaurant, and the lobby are decorated in modern/traditional Mexican style, with warm tones of yellow and red. The rooms are carpeted and come with two double beds or one king-size. They have good lighting, electric heaters, and spacious bathrooms. Guests are welcome to use the sauna, and inexpensive massages can be arranged. The hotel handles a lot of large tour groups; it can be quiet and peaceful one day, full and bustling the next. There is a new addition to the hotel across the street, but I like the doubles in the original section better. This hotel is 3 blocks north of the main plaza.

28 de Agosto 1 (at Utrilla), 29200 San Cristóbal de las Casas, Chi. ℂ **967/678-1348,** -0698. Fax 967/678-2627. www.hotelcasamexicana.com. 55 units. High season $105 double, $160 junior suite, $180 suite; low season $85 double, $140 junior suite, $170 suite. AE, MC, V. Free secure parking 1½ blocks away. **Amenities:** Restaurant; bar; babysitting; room service; sauna. *In room:* TV, hair dryer (on request).

Hotel Casavieja The Casavieja is aptly named: It has a charming old feel that is San Cristóbal to a T. Originally built in 1740, it has undergone restoration and new construction faithful to the original design in essentials such as wood-beam ceilings. One nod toward modernity is carpeted floors, a welcome feature on cold mornings. The rooms also come with electric heaters. Bathrooms vary, depending on what section of the hotel you're in, but all are adequate. The hotel's restaurant, Doña Rita, faces the interior courtyard, with tables on the patio and inside, and offers good food at reasonable prices. The hotel is 3¹/₂ blocks northeast of the plaza.

María Adelina Flores 27 (btw. Cristóbal Colón and Diego Dujelay), 29200 San Cristóbal de las Casas, Chi. ℂ/fax **967/678-6868**, -0385. www.casavieja.com.mx. 39 units. 730–900 pesos double. AE, MC, V. Free parking. **Amenities:** Restaurant; bar. *In room:* TV.

Hotel El Paraíso For the independent traveler, this is a safe haven from the busloads of tour groups that can disrupt the atmosphere and service at other hotels. Rooms are small but beautifully decorated. They have comfortable beds and good reading lights; some even have a ladder to a loft holding a second bed. Bathrooms are small, too, but the plumbing is good. The entire hotel is decorated in terra cotta and blue, with beautiful wooden columns and beams supporting the roof. The hotel's restaurant, El Edén (see "Where to Dine," below), serves good food.

Av. 5 de Febrero 19, 29200 San Cristóbal de las Casas, Chi. ℂ **967/678-0085**, -5382. Fax 967/678-5168. www.hotelposadaparaiso.com. 14 units. 700–850 pesos double. AE, MC, V. No parking. **Amenities:** Restaurant; bar; room service. *In room:* TV.

Mansión de los Angeles This hotel with a good location offers good service and tidy rooms and public areas. Guest rooms are medium- size and come with either a single and a double bed or two double beds. The rooms are warmer and better lit than at most hotels in this town. They are also quiet. Some of the bathrooms are a little small. Most rooms have windows that open onto a pretty courtyard with a fountain. The rooftop sun deck is a great siesta spot.

Calle Francisco Madero 17, 29200 San Cristóbal de las Casas, Chi. ℂ **967/678-1173**, -4371. hotelangeles @prodigy.com.mx. 20 units. 550–830 pesos double. MC, V. Limited street parking. *In room:* TV.

Inexpensive

Hotel Don Quijote Rooms in this three-story hotel (no elevator) are small but quiet, carpeted, and well lit, but a little worn. All have two double beds with reading lamps over them, tiled bathrooms, and plenty of hot water. There's complimentary coffee in the mornings. It's 2¹/₂ blocks east of the plaza.

Cristóbal Colón 7 (near Real de Guadalupe), 29200 San Cristóbal de las Casas, Chi. ℂ **967/678-0920.** Fax 967/678-0346. 24 units. 300–480 pesos double. MC, V. Limited street parking. *In room:* TV.

Hotel Palacio de Moctezuma This three-story hotel has open courtyards and more greenery than others in this price range. Fresh-cut flowers tucked around tile fountains are its hallmark. The rooms have carpeting and tiled bathrooms with showers; many are quite large but, alas, can be cold in winter. The restaurant looks out on the interior courtyard. On the third floor is a solarium with comfortable tables and chairs and great city views. The hotel is 3¹/₂ blocks southeast of the main plaza.

Juárez 16 (at León), 29200 San Cristóbal de las Casas, Chi. ℂ **967/678-0352**, -1142. Fax 967/678-1536. 42 units. 360–480 pesos double. MC, V. Free limited parking. **Amenities:** Restaurant. *In room:* TV, no phone.

Hotel Real del Valle (Value) This hotel has a great location just off the main plaza. The rooms in the back three-story section have new bathrooms, big closets, and tile floors. The beds are comfortable, and the water is hot—all for a good price. In winter the rooms are a little cold. Amenities include a rooftop solarium.

Real de Guadalupe 14, 29200 San Cristóbal de las Casas, Chi. ℂ **967/678-0680.** Fax 967/678-3955. hrvalle@mundomaya.com.mx. 36 units. 280–440 pesos double. No credit cards. Free parking. In room: TV, no phone.

WHERE TO DINE

San Cristóbal is not known for its cuisine, but you can eat well at several restaurants. For baked goods, try the **Panadería La Hojaldra,** Insurgentes 14 (ℂ **967/678-4286**). It's open daily from 8am to 9:30pm. In addition to the restaurants listed below, consider making reservations for dinner at **Casa Na-Bolom** (see "Attractions in Town," earlier in this chapter).

Moderate

El Edén ★ INTERNATIONAL This is a small, quiet restaurant where the food is prepared with more devotion to the final outcome than in most restaurants in San Cristobal; most anything except Swiss rarebit is good. The meats are especially tender, and the margaritas are especially dangerous (one is all it takes). Specialties include Swiss cheese fondue for two, Edén salad, and brochette. This is where locals go for a splurge. It's 2 blocks from the main plaza.

In the Hotel El Paraíso, Av. 5 de Febrero 19. ℂ **967/678-5382.** Breakfast 50 pesos; main courses 60–150 pesos. AE, MC, V. Daily 8am–9pm.

La Paloma ★ INTERNATIONAL/MEXICAN La Paloma I particularly like in the evening because the lighting is so well done. Both the Mexican and the other dishes are much more mainstream than what you get at Los Barrios—fewer surprises. For starters, I enjoyed the quesadillas cooked Mexico City style (small fried packets of *masa* stuffed with a variety of fillings). Don't make my mistake of trying to share them with your dinner companion; it will only lead to trouble. Mexican classics include *albóndigas en chipotle* (meatballs in a thick chipotle sauce), Oaxacan black *mole,* and a variety of chiles rellenos. Avoid the *profiteroles.*

Hidalgo 3. ℂ **967/678-1547.** Main courses 80–190 pesos. MC, V. Daily 9am–midnight.

Pierre ★ FRENCH Who would have thought that you could get good French food in San Cristóbal? And yet Frenchman Pierre Niviere offers an appealing selection of traditional French dishes, simplified and tweaked for the tropical surroundings. I showed up on a Sunday, enjoyed the fixed menu, and left well satisfied.

Real de Guadalupe 73. ℂ **967/678-7211.** Main courses 75–200 pesos; Sun fixed menu 130 pesos. No credit cards. Daily 1:30–11pm.

Inexpensive

Emiliano's Moustache (Finds) MEXICAN/TACOS Like any right-thinking traveler, I initially avoided this place on account of its unpromising name and some cartoonlike figures by the door. But a conversation with some local folk overcame my prejudice and tickled my sense of irony. Sure enough, the place was crowded with *coletos* enjoying the restaurant's highly popular *comida corrida* and delicious tacos, and there wasn't a foreigner in sight. The daily menu is posted by the door; if that doesn't appeal, you can choose from a menu of taco plates (a mixture of fillings cooked together and served with tortillas and a variety of hot sauces).

Crescencio Rosas 7. (C) **967/678-7246.** Main courses 50–75 pesos; *comida corrida* 48 pesos. No credit cards. Daily 8am–midnight.

La Casa del Pan Papalotl VEGETARIAN   This place is best known for its vegetarian lunch buffet with salad bar. The vegetables and most of the grains are organic. Kippy, the owner, has a home garden and a field near town where she grows vegetables. She buys high-altitude, locally grown, organic red wheat with which she bakes her breads. These are all sourdough breads, which she likes because she feels they are easily digested and have good texture and taste. The pizzas are a popular item. The restaurant shares space with other activities in the cultural center El Puente, which has gallery space, a language school, and cinema.

Real de Guadalupe 55 (btw. Diego Dujelay and Cristóbal Colón). (C) **967/678-7215.** Main courses 70–120 pesos; lunch buffet 60–70 pesos. No credit cards. Mon–Sat 9am–10pm, lunch buffet 2–4pm.

Madre Tierra INTERNATIONAL/VEGETARIAN   A lot of vegetarians live in this town, and they have many options. This one is almost an institution in San Cristóbal. The restaurant is known for its baked goods, pastas, pizza, and quiche. They also offer fresh salads and international main courses that are safe and dependable. Good for breakfast, too. Madre Tierra is 3$^{1}/_{2}$ blocks south of the plaza.

Av. Insurgentes 19. (C) **967/678-4297.** Main courses 50–75 pesos; *comida corrida* (served after noon) 85 pesos. No credit cards. Restaurant daily 8am–9:45pm. Bakery Mon–Sat 9am–8pm; Sun 9am–2pm.

Normita's MEXICAN   Normita's is famous for its *pozole,* a hearty chicken and hominy soup to which you add a variety of things. It also offers cheap, dependable, short-order Mexican mainstays. Normita's is an informal "people's" restaurant; the open kitchen takes up one corner of the room, and tables sit in front of a large mural of a fall forest scene from some faraway place. It's 2 blocks southeast of the plaza.

Av. Juárez 6 (at Dr. José Flores). No phone. Breakfast 30–40 pesos; *pozole* 35 pesos; tacos 30 pesos. No credit cards. Daily 7am–11pm.

Restaurant Tuluc (Value) MEXICAN/INTERNATIONAL   A real bargain here is the popular *comida corrida*—it's delicious and filling. Other favorites are sandwiches and enchiladas. The house specialty is *filete Tuluc,* a beef filet wrapped around spinach and cheese served with fried potatoes and green beans; while not the best cut of meat, it's certainly priced right. The Chiapaneco breakfast is a filling quartet of juice, toast, two Chiapanecan tamales, and coffee. Tuluc also has that rarest of rarities in Mexico, a smoke-free section. The restaurant is 1$^{1}/_{2}$ blocks south of the plaza.

Av. Insurgentes 5 (btw. Cuauhtémoc and Francisco León). (C) **967/678-2090.** Breakfast 35–50 pesos; main courses 45–65 pesos; *comida corrida* (served 2–4pm) 45 pesos. No credit cards. Daily 7am–10pm.

Coffeehouses

Because Chiapas-grown coffee is highly regarded, it's not surprising that coffeehouses proliferate here. Most are concealed in the nooks and crannies of San Cristóbal's side streets. Try **Café La Selva,** Crescencio Rosas 9 ((C) **967/678-7244**), for coffee served in all its varieties and brewed from organic beans; it is open daily from 9am to 11pm. A more traditional-style cafe, where locals meet to talk over the day's news, is **Café San Cristóbal,** Cuauhtémoc 1 ((C) **967/678-3861**). It's open Monday to Saturday from 9am to 10pm, Sunday from 9am to 9pm. There is also a coffee museum with a cafe inside with the confusing name **Café Museo Café.** It's at María Adelina Flores 10 ((C) **967/678-7876**).

SAN CRISTÓBAL AFTER DARK

San Cristóbal is blessed with a variety of nightlife, both resident and migratory. There is a lot of live music, surprisingly good and varied. The bars and restaurants are cheap. And they are easy to get to: You can hit all the places mentioned here without setting foot in a cab. Weekends are best, but on any night you'll find something going on.

Almost all the clubs in San Cristóbal host Latin music of one genre or another. **El Cocodrilo** (© 967/678-1140), on the main plaza in the Hotel Santa Clara, has acoustic performers playing Latin folk music *(trova, andina)*. Relax at a table in what usually is a not-too-crowded environment. After that, your choices are varied. For Latin dance music, there's a place just a block away, on the corner of Madero and Juárez, called **Latino's** (© 967/678-9972)—good bands playing a mix of salsa, merengue, and cumbia. On weekends it gets crowded, but it has a good-size dance floor. Another club, **Blue** (© 967/678-2000), is in the opposite direction on the other side of the main square. It has live music on weekends playing salsa, reggae, and some electronic music. The place is dark and has just a bit of the urban edge to it. From there, you can walk down the pedestrian-only 20 de Noviembre to visit a couple of popular bars—**Revolución** and **El Circo.**

ROAD TRIPS FROM SAN CRISTÓBAL

For excursions to nearby villages, see "The Nearby Maya Villages & Countryside," earlier in this chapter; for destinations farther away, there are several local travel agencies. But first you should try **Alex and Raúl** (p. 270). You can also try **ATC Travel and Tours,** Calle 5 de Febrero 15, at the corner of 16 de Septiembre (© 967/678-2550; fax 967/678-3145), across from El Fogón restaurant. The agency has bilingual guides and reliable vehicles. ATC regional tours focus on birds and orchids, textiles, hiking, and camping.

Strangely, the cost of the trips includes a driver but not necessarily a bilingual guide or guided information of any kind. You pay extra for those services, so when checking prices, be sure to flesh out the details.

Palenque, Bonampak & Yaxchilán

For information on these destinations, see the section on Palenque, earlier in this chapter.

Chincultic Ruins, Comitán & Montebello National Park

Almost 160km (99 miles) southeast of San Cristóbal, near the border with Guatemala, is the **Chincultic** archaeological site and **Montebello National Park,** with 16 multicolored lakes and exuberant pine-forest vegetation. Seventy-four kilometers (46 miles) from San Cristóbal is **Comitán,** a pretty hillside town of 40,000 inhabitants known for its flower cultivation and a sugar cane–based liquor called *comitecho.* It's also the last big town along the Pan-American Highway before the Guatemalan border.

The Chincultic ruins, a late Classic site, have barely been excavated, but the main **acropolis,** high up against a cliff, is magnificent to see from below and is worth the walk up for the view. After passing through the gate, you'll see the trail ahead; it passes ruins on both sides. More unexcavated tree-covered ruins flank steep stairs leading up the mountain to the acropolis. From there, you can gaze upon distant Montebello lakes and miles of cornfields and forest. The paved road to the lakes passes six lakes, all different colors and sizes, ringed by cool pine forests; most have parking lots and lookouts. The paved road ends at a small restaurant. The lakes are best seen on a sunny day, when their famous brilliant colors are optimal.

Most travel agencies in San Cristóbal offer a daylong trip that includes the lakes, the ruins, lunch in Comitán, and a stop in the pottery-making village of Amatenango del

TABASCO & CHIAPAS

9

SAN CRISTÓBAL DE LAS CASAS

Valle. If you're driving, follow Hwy. 190 south from San Cristóbal through the pretty village of Teopisca and then through Comitán; turn left at La Trinitaria, where there's a sign to the lakes. After the Trinitaria turnoff and before you reach the lakes, there's a sign pointing left down a narrow dirt road to the Chincultic ruins.

4 TUXTLA GUTIÉRREZ

82km (51 miles) W of San Cristóbal; 277km (172 miles) S of Villahermosa; 242km (150 miles) NW of Ciudad Cuauhtémoc on the Guatemalan border

Tuxtla Gutiérrez (altitude 557m/1,827 ft.) is the commercial center of Chiapas. Coffee is the basis of the region's economy, along with recent oil discoveries. Tuxtla (pop. 350,000) is a business town, and not a particularly attractive one. For travelers, it's mainly a way station en route to San Cristóbal or the Sumidero Canyon.

ESSENTIALS
Getting There & Departing
BY PLANE　Aviacsa (℃ **01-800/284-2272** in Mexico; www.aviacsa.com) can get you to several cities in Mexico, but all flights go through Mexico City—even flights to Cancún, Chetumal, Mérida, Guatemala City, Villahermosa, and Oaxaca. **Click,** a subsidiary of Mexicana (℃ **01-800/122-5425** in Mexico; www.clickmx.com), has nonstop flights to and from Mexico City and Oaxaca.

Tuxtla's main airport is called Angel Albino Corzo (airport code: TGZ). It's 45 minutes south of the city. There is taxi service at the airport.

BY CAR　From Oaxaca, you'll enter Tuxtla by Hwy. 190. From Villahermosa, or Palenque and San Cristóbal, you'll enter at the opposite end of town on the same highway from the east. In both cases, you'll arrive at the large main square at the center of town, La Plaza Cívica (see "City Layout," below).

From Tuxtla to Villahermosa, take Hwy. 190 east past the town of Chiapa de Corzo; soon you'll see a sign for Hwy. 195 north to Villahermosa. To San Cristóbal and Palenque, take Hwy. 190 east. The road is beautiful but tortuous. It's in good repair to San Cristóbal, but there may be bad spots between San Cristóbal and Palenque. The trip from Tuxtla to Villahermosa takes 8 hours by car; the scenery is beautiful.

BY BUS　The first-class **bus station** (℃ **961/612-2624**) is at the corner of calles 2 Norte and 2 Poniente (see "City Layout," below). All bus lines serving this station and the deluxe section across the street (Uno, Maya de Oro, Cristóbal Colón, Servicios Altos) belong to the same parent company, ADO. The main station sells tickets for all buses. All buses are air-conditioned and have bathrooms. There are two levels of first class; the first-class *económico* has less legroom. Then there's deluxe, which features a few extras: slightly better seats, better movies, and free coffee and soda. There are buses every half-hour to San Cristóbal, eight buses a day to Villahermosa, three or four buses a day to Oaxaca, and five to Palenque. There's usually no need to buy a ticket ahead of time, except during holidays.

Orientation
ARRIVING　Take a taxi from the airport to town. The ADO/Cristóbal Colón bus terminal is downtown.

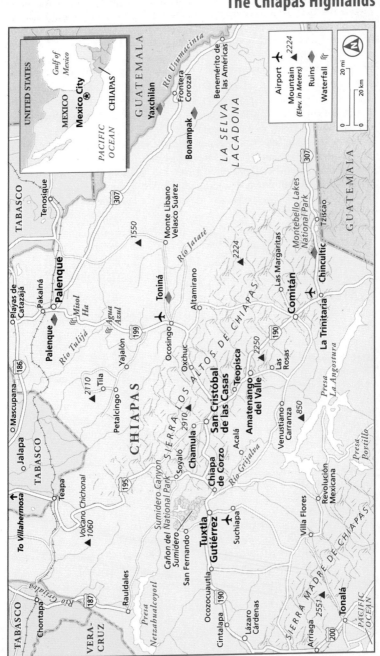

VISITOR INFORMATION The **Tourist Office** (℃ **01-800/280-3500** in Mexico, or 961/617-0550, ext. 35089) is in the Secretaría de Fomento Económico building, formerly the Plaza de las Instituciones, on Avenida Central/Bulevar Domínguez, near the Hotel Bonampak Tuxtla. It usually isn't of much help to visitors, but some of the staff at the information booths at the **international airport** (staffed when flights are due) and at the **zoo** (see below; Tues–Sun 9am–3pm and 6–9pm) can be helpful with logistics questions.

CITY LAYOUT Tuxtla is laid out on a grid. The main street, **Avenida Central,** is the east–west axis and is the artery through town for Hwy. 190. West of the central district, it's called **Bulevar Belisario Domínguez,** and in the east, it's **Bulevar Angel Albino Corzo. Calle Central** is the north–south axis. The rest of the streets have names that include one number and two directions. This tells you how to get to the street. For example, to find the street 5 Norte Poniente (5 North West), you walk 5 blocks north from the center of town and turn west (which is left). To find 3 Oriente Sur, you walk 3 blocks east from the main square and turn south. When people indicate intersections, they can shorten the names because it's redundant. The bus station is at the corner of 2 Norte and 2 Poniente.

GETTING AROUND **Buses** to all parts of the city converge upon the Plaza Cívica along Calle Central. **Taxi** fares are higher here than in other regions.

FAST FACTS The telephone **area code** is **961.** If you need medical help, the best **clinic** in town is Sanatorio Rojas, Calle 2 Sur Poniente 1847 (℃ **961/611-2079** or 612-5414).

EXPLORING TUXTLA

Most travelers simply pass through Tuxtla on their way to San Cristóbal or Oaxaca. The excellent zoo and the Sumidero Canyon are the top sights, and you might also visit the Parque Madero and its anthropology museum.

Miguel Alvarez del Toro Zoo (ZOOMAT) ★ Located in the forest called El Zapotal, ZOOMAT is one of the best zoos in Mexico. The collection of animals and birds indigenous to this area gives the visitor a tangible sense of what the wilds of Chiapas are like. The zoo keeps jaguars, howler monkeys, owls, and many more exotic animals in roomy cages that replicate their home terrain; the whole zoo is so deeply buried in vegetation that you can almost pretend you're in a natural habitat. Unlike at other zoos I've visited, the animals are almost always on view.

Bulevar Samuel León Brinois, southeast of downtown. No phone. Free admission; donations solicited. Tues–Sun 9am–5:30pm. The zoo is about 8km (5 miles) southeast of downtown; catch a bus along Av. Central and at the Calzada.

SHOPPING

The government-operated **Instituto de las Artesanías,** Bulevar Domínguez 2035 (℃ **961/612-2275**), is a shop and gallery. The two stories of rooms feature an extensive collection of crafts grouped by region and type from throughout the state of Chiapas. It's open Monday to Saturday from 10am to 8pm.

WHERE TO STAY

As Tuxtla booms, the center of the hotel industry has moved out of town, west to Hwy. 190. As you come in from the airport, you'll notice the new motel-style hotels, such as the **Hotel Flamboyán, Palace Inn, Hotel Laganja,** and **La Hacienda.** All of these are more expensive than those listed here, which are within walking distance of all the downtown attractions.

Hotel Bonampak Tuxtla   This hotel is almost a mile from the town's main square. It's one of those hotels in Mexico to which change comes slowly. This gives it character, and the place is well maintained. The furniture is an old, heavy style, but the mattresses are new and comfortable. The rooms could use a bit more light but they are of good size, with ample bathrooms and closet space.

Bulevar Domínguez 180, 29030 Tuxtla Gutiérrez, Chi. ✆ **961/602-5916.** 70 units. 900–1,220 pesos double. AE, MC, V. Free secured parking. **Amenities:** Restaurant; bar; pool; room service (until midnight). *In room:* A/C, TV.

Hotel María Eugenia   This five-story hotel on Avenida Central in the middle of town is well maintained. Rooms are medium- size, with bathrooms to match. Most of the mattresses are firm.

Av. Central 507, 29030 Tuxtla Gutiérrez, Chi. ✆ **961/613-3767** or 01-800/716-0149 in Mexico. 83 units. 850 pesos double. AE, MC, V. Free guarded parking. **Amenities:** Restaurant; bar; pool; room service; smoke-free rooms. *In room:* A/C, TV, Wi-Fi.

Hotel Regional San Marcos   For a discount hotel, this was by far the best I could find in central Tuxtla. It's in the downtown zone and very close to the *colectivos* that go to Chiapa de Corzo. Rooms are distributed on four floors (no elevator). They are medium in size but cheerful. All come with two beds: a double and a twin. The air-conditioning window units are a bit noisy, but at this rate, it's a minor inconvenience.

1 Sur Oriente 176, 29030 Tuxtla Gutiérrez, Chi. ✆ **961/613-1940,** -1887. hotelsanmarcos@prodigy.net. mx. 40 units. 500 pesos double. Anyone showing a Frommer's book receives a 10% discount. MC, V. Free parking. **Amenities:** Restaurant; bar; room service (until 11pm). *In room:* A/C, TV.

WHERE TO DINE

For a full sit-down meal, you can try local Chiapan food at **Las Pichanchas,** Av. Central Oriente 837 (✆ **961/612-5351**). It's festively decorated and pretty to look at. The emphasis is on meat, with several heavy dishes on the menu. I would recommend the *filete simojovel* (a thin steak in a not-spicy chile sauce) or the *comida grande,* which is beef in a pumpkin-seed sauce. Eating here is a cultural experience, but I usually head over to the **Flamingo,** 1 Poniente 168, just off Avenida Central (✆ **961/612-0922**), which serves standard Mexican dishes: enchiladas, *mole,* roast chicken. The restaurant is owned by a Spaniard, who also owns a decent steakhouse called El Asador Castellano, which is on the west side of town. Take a taxi.

If all you want is tacos, there are several good places around the plaza called **El Parque de la Marimba.** This plaza has free *marimba* music nightly and is enjoyable. There you'll find a couple of local taco restaurants bordering the plaza, **Parrilla Suiza** and **El Fogón Norteño.** Both have good grilled tacos. The Parque de la Marimba is on Avenida Central Poniente, 8 blocks west of the main square.

ROAD TRIPS FROM TUXTLA GUTIERREZ: CHIAPA DE CORZO & THE SUMIDERO CANYON

The real reason to stay in Tuxtla is to take a boat trip through the **Canyon of El Sumidero** ★★. The canyon is spectacular, and the boat ride is fun. Boats leave from the docks in **Chiapa de Corzo,** a colonial town of about 50,000 inhabitants that bumps up to Tuxtla. To get there, take a taxi or hop on the *colectivo* operated by Transportes Chiapa-Tuxtla (2nd Oriente at 2nd Sur; ✆ **961/616-1339**). Buses leave every half-hour from 5:30am to 9:30pm. Cost is 10 pesos. The ride takes a half-hour. Ask to get off at the main square (*parada del parque*). Chiapa de Corzo has a large main square. The two main boat cooperatives have ticket booths under the archways bordering the square. But you don't have to look for these; just go straight to the boats at the embarcadero 1¹/₂ blocks below the square.

As you pass the church of Santo Domingo, you'll see a large **ceiba** tree shading the churchyard. In better circumstances these trees get even larger than this, but this one has taken up an interesting position in front of the church. The Maya felt that these trees embodied the connection between the heavens, the world of men, and the underworld because they extend into all three realms.

The **two cooperatives** (the reds and the greens identified by the color of their boats) offer the same service. They work together sharing passengers and such. Boats leave as soon as a minimum of 12 people show up. The interval can be up to an hour or as short as 10 minutes, depending on the season. The cost is 150 pesos. The ride takes 2 hours. Besides the canyon vistas, you're likely to see some crocodiles and other things of interest. The boat's pilot will explain a few things in Spanish, but much of what he says adds little to the tour. At the deepest point in the canyon, our pilot said the walls stretch up vertically 1,000m (3,280 ft.) above the water, which, in turn, is about 100m (328 ft.) deep at that point. I wasn't about to double-check this statement—all I know is that the view was really something. There are some interesting things happening on the walls; water seeps out in places, creating little micro-environments of moss, grass, and mineral deposits. One of these places is called the Christmas Tree, for its form. Our boat glided slowly by as a fine mist fell on us from the plants.

The boats operate from 8am to 4pm. They are fast, and the water is smooth. The best times to see the canyon are early or late in the day, when the sun is at an angle and shines on one or the other of the canyon walls. The boats are necessarily open, so you should take an adjustable cap or a hat with a draw string or some sunscreen. A pair of earplugs would probably be nice to have, too, especially if they are connected to an iPod playing some kind of dramatic music to complement the rugged vistas. This river is the Grijalva, which flows to the Gulf of Mexico from Guatemala and is one of Mexico's largest.

If you'd rather stay in Chiapa de Corzo than Tuxtla, check out the simple but nice hotel off the main square: **Hotel Los Angeles,** at Av. Julián Grajales 2 (© **916/616-0048**). It offers rooms with or without air-conditioning for 300 to 400 pesos per night.

Fast Facts

1 FAST FACTS: YUCATÁN, TABASCO & CHIAPAS

BUSINESS HOURS Most businesses in larger cities are open between 9am and 7pm; in smaller towns many close between 2 and 4pm. Most close on Sunday. In resort areas stores commonly open in the mornings on Sunday, and shops stay open late, until 8 or even 10pm. Bank hours are Monday through Friday from 9 or 9:30am to anywhere between 3 and 7pm. Banks open on Saturday for at least a half-day.

DRINKING LAWS The legal drinking age in Mexico is 18; however, asking for ID or denying purchase is extremely rare. Grocery stores sell everything from beer and wine to national and imported liquors. You can buy liquor 24 hours a day, but during major elections, dry laws often are enacted by as much as 72 hours in advance of the election—and they apply to tourists as well as local residents. Mexico does not have laws that apply to transporting liquor in cars, but authorities are beginning to target drunk drivers more aggressively. It's a good idea to drive defensively.

It's illegal to drink in the street; but many tourists do. If you are getting drunk, you shouldn't drink in the street, because you are more likely to get stopped by the police.

DRIVING RULES See "Getting There & Getting Around," p. 50.

ELECTRICITY The electrical system in Mexico is 110 volts AC (60 cycles), as in the United States and Canada. In reality, however, it may cycle more slowly and overheat your appliances. To compensate, select a medium or low speed on hair dryers. Many older hotels still have electrical outlets for flat two-prong plugs; you'll need an adapter for any plug with an enlarged end on one prong or with three prongs. Many better hotels have three-hole outlets (*trifásicos* in Spanish). Those that don't may have loan adapters, but to be sure, it's always better to carry your own.

EMBASSIES & CONSULATES They provide valuable lists of doctors and lawyers, as well as regulations concerning marriages in Mexico. Contrary to popular belief, your embassy cannot get you out of jail, provide postal or banking services, or fly you home when you run out of money. Consular officers can provide advice on most matters and problems, however. Most countries have an embassy in Mexico City, and many have consular offices or representatives in the provinces.

The Embassy of the **United States** in Mexico City is at Paseo de la Reforma 305, next to the Hotel María Isabel Sheraton at the corner of Río Danubio (✆ **55/5080-2000**); hours are Monday through Friday from 8:30am to 5:30pm. Visit **http://www.usembassy-mexico.gov** for information related to U.S. Embassy services. There are U.S. Consulates at Paseo de la Victoria #3650, Ciudad Juárez (✆ 656/227-3000); Progreso 175, Col. Americana, Guadalajara (✆ 333/268-2100); Av. Constitución 411 Poniente, Monterrey (✆ 818/345-2120); Av. Tapachula 96,

Tijuana (© 664/622-7400); Calle Monterrey 141 Poiniente, Hermosillo (© 662/289-3500); Primera 200 y Azaleas, Matamoros (© 868/812-4402); Calle 60 No. 338 K x 29 y 31, Col. Acala Martin, Mérida (© 999/942-5700); Calle San Jose, Fraccionamiento "Los Alamos" Nogales, (© 631/311-8150); and Allende 3330, Col. Jardin, Nuevo Laredo (© 867/714-0512). In addition, there are consular agencies in Acapulco (© 744/469-0556 or 484-0300), Cabo San Lucas (© 624/143-3566), Cancún (© 998/883-0272), Cozumel (© 987/872-4574); Ixtapa/Zihuatanejo (© 755/553-2100), Mazatlán (© 669/916-5889), Oaxaca (© 951/516-2853 or 514-3054), Puerto Vallarta (© 322/222-0069), Reynosa © 882/823-9331), San Luis Potosí (© 444/811-7802, -7803), and San Miguel de Allende (© 415/152-2357).

The Embassy of **Canada** in Mexico City is at Schiller 529, Col. Polanco (© **55/5724-7900** or for emergencies 01-800/706-2900); it's open Monday through Friday from 9am to 1pm and 2 to 5pm. Visit www.dfait-maeci.gc.ca or www.canada.org.mx for addresses of consular agencies in Mexico. There are Canadian consulates in Acapulco (© 744/484-1305), Cancún (© 998/883-3360), Guadalajara (© 333/671-4740), Mazatlán (© 669/913-7320), Monterrey (© 818/344-2753, -3200), Oaxaca (© 951/513-3777), Puerto Vallarta (© 322/293-0098), San José del Cabo (© 624/142-4333), and Tijuana (© 664/ 684-0461)

The Embassy of **Australia** in Mexico City is at Rubén Darío 55, Col. Polanco (© **55/1101-2200;** www.mexico.embassy.gov.au). It's open Monday through Thursday from 9:30 a.m. to noon.

The Embassy of **New Zealand** in Mexico City is at Jaime Balmes 8, 4th Floor, Col. Los Morales, Polanco (© **55/5283-9460;** www.nzembassy.com/home.cfm?c=50). It's open Monday through

Thursday from 8:30am to 2pm and 3 to 5:30pm, and Friday from 8:30am to 2pm.

The Embassy of the **United Kingdom** in Mexico City is at Río Lerma 71, Col. Cuauhtémoc (© **55/5207-2089** or 5242-8500; http://ukinmexico.fco.gov.uk/en). It's open Monday through Thursday from 8am to 4pm and Friday from 8am to 1:30pm.

The Embassy of **Ireland** in Mexico City is at Cda. Boulevard Manuel Avila Camacho 76, 3rd floor, Col. Lomas de Chapultepec (© **55/5520-5803**). See www.dfa.ie/home/index.aspx?id=5495. It's open Monday through Friday from 9am to 5pm.

The **South African** Embassy in Mexico City is at Andrés Bello 10, Edificio Fórum, 9th floor, Col. Polanco (© **55/5282-9260**). It's open Monday through Friday from 8am to 4pm.

EMERGENCIES In case of emergency, dial © **060** from any phone within Mexico. Dial © **065** for the Red Cross. For police emergency numbers, turn to the "Fast Facts" sections in each of the individual chapters. The 24-hour **Tourist Help Line** in Mexico City is © **01-800/987-8224** or 55/5089-7500, or you can now simply dial © **078.** The operators don't always speak English, but they are always willing to help.

GASOLINE (PETROL) There's one government-owned brand of gas and one gasoline station name throughout the country—**Pemex** (Petroleras Mexicanas). There are two types of gas in Mexico: *magna,* 87-octane unleaded gas, and *premio,* which is 93-octane. In Mexico, fuel and oil are sold by the liter, which is slightly more than a quart (1 gal. equals about 3.8 liters). Many franchise Pemex stations have bathroom facilities and convenience stores—a great improvement over the old ones. Gas stations accept both credit and debit cards for gas purchases.

HOLIDAYS For schedules, see "Calendar of Events," in chapter 3.

INSURANCE For information on traveler's insurance, trip cancelation insurance, and medical insurance while traveling visit www.frommers.com/planning.

LANGUAGE Spanish is the official language in Mexico. English is spoken and understood to some degree in most tourist areas. Mexicans are very accommodating with foreigners who try to speak Spanish, even in broken sentences. See the appendix for a glossary of simple phrases for expressing basic needs.

MAIL Postage for a postcard or letter is 11 pesos; it may arrive anywhere from 1 to 6 weeks later. The price for registered letters and packages depends on the weight, and unreliable delivery time can take 2 to 6 weeks. The recommended way to send a package or important mail is through FedEx, DHL, UPS, or another reputable international mail service.

NEWSPAPERS & MAGAZINES The English-language newspaper the *Miami Herald* is published in conjunction with *El Universal.* You can find it at most newsstands. *The News* is a new English-language daily with Mexico-specific news, published in Mexico City. Newspaper kiosks in larger cities also carry a selection of English-language magazines.

PASSPORTS See www.frommers.com/planning for information on how to obtain a passport.

POLICE Several cities, including Cancún, have a special corps of English-speaking Tourist Police to assist with directions, guidance, and more. In case of emergency, dial © **060** from any phone within Mexico. For police emergency numbers, turn to "Fast Facts" in the individual chapters.

SMOKING See p. 60 in chapter 3.

TAXES The 15% IVA (value-added) tax applies on goods and services in most of Mexico, and it's supposed to be included in the posted price. This tax is 10% in Cancún, Cozumel, and Los Cabos. There is a 5% tax on food and drinks consumed in restaurants that sell alcoholic beverages with an alcohol content of more than 10%; this tax applies whether you drink alcohol or not. Tequila is subject to a 25% tax. Mexico imposes an exit tax on every foreigner leaving the country by plane.

TELEPHONES See p. 69 in chapter 3.

TIME Central Time prevails throughout the Yucatán, Tabasco, and Chiapas. All of Mexico observes **daylight saving time.**

TIPPING Most service employees in Mexico count on tips for the majority of their income, and this is especially true for bellboys and waiters. Bellboys should receive the equivalent of 5 to 15 pesos per bag; waiters generally receive 10% to 15%, depending on the level of service. It is not customary to tip taxi drivers, unless they are hired by the hour or provide touring or other special services.

TOILETS Public toilets are not common in Mexico, but an increasing number are available, especially at fast-food restaurants and Pemex gas stations. These facilities and restaurant and club restrooms commonly have attendants, who expect a small tip (about 5 pesos).

VISAS See p. 48 in chapter 3, "Planning Your Trip to Mexico".

VISITOR INFORMATION The **Mexico Tourism Board** (© **800/446-3942;** www.visitmexico.com) is an excellent source for general information; you can request brochures and get answers to the most common questions from the exceptionally well-trained, knowledgeable staff.

The **Mexican Government Tourist Board's** main office is in Mexico City (© **55/5278-4200**). Satellite offices are in the U.S., Canada, and the U.K. In the **United States:** Chicago (© **312/228-0517**), Houston (© **713/772-2581**), Los

Online Traveler's Toolbox

Veteran travelers usually carry some essential items to make their trips easier. Following is a selection of handy online tools to bookmark and use.

- **Regional Travel** (www.travelyucatan.com; www.yucatantoday.com; www. sac-be.com; www.cozumelmycozumel.com)
- **Regional Airports** (www.asur.com.mx)
- **Cancún Convention & Visitor's Bureau** (www.cancun.info)
- **Riviera Maya Tourism Board** (www.rivieramaya.com)
- **Yucatán Tourism Board** (www.mayayucatan.com.mx)
- **Campeche Tourism Board** (www.campeche.info)
- **Expat Life on the Peninsula** (www.locogringo.com; www.yucatanliving. com)
- **Local Government** (www.yucatan.gob.mx; www.qroo.gob.mx; www.portal. camp.gob.mx; www.chiapas.gob.mx; www.tabasco.gob.mx)
- **Travel Warnings** (www.state.gov; www.fco.gov.uk/travel; www.voyage. gc.ca; www.smartraveller.gov.au)

Angeles (© 310/282-9112), Miami (© 786/621-2909), and New York (© 212/308-2110).

In **Canada:** Toronto (© 416/925-0704). In the **United Kingdom:** London (© 020/7488-9392).

The **Chiapas Tourism Board** is at Blvd. Belisario Dominguez 950, CP29060 Tuxtla Gutiérrez, Chiapas (© 961/613-9396). The **Quintana Roo Tourist Board** is at Carr. a. Calderitas 622, CP77010 Chetumal, Quintana Roo, (© 983/835-0860). The **Tabasco Tourism Board** is at Av. Los Rios s/n, Tabasco 2000, CP86035 Villahermosa, Tabasco (© 993/316-5134). The **Yucatán Tourism Board** is at Calle 59 No. 514, Centro, CP97000 Mérida, Yucatán (© 999/924-9389).

The **Mexican Embassy** in the **United States** is at 1911 Pennsylvania Ave. NW, Washington, DC 20006 (© 202/728-1600).

The **Mexican Embassy** in **Canada** is at 055 Rue Peel, Ste. 1000, Montreal, QUE, H3A 1V4 (© 514/288-2502); Commerce Court West, 199 Bay St., Suite 4440, Toronto, ON, M5L 1E9 (© 416/684-3522); 411-117 W. Hastings Street, 4th Floor, Vancouver, BC, V6E2K3 (© 604/684-1859); and 1500-45 O'Connor St., Ottawa, ON, K1P 1A4 (© 613/233-8988; fax 613/235-9123).

The **Mexican Embassy** (Consular Section) in the **United Kingdom** is at 16 Georges Dr., London, W1S1FD (© 020/7235-6393).

WATER Tap water in Mexico is generally not potable and it is safest to drink purified bottled water. Some hotels and restaurants purify their water, but you should ask rather than assume this is the case. Ice may also come from tap water and should be used with caution.

2 AIRLINE, HOTEL & CAR RENTAL WEBSITES

MAJOR AIRLINES

AeroMéxico
www.aeromexico.com

Alaska Airlines/Horizon Air
www.alaskaair.com

American Airlines
www.aa.com

British Airways
www.british-airways.com

Continental Airlines
www.continental.com

Delta Air Lines
www.delta.com

Iberia Airlines
www.iberia.com

North American Airlines
www.flynaa.com

Northwest Airlines/KLM
www.nwa.com

United Airlines
www.united.com

US Airways
www.usairways.com

Virgin America
www.virginamerica.com

Virgin Atlantic Airways
www.virgin-atlantic.com

BUDGET AIRLINES

Click Mexicana
www.clickmx.com

Frontier Airlines
www.frontierairlines.com

Interjet
www.interjet.com.mx

JetBlue Airways
www.jetblue.com

Volaris
www.volaris.com.mx

MAJOR HOTEL & MOTEL CHAINS

Best Western International
www.bestwestern.com

Courtyard by Marriott
www.marriott.com/courtyard

Crowne Plaza Hotels
www.ichotelsgroup.com/crowneplaza

Embassy Suites
www.embassysuites.com

Four Seasons
www.fourseasons.com

Hilton Hotels
www.hilton.com

Holiday Inn
www.holidayinn.com

Hyatt
www.hyatt.com

InterContinental Hotels & Resorts
www.ichotelsgroup.com

Marriott
www.marriott.com

Omni Hotels
www.omnihotels.com

Radisson Hotels & Resorts
www.radisson.com

FAST FACTS

AIRLINE, HOTEL & CAR RENTAL WEBSITES

Ramada Worldwide
www.ramada.com

Renaissance
www.renaissancehotels.com

Sheraton Hotels & Resorts
www.starwoodhotels.com/sheraton

Westin Hotels & Resorts
www.starwoodhotels.com/westin

Wyndham Hotels & Resorts
www.wyndham.com

CAR RENTAL AGENCIES

Advantage
www.advantage.com

Alamo
www.alamo.com

Auto Europe
www.autoeurope.com

Avis
www.avis.com

Budget
www.budget.com

Dollar
www.dollar.com

Enterprise
www.enterprise.com

Hertz
www.hertz.com

Kemwel (KHA)
www.kemwel.com

National
www.nationalcar.com

Thrifty
www.thrifty.com

Appendix: Survival Spanish

Most Mexicans are very patient with foreigners who try to speak their language; it helps a lot to know a few basic phrases. Included here are simple phrases for expressing basic needs, followed by some common menu items.

1 ENGLISH-SPANISH PHRASES

English	Spanish	Pronunciation
Good day	**Buen día**	Bwehn *dee*-ah
Good morning	**Buenos días**	*Bweh*-nohs *dee*-ahs
How are you?	**¿Cómo está?**	*Koh*-moh eh-*stah*
Very well	**Muy bien**	Mwee byehn
Thank you	**Gracias**	*Grah*-syahs
You're welcome	**De nada**	Deh *nah*-dah
Goodbye	**Adiós**	Ah-*dyohs*
Please	**Por favor**	Pohr fah-*bohr*
Yes	**Sí**	See
No	**No**	Noh
Excuse me	**Perdóneme**	Pehr-*doh*-neh-meh
Give me	**Déme**	*Deh*-meh
Where is . . . ?	**¿Dónde está . . . ?**	*Dohn*-deh eh-*stah*
the station	**la estación**	lah eh-stah-*syohn*
a hotel	**un hotel**	oon oh-*tehl*
a gas station	**una gasolinera**	*oo*-nah gah-soh-lee-*neh*-rah
a restaurant	**un restaurante**	oon res-tow-*rahn*-teh
the toilet	**el baño**	el *bah*-nyoh
a good doctor	**un buen médico**	oon bwehn *meh*-dee-coh
the road to . . .	**el camino a/hacia**	el cah-*mee*-noh ah/*ah*-syah
To the right	**A la derecha**	Ah lah deh-*reh*-chah
To the left	**A la izquierda**	Ah lah ees-*kyehr*-dah
Straight ahead	**Derecho**	Deh-*reh*-choh
I would like	**Quisiera**	Key-*syeh*-rah
I want	**Quiero**	*Kyeh*-roh
to eat	**comer**	koh-*mehr*
a room	**una habitación**	*oo*-nah ah-bee-tah-*syohn*

English	Spanish	Pronunciation
Do you have . . . ?	¿Tiene usted . . . ?	Tyeh-neh oo-*sted*
a book	un libro	oon *lee*-broh
a dictionary	un diccionario	oon deek-syoh-*nah*-ryoh
How much is it?	¿Cuánto cuesta?	*Kwahn*-toh *kweh*-stah
When?	¿Cuándo?	*Kwahn*-doh
What?	¿Qué?	Keh
There is (Is there . . . ?)	(¿)Hay (. . . ?)	Eye
What is there?	¿Qué hay?	Keh eye
Yesterday	Ayer	Ah-*yer*
Today	Hoy	Oy
Tomorrow	Mañana	Mah-*nyah*-nah
Good	Bueno	*Bweh*-noh
Bad	Malo	*Mah*-loh
Better (best)	(Lo) Mejor	(Loh) Meh-*hohr*
More	Más	Mahs
Less	Menos	*Meh*-nohs
No smoking	Se prohibe fumar	Seh proh-*ee*-beh foo-*mahr*
Postcard	Tarjeta postal	Tar-*heh*-tah poh-*stahl*
Insect repellent	Repelente contra insectos	Reh-peh-*lehn*-teh *cohn*-trah een-*sehk*-tohs

MORE USEFUL PHRASES

English	Spanish	Pronunciation
Do you speak English?	¿Habla usted inglés?	*Ah*-blah oo-*sted* een-*glehs*
Is there anyone here who speaks English?	¿Hay alguien aquí que hable inglés?	Eye *ahl*-gyehn ah-*kee* keh *ah*-bleh een-*glehs*
I speak a little Spanish.	Hablo un poco de español.	*Ah*-bloh oon *poh*-koh deh eh-spah-*nyohl*
I don't understand Spanish very well.	No (lo) entiendo muy bien el español.	Noh (loh) ehn-*tyehn*-doh mwee byehn el eh-spah-*nyohl*
The meal is good.	Me gusta la comida.	Meh *goo*-stah lah koh-*mee*-dah
What time is it?	¿Qué hora es?	Keh *oh*-rah ehs
May I see your menu?	¿Puedo ver el menú (la carta)?	*Pweh*-doh vehr el meh-*noo* (lah *car*-tah)
The check, please.	La cuenta, por favor.	Lah *kwehn*-tah pohr fa-*borh*
What do I owe you?	¿Cuánto le debo?	*Kwahn*-toh leh *deh*-boh
What did you say?	¿Mande? (formal)	*Mahn*-deh
	¿Cómo? (informal)	*Koh*-moh

English	Spanish	Pronunciation
I want (to see) . . .	Quiero (ver) . . .	*kyeh*-roh (vehr)
a room	un cuarto or	oon *kwar*-toh,
	una habitación	*oo*-nah ah-bee-tah-*syohn*
for two persons	para dos personas	*pah*-rah dohs pehr-*soh*-nahs
with (without) bathroom	con (sin) baño	kohn (seen) *bah*-nyoh
We are staying here only . . .	Nos quedamos aquí solamente . . .	Nohs keh-*dah*-mohs ah-*kee* soh-lah-*mehn*-teh
one night.	una noche.	*oo*-nah *noh*-cheh
one week.	una semana.	*oo*-nah seh-*mah*-nah
We are leaving . . .	Partimos (Salimos) . . .	Pahr-*tee*-mohs (sah-*lee*-mohs)
tomorrow.	mañana.	mah-*nya*-nah
Do you accept . . . ?	¿Acepta usted . . . ?	Ah-*sehp*-tah oo-*sted*
traveler's checks?	cheques de viajero?	*cheh*-kehs deh byah-*heh*-roh
Is there a	¿Hay una	Eye *oo*-nah
laundromat . . . ?	lavandería . . . ?	lah-*bahn*-deh-*ree*-ah
near here?	cerca de aquí?	*sehr*-kah deh ah-*kee*
Please send these clothes to the laundry.	Hágame el favor de mandar esta ropa a la lavandería.	*Ah*-gah-meh el fah-*bohr* deh mahn-*dahr* eh-stah *roh*-pah a lah lah-*bahn*-deh-*ree*-ah

NUMBERS

1 uno (*ooh*-noh)
2 dos (dohs)
3 tres (trayss)
4 cuatro (*kwah*-troh)
5 cinco (*seen*-koh)
6 seis (sayss)
7 siete (*syeh*-tay)
8 ocho (*oh*-choh)
9 nueve (*nway*-bay)
10 diez (dee-ess)
11 once (*ohn*-say)
12 doce (*doh*-say)
13 trece (*tray*-say)
14 catorce (kah-*tor*-say)
15 quince (*keen*-say)
16 dieciseis (de-*ess*-ee-sayss)

17 diecisiete (de-*ess*-ee-*syeh*-tay)
18 dieciocho (dee-*ess*-ee-*oh*-choh)
19 diecinueve (dee-*ess*-ee-*nway*-bay)
20 veinte (*bayn*-tay)
30 treinta (*trayn*-tah)
40 cuarenta (kwah-*ren*-tah)
50 cincuenta (seen-*kwen*-tah)
60 sesenta (say-*sen*-tah)
70 setenta (say-*ten*-tah)
80 ochenta (oh-*chen*-tah)
90 noventa (noh-*ben*-tah)
100 cien (see-*en*)
200 doscientos (*dos*-se-en-tos)
500 quinientos (keen-ee-*ehn*-tos)
1,000 mil (meal)

TRANSPORTATION TERMS

English	Spanish	Pronunciation
airport	Aeropuerto	Ah-eh-roh-*pwehr*-toh
flight	Vuelo	*Bweh*-loh

English	Spanish	Pronunciation
rental car	**Arrendadora de autos**	Ah-*rehn*-da-doh-rah deh *ow*-tohs
bus	**Autobús**	Ow-toh-*boos*
bus or truck	**Camión**	Ka-*myohn*
lane	**Carril**	Kah-*reel*
nonstop (bus)	**Directo**	Dee-*rehk*-toh
baggage (claim area)	**Equipajes**	Eh-kee-*pah*-hehss
intercity	**Foraneo**	Foh-rah-*neh*-oh
luggage storage area	**Guarda equipaje**	*Gwar*-dah eh-kee-*pah*-heh
arrival gates	**Llegadas**	Yeh-*gah*-dahss
originates at this station	**Local**	Loh-*kahl*
originates elsewhere	**De paso**	Deh *pah*-soh
Are seats available?	**Hay lugares disponibles?**	Eye loo-*gah*-rehs dis-pohn-*ee*-blehss
first class	**Primera**	Pree-*meh*-rah
second class	**Segunda**	Seh-*goon*-dah
nonstop (flight)	**Sin escala**	Seen ess-*kah*-lah
baggage claim area	**Recibo de equipajes**	Reh-*see*-boh deh eh-kee-*pah*-hehss
waiting room	**Sala de espera**	*Sah*-lah deh ehss-*peh*-rah
toilets	**Sanitarios**	Sah-nee-*tah*-ryohss
ticket window	**Taquilla**	Tah-*kee*-yah2 Dining Terminology

MEALS

desayuno   breakfast
comida   main meal of the day, taken in the afternoon
cena   supper

COURSES

botana   a small serving of food that accompanies a beer or drink, usually served free of charge
entrada   appetizer
sopa   soup course (Not necessarily a soup—it can be a dish of rice or noodles, called *sopa seca* [dry soup].)
ensalada   salad
plato fuerte   main course
postre   dessert
comida corrida   inexpensive daily special usually consisting of three courses
menú del día   same as *comida corrida*

DEGREE OF DONENESS

término un cuarto   rare, literally means one-fourth
término medio   medium rare, one-half
término tres cuartos   medium, three-fourths
bien cocido   well-done

Note: Keep in mind, when ordering a steak, that *medio* does not mean "medium."

cucharra spoon
cuchillo knife
la cuenta the bill
plato plate
plato hondo bowl
propina tip
servilleta napkin
tenedor fork
vaso glass
IVA value-added tax
fonda Strictly speaking, a food stall in the market or street, but now used in a loose or nostalgic sense to designate an informal restaurant.

POPULAR MEXICAN & YUCATECAN DISHES

A la tampiqueña (Usually *bistec a la t.* or *arrachera a la t.*) A steak served with several sides, including but not limited to an enchilada, guacamole, rice, and beans.

Achiote Small red seed of the *annatto* tree, with mild flavor, used for both taste and color.

Adobo Marinade made with chiles and tomatoes, often seen in adjectival form *adobo/adobada.*

Agua fresca Any sweetened fruit-flavored water, including *limonada* (limeade), *horchata* (see below), *tamarindo* (see below), *sandía* (watermelon), and *melón* (cantaloupe).

Alambre Brochette.

Albóndigas Meatballs, usually cooked in a *chile chipotle* sauce.

Antojito Literally means "small temptation." It's a general term for tacos, *tostadas, quesadillas,* and the like, which are usually eaten for supper or as a snack.

Arrachera Skirt steak, fajitas.

Arroz Rice.

Atole A thick, hot drink made with finely ground corn and flavored with fruit usually, but also can be flavored with chile, chocolate, or spices.

Bistec Steak.

Bolillo Small bread with a crust much like a baguette.

Buñuelos Fried pastry dusted with sugar. Can also mean a large, thin, crisp pancake that is dipped in boiling cane syrup.

Café con leche Hot coffee with milk. In cheap restaurants, often made with powdered instant coffee.

Cajeta Thick caramel sauce made from goat's milk.

Calabaza Zucchini squash.

Caldo tlalpeño Chicken and vegetable soup, with rice, *chile chipotle, avocado,* and garbanzos. Its name comes from a suburban community of Mexico City, Tlalpan.

Caldo xochitl Mild chicken and rice soup served with a small plate of chopped onion, chile serrano, avocado, and limes, to be added according to individual taste.

Camarones Shrimp. For common cooking methods, see **pescado.**

Carne Meat.

Carnitas Slow-cooked pork dish from Michoacán and parts of central Mexico, served with tortillas, guacamole, and salsa or pickled jalapeños.

Cebolla Onion.

Cecina   Thinly sliced pork or beef, dried or marinated, depending on the region.

Ceviche   Fresh raw seafood marinated in fresh lime juice and garnished with chopped tomatoes, onions, chiles, and sometimes cilantro.

Chalupas poblanas   Simple dish from Puebla consisting of handmade tortillas lightly fried but left soft, and topped with different chile sauces.

Chayote   A type of spiny squash boiled and served as an accompaniment to meat dishes.

Chilaquiles   Fried tortilla quarters softened in either a red or a green sauce and served with Mexican sour cream, onion, and sometimes chicken *(con pollo)*.

Chile   Any of the many hot peppers used in Mexican cooking, in fresh, dried, or smoked forms.

Chile ancho   A dried *chile poblano,* which serves as the base for many varieties of sauces and *moles.*

Chile chilpotle (or **chipotle**)   A smoked jalapeño sold dried or canned in an *adobo* sauce.

Chile en nogada   *Chile poblano* stuffed with a complex filling of shredded meat, nuts, and dried, candied, and fresh fruit, topped with walnut cream sauce and a sprinkling of pomegranate seeds.

Chile poblano   Fresh pepper that is usually dark green in color, large, and not usually spicy. Often stuffed with a variety of fillings *(chile relleno).*

Chile relleno   Stuffed pepper.

Chimichurri   Argentine sauce made with olive oil, oregano, parsley, and garlic, served with grilled meats.

Chivo   Kid or goat.

Churro   Fried pastry dusted with sugar and served plain or filled. The Spanish equivalent of a donut.

Cochinita pibil   Yucatecan dish of pork, pit-baked in a *pibil* sauce of *achiote,* sour orange, and spices.

Col   Cabbage. Also called *repollo.*

Consomé   Clear broth, usually with rice.

Cortes   Another way of saying steaks; in full, it is *cortes finas de carne* (fine cuts of meat).

Cuitlacoche   Variant of *huitlacoche.*

Elote   Fresh corn.

Empanada   For most of Mexico, a turnover with a savory or sweet filling. In Oaxaca and southern Mexico, it is corn masa or a tortilla folded around a savory filling and roasted or fried.

Empanizado   Breaded.

Enchilada   A lightly fried tortilla, dipped in sauce and folded or rolled around a filling. It has many variations, such as *enchiladas suizas* (made with a cream sauce), enchiladas del portal or enchiladas placeras (made with a predominantly *chile ancho* sauce), and enchiladas verdes (in a green sauce of tomatillos, cilantro, and chiles).

Enfrijoladas   Like an enchilada, but made with a bean sauce flavored with toasted avocado leaves.

Enmoladas   Enchiladas made with a *mole* sauce.

Entomatadas   Enchiladas made with a tomato sauce.

Ensalada   Salad.

Escabeche   Vegetables pickled in a vinegary liquid.

Fideo   Angel hair pasta.

Flan   Custard.

Flautas   Tortillas that are rolled up around a filling (usually chicken or shredded beef) and deep- fried; often listed on a menu as *taquitos* or *tacos fritos.*

Frijoles refritos   Beans mashed and cooked with lard.

Gorditas   Thick, fried corn tortillas, slit open and stuffed with meat or cheese filling.

Horchata   Drink made of ground rice, melon seeds, ground almonds, or coconut and cinnamon.

Huazontle   A vegetable vaguely comparable to broccoli, but milder in taste.

Huevos mexicanos   Scrambled eggs with chopped onions, *chiles serranos,* and tomatoes.

Huevos rancheros   Fried eggs, usually placed on tortillas and bathed in a light tomato sauce.

Huitlacoche   Salty and mild-tasting corn fungus that is considered a delicacy in Mexico.

Jitomate   Tomato.

Lechuga   Lettuce.

Limón   A small lime. Mexicans squeeze these limes on everything from soups to tacos.

Lomo adobado   Pork loin cooked in an ***adobo.***

Masa   Soft dough made of corn that is the basis for making tortillas and tamales.

Menudo   Soup made with beef tripe and hominy.

Milanesa   Beef cutlet breaded and fried.

Molcajete   A three-legged mortar made of volcanic stone and used for grinding. Often used now as a cooking dish that is brought to the table steaming hot and filled with meat, chiles, onions, and cheese.

Mole   Any variety of thick sauce made with dried chiles, nuts, fruits or vegetables, and spices. Variations include *m. poblano* (Puebla style, with chocolate and sesame), *m. negro* (black *mole* from Oaxaca, also with chocolate), and *m. verde* (made with herbs and/or pumpkin seeds, depending on the region).

Pan   Bread. A few of the varieties include *p. dulce* (general term for a variety of sweet breads), *p. de muerto* (bread made for the Day of the Dead holidays), and *p. Bimbo* (packaged sliced white bread).

Panuchos   A Yucatecan dish of *masa* cakes stuffed with refried black beans and topped with shredded turkey or chicken, lettuce, and onion.

Papas   Potatoes.

Papadzules   A Yucatecan dish of tortillas stuffed with hard-boiled eggs and topped with a sauce made of pumpkin seeds.

Parrillada   A sampler platter of grilled meats or seafood.

Pescado   Fish. Common ways of cooking fish include *al mojo de ajo* (pan seared with oil and garlic), *a la veracruzana* (with tomatoes, olives, and capers), and *al ajillo* (seared with garlic and fine strips or rings of *chile guajillo*).

Pibil   See ***cochinita pibil.*** When made with chicken, it is called *pollo pibil.*

Picadillo   Any of several recipes using shredded beef, pork, or chicken and onions, chiles, and spices. Can also contain fruits and nuts.

Pipián   A thick sauce made with ground pumpkin seeds, nuts, herbs, and chiles. Can be red or green.

Poc chuc   Pork with onion marinated in sour orange and then grilled; a Yucatecan dish.

Pollo   Chicken.

Pozole   Soup with chicken or pork, hominy, lettuce, and radishes, served with a small plate of other ingredients to be added according to taste (onion, pepper, lime juice, oregano). In Jalisco it's red *(p. rojo)*, in Michoacán it's clear *(p. blanco)*, and in Guerrero it's green *(p. verde)*. In the rest of Mexico, it can be any one of these.

Puerco   Pork.

Pulque   A drink made of fermented juice of the maguey plant; most common in the states of Hidalgo, Tlaxcala, Puebla, and Mexico.

Quesadilla   Corn or flour tortillas stuffed with white cheese and cooked on hot griddle. In Mexico City, it is made with raw masa folded around any of a variety of fillings (often containing no cheese) and deep- fried.

Queso   Cheese.

Res   Beef.

Rompope   Mexican liqueur, made with eggs, vanilla, sugar, and alcohol.

Salbute   A Yucatecan dish much like a *panucho*, but without bean paste in the middle.

Solomillo   Filet mignon.

Sopa azteca   Tortilla soup.

Sopa tarasca   A blended soup from Michoacán made with beans and tomatoes.

Sope   Small fried masa cake topped with savory meats and greens.

Tacos al pastor   Small tacos made with thinly sliced pork marinated in an *adobo* and served with pineapple, onion, and cilantro.

Tallarines   Noodles.

Tamal   (Not "tamale.") *Masa* mixed with lard and beaten until light and folded around a savory or sweet filling, and encased in a cornhusk or a plant leaf (usually corn or banana) and then steamed. *Tamales* is the plural form.

Taquitos   See *flautas.*

Tinga   Shredded meat stewed in a *chile chipotle* sauce.

Torta   A sandwich made with a bolillo.

INDEX

See also Accommodations and Restaurant indexes, below.

GENERAL INDEX

Academic trips and language classes, 67–68
Acanceh, 219
Accommodations, 70–71, 287–288. *See also* Accommodations Index
  Akumal, 167–168
  best, 11–13
  best places to get away from it all, 9
  Campeche, 234–235
  Cancún
    Ciudad Cancún, 99–100
    Isla Cancún, 92–99
    prices, 94
  Chetumal, 182–183
  Chichén Itzá, 241–242
  Cozumel, 138–141
  green-friendly, 67
  Isla Mujeres, 123–125
  Majahual, 179–180
  Mérida and environs, 198–204
    haciendas, 200–201
  Ocosingo, 263
  Paamul, 165
  Palenque, 259–260
  Playa del Carmen, 156–160
  Puerto Aventuras, 166
  Puerto Morelos and vicinity, 150–153
  Río Bec area, 184–185
  Río Lagartos, 246
  San Cristóbal, 273–275
  Tulum, 172–174
  Tuxtla Gutiérrez, 280–281
  Uxmal, 223–224
  Valladolid, 245
  Villahermosa, 253–254
Achiote, 31
Active vacations, best, 8
Adobo, 212
ADO buses (Cozumel), 131
ADO/Cristóbal Colón (Palenque), 257

Adventure trips, 68
Aerolitoral
  Mérida, 192
  Villahermosa, 250
AeroMéxico, 52
  Campeche, 230
  Cancún, 86
  Mérida, 192
  Villahermosa, 250
Agua Azul waterfalls, 263
Aguacatenango, 264, 271
Aguas frescas, 30
AIM-Adventures in Mexico, 64
A(H1N1) influenza (swine flu), 1, 57
Air Ambulance, 90
Airport taxes, 53
Air travel, 50, 52–53, 287. *See also specific airlines*
  Campeche, 230
  Cancún, 86
  Chetumal, 181
  Cozumel, 128–129
  Mérida, 192, 195
  Playa del Carmen, 154
  Tuxtla Gutiérrez, 278
  Villahermosa, 250, 252
AITO (Association of Independent Tour Operators), 67
Akab Dzib (Temple of Obscure Writing; Chichén Itzá), 241
Aktun Chen, 168
Akumal, 146, 167–168
Akumal Dive Adventures, 167
Akumal Dive Shop
  Playa del Carmen, 148
  Puerto Aventuras, 167
Akumal Vacations, 167
Alacrán (scorpion), 59
Alamo, 87
Alaska Airlines, Cancún, 86
Allende, Ignacio, 23
All-inclusive resorts. *See also* Accommodations
  Riviera Maya, 162
  Xpu-Ha, 166
All Sports Bar (Cozumel), 144

Alltournative (Riviera Maya), 149
Alma Libre (Puerto Morelos), 152
Alpargatas, 244
Altitude sickness, 58–59
Alux (Playa del Carmen), 163
AMAT (Cancún), 90
Amate Books (Mérida), 197
Amatenango del Valle, 264, 271
Ambriz, Dr. G., 156
American Airlines (Cancún), 86
American Cetacean Society, 66
AMTAVE (Asociación Mexicana de Turismo de Aventura y Ecoturismo, A.C.), 68
Anexo Este (Chichén Itzá), 241
"Angeles Verdes," 53
Animal-rights issues, 66, 67
Año Nuevo, 44
Anthropology museums
  best, 9–10
  Museo de la Cultura Maya (Chetumal), 181, 182
  Museo Regional de Antropología (Mérida), 210, 211
  Museo Regional de Antropología Carlos Pellicer Cámara (Villahermosa), 10, 252–253
  Villahermosa, 252–253
Aquarius Travel Fishing (Cozumel), 134
Aqua Safari (Cozumel), 133
Aquaworld (Cancún), 107, 108
Aqua World (Cozumel), 134
Archaeological Conservancy, 68
Archaeological museums and exhibits
  Museo de la Cultura Maya (Chetumal), 181, 182
  Museo del Pueblo Maya (Dzibilchaltún), 216–217

Archaeological sites and ruins
Acanceh, 219
Balamkú, 189
Becán, 187
best, 5, 8
Bonampak, 8, 262
Calakmul, 5, 188–189, 229
Chicanná, 187–188
Chichén Itzá, 236
Chincultic, 277
Cobá, 176–177
Comalcalco, 255–256
Cozumel, 137
Dzibanché (Tzibanché), 185–186
Dzibilchaltún, 73, 191, 216–217
Edzná, 228–229
Ek Balam, 8, 148, 246
Isla Mujeres, 122
Kabah, 224–225
Kinichná, 186
Kohunlich, 186
Labná, 226
Mayapán, 219
Muyil, 177
Palenque, 8, 257–259
Puuc Maya Route, 224–229
Río Bec area, 177, 180–185, 229
Riviera Maya, 148
Sayil, 226
side trips from Chetumal to, 183–189
suggested itineraries, 77–84
Tecoh, 219
Toniná, 263–264
tours, 68, 149
Tulum, 5, 8, 146, 148, 170–172
Uxmal, 221–223
Xcambó, 217
Xpujil, 187
Yaxchilán, 262
Architecture, 33–35
books about, 39
Art, 33, 35
books about, 39
tours, 68
Arts and crafts. *See* Crafts
Ash Wednesday, 45
Association of Independent Tour Operators (AITO), 67
Assumption of the Virgin Mary, 46
ATC Tours and Travel, 68, 277
Atlantis Submarines
Cancún, 109–110
Cozumel, 134

ATMs (automated teller machines), 56
ATV (all-terrain-vehicle) jungle tours, 109
Australia
customs regulations, 49
Embassy of, 284
sustainable tourism, 67
Autobuses Riviera (Playa del Carmen), 155
Auto insurance, 51–52, 54
Avenida Juárez (Playa del Carmen), 156
Aventuras XTC (Xcalak), 178
Aviación de Chiapas (Villahermosa), 250
Aviacsa, 52
Cancún, 86
Chetumal, 181
Mérida, 192
Tuxtla Gutiérrez, 278
Avis, 87
Cozumel, 131
Avocado, 28
Ayuntamiento (Palacio Municipal; Mérida), 208
Aztecs, 22

Bacab, 36
Bacalar, 180–181
Bacalar Lake, 180–181
Bahía Dive Shop (Isla Mujeres), 120
Baird, David, 61
Balam, 36
Balamkú, 189
Balankanché, Cave of (near Chichén Itzá), 243–244
Ball court (*juego de pelota***)**
Chichén Itzá, 238
Cobá, 176
Palenque, 259
Uxmal, 222
Baluarte de la Soledad (Campeche), 232
Baluarte de San Carlos/ Museo de la Ciudad (Campeche), 232–233
Baluarte de Santiago (Campeche), 233
Banderas reef, 120
Banks, 56
Barcos México, 129
Bargaining, tips on, 10
Bar Hopper Tour (Cancún), 112
Bazaar de Artesanías (Mérida), 212

Beaches. *See also specific beaches*
best beach vacations, 4–5
Cancún, 4, 106
Cozumel, 4, 136–137
Isla Holbox, 247
Isla Mujeres, 4, 119–120
Paamul, 165
Playa del Carmen, 4
Puerto Morelos, 151
Tulum, 5, 171, 172
Xpu-Ha, 166–167
Becán, 184, 187
Beer, 31
Beverages, 30–31
Biking and bike rentals
Isla Mujeres, 116, 118
San Cristóbal, 267
Tulum, 171
Biodegradable sunscreen, 65
Birds and bird-watching, 8, 37
Celestún National Wildlife Refuge, 215–216
Huitepec Cloud Forest, 272
Yucatán Bird Festival (Festival de las Aves de Yucatán), 46
Black beans, 28
Bling (Cancún), 113
Blue (San Cristóbal), 277
Blue Parrot (Playa del Carmen), 163
Blue Ray (Cancún), 108
Boat excursions and cruises. *See also* Ferries
Cancún, 108–110
Chiapa de Corzo and Sumidero Canyon, 281–282
Cozumel, 134
dinner cruises (Cancún), 100
BOB Submarines (Cancún), 107
Boca Paila Fishing Lodge (between Tulum and Punta Allen), 148
Bonampak, 8, 262
Books, recommended, 39–40, 185
Bookstores
Mérida, 197
San Cristóbal, 268
Bribes and scams, 62
Brisas Hotels & Resorts, 70
Buceo Médico Mexicano (Cozumel), 132
Budget, 87
Bugs and bites, 59
Buho's (Isla Mujeres), 127

Bullfighting, 66
Bus hijackings, 54
Business hours, 283
Bus tours, Mérida, 207
Bus travel, 52, 55, 62
    Campeche, 230
    Cancún, 87–89
    Chetumal, 182
    Chichén Itzá, 237
    Cozumel, 131
    Maya heartland, 190
    Mérida, 194–195, 197
    Palenque, 257
    Playa del Carmen, 155
    San Cristóbal, 266
    Tuxtla Gutiérrez, 278
    Uxmal, 221
    Valladolid, 244
    Villahermosa, 250, 252

Cabs. See Taxis
Calakmul, 5, 188–189, 229
Calakmul Biosphere Reserve, 73, 189
Calderón, Felipe, 25–26
Calendar of events, 44–47
The California Native, 68
Calle 60 (Mérida), 210
Calmecac, 70
Cambios Portales (Mérida), 197–198
CAME bus station (Mérida), 194
Campeche, 192, 229–236
    en route to, 228–229
Canada
    consulate, Cancún, 89
    customs regulations, 49
    Embassy of, 284
    sustainable tourism, 67
    visitor information in, 286
Cancún, 85–114
    accommodations, 91–100
        Ciudad Cancún, 99–100
        Isla Cancún, 92–99
        prices, 94
    area code, 89
    average temperatures, 44
    beaches, 4, 106
    brief description of, 72
    climate, 89
    consulates, 89
    crime, 90
    currency exchange, 90
    drugstores, 90
    emergencies, 90
    finding an address in, 88
    getting around, 88–89

Internet access, 90
layout of, 88
luggage storage and lockers, 90
newspapers and magazines, 90
nightlife, 11, 112–114
orientation, 86–91
outdoor activities and attractions, 110–111
police, 90
post office, 91
restaurants, 100–106
    Ciudad Cancún, 104–106
    dinner cruises, 100–101
    Isla Cancún, 101–104
seasons, 91
shopping, 10, 111–112
traveling to, 86
watersports, 106–108
websites, 87
what's new in, 2
Cancún Golf Club at Pok-Ta-Pok, 110
Cancún Hideaways, 91
Cancún Jazz Festival, 45
Cancún Mermaid, 108–111
    Puerto Morelos, 152
Cancún Municipal Tourism Office, 88
Cancún Tips, 88
Candlemas, 44
Canyon of El Sumidero, 281
Captain Hook Lobster Dinner Cruise (Cancún), 100–101
Capt. Rick's Sportfishing Center (Puerto Aventuras), 166
Car accidents, 53–54
Carbon offsetting, 67
Car breakdowns, 53
Cárdenas, Lázaro, 25
Car documents, 50, 51
The Caribbean Coast (Riviera Maya), 145–189
    activities along, 146, 148–149
    all-inclusive resorts, 162
    between Cancún and Playa del Carmen, 149–151
    coastal stops north to south, 146
    driving along, 157
    exploring, 145–149
    what's new in, 2
Caribbean Savage (ferry), 109
Caribbean Village (Isla Mujeres), 122

Carlos 'n' Charlie's (Cozumel), 299 144
Carnaval, 45
    Cozumel, 133
Carranza, Venustiano, 25
Car rentals, 54, 288
    Cancún, 87
    Cozumel, 131
    San Cristóbal, 267
Carretera Santa Pilar (Cozumel), 139
Car travel, 53–54
    Campeche, 230
    Cancún, 88
    Chetumal, 182
    Chichén Itzá, 237
    Cobá, 176
    highway safety, 62
    Mérida, 192, 194
    to Mexico, 50–51
    Palenque, 256–257
    Playa del Carmen, 154
    along Riviera Maya, 157
    San Cristóbal, 266
    Tuxtla Gutiérrez, 278
    Uxmal, 220
    Valladolid, 243
    Villahermosa, 250
Casa Bonita (Cancún), 112
Casa de Artesanías Amanecer (San Cristóbal), 272
Casa de Artesanías Tukulná (Campeche), 233
Casa del Alguacil (Magistrate's House; Mérida), 208
Casa de las Artesanías (Mérida), 212
Casa de los Jipis (Mérida), 214
Casa de los Metates (Temple of the Grinding Stones; Chichén Itzá), 240
Casa de los Sueños Resort and Zenter (Isla Mujeres), 121
Casa Na-Bolom (San Cristóbal), 269
Casa no. 6 Centro Cultural (Campeche), 233
Casanova, Victor, 134
Casas de cambio (exchange houses), 56. See also Currency and currency exchange
Castillo
    Chichén Itzá, 237–238
    Cobá, 176
    Labná, 226
    Muyil, 177
    Tulum, 171–172

300

Cathedral
Mérida, 207
San Cristóbal, 269
Catholicism, 35
Cave of Balankanché (near Chichén Itzá), 243–244
Cave of the Sleeping Sharks, 107
Cavern diving. *See* Cenotes and cenote diving
Caves of the Sleeping Sharks (Cuevas de los Tiburones), 120
Ceiba trees, 37, 182, 218, 253, 259, 282
Celestún National Wildlife Refuge, 191, 215–216
Celestún Wildlife Refuge, 73
Cellphones, 69
Cellular Abroad, 69
Cenote Dzitnup (Cenote Xkekén; near Valladolid), 245–246
Cenotes and cenote diving, 8, 37–38, 133–134
Hidden Worlds Cenotes Park (near Xel-Ha), 164
Ik-Kil, 243
Valladolid area, 244–246
Cenote Xtoloc (Chichén Itzá), 240
Cenote Zací (Valladolid), 244
Centers for Disease Control and Prevention (CDC), 57
Central Group (Dzibil-chaltún), 217
Centro Bilingüe (San Cristóbal), 268
Centro Cultural y Artesanal (Izamal), 215
Centro de Idiomas del Sureste (Mérida), 211
Centro de Investigaciones Pesqueras (Isla Mujeres), 121
Centro de Salud (Isla Mujeres), 119
Centro Ecológico de Sian Ka'an, 175
Centro Médico Cozumel, 132
Centro Médico de las Américas (Mérida), 198
Centruroides, 59
Ceramics and pottery
Amatenango del Valle, 271
Muna, 218
Chaac, 36, 221, 226
Chamula, 264, 271
Chankanaab National Park (Cozumel), 136

Chen Río (Cozumel), 137
Chetumal, 181–183
side trips to Maya ruins from, 183–189
Chiapa de Corzo, 281–282
Chiapas, 3, 66, 249
Chiapas Tourism Board, 286
Chiapas Tourism Secretariat, 66
Chicanná, 187–188
Chichanchob (Little Holes; Chichén Itzá), 240
Chichén Itzá, 8, 148, 191, 236–243
accommodations, 241–242
boat trips to, from Cozumel, 138
exploring the ruins, 237–241
itineraries, 77–79, 82
other attractions near, 243
restaurants, 242
traveling to/from, 237
what's new in, 3
Chichén Viejo (Old Chichén), 241
Chicle, 27
Children, families with
information and resources, 63–64
traveling with minors, 49
Chiles, 28, 30
Chinchorro Reef Underwater National Park, 178
Chincultic, 277
Chocolate, 28
Christmas, 47
Christmas Posadas, 47
The Church (La Iglesia; Chichén Itzá), 241
Cinco de Mayo, 45
Cine Hollywood (Playa del Carmen), 163
Cinemas
Cozumel, 144
Mérida, 208, 214
Playa del Carmen, 163
Cine Mérida, 208, 214
Cinépolis (Cozumel), 144
The City (Cancún), 113
City Museum (Museo de la Ciudad)
Campeche, 232–233
Mérida, 210
Ciudad Cancún (Cancún City), 88
accommodations, 99–100
restaurants, 104–106
The Classic Period, 18–19
Click Mexicana, 52
Cancún, 86
Chetumal, 181

Mérida, 192
Tuxtla Gutiérrez, 278
Villahermosa, 250
Cliff of the Dawn (Isla Mujeres), 122
Climate, 43–44
Cozumel, 132
Mérida, 197
Palenque, 257
San Cristóbal, 268
Clinics. *See* Hospitals and clinics
Club and music scene, Cancún, 112–114
Club Nitrox (Isla Mujeres), 128
Cobá, 148, 175–178, 246
boat trips to, from Cozumel, 138
CoCo Bongo (Cancún), 113
Cocos Cozumel (Cozumel), 137
Coffee, 30
Columbus Day, 46
Comalcalco, 255–256
Comitán, 277
Community Tours Sian Ka'an, 175
Conjunto Las Pinturas (Cobá), 176
Constitution Day, 44–45
Consumer protection, Isla Mujeres, 119
Continental Airlines
Cancún, 86
Mérida, 192
Continental ExpressJet, 250
"The Convent Route" (Highway 18), 218–219
Cool (Isla Mujeres), 126
Coral Negro (Cancún), 111
Coral Reef Alliance (CORAL), 65, 66
Coral reefs. *See* Reefs
Coral Scuba Center (Isla Mujeres), 120
Corbelled arch (Labná), 226
Corn, 28
Corpus Christi, 46
Cortez, Hernán, 22–23
Costa Maya, 3, 146
Country code for Mexico, 69
Cozumel, 128–144
accommodations, 138–141
all-inclusive vacations in, 130
area code, 132
beaches, 4, 136–137
climate, 132
clinics, 132

currency exchange, 132
emergencies, 132
exploring, 133–138
fishing, 134
getting around, 131
Internet access, 132
layout of, 131
nightlife, 144
post office, 132
recompression chamber, 132
restaurants, 141–144
seasons, 132
shopping, 138
snorkeling, 134
tours, 137
traveling to, 128–131
trips to the mainland, 138
visitor information, 131
watersports, 133–134
what's new in, 2
Cozumel Country Club, 138
Cozumel Vacation Villas and Condos, 139
Crafts, 10
Aguacatenango, 271
Amatenango del Valle, 271
Campeche, 233
Cancún, 111, 112
Cozumel, 138
Mérida, 212
Muna, 218
Puerto Morelos, 152
San Cristóbal, 272–273
Tenejapa, 271–272
Tuxtla Gutiérrez, 280
Valladolid, 244
Credit cards, 56–57
Crime, 60–62
Cristo de las Ampollas **(Mérida), 207–208**
CrocoCun (near Puerto Morelos), 150
Croozy Scooters (San Cristóbal), 267
The Cross of the Bay, 120
Cruises and boat tours. *See* **Boat excursions and cruises**
Cruise ships and lines, 52
CruisesOnly, 52
Cruz Roja (Red Cross)
Cancún, 90
Mérida, 198
Cuevas de los Tiburones (Caves of the Sleeping Sharks), 120
Cuisine. *See* **Food and cuisine**
Culinary Adventures, 68
Cultural experiences, best, 5

Currency and currency exchange, 55–56
Cancún, 90
Cozumel, 132
Isla Mujeres, 119
Mérida, 197–198
Playa del Carmen, 156
San Cristóbal, 268
Customs regulations, 49–50
Cyber Isla Mujeres.com, 119

Dady'O (Cancún), 113
Dady Rock Bar and Club (Cancún), 113
Daylight saving time, 285
Day of the Dead, 46
Deep-sea fishing. *See* **Fishing**
Delta Airlines, Cancún, 86
Día de la Candelaria, 44
Día de la Constitución, 44–45
Día de la Marina, 46
Día de la Raza, 46
Día de los Muertos, 46
Día de los Reyes, 44
Día de San Pedro, 46
Díaz, Porfirio, 24
Dietary red flags, 58
Dining. *See also* **Restaurants Index**
Akumal, 168
Bacalar Lake, 181
best, 13–14
Campeche, 235–236
Cancún, 100–106
Ciudad Cancún, 104–106
dinner cruises, 100–101
Isla Cancún, 101
Chetumal, 183
Chichén Itzá, 242
Cozumel, 141–144
dining service tips, 32
Isla Mujeres, 126–127
Mérida, 204–206
Oxkutzcab, 227
Paamul, 165
Palenque, 260–262
Playa del Carmen, 160–161, 163
Puerto Morelos, 153
Río Bec area, 185
San Cristóbal, 275–276
Tulum, 174
Tuxtla Gutiérrez, 281
Uxmal, 224
Valladolid, 245
Villahermosa, 255

Disabilities, travelers with, 63
Dive In Puerto Morelos, 152
Diving god, 171
Doctors. *See also* **Hospitals and clinics**
Playa del Carmen, 156
San Cristóbal, 268
Dollar, 87
Dolphin Discovery
Cancún, 110
Cozumel, 136
Isla Mujeres, 121
Puerto Aventuras, 165–166
Riviera Maya, 149
Dolphins, swimming with, 66
Cancún, 110
Cozumel, 136
Isla Mujeres, 121
Puerto Aventuras, 165–166
Riviera Maya, 149
Xel-Ha, 169
The Dovecote (Uxmal), 223
Drinking laws, 283
Drinks, 30–31
Drugstores
Cancún, 90
Isla Mujeres, 119
Mérida, 198
Playa del Carmen, 156
Dry season, 43
Dulcería y Sorbetería Colón (Mérida), 208
Duty-free shops, Cancún, 10
Dzibanché (Tzibanché), 185–186
Dzibilchaltún, 73, 191, 216–217

East Group (Kabah), 225
Eating and drinking, 27–33
Eco-adventure itineraries, 80–82
Ecochiapas, 66
Eco-theme parks and nature reserves, Huitepec Cloud Forest, 272
Eco-theme parks and reserves
Aktun Chen, 168
Calakmul Biosphere Reserve, 189
Celestún National Wildlife Refuge, 215–216
Sian Ka'an Biosphere Reserve, 73, 149, 175
Xel-Ha, 168–169
Ecotourism, 65–66

Ecotours, Mérida, 211–212
Ecoturismo Yucatán (Mérida), 211–212
Edificio de las Monjas (Edifice of the Nuns; Chichén Itzá), 240–241
Edventure Tours (Tulum), 149
Edzná, 228–229
Ek Balam, 8, 148, 246
El Ayuntamiento (Valladolid), 244
El Caracol (Ek Balam), 246
El Caracol (Observatory; Chichén Itzá), 240
El Castillo
    Chichén Itzá, 237–238
    Cobá, 176
    Labná, 226
    Muyil, 177
    Tulum, 171–172
El Centro (Parque Francisco Cantón Rosado; Valladolid), 244
El Centro (Plaza Mayor; Mérida), 195, 207–208, 210
El Cocodrilo (San Cristóbal), 277
Electricity, 283
Elements of the Island (Isla Mujeres), 121
El Encuentro (San Cristóbal), 272
Elevation sickness, 58–59
El Garrafón Natural Park (Isla Mujeres), 107, 108, 121–122
Elios (Valladolid), 244
Elite (Mérida), 194
El Mercado (The Market)
    Chichén Itzá, 240
    San Cristóbal, 269
El Mirador
    Guatemala, 188
    Labná, 226
    Sayil, 226
El Nuevo Olimpo (Mérida), 208, 214
El Palacio
    Labná, 226
    Sayil, 226
El Palacio de los Estucos (Acanceh), 219
El Paraíso Beach Club (Tulum), 171
El Parque de la Marimba (Tuxtla Gutiérrez), 281
El Sol Golf Cart Rental (Isla Mujeres), 118
Embassies and consulates, 283–284

Emergencies, 284
    Campeche, 232
    Cancún, 90
    Cozumel, 132
    Isla Mujeres, 119
Enchiladas, 29
Entry requirements, 48–50
Exchange houses (casas de cambio), 56
Executive car rentals (Cozumel), 131
Extreme weather exposure, 58

Fall Equinox (Chichén Itzá), 46
Families with children
    information and resources, 63–64
    traveling with minors, 49
Farmacía Cancún, 90
Farmacía del Carmen (Playa del Carmen), 156
Farmacías del Ahorro (Cancún), 90
Farmacía Yza (Mérida), 198
Faro Celerain Ecological Reserve (Cozumel), 136
Feast of San Isidro, 45
Feast of the Virgin of Guadalupe, 47
Felipe Carrillo Puerto, 177–178
Ferries
    Cozumel, 129
    Isla Mujeres, 116
    Playa del Carmen, 155
Festival de las Aves de Yucatán (Yucatán Bird Festival), 46
Festival of San Cristóbal de las Casas, 47
Festivals and special events, 44–47
Fiesta Americana, 70
Fiesta Americana Coral Beach (Cancún), 114
Fiesta Inn, 70
Films
    Mexican, 40–41
    set in Mexico, 41
Fishing, 8, 47
    Cancún, 106–107
    Cozumel, 134
    Isla Mujeres, 120
    Riviera Maya, 148
Flamingos, 191, 215–216
Food and cuisine, 27–33. See also Restaurants
    drinks, 30–31
    health concerns, 58

    regional specialties, 31–33
    staples, 28–30
    tours, 68
Forum by the Sea (Cancún), 111–112
Fox, Vicente, 25
Frijoles, 29
Frontier Airlines, Cancún, 86
Fuerte-Museo San José el Alto (Campeche), 233
Fuerte-Museo San Miguel (Campeche), 233
Fun Jet, 129

Galenia Hospital (Cancún), 90
Garrafón Natural Reef Park (Isla Mujeres), 107, 108, 121–122
Garrido Canabal, Tomás, 250
Gasoline, 53, 284
Gays and lesbians, 62–63
    International Gay Festival, 45
Gnats, 59
Golf
    Cancún, 110
    Cozumel, 138
    Riviera Maya, 148
The Governor's Palace (Uxmal), 222
Gran Meliá Cancún, golf course at, 110
Great Acropolis (Edzná), 228
Great Mesoamerican Barrier Reef, 39, 65
Great Mesoamerican Reef (Gran Arrecife Maya), 107, 108
The Great Pyramid (Uxmal), 222–223
Great Temple (Kabah), 225
"Green Angels," 53
Greetings, 17
Greyhound-Trailways, 52
Grupo Cobá, 176
Guayaberas, 212–213
Guayaberas Jack (Mérida), 213
Guide to Ancient Maya Ruins (Hunter), 137
Gum chewing, 27

Häagen-Dazs (Cancún), 90
Haciendas, 200–201
Hacienda Sisal (Cancún), 114

Hacienda Sotuta de Peón (near Mérida), 200, 214–215
Hacienda Yaxcopoil, 200, 217, 218
Hamacas El Aguacate (Mérida), 213–214
Hammocks, Mérida, 213–214
Handicrafts. *See* Crafts
Hard Rock Cafe (Cozumel), 144
Health concerns, 57–60
Henequén, 24, 200
Hernández, Roberto, 201
Hertz, 87
Hidalgo, Father Miguel, 23
Hidden Worlds Cenotes Park (near Xel-Ha), 148, 164, 169
High-altitude hazards, 58–59
High season, 43
Highway 18 ("The Convent Route"), 218–219
Hilton Cancún Golf & Spa Resort, golf course at, 110
History of the Yucatán, Tabasco and Chiapas, 15–26
books about, 39
pre-Hispanic civilizations, 18–22
Holbox, 247–248
Holy Week, 45
Horseback riding
Cancún, 110–111
Cozumel, 137
Riviera Maya, 148
San Cristóbal, 270
tours, 68
Hospital de la Armada (Isla Mujeres), 119
Hospitals and clinics
Cancún, 90
Cozumel, 132
Isla Mujeres, 119
Mérida, 198
Hospitén (Cancún), 156
Hostels, 64
Hot chocolate, 30
Hoteles Camino Real, 71
Hotel Na Balam (Isla Mujeres), yoga classes, 121
Hotels, 70–71. *See also* Accommodations Index
Akumal, 167–168
best, 11–13
best places to get away from it all, 9
Campeche, 234–235

Cancún
Ciudad Cancún, 99–100
Isla Cancún, 92–99
prices, 94
Chetumal, 182–183
Chichén Itzá, 241–242
Cozumel, 138–141
green-friendly, 67
Isla Mujeres, 123–125
Majahual, 179–180
Mérida and environs, 198–204
haciendas, 200–201
Ocosingo, 263
Paamul, 165
Palenque, 259–260
Playa del Carmen, 156–160
Puerto Aventuras, 166
Puerto Morelos and vicinity, 150–153
Río Bec area, 184–185
Río Lagartos, 246
San Cristóbal, 273–275
Tulum, 172–174
Tuxtla Gutiérrez, 280–281
Uxmal, 223–224
Valladolid, 245
Villahermosa, 253–254
House rentals and swaps, 71
HSBC Bank (Isla Mujeres), 119
Huerta, Victoriano, 24
Huitepec, 76
Huitepec Cloud Forest, 272
Hunter, Bruce, 137
Hurricane Gilbert, 26
Hurricanes, 44
Hurricane Wilma, 26
Hwy. 180, 243
Hyperbaric Center of Cozumel, 132

Iglesia de Jesús (El Tercer Orden; Mérida), 210
Iglesia de Santa Lucía (Mérida), 210
Iguana Bike (Tulum), 171
Ik-Kil, 243
IMAC, 67
Immigration and customs, 50
Independence Day, 46
Indigo (Cozumel), 138
Info-Akumal, 167
Insect repellent, 59
Inspiración (Cozumel), 138
Instituto de las Artesanías (Tuxtla Gutiérrez), 280
Instituto Jovel (San Cristóbal), 268

Insurance, 285
Interactive Aquarium (Cancún), 110
InterJet, 52
Interjet, Cancún, 86
InterMar Cozumel Viajes, 133
International Gay Festival, 45
International Pier (Cozumel), 131
Internet access, 70
Campeche, 232
Cozumel, 132
Isla Mujeres, 119
Mérida, 198
Playa del Carmen, 156
Ireland, Embassy of, 284
Isla Beckons (Isla Mujeres), 123
Isla Cancún (Cancún Island), 88
accommodations, 92–99
restaurants, 101–104
Isla Contoy, 73, 107, 122
Isla Holbox, 247–248
whale sharks of, 247
Isla Mujeres, 108–110, 115–128
accommodations, 123–125
area code, 119
beaches, 4, 119–120
currency exchange, 119
emergencies, 119
fishing, 120
getting around, 118–119
hospitals, 119
Internet access, 119
layout of, 118
nightlife, 127–128
outdoor activities, 119–121
post office, 119
restaurants, 126–127
shopping, 123
taxis, 119
telephone, 119
tourist seasons, 119
traveling to, 116–117
visitor information, 117
websites, 118
what's new in, 2
Isla Mujeres Farmacía, 119
Itineraries, suggested, 77–84
Iturbide, Agustín de, 23
The Itzáes, 22
Itzamná, 36
IVA (value-added tax), 57
Ixchel, 36
Ixtab, 36
Izamal, 215

Jardín Botánico Dr. Alfredo Barrera (near Puerto Morelos), 150
Jax Bar & Grill (Isla Mujeres), 127
JetBlue, Cancún, 86
Jet skis, Cancún, 106
Joseph Bonaparte, 23
Journey into Amazing Caves (IMAX production), 169
Juárez, Benito, 23
  Birthday of, 45
Juego de pelota (ball court)
  Chichén Itzá, 238
  Cobá, 176
  Palenque, 259
  Uxmal, 222
Jungle Cruise (Cancún), 108
Jungle Spa (Puerto Morelos), 152

Kabah, 224–225
Kahlúa, 31
Kanasin, 218
Kinich, 36
Kinichná, 186
Kohunlich, 186
KoKo Nuts (Isla Mujeres), 128
Kukulcán Plaza (Cancún), 111
Kukulkán, 36
Kuzamil Snorkeling Center (Cozumel), 134

La Adelita (Isla Mujeres), 128
Labná, 226
Labor Day, 45
La Cañada (Palenque), 257
La Galería (San Cristóbal), 272
Lago Bacalar, 180–181
Lagoonview Marina & Fishing Club (Cancún), 107
Lágrimas de la Selva (San Cristóbal), 272
La Iglesia (The Church)
  Chichén Itzá, 241
  Cobá, 176
La Isla Shopping Village (Cancún), 112
La Madonna (Cancún), 113
Lamanai (Belize), 183
Landa, Diego de, 172
Language, 285. *See also* Spanish classes
La Pared (San Cristóbal), 268

La Parroquia de San Servacio (Valladolid), 244
La Punta, 120
La Ruta Maya, suggested itinerary, 82–84
Las Palapas Chimbo's (Isla Mujeres), 127
Latino's (San Cristóbal), 277
Latitud 16, 66
Le Chef (Cozumel), 141
Librería Dante (Mérida), 197
Liqueurs, 31
Liquid Blue Divers (Cozumel), 133
Literature, 40
Little Holes (Chichanchob; Chichén Itzá), 240
The Lobby Lounge (Cancún), 114
Lobster Dinner Cruise (Cancún), 100
Loco Gringo, 167
Loltún, 226–227
López Obrador, Andrés Manuel, 26
Los Cinco Soles (Cozumel), 138
Los Delfines (Cozumel), 144
Los Pingüinos (San Cristóbal), 267
Low season, 43

Mac, Juan, 244
Madero, Francisco, 24
Madonna and Child (Mérida), 210
Magdalena, 264
Magistrate's House (Casa del Alguacil; Mérida), 208
Mail, 285
Majahual, 178–180
Malls, Cancún, 111
Mama, 219
Mambo Café (Mérida), 214
Manchones reef, 120
Mariachi, 42
Marimba music, 41
Marinonis (fishing boat), 120
Marítima Chankanaab, 130
The Market (El Mercado; Chichén Itzá), 240
Maximilian of Austria, Archduke, 23
Maya culture and people, 16–18
  best cultural experiences, 5
  etiquette and customs, 17–18
  gods and goddesses, 36

The Maya Interior, what's new in, 3
Maya K'iin (Mérida), 194
Mayapán, 219
Maya ruins
  Acanceh, 219
  Balamkú, 189
  Becán, 187
  best, 5, 8
  Bonampak, 8, 262
  Calakmul, 5, 188–189, 229
  Chicanná, 187–188
  Chichén Itzá, 236
  Chincultic, 277
  Cobá, 176–177
  Comalcalco, 255–256
  Cozumel, 137
  Dzibanché (Tzibanché), 185–186
  Dzibilchaltún, 73, 191, 216–217
  Edzná, 228–229
  Ek Balam, 8, 148, 246
  Isla Mujeres, 122
  Kabah, 224–225
  Kinichná, 186
  Kohunlich, 186
  Labná, 226
  Mayapán, 219
  Muyil, 177
  Palenque, 8, 257–259
  Puuc Maya Route, 224–229
  Río Bec area, 177, 180–185, 229
  Riviera Maya, 148
  Sayil, 226
  side trips from Chetumal to, 183–189
  suggested itineraries, 77–84
  Tecoh, 219
  Toniná, 263–264
  tours, 68, 149
  Tulum, 5, 8, 146, 148, 170–172
  Uxmal, 221–223
  Xcambó, 217
  Xpujil, 187
  Yaxchilán, 262
Medical requirements for entry, 50
Médica San Miguel (Cozumel), 132
Mercado de Artesanías de Valladolid, 244
Mérida, 190–214
  accommodations, 198–204
  area code, 197
  bookstores, 197
  business hours, 197

climate, 197
consulates, 197
currency exchange, 197–198
drugstore, 198
exploring, 207–211
festivals and special
    events, 196
getting around, 197
hospitals, 198
Internet access, 198
itineraries, 78–80
layout of, 195–197
nightlife, 214
police, 198
post office, 198
restaurants, 204–206
seasons, 198
shopping, 212–214
side trips from, 214–220
street scene, 5
traveling to, 192, 194–195
visitor information, 195
what's new in, 3
Mérida en Domingo, 196
Mescal, 31
**Mesoamerican Ecotourism
    Alliance, 66**
MexGay Vacations, 63
Mexicana, 52
Cancún, 86
Mérida, 192
Villahermosa, 250
**Mexican-American War
    (1846-48), 23**
Mexican embassies, 286
**Mexican fiesta nights
    (Cancún), 114**
Mexico Art Tours, 68
Mexico Boutique Hotels, 71
Mexico Tourism Board, 285
MexicoTravel.net, 68
**Miguel Alvarez del Toro
    Zoo (ZOOMAT; Tuxtla
    Gutiérrez), 280**
Miniaturas (Mérida), 212
Misol Ha waterfalls, 263
Moctezuma II, 22
Modutel (Cozumel), 132
Money and costs, 55–57
Monte Albán, 18–19
Montebello National Park, 277
Montes Azules, 76
**Moon Palace Spa & Golf Club,
    golf course at, 110**
Moped rentals. *See also*
    Scooters
Cozumel, 132
Isla Mujeres, 116
Mordida, 62

Mosquitoes, 59
Movie theaters
Cozumel, 144
Mérida, 208, 214
Playa del Carmen, 163
Mr. Sancho's (Cozumel), 136
**Muelle Internacional
    (Cozumel), 131**
Muna, 218
**Mundaca Travel and Real
    Estate (Isla Mujeres), 123**
**Municipal Tourism Office
    (Cozumel), 131**
Murals, 35
**Museo de Arte Contemporá-
    neo Ateneo de Yucatán
    (Mérida), 208**
**Museo de la Ciudad (City
    Museum)**
Campeche, 232–233
Mérida, 210
**Museo de la Cultura Maya
    (Chetumal), 9, 181, 182**
**Museo de la Isla de Cozumel,
    137–138**
**Museo del Ambar (San
    Cristóbal), 269**
**Museo del Pueblo Maya
    (Dzibilchaltún), 216–217**
**Museo Regional de
    Antropología (Anthropol-
    ogy Museum; Mérida),
    9, 210, 211**
**Museo Regional de
    Antropología Carlos Pel-
    licer Cámara (Villaher-
    mosa), 10, 252–253**
**Museo Templo y Convento
    Santo Domingo (San
    Cristóbal), 270**
Museums. *See also* Anthro-
    pology museums; Archaeo-
    logical museums and
    exhibits
best, 9–10
Museo de Arte Contem-
    poráneo Ateneo de
    Yucatán (Mérida), 208
Museo de la Cultura Maya
    (Chetumal), 181, 182
Museo de la Isla de
    Cozumel, 137–138
Museo del Ambar (San
    Cristóbal), 269
Museo del Pueblo Maya
    (Dzibilchaltún), 216–217
Museo Templo y Convento
    Santo Domingo (San
    Cristóbal), 270

Music, 41–42
Muyil, 175, 177

Na Balam hotel bar (Isla
    Mujeres), 127
Napoleon Bonaparte, 23
National car rentals, 87
Nature preserves, 73, 76. *See
    also* Eco-theme parks and
    reserves
Navy Day, 46
**Newspapers and magazines,
    285**
New Year's Day, 44
New Year's Eve, 47
New Zealand
customs regulations, 50
Embassy of, 284
Nextel, 69
NH Hoteles, 71
Nightlife
Cancún, 11, 112–114
Cozumel, 144
hottest, 10–11
Isla Mujeres, 127–128
Mérida, 214
Playa del Carmen, 163
San Cristóbal, 277
**Nohoch Mul Group
    (Cobá), 176**
**The North Temple (Chichén
    Itzá), 238**
**Northwest Airlines
    (Cancún), 86**
**The Nunnery Quadrangle
    (Uxmal), 221–222**

Obregón, Alvaro, 25
**Observatory (El Caracol;
    Chichén Itzá), 240**
Ocosingo, 263
The Olmecs, 18, 34
Om (Playa del Carmen), 163
**Om Bar and Chill Lounge
    (Isla Mujeres), 128**
**Optima Car Rental (San
    Cristóbal), 267**
**Orange Festival (Oxkutzcab),
    227**
Outdoor activities. *See also*
    Watersports
Cancún, 110–111
Isla Mujeres, 119–121
Riviera Maya (the
    Caribbean Coast),
    146, 148–149
Over-the-counter drugs, 59
Oxkutzcab, 227

Paamul, 165
The Palace
    Palenque, 258
    Xlapak, 226
Palace Group (Kabah), 225
Palace of Masks (Kabah), 225
Palacio de Gobierno
    (Mérida), 195, 210
Palacio de las Bellas Artes
    (San Cristóbal), 270
Palacio Montejo
    (Mérida), 208
Palacio Municipal (Ayun-
    tamiento; Mérida),
    196, 208
Palancar Reef, 133
Palenque, 8, 256–264
PAN (Partido Acción
    National), 25
Panadería La Hojaldra (San
    Cristóbal), 275
Panadería La Reyna (Isla
    Mujeres), 126
Panama hats, 214
Pantanos de Centla, 73
Papaya, 28
Paradise Beach (Cozumel), 136
Paradise Cafe (Cozumel), 137
Parking, Playa del Carmen, 156
Parque Cepeda Peraza
    (Parque Hidalgo;
    Mérida), 210
Parque de la Madre
    (Mérida), 210
Parque Francisco Cantón
    Rosado (El Centro;
    Valladolid), 244
Parque-Museo La Venta
    (Villahermosa), 10, 250,
    252, 253
Parque Nacional Palenque,
    257–259
Parque Principal (Campeche),
    232
Parque Santa Ana
    (Mérida), 210
Parque Santa Lucía
    (Mérida), 210
Parroquia de San Servacio
    (Valladolid), 244
Partido Acción National
    (PAN), 25
Partido de la Revolución
    Democrática (PRD), 25
Partido Revolucionario Insti-
    tucional (PRI), 25
Pasaje Picheta (Mérida), 208
Paseo de Montejo (Mérida),
    196, 211

Passport Card, 48
Pellicer Cámara, Carlos, 250
Pemex, 53
Performing arts, Cancún, 114
PETA (People for the Ethical
    Treatment of Animals), 66
Petrol, 284
Pingüinos (Isla Mujeres),
    127–128
Pirate fortress, Isla Mujeres,
    122–123
Pisté, 237
Planning your trip, 1–2, 43–71
    accommodations, 70–71
    customs regulations,
        49–50
    entry requirements, 48–50
    getting around, 52–55
    health concerns, 57–60
    Internet access, 70
    money and costs, 55–57
    safety concerns, 60–62
    special interest trips, 67–68
    specialized travel
        resources, 62–67
    sustainable tourism, 64–66
    telephones, 69–70
    traveling to Mexico, 50–52
    when to go, 43–44
Platform of the Eagles
    (Chichén Itzá), 238
Platform of Venus (Chichén
    Itzá), 238–239
Playa Bonita (Cozumel), 137
Playa Caracol (Cancún), 106
Playacar Golf Club, 148
Playa del Carmen, 146,
    154–163
    accommodations, 156–160
    area code, 156
    beaches, 4
    boat trips to, from
        Cozumel, 138
    currency exchange, 156
    doctors, 156
    drugstore, 156
    Internet access, 156
    layout of, 156
    nightlife, 163
    orientation, 155–156
    parking, 156
    post office, 156
    restaurants, 160–161, 163
    seasons, 156–157
    shopping, 10
    south of, 163–170
    traveling to, 154–155
    what's new in, 2–3
Playa Lancheros (Isla
    Mujeres), 120

Playa Linda, ferries to Isla
    Mujeres from, 116–117
Playa Mía (Cozumel), 136
Playa Norte (Isla Mujeres),
    108, 119–120
Playa Palancar (Cozumel),
    136–137
Playa San Francisco
    (Cozumel), 136
Plaza Caracol (Cancún), 111
Plaza de Santo Domingo
    (San Cristóbal), 272–273
Plaza La Fiesta (Cancún), 111
Plaza Mayor (El Centro; Mér-
    ida), 195, 207–208, 210
Plaza Xibalba (Dzibanché), 185
Police, 285
    Cancún, 90
    Mérida, 198
Portal de Granos (Mérida), 212
Post office
    Campeche, 232
    Cancún, 91
    Cozumel, 132
    Isla Mujeres, 119
    Mérida, 198
PRD (Partido de la Revolu-
    ción Democrática), 25
Pre-Hispanic civilizations,
    18–22
PRI (Partido Revolucionario
    Institucional), 25
Profeco (Procuraduría
    Federal del Consumidor)
    Cancún, 90
    Isla Mujeres, 119
Progreso, 191, 217
Pronatura, 272
Puerta de Tierra (Campeche),
    233
Puerta Maya (Cozumel), 131
Puerto Aventuras, 146, 148,
    165–166
Puerto Calica, 165
Puerto Morelos and vicinity,
    146, 149–154
Pulque, 31
Punta Allen, 175
Punta Allen Peninsula, 170
    exploring, 174–175
Punta Langosta (Cozumel,
    Ticul), 131
Punta Morena (Cozumel), 137
Punta Sam, 116
Puuc Maya Route, 192, 194,
    220, 224–229
Pyramid of Five Stories
    (Edzná), 229
Pyramid of the Magician
    (Uxmal), 221

Pyramid of the Masks (Kohunlich), 186
Pyramid of the Painted Lintel (Cobá), 176–177

Quetzalcóatl, 19, 22
Quinta Avenida (Fifth Avenue; Playa del Carmen), 156
Quintana Roo, 73
Quintana Roo Tourist Board, 286
Quinta Real Grand Class Hotels and Resorts, 71

Rainy season, 43–44
Rancho Loma Bonita (near Puerto Morelos), 150
Rancho Palmitas (Cozumel), 137
Rancho Punta Venado (near Playa del Carmen), 148
Recompression chamber, Cozumel, 132
Reefs
    anatomy of, 134
    Cancún, 107–108
    Chinchorro Reef Underwater National Park, 178
    Cozumel, 133
    Felipe Carrillo Puerto area, 177
    Isla Mujeres, 120
    Puerto Morelos, 152
Regions in brief, 72–77
Religion, myth and folklore, 35–37
Resort clothing, 10
Restaurants. See also Restaurants Index
    Akumal, 168
    Bacalar Lake, 181
    best, 13–14
    Campeche, 235–236
    Cancún, 100–106
        Ciudad Cancún, 104–106
        dinner cruises, 100–101
        Isla Cancún, 101
    Chetumal, 183
    Chichén Itzá, 242
    Cozumel, 141–144
    dining service tips, 32
    Isla Mujeres, 126–127
    Mérida, 204–206
    Oxkutzcab, 227
    Paamul, 165
    Palenque, 260–262

Playa del Carmen, 160–161, 163
Puerto Morelos, 153
Río Bec area, 185
San Cristóbal, 275–276
Tulum, 174
Tuxtla Gutiérrez, 281
Uxmal, 224
Valladolid, 245
Villahermosa, 255
Revolution Day, 46
Río Bec area, 177, 180–185, 229
Rio Lagartos Nature Reserve, 246–247
Río Lagartos Wildlife Refuge, 73
Riviera Maya (the Caribbean Coast), 145–189
    activities along, 146, 148–149
    all-inclusive resorts, 162
    between Cancún and Playa del Carmen, 149–151
    coastal stops north to south, 146
    driving along, 157
    exploring, 145–149
    what's new in, 2
Rock music, 42
Roman Catholicism, 35
Rosca de Reyes, 44
Ruins and archaeological sites
    Acanceh, 219
    Balamkú, 189
    Becán, 187
    best, 5, 8
    Bonampak, 8, 262
    Calakmul, 5, 188–189, 229
    Chicanná, 187–188
    Chichén Itzá, 236
    Chincultic, 277
    Cobá, 176–177
    Comalcalco, 255–256
    Cozumel, 137
    Dzibanché (Tzibanché), 185–186
    Dzibilchaltún, 73, 191, 216–217
    Edzná, 228–229
    Ek Balam, 8, 148, 246
    Isla Mujeres, 122
    Kabah, 224–225
    Kinichná, 186
    Kohunlich, 186
    Labná, 226
    Mayapán, 219
    Muyil, 177
    Palenque, 8, 257–259
    Puuc Maya Route, 224–229

Río Bec area, 177, 180–185, 229
Riviera Maya, 148
Sayil, 226
side trips from Chetumal to, 183–189
suggested itineraries, 77–84
Tecoh, 219
Toniná, 263–264
tours, 68, 149
Tulum, 5, 8, 146, 148, 170–172
Uxmal, 221–223
Xcambó, 217
Xpujil, 187
Yaxchilán, 262
Ruta Maya, 82–84

Sacred Cenote (Chichén Itzá), 239
Safety concerns, 60–62
Sailboards, Cancún, 106
Sailing, Cancún, 106
St. Peter and St. Paul's Day, 46
Sammulá (near Valladolid), 246
San Andrés, 264
San Antonio de Padua (Izamal), 215
San Bernardino de Siena (Valladolid), 244
Sanborn's Mexico Insurance, 52
Sanborn Tours, 64
San Cristóbal de las Casas, 5, 264–278
    accommodations, 273–275
    area code, 267
    books about, 267–268
    bulletin boards, 268
    climate, 268
    coffeehouses, 276
    currency exchange, 268
    doctor, 268
    exploring, 268–272
    getting around, 267
    layout of, 267
    Maya villages and countryside near, 270–272
    nightlife, 277
    orientation, 266
    parking, 268
    post office, 268
    restaurants, 275–276
    road trips from, 277–278
    shopping, 10, 272–273
    telephone, 268
    traveling to, 266
    visitor information, 267

San Francisco Reef, 133
San Gervasio (booklet), 137
San Gervasio (Cozumel), 137
San Juan Chamula, 271
San Miguel (Cozumel), 128
    layout of, 131
Santa Anna, Antonio López
    de, 23
Santa Rosa Wall, 133
Savana (Tulum), 171
Sayil, 226
Scams, 62
Scooters
    Cancún, 89
    San Cristóbal, 267
Scorpion (alacrán), 59
Scuba Cancún, 107
Scuba diving, 8. *See also*
    Cenotes and cenote diving
    Akumal, 167
    Cancún, 107–108
    Chinchorro Reef Underwa-
        ter National Park, 178
    Cozumel, 132
    Isla Mujeres, 120
    Puerto Morelos, 152
    Riviera Maya, 148
Scuba-Mex (Paamul), 165
Sculptured Spaces (Isla
    Mujeres), 122
Seasons, 43–44
    Cozumel, 132
    Isla Mujeres, 119
    Mérida, 198
    Playa del Carmen, 156–157
Sea turtles, Isla Mujeres, 121
Selva del Ocote, 76
Selvática (Cancún), 149
Semana Santa, 45
Senior travel, 64
Señor Frog's, Cozumel, 144
Shopping
    best, 10
    Campeche, 233
    Cancún, 10, 111–112
    Cozumel, 138
    Isla Mujeres, 123
    Mérida, 212–214
    Playa del Carmen, 10
    San Cristóbal, 272–273
    San Cristóbal de las
        Casas, 10
    Tuxtla Gutiérrez, 280
    Valladolid, 244
Sian Ka'an Biosphere
    Reserve, 73, 149, 175
Smoking, 60
Sna Jolobil (San Cristóbal),
    273

Snorkeling
    Akumal, 167
    Cancún, 107–108
    Cozumel, 134, 136
    Isla Mujeres, 120–121
    Puerto Morelos, 152
    Riviera Maya, 148
    Tankah Bay, 170
    Xcaret, 164
    Xel-Ha, 168–169
Sociedad Cooperativa Turís-
    tica (Isla Mujeres), 120, 122
Sound-and-light show
    Chichén Itzá, 237
    Uxmal, 221
South Africa, Embassy of, 284
Spa del Mar (Cancún), 96
Spa Itzá (Playa del Carmen),
    148
Spanish classes
    Mérida, 211
    San Cristóbal, 268
The Spanish Institute, 67–68
Spas, Playa del Carmen, 148
Spas and spa resorts, Puerto
    Morelos and vicinity,
    150–152
Special events and festivals,
    44–47
Spring Equinox, 45
Starwood Hotels, 201
Street food, 31
Structure 6 (Dzibanché), 186
Structure 38 (Dzibilchaltún),
    217
Student travel, 64
Sub See Explorer
    Cancún, 107
    Cozumel, 134
Sun exposure, 58
Sunscreen, biodegradable, 65
Super Chomak (Akumal), 168
Sustainable tourism, 64–66
Swimming, Isla Mujeres,
    119–120
Swine flu, 1, 57

Tabasco, 3, 66, 249
Tabasco Tourism Board, 286
Tabos reef, 120
Taller de Artesanía Los
    Ceibos (Muna), 218
Tamales, 29
Tankah Bay, 169–170
Tank-Ha Dive Center (Playa
    del Carmen), 148
Taxes, 285

Taxis, 54
    Cancún, 87, 88–89
    Cozumel, 132
    Isla Mujeres, 119
    Mérida, 197
    Playa del Carmen, 155
    San Cristóbal, 266
    Villahermosa, 252
Teatro Ayala (Mérida), 214
Teatro Daniel de Ayala
    (Mérida), 210
Teatro Peón Contreras
    (Mérida), 195, 210, 214
Tecoh, 219
Tejidos y Cordeles Nacionales
    (Mérida), 214
Telcel, 69
Telephones, 285
Téllez, Luis, 183, 184
Temple 13 (Palenque), 258
Temple 14 (Palenque), 258
Temple of Jaguars (Chichén
    Itzá), 238
Temple of Obscure Writing
    (Akab Dzib; Chichén Itzá),
    241
Temple of Panels (Templo de
    los Tableros; Chichén Itzá),
    240
Temple of the Church
    (Cobá), 176
Temple of the Cormorant
    (Dzibanché), 186
Temple of the Count
    (Palenque), 259
Temple of the Cross
    (Palenque), 258
Temple of the Deer (Templo
    del Venado; Chichén
    Itzá), 240
Temple of the Foliated Cross
    (Palenque), 258
Temple of the Frescoes
    (Tulum), 172
Temple of the Grinding
    Stones (Casa de los
    Metates; Chichén Itzá), 240
Temple of the Inscriptions
    (Palenque), 258
Temple of the Macaws
    (Uxmal), 223
Temple of the Owl
    (Dzibanché), 185
Temple of the Seven Dolls
    (Dzibilchaltún), 217
Temple of the Skulls (Tzom-
    pantli; Chichén Itzá), 238
Temple of the Sun
    (Palenque), 258

Temple of the Warriors
(Templo de los Guerreros;
Chichén Itzá), 240
Templo de las Inscripciones
Iniciales (Temple of the
First Inscriptions;
Chichén Itzá), 241
Templo de los Dinteles
(Temple of the Lintels;
Chichén Itzá), 241
Templo de los Guerreros
(Temple of the Warriors;
Chichén Itzá), 240
Templo de los Tableros
(Temple of Panels;
Chichén Itzá), 240
Templo del Venado (Temple
of the Deer; Chichén
Itzá), 240
Templo de San Cristóbal
(San Cristóbal), 270
Tenejapa, 264, 271–272
Tennis
    Cancún, 110
    Riviera Maya, 148
Teotihuacán, 18–19
Tequila, 30, 31
Three Kings' Day, 44
Thrifty, 87
Ticket Bus, Cozumel, 131
Ticul, 219–220
Time zone, 285
Tipping, 285
Toilets, 285
Toll-free numbers, 69
Toll roads, 53
Toltecs, 19, 22
Tomatoes, 28
Tomb of the High Priest
(Tumba del Gran Sacer-
dote; Chichén Itzá), 240
Toniná, 263–264
Topping, 32
Tortillas, 28–29
Tourist Help Line, 284
Tourist information, 285–286
    Campeche, 230
    Cancún, 88
    Chetumal, 182
    Cozumel, 131
    Isla Mujeres, 117
    Mérida, 195
    Palenque, 257
    San Cristóbal, 267
    Tuxtla Gutiérrez, 280
    Valladolid, 244
    Villahermosa, 252
Tourist Migration Form,
48–49

Transportadora Carnaval
(Mérida), 207
Transportes Rodolfo
Figueroa
    Palenque, 257
    San Cristóbal, 266
Transportes Terrestres
(Cozumel), 131
Trek America, 68
Tricycle taxis, Isla Mujeres,
118
Tropical illnesses, 59
Tula, 19, 22
Tulum, 5, 8, 146, 148,
170–174
    beaches, 5
    boat trips to, from
    Cozumel, 138
    suggested itineraries,
    80, 81, 84
    what's new in, 3
Tumba del Gran Sacerdote
(Tomb of the High Priest;
Chichén Itzá), 240
Turista (diarrhea), 58
Tuxtla Gutiérrez, 278–282
Tzibanché (Dzibanché),
185–186
Tzompantli (Temple of the
Skulls; Chichén Itzá), 238

Ultrafemme (Cancún), 111
Ultramar (ferry), 109, 116
    Cozumel, 129
Unión Regional de
Artesanías de los Altos
(San Cristóbal), 273
United Airlines (Cancún), 86
United Kingdom
    consulate, Cancún, 89
    customs regulations, 49
    Embassy of, 284
    sustainable tourism, 67
    visitor information in, 286
United Nations Environmen-
tal Program (UNEP), 65
United States
    consulates
        Cancún, 89
        Mérida, 197
    customs regulations, 49
    Embassy of, 283
    visitor information in,
    285–286
Universidad de Yucatán
(Mérida), 210
US Airways, Cancún, 86
U.S. Department of State
travel advisories, 60

Uxmal, 8, 192, 220–224   **309**
    en route to, 217–220
    itineraries, 78, 80, 82

Vacation Rentals by Owner
(VRBO), 71
Vacation-Spot, 71
Valladolid, 191, 243–248
Value-added tax (IVA), 57
Vanilla, 28
Vaquería regional
(Mérida), 196
Ver y Wine (Cancún), 114
Viajes Na Chan Kan
(Palenque), 263
Viajes Shivalva (Palenque),
263
Villa, Pancho, 24–25
Villahermosa, 250–256
Visas, 48
Visitor information, 285–286
    Campeche, 230
    Cancún, 88
    Chetumal, 182
    Cozumel, 131
    Isla Mujeres, 117
    Mérida, 195
    Palenque, 257
    San Cristóbal, 267
    Tuxtla Gutiérrez, 280
    Valladolid, 244
    Villahermosa, 252
Viva México (Cozumel), 138
Volaris, 52
    Cancún, 86
    Mérida, 192
Volunteer travel, 67

War of the Castes, 24, 178,
226, 243
Water, drinking, 58, 286
Water skis, Cancún, 106
Watersports
    Cancún, 106–108
    Cozumel, 133–134
    Felipe Carrillo Puerto
    area, 177
    Xcaret, 164
    Xel-Ha, 168–169
Water Taxi, Isla Mujeres, 117
Weather, 43–44
Websites
    airline, hotel, and car
    rental, 287–288
    Cancún, 87
    Isla Mujeres, 118

for Mérida, Chichén Itzá,
and the Maya
interior, 191
traveler's toolbox, 286
**Weekend trips, suggested
itineraries for, 77**
**Whale and Dolphin Conser-
vation Society, 66**
**Whale sharks of Isla
Holbox, 247**
Wi-Fi access, 70
Wildlife, 38–39. *See also* Birds
and bird-watching
CrocoCun (near Puerto
Morelos), 150
Río Bec region, 183–184
Xcaret, 164
Yumká, 253
Women travelers, 64
**World Health Organization
(WHO), 1, 57**
World Wildlife Fund (WWF), 65

Xcalak, 178
Xcambó, 217
Xcaret, 149, 164–165
boat trips to, from
Cozumel, 138
Xel-Ha, 149, 168–169
Xibalba, 187
The Xiu, 22
Xlapak, 226
Xpu-Ha, 166–167
Xpujil, 187
Xtabentún, 31

Yal-ku Lagoon (Akumal), 167
Yaxchilán, 8, 262
Yoga, Isla Mujeres, 121
Yucab Reef, 133
**Yucatán, exploring the
heartland, 190–192**
Yucatán Ballet Folklórico, 196
Yucatán Bird Festival, 46
Yucatan Peninsula Travel, 123
Yucatán Today (magazine), 195
Yucatán Tourism Board, 286
**Yucatech Expeditions
(Cozumel), 133**
Yumil Kaxob, 36
Yumká, 253

Zapata, Emiliano, 24
**Zapatista Liberation Army,
249, 266**
Zapotec, 18, 19, 252

Zermatt (Cozumel), 141
Zinacantán, 264, 271
Zona Hotelera (Cancún), 88

ACCOMMODATIONS

**Acanto Hotel & Suites (Playa
del Carmen), 157**
Al Cielo (Xpu-Ha), 166
**Amar Inn (Puerto Morelos),
152**
Ana y José (Tulum), 172
Aqua (Cancún), 92
**Aventura Spa Palace
(Xpu-Ha), 162**
Azulik (Tulum), 172–173
**Balamkú Inn on the Beach
(Majahual), 179**
**Bel Air Collection Hotel & Spa
(Cancún), 98**
**Best Western Hotel Maya
Tabasco (Villahermosa),
254**
**Boca Paila Fishing Lodge
(Punta Allen Peninsula),
175**
Cabañas Paamul, 165
Cabañas Tulum, 174
**Casa Cenote (Tankah Bay),
169**
**Casa de los Sueños Resort &
Spa Zenter (Isla Mujeres),
123**
**Casa Felipe Flores (San
Cristóbal), 273**
**Casa Mexilio Guest House
(Mérida), 202**
**Casa Quetzal (Valladolid),
245**
**Casa Sandra (Isla Holbox),
248**
Casa San Juan (Mérida), 203
**Ceiba del Mar (Puerto
Morelos), 150**
**Chan-Kah Resort Village
(Palenque), 259**
**Chicanná Eco Village (near
Xpujil), 184–185**
**Coco's Cabañas (near Playa
del Carmen), 154**
**Condumel Condobeach
Apartments Value
(Cozumel), 139**
Copacabana (Xpu-Ha), 166
**Costa de Cocos Dive & Fly-
Fishing Resort (near
Majahual), 179–180**
Cozumel Palace, 130
**Cuzan Guesthouse (Punta
Allen), 175**

**Deseo Hotel + Lounge (Playa
del Carmen), 157–158**
**Dreams Cancún Resort &
Spa, 97**
El Bocadito (Cobá), 177
**El Cantil Condominiums
(Cozumel), 141**
El Cozumeleño (Cozumel), 130
**El Mesón del Marqués
(Valladolid), 245**
Esencia (Xpu-Ha), 166–167
**The Explorean (near
Kohunlich), 184**
**Fairmont hotel (Mayakobá;
near Playa del Carmen), 153**
**Fiesta Americana Grand
Coral Beach (Cancún), 92**
**Fiesta Americana Mérida,
198, 200**
Flamingo Cancún, 98–99
**Flycatcher Inn B&B (Uxmal),
223**
**Freedom Paradise (Tulum),
162**
**Genesis Retreat Ek Balam
(Valladolid), 245**
**Hacienda Blanca Flor (near
Mérida), 201**
**Hacienda Chichén Resort
(Chichén Itzá), 241**
**Hacienda Petac (near
Mérida), 201**
**Hacienda Puerta Campeche,
234**
**Hacienda San Antonio (near
Mérida), 201**
**Hacienda San José Cholul
(near Mérida), 201**
**Hacienda San Miguel
(Cozumel), 140**
**Hacienda San Pedro Nohpat
(near Mérida), 201**
**Hacienda Santa Rosa (near
Mérida), 201**
**Hacienda Uxmal and The
Lodge at Uxmal, 223**
**Hilton Cancún Golf & Spa
Resort, 92, 94**
**Holiday Village White Sands
(Cozumel), 130**
**Hospedaje Esmeralda
(Ocosingo), 263**
Hotel 49 (Río Lagartos), 246
**Hotel Akumal Caribe,
167–168**
**Hotel & Bungalows Maya-
land, The Lodge at Chichén
Itzá, 242**
**Hotel Baluartes (Campeche),
234**

Hotel Básico (Playa del Carmen), 158

Hotel Belmar (Isla Mujeres), 125

Hotel Bonampak Tuxtla (Tuxtla Gutiérrez), 281

Hotel Cabañas María del Mar (Isla Mujeres), 124

Hotel Caribe (Mérida), 202

Hotel Casa Mexicana (San Cristóbal), 273

Hotel Casavieja (San Cristóbal), 274

Hotel Central (Ocosingo), 263

Hotel Ciudad Real (Palenque), 260

Hotel Colonial (Campeche), 234–235

Hotel Copacabana (Xpu-Ha), 162

Hotel Cozumel & Resort, 130

Hotel Del Mar (Campeche), 234

Hotel D'Gomar (Isla Mujeres), 125

Hotel Dolores Alba (Chichén Itzá), 242

Hotel Dolores Alba (Mérida), 203

Hotel Don Quijote (San Cristóbal), 274

Hotel Eco Paraíso Xixim (Celestún), 216

Hotel El Paraíso (San Cristóbal), 274

Hotel Francis Arlene (Isla Mujeres), 125

Hotel Francis Drake (Campeche), 234

Hotel Holiday Inn Puerta Maya (Chetumal), 182

Hotel Lab Nah (Playa del Carmen), 159

Hotel Laguna (Bacalar), 180–181

Hotel Los Angeles (Chiapa de Corzo), 282

Hotel Lunata (Playa del Carmen), 158–159

Hotel Maison Lafitte (Mérida), 202–203

Hotel María Eugenia (Tuxtla Gutiérrez), 281

Hotel Marionetas (Mérida), 202

Hotel Maya Tucán (Palenque), 260

Hotel Maya Tulipanes (Palenque), 260

Hotel MedioMundo (Mérida), 203

Hotel Mucuy (Mérida), 203–204

Hotel Na Balam (Isla Mujeres), 124

Hotel Nachancán (Chetumal), 183

Hotel Palacio de Moctezuma (San Cristóbal), 274

Hotel Plaza (Ticul), 220

Hotel Plaza Independencia (Villahermosa), 254

Hotel Posada del Mar (Isla Mujeres), 125

Hotel Provincia Express (Villahermosa), 254

Hotel Real del Valle (San Cristóbal), 275

Hotel Regional San Marcos (Tuxtla Gutiérrez), 281

Hotel Tierra Maya (near Majahual), 180

Hotel Villa Rolandi Gourmet & Beach Club (Isla Mujeres), 123–124

Hotel Xibalba (Palenque), 260

Hotel Zací (Valladolid), 245

Hyatt Villahermosa, 254

Iberostar Cozumel, 130

Ibero-star Quetzal (Tucán; Playa del Carmen), 162

Jardín de Marieta (Playa del Carmen), 159–160

JW Marriott (Cancún), 94

La Casona Real (Cozumel), 140

La Hacienda Xcanatún (Mérida), 200–201

Le Méridien Cancún Resort & Spa, 96

Los Itzaes (Playa del Carmen), 159

Mansión de los Angeles (San Cristóbal), 274

Maroma (near Puerto Morelos), 150–151

Marriott Casa Magna (Cancún), 97–98

Mayakoba Residential Golf & Spa Resort (near Playa del Carmen), 153

ME (Cancún), 98

Meliá Cozumel, 130

Misión Palenque, 259

Occidental (Cozumel), 130

Omni Puerto Aventuras, 166

Petit Lafitte Hotel (near Puerto Morelos), 153

Playa Azul Golf-Scuba-Spa (Cozumel), 139

Playa Maya Value (Playa del Carmen), 159

Posada Dos Ceibas (Tulum), 173–174

Posada El Moro (Puerto Morelos), 152–153

Posada Lucy (Río Lagartos), 247

Presidente InterContinental Cozumel, 141

Puerta Calakmul (near Calakmul), 185

Radisson Hacienda Cancún, 99

Rancho Encantado Cottage Resort (Carretera Bacalar-Felipe Carrillo Puerto), 181

Rancho Sol Caribe (Punta Allen), 175

Rey del Caribe Hotel (Cancún), 99–100

Río Bec Dreams (near Xpujil), 185

Ritz-Carlton Cancún, 96

Riu Palace Las Américas (Cancún), 96–97

Royal (Cancún), 97

Sandos Playacar (Playa del Carmen), 162

Secreto (Isla Mujeres), 124

Shangri-La Caribe (Playa del Carmen), 158

Sol y Luna (Cancún), 100

Suites Vima (Cozumel), 140

Temozón (near Mérida), 201, 204

Temptation Resort & Spa Cancún, 99

The Tides Riviera Maya (formerly Ikal del Mar; Playa Xcalacoco), 151

Uayamón, 201

Villas Arqueológicas Chichén Itzá, 242

Villas Arqueológicas Cobá, 177

Villas Arqueológicas Uxmal, 223–224

Villas Delfines (Isla Holbox), 247–248

Villas Flamingo (Akumal), 167

Villas Flamingos (Isla Holbox), 247

Vista del Mar (Cozumel), 140

Vista del Mar Hotel and Condos (Akumal), 168

Wyndham Cozumel Resort, 130

Xbalamqué (Cancún), 100

Xpu-Ha Palace (Xpu-Ha), 166

312 Zamas (Tulum), 174
Zoetry Paraíso de la Bonita (near Puerto Morelos), 151

RESTAURANTS

Aioli (Cancún), 101
Alberto's Continental (Mérida), 205
Amaro (Mérida), 205
Angelo (Isla Mujeres), 126
Azafrán (Tulum), 174
Bazar Municipal stalls (Valladolid), 245
Bodo's (Puerto Morelos), 153
Cabaña del Pescador (Lobster House; Cozumel), 142
Cactus (Campeche), 235
Café Alameda (Mérida), 206
Café Cito (Isla Mujeres), 127
Café de Yara (Palenque), 262
Café La Selva (San Cristóbal), 276
Café Museo Café (San Cristóbal), 276
Café San Cristóbal, 276
Capicúa (Cozumel), 143
Casa de Frida (Mérida), 205
Casa de las Margaritas (Cancún), 101–102
Casa Mediterránea (Playa del Carmen), 160–161
Casa Rolandi (Cancún), 102
Casa Rolandi (Isla Mujeres), 126
Casa Vieja (Campeche), 235
Cenaduría Portales (Campeche), 235–236
Charlie's (Tulum), 174
Club Grill (Cancún), 101
Cocos Cozumel, 143–144
Comida Casera Toñita, 141
Copal (Tulum), 174
David Lau's (Puerto Morelos), 153
Doña Tina (Tulum), 174
Don Cafeto's (Tulum), 174
Eladio's (Mérida), 206
El Amigo Mario (Cozumel), 141
El Asador de Manolo (Playa del Carmen), 161
El Buen Gusto (Chetumal), 183
El Chaac Mool (Santa Elena), 220
El Edén (San Cristóbal), 275
El Fogón Norteño (Tuxtla Gutiérrez), 281
El Mesón del Marqués (Valladolid), 245
El Moro (Cozumel), 143

El Oasis (Playa del Carmen), 160
El Pirata (Puerto Morelos), 153
El Príncipe Tutul Xiú (Mérida), 205
El Shrimp Bucket (Cancún), 104
El Templo (Mérida), 205
Emiliano's Moustache (San Cristóbal), 275–276
Fiesta (Chichén Itzá), 242
Flamingo (Tuxtla Gutiérrez), 281
French Quarter (Cozumel), 142
Guido's (Cozumel), 142
Gustino (Cancún), 102
Harry's (Cancún), 102–103
Hotel Básico (Playa del Carmen), 160
Jangada (Villahermosa), 255
John Gray's (Puerto Morelos), 153
Labná (Cancún), 105
La Buena Vida (Akumal), 168
La Casa del Agua (Playa del Carmen), 160
La Casa del Pan Papalotl (San Cristóbal), 276
La Choza (Cozumel), 143
La Cocay (Cozumel), 142
La Cueva del Chango (Playa del Carmen), 161
La Destilería (Cancún), 104
La Flor de Santiago (Mérida), 206
Laguna Grill (Cancún), 103
La Habichuela (Cancún), 104–105
La Ideal (Chetumal), 183
La Nave (Tulum), 174
La Paloma (San Cristóbal), 275
La Parrilla (Playa del Carmen), 160
La Parroquia (Campeche), 236
La Pigua (Campeche), 235
Las Campanas (Valladolid), 245
La Selva (Palenque), 262
Las Pichanchas (Tuxtla Gutiérrez), 281
La Suegra (Puerto Morelos), 153
La Tarraya Restaurant/Bar (Playa del Carmen), 161, 163
La Vagabunda (Playa del Carmen), 161
Le Café d'Amancia (Puerto Morelos), 153

Lorenzillo's (Cancún), 101
Los Carboncitos (Playa del Carmen), 163
Los Pelícanos (Puerto Morelos), 153
Los Tulipanes (Villahermosa), 255
Madre Tierra (San Cristóbal), 276
Media Luna (Playa del Carmen), 161
Normita's (San Cristóbal), 276
100% Natural (Cancún), 105
Oscar y Lalo's (Punta Solimán Bay), 169
Paloma Bonita (Cancún), 103
Parrilla Suiza (Tuxtla Gutiérrez), 281
Périco's (Cancún), 105
Pierre (San Cristóbal), 275
Pingüinos (Isla Mujeres), 126–127
Pizza Rolandi (Cancún), 105–106
Prima (Cozumel), 142–143
Puerto Madero (Cancún), 103
Restaurant del Museo (Cozumel), 144
Restaurante Cenote Azul (Bacalar), 181
Restaurante Kantún (Mérida), 206
Restaurante Pantoja (Chetumal), 183
Restaurant Los Almendros (Mérida), 206
Restaurant Maya and Maya Cañada (Palenque), 262
Restaurant Tuluc (San Cristóbal), 276
Restaurant y Hotel Calakmul (Xpujil), 185
Rolandi's (Isla Mujeres), 127
Roots (Cancún), 106
Sanborn's (Villahermosa), 255
Su Cabaña Suiza (Oxkutzcab), 227
Sunset Grill (Isla Mujeres), 126
Super Carnes H C de Monterrey (Playa del Carmen), 160
Thai (Cancún), 103–104
Turtle Bay Café and Bakery (Akumal), 168
VIPS (Villahermosa), 255
Vito Corleone (Mérida), 204
The Wynston (Cozumel), 142
Yaxché (Playa del Carmen), 160
Zamas (Tulum), 174
Zazil Ha (Isla Mujeres), 127